PEARL

HARBOR

From INFAMY *to* GREATNESS

CRAIG NELSON

SCRIBNER

New York   London   Toronto   Sydney   New Delhi

Scribner
An Imprint of Simon & Schuster, Inc.
1230 Avenue of the Americas
New York, NY 10020

First Scribner hardcover edition September 2016

SCRIBNER and design are registered trademarks of The Gale Group, Inc.,
used under license by Simon & Schuster, Inc., the publisher of this work.

For information about special discounts for bulk purchases,
please contact Simon & Schuster Special Sales at 1-866-506-1949
or business@simonandschuster.com.

The Simon & Schuster Speakers Bureau can bring authors to your live event.
For more information or to book an event, contact the Simon & Schuster Speakers Bureau
at 1-866-248-3049 or visit our website at www.simonspeakers.com.

Manufactured in the United States of America

1   3   5   7   9   10   8   6   4   2

Library of Congress Cataloging-in-Publication Data
Names: Nelson, Craig, [date] author.
Title: Pearl Harbor : from infamy to greatness / Craig Nelson.
Description: New York : Scribner, an imprint of Simon & Schuster, [2016] |
Includes bibliographical references.
Identifiers: LCCN 2016018490 (print) | LCCN 2016018644 (ebook) |
ISBN 9781451660494 | ISBN 9781451660517
Subjects: LCSH: Pearl Harbor (Hawaii), Attack on, 1941.
Classification: LCC D767.92 .N46 2016 (print) | LCC D767.92 (ebook) | DDC
940.54/26693—c23
LC record available at https://lccn.loc.gov/2016018490

ISBN 978-1-4516-6049-4
ISBN 978-1-4516-6051-7 (ebook)

On the cover: An armor-penetrating Japanese shell strikes destroyer USS *Shaw*'s forward
magazine and ignites its cache of ammunition at 0912 on December 7, 1941, in a direct echo
of the single blow that, minutes before, killed over a thousand men aboard the USS *Arizona*.

PHOTO INSERT CREDITS: Photos courtesy of the National Archives and
Naval History and Heritage Command, except 1: courtesy of the FDR Library;
2: courtesy of the National Diet Library; 4 and 7: courtesy of the author.

On April 4, 1968, Robert Kennedy was giving a speech in Indiana when he was told that Martin Luther King Jr. had been assassinated. After sharing the news with his shocked and tearful audience, he quoted Aeschylus:

> Even in our sleep, pain which cannot forget
> falls drop by drop upon the heart,
> until, in our own despair,
> against our will,
> comes wisdom
> through the awful grace of God.

CONTENTS

CONTENTS

DREADNOUGHTS AND HOLYSTONES

On February 13, 1940, thirteen days before he turned eighteen, San Antonio high school football player James Lawson volunteered to join the United States Navy. Like everyone else at that moment at the bottom of the barrel in the Department of War, he was paid a princely $21 a month, but getting three hots and a cot was an economic toehold in an America just financially rousing itself from the Great Depression. The services had so slimmed down from their Great War peaks that it was a leap to get in, though civilians commonly looked down on sailors as unsavory ne'er-do-wells whom they called squids. First Lady Eleanor Roosevelt had made a quip—"The cleanest bodies and the dirtiest minds in the world"—while Norfolk, Virginia, had signs in its city parks: SAILORS AND DOGS KEEP OFF THE GRASS.

After San Diego boot camp, Seaman 2nd Class Lawson rode a supply ship across the Pacific, arriving in Oahu at Ford Island's quay Fox 8 in May of 1940. He never forgot crossing the plank for his very first day aboard the USS *Arizona*, a moment when, so awed by the thirty-thousand-ton dreadnought's grandeur and majesty, he forgot to salute: "I was just overwhelmed by the size of it. New sailors are like that. You go up that gangway for the first time, and you been trained to ask permission to come aboard and salute the flag at the stern, but the new seamen second come aboard and right away they forget."

Lawson's first assignments were brute labor—chipping paint; polishing brass; swabbing—and the most dreaded of all, holystoning. The decks of the ship were planked in teak, and the muscular technique the USN devised to polish them to a sheen was to take a sandstone brick with a hole drilled in it—the bricks originally came from churchly ruins, thus holystones—and use a broomstick in the hole to soothe the

1

deck. Lawson's bed his first year aboard was a hammock hung six feet in the air so "people could walk underneath it," as fellow sailor Galen Ballard remembered. "It rocked nice and put you to sleep, but it was very easy to fall out of. . . . That's a long way to fall."

Promoted to messcook—better to peel potatoes than holystone decks—Lawson was promoted again after a few months, to gunner's mate 3rd class, Deck Division 4. He lived in the stern, working the port quarterdeck's Turret 4 as well as the No. 2 catapult, which threw scouts into the sky: "The [float] plane sat on top of the catapult on a cradle, with a long cable that ran along the tracks of the catapult. Usually the plane went off the port side. As the ship turned and faced into the wind, we get the word to fire. We'd hit the firing key, it was just like firing a gun. The firing mechanism would fire off that five-inch cartridge, basically a can full of powder, and when that charge expanded the gas, it fired the plane, it would run on the cradle all the way to the end of the catapult. By the time it hit the catapult it was at takeoff speed. We had trained to rotate the catapult so that when planes left the ship, they'd be headed into the wind, which was takeoff position for aircraft. When they would come back in, the ship would have to swing around to make a slick. The big ship turning this way or that would flatten out the waves enough for the aircraft to sit down in the water. The plane would taxi up close to where the boatswain's mates could swing the crane out to hook on to the plane to hoist it back aboard and over onto the catapult."

In that dawn-of-radar era, a battlewagon's scout planes sent target coordinates back to her control room, and Lawson, as a pointer, controlled the elevation of his great Turret 4 guns, while the trainers ruled their horizontal. Their 179,614-pound cannon could blast 1,400-pound, armor-busting projectiles at an angle of fifteen degrees for a range of twenty miles . . . so far that they could pierce the horizon to strike enemies unseen: "It was a thrill: pulling the trigger and knowing it was going after somebody across the horizon with another twenty-five hundred to three thousand pounds of high explosives. . . . Every time I'd press the firing key in that turret and hear those big bullets going *shreeeeeeeeeooooooooooooo* twenty miles across the water, I was thinking, 'Here's another one for Tojo'—that was what the head honchos called the Japanese in those days. We figured that, with our superior forces, our superior ships, our superior gunnery, we'd take 'em."

The ship was so huge that it could be depersonalizing—Lawson called everyone "Guns" since he knew so few of the other men by name—but the navy knew how to build camaraderie, as *North Carolina*'s John Rampley explained: "A man's name was presented by the senior petty officer to the whole gun crew. If any of them didn't like him or [thought] that he would be incompatible, he didn't get in. So if you did make it, you felt you were part of a select group." Clint Westbrook, originally from the Bronx, was one of the powder men working with Lawson at Turret 4, using hoists to transfer sixty-pound powder bags and shells up from the magazine deep below, across the scuttle of the fireproof hatch, and then up to the turret. Westbrook assumed that war was near . . . but that it would strike, not in their Pacific, but in the Atlantic. "I signed up for a six-year peacetime stint," he said.

Lawson eventually qualified as a helmsman, taking wheel watch on alternate days, meeting the boss, Captain Franklin Van Valkenburgh, and working the ship's three methods of steering—electric; steam; auxiliary—to make sure she was ready for anything. Auxiliary meant brute muscle force, a tag team of crew using their full body weight against enormous cranks: "You'd run down a long hallway and grab one of those big spokes and ride that sucker down. Somebody'd go right behind you and ride the next one down. It was a constant run, one man at a time." But besides that method of power and the dreaded holystoning, Lawson loved his life at sea, especially serving on a battleship: "We were kingpins of the navy in those days. We looked down on the destroyer sailors. It was like living in a big city."

The *Arizona*'s keel was laid at the Brooklyn Navy Yard in New York City on March 16, 1914, when she was then known only as No. 39. The keel is the spine of a ship's hull, which, like a human spine, serves as the structural foundation; the vessel's backbone. "Laying the keel" places that spine in the cradle where the ship will be constructed around it and is the official moment of birth. Since No. 39 with her sister ship, *Pennsylvania*, would be the "biggest fighting ship, built or building, for any navy," according to the *New York Times*, "the ceremony of laying the keel was . . . postponed until 11 o'clock yesterday morning in order to make possible the presence of Assistant Secretary Roosevelt [in a greatcoat, bowler hat, and gold pince-nez]. . . . The firing of a salute of seventeen guns from the superdreadnought *North Dakota* announced his coming [then] the giant traveling crane above the cradle of the battleship-to-be began to move. It carried a massive steel plate and dropped it at the spot designated by the constructors. Then Mr. Roosevelt stepped forward. Capt. Gleaves handed him a silver-plated bolt. Mr. Roosevelt quickly hammered it into place while the band played the National Anthem and the crowd stood with bared heads."

Through his mother, Sara, Assistant Secretary of the Navy Franklin Delano Roosevelt was descended from a family that had made its fortune in seafaring, his grandfather Warren Delano having prospered in the trade of Chinese tea and opium. Franklin as a teenager learned to sail the Hudson River aboard the family's sixty-foot schooner, *Half Moon*, and at the age of five, he accompanied his influential father, who had made a great fortune in rail and coal, to the White House, where President Grover Cleveland told the boy, "My little man, I am making a strange wish for you. It is that you may never be president of the United States."

As a New York state senator, Franklin publicly campaigned for Woodrow Wilson against his fifth cousin Teddy. When Wilson won, he appointed FDR assistant secretary of the navy in 1913, and Roosevelt would have this job when, on April 6, 1917, America joined the Great War. He nagged Navy Secretary Josephus Daniels to grant him a commission, but was turned down because Daniels judged Roosevelt's administrative duties—overseeing procurement and shipping—as too important.

FDR would forever after love the United States Navy with an unimaginable passion. During his presidency, he personally selected the service's flag officers, raised its budget every year, and called the navy "us" and the army "them" until General George Marshall insisted he stop. At his White House breakfast meetings, the nation's chief executive often sat in bed, his shoulders draped in a blue navy cape, surrounded by his collections of postage stamps and naval memorabilia. Admiral Ernest King, chief of naval operations after Pearl Harbor, remembered a visit to the cruiser *Houston* on the afternoon of February 28, 1939; Roosevelt "was in high spirits, for he loved the Navy and always visibly expanded when at sea. As the admirals greeted him, he would have some pleasant, half-teasing personal message for each."

During FDR's tenure with the navy in World War I, Winston Churchill was Great Britain's first lord of the admiralty, and Roosevelt saw their careers as taking similar paths. Eventually he wrote to Churchill in 1939 that you "should keep me in touch personally about anything you want me to know about." When Joseph Kennedy, ambassador to

England, asked about their relationship, FDR said, "I have always disliked him since the time I went to England in 1918. He acted like a stinker at a dinner, lording it all over us. . . . I'm giving him attention now because there is a strong possibility that he will become the prime minister and I want to get my hand in now." Cabinet member Frances Perkins called Roosevelt "the most complicated human being I ever knew."

On August 10, 1921, Roosevelt was on vacation with his family at Campobello, his father's island estate off the New Brunswick coast. FDR and his sons were out sailing when they spotted a fire in the woods and docked to help put it out. At dinner that night, Roosevelt didn't feel well and went to bed early; in the morning, he found he could barely walk. By that night, his back and legs were wracked with pain, his temperature had soared to 102 degrees, and eventually he was diagnosed with poliomyelitis and was paralyzed from the waist down. He now had to be carried by attendants up and down stairs; had a Ford convertible modified so it could be driven entirely by hand; and on being elected governor of New York in 1928 and president of the United States in 1932, developed a gentleman's agreement with the press (especially the photographers) for him not to be seen as helpless. He had trained himself to appear to walk in public through a remarkable feat: holding on to a cane with one hand and the arm of an aide or a son with the other, he would tilt his useless legs (held rigid by steel braces) from side to side, inching forward like an acrobat on the parallel bars, powered entirely by his arms and shoulders. It was such an incredible performance that few Americans ever knew their longest-serving president was completely paralyzed from the waist down. The disease also awoke in him a sympathy for the ignored, the underprivileged, and the dismissed in American society—he told America's first female cabinet secretary, Frances Perkins, "We are going to make a country in which no one is left out"—and he founded the March of Dimes, which ultimately led to polio vaccines, which may soon eradicate polio entirely.

His paralysis meant FDR needed to keep nearby anything he needed throughout the day, leading to a life of monumental clutter. He ran the nation not from the Oval Office, but from the Oval Study, a small room next to the presidential bedroom on the White House's second floor, filled with model ships and furniture from the yacht the *Mayflower*. One corner of the room was taken up by a pipe organ, while shelves were devoted to the 150-volume Roosevelt stamp collection, and the walls were festooned with portraits of his mother, his wife, and historic sailing ships. Using these three adjoining rooms of bed, bath, and study, FDR required no help. The suite was so significant that, in case of a power failure, backup generators would keep the electricity going there, but not in the Oval Office itself.

The USS *Arizona*'s array of four turrets, each hosting three fourteen-inch guns, made up her signature artillery (fourteen-inch/45-caliber meaning the inner diameter of the bore), but she was additionally provisioned with twenty-two five-inch/51-caliber guns, four three-inch/50-caliber antiaircraft guns, thirty-nine .45-caliber machine guns, and two twenty-one-inch torpedo tubes. Like her great historic predecessor, HMS *Dreadnought*, *Arizona* reached a maximum speed of twenty-one knots driven by four shafts, each powered by a Parson turbine fed by three Babcock and Wilcox boilers, but unlike her British ancestor, she supped oil, not coal.

Arizona's crew nicknamed her *At 'em Maru*—combining *up and at 'em* with the Japanese word for "ship"—and Herbert Hoover rode her on a presidential tour of the Caribbean. Then after nine years based in San Diego, she sailed, along with the rest of the American fleet, to Pearl Harbor, in June 1940.

The two stars of the fleet in Hawaii, *Arizona* and *Pennsylvania*, were as good as you could get in battlewagons in their day, the result of a revolution in warfare that navies around the world believed would be, forever after, the ways of their world. For three prior centuries, ending with the Age of Sail, nations had built ships of the line that pounded at each other broadside with batteries of gun and cannon mounted in rows in deck upon deck . . . but from no more than a few hundred yards, with their firepower and maneuverings defined by the speed and direction of the wind. France introduced steam propulsion to her of-the-line vessels in 1850 with *Napoléon*; armoring with iron in 1859 with *Gloire*; and pioneering steel construction in 1876 with *Redoubtable*. These innovations triggered an arms race with Britain and Germany, culminating in 1906 with the English ship that would render all others obsolete: HMS *Dreadnought*. Powered by steam turbines to an astonishing twenty-one knots, protected by an eleven-inch armor belt, and bristling with ten twelve-inch cannons mounted on five turrets, *Dreadnought* was so revolutionary and so powerful that she indeed feared nothing, as her title proclaimed; her global descendants would be called dreadnoughts and their progeny, superdreadnoughts.

While US battleships averaged crews of around sixteen hundred, it took twenty-one hundred to man the fleet's other giants, aircraft carriers. Carrier warplanes included the fighter (used for both offense and defense), the dive-bomber (which zeroed in on its target at close range for greater accuracy), the high-level bomber (which dropped heavier ordnance than a diver from a defensive altitude and used gravity to increase its devastation), and the torpedo bomber (which skimmed low over the waters). Vulnerable carriers set sail surrounded by a task force that included the more lightly armored and thus faster cruisers, which screened the formation and scouted foes, and destroyers, which were originally designed to attack torpedo boats and were known as torpedo boat destroyers. One bell-bottom joked that their real name should have been "destroyeds," since their mission was more often than not to be first to reveal the enemy by taking a hit.

One of the maneuvers all sailors needed to learn at this time was zigzagging to evade torpedo strikes. During one practice zigzag, *Oklahoma* smashed into *Arizona*'s bow, leaving a gash thirty feet high and twenty feet wide, which was quickly repaired in dry dock. One sailor would later say, "You can't hurt a battleship much."

If the navy's capital ships were state-of-the-art for their era—in December of 1940, one midshipman wrote home, "Well, Mother, a battleship is about as safe a vessel as you can find in a fleet, so you don't have to worry about my well-being!"—the same could not be said for America's army forces based just down the road, charged with both defending the American territory of Hawaii and the US Fleet when she was at anchor. These soldiers were still armed with bolt-action Springfields, their heads protected by "dishpan" helmets with cotton liners that took a good half hour to thread into place.

While presenting awards to the various Fleet sports teams at the start of December 1941, Admiral Isaac Kidd made a special announcement: "I think I know what all you men want for Christmas, and you're going to get that." "We all wanted leave," John Rampley remembered. "After he said that, scuttlebutt started floating around the ship that we were scheduled to leave Monday the eighth for R and R in San Diego." Galen Ballard, with a week of duty left on his ticket, was told he'd be going home on December 13: "I don't think any of us had any idea whatsoever that anything was going to happen. We were happy as larks."

They were, on the whole, happier than larks. Some places in the world are so beautiful it's impossible to believe they haven't been retouched by Hollywood or Photoshop, and one of these is a swath of volcanic peaks shimmering in the midst of a too-blue-to-be-true Pacific. Today, California likes to think she's the prettiest one, but she is wrong; the most beautiful state in America is both a glorious archipelago and a military stronghold, with an ocean undulating in cobalt blue and Coke-bottle green; butter-yellow sands; creamy-white surf; hell-black lava; pencil-thin waterfalls; primordial canyons; and even a snowcap. She is home to marine-mammal leviathans, and the planet's most active volcano, belching white smoke and fiery red magma; and she is a territory of flowers: orchids and jacaranda; hibiscus and bougainvillea; lavender and oleander; the latter with such strong perfumes they stop passersby in their tracks. In case you can't tell, I love her like Christmas, and Charles Lindbergh loved her so much, he arranged to die there.

Hawaii is a salting of 130 islands and atolls over fifteen hundred miles of the Pacific. Her first arrivals were Polynesians from the Marquesas, bringing gods that were tall and lean and grimacing, as well as a society with a code of behavior and relationships called *kapu*, which included wife swapping, torture, human sacrifice, and a worship of gods and spirits found in such things as canoes, mists, odd noises, and lunatics. The first European arrival was James Cook, who returned a year later to retrieve a stolen boat, but came under attack by two hundred warriors and died in combat. Over the next hundred years, Cook's fellow travelers, lured to this crossroads of the Pacific, would wreak a kind of vengeance, as 90 percent of the archipelago's population died of European diseases.

Records portray the first American and British visitors to what were then known as the Sandwich Islands as concentrating on Maui, Kauai, and the big island of Hawaii. In 1794, US merchant ship *Lady Washington* used her cannon to help the king of Oahu win a victory at Rabbit Island and Wai-Momi—today's Ford Island and Pearl Harbor. Fifteen years later, the first King Kamehameha united the archipelago into a Polynesian state, and ten years after that, the Congregationalist Church sent the first of a dozen missionaries to his kingdom. By 1820, an "Agent of the United States for Commerce and Seamen" was stationed at Honolulu to assist the great fleets of American whalers and merchants, which numbered forty-two out of the forty-eight ships in the city's harbor by November of 1867. On January 20, 1887, the US Senate amended its treaty with Hawaii to include that "His Majesty the King of the Hawaiian Islands, grants to the Government of the U.S. the exclusive right to enter the harbor of Pearl River, in the Island of Oahu, and to establish and maintain there a coaling and repair station for the use of vessels of the U.S. and to that end the U.S. may improve the entrance to said harbor and do all things useful to the purpose aforesaid." Maui's Lahaina became practically an American city, she was so filled with whaling crew, and the isle of Molokai became a notorious leper colony. Sufferers were taken by boat and forced into the waves after being told, "Prepare for Molokai as for the grave."

Establishing schools and creating a written Hawaiian language, missionaries converted Queen Keopuolani on her deathbed in 1823, beginning a protected niche for haole (whites) in the islands, many of whose descendants made their fortunes in white gold—sugar. In 1850, the general population was bequeathed ownership of their lands, and the Alien Land Ownership Act was passed, letting them sell said lands to outsiders. As whaling declined, sugar roared, as did a Hawaiian craze for American clothing and furniture, paid for by devastating the archipelago's groves of sandalwood. In an 1893 coup led by the American Annexation Club (composed of the "Big Five" sugar executive haoles—onetime missionaries who'd tried to outlaw surfing and that "vile obscenity," hula dancing) and supported by marines invading from a ship in the harbor, Queen Lili'uokalani was deposed. She appealed to the White House, but refused to promise leniency for the guilty Americans, and the Hawaiian throne fell to a shameful swipe by colonial plutocrats.

After five years as a republic under President Sanford Dole, the onetime kingdom was annexed to the United States as a territory in 1898, with the official ceremony on August 12 at Iolani Palace attended by no one of native birth; Lili'uokalani's niece called that moment "bitterer than death to me." The following year the United States Navy started building on Oahu its keystone for operations in the Pacific, and by 1935 the *New York Times* could report, "An armada of 160 ships, the greatest fleet ever to visit Pearl Harbor, was moored or anchored in the east and west lochs tonight. Twelve battleships, two flotillas of destroyers, about thirty submarines, twelve heavy and seven light cruisers and several score auxiliaries were 'home from the sea.' . . . Only the large aircraft carriers, the *Lexington*, the *Ranger*, and the *Saratoga*, lay at anchor in the open roads off Honolulu. . . . It is the first time such a large number of ships has ever been, and their presence definitely indicates that Pearl Harbor has assumed first rank as a naval base."

With Admiral James Richardson in command, the US Fleet was dispatched to Hawaii in the spring of 1940 for its annual maneuvers known as Fleet Problem XXI. Less than a week before they were to return to California on May 9, however, Richardson was ordered to instead remain in Hawaii by Chief of Naval Operations Harold "Betty" Stark.* Two weeks later, Richardson complained to Stark that Pearl Harbor's facilities were inadequate: "My objections for remaining there were, primarily, that you only had one port, secure port, and very crowded, no recreation facilities for the men, a long distance from Pearl Harbor to the city of Honolulu, inadequate transportation, inadequate airfields. A carrier cannot conduct all training for her planes from the carrier deck. In order to launch her planes she must be underway at substantial speed, using up large amounts of fuel. So that wherever carriers are training their squadrons there must be flying fields available, so that while the ship herself is undergoing overhaul, or repair, or upkeep, the planes may conduct training, flying from the flying fields. There were inadequate and restricted areas for anchorages of the fleet; to take them in and out of Pearl Harbor wasted time."

With one of the signature "on the one hand, on the other" cables that would eventually get him demoted, CNO Stark replied on May 27, "You are there because of the deterrent effect which it is thought your presence may have on the Japs going into the East Indies. . . . Suppose the Japs do go into the East Indies? What are we going to do about it? My answer is I don't know and I think there's nobody on God's green earth who can tell you."

On June 17, the US War Department, believing that an aggressive Tokyo, having concluded a treaty with Moscow, was now setting its sights on Hawaii, cabled Major General Charles D. Herron, the army's Hawaiian Department commander, with the first of a stream of warn-

---

*Stark's nickname Betty was a joke about Revolutionary War hero John Stark's wife begun by classmates at Annapolis, though Secretary of War Henry Stimson saw it as more than that, calling Stark "timid and ineffective . . . the weakest one of all."

ings: "Immediate alert. Complete defensive organization to deal with possible transpacific raid. . . . Maintain alert until further orders." The warning was held for a number of months, then faded away.

After Stark refused to reconsider Richardson's orders to remain in Hawaii, the Commander-in-Chief, United States (known as CIN-CUS) came to Washington to make his case directly. "On October 7, I talked with Stark, Nimitz, Knox," Richardson said. "And while here I lunched with the President. Had a long talk with him. The President stated that the fleet was retained in the Hawaiian area in order to exercise a restraining influence on the actions of Japan. I stated that in my opinion the presence of the fleet in Hawaii might influence a civilian political government, but that Japan had a military government which knew that the fleet was undermanned, unprepared for war, and had no train of auxiliary ships without which it could not undertake active operations. Therefore, the presence of the fleet in Hawaii could not exercise a restraining influence on Japanese action. . . .

"The President said in effect, 'Despite what you believe, I know that the presence of the fleet in the Hawaiian area, has had, and is now having, a restraining influence on the actions of Japan.'

"I said, 'Mr. President, I still do not believe it, and I know that our fleet is disadvantageously disposed for preparing for or initiating war operations.'

"The President then said, 'I can be convinced of the desirability of returning the battleships to the west coast if I can be given a good statement which will convince the American people and the Japanese Government that in bringing the battleships to the west coast we are not stepping backward.'"

Secretary of State Cordell Hull, among others, took issue with Richardson's version of events. "Now, someone suggested that the government was trying to bluff the Japanese," Hull later testified. "The whole truth is that we were in our own waters, in our territory, on our own side of the Pacific, and that we were pursuing a perfectly peaceful and defensible course. In all our talks with the Japanese and all of our representations, we were pleading with them for peaceful relations and their continuance. If we happened to have a double-barreled shotgun sitting back in the corner somewhere in the house when we are talking to a desperado, it does no harm, to say the least. I always feel a little better and I think he would feel a little worse if he could see the outlines of that gun back there. It is a psychological thing that nobody can escape."

Another Washington official taken aback by Richardson's statements was Fleet Admiral William Leahy. "The President asked me to have luncheon with him on October 8," Leahy recalled. "I found after I arrived that Admiral Richardson was also to be at lunch. . . . My memory in that matter is good, principally because I was exceedingly surprised to learn that the commander in chief of the fleet did not consider the fleet prepared for war and at that time I was apprehensive in regard to an early war situation in the Pacific, although I was very far from sources of information and I had no late information in regard to that matter.

"[Richardson] said the ships did not have their war complements; that the facilities in Pearl Harbor were not sufficient to keep the ships in a top condition at all times; that he had not a sufficient number of fuel ships to make it possible for him to operate the fleet at any distance from the Hawaiian Islands; that the personnel of the fleet, the officers and the crews, did not know why they were in the Hawaiian Islands; that apparently nobody expected to be called upon for war duty; that the families of the men and officers were in the continental United States and they wanted to get home and see their families; that the recreation facilities and the means for taking care of his men when they were on shore in Honolulu were almost nonexistent, at least they were entirely insufficient and that he felt that if there was a prospect of calling upon the fleet for war service it could be done much more advantageously in a port on the Pacific Coast of the United States where he could clear his ships for action, get the additional things that would be needed and reinforce his peacetime crews. . . . I expressed to Admiral Richardson my surprise to find that the fleet was in the condition which he had stated to the President and I said that I hoped he would manage to correct as many of the deficiencies as possible without any delay because I had been telling the Congress and the people of this country for some time that the Navy was ready for war and I was distressed to find that it was not."

The Japanese had in fact taken notice of the American fleet remaining at Pearl Harbor, but their reaction was not what FDR had presumed. Japanese admiral Isoroku Yamamoto: "Conversely, we're within striking distance [of Hawaii], too. In trying to intimidate us, America has put itself in a vulnerable position. If you ask me, they're just that bit too confident."

Admiral Richardson and President Roosevelt had their difference of opinion solved in ninety days. "In early January, a dispatch came in ordering Richardson to be relieved by Admiral Husband E. Kimmel," Vice Admiral George Dyer remembered. "Richardson's remark was 'My God, they can't do that to me.' But, of course, they could and did." The by-the-books, humorless, hardworking, and picture-perfect Rear Admiral Kimmel arrived in Oahu on February 1, 1941, with the dual title of commander in chief, United States Fleet, and commander in chief, Pacific Fleet. While Admiral Isoroku Yamamoto would be known for a temper that left the elfin man stomping his office floors so hard the furniture quaked, Kimmel—called by his friends Kim or Mustapha—would throw his hat on the ground and stomp on it while screaming . . . and he had a hat on standby to be used in such circumstances. In his first months after taking command, Kimmel moved his administration out of the USS *Pennsylvania* and into an office on the second floor of the Fleet Headquarters building at the submarine base opposite Ford Island, not for the admiral's comfort, but for the battleship to be readied for war instead of pomp. Yamamoto never did this, making in turn his flagships *Nagato* and *Yamato* residences instead of the dreadnoughts they were built to be.

While Richardson had alternated half the fleet at sea and half in port, Kimmel started three task forces under William Pye, William Halsey, and Wilson Brown, resulting in ships spending 60 percent of their time in port and 40 percent at sea. Kimmel had wanted to regularly have two task forces on the prowl at a time, but Hawaii didn't have the fuel reserves to allow it. One key drawback of basing the US Fleet in Hawaii was that all of Pearl Harbor's fuel had to be tankered across the Pacific from the American mainland.

Oahu's other significant drawback, one shared by the majority of America's military installations, was its paucity of surveillance aircraft. On January 16, 1941, Naval Base Defense Air Force commander Admiral Patrick Bellinger wrote CNO Harold Stark, "After taking over command of Patrol Wing Two and looking over the situation, I was surprised to find that here in the Hawaiian Islands, an important naval advanced post, we were operating on a shoestring and the more I look the thinner the shoestring appeared to be [which] indicates to me that the Navy Department as a whole does not view the situation in the Pacific with alarm." After meeting with Kimmel, Bellinger was ordered to work with Hawaiian Air Force commander General Frederick Martin to draft a plan coordinating army and navy air operations in the event of an attack on Oahu. On March 31, 1941, their memorandum warned:

> (a) A declaration of war might be preceded by:
> 1.   A surprise submarine attack on ships in the operating area.
> 2.   A surprise attack on OAHU including ships and installations in Pearl Harbor.
> 3.   A combination of these two.
> (b) It appears that the most likely and dangerous form of attack on OAHU would be an air attack. It is believed that at present such an attack would most likely be launched from one or more carriers which would probably approach inside of 300 miles.
> (c) A single attack might or might not indicate the presence of more submarines or more planes awaiting to attack after defending aircraft have been drawn away by the original thrust.
> (d) Any single submarine attack might indicate the presence of a considerable undiscovered surface force probably composed of fast ships accompanied by a carrier.
> (e) In a dawn air attack there is a high probability that it could be delivered as a complete surprise in spite of any patrols we might be using and that it might find us in a condition of readiness under which pursuit would be slow to start, also it might be successful as a diversion to draw attention away from a second attacking force. The major disadvantage would be that we could have all day to find and attack the carrier. A dusk attack would have the advantage that the carrier could use the night for escape.

What would later be known in Pearl Harbor history as the remarkably prescient Martin-Bellinger Report concluded, "The aircraft at present available in Hawaii are inadequate to maintain . . . a patrol extensive enough to insure that an air attack from an Orange [Japanese] carrier cannot arrive over Oahu as a complete surprise."

On February 4, Kimmel's army counterpart, Lieutenant General Walter Short, arrived to replace Herron as commander of the Hawaiian Department, and despite their services' decades of vicious rivalry, the admiral and the general quickly began a tradition of playing golf together on alternate Sundays. Just as quickly, since Short's army was supposed to protect Kimmel's navy while it was anchored in Hawaii, Kimmel complained to CNO Harold Stark that the army was under-armed and understaffed for the assignment, notably in the category of aerial patrols. In response, army chief George Marshall said that, just as every army base and command had been shortchanged through years of disastrous economic depression, so it was in Honolulu, but that "Hawaii is on a far better basis than any other command in the Army."

One man who did not think much of the newly arrived Walter Short was the general's predecessor, Major General Charles Herron, who'd commanded Hawaii for the army since 1937. Herron's opinion began with their first meeting. Since Herron would be returning to the mainland on February 7 aboard the same ship that had brought Short and his wife to Hawaii on the fourth, they had about two days to work out the transfer of command and fully brief Short on his new position. To help with this, Herron had his staff create a briefing book, which was sent to Short in San Francisco to read on the voyage to Oahu. "Upon my meeting Short when he arrived" on February 7, Herron said, "I asked him whether he had read the papers and material. He replied that . . . he had not given them much time while en route." Instead he'd read the Kenneth Roberts novel *Oliver Wiswell*.

Herron would also say that Walter Short and his wife, Isabel, were insulted by being posted to Hawaii, believing that he deserved a spot in Washington or at the Presidio in San Francisco. Mrs. Short was additionally angered at being taken away from her friends and family to live in the middle of nowhere. Herron concluded, "Following my talks with General Short at the time, he did not ever ask my opinion, or for information, or correspond with me on the subject of command or related problems."

As news of Japanese attacks in Asia reached a crescendo over the start of 1941, many officers and FBI agents on Oahu, knowing that 155,000 residents were of Japanese ancestry—a third of the population—became convinced that a fifth column lurked behind the scenes in Honolulu, sabotaging the territory and infecting the populace in preparation for Tojo's invasion. No evidence was ever found. Instead, historian Thurston Clarke theorizes that the fifth column sabotaging American defenses wasn't Japanese immigrants and their children, but the glories of Hawaii itself: "Cables from the Navy Department might have declared, 'This dispatch is to be considered a war warning,' but when their recipients looked out windows and up from breakfast tables, they saw paradise. They rose to soft and flower-scented breezes, ate papaya or mango from backyard trees, and took cool showers, because in a climate that may be the most perfect on earth, many houses lacked water heaters. On weekends, women dressed in loose-fitting muumuus or kimonos, and men wore aloha shirts, a recent invention of a local Japanese tailor, who made them from the colorful silk fabrics used for children's clothing in Japan. On weekdays, people worked in the mornings and relaxed in the afternoons. After the attack, a captain commanding a field artillery battery at Schofield Barracks told the army board of inquiry, 'Because it was in the tropics we did very little work in the afternoon. It was just the opposite of a warlike attitude.'"

Pearl Harbor itself was then a tourist destination, with each capital ship looking like the industrialized skyline of a small town from the future. So many of them massed in one harbor was thrilling to behold. In the Pacific sun, the navy's dress whites shone, and while that service's blues matched the ocean itself, the army's khaki browns and greens faded into the jungle. James Jones's *From Here to Eternity* captures that time, when American officers wore white gloves, gazed over manicured lawns, and presented engraved calling cards, while granting their men "Cinderella liberty"—back aboard by midnight. The 1941 slogan for the city of Honolulu? "A World of Happiness in an Ocean of Peace." The town had no stoplights; instead, policemen either sat under umbrellas with leis draped across their shoulders flipping Stop levers and Go levers or waved cars through with their gloved hands, while shimmying a hula.

Yet, some signs couldn't be ignored. "During the spring and summer of 1941 we saw a death ship," Lawson remembered. "It was a British cruiser, and it had just a makeshift bow they had put on in the Philippines. And the ship stunk to high heaven, because they had had to seal off a couple of frames to make the ship seaworthy, but inside those frames was a whole bunch of their crew dead and rotting, and you could smell it all over the harbor. They were dead from a torpedo they took somewhere in the South Pacific."

On what would be the last sail of *Arizona*'s life from late November to December 5, 1941, Japanese subs followed the fleet around the Hawaiian Islands. Lawson: "Long about one o'clock in the morning the general alarm went off—'Man your battle stations!' The picket submarines and picket destroyers had detected a bunch of sonar contacts. Every man aboard knew that meant Japanese submarines." But such reminders of hostilities were all too rare, and the warnings of what was to come seemed so distant. Lieutenant Albert Brower: "We'd have a few beers at the Officers' Club. Talk would get around to the war in Europe. And we kept patting each other on the back saying that, in case of war, this is the place to be. We have it made! Look at all this water around us, protected by the United States Navy. We have it made." "Nobody talked about the possibility of war. That was the farthest thing from our minds," Naval Hospital nurse Lenore Rickert said. "I met my husband, Albert, at that time. He had been a patient in the wars there. We weren't supposed to go with patients, of course. I remember he was stationed at the marine base right next door to us. So I would go down the road and I would flash my light so he would step out from the bushes, knowing that it was me that was coming."

Though their routine chores may have been stultifying, the soldiers and sailors of Oahu were living the life of *Mutiny on the Bounty*'s Fletcher Christian, with their ironwood trees and breadfruit groves; their warm and hibiscus-kissed breezes; and their light daily rain. *West Virginia* bugler Richard Fiske: "It was actually my first time to have any distance away from home. I'd just made my eighteenth birthday and I'm thinking about a lot of hula girls in just grass skirts. It had all the enchantment that a person could imagine by reading books. . . . We had ice cream parlors, and a few bars where we could get a cold beer for twenty-five cents. It was a great place. You could go down to Waikiki Beach and you could see the bathing beauties. You could sleep on Waikiki beach and nobody would even bother you." Their life was evoked by the most popular song in Hawaii four years in a row, the one played by all the local bands of Honolulu, an Oscar winner from the 1937 movie *Waikiki Wedding*, "Sweet Leilani," which had turned into a number one hit single for Bing Crosby:

> Sweet Leilani, heavenly flower
> I dreamed of paradise for two
> You are my paradise completed
> You are my dream come true.

PART I

THE ROADS TO WAR

CHAPTER ONE

CONCEIVING THE INCONCEIVABLE

One of the world's most beautiful countries, Japan is so crowded she has developed both a unity of social grace and a national impulse of exceeding kindness to strangers. Those of us who love her and have been treated so well by her find it impossible to imagine her war crimes of World War II, just as after so many decades as allies, it is impossible for most Americans to imagine our two countries at war. It was, in fact, nearly as difficult for Americans to imagine such a thing in 1941, part of the reason that Pearl Harbor came as such a shock. Yet, in the decades leading up to the attack, the one word for the two nations' history was *fraught*—and this querulous state began at their first encounter.

On February 3, 1867, four weeks after his father's sudden death, a teenager named Mutsuhito was crowned emperor of Japan. For centuries, his nation had been governed by a shogunate, a feudal military clique led by the greatest of the nation's warlords, each of whom employed private armies of samurai constantly warring with each other, with their greatest honor being to die for their master. The shogun ran the country from the city of Edo, while the symbolic head of state, the emperor, resided in the ancient capital of Kyoto, devoting his life to a contemplation of poetry, philosophy, and calligraphy . . . not politics.

In the 1600s, after a string of Catholic missionaries had appeared and tried to convert the citizenry, the shogun decreed *sakoku*—"closed nation"—a foreign policy pioneered by the Chinese. Beyond a select group of Dutch and Japanese merchants restricted to the island of Dejima, any foreigners trying to enter the country would be executed. *Sakoku* was the rule of law for 250 years, until 1853, when Mutsuhito was all of one year old, and the commandant of Brooklyn's New York

21

Naval Shipyard and the father of the American steam navy, Commodore Matthew Calbraith Perry, appeared in Tokyo Bay with a letter from American president Millard Fillmore, a white flag, the seven cannon-festooned gunboats of the East India Squadron (including his black-pitch-hulled frigate, *Susquehanna*), and a regiment of US marines. President Fillmore wanted commercial access to Japan to globally strengthen America's whaling and merchant businesses, and the president's letter promised that, if Edo did not revoke *sakoku* and allow American entry, the United States would destroy the country. With one look at Perry's boats, which could sail upwind, armed with state-of-the-art Paixhans guns firing explosive shells that could demolish anything along the way, the shogun knew he could not win and signed a treaty acceding to Fillmore's demands.

In the years that followed, many in Japan refused to accept the forced presence of foreign barbarians, especially a group of young samurai known as *shishi*—"men of high purpose"—who believed such conditions evidenced a faltering society, a culture that could only be repaired through violent revolution, including the death or expulsion of foreigners, and the downfall of the ruling clique (Mutsuhito's grandson, Hirohito, will face an almost identical constellation of social forces across the 1930s and 40s). Emperor Komei, Mutsuhito's father, was thirty-five years old, and in excellent health. Suddenly in January of 1867 he turned grievously ill, dying on the thirtieth. Many of the era's scholars believe he was poisoned, but it meant the fifteen-year-old Mutsuhito inherited the throne. Riding the revolutionary sentiment streaking through his country, he would turn everything upside down.

Crowned as Meiji, the emperor hired foreign immigrants to build railroads, shipyards, spinning mills, port facilities, and foundries. When each business was up and running, it was sold to a Japanese family. He moved his palace from Kyoto to Edo, renamed that city Tokyo, abolished the feudal land system, and created a government with a constitution, a cabinet, and a legislature. As more and more examples of Western science, business, and culture appeared, the Japanese underwent a cultural upheaval similar to the West's Enlightenment—the Meiji Restoration. Top-ranking Tokyo students traveled to London to study shipping, to Paris for law, to Germany for medicine, and to the United States for business. Every innovation of the past three hundred years—from lightbulbs to hansom cabs—was immediately imported. While wearing Western clothes and eating Western food, however,

Meiji saluted his ancestry by composing one hundred thousand *waka* verse, one of which would be quoted by his grandson as Hirohito's most significant stand against fascism:

> The seas of the four directions—
> all are born of one womb:
> why, then, do the wind and waves rise in discord?

Emperor Meiji chose for his tutor the son of a samurai, an admiral who would become a legendary naval hero: Heihachiro Togo. In 1876, Meiji dispatched gunboats to Korea to force it to sign commerce agreements—exactly what Millard Fillmore and Matthew Perry had done to the Japanese in 1853. Japan then won its first two wars back-to-back, against the China of the Qing, and the Russia of the czar. One news item displayed on the bulletin boards of Japanese elementary schools announced, "Japanese troops defeat Chinese at P'yongyang and win a great victory. Chinese corpses were piled up as high as a mountain. Oh, what a grand triumph! Chinka, Chinka, Chinka, Chinka, so stupid and they stinka."

Across the Pacific at that moment, America had similar feelings. Beginning in the 1850s with settlers from Guangdong hoping to pan their fortune out of California's gold rush, the American West swelled with Chinese immigrants, peaking when the Transcontinental Railroad imported hordes of manual laborers to work its desert and mountain track. After that great feat was completed in 1869, however, many Americans came to believe that their states were infested with Asian immigrants taking their jobs and engaging in criminal enterprise, a belief that grew into a mass panic known as yellow peril. The *San Francisco Chronicle* ran stories such as "Brown Asiatics Steal Brains of Whites," and *New-York Tribune* editor Horace Greeley—he of "Go west, young man" fame—complained "The Chinese are uncivilized, unclean, and filthy beyond all conception without any of the higher domestic or social relations; lustful and sensual in their dispositions; every female is a prostitute of the basest order." An estimated two hundred Asians were lynched by white mobs in the 1870s and 1880s, leading to the colloquialism *a Chinaman's chance*—i.e., no chance. Meanwhile, so much of Chinese culture would permeate into America that it became invisible, such as the US Marine Corps slogan *gung ho*—a version of the Chinese for "work together."

On May 27, 1905, the Japanese Imperial Navy made history, using its twelve-inch guns imported from England to battle the czar. It would prove a field test of the new battleships' value and would echo, in detail upon detail, with another historic battle—that of December 7, 1941. Russia and Japan were then competing in imperial designs on China and Korea—Japan wanted natural resources, and Russia yearned for a warm-water Pacific base for both defense and trade, to complement its seasonal port at Vladivostok. Japan offered to settle their quarrels by splitting the difference, giving Russia preeminence in Manchuria if Japan was given free rein in Korea. Moscow, knowing her navy was far more powerful than Tokyo's, refused, and Tokyo interpreted this bellicosity as a threat. On the night of February 8, 1904, an Imperial Japanese squadron of destroyers launched a surprise attack against the Russian fleet at Manchuria's Port Arthur. Two days after, Japan declared war, and by May, Japanese army troops were invading the peninsula. Russia massed her own troops across the Trans-Siberian Railway and, on October 15, sent five divisions of her Baltic Fleet around the Cape of Good Hope to Vladivostok through the strait that lay between Korea and Japan—Tsushima.

On the night of May 26, 1905, Russia's Second Pacific Squadron entered these narrows, camouflaged by heavy fog. In the dark murk, hospital ship *Oryol* came across an auxiliary cruiser, and the two vessels signaled their identities to each other, with *Oryol* helpfully adding that other Russian ships were nearby. But the cruiser was not Russian, but Japanese, and in one of the first uses of wireless radio in a naval clash, the ship cabled her commander and Mutsuhito's mentor, Admiral Heihachiro Togo, "Enemy is in square 203." By 0500, the Russians in turn had intercepted the Japanese messages and knew they had been discovered.

Togo would now risk forty ships—nearly the whole of Japan's navy—in this one-throw-of-the-dice battle. He wrote a message to the naval ministry, which would echo through Japanese military history for its daring confidence and lace of sangfroid: "In response to the warning that enemy ships have been sighted, the Combined Fleet will immediately commence action and attempt to attack and destroy them. Weather today fine but high waves." At 1355, the admiral ordered a Z flag to rise, which signaled to his crew, "The Empire's fate depends on the result of this battle. Let every man do his utmost duty."

If Togo's first great asset was his nerve, the second was his fleet's radio, as he described this technological miracle: "Though a heavy fog covered the sea, making it impossible to observe anything at a distance of over five miles, [through radio reports] all the conditions of the enemy were as clear to us, who were thirty or forty miles distant, as though they had been under our very eyes." A third asset was that the Russians had trawled eighteen thousand miles to war, but hadn't been able to maintain their ships' power systems along the way, and their speeds were now greatly reduced, and a fourth was that, because of his attack on Port Arthur, Togo was the world's only admiral with dreadnought experience in an actual engagement. But perhaps the greatest asset of all for the Japanese was that all of these advantages united into Togo's perfect execution of one of the great naval strategies of all time, which he executed twice at Tsushima: crossing the T.

For three hours, beginning at 2000, Togo sent twenty-one destroyers and thirty-seven torpedo boats to continually barrage the Russian fleet from every direction. While the enemy's attentions were focused on defending itself, Togo then turned his battleships, one by one, so they were broadside, facing the front line of Russia's navy, enabling the whole of Japan's aquatic arsenal to be used against Russia, while only Russia's forward guns could be fired against Japan. In a mere ninety minutes, *Oslyabya* became history's first armored battleship to be sunk by gunfire alone, with Commander Vladimir Semenoff reporting "The steel plates and superstructure on the upper decks were torn to pieces, and the splinters caused many casualties. Iron ladders were crumpled up into rings, guns were literally hurled from their mountings. In addition to this, there was the unusually high temperature and liquid flame of the explosion, which seemed to spread over everything. I actually watched a steel plate catch fire from a burst."

The six remaining Russian ships were ordered to give up. They raised XGE flags, international codes for surrender, but the Japanese didn't recognize those and kept firing. The Russians then raised white tablecloths up their flagpoles, but Togo had lost a ship eleven years before to Chinese sailors using a white flag as a ruse, and the Japanese kept firing. Finally, the Russians stopped their motors dead in the water and raised Japanese naval flags up their mastheads to signal their complete and unconditional surrender.

For the first time in modern history, an Asian nation had devastated a European navy. The czar's flagship was lost, as were all of Russia's battleships, most of its cruisers and destroyers, and 4,380 sailors.

In victory, however, Togo retained his grace. Visiting his counterpart, the gravely wounded Admiral Rozhestvensky, Togo offered a kindness, insisting, "Defeat is a common fate of a soldier. There is nothing to be ashamed of in it. The great point is whether we have performed our duty." In decades to come, Togo would be so revered that, even among the Japanese immigrants working in Hawaii, a brand of sake was named for the admiral and labeled with his portrait.

Some historians theorize that Russians' discontent with the Romanov military disaster at Tsushima was a major impetus for their revolution, and the consensus is that, with this one battle, Japan vaulted herself into the league of global powers. However, British historian Geoffrey Regan posited that Tsushima had unforeseen consequences, creating "a legend that was to haunt Japan's leaders for forty years [when] victory over one of the world's great powers convinced some Japanese military men that with more ships, and bigger and better ones, similar victories could be won throughout the Pacific. Perhaps no power could resist the Japanese navy, not even Britain and the United States."

Aboard one of those torpedo boats attacking the Russian fleet in the fogs of Tsushima was a twenty-one-year-old, five-foot-three-inch-tall ensign who would in years to come be the most studied Japanese man in American history. Isoroku, which means "5-10-6," was the son of schoolteacher Teikichi Takano, who was fifty-six years old at the time of his sixth son's birth. As was tradition in Japan for the lucky, the child was in time adopted by a wealthy family and grew to become the great military visionary Admiral Isoroku Yamamoto, who would remember the triumph of Tsushima for the rest of his life, as his abdomen was scarred with its shrapnel, and the second and third fingers of his left hand had to be amputated, leading Tokyo geishas to nickname him Eighty Sen (a manicure then cost one hundred sen). They knew him well, for the admiral had a decade-long love affair with the remarkable temptress Plum Dragon, to whom he wrote letters of transforming passion. Yamamoto would call his attack on Pearl Harbor Operation Z and would order Togo's Z flag raised at the time of battle to remind his men of their victorious heritage. Like Roosevelt decades later, Yamamoto was determined to never let his handicap hold him back. He insisted on no special treatment in the service, trained himself to play catch with his son using the three-fingered hand, and perhaps, like Roosevelt, his difference from others inspired him to new ideas.

When Emperor Meiji died in 1912—the same year that Tokyo's mayor gave America's capital city her Tidal Basin's voluptuous cherry trees, their petals so quick to fall—his rule had lasted forty-five years, longer than even that of Queen Elizabeth I. As a child, his country was feudal and backward; now, it had all the hallmarks of a modern nation: universities; rail transit; even a national post office. But his greatest achievement, Mutsuhito believed, was his modernization of the country's armed forces.

After her victory over Russia at Tsushima, Japan expected a treasure of concessions. Instead, the peace treaty arbitrated by Theodore Roosevelt (who won the Nobel Peace Prize for his efforts) offended the winners when they didn't get the reparations payments or Manchurian territory they'd expected. This was followed by the post–Great War Washington Naval Conference of 1922, a treaty which forced Tokyo to accept a 10:10:6 ratio of US:UK:Japan tonnage for battleships and aircraft carriers. Many Japanese officials considered this concession proof that their country would never be considered an equal by Britain and America, whom they called the Anglo-Saxons. With the treaty's conclusion, chief naval adviser Kanji Kato was seen sobbing and shouting, "As far as I am concerned, war with America starts now. We'll get our revenge over this, by God!" The day after the Pearl Harbor attack, Japan's home minister, Admiral Nobumasa Suetsugu, said the carnage in Hawaii had been birthed in 1922: "Ever since the ten:six ratio was imposed by the Washington treaty, we have endured unspeakable drills for over twenty years, and today we must say these drills produced a wonderful result. Furthermore we may say that these drills and pent-up resentment exploded today to produce this success." One of the attack's architects, Minoru Genda, explained that 1922's limitations produced the technological innovations that would make December 7 a triumph: "Throughout the history of Japanese naval aviation, the prevailing philosophy was to emphasize attack, particularly by torpedoes. . . . We introduced dive-bombing and found it to be highly destructive and superior as a method of surprise attack. It also enabled us to put more stress than previously on the offensive potential of carrier planes."

In 1922, the US Supreme Court ruled that Japanese immigrants could not become American citizens and, the following year, held as constitutional a ban against Japanese owning American real estate—at a time when Japanese immigrant farmers were producing 10 percent of California's produce on 1 percent of its farmland. In 1924, after Congress imposed national immigration quotas, with a quota for Japan of zero, fifteen Tokyo newspapers attacked the Americans' insulting behavior, and soon after, the Japanese Army and Navy General Staff's Imperial National Defense Policy appointed the United States as enemy number one.

At the same time that Japan felt disrespected by Americans and Europeans, she saw herself encircled by their colonies. Hong Kong, the Malay Peninsula, Singapore, and a part of Shanghai were British; China's Shantung Province was German; another district of Shanghai was French; the Dutch had their vast East Indies holdings; Hawaii, Midway, Guam, and the Philippines were American; and even the Russians were moving into Manchuria and the Liaotung Peninsula. In the years before Pearl Harbor, Japan's leaders would continue to complain of this foreign encirclement, even though after victory in the Great War, Tokyo was awarded the German possessions of Tsingtao, the Marianas, the Carolinas, and the Marshall Islands, while her own military successes brought her Korea, Taiwan, Sakhalin, the Ryukyus, the Bonins, the Pescadores, and the Kuril Islands; as well as parts of Manchuria. Long before 1931's start of the Great East Asia War (what the Japanese call World War II), she was on her way to empire.

In 1925, *London Daily Telegraph* naval correspondent Hector C. Bywater published *The Great Pacific War*, reviewed by the *New York Times Book Review* on its front page with the headline "If War Comes in the Pacific." Bywater's novel described a Japanese surprise attack on the American fleet in Pearl Harbor, with simultaneous assaults on Guam, and on the Philippines at Lingayen Gulf and Lamon Bay. Though no paper trail ties this novel to Japanese military strategy, it predicted exactly what would happen in the closing weeks of 1941. An additional quirk of the Bywater coincidence is that one of the architects of the Pearl Harbor attack, Isoroku Yamamoto, was serving as a naval attaché in the United States when *The Great Pacific War* was published.

Until that moment, Yamamoto's life had paralleled in lockstep that of another historic Japanese figure of the era, General Hideki Tojo. In World War II American eyes, Yamamoto and Tojo would become Asian Adolf Hitlers. *Time* magazine's cover of December 22, 1941, called Yamamoto "Japan's Aggressor," portraying the admiral as sinister and treacherous, with slitted eyes and yellowed skin, while highlighting his boast to "dictate the terms of peace in the White House." That boast was, in fact, made to try to talk the Japanese out of going to war with the United States, as Yamamoto was so in favor of Tokyo's remaining friendly with Washington that he would repeatedly be targeted for assassination by ultranationalist fascists.

Both Yamamoto and Tojo were born in 1884 in their country's northern provinces to families descended from samurai, and both were rewarded for their hard work and dedication in the armed forces with foreign postings, the army flying Tojo to Berlin, and the navy sailing Yamamoto to Washington. With those foreign educations, however, the similarities ended. The admiral was confident, charismatic, fun loving, with a nearly childlike enthusiasm about the world, and utterly inspirational to his subordinates, breaking the formalities of Japanese tradition with games of *shogi*, poker, and bridge. He did not drink, but loved women and gambling, the latter for high stakes. He was rumored to have won so much playing roulette in Monte Carlo that he was forbidden from ever returning to its great casino, and one of his closest staff officers remembered, "In all games Yamamoto loved to take chances just as he did in naval strategy. He had a gambler's heart."

During his years in America, the young officer traveled the country on his naval stipend, staying in fleabag hotels and skipping meals, becoming such a devotee of Abraham Lincoln that he struggled with his rough command of English through presidential biographies to further understand someone who rose from rural poverty to become Yamamoto's highest ideal—"a champion [of] human freedom." As commander, Yamamoto regularly urged his staff to read Carl Sandburg's life of Lincoln to improve their English.

At this time, both Japanese and American military chiefs were wholly convinced that their nations' great Pacific conflict would be waged according to the groundbreaking turn-of-the-century battle theories of an American Civil War lieutenant who had avoided as much naval duty as possible, since he found steamships unpleasant. To write *The Influence of Sea Power upon History, 1660–1783*, Alfred Thayer Mahan had extensively studied the nineteenth-century navies of Britain and France and decided that a navy was the most important engine of both national defense and global stature for any country, with "command of the sea . . . attained by the defeat of the enemy's fleet in a decisive battle, after which the enemy's coast and ports would be subject to blockade and perhaps invasion." Mahan urged America to acquire Hawaii to curb Japanese territorial aggression.

American leaders so believed in a decisive battle won by state-of-the-art battleships that Theodore Roosevelt gave *The Influence of Sea Power upon History* to his navy-loving cousin Franklin for the lad's fifteenth birthday in 1897. As Japan had won her wars against Russia and China with decisive Mahanian battles, her admirals became his biggest acolytes, with more of his works translated into Japanese than any other language. After the forced reduction in their capital ships from 1922, the Japanese dramatically improved their carrier and submarine technologies and created a Mahan-inspired war plan—the Kantai Kessen—the decisive battle. If the United States tried to sail a great fleet in the Pacific, Tokyo's submarines would decimate it as it traveled west, and planes from her bases on her League of Nations mandate islands would attack it from the air. Finally, her main naval warships would utterly defeat it in Japan's home waters.

During his eight years (1919–27) as an attaché in America, however, Isoroku Yamamoto came under the spell of the gospel of air power as taught by the great visionary Brigadier General William Mitchell. A decorated commander of America's pilots defending the skies of France in the Great War, General Mitchell convinced Congress to let him run tests against a flotilla of targets captured from the kaiser, including submarine *U-117*, destroyer *G-102*, light cruiser *Frankfurt*, and battleship *Ostfriesland*. After Mitchell's air crews struck the battleship with six two-thousand-pound bombs, it was sunk in a mere twenty minutes.

While America's generals and admirals sputtered about how this test didn't reflect real-world battle conditions, Mitchell biographer Alfred Hurley noted a "basic fact which deeply impressed itself on the public's mind. Mitchell had sunk a battleship, as he claimed he could." When Congress then asked why the Department of War was still pursing expensive battleships instead of inexpensive planes, the Joint Army Navy Board, created to squelch the constant interservice rivalries of American defense forces, issued a report signed by General Pershing that concluded: "The Battleship is still the backbone of the fleet and the nation's defenses." Three years later, Mitchell testified before the House Select Committee of Inquiry into Operations for the United States Air Service, "It is a very serious question whether airpower is auxiliary to the army and the navy, or whether armies and navies are not actually auxiliary to airpower." These outspoken declarations enraged his superiors, and in March 1925, he was demoted. But Mitchell would not be deterred from his great dream; when the end of that year brought two naval air disasters, he returned to the newspapers, claiming the Navy and War Departments were suffering from "incompetency, criminal negligence and almost treasonable administration of the National Defense." In October 1925, the War Department court-martialed Billy Mitchell, and he resigned from the service.

Regardless of this turn of events, Yamamoto and his colleague at Japan's naval air command Admiral Shigeyoshi Inoue became proselytizers of such Mitchell nostrums as "with the advent of aircraft, the battleship has become window dressing, [for] he who commands the air commands the sea." They essentially came to believe that the navy should turn itself into a floating air force, with Inoue predicting that if Japan controlled the skies of the Pacific, the United States could not attack it, and that a naval contest between the two nations would focus on the islands stretching from Hawaii to Malaysia that were big enough for airstrips. His predictions came true, for after Pearl Harbor, Japan didn't control her airways, the United States attacked, and World War II's Pacific theater focused on islands big enough for airstrips stretching from Hawaii to Malaysia.

On his return to Tokyo from Washington in 1927, Yamamoto tried to warn his nation's militant fascists that they were underestimating the United States: "Anyone who has seen the auto factories in Detroit and the oil fields in Texas knows that Japan lacks the national power for a naval race with America." After being promoted to admiral, Isoroku Yamamoto would publicly belittle his superiors' prized superdreadnoughts *Yamato* and *Musashi*, calling them "as useful as a samurai sword," and relentlessly criticize his superiors' beloved strategy of Kantai Kessen. When Yamamoto was then promoted to vice minster of the navy, it became publicly known he was a member of the service's moderate "treaty faction," which considered war a last instead of a first resort. Called an Anglo-Saxon "running dog" by the fascists, Yamamoto was threatened with punishment "on heaven's behalf." A bounty was offered for his murder, and a terrorist scheme to blow up a bridge as he crossed it was uncovered. During the whole of his tenure in the ministry, Yamamoto's residence had to be patrolled by armed guards.

One of the great architects of Pearl Harbor was thus the Japanese leader least enthusiastic about war with America. His position stood out, for across the first decades of the twentieth century the two countries' armed forces had regularly planned to attack each other. Along with the Panama Canal Zone, Oahu became America's most significant post–Great War foreign military base. The navy spent about $75 million a year in Hawaii, and the army more than $150 million, eventually making the Oahu garrison its largest and, for the most part, its best equipped.

In 1936, the Japanese Navy War College published "Study of Strategy and Tactics in Operations against the United States," which noted, "In case the enemy's main fleet is berthed at Pearl Harbor, the idea should be to open hostilities by surprise attacks from the air." From February 1 to 14, 1932, the Americans' Grand Joint Exercise Number Four war games simulated the US navy attacking Hawaii with the islands defended by the army, notably her Air Corps. With an assault beginning at dawn on Sunday, February 7, the navy achieved complete surprise and won the game easily. Admiral Arthur Radford remembered, "The general nature of the exercise was pretty well publicized [and] apparently, the Japanese read all this publicity in great detail. Their attack on Pearl Harbor, which came within two months of being exactly ten years later, was almost a perfect duplicate."

On January 10, 1938, Colonel Edward Markham completed his survey of Hawaiian military strength for the War Department that concluded, "War with Japan will be precipitated without notice. One of the most obvious and vital lessons of history is that Japan will pick her own time for conflict. The very form of its government lends itself to such action in that its military and naval forces can, under the pretext of an emergency, initiate and prosecute military and naval operations independently of civil control. . . . If and when hostilities develop between the United States and Japan, there can be little doubt that the Hawaiian Islands will be the initial scene of action, and that Japan will apply her available man-power and resources in powerful and determined attacks against these islands."

How could nations with such long traditions of culture and civility as Japan and Germany fall under the sway of fascist thugs? Is civilization so light and so precarious that it can be tossed off like an old sweater? The stories of both nations' fall began in social chaos. When the Great Depression surged, and with it many countries' shortsighted fix of stringent import tariffs, Japan found itself in an especially sorry state. She couldn't sell her products, notably silk, to other nations, and she soon enough couldn't afford to buy anything, either—notably petroleum. By 1932, as around 20 million Germans faced starvation, four-fifths of Japan's college graduates were unemployed, and its rural population suffered such constant crop failure that rice—the signature foodstuff of the nation—had to be rationed and could only be bought with coupons, leading to such endemic poverty that daughters were sold into brothels, and sons believed, like the samurai *shishi* from the great era of Meiji, that their nation required revolutionary political change. The most successful of those rural sons ended up in the Imperial Japanese Army and Navy, where exactly that revolution could be wrought. As historian Donald Goldstein commented, "In the 1920s and 30s, the best and brightest in America didn't go into the military. But in Japan, to be in the military was the best that one could do."

Just as Meiji's father had fallen to revolutionaries, so would his grandson Hirohito be beset by radical militarists who wanted to forge a new nation, Dai Nippon Teikoku—the Great Empire of Japan. In October 1921, four officers known as "the pillars of the army" met in the Black Forest resort of Baden-Baden to secretly engineer a pact. This group, which would be known as the ruthlessly pragmatic Control Faction, would radically reorganize the management and personnel of the Imperial Japanese Army. In their great dream, Japan would be purged of corrupt politicians and business interests, and its people would be led by the divine presence, the emperor, wholly supported by a vast army without rules, a fighting force whose generals would be key figures in the nation's political life, and whose troops were always ready for total war. One founding father of the Control Faction was a main backer of the ultranationalistic terrorist group Imperial Way, and another was the man who would one day lead his country into World War II: Hideki Tojo.

On June 4, 1928, Manchurian warlord Marshal Chang Tso-lin was traveling by rail through the Kwantung Peninsula, a sliver of Chinese land won by Japan after its 1905 victory over Russia as negotiated by Teddy Roosevelt. A bomb exploded on the train, and the warlord was assassinated. On September 18, 1931, another explosion struck the same Japanese railway. Blaming these attacks on Chinese rebels, troops of Japan's Kwantung Army—a regiment that defended the protectorate's bureaucrats, expatriates, and businesses—invaded the town of Mukden. They were ordered to withdraw by their Tokyo commanders, but instead, under "insubordination in service to the nation," within five months they took over all of Manchuria, turning it into a colony, providing Japan with such key commodities as iron, coal, and rice, as well as serving as a buffer against Russia.

Though Japanese newspaper editors knew full well that both railroad bombs were detonated by Kwantung Army troops, they watched their circulations soar with such headlines as "Our Army Heroically Marches from Changchun to Jilin" and "Our Imperial Army Charges into Qiqihar, Its Great Spirit Piercing through the Sky!" On March 1, 1932, Japan officially renamed Manchuria Manchukuo, and in time, half a million Japanese immigrants would settle there, with the "last emperor" of China, Pu Yi, installed as the colony's governor.

On January 28, 1932, a Chinese mob attacked five Japanese Buddhist priests in Shanghai, killing one. The Kwantung retaliated by bombing the city, killing hundreds of thousands. That same year in Tokyo, a group of army and navy cadets loyal to the Kwantung assassinated the "corrupted" leaders who had opposed the invasion of Manchuria, including the prime minister, the finance minister, and the chief of military affairs.

The Imperial Japanese Army's legendary brutality began at this time, with the Kwantung's training of green recruits. From his days in Manchukuo, Second Lieutenant Shozo Tominaga remembered, "We planned exercises for these men. As the last stage of their training, we made them bayonet a living human. Prisoners were blindfolded and tied to poles. The soldiers dashed forward to bayonet their target at the shout of 'Charge!' Some stopped on their way. We kicked them and made them do it. After that, a man could do anything easily. The army created men capable of combat. . . . Human beings turned into murdering demons. Everyone became a demon within three months. Men were able to fight courageously only when their human characteristics were suppressed."

The Japanese public, meanwhile, wouldn't know the truth about their military's overseas machinations for fifteen years.

Across this decade, the US ambassador to Japan was the exceedingly temperate and insightful Joseph Grew, a Boston Brahmin. He had, like Franklin Roosevelt and Assistant Secretary of State Sumner Welles, attended Groton and Harvard and was a member of Washington's cosmopolitan internationalist wing, believing that the United

States needed to stop isolating itself between the Atlantic and Pacific Oceans and wholly engage with the community of nations for both commercial and defensive gain. Joseph Grew had served as ambassador to Denmark, to Switzerland, and to Turkey, but after eight years in Japan, he and his wife, Alice—a grandniece to Commodore Matthew Perry and fluent in Japanese—had ascended to the peaks of Tokyo society. Ambassador Grew had developed deep insights into the complications of Japanese politics, insights that were wholly ignored by Washington.

On August 13, 1932, Grew sent a memorandum to Secretary of State Henry Stimson on Japan's Chinese aggressions, which included, "This situation reminds me strongly of the efforts of the German Government, by calumniating foreign nations, to build up a public war psychology in 1914, the effort being repeated whenever some new venture, such as the indiscriminate submarine warfare, was about to be launched. Here in Japan the deliberate building up of public animosity against foreign nations in general and the United States in particular has doubtless a similar purpose—to strengthen the hand of the military in its Manchurian venture in the face of foreign, and especially American, opposition. I believe that on the part of the Japanese it is a sign of weakness, not of strength. The internal economic and financial situation in Japan is serious and may become desperate. The plight of the farmers is very bad, many industries are at low ebb, unemployment is steadily increasing. . . . Such a national temper is always dangerous. The German military machine, supported by a carefully nurtured public war psychology, took the bit in its teeth and overrode all restraining influences in 1914. The Japanese military machine is not dissimilar. It has been built for war, feels prepared for war and would welcome war. It has never yet been beaten and possesses unlimited self confidence. I am not an alarmist but I believe that we should have our eyes open to all possible future contingencies. The facts of history would render it criminal to close them."

Grew's boss had an more hawkish view. President Herbert Hoover had declared a new American doctrine on August 11—"That we do not and never will recognize title to possession of territory gained in violation of the peace pacts"—a policy drafted by his secretary of state, Henry Stimson. This policy's ensuing categorical refusal by Washington to accept any Japanese government in China would be known as the Stimson Doctrine. In Japan's view, the Stimson Doctrine was pure hypocrisy, since America's own Pacific territories were acquired by force. When Hoover lost to Roosevelt in 1932, Stimson joined FDR's cabinet as secretary of war, a position he'd also held under William Howard Taft, and the Stimson Doctrine continued as such a key tenet of America's Asian foreign policy that it led directly to Pearl Harbor.

On February 24, 1933, delegates of the forty-member League of Nations met on the shore of Lake Geneva in Switzerland's Palais Wilson to consider Japan's Manchurian expeditions. The League voted 42–1 that Japan should withdraw its armies and return sovereignty to the Chinese, the one opposing vote being Japan's. The head of her delegation, Yosuke Matsuoka, then approached the podium. As a child, Matsuoka's family was too poor to support him, so at the age of thirteen he became a ward of Methodist missionaries in Portland, Oregon. There he would be called Frank and work as a farmhand, janitor, busboy, rail worker, and substitute pastor, escaping destitution but facing racial prejudice. He would rise to become vice president of the South Manchurian Railway Company and then foreign minister of Japan, where he would in time try to create a new political party in the style of Mussolini's Fascists and would engineer the Tripartite Pact uniting Tokyo with Berlin and Rome into the Axis powers. All the same, in 1938 Matsuoka would rescue Jewish refugees with a safe harbor in Japanese-controlled Shanghai.

On that evening at the Palais Wilson, Matsuoka in his trim white tie and tails, with a mustache notably similar to Hitler's, announced that Japan, which had been one of the League of Nation's Big Five framers and which had contributed more than its share of financial and diplomatic support, would quit the League. Matsuoka privately disagreed with Tokyo's order to exit but on coming home, he discovered that his spirited declaration in Switzerland had made him a national hero as a man who had stood up to the racist and arrogant West. Exiting the League, however, also meant losing a restraint that the civilian government held over her military forces. With no global organization castigating the Japanese for their war crimes in Asia, the Imperial Japanese Army was unleashed to conquer an empire, and the fascist revolution was reignited.

In February 1936, a cadre of fifteen hundred servicemen assassinated the nation's finance minister, the lord keeper of the privy seal, and the prime minster's brother-in-law by mistake; they were trying to kill the prime minister. The terrorists stormed and occupied the War Ministry and Diet buildings, forcing legislators to flee for their lives, and published a manifesto: "The national essence of Japan, as a land of the gods, exists in the fact that the Emperor reigns with undiminished power from time immemorial into the farthest future in order that the natural beauty of the country may be propagated throughout the universe, so that all men under the sun may be able to enjoy their lives to the fullest extent. . . . In recent years, however, there have appeared many persons whose chief aim and purpose have been to amass personal material wealth, disregarding the general welfare and prosperity of the Japanese people, with the result that the sovereignty of the Emperor has been greatly impaired. . . . The senior statesmen, military cliques, plutocrats, bureaucrats, and political parties are all traitors who are destroying the national essence."

These rebels were quickly surrounded, taken into custody, tried, and executed. Even so, many in the press and the public revered their "selfless" acts. The public reaction meant the Japanese government had fallen beneath the thumb of extremists who could blackmail with threats of assassination and coup d'état. The nation's military now believed it could defeat any enemy, while its populace as a whole came to believe in *kokutai*, the idea that the Japanese were a unique race with a unique culture governed directly by a godlike emperor. Starting in 1936, the nation's secret police could imprison those acting contrary to *kokutai* with that year's Law for Protection against and Surveillance of the Holders of Dangerous Thoughts.

Outsiders learning of *kokutai* and *tenno heika banzai*—"long live the emperor"—would understandably think that Japan's head of state was divine and his rule, absolute, especially considering the sacred talismans accompanying the Chrysanthemum Throne—the sword, the jewel, and the mirror, representing courage, benevolence, and wisdom— bequeathed at the dawn of Japanese society from the Sun Goddess to her grandson, the first emperor, for his descent to the earth. In reality, after her legislature, military leaders, prime minister, and cabinet had agreed on government policy, it was both tradition and expectation that Japan's emperor had to concur; the consensus policy was then revealed to the nation as his personal decision.

When he was crown prince, Hirohito's tutor for ten years impressed on his charge the principle that meddling in politics would damage the imperial family's reputation and its unique and lofty position as the spiritual embodiment of the Japanese race. Crippled by this tradition and by his own social awkwardness, as ruler Hirohito disliked, in turn, nearly every one of his generals, admirals, ministers, and advisers. Emperor Showa wanted to be a marine biologist, not a monarch; he liked whiskey more than sake, listened to Western classical music, and loved golf. His face was covered in moles, which to the Japanese signified good luck, but Hirohito was also a notorious tightwad, using pencils to their nubs, and wandering the palace grounds in ragged clothes with buttons fastened in the wrong places. All of this resulted in a leader who would only speak his opinions in the vaguest of terms. Subordinates had to interpret his cryptic, expressionless utterances, which usually took the form of poetry, or quotations from his ancestors. This vague lack of command allowed military hard-liners to do exactly as they wished, all in the name of the emperor . . . and yet Hirohito had faced assassination attempts in both 1923 and 1932.

On November 25, 1936, Japan and Germany signed the Anti-Comintern Pact, joining together to fight the menace of communism. Though Grew reported to Washington that Japan's foreign office had categorically denied any military element to this agreement, many in the diplomatic community knew that Japanese and Nazi officers had come to a secret understanding. The Japanese navy, however, was still pro-Anglo-Saxon. Naval air visionary Shigeyoshi Inoue read Hitler's *Mein Kampf* in German and was shocked to see that its anti-Asian and anti-Japanese diatribes had been left out of the Japanese translation.

On July 7, 1937, Chinese and Japanese soldiers were practicing maneuvers near the Marco Polo (Lugou) Bridge in Tientsin near Peking. Shots were fired. On the morning of July 8 a Japanese officer was discovered missing. Truce negotiations were begun, but then, more shots were fired—by whom is unclear. The Japanese thought it was a plot by Communist agents, while the Chinese believed that the Japanese were triggering incidents similar to the Manchurian railway bombings. Sporadic, chaotic, incidental skirmishes turned into battles, and both Peking and the port of Tientsin fell into Japanese hands.

Many Japanese leaders saw their imperial ambitions as mirroring not the path of Germany, but of the United States, echoing in 1823's Monroe Doctrine, which declared that any attempts to colonize the western hemisphere would be considered hostile by the United States and be countered by American military action. Japan's "Asia for Asians and Japan above all" philosophy began that same year with political scientist Sato Nobuhiro's *Kondo Hisaku (A Secret Strategy for Expansion)*, which held that "Japan is the foundation of the world" and described how the conquest of Manchuria and then the whole of China would begin Japan's inexorable process of making the rest of the globe her "provinces and districts." In the 1920s, politician Kijuro Shidehara explained this philosophy of *hakko ichiu*—"bringing the eight corners of the world under one roof"—as "the four races of Japan, China, Korea, and Manchuria will share a common prosperity through a division of responsibilities: Japanese, political leadership and large industry; Chinese, labor and small industry; Koreans, rice; and Manchus, animal husbandry." Then in the same year that Teddy Roosevelt brought peace to Moscow and Tokyo with the treaty that embittered so many Japanese, he suggested to his Harvard classmate, reporter Kentaro Kaneko, that Japan should pursue her own version of the Monroe Doctrine. In the 1930s, junior officers in the navy and army passed around the demagogue Ikki Kita's pamphlet "A General Outline of Measures for the Reconstruction of Japan," which explained, "Seven hundred million brethren in India and China cannot gain their independence without our protection and leadership. . . . The only possible international peace, which will come after the present age of international wars, must be a feudal peace. This will be achieved through the emergence of the strongest country, which will dominate all other nationals of the world."

In the World War II era, Japan would use this version of Monroe to justify her military aggression in Asia and its name—the Greater East Asia Co-Prosperity Sphere—would come from the man who'd walked out of the League of Nations and who was now the nation's foreign minister, Yosuke Matsuoka. On December 23, 1935, a key official of the foreign office, Saburo Kurusu—who will appear again in this story, as he will arrive in Washington as the crisis between America and Japan escalates—met with American consular staff in Tokyo and explained this new thinking. He said that Great Britain was degenerating and that the Soviet Union was a bunch of dreamers who would never amount to anything, leaving one power in the West: the United States. Japan's fate was to be the leader of an oriental civilization—the "boss of China, India, the Netherlands East Indies, etc."—as the

United States would become the leader of the occidental civilization. And, he insisted, these two great new world powers must never fight. That would be suicide.

If it is difficult for Americans today to imagine 1930s Japanese as enemies, it is just as hard to imagine 1930s Chinese as our closest friends. In fact, a 1938 poll revealed that 80 percent of Americans considered the Chinese to be their natural allies in the fight against global fascism, versus 40 percent who thought of the British in that way. For decades, US missionaries had crossed China seeking converts to Christianity in a campaign financed by children's donations, similar to the March of Dimes. This vast network of Christian missionaries and their stateside fund-raising endeavors resolutely portrayed the country as a hardworking and earnest little brother trying to follow in America's democratic footsteps. China's American proselytizers included media baron (and child of American missionaries preaching in China) Henry Luce and bestselling Nobel laureate Pearl S. Buck. Luce's coverage of Chinese resistance to Japan's brutal invasion in *Time*, *Life*, and *Look* rang with analogies to Americans fighting for their own freedom in the Revolutionary War, while American newsreels, projected before the entertainment in movie theaters, showed Japanese airmen—their padded cotton helmets and full-face goggles making them look more like robots than people—gleefully strafing rice paddies and water buffalo while vicious soldiers on the ground manhandled defenseless Chinese peasants and set their meager daub-and-straw dwellings on fire. The Depression-era American public was dazzled by the alluring Soong sisters, Madame Chiang (wife to the current leader, Chiang Kai-shek), and Madame Sun (wife to the father of the nation, Sun Yat-sen), and so loved China that the first US paperback book, test-marketed by Pocket in 1938, was Buck's three-hankie weeper of striving Chinese peasants and devious landlords, *The Good Earth*. Yet this unswerving dedication to the Chinese baffled any number of American officials who found no reason for it besides a moral high ground. "We have large emotional interest in China, small economic interest, and no vital interests," a perplexed US ambassador to France, William Christian Bullitt, pointed out to Roosevelt.

As highly as Americans regarded China at this time, they held Japan in low regard, thinking them slow brained, irrational, primitive, neurotic, compulsive, and mechanically incompetent, with inner-ear defects, extreme nearsightedness, and buckteeth—racially inferior. A significant element in the surprise at Pearl Harbor was the great number of Americans who couldn't conceive of Japan successfully attacking the United States. The most influential Asianist in the American State Department was a man who'd spent five years teaching in China before being named consul general to a city at the heart of Japanese aggression: Mukden. Stanley Hornbeck insisted that no matter what Washington demanded of Tokyo, the timid Japanese would never attack. When, as late as November 23, 1941, Foreign Service officer John K. Emmerson returned to Washington from a Tokyo posting to tell Hornbeck that if the United States kept pushing Japan into a corner, her militarists would insist on fighting, Hornbeck insouciantly replied, "Tell me of one case in history when a nation went to war out of desperation." In fact, nearly this exact phrase had appeared in an October 7, 1941, letter from Yasaka Takagi to Joseph Grew, which Grew had forwarded to State: "The danger of war is by far the greatest . . . when [Japan] feels, rightly or wrongly, that she is driven into a corner, and, therefore, desperately strikes back defying consequences." Hornbeck's hard stance was mirrored by FDR's secretary of war Henry Stimson, who insisted that he understood "the Oriental mind" from his experience as governor-general of the Philippines. Stimson advised, "To get on with Japan, one had to treat her rough, unlike other countries."

Five decades after December 7 and eight years before 9/11, Central Intelligence Agency analyst A. R. Northridge summarized these attitudes in a September 22, 1993, Pearl Harbor report: "It seems clear to me that we failed to foresee the Japanese assault largely because we were influenced by a faulty stereotype of what was an adversary nation. Today, progress in the arts of weaponry and technical intelligence collection make unlikely another Pearl Harbor kind of surprise attack, but the faulty stereotypes that can lead to grave miscalculation of an adversary's capability and intent remain with us, almost as a human condition. . . . What sort of people did Americans, at the time of Pearl Harbor, believe the Japanese to be, and what did they believe about Japanese intentions toward themselves? . . . 'The Japanese people, given the conflicts of interest between us, will quite likely—or maybe only possibly—do us a mischief if they can; but they lack the capacity to harm us seriously, and they know that this is so. On the other hand, they are so cultivated and mannerly that it really is, after all, inconceivable that they would even try to harm us.'"

The Japanese, meanwhile, shared this cultural and racial blindness.

As historian Donald Goldstein described it, while Americans viewed the Japanese as "at a lower order of the human evolution, the Japanese saw the Americans ironically almost in the same light. To the Japanese, the Americans were not pure. Their view was what they saw in the motion pictures. The Americans to them were gangsters and bums and prostitutes." The Japanese also believed the United States was a nation governed of the rich, by the rich, and for the rich. Colonel Masanobu Tsuji, the member of the Control Faction who will plan his country's astounding 1941 military assault on Southeast Asia (including Pearl Harbor), Operation Number One, assumed, like many of his fellow officers, that the Great East Asia War would end quickly with Japan's victory: "Our candid ideas at the time were that the Americans, being merchants, would not continue for long with an unprofitable war."

For thirteen years, American leaders met for cocktails each twilight at the White House's library office, the drinks made badly by Roosevelt himself from a wet bar on wheels. This second-floor room next to the elevator included a card table for FDR's solitaire game of Miss Milligin, shelves for his stamp collection, and practically a museum's-worth collection of paintings and carvings of schooners, steamboats, dreadnoughts, and barques. The conversation was limited to good jokes, great stories, and the latest gossip about everyone from Sonja Henie to Shirley Temple, since during the day that same room was the meeting ground for the men and women who ran the United States during what was likely its grimmest era.

Along with secretary of war Henry Stimson and presidential aide Harry Hopkins, the men who met daily in the White House library office included Roosevelt's military aide and appointments secretary, General Edwin "Pa" Watson; secretary of the navy Frank Knox; the chief of naval operations, Admiral Harold "Betty" Stark; the commander in chief of the US Fleet, Admiral Ernest J. "Ernie" King; the army air corps chief of staff, General Henry "Hap" Arnold; and the army chief of staff, General George Catlett Marshall. A more disparate band of headstrong individuals could only be found in the cabinet of Abraham Lincoln. While Roosevelt was constantly laughing and joking, waving his cigarette holder, his favorite reaction "I love it! I love it!," Marshall was notoriously humorless. Stimson said that listening to FDR "was very much like chasing a vagrant beam of sunshine around an empty room," while Marshall's conversation was marked by austerity and a need to cut to the quick. "Unsmiling and unbending, the tall, ramrod-straight general [Marshall], formal in manner and manners, was disciplined and organized, and was offended aesthetically by his commander in chief [Roosevelt], who was none of these things," noted biographer David Fromkin. "And he refused to laugh at the president's jokes."

On July 12, 1937, Roosevelt's secretary of state, Cordell Hull, lectured Japan's ambassador to Washington, Hiroshi Saito, that war was futile—as it damaged both the victor and the vanquished—so a first-class power such as Saito's could afford to exercise self-restraint while emphasizing trade and business, the keys to peace and prosperity, and one of Hull's Eight Pillars of Peace, a compilation he considered as significant as the Ten Commandments. Hull asked Saito if instead of squabbling over provinces in China, Japan would partner with the United States in leading the Pacific to a stable future of peace and prosperity through a program of amity similar to the Declaration of Principles of Inter-American Solidarity and Cooperation, which the nations of North and South America had negotiated at Buenos Aires in December 1936.

Secretary Hull was a log-cabin-born, sixty-nine-year-old Tennessee mountaineer who had been a circuit court judge, a congressman, and a senator, but though he'd spent decades in Washington and developed the hair of an éminence grise, he wasn't highly regarded; his plodding and his earnestness produced the nickname Parson Hull. Within the cabinet chain of command, Hull found himself repeatedly undercut by Roosevelt's playing favorites with Undersecretary Sumner Welles, and since the president was focused on Europe and considered Japan a sideshow—if Roosevelt bears any responsibility for Pearl Harbor, it is through this failing—the secretary was stuck in the thickets of Asian diplomacy. Hull also had a speech impediment, which amused his boss. "If Cordell says, 'Oh, Chwist,' I'm going to scream," FDR told Frances Perkins. "I can't stand profanity with a lisp."

At times stubborn, willful, thin-skinned, and hot tempered, the American secretary of state conducting negotiations with Japan believed that Japanese cultural politeness bordered on criminal hypocrisy. Hull referred to Tokyo's envoys as "pissants" and described his Japanese counterpart, Foreign Minister Matsuoka, "as crooked as a bundle of fishhooks." Even so, Secretary Hull worked tirelessly and patiently trying to achieve a peaceful accord with Japan's fascists in order to, at the least, keep the United States out of any overseas conflict until her army and navy were ready to fight.

Instead of following Hull's suggestion on friendship, in August 1937 Japanese troops invaded Shanghai. Chinese resistance was strong, and it took four months for the Imperial Japanese Army to triumph. The Japanese then burned the town of Sung-chiang to the ground, killing 100,000 civilians, and slaughtered nearly the whole 350,000 population of ancient Suzhou on November 19. "Smoldering ruins and deserted streets present an eerie spectacle, the only living creatures being dogs unnaturally fattened by feasting on corpses," Manchester's *Guardian* reported.

Surging up the Yangtze River, the Imperial Japanese Army was by the second week of December assaulting Chiang's capital, Nanking. As the Chinese abandoned their homes and the last of the Americans were extricated from the city by embassy staff, the American gunboat *Panay* waited at anchor in Nanking harbor to escort the last of the US consulate to safety. After the evacuees boarded on December 11, *Panay* sailed upriver to avoid the barrage of gunfire.*

On December 12, Japanese pilots were ordered to attack "any and all ships" in the river above Nanking. Knowing *Panay* was there, the aviators asked for confirmation of the order. It was confirmed. For twenty minutes, the Japanese bombed and strafed the American gunboat, injuring the captain and several others. Finally *Panay* was abandoned, as were two of her accompanying tanker barges. Survivors reported that the Japanese even strafed the reeds along the riverbanks where they were swimming to shore.

The crew and embassy staff were cared for by local Chinese for two days until they could be taken aboard HMS *Ladybird* and USS *Oahu*. The final tally was three dead, with an additional forty-three sailors and five civilians wounded. Instead of any military retaliation, though, the United States requested the Japanese pay $2.2 million in reparations and make "a formally recorded expression of regret, an undertaking to make complete and comprehensive indemnifications; and an assurance that definite and specific steps have been taken which

---

Panay's launch, on November 1, 1927, had been ominous. Chinese bandits had stolen the grease to be used to slip her from Shanghai's Kiangnan Dockyard and Engineering Works into the water, substituting a cheap replacement. Instead of launching stern-first, *Panay* slid sideways out of dry dock, coming to a stop halfway down the rails. This, as any sailor knows, is a dark portent.

will insure that hereafter American nationals, interests and property in China will not be subjected to attack by Japanese armed forces or unlawful interference by any Japanese authorities or forces." The US State Department explained, "The overwhelming endorsement given by the people of the United States to the manner in which the *Panay* incident was settled attested to their earnest desire to keep the United States out of war."

When the Nationalist capital fell on December 13, 1937, fifty thousand Japanese soldiers took control of a metropolis of half a million. Posters were tacked on street corners: TRUST OUR JAPANESE ARMY— THEY WILL PROTECT AND FEED YOU. Going neighborhood by neighborhood, the conquerors eased Chinese civilians into surrender and divided them up into groups of around 150. The new commander in chief of the Nanking area army was a prince, Lieutenant General Yasuhiko Asaka, given the job by his nephew Hirohito. His order: "Kill all captives."

Historian Iris Chang: "The Japanese would take any men they found as prisoners, neglect to give them water or food for days, but promise them food and work. After days of such treatment, the Japanese would bind the wrists of their victims securely with wire or rope and herd them out to some isolated area. The men, too tired or dehydrated to rebel, went out eagerly, thinking they would be fed. By the time they saw the machine guns, or the blooded swords and bayonets wielded by waiting soldiers, or the massive graves, heaped and reeking with the bodies of the men who had preceded them, it was already too late to escape."

Kuomintang forces fled to inland Chongqing, and Japanese soldiers rampaged through the streets of Nanking for months on end in what became known as Nanjing Datusha—the Rape of Nanking—killing somewhere between 260,000 and 350,000 civilians . . . the exact number is still unknown. Japanese military correspondents reported back to their Tokyo readers, "One by one the prisoners fell down to the outside of the wall. Blood splattered everywhere. The chilling atmosphere made one's hair stand on end and limbs tremble with fear. I stood there at a total loss and did not know what to do. . . . There was the dark silhouette of a mountain made of dead bodies. About fifty to one hundred people were toiling there, dragging bodies from the mountain of corpses and throwing them into the Yangtze River. The bodies dripped blood, some of them still alive and moaning weakly, their limbs twitching. . . . After a while, the coolies had done their job of dragging corpses and the soldiers lined them up along the river. Rat-tat-tat machine-gun fire could be heard. The coolies fell backwards into the river and were swallowed by the raging currents. . . . Those in the first row were beheaded, those in the second row were forced to dump the severed bodies into the river before they themselves were beheaded. The killing went on nonstop, from morning until night. . . . I've seen piled-up bodies in the Great Quake in Tokyo, but nothing compared to this."

A Japanese veteran of Nanking, Hakudo Nagatomi, remembered the details: "Few know that soldiers impaled babies on bayonets and tossed them still alive into pots of boiling water. They gang-raped women from the ages of twelve to eighty and then killed them when they could no longer satisfy sexual requirements. I beheaded people, starved them to death, burned them, and buried them alive, over two hundred in all. It is terrible that I could turn into an animal and do these things. There are really no words to explain what I was doing. I was truly a devil. . . . Soldiers would force one group of Chinese captives to dig a grave, a second group to bury the first, and then a third group to bury the second, and so on. . . . One method of entertainment was to drive mobs of Chinese to the top stories or roofs of buildings, tear down the stairs, and set the bottom floors on fire. . . . Another form of amusement involved dousing victims with fuel, shooting them, and watching them explode into flame. . . . Many women in their eighties were raped to death. . . . Chinese witnesses saw Japanese rape girls under ten years of age in the streets and then slash them in half by sword. In some cases, the Japanese sliced open the vaginas of preteen girls in order to ravish them more effectively. . . . After gang rape, Japanese soldiers sometimes slashed open the bellies of pregnant women and ripped out the fetuses for amusement. . . . The Japanese raped a barber's wife and then stuck a firecracker in her vagina. It blew up and killed her."

Beyond raping somewhere between twenty thousand to eighty thousand women, the Japanese disemboweled them, cut off their breasts, tried to see how deeply they could punch their way inside their vaginas, had fathers rape daughters and sons rape mothers while the rest of the family watched, nailed women to walls, carved organs out of the bodies, hung women from hooks by their tongues, and buried young men up to their waists for the sport of unleashing German shepherd attack dogs to tear them apart. Raping a virgin, some believed, made you stronger; carrying a packet of their pubic hair could protect you from injury. After raping, Nagatomi remembered, "We always stabbed and killed them. Because dead bodies don't talk. . . . Perhaps when we were raping her, we looked at her as a woman, but when we killed her, we just thought of her as something like a pig." In time the Imperial Japanese Army would establish "comfort houses," or brothels, stocked by captured Taiwanese, Korean, and Chinese women, who were referred to as "public toilets."

An anonymous soldier remembered, "I personally severed more than forty heads. Today, I no longer remember each of them well. It might sound extreme, but I can almost say that if more than two weeks went by without my taking a head, I didn't feel right. Physically, I needed to be refreshed. I would go to the stockade and bring someone out, one who looked as if he wouldn't live long. I'd do it on the river-bank, by the regimental headquarters, or by the side of the road. . . . A good sword could cause a head to drop with just an easy motion. But even I sometimes botched the job. . . . Sometimes I'd hit the shoul-der. Once a lung popped out, almost like a balloon. I was shocked. All I could do was hit the base of the neck with my full strength. Blood spurted out. Arteries were cut, you see. The man fell immediately, but it wasn't a water faucet, so it soon stopped. Looking at that, I felt ecstasy. . . . It was almost like being addicted to murder. When I met people, I often looked at their necks and made a judgment. Is this an easy neck, or hard to cut?"

While the Japanese military and her civilian government would frequently give speeches promoting their policy of "Asia for Asians," the Rape of Nanking would instead turn out to be one element in a cavalcade of gruesome Japanese war crimes against Asians. Starting in 1937, the Imperial Japanese Army began using chemical weapons on the Chinese, escalating to lewisite, phosgene, chlorine, and nausea red gases in 1938, and then mustard gas in 1939. Over the ensuing decade, the Japanese army built and staffed a "water purification unit" outside the Manchurian city of Harbin, which was in fact a testing ground for bacterial warfare, using prisoners as living guinea pigs to be infected with bubonic plague, pneumonia, epidemic hemorrhagic fever, typhoid, and syphilis. Founded by an army medical lieutenant general, Shiro Ishii, it was known as Unit 731.

Where did this barbarism come from? One Asian scholar, Robert Edgerton, believes that Japanese soldiers were once among the world's finest, but their attitudes changed in the 1930s. Bushido, their military code of honor inherited from the samurai, was now interpreted as meaning no soldier would be held accountable for crimes committed against an enemy. Many found guidance from Tsunetomo Yamamoto's eighteenth-century *Book of the Samurai*: "Meditation on inevitable death should be performed daily. Every day when one's body and mind are at peace, one should meditate upon being ripped apart by arrows, rifles, spears, and swords, being carried away by surging waves, being thrown into the midst of a great fire, being struck by lightning, being shaken to death by a great earthquake, falling from a thousand-foot cliff, dying of disease, or committing seppuku [suicide by disembowelment] at the death of one's master. And every day without fail one should consider himself as dead."

The Imperial Japanese Army had allied with Britain in the Great War, but it felt shabbily treated by the armistice and decided afterward to send its officers for training to Berlin instead of London. Aligning with a German spirit, the Army Ministry's September 1, 1934, pamphlet *Kokubo no hongi to sono kyoka no teisho* (*On the Essence and Improvement of National Defense*) began with inspiring words from Prussian general Carl Philipp Gottfried von Clausewitz: "War is the father of creation and the mother of civilization." The IJA also adopted the peculiar German innovation that midlevel staff officers should hold the key role in forming military policy, reaching decisions, and preparing documents for their commanders to sign. Decisions rose up from lieutenants known as the *bakuryo*—"officers behind the curtains"—instead of down from generals. By the late 1930s, the two most influential *bakuryo* were the chief of the Army General Staff's Operations Division, Shinichi Tanaka, and a section chief in the Navy Ministry's Military Affairs Bureau, Shingo "Wild Shot" Ishikawa. Tanaka was so ardent in his convictions that he became Japan's squeaky-wheel leader in setting military policy, while by the end of 1940, Wild Shot had become the head of the Arms Division and could boast, "I am the one who brought Japan to the war course."

These Japanese lieutenants, wholly in control of their nation's army, had spent most of their lives isolated from civilian society and came to believe they had unique talents as heirs to the samurai warrior tradition, a tradition that emphasized immediate and resolute action. They developed a self-confidence far beyond their achievements as well as a belligerence that ignored the opinions of those outside their clique.

They were also distinct in the samurai thinking that, should soldiers be inspired by patriotism and the need for action that would enrich all Japan—*gekokujo*, insubordination in service to the nation—it was their right to move forward and do whatever needed to be done, regardless of their commanding officers, their standing orders, or their country's civilian leaders. The *bakuryo* system produced a fighting force that lurched from decision to decision instead of following a coherent long-term strategy.

This self-absorbed and belligerent fervor coincided with the unique status of the armed forces within the Japanese government. Instead of serving under the civilian legislature or prime minister, the army and navy reported directly to the emperor in what was called "the independence of the supreme command." During audiences at the Imperial Palace between admirals, generals, and the emperor, to keep defense of the nation free from the taint of politics, the prime minister and other members of the civilian government, and even Hirohito's own political adviser, Lord Privy Seal Koichi Kido, were not invited, except for rare and momentous occasions. The armed forces' civilian leaders were, meanwhile, chosen by the minister of war, the inspector general for training, and the general staff chief, giving the military effective control of the civilian cabinet—by withdrawing their ministers, they could bring down a government and force a new prime minster into office, one who needed their approval to form a new cabinet. This essentially led to a system of two governments, military and civilian, each with its own foreign policy.

Within the military, the army and the navy were always at odds with each other, their struggles creating further chaos. From 1937 to 1941, the only significant opposition to a rampage across Asia by the Imperial Japanese Army was found not in the civilian leadership, but in the Imperial Japanese Navy. That service would try until the very last to keep the country out of an ever-expanding global war.

Japan, then, had the appearance of a civilian government, but it was a de facto military dictatorship. Yet, unlike the smooth governance offered by other fascists, all of this resulted in anarchy. In the fourteen years of the Great East Asia War—from 1931's Manchurian Incident, to 1945's unconditional surrender—Japan was led by fifteen different prime ministers. This wasn't just a fascistic and chaotic government; it was one so marred by threats of domestic violence that even the revered emperor regularly feared his assassination. One simple explanation for Pearl Harbor, then, is the great difficulty American leaders had in crafting an effective defense strategy against an enemy that had lost its mind.

After an eleven-day sojourn aboard Vincent Astor's yacht, President-elect Franklin Delano Roosevelt made a brief speech in Miami, Florida, on February 15, 1933, and then met with the visiting mayor of Chicago, Anton Cermak. There was the crack of a rifle. Cermak fell. The Secret Service reflexively began speeding the convertible away, but Roosevelt made them stop and turn around, insisting they carry Cermak to the hospital. "Tony, keep quiet—don't move. It won't hurt you if you keep quiet," Roosevelt said, cradling the dying man.

That night, the Secret Service drove Roosevelt back to Astor's yacht. Waiting for him was speechwriter Raymond Moley, who remembered expecting to see some reaction in a human being who'd just survived an assassination attempt and who had held a dying man in his arms. But there was nothing—"not so much as the twitching of a muscle, the mopping of a brow, or even the hint of a false gaiety—to indicate that it wasn't any other evening in any other place. Roosevelt was simply himself—easy, confident, poised, to all appearances, unmoved."

That same year, *Mein Kampf* was published in the United States, and FDR, like Inoue, was shocked to see how edited the translation was from the German, writing on the flyleaf, "A wholly false view of what Hitler really is or says. The German original would make a different story." He told his State Department, "Hitler is a madman and his counselors, some of whom I personally know, are even madder than he is." One of Hitler's closest friends, Nazi philosopher Alfred Rosenberg, had recently commented on how much he would enjoy seeing, from the train window on his journey from Berlin to the North Sea, a Jew's head atop each telephone pole.

As the 1930s ended, American defense forces were notably meager and her military technology out-of-date, since the nation was still broke. When FDR won his first election to the Oval Office, the unemployment rate was 25 percent. By March 4 and his inauguration, thirty-eight states had closed their banks, and the remaining ten were moving to follow suit. During a period when the president judged one-third of the nation as "ill-housed, ill-clad, ill-nourished," the US Army totaled 185,000 men, smaller than the defenses of Sweden, or even Switzerland,

and the world was shrinking in two ways at once. Just as Japan had once felt itself encircled by Western colonies, so now the United States felt surrounded by fascist imperialists.

The month after Mussolini's forces invaded Ethiopia in October of 1935, Pan American Airways' *China Clipper*—a Martin M-130 flying boat decked out as a hotel lobby, with stuffed armchairs and elaborate meals—lifted from the waters of San Francisco on its maiden voyage on November 22. It puddle-jumped for nearly sixty hours across the new bases that Pan Am's founder, Juan Trippe, had built for it—Pearl Harbor's Middle Loch; Midway; Wake; Guam—before berthing in the Philippine capital of Manila on the island of Luzon on the twenty-ninth. Pearl Harbor; Midway; Wake; Guam; Luzon—these were America's links to Asia and Australia, sea routes established by New England whaling schooners, and now, air routes created by Pan Am. They would in five years to come be the route of victory in MacArthur and Nimitz's Pacific theater, and of revenge for Pearl Harbor. The regular passenger and mail service the *Clipper* provided, though, informed those with foresight how little their oceans now protected the United States.

Over one hundred Pan Am employees would die in World War II.

In 1938, Admiral Isoroku Yamamoto instituted a Japanese navy training program that was so rigorous, it begat a motto: "Death in training is a hero's death." By 1939, however, he was so publicly known as being in favor of Washington and against Berlin that guards outside his residence weren't enough; naval minister Admiral Mitsumasa Yonai promoted him to commander in chief, Combined Fleet, and sent him to sea duty. Far from Tokyo, he was protected from assassination.

By the middle of 1939, Japan controlled five northeastern Chinese provinces as well as China's Pacific coast, but as Cordell Hull had foretold, military conquest, instead of civilian trade and treaty, had significant costs. The solution to the Japanese was as it had been to the Nazis: more conquest.

In July, Hirohito gave the go-ahead for the army to invade Britain's Asian colonies, but refused to approve of a Tripartite alliance with Germany and Italy even though his brother Prince Chichibu had campaigned for it ardently. The emperor believed the army was using the threat of America and England as a smoke screen to divert the Japanese public from its Chinese quagmire, and refused to accommodate it. The Chinese, meanwhile, told the Western press that Japanese colonial representatives ran "opium governments," since for all the talk of coprosperity spheres, that turned out to be their colonies' principal revenue stream.

As the Japanese army took over the nation's government, so it took over her culture. Toy shops sold out of miniature tanks and soldiers; boys' clothing included helmets, rifles, bugles, antiaircraft guns, and howitzers. One common children's game was to tie a bag of logs to your back to simulate the human bombers who went on suicide missions. The story is told of a 1930s youngster bursting into tears when faced with dissecting a frog. His teacher screamed, "Why are you crying about one lousy frog? When you grow up, you'll have to kill one hundred, two hundred Chinks!"

After Hitler invaded Poland on September 1, 1939, and war was declared by France and Great Britain, on February 9, 1940, President Roosevelt sent his State Department favorite, Undersecretary Sumner Welles, to Berlin, London, Rome, and Paris, hoping to negotiate a peace for Europe. In Rome, though many of Italy's leaders fervently hoped to avoid war, Mussolini refused to consider any negotiations with Welles, and in Berlin, after being assaulted by a two-hour lecture from German foreign minister Joachim von Ribbentrop, Welles concluded, "The man is saturated with hate for England."

On March 1, Welles met Hitler. The Führer was fretful that the Americans might convince Mussolini to stay out of the conflict, so Welles bluffed, reporting that he and Il Duce had a "long, constructive, and helpful" conversation, with Mussolini agreeing "there was still a possibility of bringing about a firm and lasting peace." Hitler in a fury insisted the fault lay with Paris and London, that there would indeed be peace . . . after fascists ruled the whole of Europe.

Even with twenty-twenty hindsight, it is difficult to comprehend the fury and speed of the Nazi blitzkriegs. On April 9, 1940, German troops conquered Denmark and, a few weeks later, Norway. On May 10, 1940, they began their assaults on Belgium, the Netherlands, and France, all of which surrendered in thirty-eight days. The US public had been so hostile to Americans fighting another European war that Washington legislators had almost annually passed "neutrality" laws. But the fall of France provoked a sea change. In May 1940, 35 percent of Americans favored supporting the Allies; by August, 60 percent did, enabling FDR to get through Congress a nearly tenfold increase in the War Department's budget.

Nazi foreign minister von Ribbentrop on May 22 informed Tokyo that Hitler "was not interested in the problem of the Netherlands East Indies," meaning that the territory was free for Japan to invade. In June, Japan told the conquered French to give her permission to post a military base in Vichy Indochina (today's Vietnam, Cambodia, and Laos); told the Netherlands East Indies (today's Indonesia) to guarantee her a flow of raw materials; and said that if Britain did not remove its troops from Shanghai and close the borders between China, Burma (today's Myanmar), and Hong Kong, there would be war.

An Imperial Japanese Army war plan drafted soon after included building air bases in Indochina and Thailand and attacks on the Netherlands East Indies, Hong Kong, and Malay, but "war with America was to be avoided as much as possible . . . although preparations must proceed in anticipation of a probable military clash." Those preparations included Combined Fleet Commander Yamamoto, now fifty-six years of age with a crew cut gone silver, saying to one of his lieutenants, "I wonder if an aerial attack can't be made on Pearl Harbor." The following year he would begin plans for Operation Hawaii, also known as Operation Z.

For all its outward show of military force, Japan was so internally chaotic that political assassinations were an open topic of conversation. Prime Minister Yonai created a plan to save the emperor aboard a battleship if the Imperial Palace was attacked. These fears escalated when it was discovered that, in the first days of July, members of the secret police plotted to murder anyone who championed friendship with Britain and the United States, including Prime Minister Yonai and Lord Privy Seal Kido. The traitors were discovered and captured; the army and police acted as they should—but it was another grave turn of events.

On July 16, the army brought down Yonai's government, and Prince Fumimaro Konoye returned as prime minister. During his prior reign, each time the world learned of new Japanese war atrocities, Konoye would offer his deepest lamentations and then do nothing to stop the carnage. Lean and mustachioed, with a driving need to keep everyone happy, Konoye came from a lineage as lofty as Franklin Roosevelt's as he was a Japanese prince descended from one of the country's four noble clans whose daughters served as royal concubines from whom all emperors were birthed. The prince was notorious for his extremely picky eating habits. Arriving at a lavish dinner offering the choicest of raw fish, a geisha would follow him to the table with a bowl of boiling water. She would, piece by piece, shabu-shabu the sushi, then use her chopsticks to place the food into the prince's mouth. Also, like Roosevelt, Konoye enjoyed talking directly to his citizens over the radio, which was convenient as he was president of the nation's leading broadcaster, NHK, and his sonorous voice—a melancholy tenor—was captivating.

Konoye's new cabinet included at least two avowed foes of the Anglo-Saxons, Foreign Minister Yosuke Matsuoka and War Minister Hideki Tojo. In the face of Japan's continued military rumblings, while Joseph Grew and Sumner Welles urged moderation, Chief of Naval Operations Harold Stark, Navy Secretary Frank Knox, Interior Secretary Harold Ickes, and War Secretary Henry Stimson urged FDR to take the hardest possible line with Tokyo.

The president found an answer from the other side of the world. In October 1937, the US Asiatic Fleet commander, Admiral Harry Yarnell, had written a letter to his superiors pointing out Japan's reliance on imports, a letter that eventually made its way to the White House. The admiral suggested that the United States, Britain, France, the Netherlands, and the Soviet Union cut off all trade with Japan, battling the Asian fascists with commerce instead of troops. The idea reminded FDR of when America used a similar technique against Tripoli in the Barbary Wars, the subject of an article he'd published in *Asia* magazine in 1923, an article he had hoped at the time would strengthen ties between Tokyo and Washington.

Yarnell's logic was so convincing that it begat a new foreign policy, the thinking that, with its oil, iron, and other material exports, the United States was providing Japan with the materials it needed to subjugate the Chinese and, in time, the whole of East Asia. In 1938, the State Department announced its vigorous opposition to the sale of American-manufactured aeronautical equipment to nations employing airplanes to attack innocent civilians and, in 1939, extended this "moral embargo" to production methods for aviation-grade gasoline.

The Japanese immediately noticed, even the new commander in chief of the Combined Fleet, the navy's highest-ranking seagoing officer, Admiral Isoroku Yamamoto, living aboard flagship *Nagato*, anchored in Hiroshima Bay next to the military port of Kure. Yamamoto wrote Vice Admiral Shigetaro Shimada in September 1939 that, as Japan imported most of its oil and steel from the Anglo-Saxons, losing them as allies was foolish, especially since "there is no chance of winning a war with the United States for some time to come."

Ambassador Grew, meanwhile, foresaw the unintended consequences of economic weaponry in October: "In both my talks with the President I brought up clearly my view that if we want to start sanctions against Japan we must see them through to the end, and the end may conceivably be war. I also said that if we cut off Japanese supplies of oil and that if Japan then finds that she cannot obtain sufficient oil from other commercial sources to ensure national security, she will in all probability send her fleet down to take the Dutch East Indies."

Roosevelt didn't listen to Grew's cautions; instead in January 1940, he ordered Hull to inform Japan that the United States would now withhold key petroleum exports since "so many countries were engaged in fighting in various parts of the world . . . that my Government felt that it should undertake to conserve quite a number of commodities and products in order to be able better to defend itself in case it should be attacked," as the secretary phrased it. Hull would later tell the American public that the Japanese "have in a large number of instances resorted to bombing and machine-gunning of civilians from the air at places near which there were no military establishments or organizations. Furthermore, the use of incendiary bombs has inflicted appalling losses on civilian populations. Japanese air attacks in many instances have been of a nature and apparent plan which can be comprehended only as constituting deliberate attempts to terrorize unarmed populations."

In the spring of 1940, Grew wrote Hull that three Japanese groups were now arguing over their country's future. One wanted to negotiate with the Kremlin to divvy up China; another wanted to join Hitler and battle Churchill; the third wanted to negotiate a peace with the Anglo-Saxons and end the war in East Asia. The latter was the weakest group and needed help, so Grew proposed that he be allowed to tell the government that, as soon as Japan made clear steps to begin a withdrawal of military forces from China, America would grant it economic benefits.

Hull on June 4 vetoed this. Instead, on July 18, 1940, Stimson and Knox had dinner with representatives of Britain and Australia, Stimson noting in their conversation, "We now had an opportunity under the new legislation of stopping the supplies of oil to Japan." The group decided that the United States should halt petroleum exports, with

Britain and the United States buying up any surplus; the Dutch should destroy their East Indies oil wells; and a bombing campaign would stop production at Germany's synthetic-oil plants. Without fuel for their war machines, the rampaging fascists would be stopped in their tracks. At a White House meeting of Stimson, Knox, and Welles the next day, Stimson remembered, "The president . . . finally came to the conclusion that the only way out of the difficulties of the world was [limiting export of] the supply of fuel to carry on the war."

On July 25, 1940, FDR announced that scrap metal and oil exports would be subject to license, and that same day, navy chief Harold Stark and army chief George Marshall warned Admiral Kimmel and General Short in Hawaii of the embargo, but added that they "do not anticipate immediate hostile reaction by Japan through the use of military means but you are furnished this information in order that you may take appropriate precautionary measures against possible eventualities." Washington informed Tokyo the next day that it would also terminate their Treaty of Commerce and Navigation, meaning that in six months at its expiry, additional controls and limits would be placed on Japan's American imports. The hawks in FDR's cabinet—Stimson, Treasury Secretary Henry Morgenthau Jr., and Harold Ickes—wanted to halt the export of all petroleum products to Japan, but the president, mindful of the Nazi's Atlantic U-boat patrols, said that might trigger "the wrong war in the wrong ocean at the wrong time." His aviation and iron embargoes, though, would allow him to "slip the noose around Japan's neck, and give it a jerk now and then."

The government-dominated press in Japan reacted vehemently. "It seems inevitable," reported Tokyo's biggest daily paper, *Asahi Shimbun*, "that a collision should occur between Japan, determined to establish a sphere of interest in East Asia . . . and the United States, which is determined to meddle in affairs on the other side of a vast ocean." Yamamoto wrote Shimada that the Konoye government's "action in showing surprise now at America's economic pressure and fuming and complaining against it reminds me of the aimless account of a schoolboy which has no more consistent motive than the immediate need or whim of the moment" and warned Prime Minister Konoye, "If you tell me that it is necessary that we fight, then, in the first six months to a year of war against the U.S. and England I will run wild, and I will show you an uninterrupted succession of victories; I must also tell you that, should the war be prolonged for two or three years, I have no confidence in our ultimate victory. . . . I hope at best you'll make every effort to avoid war with America."

Joseph Grew wrote Secretary Hull on September 12 that the military and nationalist elements in Japan saw in Europe's turmoil a "golden opportunity" to create an empire in Asia, as Germany's many victories, "like strong wine," had gone to their heads. Others in Tokyo believed it likely that Germany would never conquer Great Britain; that the union of London and Washington would turn out to be a formidable force; and that if Germany succeeded in taking over all of Europe, it might next turn its eyes toward Asia. Grew continued that, if the Japanese military felt that American commercial embargoes kept it from victory, its "do or die" temperament would lead to some form of retaliation, probably some sudden strike by the navy or army, possibly without either knowledge or permission from Tokyo. Japan's imperial ambitions, he concluded, were a clear threat to American interests in Asia and the Pacific.

It was a significant threat. The Japanese had a two-foot-long, oxygen-powered torpedo that could travel twenty-four miles and was twice as effective in speed, in distance, in targeting, and in explosive power as anything American-made. Their Zero fighter, which could take off from a carrier and reach 330 mph while maneuvering the currents like a raptor, was outfitted with two machine guns and two twenty-millimeter cannon and was dramatically superior to any fighter that America then produced. In the plane's premier engagement on September 13, 1940, thirteen Zeros took down twenty-seven Chinese flying Russian-built Polikarpov I-15 and I-16 fighters . . . in thirty minutes . . . without a single Japanese loss.

Years of economic hardship and political gamesmanship had meanwhile left American defenses in decay. America's top field commanders were all veterans of the 1898 Spanish-American War. The average recruit—there were only 243,500 of them in 1940—was issued a Springfield rifle, designed in 1903. Many of their uniforms were Great War leftovers smelling of mothballs along with tin hats and puttees—canvas strips for wrapping around the tops of shoes to keep them dry. As late as October 27, 1941, *Time* magazine reported, "The worst example of the [Army Ordnance Department's] doodling in the peacetime years is the U.S. soldier's steel helmet. Knowing full well that the helmet exposed the wearer's neck to shell fragments and was also uncomfortable, Ordnance delayed adoption of a better helmet. Today, 20 years later, with a crackerjack design in its pocket, Ordnance is delayed in getting production because it can't get enough manganese steel to make it."

On September 23, 1940, the die was cast. Japanese troops invaded what are today the nations of Malaysia, Vietnam, Cambodia, and Indonesia, and what were then the resource-rich Southeast Asian colonies of Europe. Japan now controlled British Malaya's acres of rubber plantations, French Indochina's sinuous veins of tin, and most important, the Dutch East Indies' bounteous cache of oil. Washington's hawks saw their worst fears confirmed: Japan had turned into Germany's criminal little brother, treating the Chinese as the Germans were treating the Jews, rampaging across a continent with no regard to international law. Even civilian life in Japan seemed to be following in the Nazis' footsteps, with that autumn's mandatory creation of neighborhood associations, which trained civilians to defend the nation in case of direct attack, helped fight fires, organized patriotic rallies, and distributed rationed items. The Special Higher Police, which brutally attacked thought crimes, had informers in each of these groups.

Joseph Grew: "I reported to the State Department that our Japanese contacts, sources of information, were falling away simply because they were being very carefully watched by the secret police and most of them did not dare come to the Embassy any more, they did not dare meet me outside, and even when I went to the Tokyo Club, which was sort of a neutral meeting ground for Japanese and foreigners, I found the Japanese I knew would quietly slip away into other rooms or corners. They just did not want to be seen talking to me; they did not dare. Therefore, it was extremely difficult, under those circumstances, for us to keep in touch with everything that was going on there."

Four days after the invasion of Southeast Asia on September 27, Japanese foreign minister Yosuke Matsuoka arrived in Berlin to thunderous drumrolls, cries of "Heil Hitler! Heil Matsuoka!," and the Swastika and Rising Sun waving side by side in unison. After signing the Tripartite Pact with Hitler's eager representatives, Matsuoka was next received in Rome by Mussolini and Pope Pius XII, with Matsuoka telling the pope, "Of all the world's statesmen, there is nobody before or after me who understands and loves Christianity as much as I do." Il Duce insisted that the Japanese must have a clear focus on their mutual enemies, and enemy number one would now be the United States.

Both Hitler and Matsuoka hoped the treaty would frighten America from interfering with their global conquests, as the Tripartite Pact's central tenet was that Japan, Germany, and Italy would aid each other if attacked "by a power not already engaged in war."

For years, the Imperial Japanese Army had supported an alliance with Hitler, who was seen as being both unbeatable and an ally who might make Joseph Stalin think twice about meddling against Japan in China. But Japanese admirals, including Yamamoto, worried that officially joining the Axis would trigger war with Britain and the United States. "Our opposition to the alliance was like desperately paddling against the rapids only a few hundred yards upstream from the Niagara Falls," Admiral Yonai later explained. When asked whether he would have opposed the treaty if he'd still been minister of the navy or prime minister, he replied, "Of course, but we would have been assassinated." The alliance so worried Hirohito he uncharacteristically made his personal opinion known. As he pressed his seal of acquiescence into the pact with the Nazis, the emperor darkly told Prime Minister Konoye, "You must, therefore, share with me the joys and sorrows that will follow."

After signing a neutrality agreement with Moscow the following spring, a triumphant Foreign Minister Matsuoka was waiting to board the first-class car of the Trans-Siberian Railway's *Red Arrow* when who came out of the fog to bid him adieu but Stalin and Foreign Minister Vyacheslav Molotov. It was an immense honor, as Stalin almost never appeared in public and had found himself at his last encounter with Matsuoka on the receiving end of his typical lecture on the benefits and perils of communism. With his farewell, Stalin explained, "You see, I am an Asian. I am from Georgia! We are brothers, so we must work together!" On the ride home, plied generously with vodka and caviar, Matsuoka explained to his staff that "he would make puppets of Hitler and Stalin" and wrote poems "full of subtle twists of thought." "To shake hands with Germany is a temporary excuse to shake hands with the Soviet Union," he told his secretary. "But that handshaking with the Soviet Union is also nothing more than an excuse to shake hands with the United States," meaning the strength of Japan's new alliance would force Washington into a more conciliatory posture. Sumner Welles, among other American and British leaders, said only one word described the Soviet-Japanese treaty: "sinister."

On October 16, 1940, every American man of at least five feet in height and 105 pounds in weight with fixable vision, but no VD, hernias, or flat feet, appeared before one of the nation's sixty-five hundred Selective Service boards to receive urine tests, a cursory medical inspection, and a one-minute psychiatric exam—"flies spread disease, so keep yours buttoned" was one admonition—and then registered for the first peacetime draft in US history. Anyone under the age of forty had to march, in full equipment, for at least twenty-five miles and be able to complete an obstacle course with a rifle and a thirty-pound pack: assaulting an eight-foot wall, shimmying down a ten-foot pole, jumping across flaming trenches, crawling through water mains, climbing one rope and then swinging on another across a ditch, and swinging hand-over-hand on a rope ladder—in less than 3.5 minutes. On October 29, a blindfolded Secretary of War Henry Stimson fished numbers out of a ten-gallon glass bowl. The first was handed to President Roosevelt, who announced, by radio, number 158. The 6,175 draftees holding number 158 immediately received Selective Service telegrams that began, "Greetings."*

On the night of November 11–12, 1940, Britain's Royal Navy launched twenty-one obsolete Fairey TSR Swordfish biplane torpedo and dive-bombers from the carrier HMS *Illustrious* to attack Italy's fleet, then anchored in the shallow Mediterranean harbor of Taranto. The British lost two planes, with two men dead, and two taken prisoner. The Fascists lost thirty-two men and three battleships, nearly half of its capital fleet, and had to sail to Naples to avoid another devastating assault, giving the British the upper hand in Mediterranean naval power. The night's victor, Admiral Andrew Cunningham, concluded, "Taranto, and the night of November 11–12, 1940, should be remembered for ever as having shown once and for all that in the Fleet Air Arm the Navy has its most devastating weapon."

Learning of this great triumph, on November 22, CNO Stark recommended to then-CINCPAC (Commander in Chief, Pacific Command) James Richardson that antitorpedo nets be installed in Pearl Harbor. Richardson replied, "Torpedo nets within the harbor are neither necessary nor practicable," reasoning that "ships, at present, are not moored within torpedo range of the entrance." After the war, Richardson admitted, "I had not considered that it was likely that the fleet would be attacked by a carrier raid," ignoring the great naval lesson of

---

*In a year's time, the army would meet its quota of 900,000 and retire the fishbowl, but eventually, 9,818,977—one-sixth of America's males—would serve in World War II.

Taranto. When Henry Stimson mentioned torpedo nets to Richardson's replacement, Husband Kimmel, Kimmel also demurred, saying, "It would restrict boat traffic by narrowing the channel."

Those in Washington had good reason to be concerned by Taranto. An assistant naval attaché in Germany, Lieutenant Commander Takeshi Naito, flew to the site to make a report, as did a Japanese naval mission. The lead pilot against Pearl Harbor, Mitsuo Fuchida, later said, "The most difficult problem was torpedo launching in shallow water. We learned from when the British navy attacked the Italian fleet at Taranto."

Taranto came as such a surprise that CNO Stark, for one, couldn't stop reflecting on its implications, especially in regard to Hawaii. He assigned Rear Admiral Walter Ansel to do a study and then on January 24 cabled War Secretary Stimson and Hawaii's Kimmel, Short, and Rear Admiral Claude Bloch on the conclusions:

> The security of the U.S. Pacific Fleet while in Pearl Harbor, and of the Pearl Harbor Naval Base itself, has been under renewed study by the Navy Department and forces afloat for the past several weeks. This reexamination has been, in part, prompted by the increased gravity of the situation with respect to Japan, and by reports from abroad of successful bombing and torpedo plane attacks on ships while in bases. If war eventuates with Japan, it is believed easily possible that hostilities would be initiated by a surprise attack upon the Fleet or the Naval Base at Pearl Harbor.
>
> In my opinion, the inherent possibilities of a major disaster to the fleet or naval base warrant taking every step, as rapidly as can be done, that will increase the joint readiness of the Army and Navy to withstand a raid of the character mentioned above.
>
> The dangers envisaged in their order of importance and probability are considered to be:
> (1) Air bombing attack.
> (2) Air torpedo plane attack.
> (3) Sabotage.
> (4) Submarine attack.
> (5) Mining.
> (6) Bombardment by gun fire. . . .

Originally believing the United States would battle one enemy at a time, the American War Department's War Plans Division had designed "color plans"—Japan was orange; England was red—but the rise of the Axis powers made it clear that the army and the navy would have to fight on multiple fronts at once. Five "Rainbow" plans were drafted, and with the fall of France, it became clear that if Britain was lost, the United States would need to fight Germany, Italy, and Japan on its own—a dark and terrifying prospect. Stark submitted a memo to the president on November 12, 1940, extending an earlier Rainbow plan of military operations, setting forth a series of options—

A. Defend the western hemisphere.

B. Go on the offensive in the Pacific against Japan while remaining on the defensive in the Atlantic.

C. Fight equally committed in both the Atlantic and the Pacific.

D. Go on the offensive in the Atlantic (against Germany and Italy) while remaining on the defensive in the Pacific.

—and recommending the last. Known as Plan D (or Plan Dog), the memo would crystallize the "Europe first" leanings of both Stark and the army's chief of staff, George Marshall, which held that America must help England in any way possible, giving priority to the Atlantic in the escalating global conflict. The most powerful Republicans in FDR's cabinet, Henry Stimson and Frank Knox (who had been a Rough Rider with FDR's cousin Theodore), aggressively concurred on pursuing a muscular foreign policy that included fully supporting Churchill. A fundamental belief of Henry Stimson's was that the world would be dramatically improved if the United States were a global superpower, and the efforts he oversaw as FDR's secretary of war would make that dream come true. Roosevelt, meanwhile, believed in Plan Dog wholeheartedly, saying, "If Great Britain goes down, all of us in the Americas would be living at the point of a gun."

Even those without knowledge of Plan Dog pondered, how could the United States defend itself on two oceans at once? The prospect seemed overwhelming, and insurmountable. On December 14, 1940, Ambassador Grew wrote the president:

DEAR FRANK:

About Japan and all her works. It seems to me to be increasingly clear that we are bound to have a showdown some day, and the principal question at issue is whether it is to our advantage to have that showdown sooner or to have it later. . . . After eight years of effort to build up something permanently constructive in American-Japanese relations, I find that diplomacy has been defeated by trends and forces utterly beyond its control, and that our work has been swept away as if by a typhoon, with little or nothing remaining to show for it. Japan has become openly and unashamedly one of the predatory nations and part of a system which aims to wreck about everything that the United States stand for. . . . It is important constantly to bear in mind the fact that if we take measures "short of war" with no real intention to carry those measures to their final conclusion if necessary, such lack of intention will be all too obvious to the Japanese, who will proceed undeterred, and even with greater incentive, on their way. Only if they become certain that we mean to fight if called upon to do so will our preliminary measures stand some chance of proving effective and of removing the necessity for war.

At the start of 1941, rumors of war began to circulate in Japan's diplomatic community. A book published in Tokyo predicting war between Japan and the United States and analyzing its course—the winner: Japan—sold fifty-three thousand copies in its first month on sale. At the same time that the United States began recalling her consulate staff's families, Japan replaced her American ambassador with onetime foreign minister Admiral Kichisaburo Nomura. In fact an attempt to improve the relationship since Nomura had gotten to know Assistant Secretary of the Navy Franklin Delano Roosevelt while serving as a naval attaché in Washington. In the telling of the drama of Pearl Harbor, it has been common for Americans to portray Nomura as either a dupe of the warmongers or as a duplicitous agent who knew full well of the attack, and for the Japanese to portray him as an incompetent stooge. Instead, Admiral Nomura was as honorable, and as unlucky, as Messrs. Kimmel and Short.

At six feet, the Japanese admiral was strikingly tall, but that wasn't his only distinguishing physical feature. On April 29, 1932, Chinese rebels had thrown a bomb into the middle of attendees at a ceremony in Shanghai, leaving him with a limp, and destroying his right eye.

Originally, Nomura refused his orders to Washington, reasoning that "it is impossible to rectify diplomatic relations between Japan and the United States by trying to juggle both Germany and the United States at the same time, I could not accomplish any purpose were I to go to the United States." But Nomura came to believe that his country needed a steadying hand to avoid war, so he departed for the United States on January 23. On his layover in San Francisco, Nomura met with American naval intelligence officer Ellis Zacharias who had been stationed in Tokyo in the 1920s and '30s, where he became friendly with both Nomura and Yamamoto. In what Zacharias remembered as an "amazingly frank" conversation, Nomura said he was fearful of how power in Japan had been concentrated in the war extremists, who were pushing to battle the United States. The admiral felt this conflict was becoming both inevitable and, for Japan, suicidal.

The year before, Zacharias had been told by a confidential informant that the Japanese were planning an October 17 surprise attack against the American naval base in San Pedro, California. The threat did not come true, but that information combined with Nomura's revelations convinced Zacharias that Japan would go to war with America, a war that would begin with a sneak attack.

At the end of March 1941, Zacharias warned Hawaii's Admiral Kimmel that Japan "would begin with an air attack on our fleet on a weekend and probably on a Sunday morning; the attack would be for the purpose of disabling four battleships." Zacharias predicted carrier-based planes would arrive from the north of Oahu to take advantage of the prevailing winds, preceded by submarine patrols. Kimmel asked what should be done to make sure this didn't happen, and Zacharias said, "The only possible way of doing it would be to have a daily patrol out to five hundred miles" for surveillance. When Kimmel said he didn't have the men or the planes to do that, Zacharias said, "Well, Admiral, you better get them because that is what is coming."

After the war, when asked by congressional investigators about this conversation, Kimmel claimed no memory of it, while another man at this meeting, Captain W. W. "Poco" Smith, said there was no talk of air attack, and that Zacharias was suffering from "clairvoyance operating in reverse."

When Admiral Kichisaburo Nomura arrived in Washington on February 11, meanwhile, Roosevelt at a press conference tried to be welcoming: "Nomura is an old friend of mine. . . . There is plenty of room in the Pacific area for everybody. It would not do this country any good nor Japan any good, but both of them harm, to get into war."

An American with a great deal of business interests in Tokyo at this moment was Kuhn, Loeb & Co. Wall Street banker Lewis Strauss. Strauss decided it would be a good idea to introduce three of his friends—the postmaster general of the United States, Frank C. Walker; the vicar general of the Roman Catholic Foreign Mission Society of America at Maryknoll, James M. Drought; and James E. Walsh, the superior general of Maryknoll (which to this day has extensive missionaries and charities in Asia)—to Japanese business colleague Tadao Ikawa, a banker who himself had many friends in high places, notably Prince Fumimaro Konoye. Calling themselves the John Doe Associates, this American group thought they could succeed in bringing peace to Asia where the US State Department and the Japanese Foreign Ministry had failed.

In January 1941, the John Doe Associates met with Hull and Roosevelt to insist that, if Washington restored trade, Tokyo would withdraw from China and renounce Hitler. FDR and Hull didn't believe it, but asked the JDA to get a treaty offer in writing. On April 9, 1941, a draft said to be supported across the whole of Japan's leadership was delivered to Cordell Hull. It was far from what had been promised, including such provisions as American recognition of Japanese rule in Manchukuo; Japanese troops remaining in China; and the halt of US aid to the Chinese Nationalists until Chiang agreed to merge his leadership with that of Japan's Manchukuo governor, Pu Yi.

At a meeting at Hull's Wardman Park apartment, Ambassador Nomura explained that he was a collaborator on this plan and eagerly hoped it would be the beginning of a new dialogue with the United States. Hull replied that Washington could accept neither Japanese troops ruling the Chinese by force, nor the demand to halt further American aid to China. Additionally, Japan had to agree on Hull's four points: respect for the territorial integrity of all nations; noninterference in their internal affairs; equality of opportunity including trade; and nondisturbance of the status quo, except by peaceful means. The secretary then "said that I had observed every phase of Hitler's conduct and utterances . . . and that I, in common with many others, have absolutely no faith in any statement or promise that he makes, but any world, subjected to his methods and his philosophies, which are rooted largely in barbarism, would be an unthinkable world in which to live; that he has no real friends anywhere and that he is not a real friend to anyone; that he would abandon overnight the most solemn obligation taken the day before, if it suited his purpose in the least. I then added that this Government cannot conscientiously sit still and see this unthinkable brand of government fastened on the world."

In Japan, the JDA treaty draft was received on April 15 with great joy since, when Ambassador Nomura sent it to Tokyo, he left out Hull's four points, making it more palatable to the government's right wing. Only Foreign Minister Matsuoka realized something was wrong, telling an underling, "The draft understanding that came from America is appalling. . . . That thing has been written by Japanese. Everyone, including Prince Konoye, seems to think that the hardest part is over, that we just need to give the United States a positive reply. What fools! . . . I guarantee you, once we start negotiating, all sorts of problems are bound to emerge. . . . With the China Incident still going on, we cannot negotiate [with Washington] properly. . . . And if the negotiation fails, that will have given the military an excuse to start a war."

CHAPTER TWO

A SINISTER WIND

At the same time that Tokyo's Foreign Ministry was arranging for Admiral Nomura to become the newest Japanese ambassador to America, Admiral Yamamoto began planning to attack Pearl Harbor. On January 7, 1941, from his cabin aboard the thirty-two-thousand-ton battleship *Nagato* in Hiroshima Bay, Yamamoto composed a letter to Navy Minister Koshiro Oikawa that predicted "A conflict with the United States and Great Britain is inevitable." After his cross-country American travels, the admiral concluded that Japan could not win a traditional war against a nation so mighty with industry, and so he could "see little hope of success in any ordinary strategy." His plan, which he called Operation Z or Operation Hawaii, was "conceived in desperation."

The admiral wanted a naval blitzkrieg to "fiercely attack and destroy the US main fleet at the outset of the war, so that the morale of the US Navy and her people [will] sink to the extent that it cannot be recovered." Japan's navy must "decide the fate of the war on the very first day. . . . In case the majority of the enemy's main force is at Pearl Harbor, attack it vigorously with our air force, and blockade the harbor . . . on a moonlight night or at dawn." All of Japan's forces would have to be "firmly determined to devote themselves to their task even at the sacrifice of their lives," including himself: "I sincerely desire to be appointed commander in chief of the air fleet to attack Pearl Harbor so that I may personally command that attack force [and thereby] devote myself exclusively to my last duty to our country." As for any of his fellow naval officers who might criticize this plan as too risky, they needed to consider "the possibility that the enemy would dare to launch an attack upon our homeland to burn down our capital and other cities," a devastation for which the navy's cowardice would be blamed. Combined with the pressing need to fight Hitler on the opposite side of the world, this devastating strike, he was certain, would convince America to forfeit Asia to Japan.

Yamamoto's plan was so inconceivably daring that it met with tremendous criticism from his fellow officers. Vice Admiral Chuichi Nagumo summarized that, taking into account the enormity of America's fleet, the great distance of Oahu from the Japanese mainland, and Pearl Harbor's shallow waters, Yamamoto's scheme was absurd. Instead, the Imperial Japanese Army should first invade Southeast Asia, then wait patiently for the Anglo-Saxons to draw nigh, where they would be annihilated in the battle that Japanese sailors had spent their lives training for, Alfred Thayer Mahan's decisive confrontation of dreadnoughts, the Kantai Kessen.

Nagumo's position was widely supported, even by Yamamoto's chief of staff, Vice Admiral Shigeru Fukudome. When Yamamoto first told Fukudome of his Operation Z thinking in the spring of 1940, the vice admiral said that a much better strategy would be a decisive maritime battle between the fleets of Japan and America, followed by an air attack on Oahu. Some Imperial Japanese Navy leaders, though, considered Yamamoto's scheme so crazy that it would come as a stunning surprise to the Americans—who in their right mind could ever imagine such a thing?—and therein lay its only chance for success. Even so, they expected their task force to lose a third of its ships to counterstriking US bombers.

Coincidentally on that same January 7 that Yamamoto wrote Oikawa, Pearl Harbor's commander Admiral Richardson memoed CNO Stark on the subject "Situation Concerning the Security of the Fleet and the Present Ability of the Local Defense Forces to Meet Surprise Attacks," which included, "Aircraft attacking the base at Pearl Harbor will undoubtedly be brought by carriers. Therefore, there are two ways of repelling attack. First, by locating and destroying the carrier prior to launching planes. Second, by driving off attacking bombers with anti-aircraft guns and fighters. The Navy component of the local defense forces has no planes for distant reconnaissance with which to locate enemy carriers and the only planes belonging to the local defense forces to attack carriers when located would be the Army bombers . . . [of which] neither numbers nor types are satisfactory for the purpose intended. . . . To drive off bombing planes after they have been launched will require both fighting planes and anti-aircraft guns. The Army has in the Hawaiian area 36 pursuit planes, all of which are classified as obsolete. . . . The ideal defense against submarines would be conducted by patrol vessels and aircraft working in conjunction. The district has no aircraft for this purpose."

Navy Secretary Frank Knox sent a similarly alarming January 24 letter to War Secretary Harold Stimson, which predicted a carrier strike of bombs or torpedoes attacking the fleet "without warning prior to a declaration of war."

Isoroku Yamamoto then followed up his original thoughts to the ministry with a more detailed proposal sent to the Eleventh Air Fleet chief of staff, Rear Admiral Takijiro Onishi, aboard aircraft carrier *Kaga*: "If we are to have war with America, we will have no hope of winning unless the US Fleet in Hawaiian waters can be destroyed. . . . This will not be easy to carry out. But I am determined to give everything to the completion of this plan, supervising the aerial divisions myself. I would like you to research the feasibility of such a plan in detail."

Echoing the thrashing back and forth in the mind of Japanese leaders, however, the same Yamamoto planning this belligerent and unexpected attack on the United States wrote an anti-war letter on January 26 to the ultranationalist Ryoichi Sasakawa, pointing out exactly how foolish he and his political colleagues urging the fight against America were: "Should hostilities break out between Japan and United States, it would not be enough that we take Guam and the Philippines, nor even Hawaii and San Francisco. To make victory certain, we would have to march into Washington and dictate the terms of peace in the White House. I wonder if our politicians, among whom armchair arguments about war are being glibly bandied about in the name of state politics, have confidence as to the final outcome and are prepared to make the necessary sacrifices."

Moving forward with Operation Z, Onishi turned to his expert in aerial torpedo warfare, Commander Kosei Maeda. Maeda said that it would be extremely difficult for a great fleet to travel all the way from Japan to Hawaii without notice, and that it was technically impossible to use torpedoes in Pearl Harbor's shallow waters, concluding, "Unless a technical miracle can be achieved in torpedo bombing, this type of attack would be altogether impractical. Such a difficult operation might conceivably be possible if parachutes could be fastened to the torpedoes to keep them from sinking too deeply into the water and lodging in the soft mud below, or if they could be launched from a very low level."

In February, Onishi revealed Yamamoto's plans to *Kaga*'s First Aerial Division staff officer Minoru Genda. As famous as any movie star, the thirty-six-year-old Genda was both an ace of the wars with China and the featured attraction of Genda's Flying Circus, a squadron of stunt fliers that performed breathtaking feats of aerial derring-do. If Yamamoto was the most magisterial of the Japanese military leaders in this history, and lead pilot Mitsuo Fuchida the most indicative, Minoru Genda, as important to Japan's victory as anyone else, was the most interesting, the wild card, and the man who would become, even beyond Isoroku Yamamoto, the key architect of the Pearl Harbor attack.

Fuchida called Genda "reckless," and though he was first in his class at Etajima Naval Academy, more than a few of his fellow cadets thought him insane; his nickname among naval aviators was Mad Genda. Like Yamamoto, Genda believed the potential of airpower was woefully underestimated by the navy, which to take one example, employed Zeros only to defend. Genda thought fighters should fight—defending carriers, accompanying bomber sorties, and strafing the enemy with their machine guns. This naval use of aggressive airpower, combined with an offensive posture focusing on carriers, destroyers, and submarines, would become famous in Japan as Gendaism.

When Onishi handed over Operation Z's orders, Genda immediately recognized the distinctive lyrical brush of calligraphy as Yamamoto's. The pilot finished reading the admiral's scheme and didn't know what to say, so he politely commented, "What an idea!" and in true Japanese fashion, praised "Yamamoto's daring plan and brave spirit." When Onishi then said, "I want you to find out if it could be done or not," Mad Genda had an immediate answer: "The plan is difficult but not impossible."

Onishi and Genda then remembered a conversation from 1936, when both were at the Yokosuka Air Corps base. Genda had brought up the idea of attacking Pearl Harbor with flattops, having been inspired by a newsreel of four American carriers sailing in concert: "A new concept suddenly hit me. If several carriers were concentrated in one group, the time necessary for all of [their] planes to join up in a giant formation would be relatively short. . . . I saw this concentrated grouping as a rather good policy in order to prove a decisive blow against the enemy." If the Japanese navy massed its carriers, it could launch "two big attack waves" of "about eighty bombers and approximately thirty fighter planes for protection."

Genda wanted every carrier in Japan's navy assigned to Operation Z, as he planned to include all three types of bombing—high-level horizontal; torpedo; and dive—as well as fighters. Such a great task force traversing the western Pacific without drawing notice, however, seemed an insurmountable problem—absolute secrecy, he realized, would be a necessity—and equally problematic was refueling at sea, a practice then still in its primitive stages. Genda also wanted, like Yamamoto, to re-create the great victory of Tsushima with a surprise dawn attack, since Japanese bombing technology wasn't yet sophisticated enough to strike under cover of night. His plan was to begin with a devastating aerial assault, followed by a full Imperial Japanese Army invasion of Hawaii. He and Yamamoto were both fervently opposed to the one-way attack strategy then popular among Japan's naval officers—notably the nonflying branch—which would keep their prized carriers five hundred miles away from the target and let any surviving air crews be recovered by submarines or destroyers.

Genda immediately ran into an argument over targets—"Aviation experts considered enemy carriers to be the primary targets," he said, "while the gunnery staffs emphasized going after enemy battleships"— as well as the insurmountable engineering problem Maeda had warned about. The waters of Pearl Harbor averaged thirty-nine feet deep, but Japan's best torpedoes dropped by its ace pilots needed ninety-eight feet of clearance before they leveled to begin their run to target. In shallow depths, torpedoes would propel themselves into the mud and be useless.

Two months after receiving Yamamoto's orders, Onishi replied in March with Genda's recommendations, which gave up on torpedoes and relied solely on dive-bombing and high-altitude level bombing. Yamamoto was deflated, telling his staff, "Since we cannot use a torpedo attack because of the shallowness of the water, we cannot expect to obtain the results we desire. Therefore, we probably have no choice but to give up the air-attack operation." The commander said none of this to Genda and Onishi, though; instead, he criticized their shortsightedness, insisting that torpedoes could be adjusted, and pilots could be trained.

Under Genda's plan, the Imperial Japanese Navy created the First Air Fleet on April 10. Gendaism had carried the day, with over two hundred planes assigned to his one strike force, which united the first carrier division of *Akagi* and *Kaga* (each weighing just shy of twenty-seven thousand tons and sailed by two-thousand-man crews) with the second carrier division of *Soryu* and *Hiryu*. Each division included four destroyers.

That same month, Japanese navigators studied which ships had crossed the Pacific over the past ten years. They discovered that not one had traveled in November and December at latitude forty degrees north because the seas on that route were so rough.

Yamamoto's staff officer, Captain Kameto Kuroshima, would be the third key to Operation Z's success. The son of a poor Hiroshima mason, Kuroshima was tall, gaunt, and bald, with such a severe mien that his fellow officers called him Ganji (Gandhi). He rarely bathed, smoked until he left a trail of ash everywhere he went, and when he needed to concentrate, Ganji spent days, naked, in an incense-filled room. But these eccentricities were part of a mind unlike others in the Japanese navy, and Yamamoto prized Kuroshima for his creativity and his refusal to be just another saluting yes-man. When it came to Operation Z, Kuroshima was nearly alone in sharing Yamamoto's unbridled enthusiasm and would prove essential in working the political levers of the navy's senior hierarchy. The newest obstacle they faced was the admiral given command of the First Air Fleet that would execute Operation Z; a staunch traditionalist who had indeed been one of the harshest of Yamamoto's critics: Chuichi Nagumo

In April, Kuroshima went to Tokyo to discuss the plan with the operation section headed by Captain Sadatoshi Tomioka, who was wholly negative, telling Kuroshima that Yamamoto's scheme was an inadmissible risk, and that Operation Number One could not spare the ships required for an attack on Hawaii, especially considering that Japanese carriers had no experience in refueling on the high seas. The Naval General Staff instead planned a modified version of the great all-out battle that would ensue when the US Pacific Fleet sailed westward to block Japan's southern advance. This included sending a sizable submarine force to Hawaiian waters to pick off pieces of the American fleet as she journeyed across the Pacific.

Yamamoto ordered Vice Admiral Mitsumi Shimizu, commander in chief, Sixth Fleet, to lead his submarines as part of the First Air Fleet's

Kido Butai (mobile force), saying on July 29, "Under present conditions I think war is unavoidable. If it comes, I believe there would be nothing for me to do but attack Pearl Harbor at the outset, thus tipping the balance of power in our favor."

Shimizu would commandeer a large force of twenty-five fleet and five midgets—a high percentage of the sixty-three subs in the entire Japanese fleet—whose assignments would include reconnaissance, interception of American reinforcements, attacking ships attempting to sortie from the anchorage, and rescuing downed pilots. The midgets were ordered to penetrate the harbor and torpedo any warships that had escaped the First Air Fleet's bomb and torpedo strikes. Japan had used midget submarines before, but those had been launched from surface ships; they now modified fleet submarines to ferry the midgets to within ten miles of Pearl Harbor. There, the midgets' size would let them stealthily cruise into Pearl's lochs, lurk beneath the surface of her shallow waters, then rise to attack American warships.

The midgets were all of seventy-eight feet long, weighed forty-six tons, and were armed with two torpedoes powerful enough to bring down a battleship. Crewed by two men operating from a control room the size of a coat closet with internal temperatures spiking at 150 degrees, they had a range of eighty miles surfaced and eighteen submerged. During the nights of their voyage when the mother subs surfaced, the crewmen could inspect their charges. In the rocking seas, they were roped to the ship with safety harnesses, and twice, Ensign Kazuo Sakamaki was pulled overboard by waves and had to be hauled back aboard.

Theoretically the crews of the midget subs had a chance to survive their mission, but no one—least of all the crews themselves—harbored illusions about the odds against these tiny craft escaping through Pearl Harbor's narrow channel in the aftermath of the attack. Ensign Sakamaki, who will be the sole survivor of the ten crewman, summed up their predicament: "None of us was a volunteer; we had all been ordered to our assignment. That none of us objected goes without saying. We knew that punishment would be very severe if we objected; we were supposed to feel highly honored."

In the middle of January 1941, Peru's ambassador to Japan, Ricardo Rivera-Schreiber, heard a rumor that made him go directly to the American embassy and on January 27, Ambassador Grew cabled his revelation to the State Department: "My Peruvian colleague told a member of my staff that he had heard from many sources including a Japanese source that the Japanese military forces planned, in the event of trouble with the United States, to attempt a surprise mass attack on Pearl Harbor using all of their military facilities. He added that although the project seemed fantastic the fact that he had heard it from many sources prompted him to pass on the information."

On February 1, 1941, Chief of Naval Operations Harold Stark cabled this news to Commander in Chief of the Pacific Fleet Husband Kimmel, and then said, "The Division of Naval Intelligence places no credence in these rumors. Furthermore, based on known data regarding the present disposition and employment of Japanese Naval and Army forces, no move against Pearl Harbor appears imminent or planned for in the foreseeable future." Kimmel replied that he was making defensive plans anyway, since "I feel that a surprise attack (submarine, air, or combined) on Pearl Harbor is a possibility. We are taking immediate practical steps to minimize the damage inflicted and to ensure that the attacking force will pay."

In February, a squadron of Japanese warships arrived in the Gulf of Siam, with Tokyo claiming its purpose was to resolve border clashes between French Indochina and Thailand. American diplomats in Japan warned the vice minister of foreign affairs that if Japan threatened the British, it "would have to expect to come into conflict with the United States." A shocked official asked for clarification: "Do you mean to say that if Japan were to attack Singapore, there would be war with the United States?" Embassy counselor Eugene Dooman replied, "The logic of the situation would inevitably raise that question." On February 6, Roosevelt threatened that if Japan attacked the Soviets, the United States would have to intervene. On the seventh, an irritated Matsuoka asked for a straight-up answer: Was the United States ready to fight?

Over the course of the following months, President Roosevelt met at least five times with his admirals to explore sailing an expeditionary force to Europe. Though America would become the powerhouse arsenal of democracy for the Allied cause in a mere eighteen months, at that moment she lacked the men, transports, and warships needed for such a vast undertaking. In January of that year, US factories produced 159 bombers and 248 fighters, which were divvied out as seventy-seven to the US Navy; fifteen to the US Army; and 315 to the United Kingdom. It wasn't bad, but it wasn't enough to beat Hitler.

On February 14, Japanese ambassador Nomura met with Hull and Roosevelt at the White House. The president bought up his and Nomura's "association of some twenty-odd years ago" and asked if, instead of ambassador, could the president call him admiral? FDR went on to say that the United States and Japan "were friends that could at all times talk candidly as friends about the relations and the related affairs of the two countries," but present relations were "deteriorating," and that if Hull and Roosevelt "had not almost instantly played down the *Panay* incident, there would in all probability have been a terrific inflammation of public sentiment in this country."

On February 25, Stark forwarded to Kimmel his analysis of the situation in Southeast Asia. As the US Department of War had determined that Japan didn't have enough men or ships to invade French Indochina, Thailand, British Singapore, and the American Philippines simultaneously, Stark concluded that Japan could only strike the British, the Dutch, and the American territories one at a time, meaning Tokyo posed little threat to US interests at that moment.

In early March, perhaps linking Taranto with the Peruvian rumor in his thoughts, Marshall asked Short what defenses Pearl Harbor had against carrier-based torpedo planes. The answer was convoluted, because in Hawaii, the Department of War had the army's troops guarding the navy's fleet when it was anchored at Pearl Harbor. Yet, the army's Hawaiian Department chief of staff, Colonel Walter Phillips, would later testify, "We felt secure against a raid, particularly with the Fleet here." The Army Air Corps was to additionally coordinate short-range aerial surveillance while the navy performed long-range scouting, but Phillips said, "I never knew what the navy had [in its scout-plane arsenal]." Similarly, the army man in charge of defending the navy's ships at harbor, General Walter Short, said that the Fleet, as well as the bases of Wake and Midway, were a far more formidable defense than his troops would ever be.

On March 8, Cordell Hull, with his speech impediment, had his first long-running one-on-one conversation with Ambassador Nomura, whose English was less than fluent and who was partially deaf. Hull and Nomura would meet fifty times over the next nine months, with Hull telling colleagues that the Japanese were notoriously two-faced, and nothing they said could be trusted.

To begin their dialogue, Hull asked Nomura if the military groups running Japan expected the United States "to sit absolutely quiet while two or three nations before our very eyes organized naval and military forces and went out and conquered the balance of the earth, including the seven seas and all trade routes and the other four continents"? Nomura replied that he didn't think Japan would make any further military moves unless American embargoes forced its hand. When on March 14, Hull and Nomura met again with FDR at the White House, "The Ambassador proceeded to say [that] none of his people, with few exceptions, desired war between our two countries," Hull noted; "that Matsuoka talks loudly for home consumption because he is ambitious politically, but Japan herself cannot maintain such ambitious plans." The president "proceeded to emphasize vigorously the dangerous effects of this [Tripartite] agreement and the utter lack of any sound reason for Japan to enter into it from every standpoint of her welfare. The Ambassador rather lamely remarked that this country was pressing Japan with embargoes and trade restrictions, and they were in a way forced into this Tripartite arrangement."

Though American armed forces weren't ready for a global conflict, Washington had a remarkable secret weapon that no Axis leader in Tokyo, Rome, or Berlin knew anything about. The weapon had been born on Friday, September 20, 1940, when thirty-two-year-old Frank Rowlett arrived at his job at DC's Munitions Building an hour early, as he did every workday. He was allowed past the steel gate and armed guards to his offices in rooms 3416 and 3418, guarded and gated since Rowlett was a civilian in charge of the team trying to break the code of the highest level of Japan's diplomatic ciphers.

This was all part of a remarkable history, in that America had historically been poor in spy talent, but rich in code breakers. After the Versailles accords, the US Army continued to run an intelligence unit specializing in aerial photography (and, in time, radar). Backed by money from the army and State, Herbert Yardley then began a secret government program of diplomatic code-cracking in the autumn of 1919—the Black Chamber—which gave American diplomats an edge in negotiations with Japan in the Washington Conference of 1921–22. In 1923, American naval intelligence agents rifling though the luggage of a Japanese officer stationed in New York found the Secret Operating Code cookbook used by Japan's navy in the Great War. When the American navy's Research Desk used it to decrypt Japanese traffic, they kept the results in red folders to indicate their top-secret status, and the broken codes within were called RED.

Believing that "gentlemen do not read each other's mail," Herbert Hoover's Secretary of State Henry Stimson canceled the Black Chamber's funding in 1929, but the efforts continued at the Department of War, where an Army Signal Intelligence Service team was cracking code after code, while the Office of Naval Intelligence Research Desk at OP-20-G monitored radio traffic and ship positions across the Pacific. At least three times during this era, ONI arranged to "borrow" ciphers from Japan's New York consulate, but when in 1930 the Japanese changed their codes, it took two years for the navy's operation to crack them. Keeping with tradition, they called it BLUE.

In 1938, when Japan changed her code again, ONI hired a cryptanalyst abandoned by State, the onetime music and mathematics teacher Agnes "Miss Aggie" Meyer Driscoll. By learning the names of every major ship and frequently used phrases of Japan's forces and paging through a photographic reproduction of the codebook's pages with the tip of her pencil's eraser, Miss Aggie cracked the code, now called BLACK.

One cracker explained his craft's eureka breakthroughs: "It first off involved what I call the staring process. You look at all of these messages that you have; you line them up in various ways; you write them one below the other; you'd write them in various forms and you'd stare at them. Pretty soon you'd notice a pattern; you'd notice a definite pattern between these messages. This was the first clue."

On March 20, 1939, the Americans intercepted a new Japanese diplomatic cryptosystem, and by the summer it had so replaced RED and BLACK that little traffic could be read. Frank Rowlett was in charge of breaking this new code, and on that September 20, 1940, a twenty-six-year-old cryptanalyst, Genevieve Grotjan, unlocked what Washington would call PURPLE. Rowlett took notes: "Grotjan enters room, obviously excited, politely interrupts, asks if she can show us what she has found. She takes us to her desk in next room, lays out worksheets, points to one example, then another, then a third. She stands back, with eyes tranced behind her rimless glasses. Small dashes around the room, hands clasped above his head like a victorious prizefighter. 'Whoopee!' he yells. Ferner, the quiet one, clasps his hands, shouting, 'Hooray, Hooray.' I jump up and down—'That's it! That's it!' The room gets crowded; everyone in section suddenly in room. Friedman comes in and asks, 'What's all the noise about?' I settle down and say, 'Look what Miss Grotjan has just discovered.' Gene wipes her eyes, tries to regain her composure. I point to the worksheets—'Gene's found what we've been looking for. Look here, and here, and here.'"

Once again, a woman who would remain unrecognized by her country had delivered a behind-the-scenes breakthrough that would lead to victory in World War II. As countless American nerd geniuses would do in decades to come, the team celebrated their great achievement by ordering in bottles of Coke.

Before Pearl Harbor, anyone with ambitions for a high-ranking career in the US military avoided intelligence, which was universally dismissed as a desk job for those lacking in courage. Before PURPLE, any intelligence cooperation between the US Army and Navy was more a matter of individual initiative than of concerted policy. Now, Japan's consular cables were intercepted by military listening stations in Alaska, Washington State, Hawaii, Guam, and Luzon, as well as collected at the cable companies' offices, except for many years in Honolulu, where intercepting cables was judged illegal.* The intercepted messages were forwarded to Washington, frequently by mail, and then decoded, translated, and evaluated by army and navy intelligence. Those results went to the navy's Rear Admiral Richmond Kelly Turner and the army's Brigadier General Leonard T. Gerow, who selected the most significant for a locked briefcase, carried daily by a distributing officer to the secretaries of navy, war, and state; the army's chief of staff; the chief of naval operations; and the president. Each US official read the decoded and translated materials with the officer standing by, then returned the documents to G-2, where they were burned.

By the fall of 1941, American cryptographers would know about Japan's foreign policy before its ambassadors to America (a situation that would be echoed at war's end when Stalin knew more about the development of the atomic bomb than Truman). It was so astonishing that someone—many swear it was FDR—called it magic, and MAGIC was and remains one of the few joint operations between the American army and navy that worked well, with an astonishing 97 percent success rate. In one more example of FDR's passion, he arranged for only the navy to deliver his MAGIC to the White House—never the army.

A leak occurred in April of 1941, with information revealed by MAGIC passed over to Britain's ambassador, who then transmitted

---

*As the threats from Japan grew, however, in the first week of December 1941, RCA chief David Sarnoff agreed to have his company cooperate.

it in a code the Nazis had cracked. On May 5, the Foreign Ministry cabled Nomura, "According to a fairly reliable source of information it appears almost certain that the United States Government is reading your code messages. Please let me know whether you have any suspicion of the above." As Nomura was a former chief of the Intelligence Bureau of the Naval General Staff, he knew better than most consuls how to safeguard his nation's secrets. He replied that his office took "the most stringent precautions" to protect "codes and ciphers, as well as other documents" and requested "any concrete instance or details which may turn up." On May 20, Nomura confirmed to Tokyo, "Though I do not know which ones, I have discovered the United States is reading some of our codes. As for how I got the intelligence, I will inform you by courier or another safe way."

We don't have further details on how Nomura learned about American codebreaking, but since the Foreign Office did not recalibrate its codes after the leak, the United States kept reading them. Unfortunately, just as the Japanese believed wholeheartedly that PURPLE could never be decrypted, American military chiefs believed MAGIC told them everything they needed to know about Japan. Despite MAGIC's magic, it never found a message specifically detailing an attack on Hawaii because the Japanese foreign office never sent such a message . . . the Japanese military made sure to keep its greatest secrets away from the foreign office. Instead, when it came to potential Japanese military targets in the Pacific, the American War Plans Division had to speculate about a three-thousand-mile geographic area ranging from the borders of Siberia to the shores of Thailand. Except for a limited number of cables that will be discussed below, nothing about Pearl Harbor was ever found in PURPLE.

MAGIC was also less than magical in that its information suffered delays, given the military's security decision to transport top-secret documents by air, sea, trucks, and trains instead of by wireless. Plus, the overwhelming need to keep MAGIC secret greatly reduced its effectiveness. Harold Stark believed, in one example, that Husband Kimmel had a PURPLE machine at Pearl Harbor, when, instead, the commander in chief of the Pacific Fleet knew nothing at all about MAGIC or PURPLE. In fact, Grew, Kimmel, and Short all lacked direct evidence of the growing Japanese menace since they had been refused clearance for MAGIC. But even if they had been part of the select few reading decrypts, MAGIC was frankly not all that useful in helping American defense forces prepare for the great Japanese assault across East Asia. Douglas MacArthur's PURPLE machine did nothing to help him successfully defend his Philippines, and those Washington insiders who daily knew MAGIC's revelations would be just as surprised by December 7 as Kimmel and Short.

Additionally, the Americans had no idea that starting in 1936 the Imperial Japanese Army's intelligence had been decoding much of America's own diplomatic communications traffic. The IJA had cracked all three of the US State Department's codes—the Gray, the Brown, and the Strip Cipher (which was remarkable, as neither the British nor the Germans had been able to crack that Strip Cipher). But neither Washington nor Tokyo had succeeded in cracking each other's military codes. During their between-the-wars lull, the US Army's Signal Intelligence Service couldn't get enough intercepts to crack Japanese army messages, and by December 1941, with Miss Aggie and Lieutenant Prescott Currier leading the efforts, the navy had only revealed about 10 percent of the 1939 Japanese Fleet General Purpose System (which the Americans called, in turn, JN-25 and JN-25b).*

If America's secret weapons of World War II were radar and code-cracking, Japan's were its spies. On March 27, 1941, Honolulu's Japanese-language *Nippu Jiji* newspaper reported that "Tadashi Morimura, newly appointed secretary of the local Japanese consulate general, arrived here this morning on the *Nitta Maru* from Japan. His appointment was made to expedite the work on expatriation applications and other matters." In fact, no person of that name was listed in Japan's foreign registry, for Tadashi Morimura was no embassy clerk, but a naval officer whose career was struck short by illness and who had been reassigned into a civilian job with naval intelligence. Takeo

---

*In time, Miss Aggie and her colleagues would crack it well enough for breakthrough victories at the Coral Sea and Midway—as well as to use it to assassinate Admiral Isoroku Yamamoto—while December 7 would dramatically change the manpower given to American code-cracking. During the war, military decrypt teams would grow to a population of sixteen thousand in Washington alone and in 1952, it would become the National Security Agency—the NSA. One aspect of MAGIC, however, remains current and controversial. Did its revelations of Tokyo's recruitment of those living in the United States to serve as spies, combined with Washington's knowledge of Nazi-allied fifth columnists in France, Belgium, the Netherlands, and the Balkans, lead directly to February 19, 1942's Executive Order 9066—the interning of Japanese American citizens?

Yoshikawa: "Since I had been studying English, I was assigned to the sections dealing with the British and American navies. I became the Japanese navy's expert on the American navy. I read history, too. Like the works of Mahan, the famous American admiral." After using *Jane's Fighting Ships* to memorize the silhouettes of American naval warcraft, Morimura/Yoshikawa appeared in Honolulu in the spring of 1941 with $600 in cash. At the embassy, he developed a reputation as a drinker and a slacker who worked extremely odd hours, an act he called Bobby Make-Believe, to make his embassy colleagues dismiss the rumors that he was an officer of the Imperial Japanese Navy. No one in the navy, they knew, would ever behave like that.

Publicly dressed in the tourist uniform of linen trousers and aloha shirt, Yoshikawa regularly signed up for aerial sightseeing excursions, including a flight to Maui, where he watched the naval traffic at Lahaina. He went swimming near the outer edge of Pearl Harbor, looking for submarine and torpedo nets. Along with several women from the consulate, he took a glass-bottom-boat tour of Kaneohe harbor and noted its various depths. At a Japanese fencing club popular with US military officers, he became known as an "attentive listener," while at the Shuncho-Ro teahouse on Alewa Heights, he drank and ate to his heart's content while attended to by geishas and used the telescope the owner had installed for tourists on the second floor. Yoshikawa: "From there I saw the fleet in Pearl Harbor. Sometimes I went around Pearl Harbor by taxi, or bus. Sometimes I walked along, drinking a beer, to get information. I did you know 'fishing' to mark the depths of the sea. But it was very dangerous." Disguised as a Filipino, he washed dishes in the Pearl Harbor officers' club and went hiking through the Aiea Heights sugarcane fields, with their picture-postcard views of the American fleet. It was not exactly 007 derring-do, but Yoshikawa's humdrum tasks would generate detailed reports that gave crucial information to Japanese fighter, bomber, and torpedo pilots as they decimated Oahu.

Consul General Nagai Kita oversaw Yoshikawa's espionage work, and according to the army's General Charles Herron, "It was a matter of common knowledge that the Japanese consulate in Honolulu was the hotbed of espionage in Oahu." Though the United States had shut down German and Italian consulates by that time, Japan's embassies remained open, since the Americans thought it might upset ongoing treaty negotiations to expel them, and because it was believed Japanese foreign agents were too mentally and physically incompetent to pose a threat.

Of Hawaii's residents in 1941, 158,000 were of Japanese ancestry, a full 40 percent of the territory's populace. This enclave had originated with the sugarcane plantations' importing of Japanese workers for cheap manual labor, and its size meant that Honolulu was—and still is—the most Japanese city outside Japan. Half of Hawaii's 1941 restaurateurs and grocers, most of its construction workers, most of its car mechanics, nearly all of its retail clerks, and 100 percent of its fishermen were Japanese. Many patriotically supported their soldiers in the China Incident, buying Japan's war bonds, sending comfort packages to overseas troops, and contributing to Japan's Red Cross campaign to outfit a floating hospital (unknown to these Americans, that money never went to any shipyard, but was instead used to build a bomber named *Hawaii*).

Those census figures worried US military commanders, such as the Hawaii Department's intelligence chief from 1935 to 1937, Lieutenant Colonel George Patton, who prepared an undated memorandum, "Initial Seizure of Orange Nationals," which named 120 prominent local Japanese—doctors, priests, politicians, lawyers, publishers, businessmen, and consular staff—who would be detained if war was declared. The focus was so great on saboteurs that across nine Pearl Harbor investigations, Yoshikawa's espionage activities were never revealed. Then in the 1980s after the Japanese Hawaiian agent himself came forward and confessed, FBI agent J. Harold Hughes sniped, "We all knew he was a spy. . . . I'm just so tired of reading this kind of story about 'Master Spy' Yoshikawa. It just isn't so, by dang." However, while the FBI and army intelligence worked to ferret out evidence of fifth columnists among Honolulu's locals—evidence they never found—Yoshikawa continued his grunt-work surveillance of Oahu, by dang.

Even though the FBI agent in charge of Hawaii, Robert Shivers, testified he could not get any useful intelligence about the local Japanese populace from Caucasians, the Bureau had only one employee of Japanese descent—a translator. At one meeting with Consul General Kita, Shivers coyly said, "Go ahead, Mr. Kita. Cruise around the island and see what you can see." "Oh, no," Kita said, smiling. "Then you would follow me and chase me."

During this time, warning after warning was sent between Washington and Oahu. On April 1, 1941, CNO Stark cabled his naval district commanders (including Kimmel), "Personnel of your naval intelligence service should be advised that because of the fact that from past experience shows the Axis powers often begin activities in a particular field on Saturdays and Sundays or on national holidays of the country concerned, they should take steps on such days to see that proper watches and precautions are in effect."

With twenty-twenty hindsight, it is mystifying to read again and again of how insistent military officers in Hawaii were before December 7 that nothing was a threat to them, yet this was a broadly held sentiment in the United States before the shock of Pearl Harbor. Minnesota congressman and Marine Corps reservist Melvin Maas returned from active duty in Hawaii to report, "Japan is deathly afraid of the American fleet," and that US forces in the territory could defend "against any combination of forces that might challenge our interest." The *New York Times* called the islands "Our Gibraltar in the Pacific"; and *Collier's* magazine reported that Pearl Harbor was "impregnable." Clark Beach in the *Honolulu Star-Bulletin* editorialized, "A Japanese attack on Hawaii is regarded as the most unlikely thing in the world, with one chance in a million of being successful. . . . American naval men would like nothing better than to see the Japanese fleet outside of Pearl Harbor where they could take it on."

In the spring of 1941, after George Marshall had completed a tour of Hawaii's military installations, Marshall told Stimson, "With our heavy bombers and our fine new pursuit planes, the land forces could put up such a defense that the Japs wouldn't dare attack Hawaii." When Stimson passed this along to Roosevelt, the president asked for a White House meeting at noon the next day. On April 24, Stimson told FDR that Marshall "felt that Hawaii was impregnable whether there are any ships left there are not; that the land defense was amply sufficient, together with the air defense, to keep off the Japanese, and the air defense could always be reinforced from the mainland of America."

Stimson then gave FDR a memorandum from Marshall which included, "The island of Oahu, due to its fortification, its garrison, and its physical characteristics, is believed to be the strongest fortress in the world. [To invade it] the enemy must transport overseas an expeditionary force capable of executing a forced landing against a garrison of approximately 35,000 men, manning 127 fixed coast defense guns, 211 anti-aircraft weapons, and more than 3,000 artillery pieces and automatic weapons available for beach defense. Without air superiority this is an impossible task. . . . With adequate air defense, enemy carriers, naval escorts and transports will begin to come under air attack at a distance of approximately 750 miles. This attack will increase in intensity until when within 200 miles of the objective, the enemy forces will be subject to attack by all types of bombardment closely supported by our most modern pursuit. . . . Including the movement of aviation now in progress Hawaii will be defended by 35 of our most modern flying fortresses, 35 medium range bombers, 13 light bombers, 150 pursuit of which 105 are of our most modern type. In addition Hawaii is capable of reinforcement by heavy bombers from the mainland by air. With this force available a major attack against Oahu is considered impracticable."

In fact, Oahu did not have patrol planes that could fly out on a 750-mile arc; she did not have sufficient bombers to bring the enemy under attack at such range; and as of December 7, 1941, General Short would not have thirty-five B-17s; he would have twelve—only six of them operational. The key matériel problem that plagued Hawaii—not enough planes to thoroughly search 360 degrees—held true for all of America's military forces at that moment, a problem that nearly got Army Air Corps commanding general Hap Arnold fired. From 1939 to 1940, Arnold had made his position clear: FDR's enthusiastic policy of shipping planes to Britain was weakening American defense. Arnold got so vociferous with his complaints that Roosevelt told Assistant Secretary of War Louis Johnson that "either Arnold cut it out or he would be removed as head of the Air Corps."

George Marshall's optimism, meanwhile, was widely shared in his War Department, compounded by the US being as ignorant of Japan's fighting forces as she was of theirs. After the war, army intelligence officer Colonel George Bicknell remembered: "Practically every person on the island of Oahu had been lulled into a sense of false security through the constant reiteration of the belief that the defenses of the island made it practically impregnable. In addition, it had been constantly stated that Japan, as a military and naval power, amounted to nothing when pitted against the superior equipment, personnel, and tactics of our own army and navy. . . . Little was actually known about Japanese airpower, although, again, there were many stories about the poor quality of Japanese aircraft, the lack of proper equipment, and the alleged fact that the Japanese made poor aviators and would never be as good as occidentals in this field."

Some, however, knew of the military's failings; a special investigation of Hawaiian forces prepared in July 1941 by the onetime commanding officer of Hickam Field, Colonel Harvey Burwell, concluded that after years of living a tropical island life, the army's soldiers had lost their "aggressive initiative," while their commanders, backed by such an enormous force of troops, had no "critical concern for the future," with few having thought through a detailed response to enemy attacks, especially when it came to "an abrupt conflict with Japan."

The chief of the Far East Section in the Office of the Chief of Naval Operations, Rear Admiral Arthur McCollum, admitted that Washington was woefully uninformed about the Japanese. After McCollum presented a study of Japanese naval airmen and their technology in 1941 to the Navy's General Board to demonstrate that a significant threat was coming out of Asia and to "tell these people that the Japanese aviators were darned good," his warnings were utterly ignored, he said, because his fellow officers could only think of Japanese as "funny little people."

In Tokyo, the prime minister, the foreign, army, and navy ministers, and the vice chiefs of both services' general staff argued over the future course of the nation at the May 3 and May 8 liaison conferences, with Foreign Minister Matsuoka repeatedly demanding that Japan attack Singapore as soon as possible to gain a tactical advantage. It would help their Nazi allies by requiring England to fight on two oceans at once, and a great Japanese victory over the British would serve to cow the American president. "Roosevelt is keen to go to war. You see, he is a huge gambler," Matsuoka explained. "If Britain surrenders an hour before the United States enters the war in Europe, the United States would change its mind and refrain from going to war. [But] if Britain surrenders an hour after the United States enters the war, the United States would continue fighting. . . . If the United States were ever to enter this war, the war will be prolonged, and the world civilization will be destroyed." The foreign minister's enthusiasm was so excessive that Hirohito darkly concluded to Privy Seal Kido, "Matsuoka has been likely bribed by Hitler," and the emperor immediately had a private meeting with Prime Minister Konoye to make sure that he didn't agree with the foreign minister's extremist views.

On May 12, Ambassador Nomura gave State Secretary Hull a new treaty draft that asked Washington to "request the Chiang Kai-shek regime to negotiate peace with Japan" and if Chiang refused, for America to "discontinue her assistance to the Chiang Kai-shek regime." It offered a "withdrawal of Japanese troops from Chinese territory in accordance with an agreement to be concluded between Japan and China," but, as part of a joint defense against communism, included the right of Japan to station troops in China. America and Japan would resume their most-favored-nation status in commerce, and as "Japanese expansion in the direction of the southwestern Pacific area is declared to be of peaceful nature, American cooperation shall be given in the production and procurement of natural resources (such as oil, rubber, tin, nickel) which Japan needs." To cap these outrageous terms, Tokyo threw Hull's diatribes about Japanese colonialism back in the American's lap by suggesting the United States and Japan "jointly guarantee the independence of the Philippine Islands on the condition that the Philippine Islands shall maintain a status of permanent neutrality."

Hull made Nomura a counteroffer a month later. The United States needed to know what treaty terms Japan proposed to offer China before it could urge Chiang to do anything; Tokyo and Washington both would offer "access by peaceful means to supplies of natural resources which each needed" and "mutual affirmation that the basic policy of each country was one of peace throughout the Pacific area and a mutual disclaimer of territorial designs." Hull finished by telling Nomura that Japan could join the rest of the world by adhering to his principles of peace through commerce—or find herself alone and besieged.

Leaders in Tokyo, expecting a few minor changes from the original Maryknoll terms, were appalled. Couldn't Washington at the very least recognize Japan's dominion in China, if not the whole of Southeast Asia? Matsuoka told Nomura that it was high time the United States stopped trying to police the globe and interfere in other nations' "spheres of living."

Even though American officials expected that something might happen, at any time, in the Pacific—with Stimson writing on May 23, "The president shows evidence of waiting for the accidental shot of some irresponsible captain on either side to be the occasion of his going to war"—Kimmel lost nearly a quarter of his fleet in that year's transfers from the Pacific to the Atlantic: carrier *Yorktown*; battleships *Mississippi*, *Idaho*, and *New Mexico*; four light cruisers, seventeen destroyers, three oilers, three transports, and ten auxiliaries—more than he would lose on December 7. In the wake of this order, Kimmel wrote CNO Stark on May 26 an eleven-page cable that included: "With the recent detachment of many of the most modern and effective units, the adequacy and suitability of the forces remaining to accomplish the tasks to which they may be assigned is very doubtful. . . . The defense of the Fleet base at Pearl Harbor is a matter of considerable concern. . . . The naval forces available to the Commandant are meager to the point of non-existence."

Like his predecessor at Pearl Harbor, James Richardson, a concerned Admiral Husband Kimmel then came to Washington to make clear the many weaknesses of Pearl Harbor to Stark, Knox, and King at lunch, notably the "congestion of ships, fuel oil storage, and repair facilities," which invited "attack, particularly from the air." The "single entrance channel . . . exposed them to submarine attack. . . . In case of attack by air or otherwise with the Fleet in port, it would take at least three hours to complete a sortie. . . . The only real answer was for the Fleet not to be in Pearl Harbor when the attack came."

On June 9, the admiral met with the president at the White House for ninety minutes. They'd known each other casually for decades; Kimmel had even been an aide to Navy Undersecretary Franklin Roosevelt for ten days in 1915. FDR told CINCPAC that officials in the State Department "were carrying on informal talks with certain Japanese and others concerned looking forward to a peaceful Pacific for one hundred years;" Kimmel considered this "a considerable amount of wishful thinking." Roosevelt also asked the admiral's opinion on "further reducing the Pacific Fleet by three battleships," since Knox had told him that "six battleships could raid Japanese communications and defend Hawaii," and Stark thought that "three battleships is enough to defend Hawaii." Kimmel said, "That's crazy!" Roosevelt, as always, agreed with whoever was in the room at the moment: "It sounds silly to me. I told Knox it was silly." Kimmel said that he "was convinced that such further reduction would be an invitation for Japan to come into the war." "That's right," Roosevelt said.

On June 13, CNO Stark's deputy Rear Admiral Royal Ingersoll sent a memo to all naval district commanders that pointed out, though it was commonly believed that aerial torpedoes required seventy-five feet to launch, "recent developments have shown that United States and British torpedoes may be dropped from planes at heights of as much as three hundred feet, and in some cases make initial dives of considerably less than seventy-five feet, and make excellent runs. [So] it cannot be assumed that any capital ship or other valuable vessel is safe at anchor from this type of attack if surrounded by water at a sufficient distance to permit an attack to be developed and a sufficient run to arm the torpedo." Husband Kimmel read this memo, but still decided that it was impossible that "aerial torpedoes could run in Pearl Harbor."

On July 5, Stimson received from Marshall "a very interesting piece of news that had come along through authentic channels of something that Matsuoka in Tokyo had been telling Ribbentrop—about how well they had been fooling the Americans in keeping our Fleet in the Pacific. This was the last straw for me in proof of the futility of the final late efforts of the State Department." That morning at eleven o'clock he showed it to Roosevelt, who said that it "had better signalize the end of our efforts in appeasement in the Pacific."

On June 12, code breakers at England's Bletchley Park decrypted a conversation between Adolf Hitler and Japan's ambassador to Germany that said Russia would be the Nazis' next target. Five days later, another decrypt revealed Tokyo requesting German help in forcing the Vichy French to give it air and sea bases across French Indochina in Saigon, Siem Reap, and Phnom Penh.

Just before dawn on June 22, Nazi troops invaded the Soviet Union with twenty-seven hundred tanks in an immense wedge that pushed aside Russian defense forces. Within two days, the Soviets had lost over two thousand aircraft, and within a month the Nazis were triumphant, the Wehrmacht a mere 130 miles from the nation's political heart: the Kremlin. It was one more of Hitler's immensely triumphant blitzkriegs.

Now extending from the shoals of France in the west to the onion domes of Moscow in the east, and from the midnight sun of the Barents Sea in the north to the Arab Sahara of Africa in the south, the Nazi empire, conquered and amassed in a bare three years, was incomprehensibly vast, and menacing.

The effect in Tokyo of Hitler's invasion of the Soviet Union was political consternation. Matsuoka called for an immediate audience with the emperor and insisted Japan should fight simultaneously with the Germans against the Soviets in the north and against the Anglo-Saxons to the south. This meeting so upset Hirohito that he concluded the foreign minister had become unhinged and immediately suggested to the prime minister that Matsuoka be removed from the cabinet. Prince Konoye received this news enthusiastically. Originally a strong supporter of the Tripartite Pact, he had, by that summer of 1941, turned entirely against the Axis and wanted to dramatically improve relations with the United States. He assumed Matsuoka's exit would do just that, but under the constitution, Japan's prime minister couldn't dismiss a cabinet member, and Matsuoka refused to resign.

Prime Minister Konoye asked the Cabinet Planning Board's general director, Teiichi Suzuki, to meet with War Minister Hideki Tojo to ask him if, since the Nazis had so viciously abrogated their treaty with the Soviet Union, couldn't Japan now ignore the Tripartite Pact and negotiate treaties of nonaggression with Britain and America? Tojo was grievously offended, shouting at Suzuki, "Do you really think we can act in such an immoral way, against humanity and justice?"* Days later, a Naval Affairs Bureau officer begged Navy Minister Osami Nagano not to let the army push the navy into joining Hitler in the war against Russia. Nagano, knowing the army's vehement reaction to Hull's treaty terms, snorted, "You're telling me. We're on the verge of war with the United States!"

One military faction now urged a "green persimmon" policy—based on the idea that shaking the tree, and getting green persimmons, was a better harvest strategy than waiting for the fruit to ripen and fall—meaning, Japan should join Hitler and attack Russia. The opposition, those in favor of the "ripe persimmon" strategy, pointed out that, if an attack began in June 1941, twelve divisions and eight hundred Japanese planes would face thirty Russian divisions and twenty-eight hundred planes. Naval Minister Osami Nagano additionally noted that attacking the Soviet Union would assuredly mean war with Great Britain and the United States, and that if the army's southward advance continued, another American embargo would result, forcing a seizure of the Netherlands East Indies' oil fields, leading directly to war with the Americans, the British, and the Dutch.

---

*Hideki Tojo was so ramrod by-the-books and so harsh to his subordinates that he was nicknamed the Razor. When he became prime minister, one of his first orders of business was to look through people's garbage on his morning walks, which he told the press was to ensure that wartime rations were working effectively. If this was PR, it wasn't successful, as he was quickly called the Dumpster Minister. His pretentious speeches, filled with *therefore*s and *thus*es, were so odd, schoolchildren made a game of imitating them.

The persimmon debate seemed abstract enough, but its framing led Japan's leaders into a collective and fatalistic belief that war was inevitable. They only needed to answer one question: Who would be the enemy?

The moderates did have some reassuring news; using diplomacy instead of conquest, Japan had succeeded in taking over the northern section of French Indochina, and had even mediated a territorial dispute in Thailand's favor. That June, the army sided with the navy in pushing for expanding into the rest of the French colony using the same method of diplomacy to allow more access to rice, tin, and rubber, as well as to be able to extort the Netherlands East Indies for more oil. With this compromise, the army stopped insisting on an all-out war in China against both the Chinese and the Soviets, but left open the option of attacking if an opportunity—say, a great exodus of Russian troops from the Pacific theater to fight the Nazis on the Western Front—arose.

Later that month, the army's war guidance officer noted in the *Confidential War Journal*:

No new developments
Days of agonies and ruminations continue
One day's delay means waste of so much oil
One day's delay means sacrifice of so much blood
Yet they say we must avoid a hundred years' war with America!

Across 1941, the Imperial Japanese Army regularly advocated war against the United States, while the civilian government equivocated, and the navy opposed. Yet the army did little to get ready for such a great step, its war plan cavalierly stating, "Operations against the United States were primarily the responsibility of the Navy and victory or defeat was to be determined in an all-out battle between the main naval forces of the two nations; therefore operations involving the Army would be limited." Japan's generals hoped that by taking over the great natural resources of Southeast Asia, their Chinese catastrophe could be forgiven and forgotten, while the navy's plan was that Britain would fall to the Nazis and the Americans would give up, conceding to Japan her Asian territories. If there was one great moment of Japanese fascist insanity, it was this, for no further details of strategy, operations, technology, or economics for victory in a titanic war against the United States were developed by either service.

On July 2, in the Meiji Palace's First Eastern Hall conference room bedecked with European chandeliers and purple Asian silks, Japan's Privy Council president met the nation's leaders at what would be the first of four imperial conferences leading to December 7. While the emperor sat silently by, listening in, generals, admirals, and ministers were questioned in detail on their plans and expectations.

"Imperial conferences were a curious thing," Hirohito later explained. "The emperor had no deciding power, unable [even] to dictate the atmosphere of the conference." This system rendered political decisions apolitical, turning the crafting of policy into a group consensus, and relieving individuals of responsibility for their decisions. The question that day continued the persimmon debate: Should Japan attack Russia or occupy southern Indochina? The answer was a compromise both expedient and opportunistic. While preparing to invade the south and "construct the Great East Asian Co-Prosperity Sphere regardless of the changes in the world situation," if it looked as though the Russians were clearly losing to the Germans, Japan would attack them, too.

Included in the imperial conference policy statement that day was "War preparations against Great Britain and the United States [must] be stepped up [and] the Empire shall not flinch from war with Britain and the United States." When the navy's chief of staff, Osami Nagano, returned from the conference and faced his officers, he found they were stunned that he had agreed to this clause, with Second Fleet commander Mineichi Koga in near hysterics: "How could you have endorsed such a critical policy without consulting us? What if a war really broke out? You can't just tell us then, 'Okay, you go ahead and fight.' We won't win!" Isoroku Yamamoto diplomatically asked the key question—"Are we really ready for an aerial war?"—knowing that the answer was no. Though he'd actively politicked against the army's plans, Nagano now employed the imperial conference excuse with his men: "What can I say? The government decided on it."

On July 4, the US State Department directly asked Prime Minister Konoye to address rumors it had heard from "various sources" that Japan would attack Russia. On the eighth, Japan replied that she hadn't yet considered the possibility and always desired peace in the Pacific.

On July 14, Walter Short began a six-to-eight-week infantry training of Hawaiian Air Force enlistees, telling Marshall that since full combat required only 3,885 of the Air Corps' 7,229 men, 3,344 had nothing to do during maneuvers and would need to be turned into infantry if the islands were invaded and all their aircraft destroyed. In fact, what these air crews needed was aerial gunnery training, which they wholly lacked, as well as flight time, having averaged a mere two hundred to three hundred hours.

During this period, Interior Secretary Harold Ickes was overseeing petroleum production for national defense and needed to ration New England's supply of heating oil. On June 23, he wrote the president, "To embargo oil to Japan would be as popular a move in all parts of the country as you could make. There might develop from the embargoing of oil to Japan such a situation as would make it, not only possible but easy, to get into this war in an effective way. And if we should thus indirectly be brought in, we would avoid the criticism that we had gone in as an ally of communistic Russia."

In what should be a clear refutation for "back door to war" conspiracists, Roosevelt's answer to Ickes on July 1 explained that a great argument was raging among Japan's leaders at that moment about whether to fight the Soviets, to attack Southeast Asia, or to "sit on the fence and be more friendly with us. . . . Please let me know if this would continue to be your judgment if this were to tip the delicate scales and cause Japan to decide either to attack Russia or to attack the Dutch East Indies. . . . It is terribly important for the control of the Atlantic for us to keep peace in the Pacific. I simply have not got enough Navy to go round—and every little episode in the Pacific means fewer ships in the Atlantic."

After continually telling Washington of its peaceful intentions, 125,000 Japanese troops invaded the southern districts of French Indochina on July 22 to erect air and naval bases. This infuriated Roosevelt, and he had Sumner Welles tell Nomura the next day that American-Japanese negotiations were finished. When Nomura said that the Imperial Japanese Army's invasion was merely taken to ensure a steady flow of rice and other raw materials, Welles replied that, since the only reason this arrangement was made was through threats of force, the United States believed its real purpose was "offering assistance to Germany's policy of world domination and conquest."

In the escalating crisis, Nomura met with Roosevelt and Welles at 5:00 p.m. in the White House on July 24. After the admiral described how Tokyo felt itself encircled by what it called the ABCD powers, the president said it was absurd to think that China, Great Britain, the Netherlands, or the United States was threatening Japan, and that American leaders were nearly unanimous in thinking Hitler was behind Japan's military expansion to the south. Nomura claimed this was not so. The president then said that if Japan tried to take the Dutch oil fields by force, there would be more economic sanctions, and perhaps war.

Nomura insisted that he was personally opposed to the country's course in Indochina, and according to Welles's notes, FDR replied, "That the Japanese Government did not understand as clearly as we that Hitler was bent upon world domination; that if Germany succeeded in defeating Russia and dominating Europe and Africa, Germany thereafter would turn her attention to the Far East and to the Western Hemisphere; and that it was entirely possible that after some years the Navies of Japan and of the United States would be cooperating against Hitler as a common enemy. . . .

"[The president then explained that] had Japan undertaken to obtain the supplies she required from Indochina in a peaceful way, she not only would have obtained larger quantities of such supplies, but would have obtained them with complete security and without the draining expense of a military occupation. . . . [and] if the Japanese government would refrain from occupying Indochina . . . [President Roosevelt] would do everything within his power . . . to regard Indochina as a neutralized country in the same way in which Switzerland had up to now been regarded by the powers as a neutralized country. . . . Japan would be afforded the fullest and freest opportunity of assuring herself of the source of food supplies and other raw materials in Indochina which she was seeking to secure." Nomura replied that "such a step would be very difficult at this time on account of the face-saving element involved on the part of Japan and that only a very great statesman would reverse a policy at this time."

Just after this meeting, Roosevelt wrote Harry Hopkins, then on a diplomatic mission in London, "Tell [Churchill] also in great confidence that I have suggested to Nomura that Indo-China be neutralized . . . [and] I have no answer yet. When it comes it will probably be unfavorable but we have at least made one more effort to avoid Japanese expansion to South Pacific." Churchill replied to Roosevelt that he was absolutely certain Japan didn't have the wherewithal to simultaneously attack America and Britain, that instead Tokyo would wait for London to fall to Berlin, then strike the United States.

In reporting to Tokyo on FDR's offer to Switzerlandize Indochina, Nomura said that he'd "received the impression that some kind of an economic pressure will be enforced in the near future." On July 25, the president froze Japanese assets in the United States, a policy adopted in turn by Great Britain, Canada, New Zealand, the Dutch East Indies, and the Philippines.

Japanese leaders had been so focused on their imperial dream of what part of the world to conquer next, whether to drive communist Russia out of Asia or to take control of the whole of the Southeast Asian subcontinent, that they hadn't thought through the global repercussions. The asset freeze threw them into collective shock, with Tokyo newspaper *Miyako* calling it "a declaration of economic war." "We had no inkling that the United States would be so angry over our going into southern French Indochina," First Division of Military Affairs Chief Toshitane Takada said. "We, myself included, thought that advancing as far as southern French Indochina would—and should—be all right. It was a groundless conviction."

On the twenty-sixth, Roosevelt ordered a change in policy; now, each time Japan wanted to buy American oil or gas, she would need an export license, meaning that Washington could refuse to issue the license and cut off the supply at any time. The president then sailed to meet with Churchill off the coast of Newfoundland to coordinate the Allies' defense in what would be known as the Argentia Conference. When this new export licensing system went into effect, however, Assistant Secretary of State for Economic Affairs Dean Acheson and Treasury Secretary Henry Morgenthau Jr. worked in concert so that Japan's frozen funds would not be released to buy American petroleum, creating a full embargo. Hull and Roosevelt did not understand what had happened until early September, and Roosevelt was talked out of reversing the policy by the cabinet's hard-liners, who said doing so would look like a sign of weakness to the Japanese.

Joseph Grew's diary summary for July 1941: "The vicious circle of reprisals and counter-reprisals is on. . . . Unless radical surprises occur in the world, it is difficult to see how the momentum of this downgrade movement in our relations can be arrested, nor how far it will go. The obvious conclusion is eventual war."

On July 30, a squadron of Japanese naval planes was flying over Chongqing when one pilot pulled away from formation and bombed US gunboat *Tutuila* as she anchored in the river next to the American embassy. Joseph Grew reported, "By the grace of heaven the bomb missed the *Tutuila* by about eight yards, although the ship was damaged and another bomb again came dangerously near our Embassy. Fatalities were escaped only by a miracle." Japan promptly apologized, and the United States accepted.

The next day, Tokyo's foreign office sent Berlin a message to soothe her Nazi allies: "Our Empire must immediately take steps to break asunder this ever-strengthening chain of encirclement which is being woven under the guidance and with the participation of England and the United States, acting like a cunning dragon seemingly asleep. This is why we decided to obtain military bases in French Indo-China and to have our troops occupy that territory. . . . I know the Germans are somewhat dissatisfied over our negotiations with the United States, but we wished at any cost to prevent the United States from getting into the war." When Stimson showed the MAGIC version of this memo to Cordell Hull, the head of the American state department "made up his mind that we have reached the end of any possible appeasement with Japan and that there is nothing further that can be done with that country except by a firm policy and, he expected, force itself."

Prime Minister Konoye told his war and navy ministers that Japan was "only a step this side of entering into a major war" with the Anglo-Saxons. War and navy insisted the asset freeze was an act of war, and it should be met with an act of war. The timing would be based on when Japan ran out of oil, meaning the military had four months to create a strategy of attack.

When Roosevelt during this period suggested ending the crisis by giving up China, he was harshly rebuked by Churchill, Chiang, Morgenthau, Ickes, and Stimson. In the conflict between Japan and the United States that would become World War II's Pacific theater, China held a similar position to the assassination of Archduke Ferdinand in World War I. What is incomprehensible now was once so crucial, so important, so decisive. But the benefit was, at the very least, that China bogged down Japan, in the same way that Russia engulfed the Nazis, giving the Anglo-Saxons what they needed most: time.

CHAPTER THREE

AUTUMN 1941

On August 7, "Ganji" Kuroshima met at the Naval General Staff headquarters with Operations chief Tomioka to again discuss the details of Yamamoto's Operation Z. The general staff remained unconvinced. How could a large force moving across the Pacific avoid "enemy ships or aircraft or ships of neutral countries on the way [or] aerial reconnaissance?" Tomioka wondered. Wouldn't the US Pacific Fleet detect the task force and then attack it in coordination with her land-based aircraft? If Kimmel's ships weren't in port once the Japanese reached Hawaii, the First Air Fleet did not have enough scouts to search for them. Pearl Harbor's shallow waters meant that torpedoes would not work, making the attack reliant on Japan's notoriously ineffective horizontal bombers. Besides, what about the untested method of refueling at sea, and, what about the weather? Finally, the operation meant reducing the number of carriers available for Japan's great gamble, Operation Number One. Tomioka concluded: "This Hawaii Operation is speculative and has little chance for success. In the worst case we may even lose our forces, which are like tiger cubs now."

None of these arguments dissuaded Yamamoto and Ganji, who responded just as aggressively. To force the general staff into agreement, Kuroshima moved up the navy's annual war games to September from November and included a private analysis of Operation Z.

Prime Minister Fumimaro Konoye at this moment realized that the only way he could avoid war with America was through a personal, face-to-face meeting with Roosevelt. Knowing that War Minister Hideki Tojo would be opposed to such a strategy, Konoye sent General Naruhiko Higashikuni, an uncle of the emperor's who had spent his childhood in France, to talk sense to the army minister. At their meeting, Higashikuni shared with Tojo that French general Marshal Pétain and Premier Georges Clemenceau had predicted that, because of the power struggle in the Pacific, the United States and Japan were destined to go to war, a war Japan was destined to lose due to America's greater industrial power. Tojo replied that if the present course of history continued, Japan as a nation would disappear; that the chance of winning a war was fifty-fifty; and that it was better to fight than to do nothing and lose one's country. Higashikuni then said that since both Hirohito and Konoye wanted a meeting with Roosevelt, that Tojo should accede to their wishes. Tojo grudgingly agreed, telling Konoye that, if things did not go as the prime minister hoped, "You shall not resign your post as a result of the meeting on the grounds that it was a failure. Rather, you shall be prepared to assume leadership in the war against America."

Konoye ordered Nomura on August 7 to arrange a summit with FDR, but the ambassador immediately ran into obstacles. Americans had a very low opinion of the prince since he had previously been prime minister when the army committed its barbaric war crimes and he was originally a vociferous supporter of allying with the Nazis. Even the sympathetic Joseph Grew said that Konoye was "saddled with the responsibility for some of the worst acts of banditry on the part of Japan which have been recorded in international history." Combining this résumé with their thinking that the Japanese were racially duplicitous—a viewpoint seemingly confirmed both by MAGIC and by the betrayal of Nomura's diplomatic negotiations with the invasion of Indochina—Cordell Hull and Henry Stimson didn't consider Konoye's summit offer sincere, saying, "The invitation is merely a blind to try and keep us from taking definite action." They knew the prime minister didn't have the full force of the government behind him and assumed that, regardless of the results of any meeting with Roosevelt, Japan's generals wouldn't significantly alter their battle plans.

Roosevelt told Nomura on August 17 that if peace could be brought to the Pacific, he would meet with the prime minister, but if Japan kept trying to negotiate nonaggression pacts with the United States while at the same time invading Asia, "we could not think of reopening the conversations."

Nomura insisted that Konoye was sincere, and on the twenty-eighth, he met with Hull to plan a summit. The prime minister had offered to meet halfway in Hawaii, but the president said that this was too far for him to travel, and he suggested they meet on a battleship anchored off Juneau, Alaska. Konoye accepted and secretly arranged for a ship to be prepared and waiting for him in Yokohama harbor so that he could leave at once to meet with Roosevelt.

Akiho Ishii, the senior staff officer in charge of operations for the Southern Area Army, would be accompanying the prime minister to Alaska and was certain as to the outcome. The president and prime minister would begin at loggerheads, due to the terms preapproved by Japan's military leaders. Then, at the last moment, when everything seemed destined for the brink of war, the emperor would assume command, castigate the generals for their poor behavior, and even though it would mean the embarrassment of troop withdrawals from Indochina and China, insist on peace with America.

One of the few direct warnings given American officials about Pearl Harbor then occurred on August 12, when triple agent Dusan Popov (who worked for Yugoslavian intelligence under the code name Dusko, for Britain's MI6 foreign spy operations as Tricycle, and for Germany's Abwehr as Ivan) appeared in the offices of the US Federal Bureau of Investigation. He wanted to offer the FBI details on the spy network he was setting up in the United States on behalf of the Nazis. Besides a goodly sum of money, the Germans had given Popov—a wealthy cosmopolitan playboy and inspiration for Ian Fleming's James Bond—a three-page questionnaire to answer, one full page of which requested detailed information about America's defenses at Pearl Harbor. Though MI6 had provided him with the strongest of bona fides, FBI director J. Edgar Hoover mistrusted a double agent and a womanizer who was at the moment, Hoover knew, having an affair with French movie star Simone Simon. The Bureau refused to take Popov's revelations seriously. When the Serbian operative later learned of the assault on Oahu, he was crushed: "I had the right information to forestall the attack. I had traveled thousands of miles to deliver the information, which would certainly have shortened the war by a year or more. American red tape stopped the information going through."

A week after Popov tried to convince the FBI of Axis threats against Pearl Harbor, on August 20 the army in Hawaii sent Washington the "Plan for the Employment of Bombardment Aviation in the Defense of Oahu," as prepared by Colonel William Farthing. "Our most likely enemy, Orange [Japan], can probably employ a maximum of six carriers against Oahu," Farthing determined. "An enemy should be primarily interested in obtaining the maximum cover of darkness for his carrier approach. . . . The early morning attack is, therefore, the best plan of action to the enemy." Since "the key to this plan is found in the provision for first, a complete and thorough search of the Hawaiian area daily during daylight," the colonel asked for "180 B-17 D type airplanes or other four-engine bombers with equal or better performance and operating range and 36 long-range torpedo carrying medium bombers." The Army Pearl Harbor Board later called this memo "prophetic in its accuracy and uncanny in its analysis of the enemy's intention," as indeed it was. However, as of the August date of the memo, the entire US Army had 109 B-17s, while Farthing's other great miscalculation was an idea shared by many in Hawaii—that war would be declared, and then an attack would be made. Additionally, Farthing later admitted what so many American officers believed: "I didn't think [Japan] could do it. I didn't think they had that ability."

On August 27 at Konoye's residence in Tokyo, graduate students from the Total War Research Institute spent nine hours presenting a report to the nation's ministers. After six weeks researching the government's own data on military, economic, and diplomatic history, the students concluded that if Japan attacked the Anglo-Saxons, she might win the opening salvoes, but any prolonged war would consume all her resources, and eventually she would be defeated. The students were then assigned a war game, with the theoretical condition that Japan had been economically isolated and needed to take Southeast Asian oil fields by force. The students concluded that this made the unwinnable war they'd predicted inevitable. Enemy fleets, they noted, could easily attack petroleum tankers, making the whole endeavor pointless. The students suggested that the fiasco could and should be avoided though diplomacy.

Their instructor, Colonel Horiba Kazuo, said that they had forgotten a crucial ingredient: "*Yamato-damashii* is what the United States is lacking, and that is the greatest resource of our country," he lectured, referring to "Japanese spirit," a quality shared by the people of the nation, which included discipline, hard work, and resilience. No matter their data or their conclusions, *Yamato-damashii* would ensure that Japan would win.

Navy Chief of Staff Nagano met with Hirohito at the palace on August 31 to discuss Japan's latest war plans. Before his emperor, Nagano insisted he was completely opposed to the Tripartite Pact, as it kept Japan from diplomatically moving forward with the United States, and that a war with America must be avoided. However, he now said, "If our petroleum supplies were cut off, we would lose our stock in two years. If a war broke out, we would use it all up in eighteen months." Under such circumstances, there was "no choice but to strike."

"Could we expect a big victory, such as our victory [over Russia] in the Sea of Japan?" Hirohito wondered.

"I am uncertain as to any victory," Nagano said, "let alone the kind of huge victory won in the Sea of Japan."

"What a reckless war that would be!" Hirohito exclaimed.

Meanwhile, in a sign of growing desperation, the Imperial Japanese Army had stripped away the cast-iron ornaments and fences from Tokyo's buildings to manufacture a mere nineteen hundred pounds of weaponry.

As Japan's leaders lurched between war and peace, Minoru Genda continued to develop Operation Z. To ensure that his pilots were achieving their best, he recruited a naval academy classmate with a reputation as both a fearless China War torpedo ace and a vociferous advocate of carrier warfare among his fellow naval officers, Mitsuo Fuchida. Nicknamed Tako (octopus) since he was so quick to blush—octopuses turn red when cooked—Fuchida was such a charmer that he became fast friends with both Genda and Prince Takamatsu, Hirohito's brother, at the naval academy, Etajima, Japan's Annapolis. A hotshot pilot and hard drinker born on the rural outskirts of Kyoto in 1902, the year of the tiger (*tora* in Japanese), Fuchida so admired Hitler that he groomed his mustache until it resembled the Führer's. In 1940, when he was Third Air Squadron staff officer in charge of the pilots on carriers *Ryujo* and *Shoho*, the young ensign heard another naval officer say, "How many planes do we need on the carriers to protect our battleships?" This made Fuchida—another fervent disciple of Gendaism—enraged. "Aircraft carriers should not protect battleships; it should be the other way around," he yelled. "Japan should gather all her carriers into one great squadron for massive air striking power. The battleships, cruisers, and other ships should protect the carriers."

Like many Japanese of this era, Fuchida thought Christians were treasonous and blasphemous because they wouldn't refer to the emperor as *O Gimi* (great master), an honorific they reserved for Jesus. He also believed Japan was doing the right thing in her conquest of China, since the Japanese were clearly the superior race, destined to rule over Asia. And unlike Yamamoto and Hirohito, Mitsuo Fuchida had no ethical qualms about launching a surprise attack before formally declaring war. If soldiers weren't ready to fight for their defense, he reasoned, they deserved the justice of death.

Genda appointed Fuchida commander of the First Air Fleet's air groups. Operation Z would be comprised of thirty-one vessels ferrying over four hundred aircraft within 220 miles of Oahu. Fuchida organized his squadrons into arrow-shaped formations of five high-level horizontal bombers and nine dive-bombers. He then spent the autumn of 1941 drilling these air crews again and again in trial runs outside the town of Kagoshima on the island of Kyushu, a spot remarkably similar in geography to Pearl Harbor. The trainees were shocked by the advanced torpedo course, in which they roared over the city at a little more than one hundred feet.

Two great revolutions in naval warfare would be wrought by the Japanese at Pearl Harbor. The first would be the ascendancy of the flattop coupled with the fall of the battleship; but the other has been little discussed: the torpedo. A descendant of the floating mine named by Robert Fulton after a genus of electric rays and originally developed as an accessory for his French submarine *Nautilus*, the torpedo was first granted self-propulsion (from compressed air) by English engineer Robert Whitehead, which turned it into an excellent David-versus-Goliath weapon. In the wake of HMS *Dreadnought*, battleships were heavily armed, heavily armored, and thus slow and expensive. Cheap torpedoes could be deployed by small boats, by airplanes, and even by individual frogmen. Running beneath the armored sides to strike the keel and other structural elements of a hull's underbelly, they could break the back of any warship.

Aerial torpedo technology mixed together seemingly every variable of the material world—flight; air; gravity; water; propulsion; detonation; explosion—requiring wildly complicated engineering mathematics to work effectively. In the Japanese standard technique, in which torpedoes were dropped at high speed from a height of three hundred feet, they descended one hundred to three hundred feet into the water, with some then shooting up so sharply they would porpoise over the surface, while others ran so deeply they would pass right under a target's keel. American navy officer Bradley Fiske developed a patented technique of descending in a spiraling dive to escape enemy fire, leveling at ten to twenty feet over the water while setting a course to adjust the torpedo's path, waiting to release until fifteen hundred to two thousand yards from the target, and finally executing a steep climb to avoid collision with a warship's superstructure. Fiske reported that, given enough depth and distance, ships could be sunk in their own harbors with this technique.

Genda and Fuchida ordered the fleet's finest torpedo pilots, the Yokosuka Air Group, to combine engineering with technique to prevent their Model II torpedoes from descending farther than thirty-three feet underwater. After months of experiments and drills, a wooden fin was attached to the torpedoes' tails that would break away when the missile hit the water and, in doing so, slow its dive. This fin additionally gave the torpedoes such quick steadying they could run in a narrow confine, such as a harbor. But manufacturing enough, under a deadline, was a problem; Fuchida could only have thirty by October 15, another fifty by October 31, and the final hundred would not be delivered until November 30. Between October 30 and November 4, however, only five to ten fins were available to test in Kagoshima. The results were "irregular."

Finally, however, the pilots perfected the missing ingredient: Fiske's leveling technique of skimming over the water at a shockingly low altitude. On a beautiful day that fall, three torpedoes were dropped into waters as shallow as Pearl Harbor's. One sank to the bottom and stuck there, but the other two righted themselves and barreled straight into their targets. If his airmen could maintain this same two-of-three ratio over Hawaii, Fuchida knew he could achieve a great victory. Even so, the commander decided, "We cannot rely only on torpedoes. Nor can we expect too much from dive-bombing because the missiles are too light to penetrate the heavy armor of a United States battleship. We must work on high-level bombing and train incessantly until our bombardiers are good enough." Additionally he saw that only an outbound ship could be attacked with torpedoes on a double mooring. He brought up all these technical worries about torpedo attacks with his commander. "Do it anyway!" Genda said.

Since they expected Pearl Harbor and its biggest ships to be ringed with torpedo nets, Yokosuka experimented with various methods of cutting them. Nothing worked. Fukudome later said that, faced with nets, "It was decided to make bombings only against them, giving up torpedo attacks." But that wasn't the whole truth, as Fuchida had furtively gotten Genda's approval to have pilots suicide-dive into any torpedo nets to shatter them.

The high-level bombing presented even more of a problem than the torpedoes, since the Japanese had no shells that could penetrate a battleship's high-armored decks; the ones that they did have wouldn't fall straight, and their bombsight technology was so primitive it meant a humiliating failure rate in hitting their targets. After days of experiment and failure, Fuchida's teams finally came up with the answer. By adding metal fins to a sixteen-inch, seventeen-hundred-pound battleship shell to ensure it would fall nose-first, and then dropping it from a height of eleven thousand feet, the shell's weight, combined with the power of gravity, created a bomb that could penetrate a battleship's deck. Fuchida also exchanged the traditional nine-plane high-level formation for five planes in an arrowhead, which gave him ten attack units, each of which could concentrate on its assigned target. After months of drilling, squads led by the best high-level pilots with the best bombardiers had every crew drop their ordnance when their leaders did. The hit rate improved by 70 percent.

Japanese dive-bomber pilots normally cruised at thirteen thousand feet before diving to release their ordnance at around two thousand feet. Takeshige Egusa, who would lead the divers in the second attack, suggested dropping to fifteen hundred feet before releasing the bombs. This increased the chance of a direct hit, but also increased the danger of a pilot's failing to pull out of the dive. Shortly after this change in technique, one of the dive-bombers in training crashed, resulting in serious discussions over Fuchida's head. But the change in the release point proved so effective that regardless of the danger, Nagumo agreed to it; men would be sacrificed to kill ships.

Dive-bomber pilot Zenji Abe would provide an astonishing coda in Pearl Harbor history. "I was in command of a bomber company on board the carrier *Akagi*. One day in October, all of the officers above the grade of company commander in our task force were assembled. . . . Commander Minoru Genda, the operation staff officer, came into the conference room and without formality opened the curtain on the front wall to reveal models of Pearl Harbor and Oahu Island, constructed on the full space of the wall. . . .

"One day before leaving [training in] Kyushu, a party was held in a restaurant in Kagoshima. Vice Admiral Chuichi Nagumo, commander in chief of the task force, exchanged cups of wine with each of the officers, shaking hands with them. I thought that I perceived the sparkle of a tear in his eye." The tear was from Nagumo's deep and continuing pessimism about the prospects of the mission he had been ordered to lead, and the foreboding that he would never again see these young men.

Back in Tokyo on September 5, Prime Minister Konoye met at the palace with Hirohito to prepare him for the next day's imperial conference where, following Japanese tradition, he would bless the "Essentials for Carrying Out the Empire's Policies," which the government had approved two days before. The emperor was stunned when Konoye told him that Japan needed to prepare for war since, if diplomacy didn't succeed by the first week of October, at the end of that month, the country would attack Britain, Holland, and the United States. Konoye then tried to describe the military's plans for how this war would be won: "By occupying the necessary areas to the south . . . we should be able to consolidate an invincible position; by taking advantage of conditions in the interim, we can entertain hopes of being able to bring the war to an end."

When the emperor said he wanted the policy's priorities reversed to emphasize diplomacy, Konoye said "that would be impossible." The emperor then asked how war could be so close and yet he knew nothing of it. The prime minister said it was the fault of the two chiefs of staff. The emperor immediately summoned the navy's Osami Nagano and the army's Hajime Sugiyama to the palace.

"If something happens between Japan and the United States," Hirohito asked his military chiefs after they'd arrived, "how long does the army really believe it will take to clear things up?"

"If limited to the South Seas, I would expect to clear things up in three months," Sugiyama replied.

"You were army minister at the time the China Incident broke out," Hirohito pointed out. "I remember you saying, 'The Incident will be cleared up in about a month.' But it still hasn't been cleared up after four long years, has it?"

Sugiyama: "China opens a [vast] hinterland, and military operations could not be conducted as planned."

Emperor: "If the hinterland of China is vast, isn't the Pacific even more vast? What convinces you to say three months?"

Sugiyama bowed his head, refusing to answer.

Emperor: "The high command understands that as of today the objective is to emphasize diplomacy, correct?"

Sugiyama and Nagano: "That is correct."

At the next day's imperial conference, Hirohito reclined on his throne on a platform far from the table where the ministers conferred, his divine and silent presence serving to bless the undertaking. After Konoye and the four leaders of the army and navy ministries each presented their views, the president of the Privy Council interrogated them with the emperor's concerns: "Am I right in believing that everything is being done diplomatically at present to save the situation in that war will be resorted to only when diplomatic means fail?" Oikawa said yes, but Nagano and Sugiyama said nothing, prompting the emperor, for the first time in known history, to break the tradition of the imperial conference and shock the assembled leaders by saying aloud, "President Hara's question just now was truly appropriate. It is regrettable that both chiefs of the general staff are unable to answer it."

Nagano finally admitted that Japan had a 70 to 80 percent chance of winning its first battles, which might mean a long-term peace, and that, echoing Tojo, "the government has decided that if there were no war, the fate of the nation was sealed. Even if there is war, the country may be ruined. Nevertheless a nation which does not fight in this plight has lost its spirit and is already a doomed nation." Nagano later explained the militarists' thinking: "Japan was like a patient suffering from a serious illness. . . . Should he be let alone without an operation, there was danger of a gradual decline. An operation, while it might be extremely dangerous, would still offer some hope of saving his life."

As their discussion veered more and more toward a declaration of war, the meeting was shockingly halted, as never before in history, when Hirohito unfolded a sheet of paper from the breast pocket of his uniform. In his quavering, high alto, the emperor of Japan recited verse by his grandfather Mutsuhito, the great Meiji:

> The seas of the four directions—
> all are born of one womb:
> why, then, do the wind and waves rise in discord?

The emperor had hoped the words of his legendary ancestor, so revered by the nation, would sway the government away from war and admitted later that he had read this *waka* "over and over again . . . striving to introduce into the present the emperor Meiji's ideal of international peace." After what seemed like hours of silence, Nagano said as an apology that he was "filled with trepidation at the prospect of the Emperor's displeasure with the Supreme Command [who were] conscious of the importance of diplomacy, and advocated a resort to arms only when there seemed no other way out."

Meiji had ridden the revolutionary fervor of his people to build a modern nation, but his grandson was not as talented, or as forceful, or as lucky. In fact, when War Minister Hideki Tojo, his eyes wet with tears, later recounted the reading of the *waka* to his staff, he said its meaning was to encourage Japan's soldiers and sailors to valor, even when the outcome was uncertain.

Prime Minister Konoye was now becoming desperate, as Ambassador Joseph Grew recalled. He "arranged a meeting with me on September 6 in order to discuss a meeting with President Roosevelt. . . . He, I think, saw the handwriting on the wall and realized that Japan was on the brink of an abyss and wanted, if possible, to reverse the engine. That is only opinion. Anyway, on September 6 he asked me to dinner, and he was very much afraid of any possibility of the military extremists learning of that meeting.

"Ordinarily, a Japanese Prime Minister does not consort with diplomats. The contact is always with the Foreign Minister. Most prime ministers stay off it completely. But in this case Konoye wanted to talk the thing over directly. So we proceeded to the house of a mutual friend, and automobile tags on diplomatic and official automobiles were changed so nobody could recognize us. We had the dinner. All the servants were sent out and the dinner was served by the daughter of the house. We talked for three hours." Konoye would only meet with Grew in secret because on August 15 an ultranationalist had tried to assassinate Home Minister Kiichiro Hiranuma, who publicly argued against war with the Anglo-Saxons. Even after taking six bullets from his assassin, though, Hiranuma survived.

Grew concluded his memo to State of the meeting by saying that, if a summit between Konoye and Roosevelt could not change the two nations' relationship, "The logical outcome of this will be the downfall of the Konoye Cabinet and the formation of a military dictatorship which will lack either the disposition or the temperament to avoid colliding head-on with the United States."

Hirohito was upset by a newspaper headline he read the following week, on September 10: "The British Museum Set on Fire by a German Bomber." The emperor called his lord keeper of the privy seal, Marquis Kido, to ask if "there was any possibility that Japan might intervene as mediator between Germany and Britain in order to avoid any further destruction of Britain's cultural assets." Kido patiently explained that doing so would be somewhat difficult at this time.

From September 12 to 16, fleet officers gathered at Etajima, the Naval Staff College, to war game the opening salvoes of the Great East Asia War. It was a startling rehearsal. While the Third Fleet began its attack against Borneo and Celebes, the Eleventh Air Fleet based on Formosa attacked MacArthur's air forces in the Philippines, and the Second Fleet left Mako in the Pescadores and the Southern Expeditionary Fleet left Hainan island off China's coast to attack Singapore and other cities in British Malaya, eventually landing in Hong Kong. The Twenty-Second Air Flotilla, based in Indochina, would provide scouting and air cover, while invasion units would leave Indochina to attack British Borneo. The Gilberts, Guam, and Wake would be taken by the Fourth Fleet, keeping the United States out of Japanese waters.

The whole of the sixteenth was devoted to a Pearl Harbor table run, which was universally judged a disaster. In round one, half of Japan's carriers and half of her planes were lost; in round two, the Americans lost 4 battleships and 2 carriers, but Japan lost 127 aircraft. These results were based on everything going well—that the fleet would not be detected as it approached the Hawaiian archipelago; that the weather would be favorable to Japan's aircraft and watercraft; that the US Fleet would indeed be present in total and at anchor.

One of the participants taking the role of an American defender had attended the 1930s US war games simulating an attack on Pearl Harbor. He logically sent out a reconnaissance screen, which discovered the attack force. The Japanese airmen fell to an onslaught of antiaircraft fire and US fighter planes, while the Japanese navy lost a third of its armada.

The answer, the chiefs realized, was a perfectly timed arrival near sunset at a spot 450 miles north of Oahu, followed by a mad-dash run to the south for the launch point, and then an equally brisk getaway. Success would require inadequate US reconnaissance, and a complete Japanese surprise. Minoru Genda: "The war games cut through the year 1941 like the sharp edge of a dividing line. They clarified our problem and gave us a new sense of direction and purpose. After they were over, all elements of the Japanese Navy went to work as never before, because time was running out."

On September 24. Tokyo ordered spy Takeo Yoshikawa to divide the geography of Pearl Harbor into five sections and report on which warships were anchored in each:

> Henceforth, we would like to have you make reports concerning vessels along the following lines in so far as possible:
> 1. The waters (of Pearl Harbor) are to be divided roughly into five sub-areas. (We have no objections to your abbreviating as much as you like.) . . .
> 2. With regard to warships and aircraft carriers, we would like to have you report on those at anchor (these are not so important), tied up at wharves, buoys, and in docks. (Designate types and classes briefly. If possible we would like to have you make mention of the fact when two or more vessels are alongside the same wharf.)

Why such interest in vessels docked next to each other? One pertinent reason: a torpedo could only strike the outer ship's hull, so horizontal bombers and dive-bombers would be needed to destroy the inner targets. Because the details provided by Yoshikawa could be so useful for an aerial attack, this cable later became known as the "bomb plot" message during Washington's various Pearl Harbor investigations. When MAGIC deciphered and translated the bomb-plot message on October 9, it caught the attention of army intelligence officer Colonel Rufus Bratton. He thought it meant "the Japanese were showing unusual interest in the port at Honolulu," but his army counterpart, General Miles, didn't consider it anything out of the ordinary, since Japan ran constant surveillance on American capital-ship movements, as did the United States on Japanese warships. Miles thought the most it could mean was a "Japanese intent to execute a submarine attack on these ships." The director of naval intelligence, Captain Theodore Wilkinson, among others, thought that the Japanese could have been interested in these berthing details in order to analyze how quickly the US Fleet was ready to sortie. Bratton forwarded the memo to Stimson, Marshall, and Gerow, but no one seemed unduly alarmed. The US Navy's plan, after all, was that, when war struck, "the fleet is not going to be there." It would have weighed anchor to storm the seas.

At the liaison conference on a cold, wet, and gloomy September 25 in Tokyo, chiefs of staff Sugiyama and Nagano insisted a deadline must be set for diplomacy to end and war to begin. Konoye asked, "Is the October fifteenth deadline a very rigid demand?" Tojo replied that the imperial conference had marked early October as the deadline, so the fifteenth was already a compromise. Later the prime minister met with Lord Keeper of the Privy Seal Koichi Kido, whom he'd known since childhood. "If the military insists on the October fifteenth deadline to begin war, I do not have any confidence," Konoye said. "I have no other choice but to think of resigning."

His lifelong friend was shocked. "You are the one who called the September sixth imperial conference. You cannot leave that decision hanging and just disappear. That's irresponsible. Why not propose a reconsideration of the resolution? You cannot start talking like that before crossing swords with the military. To leave the mess this way is irresponsible."

Konoye decided that, instead of immediately resigning, he would exile himself to Kamakura, a seaside resort thirty miles outside Tokyo. In the middle of a great crisis, the prime minister of Japan ran away from home.

On September 27, Foreign Minister Matsuoka called American ambassador Grew to his office to pressure him over the Konoye-Roosevelt summit and Washington's embargoes. "The key to peace or war lies in the hands of Japan and the United States," the foreign minister began. "Should these two countries go to war, it would mean the destruction of world civilization and a dire calamity to mankind. The very idea that the head of my government should meet the president of the United States is liable to give rise to [Nazi and Fascist] misunderstandings regarding Japan's ties. Such a step would entail really a great sacrifice on the part of the Japanese government. . . . From Japan's domestic standpoint, it will be an event unprecedented in history for the prime minister to go out of the country on a diplomatic mission. . . . Eager as we are for peace, we will not bow under the pressure of another country, nor do we want peace at any price. It is a characteristic trait of our people to repel, rather than submit to, external pressure."

On September 29, the navy's commander in chief of the Combined

Fleet, Isoroku Yamamoto, who had spent ten months planning a surprise attack on America, sent a warning to his service's chief of staff, Nagano: "It is obvious that a war between Japan and the United States will become protracted. So long as the war continues to Japan's advantage, the United States will not give up the fight. As a result, our resources will be depleted over the course of several years of fighting and we shall face enormous difficulties in replacing damaged fleets and ordnance. In the end, we shall not be able to stand up to them. The commanders of the First, Second, Third, and Fourth Fleets are virtually unanimous on this. . . . A war with so little chance of success should not be fought."

In Washington that same day, Ambassador Nomura gave Secretary Hull a memorandum from Tokyo saying that a meeting between the president and the prime minister would "mark an epochal turn for good in Japanese-American relations," while refusing to have that meeting could lead to "most unfortunate" repercussions. Nomura told Hull that a Konoye-Roosevelt summit would make a tremendous impact on the Japanese public, diminishing the pro-Axis faction and encouraging the pro-American one. Nomura added that "if nothing came of the proposal for a meeting between the chiefs of our two Governments it might be difficult for Prince Konoye to retain his position and that Prince Konoye then would be likely to be succeeded by a less moderate leader."

Just a few months before, Foreign Minister Yosuke Matsuoka had dreamed that his global diplomacy with the Nazis and the Soviets would leave Japan with no real threats to its imperial dreams, and she would vault into the ranks of the world's great powers. Now her biggest allies were attacking each other, very likely driving Moscow into the arms of London and Washington, while constant contact between American, British, Chinese, and Dutch officials was creating an alliance countering Japan's imperialism in Asia. When Matsuoka's Tripartite Pact and treaty with Stalin were ascendant, Konoye had used him to quell the too fervid of the army's generals. Now, he would use the military against Matsuoka. He dissolved his cabinet and formed a new one, leaving out the foreign minister. But, for Konoye to remain in power, the army's supreme command insisted that he accept the status quo and reaffirm the Axis pact. He had no choice but to agree.

Matsuoka's replacement as foreign minister, Admiral Teijiro Toyoda, came to an agreement with navy minister Osami Nagano at a meeting on October 2 that a US war needed to be circumvented. With the navy's show of support for his moderate position, Konoye announced the end of his exile. But at nine that night in Washington, Hull told Nomura that, before Konoye could meet with Roosevelt, Japan would have to agree to Hull's Four Principles, as well as provide "a clear-cut manifestation of Japan's intention in regard to the withdrawal of Japanese troops from China and French Indochina" and "further study to the question of possible additional clarification of its position" on the Tripartite Pact.

Nomura pointed out that Hull was asking for a great deal on short notice, and that such statements of high moral grounds, coming from a country with a history of allying with imperialist powers and treating its people of color poorly, seemed hypocritical to the Japanese. Troop withdrawal from China, meanwhile, was complicated by the threat of imminent Soviet invasion. Why couldn't these difficult and important issues be discussed at the Roosevelt-Konoye summit? Nomura later told Hull in regard to the Tripartite Pact, "Many Japanese, and he himself, had not much liked it, but the Japanese Government of the day had felt that in face of the situation with which they were confronted, they must collect some friends somewhere."

While in Tokyo, war fever was infecting Japan's military leaders, so, too, was doubt as to whether a war with the Anglo-Saxons could be won. The navy's chief of operations, Shigeru Fukudome, released his assessment on October 5, which concluded, "I have no confidence . . . operations. As far as losses of ships are concerned, 1.4 million tons will be sunk in the first year of the war. The results of the new war games conducted by the Combined Fleet are that there will be no ships for civilian requirements in the third year of the war. I have no confidence." Rear Admiral Takijiro Onishi said he was against Yamamoto's Operation Z because, no matter what strategies she employed, Japan was certain to lose a Pacific war with the United States. He argued that Operation Number One's attack on Southeast Asia, which included the Philippines, would make the Americans angry and perhaps even fight, but they might still be open to negotiations. If Japan attacked Pearl Harbor, however, that would make the United States "so insanely mad" that it would destroy any hope for the compromise peace that everyone else insisted would be the result. Admiral Chuichi Nagumo, the man selected to lead the First Air Fleet against Hawaii, was so relentlessly negative about Yamamoto's scheme that Fukudome tried to cheer him up by pointing out, "If you die in this operation, special shrines will be built in your memory."

Yamamoto's behavior during the whole of 1941, with his insistent demands to attack Hawaii whipsawed by qualms that a war with the United States was unwinnable, inspired American historians to call him "the reluctant admiral." In fact, his vacillation between belligerent pushes for war and impassioned arguments for peace was characteristic of nearly every Japanese leader at this moment. Two days after insisting that he wanted to avoid a fight with the Anglo-Saxons, for example, the navy's Nagano wholly reversed course, announcing at the October 4 liaison conference, "It is no longer time for discussion. We should [set a timetable for war] right away!" Possibly this flip-flopping was due to another cultural tradition, that of having different opinions in private and in public, known as *honne to tatemae*—"true voice and façade." It allowed personal disagreements to be overcome for public consensus, but also seemed to allow for everyone to agree with everyone else all the time. It made the Americans, reading their MAGIC intercepts and then listening to Nomura's equitable statements, think the Japanese were as trustworthy as the Nazis.

On the night of October 4, War Minister Tojo met Prime Minister Konoye at Tekigaiso, the prince's magnificent villa in the Tokyo suburbs, where they dined against a postcard vista of Mount Fuji. "The United States demands us to leave the Tripartite Pact, to embrace [Hull's] Four Principles unconditionally, and to stop our military occupation. Japan cannot stomach all these," Tojo began.

"The central issue is troop withdrawal [out of China]. Why not agree to withdrawal in principle but leave some troops for the purpose of protecting resources?" Konoye asked.

The war minister huffed. "That sort of thing is called *scheming*."

Two days later, a joint army/navy meeting of midlevel officers concluded, "The army is saying that there is no hope [for diplomacy]. The navy still thinks there is hope, saying that if [the army] would only reconsider the question of military occupation, there would be hope." Naval officers were developing the consensus that the army was forcing them into a pointless war against Washington to avoid taking the blame for its continuing failures in China.

The exact same debate was reflected in a cabinet meeting a day later on October 7, when Tojo told Oikawa, "I know it is painful to your ears, but I must say this. Today's economy is not a normal economy.

Nor is the current state of diplomacy. . . . It should be our top priority now to fight our way through." When Oikawa said the army was being intransigent, Tojo asked if the navy had gone back on the commitment its leaders had made at the September 6 imperial conference. "No, our mind hasn't changed," Oikawa insisted. "As far as our resolve for war is concerned, we've still got it." Tojo pressed, Was the navy chief certain of victory? "That, I am afraid, I do not have," Oikawa replied, in a brief moment of public honesty. "If the war continues for a few years, we do not know what the outcome would be." Surprisingly, the always-belligerent War Minister Tojo now turned conciliatory: "If the navy is not confident, we must reconsider it. What must be reversed must be reversed, though it of course has to be done with the humble admission of our greatest responsibilities."

On that same day, the two chiefs of staff met, and Nagano was just as bellicose as he had been on the fourth: "I don't think matters can be settled diplomatically. But if the Foreign Ministry thinks that there is still hope, I am in favor of continuing negotiations."

General Sugiyama brought up the rumors that had been swirling for weeks: "But am I to understand that the navy is not confident about war?"

"What?" Nagano exploded. "Not confident about war? That is not true. Of course, we have never said that victory is assured. I've told the emperor this, too, but we are saying that there is a chance of winning for now. As far as the future is concerned, the question of victory or defeat will depend on the total combination of material and psychological strengths. . . . As far as the deadline for deciding between war or no war is concerned, the navy wouldn't mind extending it a bit. But that's not the army's position, is it? You seem to be charging right ahead."

"That's not true," Sugiyama insisted. "We are going about it very cautiously."

Nagano then threw everything back onto the imperial system, arguing, "It's not for nothing that the emperor reached the September sixth decision. We mustn't now hesitate to pour more soldiers into southern French Indochina."

"I agree with you completely," Sugiyama said.

Tojo met that night with Konoye, again at Tekigaiso. The prime minister delicately asked once more, Couldn't the army agree in principle to withdraw from China, with the details to be determined by the commander's needs? Tojo flatly refused. Konoye tried to ease the war minister into a less rigid stance, so that peace could be found: "As far as the Four Principles are concerned, we should accept the principle of equal opportunities," Konoye began. "There are, of course, special interests in China due to our geographical proximity, but that could be acknowledged, I believe, by the United States. As for the Tripartite Pact, to pledge [withdrawal from the pact] on paper would be difficult, but I am optimistic that something could be worked out in a direct meeting with the president. There remains only the question of military occupation [in China]. Could one not go easier on military occupation and not call it that? What would you do if this question alone became the stumbling block of the negotiations? Can we not find a way to stick to the substance of military occupation and still agree to troop withdrawal?"

Tojo thought the Americans would never honor a Japanese right of special interests in China, and besides, why should the army make this huge concession with everything else about foreign policy, including this meeting with Roosevelt, being up in the air? Konoye was exasperated: "Military men take wars too lightly!"

"You say that military men take wars too lightly," an angry Tojo bellowed. "Occasionally, one must conjure up enough courage, close one's eyes, and jump off the balcony of the Kiyomizu!" (Kiyomizu, a famed Buddhist temple built in 778, lent its architecture to a phrase that means "taking the plunge.")

"Jumping into the abyss was all well and good if one were talking only about oneself," Konoye tried to reason, "but if I think of the national polity that has lasted twenty-six hundred years and of the hundred million Japanese belonging to this nation, I, as a person in the position of great responsibility, cannot do such a thing."

Meeting with Oikawa the next day, however, Tojo admitted, "We've lost two hundred thousand souls in the China Incident, and I cannot bear to give it all up just like that. And yet if we do go to war with the United States, we will lose tens of thousands more. I am thinking about withdrawing troops, but I just cannot decide."

That autumn, Minoru Genda began investigating how the immense First Air Fleet would covertly travel across the Pacific. A southern advance with a rendezvous at the Marshall Islands would mean fairly calm seas, less volatile weather, and nearness to Japanese military bases, which could provide safe haven in case of trouble. But Kimmel's task forces trained in the south, and sunny skies meant lack of cloud cover to shield the armada from US patrol planes. Going straight from Japan to Oahu on a middle route, meanwhile, meant passing the waters of Midway and a guaranteed run-in with American warships.

Genda's solution was a route across the forty-second-degree latitude a thousand miles north of Oahu, significantly distant from the popular merchant route that sailed closer to the arcing shores of China, Russia, Alaska, and Canada. Additionally, Yoshikawa had reported that American patrols were meager to the north of Pearl Harbor—regardless of the countless memoranda given Kimmel suggesting this as the obvious route for an enemy attack—and the erratic weather of the North Pacific in late autumn/early winter would make any American patrols even more difficult.

But that route came with a serious hardship. While the US Navy had bases across the Pacific to service its fleet—the perfect arc of Johnston Island, Midway, Palmyra, American Samoa, Wake Island, and Guam—the forty-two-degree northern route meant no bases at which Japan's ships could refuel. In 1941, ships were capable of refueling at sea, but it was not common practice, on top of which, the Japanese would have to master refueling technique against a forecast of rough winds and waves at that latitude.

Genda solved this with the same management technique he had used on every other Operation Z problem; he assembled the navy's best—in this case, tanker captains—outlined the problem, and ordered them to solve it. The captains soon realized that the standard method—of tankers sailing before the ship to be refueled and floating hoses back to it—was fine for destroyers and cruisers, but not for dreadnoughts and flattops, which weren't maneuverable enough. The tanker crews had to learn how to trail the bigger ships, with tanker crew aboard carriers and battleships to maneuver the hoses.

Nagumo's chief of staff, Ryunosuke Kusaka, decided to personally look into other solutions. He realized that seven ships of the task force—the biggest carriers, battleships, and destroyers—could travel from the northeast tip of Japan all the way to Oahu without refueling. Since a carrier had to drive into the wind hard enough to achieve thirty knots of wind to lift her planes, though, they needed to be fully fueled at all times. He added drums and trim tanks to every free space aboard the bigger ships, and he trained his destroyers to be refueled three at a time.

The chosen route also created a puzzle for Operation Z's supply officer, Commander Shin-Ichi Shimizu. Everyone in Japan's army and navy was, during that autumn of '41, preparing to invade the south for Operation Number One, and therefore ordering tropical supplies. Shimizu needed to requisition cold-weather gear for his northern voyage, while keeping the journey a secret. His solution was to order everything for every season and explain that, if war came, who knew where they would go?

The Imperial Army had conducted Operation Number One tabletop maneuvers from October 1 to 5 at its war college to analyze various permutations of attack and defense. Now the navy's Combined Fleet held their tabletops from October 9 to 11 on Yamamoto's flagship, *Nagato*, to iron out final details before formally issuing Combined Fleet Operation Order Number One, the Imperial Japanese Navy's master war plan. The whole of October 13 was a conference devoted to Hawaii. The conclusion was that Operation Z needed to be finished and done with before Japanese forces heading to invade the whole of Southeast Asia were detected.

Opinions and suggestions were welcome at this conclave up to a point, Yamamoto made clear; "I realize that some do not think well of my plan, but the operation against Hawaii is a vital part of Japan's grand strategy. So long as I am commander in chief of the Combined Fleet, Pearl Harbor will be attacked. I ask you to give me your fullest support. Return to your stations, and work hard for the success of Japan's war plan. Good luck!"

Prime Minister Fumimaro Konoye called his foreign, army, and navy ministers to a 2:00 p.m. meeting on October 12, his fiftieth birthday, at Tekigaiso's art deco reception hall. The prime minister had decided he now needed to be as staunch as the war minister and used the threat of resignation to stop the militarists' rush to war: "We must continue to seek a diplomatic settlement. I have no confidence in a war such as this. If we were to start a war, it has to be done by someone who believes in it."

Previously, the navy's Oikawa had told Konoye if he really wanted peace, he had to be "prepared to swallow" America's demands, and that the navy would support him. Now, Oikawa threw the decision back onto the prime minister. "We are at the crossroads of pursuing a diplomatic approach or war. The deadline is approaching. The prime minister has to decide. If he decides not to go to war, that would be fine by [the navy]." The discussion raged on, until Oikawa suddenly reversed course and announced that if Konoye was not ready to lead Japan into global war, he needed to step aside and be replaced by a prime minister who was.

Konoye met again privately with Tojo just before an October 14 cabinet meeting—one day before the deadline for the end of diplomacy, and the start of war—and used everything he had to convince the war minister to withdraw from China, admitting, "I am greatly responsible for the China Incident. After four years, the Incident has not ended. I simply cannot agree to starting yet another great war whose outlook is very vague. . . . In order to make a great leap, we must sometimes concede [to greater forces] so that we can preserve and nurture our national strength."

But Tojo adamantly refused to concede: "I believe the prime minister's argument is too pessimistic. That's because we know our country's weak points all too well. But don't you see that the United States has its own weaknesses, too?"

"It comes down to a difference in our opinions," Konoye said. "I would insist that you reconsider."

Tojo: "I would say it's a difference in our personalities."

At the cabinet meeting, Tojo passionately described how, if Japan acceded to the American demands, it would mean turning back the clock twenty years, becoming once again "Little Japan." "For the past six months, ever since April, the foreign minister has made painstaking efforts to adjust relations," he concluded. "Although I respect him for that, we remain deadlocked. . . . The heart of the matter is the imposition on us of withdrawal from Indochina and China. . . . If we yield to America's demands, it will destroy the fruits of the China Incident. Manchukuo will be endangered and our control of Korea undermined."

The navy now refused to give its formal approval, which procedurally meant that the September 6 imperial conference decision had to be overturned. Tojo said this meant the responsible cabinet should resign, and insisted that Konoye make a decision once and for all if he was ready to lead his nation into war or step aside.

The next day, the prime minister was enjoying a lunch of grilled eel with his closest advisers when the discussion turned to Hotsumi Ozaki, a Japanese newspaperman deeply knowledgeable on the subject of China, who was late for the meal. As they began eating without him, Konoye's secretary hurried into the room: "I've got some awful news! Ozaki's been arrested. They say he's been charged with spying."

The unraveling of a Tokyo nest of Soviet spies had begun five days before with the arrest of Yotoku Miyagi, a painter who'd spent his teenage years in California, where he'd joined the Communist Party of the USA. After his arrest by Japan's secret police, Miyagi tried to commit suicide by jumping out the interrogation room's window, but as this room was on the second floor, he failed and was forced instead to confess everything, including that he worked for a Russian spy ring, which is now known to have involved at least thirteen men and three women and was epically cinematic, including a Prussian radio engineer, a Serbian Jewish journalist, Okinawa painter Miyagi, and Tokyo intellectual Ozaki. Its master, Richard Sorge, was born to a German father and a Russian mother; Sorge used his Nazi Party membership and service to the fatherland in the Great War to perfectly cover his encyclopedic acumen as a Soviet spy. His cover was working as a German newspaper correspondent in Tokyo, an assignment from which he could develop close friendships in both the Nazi foreign office and the Konoye cabinet.

In May 1941, Richard Sorge tipped off Stalin that between 170 and 190 Nazi divisions would invade the Soviet Union beginning on June 20 (they were in fact two days late). Even as the Nazi consulate in Tokyo was hounding the Japanese to attack the Russians, and even on October 15 as his clandestine network was now falling apart, Sorge was able to tell the Kremlin that the Japanese were invading Southeast Asia instead of taking on the Red Army. Forty Soviet divisions, no longer needed to counter the Japanese threat, were shipped via the Trans-Siberian Railway from the Manchurian border to help defend Moscow.

On October 16 at 4:00 p.m., Marquis Koichi Kido received a call from Prime Minister Fumimaro Konoye, saying that he had all of the letters needed to abandon his government, which Kido called a "great surprise." An hour later Konoye appeared at the palace, and Hirohito accepted his resignation.

In time, Joseph Grew would be convinced that the Pacific war could have been avoided entirely if Konoye and Roosevelt had met in Alaska, thinking that, when Japanese hard-liners saw their emperor supporting the prime minister's negotiations with the Americans, they would feel honor-bound to accept the terms of a treaty. Most of FDR's cabinet, however, were too conscious of the Japanese militarists' history of ignoring their country's moderates to pursue whatever aggressive actions they wanted to share Grew's regrets.

The fall of the second Konoye government, engineered by Hideki Tojo, meant that Hideki Tojo himself was no longer army minister. On October 17 he was packing up his things to move out of the official residence when the phone rang; Hirohito was summoning him to immediately appear at the palace. As he got ready to leave, Military Affairs Bureau section chief Kenryo Sato warned, "Minister, you cornered Prince Konoye. . . . You said you would quit the post of army minister if a troop withdrawal from China was mentioned. That's why His Majesty is about to admonish you."

"I dare not argue with His Imperial Majesty," Tojo replied. "Whatever he says is final."

At their five o'clock meeting Hirohito said that he was appointing a new prime minister of Japan: Hideki Tojo. The general was so astonished he could not even speak the traditional humbled response of "Let me please have a little time to accept the command," so the emperor had to step in and offer him such time.

What seems in retrospect as the worst decision of Hirohito's reign made a great deal of sense at that moment. There had been two candidates: the navy's Oikawa and the army's Tojo. Since the army had started this crisis, Kido thought the army should resolve it, and reinforced this idea by informing Tojo immediately after the appointment that "It is the emperor's wish that in formulating the nation's policy, you would not be a slave to the September sixth imperial resolution. You must consider both domestic and external situations, deeply and broadly. The emperor wishes you to take a cautious approach."

Konoye thought the appointment made sense in that Tojo was famously devoted to the emperor, and if Hirohito encouraged him to peace, he might obey an imperial directive . . . he might in fact be willing to take that jump from the balcony, into peace. The emperor didn't want a member of the imperial family serving as prime minister if war began, ruling out Konoye or the other leading royal candidate, Prince Naruhiko Higashikuni. Finally, Hirohito had a strategic move in mind, inspired by a Chinese proverb: "One must enter the tiger's den in order to catch his cubs." By "civilizing" Hideki Tojo, the army's most powerful and staunchest chieftain, Hirohito and Kido hoped the service's warmongering fascists could be brought under control. The Imperial Japanese Army, which had always operated as the power behind the throne, sidestepping the ultimate responsibility, would now have to face the consequences of its belligerent intransigence.

The next morning, Japan's newest prime minister was visited by the man who least thought he should be Japan's newest prime minister. Prince Kinmochi Saionji was the last surviving *genro*—one of modern Japan's founding fathers—and Saionji sternly informed Tojo, "I have three things to say to you. One, you must not make Japan into a police state. Two, you must hurry to make peace with China. Three, you must see to the success of the US-Japan negotiations." Tojo, a man of much action and not much contemplation, believed his remarkable character had brought him the prime ministry and also believed he did not need guidance from anyone. "Mr. Saionji, thank you for your advice," he replied. "I shall have my secretary contact you from now on."

When Americans in 1941 imagined "funny little" Japanese men, they imagined someone like Tojo, who was five feet two inches tall, weighed about 110 pounds, and wore enormous tortoiseshell spectacles. Tenth in his class at Ichigawa's Imperial Japanese Army Academy, by 1937 he was chief of the famously rampaging Kwantung Army, and eventually the Kempeitai—the secret police. While war minister, he had a book of conduct published and issued to every recruit, *Instructions for the Battlefield*. One instruction was particularly notorious: "Do not suffer the shame of being captured alive." Cold, flinty, disciplined, petty, easily offended, strong of conviction, autocratic, and a lover of vengeance, Tojo took his nationalist beliefs seriously, commonly remarking, "A soldier serves the emperor twenty-four hours a day. Even eating is part of his duty, so that one can better serve him."

On October 16, Nagumo's chief of staff received a letter from his retired housekeeper. She told him of a lovely dream she'd had the night before, that Japanese submarines had attacked Pearl Harbor and achieved a great victory. Kusaka knew this was a bright omen. On that same day at 2:00 p.m. in Washington, FDR canceled his cabinet meeting to confer for two hours with Stimson, Marshall, Knox, Stark, Hull, and Hopkins in the wake of the Konoye government's collapse. They expected, as Stimson remembered, that Tojo would be "much more anti-American" than Konoye and noted, "The Japanese Navy is beginning to talk almost as radically as the Japanese Army, and so we face the delicate question of the diplomatic fencing to be done so as to make sure that Japan was put into the wrong and made the first bad move—overt move. . . . If war did come, it was important . . . that we should not be placed in the position of firing the first shot, if this could be done without sacrificing our safety, but that Japan should appear in her true role as the real aggressor."

Harold Stark wrote to all of his commanders including Husband Kimmel that day: "The resignation of the Japanese Cabinet has created a grave situation. If a new Cabinet is formed it will probably be strongly nationalistic and anti-American. If the Konoye Cabinet remains the effect will be that it will operate under a new mandate which will not include rapprochement with the US. In either case hostilities between Japan and Russia are a strong possibility. Since the US and Britain are held responsible by Japan for her present desperate situation there is also a possibility that Japan may attack these two powers. In view of these possibilities you will take due precautions including such preparatory deployments as will not disclose strategic intention nor constitute provocative actions against Japan."

The next day, Stark sent Kimmel a follow-up, "Personally I do not believe the Japs are going to sail into us and the message I sent you merely stated the 'possibility'; in fact I tempered the message handed to me considerably. Perhaps I am wrong, but I hope not. In any case after long pow-wows in the White House it was felt we should be on guard at least until something indicates the trend." This "on the one hand; on the other hand" style of cable from the chief of naval operations would in essence paralyze the commander in chief, Pacific Fleet. Yet, if Stark's mixed messages confused Kimmel's sense of mission, the admiral never asked for clarification.

After Tojo announced his cabinet, Ambassador Nomura cabled the new foreign minister, Shigenori Togo, "I am firmly convinced that I should retire from office along with the resignation of the previous Cabinet. From the first, the Secretary of State recognized my sincerity but it has been his judgment that I have no influence in Tokyo. So is the President's opinion, I hear. . . . I am now, so to speak, the skeleton of a dead horse. It is too much for me to lead a sham existence, cheating others as well as myself. I do not mean to run away from the battlefield, but I believe that this is the course I should take as a public man." Togo replied with his "hope that you will see fit to sacrifice all of your own personal wishes and remain in your post." If many Japanese were willing to die for their country, the ambassador to Washington was willing to do something perhaps even more difficult: be humiliated.

In mid-October, Japanese naval planners estimated that their forces outnumbered that of their foes in the Pacific, but said that in two years' time, the industrial power of the United States would change that equation and if Japan wanted to attack, it needed to strike now. The Imperial Japanese Navy's general staff then decided that Operation Number One needed more carrier support, and that of the six flattops assigned to strike Pearl Harbor, the second carrier division's three ships would have to be reassigned. The second's leader, Tamon Yamaguchi, was so enraged at this decision he told Nagumo, "If you have made a mistake, I will kill you!" On the eighteenth Kuroshima flew to Tokyo to tell Tomioka that the Combined Fleet needed "clarification" on whether the Pearl Harbor attack was approved—if it was approved, it required six carriers to be victorious—and that Yamamoto needed his decision immediately. When Tomioka and Vice Admiral Shigeru Fukudome refused to change their minds, Kuroshima said that Yamamoto was certain that the all-important Operation Number One would fail unless the Japanese navy annihilated America's Pacific Fleet, as it was a "dagger pointed at Japan's heart."

When Tomioka and Fukudome then remained intransigent, the captain announced, "Admiral Yamamoto insists that his plan be adopted. I am authorized to state that if it is not, then the commander in chief of the Combined Fleet can no longer be held responsible for the security of the Empire. In that case he will have no alternative but to resign, and with him his entire staff." Faced again with losing Yamamoto, even though he felt queasy about Operation Z's prospects, Nagano reversed course, concluding, "If he has that much confidence, it's better to let Yamamoto go ahead." A compromise was reached: if the nation declared war, and if the carriers were returned to the Southern Operation as soon as possible after their mission was completed, Yamamoto could attack Pearl Harbor just as he'd envisaged. Shigeru Fukudome: "If this seems strange, it must be remembered that Yamamoto's position and influence in the Japanese navy were unique. He was in truth a leviathan among men." Many officers in Tokyo at this moment still held on to the hope that if Togo won by diplomacy, or the emperor intervened and the war was called off, the navy could keep its ships, its planes, and its Admiral Yamamoto.

From aboard his flagship *Pennsylvania* in Pearl Harbor, Admiral Husband Kimmel sent a memo on October 14 to all of his Pacific commanders, which included:

> The security of the Fleet, operating and based in the Hawaiian Area, is predicated at present, on two assumptions:
> (a) That no responsible foreign power will provoke war, under present existing conditions, by attack on the Fleet or Base, but that irresponsible and misguided nationals of such powers may attempt
> > (1) sabotage, on ships based in Pearl Harbor, from small craft.
> > (2) to block the entrance to Pearl Harbor by sinking an obstruction in the Channel.
> > (3) to lay magnetic or other mines in the approaches to Pearl Harbor.
> (b) That a declaration of war may be preceded by;
> > (1) a surprise attack on ships in Pearl Harbor,
> > (2) a surprise submarine attack on ships in operating area,
> > (3) a combination of these two. . . .

The next day, Roosevelt sent Churchill a cable that included the detail that Hull's negotiations had given the Allies "two months of respite in the Far East."

On October 17, the commander of the Fourteenth Naval District in Hawaii, Rear Admiral Claude Bloch, having just received an obsolete gunboat, *Sacramento*, which had "no batteries to speak of, with which the vessel could fight, and no speed with which she can run," reminded Washington of Pearl Harbor's deficiencies. He required "a number of small, fast craft [with] listening gear and depth charges" and two squadrons of reconnaissance planes. His letter's conclusion: "Nearly all of the failures of the British have been caused by what may be expressed in the cliché 'too little and too late.' It is hoped that we may profit from their errors."

At that moment, the *Washington Post* asked Navy Secretary Knox if the Philippines could be defended. He exploded, "We can defend anything!"

Admiral Yamamoto wrote a letter to Navy Minister Shimada on October 24, a week after threatening to resign over not striking Hawaii, that included, "I have recently heard that there are some elements in the general staff who argue that, since the air operation to be carried out immediately upon outbreak of war was after all nothing more than a secondary operation in which the chance of success was about fifty-fifty, the use of the entire air force in such a venture was too risky to merit consideration. But even more risky and illogical, it seems to me, is the idea of going to war against America, Britain, and China following four years of exhausting operations in China and with the possibility of fighting Russia also to be kept in mind and having, moreover, to sustain ourselves unassisted for ten years or more in a protracted war over an area several times more vast than the European war theater. If, in the face of such odds, we decide to go to war—or rather, are forced to do so by the trend of events—I, as the authority responsible for the fleet, can see little hope of success in any ordinary strategy. . . . I fear with trepidation that the only thing that can save the situation now is the imperial decision." Yamamoto was holding on to the thin hope that Hirohito would order Tojo into peace, while at the same time Yamamoto's threats to resign were forcing the navy to draft its war plan for Hirohito's approval; naval secretary Nagano presented it to the emperor at the palace that third week of October.

During the last week of October in Honolulu, Japanese consul chief Kita handed agent Takeo Yoshikawa a ripped piece of paper, $14,000 in cash, and orders to meet a man at a Lanikai beach house on October 25. A German appeared at that meeting, with his own piece of paper, whose torn edge matched Yoshikawa's.

The man, Bernard Julius Otto Kuehn, was a Nazi sleeper agent sent to Hawaii in 1935 by Joseph Goebbels; the Japanese had hired Kuehn to supplement and, in time, replace Yoshikawa. Kuehn had detailed information on American military operations, which he'd acquired by being friendly with local officers, as well as through his stepdaughter, Susie Ruth, who ran a beauty parlor specializing in Pearl Harbor's wives and daughters. On December 2 he brought the Japanese embassy a plan of codes and signals that could be seen by offshore Axis submarines:

Meaning		Signal
Battleship divisions	Preparing to sortie including scouts and screening units	1
A number of carriers	Preparing to sortie	2
Battleship divisions	All departed between 1st and 3rd	3
Carriers	Several departed between 1st and 3rd	4
Carriers	All departed between 1st and 3rd	5
Battleship divisions	All departed between 4th and 6th	6
Carriers	Several departed between 4th and 6th	7
Carriers	All departed between 4th and 6th	8
Lanikai Beach House will show lights during the night as follows to		
		signal:
One light between 8:00 and 9:00 p.m.		1
One light between 9:00 and 10:00 p.m.		2
One light between 10:00 and 11:00 p.m.		3
One light between 11:00 and 12:00 p.m.		4
Two lights between 12:00 and 1:00 a.m.		5
Two lights between 1:00 and 2:00 a.m.		6
Two lights between 2:00 and 3:00 a.m.		7
Two lights between 3:00 and 4:00 a.m.		8

Want ads:

A. Chinese rug, etc., for sale, apply P.O. Box 1476 indicates signal 3 or 6.

B. A complete chicken farm, etc., apply as above, indicates signal 4 or 7.

C. Beauty operator wanted, etc. —same—indicates signal 5 or 8.

By that autumn of 1941 as, moment by moment, a Japanese strike loomed in the Pacific, the Germans were repeatedly attacking the United States on the other side of the world. Two American-owned merchant ships, the *Sessa* and *Montana*, had been sunk by Nazi submarines while ferrying cargo to Iceland; *Steel Seafarer*, a US ship traveling to Suez, was bombed in the Red Sea by German pilots; USS destroyer *Greer* was attacked by a Nazi sub while carrying mail across the Atlantic; and on Friday, October 17, USS destroyer *Kearny* was torpedoed in the North Atlantic by another Nazi submarine, killing eleven American sailors. When Roosevelt took to the radio ten days after, he said that while the United States was doing all she could to avoid foreign wars, Hitler was trying to frighten Americans out of the oceans, which was an "absurd and insulting suggestion." The president declared, "History has recorded who fired the first shot."

One merchant sailor recalled a trip out of the Gulf of Mexico: "A Nazi tin fish chased us for three days. We never seen a patrol boat or a plane the whole time. Saw one destroyer going hell-bent for election into Charleston one afternoon about dusk, but we all figured she was trying to get safe home before dark when the subs come out. We was carrying fifty thousand barrels of Oklahoma crude and fifty thousand of high-test gasoline. I thought we'd get it any minute. Man, those nights were killers! . . . with the zigzagging and the sub alarms and the lying there in your bunk, scared stiff and waiting . . . You sleep with your clothes on. Well, I don't exactly mean sleep. You lie in bed with your clothes on. . . . You try to light a cigarette if your hand don't shake too much. Not that you're scared of course. Oh, noooh!"

John Walsh was a wiper on the tanker *Empire* when she was sunk off the coast of Florida: "I was asleep when the torpedoes hit us—three of them. A torpedo connects with one of those tankers and it's just like lighting a match to cellophane. I rushed up on deck and helped get one of the lifeboats over the side. I saw our captain on a life raft. He and some of the other men were on it. The current was sucking them into the burning oil around the tanker. I last saw the captain going into a sheet of orange flame. Some of the fellows said he screamed. . . . Monroe Reynolds was with me for a while. His eyes were burned. He was screaming that he was going blind. The last time I saw him, he jumped into the fiery water. That was his finish, I guess."

On October 31, the USS *Reuben James* was sunk by a Nazi U-boat off the shores of Iceland, and only 44 of its crew of 160 were rescued. Roosevelt told his citizens, "America has been attacked [by the] rattlesnakes of the Atlantic" since, in pursuit of "world mastery," the Nazis were trying to seize "control of the oceans." As an almost wholly unprepared United States of America was being drawn into fighting wars across two oceans and three continents, the only answer, Roosevelt explained, was a policy of "shoot on sight."

CHAPTER FOUR

NOVEMBER

The new prime minister of Japan, Hideki Tojo, was overseeing the launch of Operation Number One, the titanic series of invasions that would make him the ruler of all of East Asia, until he ran into the wall that was Finance Minister Okinori Kaya, who would not let anybody go to war with anybody else until they first made their budgets. Again and again during cabinet meetings and other conferences across November, Kaya asked, "Could you explain to me in a way that I can understand? My questions are 'What would happen to the material situation if we go to war? What would happen if we do not go to war and carry on just as we are carrying on right now? What should we do if diplomatic negotiations with the United States fail?'"

The answers to Kaya's insistent questions would hold the key to Japan's ultimate downfall. The Imperial Japanese Army had previously tried to address these concerns with data provided by intelligence agent Colonel Shinjo Kenkichi, who had been operating undercover in the United States at the Mitsui import-export firm since March of 1940. Using the services of fifty other Japanese corporations based in America, Kenkichi produced a War Economy Research Office report concluding that America's industrial might was ten to twenty times that of Japan's, meaning that in war she would be ten to twenty times as powerful. But Kenkichi's far-reaching and detailed research seemed to have no impact on Japan's militarists and their dreams of global conquest. Every senior army officer in the IJA received the brief. It changed no opinions.

Such numbers, though, were confirmed by Teiichi Suzuki's Cabinet Planning Board, which coordinated wartime resources. While the Imperial Japanese Army had estimated US industry as twenty times greater than Japan's, Suzuki's numbers said it was more like seventy-four times, with such damning details as seven times as much aluminum, nine times as much copper, twelve times as much iron, and five hundred times as much petroleum—key resources for fighting battles. Suzuki later tried to explain why facts couldn't stop what was happening: "It was as though they had already decided to go to war. My task was basically to provide numbers to fit that decision."

Tojo's new foreign minister, Shigenori Togo, now stood alongside Kaya in insisting that, even if it was humiliating to withdraw from China and Indochina, avoiding a war with the United States was a national priority. He confronted nearly the whole of the government, especially his prime minister, who predicted that submitting to Western capitalists would turn Japan into a third-rate country. "Our economy would survive even if we withdrew," Togo insisted. "The sooner it is done, the better."

Kaya and Togo, the country's leaders in financial and foreign affairs, were so staunch in their positions that they forced Prime Minister Tojo into the compromise he had always refused to give Prime Minister Konoye. In a new offer for Hull, Japan agreed to withdraw troops from Hainan, northern China, and Inner Mongolia within twenty-five years, and from the rest of the country as well as Indochina within two years of a treaty concluded with the Nationalists under Chiang Kai-shek. Togo doubted that Roosevelt and Hull would agree to such generous amounts of time, but at least it was a concession from the stubborn Tojo.

Hirohito and Kido's tiger-cub strategy seemed to be working . . . so well that in the hours before their November 1 liaison conference, Tojo tried to talk the army's Sugiyama into siding with his new position of continuing diplomatic entreaties and postponing any war, an idea he said "the navy minister, the finance minister, and the director of the Cabinet Planning Board have all agreed to endorse. Since the emperor likes to do things openly and aboveboard, I think he will not hear of carrying on with deception."

By deception, Tojo meant what all of Japan's leaders were doing at that moment—the foreign offfice negotiating peace terms with Washington while the navy planned an attack on Hawaii. A number of the country's leaders, both civilian and military, began to question this, and a notion of how to remain honorable eventually took hold: What if Ambassador Nomura formally broke off negotiations with Washington exactly thirty minutes before the attack on Oahu began?

The liaison conference where this quandary was resolved lasted a grueling seventeen hours and became one of the most controversial moments in Japanese political history. The prime minister began by noting Japan had three avenues to consider: war; no war; or both war and diplomatic negotiations simultaneously. Finance Minister Kaya turned to the admirals: "If we went to war right now, would Japan still be able to continue fighting after a few years? Would the United States still be likely to attack Japan after three years if Japan didn't go to war?" Nagano said that he felt "fifty-fifty" about going to war as "The chances of victory are unclear." When Kaya more forcefully insisted, "I don't know if we could manage to win a naval war," Nagano replied that better "now rather than waiting for three years . . . because the necessary foundation for continuing the war [meaning Dutch East Indies oil] will have been under our control." Foreign Minister Togo sided with Kaya, pointing out, "I don't think that the US fleets would come to our shores. It is unnecessary to go to war now. . . . Diplomacy by nature requires many days and nights for its goals to be fulfilled. As foreign minister, I cannot conduct diplomacy without any likelihood of success. I need to be assured that I would be given the time and conditions required to make it a success. War, needless to say, must be avoided."

The army's vice chief of staff, Osamu Tsukada, argued, "We would not want the fickle conditions of diplomacy to dictate and affect our strategic plans, and therefore we demand that November 13 be the final deadline for diplomacy."

Foreign Minister Togo erupted, "November 13. That is awful! The navy is saying November 20."

After many hours of bickering, November 30 was set as the absolute deadline for Togo and Nomura to arrive at a treaty with Washington and stop the rush to war. When Togo begged for a one-day extension to December 1, Tsukada shouted, "Absolutely not. Anything more than the last day of November is out of the question. Out of the question!"

Navy Minister Shigetaro Shimada tried for a compromise: "When you say November thirtieth, what time exactly do you mean? Surely, you would give us until the twenty-fourth hour?"

Tsukada conceded, "Yes, until twelve midnight would be all right."

They took a break, during which the hawkish-before-the-generals

Nagano turned completely dovish in private conversation with the Foreign Ministry's American Affairs Bureau chief, saying, "Would the Foreign Ministry take it upon itself to settle this mess through diplomacy? If so, the navy would be glad to entrust everything to the Foreign Ministry. What do you think?" The navy had previously tried pawning off the public humiliation of being against a war on Konoye, and now they were trying again, with the foreign office. A surprised bureau chief restated his ministry's view that, considering the army's refusal to withdraw from China, it seemed unlikely that diplomacy would succeed.

Finally at one thirty in the morning of November 2, the liaison conference concluded with the decision that Foreign Minister Togo and Ambassador Nomura would have until the very last hours of November to negotiate a peace and stop the war. Tojo promised Togo that, if the United States moved forward in any way on either of their two offers—known as Plan A and Plan B—Tojo would do everything he could to compromise to make the negotiations work. The newly accommodating prime minister even told his staff, "Plan B is not a pretext for going to war; I swear to the gods that with this plan, I hope to reach an accommodation with the United States, whatever it takes."

Even so, at five that afternoon, following protocol, Nagano and Sugiyama appeared before Hirohito with a war plan prepared for his approval at an imperial conference to be held in three days' time, on November 5. This plan was so detailed it even included weather and moonlight predictions for dawn on December 7 in Hawaii. Throughout this meeting, Hirohito kept insisting that a diplomatic solution could be found and kept asking pointed questions about the military's planning, such as "You have told me that monsoons would impede the landing of our troops. . . . Would you be able to land?" But as the details sank in, it was as if the leader of the nation was helpless before the overwhelming forces of history. He finally conceded, "Perhaps it is unavoidable that we continue preparations for military operations."

Many Japanese leaders of this period would later insist that Hirohito was blameless in the drive to war, but not Fumimaro Konoye, who told his chief cabinet secretary, "Of course His Majesty is a pacifist, and there is no doubt he wished to avoid war. When I told him that to initiate war is a mistake, he agreed. But the next day, he would tell me, 'You were worried about it yesterday, but you do not have to worry so much.' Thus, gradually, he began to lean toward war. And the next time I met him, he leaned even more toward war. In short, I felt the Emperor was telling me, 'My prime minister does not understand military matters, I know much more.' In short, the Emperor had absorbed the views of the army and navy high commands."

By this time, the Navy General Staff had set X-day for December 8 (meaning December 7 in the United States, as Tokyo time is fourteen hours ahead of Washington's eastern standard time, and nineteen hours, thirty minutes, ahead of the military's then-Hawaiian time). Many factors were involved in this date. Japan's oil reserves were vanishing. America's Pacific forces, especially in the Philippines, were rising. The task force's northern route would be unfeasible by the wintry depths of January or February, while waiting until spring would mean the worst of Southeast Asia's monsoon season, which the army feared would interfere with Operation Number One's invasions. Astronomers had predicted a good moon phase for night operations that week, and on Oahu, the spy Yoshikawa had confirmed that the great majority of Kimmel's fleet regularly came home to berth on Sundays. Finally on November 2, Rear Admiral Matome Ugaki received a message asking for the Combined Fleet's blessing on the liaison conference's creation of an "Army and Navy Central Agreement." Ugaki wrote in his diary, "With this telegram, we can see that they have made up their minds at last."

That same day, all of Operation Hawaii's ships were assembled in Ariake Bay. At 1330 on the afternoon of the third, Admiral Chuichi Nagumo met with his commanders to announce, "Judging from the diplomatic situation, war with the United States seems unavoidable. In that event, we plan to attack the American fleet in Hawaii. Although final details have not been firmed up, commanders Genda and Fuchida have mapped out a general plan. They will explain it to you. If after hearing the explanation, you have any questions, feel free to ask them."

The airmen were so excited they could only exult, "I was born a boy at the right time!"

Tokyo's government-controlled newspapers began at this time to regularly attack the United States. *Nichi-Nichi*, for example, explained to its readers that America had the soul of a prostitute.

On November 3, Togo sent Nomura Plan A, with a cover note explaining that, "This time we are showing the limit of our friendship; this time we are making our last possible bargain, and I hope that we can settle all our troubles with United States peaceably. . . . I want you to follow my instructions to the letter. . . . There will be no room for personal interpretation. . . . I want you, in as indecisive yet as pleasant language as possible, to euphemize and try to impart to them the effect that unlimited occupation [in China] does not mean perpetual occupation." American officials, reading these instructions through MAGIC, had their opinion of the Japanese as two-faced hypocrites confirmed.

That same day, Nagano went to the palace to explain in detail to Hirohito what would happen to the Americans on Oahu: "At the very outset of the beginning of hostilities, as nearly as possible coinciding with the first air attacks on the Philippines and Malaya, an air attack will be made on the main enemy force stationed in Hawaii, using an expeditionary force with a nucleus of six aircraft carriers led by the commander in chief of the First Carrier Flotilla. This expeditionary force will set out after replenishing in the Kuriles a number of days before hostilities are to begin. It will approach Hawaii from the north. One or two hours before sunrise some two hundred nautical miles north of the island of Oahu the fully loaded planes—about four hundred—will be launched. The plan is to initiate a surprise attack on the aircraft carriers and battleships at their moorings as well as the aircraft there. . . . It is an extremely daring operation. Its success is dependent from the start on the fortunes of war, which can oscillate greatly. On the day of the surprise attack, depending on the enemy ships present, it will be possible to sink two or three battleships and aircraft carriers each."

On that same November 3, Ambassador Grew sent a lengthy telegram to Secretary Hull, based on the research and interpretation of Eugene Dooman, his embassy's counselor, who had gone to school with many of Japan's civilian leaders. As before, those closest to the situation were the most prescient: "[American] policy, together with the impact of world political events upon Japan brought the Japanese Government to the point of seeking conciliation with the United States. If these efforts fail, I foresee a probable swing of the pendulum in Japan once more back to the former Japanese position or even farther. This would lead to what I have described as an all-out, do-or-die attempt, actually risking national hara-kiri, to make Japan impervious to economic embargoes abroad rather than to yield to foreign pressure. . . . My purpose is only to ensure against the United States becoming involved in war with Japan because of any possible misconception of Japan's capacity to rush headlong into a suicidal struggle with the United States. While national sanity dictates against such action, Japanese sanity cannot be measured by American standards of logic. . . . Japan may resort with dangerous and dramatic suddenness to measures which might make inevitable war with the United States."

On November 4, US Fleet commanders including Husband Kimmel were cabled that Japanese merchant vessels appeared to be withdrawing from the western hemisphere. Three days later, Stark wrote Kimmel a cable that included, "Things seem to be moving steadily towards a crisis in the Pacific. Just when it will break, no one can tell. The principal reaction I have to it all is what I have written you before; it continually gets 'worser and worser!' A month may see, literally, most anything. Two irreconcilable policies cannot go on forever—particularly if one party cannot live with the set-up. It doesn't look good." A week later on November 14, Stark sent Kimmel a cable: "The plain fact is that Japanese politics has been ultimately controlled for years by the military. Whether or not a policy of peace or a policy of further military adventuring is pursued is determined by the military based on their estimate as to whether the time is opportune and what they are able to do, not by what cabinet is in power or on diplomatic maneuvering, diplomatic notes or diplomatic treaties."

On November 4 in Washington, listening-station code breakers uncovered the creation of Japan's new military group, which they decoded as *1 no koku kantai*—the First Air Fleet—which was at that moment in dress rehearsal for the attack on Pearl Harbor. The first wave of aircraft lifted off at 0700, and the second at 0830. At Fuchida's signal, the dive-bombers rose to attack level, while the torpedo planes dropped to skimming cruise. Below the strike force, the battlewagons of the Japanese fleet lay in majestic array, just as the planners hoped their counterparts would be in Pearl Harbor. After the first wave hit the enemy, the second group of level bombers and dive-bombers swooped in (no torpedo planes would participate in the second wave because by that time the element of surprise would have been lost). The high-levels tore into the airfields, while the dive-bombers concentrated on the capital ships.

By 0930 the maneuver was over, and the next morning, Fuchida and Genda compared notes. They were concerned that it took so long for the initial rendezvous, that both the approach to the target and the general deployment were haphazard, and that only 40 percent of their modified torpedoes had leveled off at the correct depth. But overall, it was a magnificent achievement.

In Tokyo behind closed doors the next day, the momentum for war was surging. No one raised any qualms over the duplicity of preparing to strike while negotiating for peace. Hideki Tojo was no longer a prime minister with second thoughts, but a devoted warrior who insisted, "If we just stand by with our arms folded and allow our country to revert to the 'little Japan' that we once were, we would be tainting its brilliant twenty-six-hundred-year history." When the conference turned to Nomura's progress with American diplomacy, Togo admitted that Washington was persecuting Japan with a brutal economic policy, and though his ambassadors had patiently tried to reach an understanding, they had consistently been rebuffed. He concluded, "If things go as they are going now, I regret that the negotiations do not have any prospect of a quick resolution." Using the language of the Pan-Asianist movement, he also spoke of how Japan's conquests were saving the continent from predatory Western powers, turning Caucasian-ruled colonial territories into strong colleagues of a resurgent Japan. With such talk, Togo gave moral authority to the war he had been opposing for so long, and one more Japanese leader fell helpless before the course of history.

When on that same day Nagano commanded Yamamoto to prepare the fleet for a war with Britain and America, to begin in thirty days, Yamamoto replied that he would be ready, but that "we must not start a war with so little a chance of success," and couldn't the Tripartite Pact be abrogated and Japanese troops be pulled from China to avoid conflict with America? Perhaps Hirohito could intervene with a "sacred decision"? Yamamoto called a US-Japanese war "a major calamity for the world" and wrote a friend, "I find my present position extremely odd, [as I'm] obliged to make up my mind and pursue unswervingly a course that is precisely the opposite of my personal views."

On November 2, 4, 5, 6, 11, 13, 15, 19, 24, 25, and 26, Togo sent the beleaguered Nomura a series of cables demanding that he bring negotiations with the Americans to a final conclusion and set a new absolute deadline of November 29. If the ambassador failed, he was warned, it would render the situation in Asia "on the brink of chaos."

As scheduled by Togo, on November 7 Nomura presented Secretary Hull with Plan A, repeating Togo's dire predictions to emphasize how crucial these negotiations had become. They were a "last effort" in a situation that was "very grave" for a friendship that had "reached the edge," with the Japanese giving their all "on the throw of this die . . . showing the limits of our friendship . . . making our last possible bargain." But the Americans had already read all of this through MAGIC and did not respond with any sense of urgency, as the two countries' points of view were now utterly out of sync. Alone among American leaders, Royal Eason Ingersoll, vice chief of naval operations under CNO Stark, intuited that the only way Plan A made any sense was if Japan was planning attacks on ABCD territories in Asia, i.e., on the Philippines, Malaya, the Dutch East Indies, Hong Kong, and Singapore. Nearly everyone else in the Departments of State and War and at the Oval Office thought such a level of warfare was far beyond the capabilities of "little Japan" and discounted Ingersoll's exceedingly accurate prediction. At a Joint Board meeting on November 3, a frustrated Ingersoll insisted that "the present moment is not the opportune time to get brash" and that the State Department was wrong in its "impression that Japan could be defeated in military action in a few weeks."

At that day's White House cabinet meeting, Secretary Hull went over the most recent deadlocked talks with Japan and concluded that "relations had become extremely critical and that we should be on the outlook for an attack by Japan at any time." "Do not let the talks deteriorate," Roosevelt practically begged his secretary of state. "Let us make no more of ill will. Let us do nothing to precipitate a crisis." He had gotten disturbing news two days before, when Marshall and Stark had sent the president a memo finally admitting that things were not so rosy in Hawaii: "At the present time the United States Fleet in the Pacific is inferior to the Japanese fleet and cannot undertake unlimited strategic offensive in the Western Pacific. . . . War between the United States and Japan should be avoided while building up defensive forces in the Far East." Hull and Acheson were convinced, however, that if Washington took a tough stance, Tokyo would back down, so while Acheson continued his full petroleum embargo, Hull ignored the president's worries and told the Japanese that they would have to withdraw entirely from the whole of China and Indochina to receive any American imports.

That night, Nagano called a meeting with his highest-level Navy General Staff officers and warned, "There must be no behavior such as to invite reproach from future generations."

On the tenth, Nomura and Hull met with Roosevelt at the White House, where the president took a new approach, saying the two countries should come to a "modus vivendi," a way of peaceably living together with competing aims, "not merely an expedient and temporary agreement, but also one which takes into account actual human existence." This heartened Nomura, who saw it as an American softening, a path to compromise.

Captain Hankyu Sasaki, commander of the First Submarine Division, was ordered to proceed to Kure Naval Station near Hiroshima to receive his ships, which had been undergoing emergency modifications, such as the installation of air-purifying equipment, antisubmarine-net protection, and telephone systems. Sasaki was disturbed by this, as these ships were new and untested, and now they were being modified without trial runs? He asked his superiors about it and was told, "This equipment is to enable you to haul midget submarines close enough to Pearl Harbor to attack the US Pacific Fleet."

On November 10, ten sailors were selected to crew the midget subs of the Special Attack Force. When crewman Kichiji Dewa first saw his I-16 submersible, he thought it looked "tiny, like a bean. . . . On October 31, 1941, I saw a map of Pearl Harbor and learned about its geography. And then I knew that we were training for Pearl Harbor. We knew that the harbor was protected by antisubmarine nets. So the midgets were to be underwater and follow American ships into the harbor. Each midget sub also had a wire cutter on its nose to cut the nets." Yamamoto himself had met with these trainees aboard *Nagato*. He told them that a dangerous operation such as theirs held the promise of great glory. They could outshine the older officers if they were diligent, courageous, and dutiful.

The five midgets essentially acted as manned torpedoes. They had limited range, and once they were inside the harbor, the chances of the crew's surviving were little to none. Special Attack Group leader Naoji Iwasa asked for permission to attack immediately after the airstrike, instead of waiting until dark, since to remain submerged for such a long time might be dangerous, and they could inflict more carnage on a confused enemy in daylight. Besides, maximum damage to the enemy was what counted, not their meager lives. Yamamoto was one of the few Japanese officers opposed to tactical suicide, and he had repeatedly rejected the plan over the previous months, but the young officers who'd developed it insisted on going forward. Finally, the admiral gave in.

On November 11, nine vessels of the Third Submarine Group

slipped from harbor near the southern end of the main island of Honshu precisely at 1111 . . . the eleventh minute of the eleventh hour of the eleventh day of the eleventh month. On December 5, Hawaii time, the Third would reconnoiter at the sheltered anchorage between Maui and Lanai known as Lahaina Roads, from where they would cable reports on naval traffic with a deadline for information of December 6. This would give Minoru Genda time to shift his attack to Lahaina if substantial American forces were anchored there. Meanwhile, Hankyu Sasaki and his First Submarine Division would release their midgets as close as possible to the main buoy just outside the entrance to Pearl Harbor on the night before X-day. The five little subs would enter the channel that night, secure their positions, and settle to the bottom.

Between November 11 and 13, Lieutenant Commander Shigeharu Murata's torpedo bombers experimented with two techniques to improve their 66 percent strike rate. Pilot Haruo Yoshino: "We were told the altitude would have to be ten meters [thirty-three feet] or under. We never used altimeters. We flew totally by the seat of our pants. You could tell if you were flying too low if the spray from the dropped torpedo could splash up and hit your wings. We really did not have much fear." The results from both techniques were so thrilling they were telegrammed to Nagumo: "Achieved 82% hits."

In mid-November, CNO Stark's office sent Curtis Munson from Washington to Hawaii to gather information on the state of the American military in the Pacific. One of Munson's interviewees was onetime intelligence officer Captain Ellis Zacharias, now commanding cruiser *Salt Lake City*. Zacharias told Munson that local Hawaiians weren't a worry, as army intelligence and the local FBI were insisting. Instead, war with Japan "would begin with an air attack on our fleet, and for that reason it would have to be conducted with the greatest secrecy, and therefore no Japanese . . . in the United States or in Hawaii would be aware of the fact that such an attack was coming. . . . The attack would conform to [Japan's] historical procedure, that of hitting before war was declared."

At 1300 on November 15 in Tokyo, army and navy leaders gathered in the headquarters room of the Imperial Palace to explain to His Majesty the "Draft Proposal for Hastening the End of the War against the United States, Great Britain, the Netherlands, and Chiang." Among the nation's goals were winning the great all-out battle—the Kantai Kessen—with the US Navy; defeating both Great Britain and China;

bringing the Soviet Union within the Axis camp; and destroying the will of the American people.

As December 7 loomed, the cable traffic between Yoshikawa and Tokyo became more and more frantic. On November 15, Tokyo told their Hawaii spy, "As relations between Japan and the United States are most critical, make your 'ships in harbor report' irregular, but at a rate of twice a week. Although you already are no doubt aware, please take extra care to maintain secrecy." On the twenty-ninth: "We have been receiving reports from you on ship movements, but in future will you also report even when there are no movements?" On December 2, the agent was told to continue with both his daily reports and "whether or not there are any observation balloons above Pearl Harbor or if there are any indications that they will be sent out. Also advice [sic] whether . . . the warships are provided with antisubmarine nets."

MAGIC decoded and translated all of these messages between Yoshikawa and Tokyo. But they were judged low priority by the grossly overworked MAGIC decoders and translators, who were paying attention to the Japanese consulate traffic coming through Washington, not Honolulu.

On November 15 in Washington, General George Marshall held an off-the-record press conference with the three wire services, the *New York Times*, the *New York Herald Tribune*, *Time*, and *Newsweek*, to "prepare them for the shock of war." He explained that by spring, the Army Air Corps would have so many bombers based in the Philippines they could annihilate the Japanese home islands: "Our aim is to blanket the whole area with airpower. Our own fleet, meanwhile, will remain out of range of Japanese airpower, at Hawaii. . . . The last thing the US wants is a war with Japan which would divide our strength. . . . The danger period is the first ten days of December."

Taking reporters' questions, Marshall insisted, "We'll fight mercilessly. Flying Fortresses will be dispatched immediately to set the paper cities of Japan on fire [with] no hesitation about bombing civilians." He was hoping that news of this aggressive stance would leak "directly to Japanese officials" so that they might reconsider their belligerent stance. But since the Philippines was not yet ready to defend herself from a Japanese attack, Marshall warned, "Nothing that I am telling you today is publishable, even in hinted form." After a correspondent pointed out that the range of the B-24 meant it could not reach Japan from the Philippines and then make it back home, the *New York Times'* Hanson Baldwin published his report "This Is a War We Could Lose."

Marshall told his senior staff the next day that Roosevelt and Hull "anticipate a possible assault on the Philippines" by Japan, but the general had a different opinion "because the hazards would be too great for the Japanese." War Plans Division chief Leonard Gerow assumed Thailand would be a target and didn't think Tokyo would attack anything that could stir up a fight with Washington. Like so many other American military officials, their thinking was too logical in the face of an enemy who had left logic far behind.

On November 17 in Japan, Admiral Isoroku Yamamoto appeared on *Akagi*'s deck to address the men of his First Air Fleet, perhaps for the last time. He sent them into history with a speech that included, "The American commander [Kimmel] is no ordinary or average man. Such a relatively junior admiral would not have been given the important position of CINCPAC unless he were able, gallant, and brave. We can expect him to put up a courageous fight. Moreover, he is said to be far-sighted and cautious, so it is quite possible that he has instituted very close measures to cope with any emergency. Therefore, you must take into careful consideration the possibility that the attack may not be a surprise after all. You may have to fight your way in to the target. . . . It is the custom of Bushido to select an equal or stronger opponent. On this score, you have nothing to complain about—the American navy is a good match for the Japanese navy. . . . Japan has faced many worthy opponents in her glorious history—Mongols, Chinese, Russians. But in this operation we will meet the strongest opponent of all. I expect this operation to be a success."

Admiral Chuichi Nagumo added his own words of encouragement: "The Empire is now going to war with an arrogant and predestined enemy [and we are] hoping to destroy the United States fleet once and for all. However difficult the situation you may face, don't lose your confidence in victory. Cope with it with calmness and composure. . . . Is there anything, no matter how difficult it may be, that cannot be done by an intrepid spirit and a burning loyalty?"

Key officers, including Genda and Fuchida, then joined their commanders in a ritual dinner of *surume* (dried cuttlefish) and *kachiguri* (walnuts), symbolizing happiness and victory. At onboard portable Shinto shrines, they toasted "Banzai!" while throwing back sake in honor of their emperor. They planned for failure—unanimously, all the pilots of Operation Hawaii assumed they would never again see Japan—but expected victory. Bomber pilot Zenji Abe held a common Japanese opinion: "We knew that the American people were made up of many races and assumed the American people had no united loyalty to their country and no desire to fight for it."

After dinner, Yamamoto returned to *Nagato*. From the deck, he watched his great fleet depart for a battle that would sear his name into history, as well as launch a global war he never wanted to fight. On that same day, Joseph Grew warned Cordell Hull, "In emphasizing the need for guarding against sudden military or naval actions by Japan in areas not at present involved in the China conflict, I'm taking into account as a possibility that the Japanese would exploit all available tactical advantages including that of initiative and surprise. It is important, however, that our government not (repeat not) place upon us, including the military and naval attachés, major responsibility for giving prior warning. . . . Our field of military and naval observation is almost literally restricted to what can be seen with our own eyes, which is negligible."

Also on that day, Hull, Roosevelt, Nomura, and a new Japanese representative, a man who was the very picture of modern urban sophistication, met at the White House for the first time. "In this dangerous emergency, one could not afford to discharge [Nomura] or to be too hesitant," Togo recalled, so he decided to supplement him with another negotiator, Saburo Kurusu, who had arrived in the United States a mere two days before his meeting with the president of the United States. Joseph Grew: "[Togo] said he had picked Mr. Kurusu to come to Washington to help Admiral Nomura, as he had the best command of English in the Japanese service. . . . Togo asked if I would arrange to get Kurusu to Washington as soon as possible on a Clipper, as it was important to carry on the conversations to a successful conclusion as soon as possible. I said I would do so.

"I had known [Kurusu] about ten years in Japan. He spoke English almost perfectly, he had an American wife, and I negotiated with him, and I had seen him in a personal way in many respects. I always regarded him as decidedly pro-American in his outlook and sentiments, and the fact that he happened to be the Japanese ambassador in Berlin at the time of the signing of the Axis agreement did not change my opinion of him very much, because after all an ambassador, when he is at a post, takes the instructions of his government and carries them out whether he approves of that particular document or not."

After reading the cables sent between Tokyo and Washington and meeting informally with Foreign Ministry colleagues, Kurusu concluded that things had been progressing moderately well between the two countries until July, when Japan invaded Indochina. He met with Hideki Tojo just before leaving and told the prime minister that "the chance of success in the negotiations with the United States is thirty percent." "Be sure to give it your best effort and come to an agreement," Tojo said, which Kurusu found encouraging. Then the prime minister continued, "But Japan could not possibly concede on the point of troop withdrawal," since that would be a dishonor to the great souls who'd died in service to the nation. Once again, Japan's leader executed a volte-face, in what was an especially troubling moment for Nomura and Kurusu, since their current offer to the Americans, Plan A, included staged withdrawals from China, while backup Plan B would offer a speedy remove from southern Indochina and a gradual exit from the rest of both countries.

As with Konoye, however, Kurusu had a public relations problem in Washington. Americans knew him from when he'd worked under Matsuoka as ambassador to Berlin, where he was photographed with Hitler and signed the Tripartite Pact. Kurusu was in fact opposed to Japan's joining the Axis and keen to negotiate a peace with Washington. He was known in Japan as so pro-American that some army officials openly said it would be a good thing if, before getting to Washington, his plane crashed and he was killed.

Nomura and Kurusu had been instructed to strictly adhere to Togo's detailed and convoluted strategy, which involved four different steps of offering various forms of Plan A and then Plan B. Kurusu, however, was able to make plain to Roosevelt that he had been sent not to pressure officials in Washington, but as an additional effort to find a peaceful solution. He asked the president if he could understand the Japanese frame of mind, and FDR brilliantly replied, "There is no last word between friends." This was a phrase from thirty years before, said by Secretary of State William Jennings Bryan to Japan's then ambassador during a period when the two countries' relationship was similarly fraught—California had passed a yellow-peril act; yet, Japan planted cherry trees on the banks of Washington's Potomac. To Japanese with any knowledge of their country's history with the West, "There is no last word between friends" held deep emotional resonance, and the two Japanese ambassadors were moved by the American president's allusion.

Like all of official Washington, Hull's office at State had ivory- and gray-painted walls; heavily padded furniture in oak or walnut, in damask or leather; thick carpets and drapes; and clocks that chimed not quite in unison every fifteen minutes. At their initial meeting, the secretary reminded the ambassadors of their nation's diplomatic history with Germany, when the Nazis signed the Anti-Comintern Pact with Japan, then turned around and signed a nonaggression pact with the Soviet Union, then turned around again and attacked Russia. Couldn't the Japanese see that it was only a matter of time before Hitler showed up in Asia to double-cross them, too?

Kurusu understood that the most important issue in FDR's mind blocking forward movement on normalizing relations was not China, but the Tripartite Pact. He explained that, though it would be hard for Tokyo to formally renounce that alliance, a "general understanding" with America would "outshine" the treaty with Nazi Germany. This salvo, though an honest reflection of Tokyo's current murky thinking, was not successful. As Kurusu was himself the one who had signed the Tripartite Pact, for the large percentage of American leaders who thought the Japanese were duplicitous, here was one more flagrant example. The meeting ended, and Hull invited the ambassadors to continue their conversation, but Kurusu, perhaps because he was tired, or needed to do more research, or was awaiting further instructions from Togo, declined. This was a grave miscall, for it hardened the secretary's feelings.

When Hull met with Kurusu and Nomura the next day, the eighteenth, Kurusu repeated that a treaty with Washington would doubtlessly "outshine" the one with Berlin, and Hull certainly knew that "big ships cannot turn around too quickly, that they have to be eased around slowly and gradually." Seeing things falling further and further apart, Nomura revealed his final option: What would happen if Japan withdrew from southern Indochina, and she and America returned to the status "before [the US] freezing measures were put into effect?" Hull did not react as expected, instead saying that the Japanese would just send those soldiers "to some equally objectionable" target, and that reversing the embargo meant the United States "believed that the Japanese were definitely started on a peaceful course and had renounced purposes of conquest." But Nomura continued, insisting Japan was tired of its pointless war in China and ready to take steps away from colonial expansion. Couldn't Hull see a way to create a détente to soothe relations, as Roosevelt had suggested with his "modus vivendi"?

This approach worked. At the end of the meeting, Hull said he would discuss Japan's offer with the British and the Dutch, meaning he was now turning to "formal negotiations." The two ambassadors were convinced that they were steps away from a great diplomatic success. Kurusu, as soon as he could, cabled Togo with the encouraging news.

The following night, Nomura and Kurusu met with Hull at his apartment, where the secretary was remarkably congenial, saying if they could come to an agreement, a pact "might enable the leaders in Japan to hold their ground and organize public opinion in favor of a peaceful course." He even allowed that this process of reversing public thinking "might take some time." It was the first hopeful meeting between the United States and Japan since 1931's Manchurian Incident, ten years before.

A First Air Fleet sailor writing under the pseudonym Iki Kuramoti remembered that momentous third week of November: "At the time of year when green leaves turn suddenly to red in the cool winds of approaching autumn, and one begins to feel the piercing breath of the North Wind—that is to say, on 18 November 1941—we left Kure harbor and sailed for the distant northern seas. The purpose of this operation was unknown to us. We had taken on board warm clothing, materials for protecting the guns against the cold, and a great quantity of sea nets, but understood nothing of this. Day after day and night after night the ships carried out target practice.

"In the newspapers that we had on board it was said that we were to attack Dutch Harbor [in Alaska's Aleutians], but we did not believe it. Why did we not believe it? Consider the moderate course of Japanese diplomacy up to that time. It seemed unlikely that Japan meant at this time to lift up her hand against Britain and America. Indeed, was there not at that moment a conference in progress at Washington between America and Japan?"

Mitsuo Fuchida: "At six o'clock on the dark and cloudy morning of 26 November, our twenty-eight-ship task force weighed anchor and sailed out into the waters of the North Pacific Ocean. . . . The crew

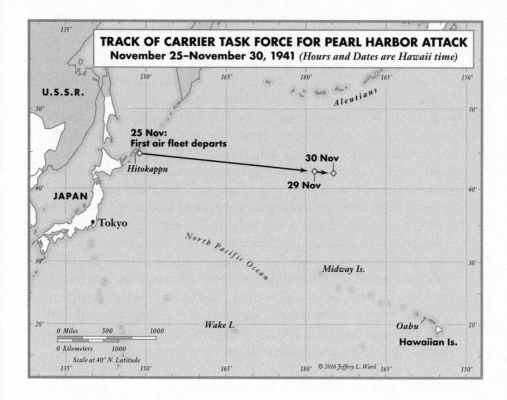

TRACK OF CARRIER TASK FORCE FOR PEARL HARBOR ATTACK
November 25–November 30, 1941 *(Hours and Dates are Hawaii time)*

U.S.S.R.

Aleutians

25 Nov:
First air fleet departs

30 Nov

Hitokappu

29 Nov

JAPAN

•Tokyo

North Pacific Ocean

Midway Is.

Wake I.

Oahu

Hawaiian Is.

0 Miles   500   1000
0 Kilometers   1000
Scale at 40° N. Latitude

© 2016 Jeffrey L. Ward

shouted 'Banzai!' as they took what might be their last look at Japan. . . .
I thought the plan should have called for complete destruction of the
US Pacific Fleet at the outset, followed by an invasion of the Hawaiian Islands to push America entirely out of the Central Pacific. . . . In
the meantime, the fleet had assumed formation. The carriers sailed
in parallel columns of three, followed by the tankers. On the outside,
two battleships and two heavy cruisers took positions, the whole group
encircled by a screen of the light cruisers and destroyers. The submarines patrolled about two hundred miles ahead of our force."

As the ships plowed into heavy Pacific swells, the commanders
enforced strict radio silence. To save fuel on that chilly journey, only
Shokaku and *Zuikaku* had heat and hot water. The tanker skippers
weren't experienced in keeping up with the fleet at night, so every
dawn, the destroyers would herd them back to the force.

Refueling in the stormy North Pacific turned out to be back-
breaking, dangerous work. As the ships bucked and lurched in the
rough seas, the big hoses connecting the oilers would break loose and

whiplash, leaking fuel. Even after a thorough cleaning of the decks, crewmen had to tie straw rope around their shoes to keep from slips and falls. Several were swept overboard and lost, but nothing could be done.

Nagumo continually worried about evading enemy and neutral eyes. If the fleet was spotted before December 6, he was to return home; after the sixth, he was to proceed with the attack; on the sixth, the call was his. He received daily updates of the US Fleet's position from Yoshikawa and Kuehn via Tokyo and especially worried about the weather. If it was bad and the seas were rough, that could make refueling impossible. Sunny skies, however, meant an extremely visible fleet traveling across hundreds of miles of empty ocean.

Akagi's engine was run by Commander Yoshibumi Tanbo and 350 men, who almost never left their charge, which was in the bowels of the ship. Their meals were brought to them—rice balls, pickled plums, and radishes, wrapped in bamboo bark. Almost none of the crew knew what they were going to do since negotiations were ongoing, and if an agreement was reached, the fleet would return to Japan and its mission would remain secret and unknown. The engineers, however, knew how much fuel was available and, calculating the distance, were certain that they were on their way to the Philippines.

On November 19, Tokyo's foreign office radioed her embassies two messages preparing them for an escalation of global war:

> Regarding the broadcast of a special message in an emergency.
>
> In case of emergency (danger of cutting off our diplomatic relations), and the cutting off of international communications, the following warnings will be added in the middle of the daily Japanese language short-wave news broadcast.
>
> (1) In case of a Japan-US relations in danger: HIGASHI NO KAZE AME [East wind, rain].
>
> (2) Japan-USSR relations: KITA NO KAZE KUMORI [North wind, cloudy].
>
> (3) Japan-British relations: NISHI NO KAZE HARE [West wind, clear].
>
> This signal will be given in the middle and at the end as a weather forecast, and each sentence will be repeated twice. When this is heard, destroy all code papers, etc. This is as yet to be a completely secret arrangement.

When our diplomatic relations are becoming dangerous, we will add the following at the beginning and end of our general intelligence broadcasts:

(1) If it is Japan-US relations, "HIGASHI" [east].

(2) Japan-Russia relations, "KITA" [north].

(3) Japan-British relations (including Thai, Malaya, and N.E.I.), "NISHI" [west].

The above will be repeated five times and included at beginning and end.

That month, a doctor and an assistant purser arrived in Honolulu aboard passenger ship *Taiyo Maru* from Yokohama. They were in fact agents of the Navy General Staff who had come to Hawaii to assemble the latest detailed information on American forces. The lead agent was the youngest lieutenant commander in the Japanese Imperial Navy, Suguro Suzuki, and the *Taiyo* would be one of the last ships making the trip between Japan and the United States, her voyage following the route the First Air Fleet would use across the North Pacific. Along the way, Suzuki prepared daily reports on visibility, direction, and velocity of the wind, pitch and roll of the ship, sea conditions, and the appearance of any foreign vessels or patrol planes. He would return to Tokyo with remarkably good news, reporting that, except for a brief storm, the weather had been fine, and no American patrols were spotted until a mere two hundred miles north of Oahu, and none whatsoever adjacent to Midway.

Honolulu consul chief Kita and other members of the embassy visited the *Taiyo* multiple times to deliver daily newspapers in Japanese, with bits of military information tucked inside. At harbor security, they were forced to flip the pages, but these men knew a flipping technique to keep the tucked-in reports hidden from American eyes.

Honolulu spy Takeo Yoshikawa was not allowed anywhere near the ship, as a safety measure. He did, however, have to answer a detailed hundred-item questionnaire brought by Suzuki on a "tiny ball of crumpled rice paper." When one consulate employee saw it, he remembered thinking, "Would it be possible for the Japanese to come all the way out here and launch a successful attack? I do not recall any statement by consulate personnel that Pearl Harbor might be attacked. But after the episode of the ship and the important questionnaire, the implications were there."

Yoshikawa had twenty-four hours to finish the queries, with Kita returning with his answers to the ocean liner. They included:

This is the most important question: On what day of the week would the most ships be in Pearl Harbor on normal occasions?

A: Sunday.

How many large seaplanes patrol from Pearl at dawn and sunset?

A: About 10, both times.

Where are the airports?

A: For this question, I was able to provide a map with every detail, plus aerial photos which I had taken . . . as late as October 21, and considerable structural detail on the hangars at Hickam and Wheeler Fields.

Are the ships fully provided with supplies and ready for sea?

A: They are not ready for combat; [they are] loaded with normal supplies and provisions only.

Yoshikawa also reported that aerial reconnaissance to the north was "at a minimum . . . poorly organized . . . downright bad." Though this was true, how he knew this is a mystery. Other agents from the *Taiyo* investigated where in Hawaii midget-sub and air crews should go in case of emergency for rescue. They decided on the privately owned, sparsely populated island of Ni'ihau. (Fuchida, researching the issue back in Japan, had arrived at the same conclusion.)

Yoshikawa also provided Suzuki with drawings, photographs, and maps. A "Souvenir of Honolulu" aerial photo of Pearl Harbor that Yoshikawa had marked up with numbered squares, similar to the ones described by the "bomb plot" message, as well as overhead photographs of the harbor he'd taken from a sightseeing plane, would be found in the cockpits of Japanese bombers brought down on December 7. Later he said, "We knew then that things were building to a climax and that my work was almost done."

The feeling of amity and hope built by Hull, Kurusu, and Nomura in their negotiations was destroyed on November 20 when a furious cable from Togo arrived. Since Hull hadn't yet responded to Plan A, Kurusu and Nomura were not authorized to offer the troop withdrawals of Plan B, and Togo excoriated Nomura for his impudence. Togo then ordered them to submit Japan's final proposal, which offered a halt to military advances beyond Indochina and withdrawal of troops from the south of that territory while requesting US help in securing Dutch East Indies oil; an American restoration of trading status back to the conditions of July; and no American intervention in Tokyo's negotiations with Chiang Kai-shek's Nationalist government.

At their meeting on that day, Hull was given Japan's final Plan B offer and took issue with the terms. He was then so stricken with flu that he couldn't work. By the twenty-third, Hull had fully recovered and refused to offer an official US reaction to Plan B. He instead said that, since the Japanese had told the American State Department in the spring that her oil purchases would be "used for normal civilian consumption," but were instead employed to invade southern Indochina, why should he trust her envoys now claiming a desire for peace? And why was the Japanese press filled with anti-American editorials? Hull later explained that the Americans saw Plan B as "condonement by the United States of Japan's past aggressions, assent by the United States to unlimited courses of conquest by Japan in the future, abandonment by the United States of its whole past position in regard to the most essential principles of its foreign policy in general, betrayal by the United States of China, and acceptance by the United States of a position as a silent partner aiding and abetting Japan in her effort to create a Japanese hegemony in and over the Western Pacific and Eastern Asia. . . . no responsible American official could ever have dreamed of accepting it."

CNO Stark cabled his fleet commanders including Husband Kimmel on the twenty-fourth, "Chances of favorable outcome of negotiations with Japan very doubtful. This situation coupled with statements of Japanese Government and movements of their naval and military forces indicate in our opinion that a surprise aggressive movement in any direction including attack on Philippines or Guam is a possibility."

The next day in a private letter to Kimmel, Stark said, "I have been in constant touch with Mr. Hull and it was only after a long talk with him that I sent the message to you a day or two ago showing the gravity of the situation. He confirmed it all in today's meeting, as did the President. Neither would be surprised over a Japanese surprise attack. From many angles an attack on the Philippines would be the most embarrassing thing that could happen to us. There are some here who think it likely to occur. I do not give it the weight others

do, but I included it because of the strong feeling among some people. You know I have generally held that it was not time for the Japanese to proceed against Russia. I still do. Also I still rather look for
an advance into Thailand, Indo-China, Burma Road areas as the most
likely. I won't go into the pros or cons of what the United States may
do. I will be damned if I know. I wish I did. The only thing I do know
is that we may do most anything and that's the only thing I know to
be prepared for; or we may do nothing—I think it is more likely to
be anything."

After the *Taiyo Maru* returned from its espionage mission, Suzuki
debriefed Nagumo, Genda, Fuchida, and other officers aboard *Akagi*.
He was full of good news about surveillance—not a single foreign
vessel was spotted in either direction across the northern route—and
a piece of bad news. Even though they spotted a number of carrier
planes in the skies, they saw no carriers in the harbor itself. He also
warned the admirals that, if they did not achieve surprise with this
mission, they could expect a vigorous American defense followed by a
vicious retribution.

Suzuki's report inspired Genda and Fuchida to create one strategy if
the Americans were caught by surprise, and another if they were found
ready and waiting. In the former case, Fuchida would fire his flare gun
once, bringing Murata and the torpedo planes to the fore to do as
much damage as possible, followed by the dive-bombers and the high-
level bombers. But if the Americans were ready to fight back, Fuchida
would shoot off two flares, bringing in the dive and horizontals first.

Genda so fretted over the shallowness of Pearl Harbor and the possible failure of his torpedoes that he came up with an novel strategy,
suggesting to Furukawa, the leader of the horizontal bombers, "If your
bomb hits directly beside the turret and if it explodes in the powder
magazine, the ship will be reduced to fragments." When Furukawa
expressed his doubts about achieving such accuracy in targeting—
since the horizontals had a hard enough time just hitting ships, much
less turrets—Genda said, "Do it with spiritual strength." Furukawa
pleaded, "Genda, don't ask such unreasonable things!" As it turned
out, the most famous and devastating high-level strikes at Pearl Harbor would be those that struck directly by a turret and exploded in
powder magazines exactly as Genda had hoped, turning the American
warships themselves into bombs.

Back in Tokyo at Operations, Tomioka now brooded over his role in all of this, how he had vociferously opposed Yamamoto's plan but, under the threat of resignation, had succumbed, agreeing to this ridiculous scheme. He decided that he could never forgive himself if disaster struck the First Air Fleet and became so certain of catastrophe at Hawaii that he decided to keep a .38-caliber revolver in the drawer of his desk. If Nagumo, Genda, and Fuchida failed in their mission, Tomioka was going to shoot himself in the head.

On November 22, a strange advertisement appeared in the *New Yorker* magazine. It pictured a group of people sheltered from an air raid, playing dice. Under the headline "Achtung, Warning, Alerte!" the copy read, "We hope you'll never have to spend a long winter's night in an air-raid shelter, but we were just thinking . . . it's only common sense to be prepared. If you're not too busy between now and Christmas, why not sit down and plan a list of the things you'll want to have on hand. . . . And though it's no time, really, to be thinking of what's fashionable, we bet that most of your friends will remember to include those intriguing dice and chips which make Chicago's favorite game: THE DEADLY DOUBLE." Scattered throughout the issue were six smaller tag ads referring back to the main copy, with the dice numbered 12 and 7, numbers on no known dice. Later during the war, navy transport pilot Joseph Bell was flying a South Pacific route when one of his passengers, an intelligence officer, told him that many in intelligence considered this ad a secret warning. He had been assigned to investigate the matter, but every lead had led to a dead end—the ad's copy had been presented in person at the magazine's offices, and the fee paid with cash. Neither the game offered in the ad, nor the company that purported to make it, ever existed.

During this state of crisis, State's Cordell Hull, Navy's Frank Knox, and War's Henry Stimson met every Tuesday morning at nine thirty. On the Tuesday morning of November 25, Hull showed them America's counteroffer of a modus vivendi to Togo's Plan B. With some restrictions, the United States would resume trade and release Japanese assets if Japan reduced its northern-Indochina troops to twenty-five thousand. This truce agreement was to last for three months, at which time it could be extended.

On that same morning in Hawaii, Kimmel and Short met with a group of army and navy officers to decide whether to send planes and crews to help defend Wake and Midway, or to keep them in Hawaii to defend Oahu. General Short insisted, "If I man these islands, I must command them."

"Over my dead body," Admiral Kimmel said. "The army should exercise no command over navy bases."

The Hawaiian Air Force's chief of staff, James Mollison, returned to Short's original point: "Our mission is to protect Oahu, and shipping out these army planes will lessen our capability to do so." Kimmel wanted details on his thinking: "Why are you so worried about this? Do you think we are in danger of attack?" When Mollison replied, "The Japanese have such a capability," the admiral argued, "Capability, yes, but possibility?"

Kimmel then asked his naval war plans officer, Rear Admiral Charles McMorris, "What do you think about the prospects of a Japanese air attack?" McMorris said, "None, absolutely none." But Mollison's comments struck a chord with the admiral. Kimmel held on to the better P-40s for Hawaii and sent the more-dated Marine F4Fs to Wake and Midway.

At noon that day in Washington, Hull, Knox, and Stimson met Roosevelt, Marshall, and Stark at the White House. They read Togo's November 22 cable to his ambassadors and were struck by the point that diplomatic efforts to reach what Togo called "the solution we desire" had to be concluded by November 29. Kurusu and Nomura were told that the "deadline absolutely cannot be changed" and, ominously, "after that, things are automatically going to happen."

Henry Stimson remembered Roosevelt saying "that we were likely to be attacked perhaps as soon as next Monday, for the Japanese are notorious for making an attack without warning. The question was how we should maneuver them into the position of firing the first shot without allowing too much danger to ourselves. It was a difficult proposition."

Washington's vague lassitude at this time was captured by analyst Roberta Wohlstetter: "A curious kind of numbness seemed to characterize these last moments of waiting, a numbness that was an understandable consequence of long association with signals of mounting danger. The signal picture had been increasingly ominous for some time, and now apparently added up to something big, but not very definitive. There was also a fundamental passivity connected with the avowed policy the United States could not strike the first blow."

That afternoon, Kimmel met with Vice Admiral William F.

Halsey Jr., whom he'd known since Annapolis days. On November 28, Halsey would depart Pearl Harbor with Task Force 8—the carrier *Enterprise*; heavy cruisers *Northampton*, *Chester*, and *Salt Lake City*; and nine destroyers—to carry twelve of those Grumman F4F-3 Wildcats to the marines stationed on Wake Island. After they read Stark's memo, Kimmel asked Halsey if he wanted to take any battleships along with him, to make his task force appear more routine. "Hell no!" Halsey retorted. "If I have to run, I don't want anything to interfere with my running!"

Kimmel's only stroke of good luck in the devastation to come was that his aircraft carriers were away from Hawaii on the morning of December 7. While Halsey was delivering Wildcats to Wake, Rear Admiral John H. Newton with Task Force 12—carrier *Lexington*; heavy cruisers *Chicago*, *Portland*, and *Astoria*; and five destroyers—was carrying eight Vought SB2U-3 Vindicators to Midway, while the third Pacific Fleet carrier, *Saratoga*, after getting overhauled at Bremerton in Washington, was just entering North Island Naval Air Station in San Diego.

In Washington, DC, Henry Stimson received an army intelligence cable that same afternoon of November 25 from "G-2 that was very disturbing. It indicated that the Japanese were embarking on a large expeditionary force of thirty, forty, or fifty ships at Shanghai and that this expedition was proceeding along the China coast south of Formosa . . . with the possibility that it might be proceeding to the Philippines or to Burma to cut off the Burma Road, or to the Dutch East Indies." By phone, Stimson told Hull the details of what he'd learned, and informed the president with a hand-delivered memorandum.

When the next morning Stimson hadn't heard any response, he called Roosevelt, who "jumped into the air, so to speak, and said he hadn't seen it," Stimson recalled. The president "fairly blew up"— Roosevelt was, indeed, entirely enraged—and "that while they were negotiating with him—negotiations in which we were asking for a withdrawal of their invading troops in China—they should be sending a further expedition down to Indo-China."

Japanese apprehensions that moving forward with both war and diplomacy at the same time would be seen as duplicitous by the Americans had come true. Cordell Hull was immediately summoned to the White House, and when he then returned to State, he seemed entirely defeated. "Those men over there do not believe me when I tell them that the Japs will attack us," he told an employee. "You cannot give an ultimatum to a powerful and proud people and not expect them to react violently."

For all of Cordell Hull's failings as secretary of state, he had been so close to achieving a great diplomatic triumph that might have saved American lives and even extracted Japan from her Axis alliance. Instead, Tokyo's double-dealing had killed Roosevelt's modus vivendi compromise. Hull later said, "The slight prospect of Japan's agreeing to the modus vivendi did not warrant assuming the risks involved in proceeding with it, especially the risk of collapse of Chinese morale and resistance, and even of disintegration in China." This moment presents one of the great what-ifs of history. If FDR had met with Konoye, or if FDR's modus vivendi had been achieved, would it have prevented the attack on Pearl Harbor? And what would America be today if she had only needed to fight World War II in Europe and North Africa?

That same morning, Kurusu, with Nomura's enthusiastic support, cabled Togo with an idea. What if they asked Roosevelt to send a message to Hirohito about peace in East Asia and Japanese-American friendship? Due to his immortal station, the emperor could not begin such a dialogue, but Hirohito could reply, and talks could restart. And if Tokyo suggested that the neutralized zone FDR had proposed for Indochina be expanded to include Thailand and the Dutch East Indies, Japan could get its oil, and military forces on both sides could be excluded. Communicating the seriousness of the matter in the same way Togo had talked to him, Kurusu "sincerely desired that the message be communicated to Privy Seal Kido and be answered urgently." Togo cabled back a refusal, but asked Kido nonetheless; the Privy Seal said that "it was not an appropriate time" for the emperor to negotiate with the president.

That afternoon, Nomura and Kurusu arrived at the State Department to receive "Steps to Be Taken by the Government of the United States and by the Government of Japan," which would be known by history as the Hull Note. Instead of a simple treaty between Washington and Tokyo, it proposed an agreement to be signed by the United States, Japan, Britain, China, Holland, the Soviet Union, and Thailand. It included, "The Government of Japan will withdraw all military, naval, air and police forces from China and from Indochina. The Government of the United States and the Government of Japan will not support—militarily, politically, economically—any government or regime in China other than the National Government of the Republic of China with capital temporarily at Chongqing." After looking it over, Kurusu said that, when the Japanese government saw this, it would "throw up its hands" as the "proposal could be interpreted as tantamount to meaning the end." It was so aggressive that Hull later admitted, "We had no serious thought that Japan would accept our proposal." On the phone later that day with Stimson, Hull "told me he had broken the whole thing off. As he put it, 'I have washed my hands of it and it is in the hands of you and Knox, the army and the navy.'"

Nomura and Kurusu tried to get the secretary to revise the document before sending it to Togo. Hull refused. When they asked for amendments, such as a gradual timeline on withdrawing from China and a bilateral treaty that the other countries could later join, Hull refused. Couldn't the United States come to terms on a temporary modus vivendi, as they had been discussing? Hull said it could not. Nomura said that since there is "no last word between friends," could they meet again directly with Roosevelt? To this, Hull said yes.

On that same November 26, the US consulate in Tokyo warned American citizens to leave Japan as quickly as possible.

On the twenty-seventh, FDR received a memo on the latest military intelligence from Army Chief of Staff Marshall and CNO Stark, concluding, "Japan may attack the Burma Road, Thailand; Malaya; the Netherlands East Indies; the Philippines; the Russian Maritime Provinces . . . The most essential thing now, from the United States viewpoint, is to gain time."

That afternoon, the president met with Hull, Nomura, and Kurusu at the Oval Office and successfully hid his anger at Tokyo's duplicity and his conviction that Japan was about to strike American soil. Instead, he was wholly gracious, beginning the meeting by a ritual offering of cigarettes. He told Nomura and Kurusu that the American people wanted a peaceful solution to the troubled Pacific, and he hadn't yet given up. But those fifty troopships invading southern Indochina were "a cold bath" to his hopes, as were the "movements and utterances of the Japanese slanting wholly in the direction of conquest by force and ignoring the whole question of a peaceful settlement and the principles underlying it."

The Hull Note and Washington's ensuing refusal to compromise

were received in Tokyo as an "ultimatum" and a "humiliating proposal" that the Japanese could never accept, the last-straw instance of a
bullying and demeaning United States that unified the country's leaders to battle against a common enemy. "I was struck by despair," Togo
said. "I tried to imagine swallowing whole [the Hull Note's terms], but
there was no way to force them down my throat." Prime Minister Tojo
told his cabinet that it meant "no glimmer for hope," and at a public
rally on November 30, he decried "the desire of Britain and the United
States to fish in the troubled waters of East Asia by pitting the East
Asiatic peoples against each other, and to grasp the hegemony of East
Asia. This is a stock-in-trade of Britain and the United States. For the
honor and pride of mankind we must purge this sort of practice from
East Asia with a vengeance." In the eyes of the militarists, though, the
Hull Note was manna from heaven, "nothing short of a miracle!" as
one Army General Staff *bakuryo* officer remembered. "This must be
divine grace; this makes it easy for the Empire to cross the Rubicon
and determine on going to war. That's great, just great!"

In fact, Hull's Note was no ultimatum, and he clarified the administration's position by telling Nomura and Kurusu directly that, when
it came to the Imperial Japanese Army's intransigence on troops in
China, "the evacuation [of Japanese forces from China and Indo-
china] would be carried out by negotiations. We are not necessarily
asking that it be effected immediately." Many historians now believe
that Japan's leadership kept the Hull Note's details secret because they
knew her people were sick of the China quagmire and might easily
have accepted its terms.

When asked after the war by Congress why he didn't try harder to
negotiate peace with Japan, an outraged Cordell Hull replied: "I knew
at the same time as a matter of psychology that the worst bandit—and
they were bandits of the most savage type, the leaders of Japan and
Germany—the worst bandit, as he prowls about and he looks about,
has always got his eyes open to see if any pistols or any guns or any
weapons are in sight. He does not like for the most innocent citizen to
point an unloaded pistol or an unloaded gun at him. None of us care
for that, as a matter of fact. And it was the same way as a matter of psychology with this bunch of overlords who were running rife over the
earth. . . . Somebody who knows little and cares less now says, 'Why
didn't the United States make concessions and save us from the war,'
when any person knows, and if you look back at the situation as it

existed during those last ten, twelve, fourteen days, any rational person knows just what the Japs were doing. They were off on this final attack and no one was going to stop them unless we yielded and laid down like cowards, and we would have been cowards to have lain down."

On that same November 27 that the president was meeting with Nomura and Kurusu, Harold Stark cabled his commanders and asked Husband Kimmel to copy Walter Short: "This dispatch is to be considered a war warning. Negotiations with Japan looking toward stabilization of conditions in the Pacific have ceased and an aggressive move by Japan is expected within the next few days. The number and equipment of Japanese troops and the organization of naval task forces indicates an amphibious expedition against either the Philippines, Thai or Kra Peninsula, or possibly Borneo."

Marshall cabled a similar message to his Western Defense commanders that day, including Short, and Stark copied it in a cable to his admirals the following day: "Negotiations with Japan appear to be terminated to all practical purposes with only the barest possibilities that the Japanese Government might come back and offer to continue. Japanese future action unpredictable but hostile action possible at any moment. If hostilities cannot repeat not be avoided the United States desires that Japan commit the first overt act. This policy should not repeat not be construed as restricting you to a course of action that might jeopardize your defense. Prior to hostile Japanese action you are directed to undertake such reconnaissance and other measures as you deem necessary but these measures should be carried out so as not repeat not to alarm civil population or disclose intent. Report measures taken. A separate message is being sent to G Two Ninth Corps Area re subversive activities in United States. Should hostilities occur you will carry out the tasks assigned in Rainbow Five so far as they pertain to Japan. Limit dissemination of this highly secret information to minimum essential officers."

Within thirty minutes, Short replied to the War Department that he had instituted Alert No. 1. Perhaps Marshall and the other leaders in Washington did not fully understand what was happening in Hawaii because, according to Washington's Standard Operating Procedure (SOP) involving alerts, No. 1 was the highest alert and No. 3, the lowest. But on November 5 Short and his staff reversed this numbering, yet never sent that revision to Washington.

The new alert system instituted by Short read:

Alert No. 1: This alert is a defense against acts of sabotage and uprising within the islands, with no threat from without.

Alert No. 2: This alert is applicable to a condition more serious than Alert No. 1. Security against attacks from hostile sub-surface, surface, and air-craft, in addition to defense against acts of sabotage and uprisings, is provided.

Alert No. 3: This alert requires the occupation of all field positions by all units, preparing for maximum defense of OAHU and the Army installations on outlying islands.

This revised SOP was first received by Washington in March of 1942. This fact led the Judge Advocate General to overrule the Army Pearl Harbor Board's censure of General George Marshall.

Stark would later testify, "We considered [the November 27 cables] an unequivocal war warning . . . that war was imminent," but unfortunately, "unequivocal" is not how it was received by General Short, for one. He thought "war warning" meant "no more than saying that Japan was going to attack someplace." The commanders in Hawaii additionally believed army intelligence's reports, which had located the Japanese fleet as either in home waters or off to invade Southeast Asia, and which had judged Japan's air forces as having no bombers capable of reaching from the nearest Japanese base to Oahu, twenty-one hundred miles away. Regardless of the naval lessons of Taranto and their own prior analyses, few in Hawaii were thinking of the dangers of carriers and winds from the north.

General Short later explained his decision in the face of a war warning: "(1) The message of November 27 contained nothing directing him to be prepared to meet an air raid or an all-out attack on Hawaii; (2) he received other messages after the November 27 dispatch emphasizing measures against sabotage and subversive activities; (3) the dispatch was a 'do-don't' message which conveyed to him the impression that the avoidance of war was paramount and the greatest fear of the War Department was that some international incident might occur in Hawaii which Japan would regard as an overt act; (4) he was looking to the Navy to provide him adequate warning of the approach of a hostile force, particularly through distant reconnaissance which was a Navy responsibility; and (5) that instituting alerts 2 or 3 would have seriously interfered with the training mission of the Hawaiian Department."

Short's excuses are especially outrageous when considering that, starting January 24, 1941, the general received fifty-six pages of warnings from Washington about Japanese attacks in the Pacific, 25 percent of them arriving between December 1 and 6, 1941, even to the point of explicit instructions from the chief of the American Army on exactly what might happen and exactly what needed to be done. On February 7, 1941, Marshall wrote Short: "My impression of the Hawaiian problem has been that if no serious harm is done us the first six hours of known hostilities, thereafter the existing defenses would discourage an enemy against the hazard of an attack. The risk of sabotage and the risk involved in a surprise raid by air and by submarine constitute the real perils of the situation. . . . Please keep clearly in mind in all your negotiations that our mission is to protect the base and the Naval concentration." This was followed up on March 5, when Marshall cabled Short: "I would appreciate your early review of the situation in the Hawaiian Department with regard to defense from air attack. The establishment of a satisfactory system of coordinating all means available to this end is a matter of first priority."

On November 29 in Washington, Secretary of the Navy Frank Knox told a vacationing president, "The news this morning indicates that the Japs are going to deliberately stall for two or three days, so unless this picture changes, I am extremely hopeful that you will get a two- or three-day respite down there [in Warm Springs, Georgia] and will come back feeling very fit." On that same day, Secretary Hull told British ambassador Viscount Halifax that it would be "a serious mistake for our country and other countries interested in the Pacific situation to make plans of resistance without including the possibility that Japan may move suddenly and with every possible element of surprise . . . this would be on the theory that the Japanese recognize that their course of unlimited conquest now renewed all along the line probably is a desperate gamble and requires the utmost boldness and risk."

Hirohito asked the nation's previous prime ministers to a palace luncheon on November 29 to discuss what Japan should do in the wake of the Hull Note. Admiral Yonai began by saying, "Excuse me for speaking my mind in crude ways, but I think we mustn't become utterly poor in our quest to avoid becoming gradually poor." Konoye agreed: "Can we not stick to the status quo? In other words, should we not wait out the hard times and see if we could break the deadlock?" But none of these onetime leaders had the determination or political strength to inspire their timid emperor to stop the nation's rush to battle, which was the entire point of the meeting.

Hirohito met with his little brother, Rear Admiral Nobuhito Takamatsu, the next day. Though raised separately due to the traditions of a Japanese imperial heir, they were close. Now the thirty-six-year-old prince repudiated his public reputation of being in favor of war by admitting to his emperor brother, "The navy cannot afford to fight. There is a feeling that, if possible, the navy would want to avoid a Japanese-American war. If we pass up this opportunity, war will be impossible to avoid. The navy will start mobilizing for combat on December 1. After that, it cannot be contained."

When the emperor admitted he was worried that Japan would lose, his brother insisted that this was one more reason that Hirohito needed to act immediately. But the emperor explained that the decision had been set by the military and the government, and that there was no legal avenue for an imperial veto: "If I did not approve of war, Tojo would resign, then a big coup d'état would erupt, and this would in turn give rise to absurd arguments for war."

It is a shame of history that Emperor Showa was no Meiji.

Beginning November 30, Tokyo cabled Manila, London, Havana, Washington, Hong Kong, and Singapore with orders to destroy all their codes and all their decrypting machines "preparatory to an emergency situation." Simultaneously, the United States was bringing citizens home, destroying codebooks and machines at its own Asian embassies, and publicly discussing both its refusal to tolerate further Imperial Japanese Army aggressions, and its pessimism about the future of negotiations with Japan's envoys. Later that same day, Tokyo cabled its Berlin ambassador, "The conversations begun between Tokyo and Washington last April during the administration of the former cabinet . . . now stand ruptured—broken. . . . In the face of this, our Empire faces a grave situation and must act with determination. Will Your Honor, therefore, immediately interview Chancellor HITLER and Foreign Minister RIBBENTROP and confidently communicate to them a summary of the developments. Say to them that lately England and United States have taken a provocative attitude, both of them. Say that they are planning to move military forces into various places in East Asia and that we will inevitably have to counter by also moving troops. Say very secretly to them that there is extreme danger that war may suddenly break out between the Anglo-Saxon nations and Japan through some clash of arms and add that the time of the breaking out of this war may come quicker than anyone dreams."

After MAGIC processed this cable, US military intelligence predicted that Japan might attack Siberia, Yunnan Province, Thailand, Burma, Malaya, the Philippines, Hong Kong, Singapore, and/or the Netherlands East Indies. . . . "The most probable line of action for Japan is the occupation of Thailand. . . . Our influence in the Far Eastern Theater lies in the threat of our Naval Power and the effort of our economic blockade. Both are primary deterrents against Japanese all-out entry in the war as an Axis partner."

During the first week of December 1941, numerous American newspaper headlines promoted the readiness of the country's West Coast defenses. The *Los Angeles Times* on December 1 wrote, "HARBOR DEFENSE TESTED BY GUARD: Eighty Men Engage in Maneuvers Aimed Against Enemy Invasion," and on the second, "ARTILLERY UNITS MOVE TODAY FOR TEST OF AIR RAID DEFENSE: Gunners to 'Defend' L.A. from 'Attack' by Enemy Planes in State-wide Maneuvers." On the third and fourth, the *Orange County Register* announced, "LAGUARDIA WARNS OF RAID DANGER" and "TROOPS FOR AIR RAID DEFENSE MANEUVERS TO ARRIVE TODAY."

Hull told Nomura and Kurusu on December 1 that, since Japan's troops in Indochina were a menace to the Philippines, the Netherlands East Indies, Burma, Malaya, and Thailand, it was forcing America and its allies to keep additional forces stationed in Asia, in effect helping Hitler. Though the United States would not be driven out of Asia, Japan had no reason to war against it; she did not need a sword to get "a seat at the head of the table." Nomura replied that the Japanese people felt the United States was treating them with disdain, and his government had directed him to ask Washington to make "a deep reflection" on what was the ultimate aim of the United States in its relationship with Japan, considering the Hull Note.

That afternoon, a weary Cordell Hull told his assistant how sick he was of the whole mess: "They all come at me with knives and hatchets. The president remarked to me that he wished he knew whether

Japan was playing poker or not. He was not sure whether or not Japan had a gun up its sleeve. My reply was that I had no doubt that sooner or later, depending upon the progress of Germany, Japan would be at our throats; as for me, when I knew that I was going to be attacked, I preferred to choose my own time and occasion. I asked the President whether he had any doubt that Japan would attack Siberia if the Germans overcame the Russians. He said that he hadn't. I felt that by going to war with Japan now we would soon be in a position where a large part of our Navy, as well as of the British Navy and of the Dutch East Indies Navy, could be released for service in the Atlantic. The President's feeling was that Japan would draw herself in and that she was too far away to be attacked. It seemed to me that the President had not yet reached the state of mind where he is willing to be aggressive as to Japan."

A fourth imperial conference convened in Tokyo that day to approve going to war against Britain, the Netherlands, and the United States. When he returned to his office, Prime Minister Tojo told his secretary, "I could see with my own eyes that the emperor highly values peace. Inexcusably in one way or another I had to request the imperial sanction. It was extremely regrettable. In a quiet voice, the emperor talked about the treaty between Japan and England [of 1902] and the warm reception he received on his visit to England [in 1921]. . . . In the imperial edict proclaiming war, the sentence 'Indeed, this is not my will' was not in the original draft. It was explicitly added at the emperor's command." The nation had stumbled into war under the most wayward of circumstances, with Tojo commenting from this period, "With war, if you don't try it, you can't know how it will turn out."

That same December 1, Husband Kimmel received from his intelligence officer Edwin Layton a radio report that the Japanese had suddenly changed their military cable signals. After Kimmel underlined one of the report's points—"the fact that service calls lasted only one month indicates an additional progressive step in preparing for operations on a large scale"—he asked Layton to follow up with information on the locations of Japan's naval forces, which Layton delivered the next day. After reading it, Kimmel asked why the IJN's Carrier Divisions 1 and 2 were missing from the report, and Layton said that it was because insufficient information was available to make a reliable call on those four carriers' locations.

Kimmel was duly alarmed. "What! You don't know where Carrier Division One and Carrier Division Two are?" he asked.

"No, sir, I do not," Layton said. "I think they are in home waters, but I do not know where they are. The rest of these units, I feel pretty confident of their location."

Kimmel: "Do you mean to say that they could be rounding Diamond Head and you wouldn't know it?"

Layton: "I hope they would be sighted before now."

Layton later explained, "When carriers or other types of vessels go into home waters, home ports, home exercise areas, they use low-power radio direct with shore station. This is then handled normally on telegraphic land lines to prevent our direction-finder stations and intercept stations from hearing their traffic."

Joseph Rochefort, commander of the navy's Combat Intelligence Service, had determined that the Japanese carrier force had remained in Kyushu for training because, in a great act of radio deception, the First Air Fleet's wireless operators had stayed behind and continued to broadcast in what was a well-known hand to American listeners. This fooled US naval intelligence into thinking the carriers were anchored in home waters instead of heading at full speed toward Hawaii.

At five in the afternoon on December 2, the emperor approved the launch of X-day. Admiral Ugaki then received a telegram from the General Staff with the authority to open Imperial Naval Order Number 12, which commanded the First Air Fleet—which was at that moment about to cross the international date line along the 180th meridian—to attack Oahu at any time after midnight on December 6. Ugaki cabled Chuichi Nagumo this order with the coded message "Niitaka yama nobore ichi-ni-rei-ya"—"Climb Mount Niitaka." At the time, Niitaka, a peak on the island of Formosa, was the highest point of the Japanese Empire.

Now all the men of Nagumo's task force could be told their mission's target. Most of them agreed with Iki Kuramoti that "at last Japan would be at war with Britain and the USA! An air attack on Hawaii! A dream come true. What will the people at home think when they hear the news? Won't they be excited! I can see them clapping their hands and shouting with joy. These were our feelings. We would teach the arrogant Anglo-Saxon scoundrels a lesson!"

Soryu bomber pilot Tatsuya Otawa remembered thinking, "If it was permitted, I would have wanted to jump up and shout, 'Hurray!' I thought then what a happy man I was, to be able to participate directly in this historic moment." But not everyone was elated; Lieutenant

Commander Sadao Chigusa remembered thinking, "I am very sorry that I should take part in the attack against Hawaii where my brother now lives." He had already written farewell letters to his parents and to his wife, thanking her for their many good years together.

In the chief of staff's cabin on *Akagi* were two platforms with large models of Oahu and Pearl Harbor. Pilot Yonnekichi Nakajima: "After we finished flight training, we gathered models of the American ships, and a pilot would ask us which model was which ship. 'How about this one? How about that one?' Even now at the age of seventy-three, I remember the ship names as if they were poems."

On December 2, the order to burn all codes was sent to Japan's diplomatic officials in "North America (including Manila), Canada, Panama, Cuba, the South Seas (including Timor), Singora, Chienmai," as well as to all Japanese officials in British and Dutch colonies. The message to Washington additionally ordered Nomura to "stop at once using one code machine unit and destroy it completely [and] at the time and in the manner you deem most proper dispose of all files and messages coming or going and all other secret documents." Nomura was told to contact the naval attaché about the procedures to be taken, as the attaché had chemicals "on hand for this purpose."

That same day, Nomura was given a message from Roosevelt asking why Japan's troops were surging through Indochina, other than for further conquest? Nomura replied that Japanese forces had to be increased in the area because of the increasing activity of Chinese troops, and that the numbers the president mentioned were exaggerated.

Yamamoto went to Tokyo on December 3 to receive his rescript—the order to lead his Combined Fleet into the war he so dreaded—directly from the emperor at the Imperial Palace and later reported that Hirohito seemed "serene after fully realizing the inevitability of going to war."

Across the whole of 1941, Japan had engineered one of the greatest military operations of all time. After six months of exhaustive planning from information gathered by spies across the Pacific, Colonel Masanobu Tsuji had sent the master blueprint for the Japanese takeover of Southeast Asia—Operation Number One—to General Staff Headquarters in Tokyo that summer. Questioned closely by the Imperial Army chief, Hajime Sugiyama, on this simultaneous invasion of Malaya, Singapore, Burma, the Philippines, Wake, Guam, Borneo, and

Java by an army that had so far failed to conquer China, Tsuji boldly insisted, "If we begin on November third, we will be able to capture Manila by the New Year, Singapore by February eleventh [of 1942], Java on March tenth, and Rangoon on April nineteenth." All of Tsuji's predictions would come true in an epic global conflict that established the Great Empire of Japan: Dai Nippon Teikoku.

Operation Number One. While Chuichi Nagumo's First Air Fleet sped toward Hawaii to protect the Imperial Japanese Navy's flank and cow the Americans from war, Vice Admiral Jisaburo Ozawa's Southern Expeditionary Fleet left Japan on November 20 in small squadrons to invade Malaya; Vice Admiral Ibo Takahashi's Philippine Invasion Force of nearly one hundred warships headed for Luzon; Vice Admiral Shigeyoshi Inoue's Fourth Fleet sailed for Guam; and Vice Admiral Nobutake Kondo's Second Fleet aimed for the Netherlands East Indies, Timor, and Burma. Packed into the holds of their transports on the way to conquest across the Pacific, Imperial Japanese Army recruits studied a pamphlet especially prepared for that night, saying their efforts in the coming days would release "a hundred million Asians tyrannized by three hundred thousand whites."

Americans in Washington hypnotized themselves watching this vast armada take shape, an operation so massive it effectively camouflaged the relatively small task force heading for Oahu. The attack on Pearl Harbor, such a vital part of American history, was for Japan at that moment merely a preemptive strike, a minor sideshow to Operation Number One. Admiral Yamamoto had predicted the empire's great continental invasion "will lead to a war in which the nation's very fate will be at stake" and remained behind with the main body of the Combined Fleet—six battleships, two light carriers, two light cruisers, and thirteen destroyers—to protect the homeland.

Across the northern Pacific, Admiral Nagumo had to vary his formation depending on the weather. The default line was a forward squadron of four destroyers, followed by heavy cruisers *Tone* and *Chikuma*, and behind them, the six carriers in two columns—*Akagi*, *Kaga*, and *Shokaku* to starboard; *Soryu*, *Hiryu*, and *Zuikaku* to port—accompanied by the three submarines. Tankers and more destroyers followed, with battleships *Hiei* and *Kirishima* in the rear. Since the slowest vessel was the oiler *Toei Maru*, at sixteen knots, that set the fleet's speed.

Since Nagumo's forces crossed the date line that day, they would have two December 3s. At the same time, the First, Second, and Third submarine fleets, along with the Special Attack Unit, were within a three-hundred-nautical-mile radius, completely encircling Hawaii. Nine subs meanwhile began prowling the West Coast of the United States, preparing to strike targets of opportunity once they heard Fuchida's signal beginning the attack on Hawaii.

At the White House that Wednesday, FDR insisted that "he had the Japanese running around like a lot of wet hens because he had asked them why they were pouring military forces into Indochina. . . . I think the Japanese are doing everything they can to stall until they are ready." The next day Roosevelt's naval aide brought him the MAGIC intercept ordering Japanese embassies to burn nearly all their "telegraphic codes," destroy one of their code machines, and to shred all confidential papers. FDR wondered when Japan would strike, and the aide suggested, "Most any time." Harold Stark would later remember that day: "We felt that war was just a matter of time."

Concerned that even after being dispatched a war warning, the Pacific Fleet command didn't fully understand the Japanese threat, OP-20-G's Captain Laurance Safford decided to send a message on the third to Kimmel and the Fourteenth and Sixteenth Naval Districts, an action that overstepped his role as an intelligence officer, broke national security by revealing a MAGIC decrypt, and even mentioned PURPLE by name: "Circular twenty four forty four from Tokyo one December ordered London, Hongkong, Singapore and Manila to destroy Purple machine. Batavia machine already sent to Tokyo. December 2 Washington also directed destroy Purple, all but one copy of other systems, and all secret documents. British Admiralty London today reports embassy London has complied."

Henry Clausen interpreted Safford's urgent cable as saying "without equivocation that Tokyo has ordered its consulates to destroy their codes and code machines. Once code machines were destroyed, there could be no turning back potential Japanese attacks. The consulates could no longer communicate effectively with Tokyo. War had to follow; it was inevitable."

Also on December 3, the FBI's telephone tap intercepted the Japanese consulate's chef telling someone in Hawaii that the consul general was burning his papers. FBI agent Robert Shivers sent this information to the navy's Mayfield and the army's Bicknell, and Bicknell said he'd revealed this news at the December 6 staff meeting.

That very same day, CNO Stark's office cabled its commanders: "Highly reliable information has been received that categoric and urgent instructions were sent yesterday to Japanese diplomatic, and consular posts at Hongkong Singapore Batavia Manila Washington and London to destroy most of their codes and ciphers at once and to burn all other important confidential and secret documents."

That night, a British intelligence agent in the Philippines—probably Colonel Gerald Wilkinson—sent an urgent cable to Honolulu British intelligence: "We have received considerable intelligence confirming following developments in Indo-China. A. 1. Accelerated Japanese preparation of air fields and railways. 2. Arrival since Nov. 10 of additional 100,000 repeat 100,000 troops and considerable quantities fighters, medium bombers, tanks and guns (75mm). B. Estimate of specific quantities have already been telegraphed Washington Nov. 21 by American military intelligence here. C. Our considered opinion concludes that Japan envisages early hostilities with Britain and U.S. Japan does not repeat not intend to attack Russia at present but will act in South. You may inform Chiefs of American Military and Naval Intelligence Honolulu."* Bicknell, Mayfield, and FBI agent Shivers were duly informed, but this cable, as well as the FBI's report, never made it back to the Navy Department. For all of Kimmel's complaints that his superiors hadn't adequately informed him about every bit of MAGIC, the admiral himself never forwarded to Washington the intelligence he acquired independently.

After receiving Safford and Stark's memos, Kimmel immediately asked Edwin Layton what this Purple machine was, and Layton said that he didn't know, but he would find out. He asked Fleet security officer Lieutenant Coleman, who explained, "It was an electrical coding machine . . . that was used in the passing of messages between Japanese consuls and diplomats and the home office. The word *purple* was to designate the type of the machine is an improvement over the old one called the *red*."

Navy intelligence's Richmond Kelly Turner assumed the admirals in Hawaii would comprehend the severity of the news: "We all considered that that was an exceedingly important piece of information to send to Admiral Kimmel and Admiral Hart, because the destruction

---

*A detailed explanation of how the Navy Department told its field commanders about information derived from MAGIC without revealing its secret is in Henry C. Clausen and Bruce Lee's *Pearl Harbor: Final Judgement*.

of codes in that manner and in those places, in my mind and experience, is a definite and sure indication of war with the nations in whose capitals or other places those codes are destroyed. . . . It indicates war within two or three days. . . . The enemy codes at Washington and Manila were to be destroyed, which definitely indicates war against the United States." But in Hawaii, after Layton told Kimmel what PURPLE was, the admiral didn't understand the significance of a hostile nation destroying cipher machines. Neither did Bloch, and neither commander forwarded the message to Short, as both assumed he had received something similar directly from Marshall.

Colonel Rufus Bratton, G-2's Far Eastern Section chief, felt similarly to Safford, telling his staff that since "something was going to blow in the Far East soon," the section would "henceforth remain open on a twenty-four-hour basis." Bratton asked McCollum about the Pacific Fleet: "Are you sure these people are properly alerted? Are they on the job? Have they been properly warned?"

McCollum confidently said, "Oh, yes, the Fleet has gone . . . to sea."

The cavalcade of warnings continued the following day when Treasury Secretary Morgenthau reported to FDR, "At five forty-five this evening I received word that the representative of the Bank of Japan in New York is closing their office tomorrow under instructions from Japan. The representative will leave New York on December 10 for Japan."

A friend of the president's, Methodist pastor Eli Stanley Jones, visited the White House that December 4 to deliver a secret message from a secretary of the Japanese consulate, Hidenari Terasaki. Three days before, Kurusu had asked Togo for permission to begin a dialogue between Roosevelt and Hirohito, a notion the privy seal had dismissed out of hand. Now desperate, and knowing time was running out, Kurusu begged Terasaki to "approach the president through an intermediary . . . and suggest that he send a cable directly to the emperor appealing for peace . . . over Tojo's head." At his meeting with Reverend Jones, Roosevelt said that he had been thinking about a direct appeal to the Chrysanthemum Throne, but worried that he might "hurt the Japanese here at Washington by going over their heads to the emperor." Jones said that, in fact, the embassy was requesting it, but since they were going behind the backs of both their foreign and prime ministers, their participation would have to be kept secret, that the president must "never refer to Mr. Terasaki in connection with the message." Roosevelt said, "You tell that young Japanese he is a brave man. No one will ever learn of his part in this from me. His secret is safe."

That same day, Nomura was informed that the majority of his staff, including Terasaki, were immediately being transferred. The ambassador asked for a postponement in the case of Terasaki's departure so he could complete his "intelligence work," but the foreign office refused. Kurusu immediately responded with a desperate plea: "I feel confident that you are fully aware of the importance of the intelligence setup in view of the present conditions of the Japanese US negotiations. I would like very much to have Terasaki, who would be extremely difficult to suddenly replace because of certain circumstances, remain here until we are definitely enlightened as to the end of the negotiations. I beg of you as a personal favor to me to make an effort along these lines. I shall have him assume his post as soon as his work here is disposed of."

In the MAGIC version of this message, OP-20-G's Translation Branch chief Captain Alvin Kramer footnoted the name Terasaki with "Second Secretary, is head of Japanese espionage in Western Hemisphere. He and his assistants are being sent to South America." Kramer considered this "a very significant point," since US naval intelligence had identified Terasaki as "an especially trained espionage man and he had a number of specially trained men with him. His chief concern during the summer wasn't setting up an espionage establishment in Latin America. The fact that he was directed to leave was a further straw in the wind." Bratton said almost exactly the same thing about this transfer order: "It meant that the time was running out, that the crisis was approaching."

The Kido Butai's size and the state of its technology led to a number of startling incidents. Secrecy was so important that plane radios were disabled, and parts of each vessel's transmitters were locked away. The ships could only communicate with each other through blinker lights and signal flags. On December 5, in one of the great remaining Pearl Harbor mysteries, the task force had its only meeting with a foreign vessel: Soviet trawler *Uritsky*, sailing between Portland and Vladivostok. We know that the First Air Fleet and the trawler spotted each other, but we don't know why Nagumo didn't order the *Uritsky* attacked until sunk. Or if *Uritsky* reported sighting Nagumo's fleet, and, if she did, what Moscow told Washington, if anything. One theory is that Stalin knew a great deal about the Japanese government through his Sorge spy ring. Though Stalin was fighting Germany, he was not yet at war with Japan, and it might have been worth keeping this information from Roosevelt if it meant peace on Stalin's eastern border.

Between 0230 and 0330 on the morning of Friday, December 5, US destroyer *Selfridge* made underwater contact with an unidentified vessel in waters near Hawaii, but lost it. Another destroyer, *Ralph Talbot*, picked it up about five miles from Pearl Harbor, identified it as a submarine, and asked permission to drop depth charges. The squadron leader aboard *Selfridge* refused, insisting the intruder was an orca. *Talbot* replied, "If this is a blackfish, it has a motorboat up its stern!"

That same day the Japanese consular officials in Honolulu received an urgent message from Tokyo asking its spies about "the movements of the fleet subsequent to the fourth." Takeo Yoshikawa returned to

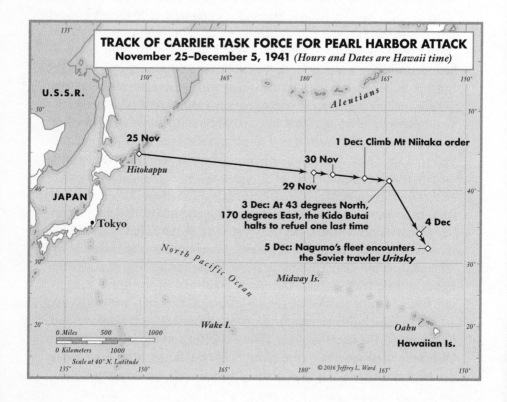

TRACK OF CARRIER TASK FORCE FOR PEARL HARBOR ATTACK
November 25–December 5, 1941 *(Hours and Dates are Hawaii time)*

the tea parlor's telescope to jot down the latest details on Kimmel's fleet: 8 battleships, 2 heavy cruisers, 6 light cruisers, 43 destroyers, and 4 submarines. At that time, 106 American vessels plied the Pacific, from Alaska to the Solomon Islands, but as before, with *Saratoga* in California, *Lexington* bringing marine planes to Midway, and *Enterprise* on the way back to Hawaii after delivering her cargo of planes to Wake, Yoshikawa saw no aircraft carriers.

Leaving his tea parlor perch, Yoshikawa taxied to the outskirts of Pearl Harbor, where he strolled about in his tourist camouflage, taking notes. By 1300 he replied to Tokyo, "At the present time there are no signs of barrage-balloon equipment [blimps hanging from metal cables to interfere with low-flying pilots]. In addition, it is difficult to imagine that they actually have any. However, even though they have made preparations, because they must control the air over the water and the land runways of the airports in the vicinity of Pearl Harbor, Hickam, Ford, and Ewa, there are limits to the balloon defense of Pearl Harbor. I imagine that in all probability there is considerable opportunity left to take advantage for a surprise attack against these places. In my opinion the battleships do not have torpedo nets. The details are not known."

Does the mention of "a surprise attack against these places" mean that he and others at the consulate in Hawaii knew in advance what was to come? Yoshikawa—who returned that night to Aiea Heights and Pearl City for one last cable that included, "It appears that no air reconnaissance is being conducted by the fleet air arm"—later insisted the "surprise attack" comment was just a coincidence.

As always, these cables were coded in PURPLE and then transmitted to Tokyo commercially, by either Mackay Radio and Telegraph or by the Radio Corporation of America—RCA. MAGIC intercepted all three December 6 messages, decrypting and processing Tokyo's on December 12, and Yoshikawa's reply on the eighth. On top of MAGIC's institutional delays, the phrase "I imagine that in all probability there is considerable opportunity left to take advantage for a surprise attack against these places" was translated as "The whole matter seems to have been dropped."

At a White House meeting that Friday, Hull said of Nomura and Kurusu, "With every hour that passes, I become more convinced that they are not playing in the open, that what they say is equivocal and has two meanings. . . . I am convinced they don't intend to make any honorable agreement with us." Frances Perkins recalled of that same meeting: "No expression of concern over Japanese attack on US. More concerned over how Japan may attack Britain through Singapore. According to Secretary of War Stimson, 'The Philippines are indefensible. We have always known it.' There was a complete sense of confidence in the American Navy. Nobody asked where it was or how it was dispersed [i.e., positioned]. It would have been extraordinarily bad form to have asked."

CHAPTER FIVE

DECEMBER 6

At about 0800 on the morning of December 6, Kimmel's intelligence officer Edwin Layton told his admiral about the alert from Washington concerning Japanese troop movements, and that this was to be taken seriously. Kimmel referred Layton to the War Plans Division officer who had drafted Plan Orange against Japan, Vice Admiral William Pye. On *California*, after Pye and his chief of staff, Captain Harold Train, had read the memo, Layton raised his key concern: "The problem is whether the Japanese will leave their flank open or whether they will take out the Philippines on their way south."

"Do you think they will leave their flank open?" Pye asked.

"They never have," Layton said.

"The Japanese will not go to war with the United States," Pye insisted. "We are too big, too powerful, and too strong." He turned to Train. "Harold, do you agree?"

"Emphatically!" Train said.

Kimmel concurred with Pye's viewpoint and dismissed any worries about enemy submarines attacking as "nil—nothing." Besides Pearl Harbor's being too shallow for torpedoes, he believed that enemy submarines couldn't fully submerge inside it. Kimmel did not even have an antisubmarine net at the entrance to the harbor, merely a crinoline that prevented torpedoes from being fired up the channel. When great ships arrived at his anchorage, in fact, they found a waterway too small for maneuvering and so anchored with bows facing landward. To prepare the Fleet for a sortie on Monday, December 8, tugboats spent all of December 6 maneuvering the great ships seaward.

At 0830, Nagumo's Kido Butai finished her last refueling, left her slow-moving oilers behind, and began ratcheting up to a full-speed

173

bore straight south toward Oahu, her tombstone-gray warships flying the flag of a bloodred sun.

Ambassador Nomura was strolling down Massachusetts Avenue that morning in Washington when he was picked up by Vice Admiral William Smedberg, driving incognito in civilian clothes, and taken to the home of Smedberg's boss, Chief of Naval Operations Harold Stark. Smedberg: "When they came out, Nomura had tears in his eyes. Stark told me afterward that Nomura was extremely worried about the possibility of the war party in Japan making some drastic decisions." The diplomat had told Stark, "If the US doesn't ease up on these sanctions against Japan, the military men in my country are going to do something desperate, in my opinion."

At the same time that Nomura and Stark were meeting secretly, a pilot cable from Togo arrived, giving Nomura advance notice that the ministry would be telegraphing a fourteen-part message in reply to the November 26 Hull Note: "I imagine you will receive it tomorrow. However, I am not sure. The situation is extremely delicate, and when you receive it, I want you to please keep it secret for the time being." Instructions as to when to present this to Hull would arrive later. "However, I want you in the meantime to put it in a nicely drafted form and make every preparation to present it to the Americans just as soon as you receive instructions. . . . There's really no need to tell you this, but in the preparation of the aide-mémoire be absolutely sure not to use a typist or any other person. Be most extremely cautious in preserving secrecy."

The Bainbridge Island naval station on Puget Sound across from Seattle intercepted the fourteen-part message—Telegram No. 902 from Togo to Nomura and Kurusu, the reply to the Hull Note, written in English. Starting around noon, the first thirteen parts were forwarded, via Teletype, to Washington.

From the beginning, Imperial Japanese Army officers planned to invade Singapore without giving prior notice to Britain, but the Imperial Japanese Navy felt differently about the United States and Operation Z. After the imperial conference on December 1, in fact, the emperor told Prime Minister Hideki Tojo repeatedly that he was not to attack the United States without warning. Naval attaché Yuzuru Sahematsu explained the sense of honor that was a hallmark of Japanese military history: "Japanese warriors never tried to assassinate a person who is sleeping. When they tried to kill him, they first kicked the pillow and woke him up. And then killed him. The same principle applied to the attack. The required time to wake America up would be approximately thirty minutes."

The story of Japan's failed warning with Togo's fourteen-part message would lead to cries of infamy in the United States—one shocked sailor on the *Monaghan* would comment, "Hell, I didn't even know they were sore at us!"—while for decades Japanese historians have explained it as wholly due to Nomura and Kurusu's inept mishandling of a simple cable. Today we know that these are not the facts. From the start, Tokyo set too tight a schedule between the cable's dispatch and the hour for presentation, with no provision for human error or mechanical interference. Togo's advance notice revealed no urgency and no time limit. Tokyo dispatched the cable in a jumble, with parts four, one, two, three, and nine sent simultaneously, followed by the pilot cable "in the late afternoon or early evening," as Colonel Bratton remembered, coming in "all mixed up." After a two-hour pause, parts six, seven, eight, eleven, twelve, and thirteen arrived together at 1451, the final pages not appearing until "sometime between nine and ten that night."

When it was finally decoded and distributed, only two Washington officials—one of them Roosevelt—interpreted the cable as a threat of war. At military intelligence, Bratton judged it as "not an ultimatum, it was not a declaration of war, nor was it a severance of diplomatic relations," and General Miles agreed: "These thirteen parts had little military significance. They concluded only with a Japanese refusal to accept the American proposal of November 26 as a basis of negotiation—a result which had been expected and discounted for some time."

That afternoon, Stark and Marshall told Stimson and Roosevelt that the army and the navy needed more than a few months before they would be ready for war, and that the Japanese sanctions needed to be eased. Smedberg: "As we left the office one of us said, 'Well, the British are sure going to catch it tomorrow at Singapore.' We didn't have the slightest suspicion that there was any threat to Pearl Harbor."

When Navy Secretary Frank Knox saw in his December 6 daily briefing that the Japanese had launched troops, he asked, "Gentlemen, are they going to hit us?" Admiral Richmond Kelly Turner replied, "No, Mr. Secretary. They are going to attack the British. They are not ready for us yet."

• • •

By 1130 Nagumo's task force had reached a speed of twenty knots. Ten minutes later, *Akagi* raised the same Z flag that the great Admiral Togo had unfurled at the Imperial Japanese Navy's finest moment: Tsushima. *Akagi* then signaled to the other ships Yamamoto's rescript ordering his men to be "firmly determined to fulfill the responsibility entrusted them by the Emperor, by destroying the US Pacific Fleet with utmost efforts. . . . The rise and fall of the Empire depends upon this battle. Every man will do his duty." As the actual attack would be inflicted by airmen two hundred miles from the fleet, for Chief Engineer Tanbo, listening on voice tube from the *Akagi*'s engine room, this was the most dramatic moment of the entire operation.

That afternoon in paradise, Sears, Roebuck Honolulu arrayed Christmas presents around its parking-lot palms, and a sellout crowd cheered for the University of Hawaii football team fighting the Willamette Bearcats. It was such a beautiful day, as so many would later remember.

At around 1400, the FBI's Japanese translator in Honolulu finished work on an extensive intercepted phone call of December 3 between a Tokyo newspaper writer and Dr. Motokazu Mori, a prominent Honolulu dentist and known Japanese agent. The journalist said, "I received your telegram and was able to grasp the essential points. I would like to have your impressions on the conditions you are observing at present. Are airplanes flying daily?" "Yes," Mori said, "lots of them fly around," and added, that the Japanese and Americans in Hawaii were "getting along harmoniously," but when the reporter asked directly about the US Navy, Mori demurred, saying, "We try to avoid talking about such matters." The conversation then changed, with Tokyo asking, "What kind of flowers are in bloom in Hawaii at present?" Mori said, "Presently, the flowers in bloom are fewest out of the whole year. However, the hibiscus and the poinsettia are in bloom now."

General Short's counterintelligence officer, Lieutenant Colonel George Bicknell, thought this transcript was "highly suspicious," but "both Colonel Fielder and General Short indicated that I was perhaps too 'intelligence conscious' and that to them the message seemed to be quite in order, and that it was nothing to be excited about." Local FBI agent Robert Shivers also found it odd and tried tracking it down, but made no headway. A cable sent to the task force from Tomioka's Operations Section, however, included, "Telephone contacts made with Japanese and civilian indicate Oahu Island was very calm with no blackout."

That afternoon in Washington, most of the staff at the Naval Cryptographic Section had already left for the weekend. One new employee, Mrs. Dorothy Edgers, decided on her own to go through the backlog of Hawaii MAGIC. She came across message after message between Tokyo and its Honolulu embassy concerning barrage balloons, airfield locations, ship movements, antitorpedo nets at Pearl Harbor, and even one report explaining how Japan's local German spy would transmit last-minute information. She showed the transcripts to Chief Ship's Clerk H. L. Bryant, but he said he couldn't get to translating them before leaving at noon, and to let the job wait for Monday. Mrs. Edgers thought the material was so important, though, that she stayed at the office and did the translating herself. That afternoon, the Translation Branch chief, Captain Alvin Kramer, came in to work and Mrs. Edgers showed him her efforts. Kramer criticized her translation and began editing it, but said he had more important things to do. Kramer remembered saying, "This needs a lot of work, Mrs. Edgers. Why don't you run along now? We'll finish the editing sometime next week." She argued with him, insisting that the job was worth finishing today. "You just go home, Mrs. Edgers," he replied. "We'll get back to this piece on Monday."

Secretary of War Henry Stimson marked the day in his diary with "The news got worse and worse and the atmosphere indicated that something was going to happen."

That afternoon, FDR decided he would try to back away from the Hull Note's tough stance by sending a conciliatory message to Hirohito that he forwarded to Hull, saying, "Shoot this to Grew. I think can go in gray code—saves time—I don't mind if it gets picked up." The president's cable asked the emperor to avoid "tragic possibilities" and continue "the long period of unbroken peace and friendship" between their two nations, years in which Japan and the United States "through the virtues of their peoples and the wisdom of their rulers" both prospered and "substantially helped humanity." Couldn't there be a way for all nations sharing the Pacific to live together without fearing "any form of military threat" and with freedom of commerce? FDR asked.

The conclusion: "I address myself to Your Majesty at this moment in the fervent hope that Your Majesty may, as I am doing, give thought in this definite emergency to ways of dispelling the dark clouds. I am confident that both of us, for the sake of the peoples not only of our own great countries but for the sake of humanity in neighboring territories, have a sacred duty to restore traditional amity and prevent further death and destruction in the world."

When Kurusu heard about FDR's cable, he publicly called it "a very clever move on the part of the [American] government" as Hirohito "could hardly say no, nor could he say yes, and that this would cause many headaches in Tokyo and give much food for thought." However, Imperial Japanese Army General Staff officers, fearing interference with Operation Number One, squelched this détente. When Army General Staff Communications Section's Major Morio Tomura learned that Roosevelt's letter to Emperor Showa had arrived at the Tokyo Central Telegraphy Office, he shook his sword to threaten the staff and ordered the office's director to reduce its urgency to delay the delivery to Ambassador Grew.

The same thing happened with the concluding cable of the fourteen-part message being sent at that moment from Togo to Nomura. The army first insisted that the fourteenth part be delayed until the president's cable was translated. They also tampered with its transmission, as evidenced by MAGIC; the original fourteen-part cable has its delivery marked "Very Urgent"; the one sent to Nomura was downgraded to "Urgent" and "Very Important." This meant that when it arrived at the Washington telegraph office in the early morning of December 7, no one called to alert the Japanese embassy, and it was left for later delivery. The original draft also announced the start of war, but the army revised the language until it merely referred to the end of diplomatic talks.

At dinner that evening, Franklin Roosevelt told his thirty-two guests, "This son of man has just sent his final message to the Son of God." Afterward, Roosevelt was meeting with Harry Hopkins when Commander L. R. Schultz, assistant to FDR's naval aide, arrived with the MAGIC intercepts of Togo's fourteen-part memo, with the fourteenth and final part not yet cabled. Roosevelt quickly read through the document and handed it to Hopkins, and when he'd finished, FDR said he interpreted the phrase that Tokyo "cannot accept the [Hull] proposal as a basis of negotiation" as "This means war." Hopkins agreed, adding,

"That since war was undoubtedly going to come at the convenience of the Japanese, it was too bad that we could not strike the first blow and prevent any sort of surprise."

Roosevelt: "No, we can't do that. We are a democracy and a peaceful people." Then according to Schultz, the president "raised his voice" to say, "But we have a good record."

FDR began to call Harold Stark, but found out he was at the theater and decided not to interrupt with a page since if Stark "left suddenly . . . undue alarm might be caused."

Rufus Bratton will testify before the army board that he had delivered the intercepts on the night of December 6. But in fact, after about half of the cable had arrived, Bratton "left and went home at about 9 p.m.," according to his assistant, Carlisle Clyde Dusenbury, who was left behind and assigned with deliveries. Instead, after the cables had been decrypted and translated, Dusenbury went home without delivering them to anyone, since "I did not wish to disturb the usual recipients who were probably at home asleep, as I did not see the implications of immediate hostilities [in the messages]." Judge Advocate General investigator Henry Clausen: "Our civilian government was being fed the most secret information by our military, but the military didn't do the job properly."

Air Corps Chief Hap Arnold was at that moment addressing the Thirty-Eighth and Eighty-Eighth Reconnaissance Squadrons, who would be crewing B-17s from California to Clark Field in the Philippines, with their first stop at Hickam Field on Oahu. "War is imminent," Arnold told them. "You may run into a war during your flight."

"If we are going into a war, why don't we have machine guns?" asked Major Truman H. Landon. Hap answered that the service was "trying to get every gallon of gas they could in the plane and they did not anticipate fighting . . . on that long hop from California to Hawaii."

At 2000 on December 6, the *Honolulu Advertiser* was printing its next morning's Sunday paper when the presses broke down. It never distributed that edition, which included one article on the revolution in warships—"By sea and by air the Navy is in fighting trim. Carrier-based aviation, which has undergone wide development in tactical scope and strategic concept, is destined to play a major role when the signal comes"—and a front-page article with the headline "U.S. Sure Pacific War Not Likely": "Official Washington believes that the tension over the Far Eastern crisis has been eased slightly, and that now there is a fairly good reason to hope that there will be no major conflict in the Pacific, at least for the next few weeks."

The *Advertiser* wasn't alone in making the wrong call. For weeks, Hawaii's newspaper headlines had seesawed back and forth between such "war is imminent" stories as "Kurusu Bluntly Warned Nation Ready for Battle," "Pacific Zero Hour Near," "U.S. Army Alerted in Manila—Singapore Mobilizing as War Tension Grows," and "U.S. Demands Explanations of Japan; Moves Americans Prepare for Any Emergency; Navy Declared Ready," and such "peace is imminent" articles as "Japan Called Still Hopeful of Making Peace with U.S.," "Hirohito Holds Power to Stop Japanese Army," "Further Peace Efforts Urged," and, on December 6, "New Peace Effort Urged in Tokyo—Joint Commission to Iron Out Deadlock with U.S. Proposal." The *Advertiser* had indeed started the week with a November 30 article—"Japanese May Strike over the Weekend"—about expected Asian targets of Japanese aggression.

That December 6, Corporal W. J. Walker was ordered to take three men and create a security checkpoint on the road into the Punchbowl, the crater of an extinct volcano just outside the city of Honolulu. After a long night, he fell asleep until 2:00 a.m. on December 7 when the private on duty called. An important admiral with an entourage of six cars and about ten motorcycles was insisting on an immediate entry. Walker explained his orders; the general, pointing to the bright lights of Pearl Harbor, belittled him with "Corporal, what in the hell do you foot soldiers think the navy is doing down there? . . . We are here to take care of anything the Nips want to start and to protect the army." Walker said he needed to check everyone's identification anyway. The admiral, far too important for a security check, cursed and stormed off.

That night, Pearl Harbor's spanking-new Bloch Recreation Center, which included a gym, a boxing ring, a jukebox, a bowling alley, and a pool hall with 3.2 percent beer, hosted "The Battle of the Bands," with troupes from the *Pennsylvania*, *Tennessee*, and *Argonne* performing swing, ballad, specialty, and jitterbug, including the hits "Take the A Train" and "I Don't Want to Set the World on Fire." That night's contest was an elimination round, pitting capital ship troupes across the whole of the Fleet against each other. For the audience, it was a night of dancing the latest steps until *Pennsylvania* was declared the winner, when everyone sang the Kate Smith hit "God Bless America." The

Pennsylvania's triumph meant that she would battle the other finalist, *Arizona*, for the championship on December 20.

Instead, every member of *Arizona*'s band would die the following day. Many Pearl Harbor survivors would, for decades, hold vivid and precise memories not so much of December 7 as of December 6, since that was the last moment they were with so many, many friends who would be taken from them.

That night a group from the *Arizona* had a big champagne blowout at a Halekulani Hotel cottage. A number were too drunk to make it back to their ship, and that's why they would survive.

Across the glittering hotels and ballrooms of Waikiki Beach that night were fox-trots, ukulele bands, and torches lighting the way to platforms for swing dancing over the sand. Lau Yee Chai, whose owners insisted was "the most beautiful Chinese restaurant in the world," with its shimmering carp ponds and artificial mountain vista, hosted a festival for the harvest moon. At a Pacific Club dinner party with her lawyer husband, Dorothy Anthony remembered the conversation with two recent arrivals from Harvard Law School: "We all knew war might break out in Asia because all the big newspapermen stopped here on their way back and forth. But that night you couldn't have gotten anyone at our party to say war would come to Hawaii."

Wheeler Field pilot Gus Ahola, his roommate, and their girlfriends spent that night drinking coffee, playing a round of cards, and watching home movies. "My God, what a way to spend that evening," he said, laughing, decades later. After driving his date home, Gus was passing by the great dreadnoughts of Pearl Harbor, twinkling in the yellow light of sodium vapor lamps, when a pilot pulled alongside and honked. The road between Honolulu and Wheeler Field was a narrow two-laner optimistically called the Kamehameha Highway, and as they would do everywhere else in the world, American pilots turned it into a drag strip. Gus: "You'd recognize another guy on that road, toot your horn, and away you'd go." Arriving at base, Gus took in the vista of Wheeler Field's glorious aircraft, illuminated by sabotage-preventing searchlights. He remembered thinking that he was part of "the best squadron in the Pacific, with the best training, the best pilots, and the best planes."

In town, the white, green, and khaki rivers of servicemen flowed across the streets and into the pool halls, the bars, and the brothels of Hotel Street. Men on their own and on the prowl have long been a feature of Honolulu's landscape, from Connecticut whalers during the era of Melville to the immigrant waves of Chinese, Japanese, and Filipino plantation workers, to American servicemen in the 1930s. For the great majority—tens of thousands of sailors and soldiers—assignment to Hawaii was tedious. The men complained about their food, the weather, their pay, and their work. It was not yet the "greatest generation"; they were lonely young men away from their families for twenty-four months, with a noticeable rate of suicide. As Japanese spy Yoshikawa had learned, the sailors practiced their maneuvers from Monday to Friday and then returned to berth on the weekends, while soldiers followed nearly an identical schedule with drills. In their time off they came to town to play Skee-Ball and cards, drink beer, buy monkeypod curios, and have their skin tattooed.

Historian Thurston Clarke: "The lonely soldiers paid to embrace Filipino taxi dancers whose heavy eye shadow melted down their faces like tears, and patronized the Hotel Street photographic studios where they paid handsomely for the pleasure of wrapping their arms around girls in grass skirts who clicked on smiles and ignored their whispered pleas for a date. They joined the double lines stretching around the block from houses of prostitution that advertised on matchbooks ('The Bell Rooms—Give the Bell a Ring!') and were so efficient that nearby taverns sold tokens good for a screw. Yet, despite the prostitution, then quaintly known as 'white-slave traffic,' and despite neighborhoods with forbidding names like Tin Can Alley, Blood Town, Mosquito Flats, and Hell's Half Acre, and despite the sneak thieves and pimps, there was a certain innocence to Hotel Street, a sense of order and propriety that later vanished from the place. The taxi-dance halls were heavily varnished, barn-like rooms reminiscent of church halls, where liquor was prohibited and dancers forbidden to leave until their mothers or husbands collected them." Army recruit Bob Kinzler: "We had no contact with the Asian population except through the Japanese lady barbers, and civilians thought we were just a bunch of bums who had enlisted in the military because we couldn't get real jobs."

Officers seldom got to enjoy a Saturday night out on the town. Rear Admiral Patrick Bellinger was at home recovering from a serious case of the flu, and Rear Admiral Claude Bloch had spent the afternoon playing golf and the evening reading; he was in bed by eight thirty. Admiral Husband Kimmel was one of many of Hawaii's leading citizens invited to a stag blowout at the Japanese consulate, but he decided to pass, as did Colonel Bicknell, who remembered Kita's affairs were "really wet parties, [with] a bottle of scotch at each place and a geisha girl pouring it out." Instead, Kimmel attended a dinner party at the Halekulani Hotel. Lieutenant General and Mrs. Short, meanwhile, were at the Schofield Barracks Officers' Club charity dinner-dance, "Ann Etzler's Cabaret." Afterward, as the couple motored by the great might of Pearl Harbor on the way home, Short remarked to intelligence officer Kendall Fielder, "What a target that would make!"

It was common to joke about a Japanese invasion of Hawaii—perhaps because, though no one seemed to take the threat seriously, they knew the threat indeed existed—and each joke made in the days before December 7 was remembered for decades. When Commander Roscoe Good had walked past Battleship Row earlier that afternoon, his thoughts matched Short's almost word for word: "What a beautiful target that would make." Mrs. James Chapman, taking in the same vista of the Kamehameha Highway as Gus Ahola, said, "If the Japanese are going to attack Hawaii, this would be the ideal time, for there sits the entire Pacific Fleet at anchor."

George Bicknell got a call at 2000 from Hawaiian Air Force signal officer Lieutenant Colonel Clay Hoppaugh, asking for help with the B-17s coming in from the mainland: "Will you put station KGMB on the air all night so planes can home in on the signal?" Bicknell was already irritated by the day's events and so responded harshly, "Why don't you have KGMB on the air every night and not just on the night we have airplanes flying? You folks have the money to do it." "We'll talk that over some other time," Hoppaugh said. Bicknell did as he was asked, with no explanation to the radio station, which was compensated by the army every time it stayed on the air. Locals noticed, however, that when the luau music played all night, planes landed in the morning.

"The mood on the mother submarine was calm, as usual," I-16 midget-sub crewman Kichiji Dewa remembered. "I went to the officers' mess, which enlisted men like me usually could not enter. We ate a farewell dinner." Afterward, he and fellow Special Attack crewmen Masaji Yokoyama and Sadamu Uyeda wrote letters to their parents, including hair and fingernail clippings to be used for their interment at Shinto shrines of honor and remembrance. "Forgive this negligent son for not writing these long months," Uyeda's letter said. "Though harvest time has come and gone, you must be pressed with work this time of year. We are soon to be dispatched to regions unknown. Should anything happen to me, do not grieve or mourn. Should I fail to write, do not be alarmed, because it means I am well and discharging my duties faithfully. Good-bye."

They donned their *fundoshi* undergarment, their leather jacket uniform, and the *hachimaki* headband of a warrior, with a final gesture of dousing themselves with perfume bought on their last night in Japan so, as Ensign Kazuo Sakamaki explained, they could die "like cherry blossoms falling to the ground." Carrying warm sweaters, bottles of sake, and a box lunch, the two-man crews followed the catwalk of the surfaced mother ships to their tiny subs, climbed up the side to the conning tower, lowered themselves within, and locked the hatch door. "We must look like high school boys happily going on a picnic," said another midget crewman, Ensign Hirowo.

The mother ships then released the men to their fates. Lieutenant Commander Hiroshi Hanabusa: "We let go of the clamps. Speaking on the telephone, I wished them success. I hoped that they would return. But Masaji Yokoyama said, 'If I come back, I'll come back with a wolf and put the mother submarine in danger.' So he knew that the Americans would follow them and get the I-16. And right away I began to miss them a little. I was thinking that they would not come back."

Ensign Sakamaki looked through the periscope at Pearl Harbor's glittering lights while talking to his commander, Hanabusa, who needed the ensign's decision on whether he would go forward. The midget's one gyrocompass had stopped working, and all attempts to repair it had failed. It would be impossible to navigate, but Sakamaki couldn't imagine missing out on this moment in history, and his crewman, Kiyoshi Inagaki, agreed. "We will go," Sakamaki declared, then shouted in a cry of courage, "On to Pearl Harbor!"

I-24 submerged, increased engine speed to give her charge a push, and at the correct depth the four clamps holding Sakamaki and Inagaki's tube to her mother were released. Almost immediately, the broken gyrocompass caused trouble. Instead of coursing level, the midget dipped. Sakamaki even had to turn off his battery-powered electric motor to try to correct it.

Sakamaki now used his periscope to discover he'd been thrown completely off track and was charging away from Pearl Harbor instead of toward it. Try as he might to keep its course true, however, the broken submarine kept turning in circles.

At around 2100, Mitsuo Fuchida met with his squadron leaders for "a little farewell drink, because we may not all be alive the next day. And I tried to sleep, but I felt that tomorrow will be the day that I would die. And I could not sleep all night." But in another version of this memory, he told his officers they all needed a good night's sleep, that he himself would be in bed within the hour: "I slept soundly. I had set up the whole machinery of attack, and it was ready to go. There was no use to worry now."

Zero pilot Iyozou Fujita: "The night before the attack, I could not sleep. I thought I would die the next day. So I drank six bottles of beer. And I couldn't get drunk. I couldn't get sleepy. I did not expect to come back alive, so I put my belongings in order. Finally I wrote a message in my scarf. I wrote something like 'I will triumph in dignity and in honor.' [After all,] I was an officer of the Imperial Japanese Navy. That means I was a samurai. It meant to act honestly and act fairly as far as fighting was concerned. To do one's best for victory." "They did not fear death," Fuchida said of his men. "Their only fear was that the attack might not be successful and that they would have to return to Japan with their mission unfulfilled." Pilot Sadamu Komachi said, "We had a mixed feeling of sorrow that we might die the next day. But also a feeling of pride, because we would die with honor."

On his flagship *Nagato* anchored in Japan's Inland Sea, Admiral Isoroku Yamamoto played *shogi* and, just before going to bed, composed a verse:

> It is my sole wish to serve the Emperor as His shield
> I will not spare my life or honor.

At 0238 December 7, Tokyo began cabling the last of the fourteen-part message, its conclusion watered down by the army: "The Japanese Government regrets to have to notify hereby the American Government that in view of the attitude of the American Government it cannot but consider that it is impossible to reach an agreement through further negotiations." MAGIC also intercepted Togo's pilot cable directing Nomura: "Will the Ambassador please submit to the United States Government (if possible to the Secretary of State) our reply to the United States at 1:00 p.m. on the seventh, your time."

At that moment in Washington, Secretary of War Henry Stimson went with Navy Secretary Frank Knox "to Secretary Hull's office at ten thirty in the morning and talked the whole matter over. This was the day on which we knew the Japanese were going to bring their answer, and Mr. Hull said he was certain that the Japanese were planning some deviltry; and we were all wondering where the blow would strike."

Since Japan's consulate in Washington had already destroyed two of their three code machines, and since Togo had forbidden the use of American typists for this English document, the staff had been kept working until 3:30 a.m., when they were sent home and told to get some sleep and come back to the office at 9:00 a.m. on Sunday.

That it was a Sunday also meant delays at the cable office handling Togo's message, which had received part fourteen and the pilot cable, but didn't get them to the consulate until 11:00 a.m. By that time, though the consul staff had finished with parts one to thirteen, their draft was messy and needed retyping, and on top of that, Tokyo forwarded additional cables filled with corrections and amendments.

Simultaneously, on the other side of the world, Joseph Grew "received a very brief, urgent message from Mr. Hull saying an important message for the Emperor was being then encoded and I should be ready to receive it. A long telegram containing the message was received in the Embassy at 10:30 p.m. The record on the face of the telegram showed it had been received in the Japanese post office at 12 noon. It was, I understand, sent from Washington 9 p.m., which would have meant 11 a.m. Tokyo time, 14 hours difference. So, in other words, the telegram appears to have been delivered to the Japanese post office, which handled telegrams, one hour after its receipt, and they held it up throughout that day. . . .

"I saw the Minister of Foreign Affairs about a quarter past twelve, about 15 minutes after midnight. I showed him the communication and I said that I wished to ask for an audience with the Emperor to present it personally. I did not want any doubt as to getting it in his hands. The Minister began to discuss the matter with me, and I said, 'I am making a definite application for an audience with the Emperor,' which is the right of every Ambassador, and Mr. Togo—not Tojo, the

Prime Minister, but [Foreign Minister Shigenori] Togo—and the Minister finally said, 'I will present your request to the Throne.'"

At a little after 2:00 a.m., Togo brought Roosevelt's message to Tojo, and after reading it, the prime minister said, "It's a good thing the telegram arrived late. If it had come a day or two earlier, we would have had more of a to-do." Togo then arrived at the Imperial Palace sometime after 3:00 a.m. Hirohito was awake, listening to a short-wave radio. Togo read him Roosevelt's cable, and then the imperial reply, which the government had already drafted for Hirohito's signature, and which insisted that peace was the emperor's "cherished desire." After hearing all this, Hirohito agreed to sign, saying his reply would "do well."

Joseph Grew: "At seven o'clock the next morning, my telephone beside my bed rang, and Mr. Kasa, the private secretary to the minister, said he had been trying to get me ever since five a.m. I said, 'That is surprising, because the telephone is right beside my bed and it has not rung.' He said, 'Please come over as soon as possible to see the minister.'

"I got to the minister's official residence about seven thirty a.m. He came into his room dressed in formal clothes. Apparently he had been with the emperor, and he had a document in his hand, he slapped it on the table, and he said, 'This is the emperor's reply to the president.' I said, 'I have asked for an audience in order to present that memorandum, that message, to the emperor personally.' Mr. Togo merely said—I remember his words—'I have no wish to stand between you and the Throne,' but nothing more was said about it. Then he read it, and he asked me to notice especially the last paragraph. He said, 'In view of the fact the conversations in Washington had made no progress, it had been decided to call them off.' That did not strike me as very serious. They had been called off before, when the Japanese first went into Indochina, and they had been resumed at a later date. So I said, 'Well, I am very sorry. I hope we can get them started again.'"

At a luncheon five months later on April 6, 1942, Prime Minister Hideki Tojo explained that he and the Japanese government on the whole had great misgivings about going to war, and that if Roosevelt's telegram had arrived three days earlier, everything would have turned out differently. In his first meeting with General MacArthur during the occupation, however, Hirohito told a very different story, saying that, if he had not approved of Japan's going to war, the army would have engineered a coup d'état, and he would have been either incarcerated in an asylum or assassinated.

Sublieutenant Iyozou Fujita was a fighter pilot aboard carrier *Soryu* who assumed that December 6, 1941, would be his last night on earth. He woke up around 0330 on the seventh, put on fresh clothing, and slipped a picture of his dead parents into his jacket pocket. He felt as though he could do no more to be ready to die; that the course of his life was now entirely in the hands of fate.

Unanimously, the pilots of Operation Z assumed they would never see Japan again. Before readying their planes, they prepared small envelopes with farewell letters, hair strands and nail clippings, so their families would have something of their departed hero to cremate. Many had "thousand-stitch" belts, a good-luck charm created by wives, mothers, or sisters who had stood on street curbs asking strangers to add a stitch apiece as a prayer for luck . . . and for battle victorious.

The pilots gathered at the portable Shinto shrines with ceramic sake decanters, candlesticks, and a miniature carved wooden temple with scrolls of prayers hanging from the eaves, which Japan provided on each of its warships. The abbreviated ceremony was a silent prayer, two handclaps, and a brisk bow, ending in ritual shots of sake.

Carrying his leather goggles, quilted jacket, and a helmet lined in rabbit fur to protect from the chill of high-altitude flying, *Akagi* dive-bomber pilot and squadron leader Lieutenant Zenji Abe prayed to the Shinto spirits of fortune, and then said to himself, "I am going now." He remembered, "I put a photo of my wife holding my six-month-old son in my uniform's inner pocket. . . . On that day, it didn't feel like we were going to war. I didn't feel fear, or such excitement as 'I'm going to beat the Americans!' Instead, I thought, 'It's just like an exercise.' I was calm, and all I cared was to follow orders."

In the dining halls that morning, instead of their standard fare of salted mackerel with rice and barley, they shared a ceremonial meal of *sekihan*—boiled rice with baby red beans. The kitchen gave each man a bento box lunch for his mission—rice ball, pickled plums, biscuit, chocolate, and amphetamines—and the airmen then assembled in their briefing rooms. Ironically, Japanese navy pilots so loved Clark

Gable in the movie *Hell Divers* that they referred to themselves by the American term *hell diver*.

Yamamoto did not believe in suicide missions, but Lieutenant Fusata Iida, commander of nine Mitsubishi A6M5 Zero fighters in the second attack wave from *Soryu*, did. He told his men that if he ran out of fuel or was about to be captured by the enemy, "I would find a target on the ground and crash into it." Pilot Iyozou Fujita: "He was very clear about this. And when he said that, everyone said okay, then we will do that, too."

After a few hours of sleep, Mitsuo Fuchida leaped out of bed at 0500, pulled on his red-dyed undergarments and shirt, then slipped on his flying suit. He and Murata had decided to wear these red clothes so that, if they were wounded, the blood wouldn't be visible to demoralize their men.

One officer was feeling optimistic, having spent the night listening to Hawaiian radio station KGMB and hearing no clues that the Americans knew what was to come. At breakfast, he said, "Honolulu sleeps."

"How do you know?" Fuchida asked.

"The Honolulu radio plays soft music. Everything is fine."

At an hour before dawn, as the task force approached its launch point, Nagumo told Genda, "I have brought the task force successfully to the point of attack. From now on the burden is on your shoulders and the rest of the flying group."

Genda replied, "Admiral, I am sure the airmen will succeed."

At 0530, cruisers *Chikuma* and *Tone* each catapulted a floatplane to scout Pearl Harbor and Lahaina Roads, then report back details of the Americans' ship locations, as well as the weather and the wind. Though the scouts could be spotted by US patrols and their reporting would mean a break in radio silence, Nagumo and Genda had decided it was worth the risk.

The *Akagi* was in charge of signaling the crews with a set of combat pennants. They now hung half-mast, meaning "Get ready." Raised to the top and then briskly dropped would mean "Launch and attack."

Carrier deck crews had already spent an hour checking the planes in their hangars, bringing them up to the deck, and towing the fighters and bombers into position. Engines rattled to life as mechanics went over them one last time.

Hiryu's Commander Amagai had the interfering pieces of paper removed from each plane's wireless, a safety precaution he'd taken during the voyage to ensure radio silence.

At 0550, 220 miles north of Oahu, these great queens of the seas raised their thrusts to twenty-four knots and turned their decks to port to face into an onrushing eastern wind. The air was glorious for flying, but the water was tough, with the ships battered by long and high swells at their bows.

Japanese aerial technology was at that time the envy of the world. Named for the final number in the year of their birth, 2600 (1940), the Mitsubishi A6M Reisen (Zero) fighter was already legendary for its quickness and nimble handling. They were not sturdy—the fuel tanks couldn't self-seal, meaning a bullet could ignite the plane—but they were otherwise superior in every way to what Americans flew in the opening years of the war. Their top speed of 310 mph and their two 20 mm cannon in the wings and two 7.7 mm machine guns in the cowling created a lethal weapon. With the belts loaded in series to maximize accuracy and damage—two armor-piercing shells; a tracer; two armor-piercing shells; a tracer; two armor-piercing shells; and an incendiary—they could pierce gas tanks, cowlings, truck engines, and ignite fires.

Even Japan's Aichi D3A dive-bomber (called "Val" by the Allies), with its top speed of 240 mph and its three 7.7 mm machine guns, could put up a serious battle against most of the Allies' fighter planes after it had released its ordnance. Dive-bombers were assigned airfield targets in the first wave and naval targets in the second. They would then join the Zeros in strafing with their two 7.7 mm forward-mounted guns in the fuselage and their 7.7 mm machine gun in the rear cockpit, each loaded with five hundred rounds.

The Nakajima B5N (known by the Allies as "Kate") would be employed against Oahu as both high-altitude horizontal bombers and as low-skimming torpedo planes. Operated by a three-man crew of pilot, bombardier, and radioman, Kates could reach 235 mph with a range of 1,237 miles and sported a 7.7 mm machine gun in the back of its cockpit, hand-operated on a flexible mount and fed from ninety-seven-round magazines. Many Kates additionally had two more machine guns in their wings, and depending on the assignment, the B5N could drop one 800-kilogram torpedo or bomb, or two 550-pounders, or six 293-pounders.

Genda and Fuchida planned a three-tier aerial attack. First, D3A dive-bombers and A6M Reisen fighters would strike American air bases at Ford Island, Ewa, Kaneohe, Wheeler, and Hickam, to annihilate the Americans' defenses. The D3As would also swoop in to decimate assorted other key naval targets, while Zeros would strafe before and mop up after.

On Battleship Row—where the ships of the Pacific Fleet would be docked in pairs as well as singly, their dark silhouettes at sunrise lit only by their anchor lights—a squadron of B5N torpedo pilots would slow their cruise to a near stall, dropping to a bare minimum altitude of twenty-five feet to release their custom torpedoes at the first, outer ring of ships. The queens of Pearl with their armored decks, as well as the ships moored to the inside, would be destroyed by horizontal-bombing B5Ns dropping their modified naval shells.

Fuchida would himself lead the first attack wave of fifty horizontal planes under his direct command, with forty torpedo bombers led by Murata, fifty-four dive-bombers led by Takahashi, and forty-five Zero fighters under Itaya. Commandeering the second wave was Fuchida's assistant, *Zuikaku*'s Lieutenant Commander Shiegkazu Shimazaki, a man unusually expert at torpedo, dive, and horizontal attacks. He would directly oversee fifty-four horizontals, accompanied by eighty-one dive-bombers under Takeshige Egusa and thirty-six fighters led by Lieutenant Saburo Shindo. Eighteen of Shimazaki's high-level planes were ferrying two 250-kilogram bombs, and the other thirty-six had one bomb of 250 kilograms, and six of 60 kilograms each (one kilogram equals 2.2 pounds). Those with multiple explosives were assigned to drop one at a time, in pairs, or all at once, depending on the size and allure of the target.

Though the bomber crews had been assigned targets with silhouettes they had memorized, Fuchida repeatedly lectured them on the great benefit to be had by sinking as many ships as possible in Pearl Harbor's tiny channel. Enough carnage there would make it impossible for the enemy's fleet to sortie and counterstrike Nagumo's ships.

The December seas were so heavy that waves swept across the carriers' decks. In the dark, the black ships crashed through, their only light the blinker lamps for communications at the top of each's superstructure. Fuchida watched with concern as, whipped by wind and spray, the flight decks tilted beyond ten degrees: "The ships pitched and rolled in the rough sea, kicking up white surf from the predawn blackness of the water. We could hear the waves splashing against the ship with a thunderous noise. Under normal circumstances, no plane would be permitted to take off in such weather. At times waves came over the flight deck, and crews clung desperately to their planes to keep them from going into the sea.

"Turning to me, Commander Shogo Masuda, the *Akagi*'s air officer, said, 'There is a heavy pitch and roll. What do you think about taking off in the dark?' The sea was rough, and there was a strong wind blowing. The sky was completely dark, and as yet the horizon was not visible. 'The pitch is greater than the roll,' I replied. 'Were this a training flight, the takeoff would be delayed until dawn. But if we coordinate the takeoffs with the pitching, we can launch successfully.'"

The airmen tied *hachimakis* around their heads emblazoned with *Hisshou*—"Certain Victory"—before climbing into their cockpits. As Fuchida readied to board his plane, *Akagi*'s senior maintenance man gave him a special white scarf, saying, "All of the maintenance crew would like to go along to Pearl Harbor. Since we can't, we want you to take this *hachimaki* as a symbol that we are with you in spirit."

"My plane was in position, its red-and-yellow-striped tail marking it as the commander's plane," Fuchida continued. "The carrier turned to port and headed into the northerly wind. The battle flag was now added to the Z flag flying at the masthead. Lighted flying lamps shivered with the vibration of engines as planes completed their warm-up. On the flight deck, a green lamp was waved in a circle to signal, 'Take off!' The engine of the foremost fighter plane began to roar. With the ship still pitching and rolling, the plane started its run, slowly at first but with steadily increasing speed. Men lining the flight deck held their breath as the first plane took off successfully just before the ship took a downward pitch. The next plane was already moving forward. There were loud cheers as each plane rose into the air."

"The ship was rolling heavily, so the takeoff was postponed for fifteen minutes," *Soryu* bomber pilot Tatsuya Otawa remembered. "It seemed like a very long time. Finally we got the signal; the fighter planes took off first. Since we were the second-wave attack unit, we waved our caps and really prayed for their success. Our flight group was very large; over a hundred planes. We were escorted by Zero fighters and so I felt secure."

Pilot Haruo Yoshino: "Our fighting spirit was high. There was no question in my mind that we would be successful. We really did not have much fear."

As the thrust of the ocean's roll raised each First Air Fleet carrier's bow, a plane struggled up and lifted away. "The wind was competing with the roar of the plane engines," dive-bomber pilot Zenji Abe recalled. "First away from the carrier were nine Zero fighters. The planes were guided by hand lamps in the dark. They moved one by one into position and took off into the black sky." In the murk just before dawn, it was impossible to see their black-green bodies marked by bright red suns. The pilots climbed to two hundred, four hundred, or five hundred meters, depending on their squadron, and continued to circle overhead until the entire wave was aloft, and then fell into formation behind their leaders.

"From the decks of the aircraft carriers, plane after plane rose, flashing their silver wings in the sunlight, and soon there were a hundred and more aircraft in the sky," Iki Kuramoti remembered. "Our Sea Eagles were now moving into a great formation. Our ten years and more of intensive training, during which we had endured many hardships in anticipation of this day—would they now bear fruit? At this thought a thousand emotions filled our hearts as, close to tears, we watched this magnificent sight. One and all, in our hearts, we sent our pleas to the gods, and putting our hands together, we prayed. Meanwhile our Sea Eagles, with the drone of their engines resounding across the heavens like a triumphal song, turned their course toward Pearl Harbor on the island of Oahu and set forth on their splendid enterprise."

In Washington, George Marshall was going to work in the Munitions Building after spending the morning on horseback: "On my arrival there Colonel Bratton handed me these intercepts which included the fourteen sections of the Japanese message, and I started reading them through. . . . When I reached the end of the document, the next sheet was the one o'clock message of December 7. That, of course, was indicative to me, and all the others who came into the room, of some very definite action at one o'clock, because that one o'clock was Sunday and was in Washington and involved the Secretary of State, all of which were rather unusual put together."

Besides the fact that diplomats meeting officially with each other on a Sunday was out of the ordinary, MAGIC had never produced an order from Japan's foreign office to its Washington embassy demanding that they meet with American officials at a specific time. This point had "immediately stunned" G-2's Rufus Bratton, who thought it "was peculiarly worded and the implication was inescapable that it was of vital importance." Bratton decided that "the Japanese were going to attack some American installation in the Pacific area," but Hawaii as a target never entered his mind: "Nobody in ONI, nobody in G-2, knew that any major element of the Fleet was in Pearl Harbor on Sunday morning the seventh of December. We all thought they had gone to sea . . . because that was part of the war plan, and they had been given a war warning."

The chief of military intelligence, General Sherman Miles, suggested they warn Panama, the West Coast, the Philippines, and Hawaii. Marshall agreed: "I think that I immediately called Admiral Stark on the phone and found he had seen [Japan's fourteen-part cable], and I proposed a message to our various commanders in the Pacific region, the Philippines, Hawaii, the Caribbean, that is the Panama Canal, and the West Coast, which included Alaska. Admiral Stark felt that we might confuse them because we had given them an alert and now we were adding something more to it."

Marshall decided to go ahead on his own. He decided the situation was serious enough to avoid using the phone for security reasons, so instead, he jotted down a note: "Japanese are presenting at one pm eastern standard time today what amounts to an ultimatum also they are under orders to destroy their code machine immediately. Just what significance the hour set may have we do not know but be on alert accordingly. Inform naval authorities of this communication. Marshall." Bratton took the general's note to the War Department's Signal Center for delivery; it was received in the Caribbean at 1200, in Manila at 1206, and at the Presidio in San Francisco at 1211, but atmospheric conditions had been blocking cables to Hawaii since 1030, and it could not get through. Lieutenant Colonel Edward French, the Signal Center's officer in charge, first thought that he should go to the navy, but then decided that using commercial carriers—from Washington to San Francisco via Western Union, and from there to Honolulu via RCA—would be faster. It went out at 1217.

Meanwhile at the navy, Captains Alvin Kramer and Arthur McCollum each used Togo's deadline to calculate what 1:00 p.m. eastern standard time would mean across the rest of the world. At his meeting with

Stark, McCollum pointed out that 1300 in Washington meant 0730 in Hawaii as well as "very early in the morning in the Far East . . . and that we didn't know what this signified, but that if an attack were coming, it looked like . . . it was timed for operations out in the Far East and possibly on Hawaii." But McCollum later insisted, "Pearl Harbor as such was never mentioned. The feeling that I had, and I think the feeling that most officers there had, was that at or near the outbreak of war with Japan, we could expect a surprise attack on the Fleet." Many at Navy in Washington believed in one scenario—war would be declared, the Fleet would go to sea, and it would be attacked—a belief so strong that they were shocked to learn, after the attack, that Kimmel and his Fleet were still sitting in Pearl Harbor on the morning of December 7.

At 0342 in Hawaii, minesweepers *Condor* and *Crossbill* were using their mechanical brooms on patrol around thirteen miles southwest of Pearl Harbor's entrance buoys when *Condor* watch officer Ensign R. C. McCloy spotted an oddly shaped white wave about a hundred yards away, moving toward the harbor. He and Quartermaster B. C. Uttrick each gave it a hard look with McCloy's binoculars, and Uttrick said, "That's a periscope, sir, and there aren't supposed to be any subs in the area." Then the periscope suddenly veered off in a 180, perhaps having spotted *Condor*.

Condor used her blinker light to message, "Sighted submerged submarine on westerly course, speed 9 knots," to the USS *Ward*, a destroyer staffed with naval reservists from Minnesota. The message was received by Lieutenant Oscar Goepner, who'd been working inshore patrol on the *Ward* for over a year but had never gotten a message like this. Goepner woke up his skipper, Lieutenant William Outerbridge; for Outerbridge, December 6 was his first night on his first patrol on his first command. From the class of Annapolis 1927, he had needed fourteen years in the peacetime navy to rise to the level of destroyer commander.

After the two ships had talked by blinker light, the *Ward* sounded general quarters, her sailors piling out of their bunks and into their battle stations. For about an hour, the destroyer searched for the white trail with lookouts, and for the submarine's metallic echo with sonar. William Outerbridge: "We searched for about an hour and didn't find anything; so I got in contact with [*Condor*] again and asked, 'What

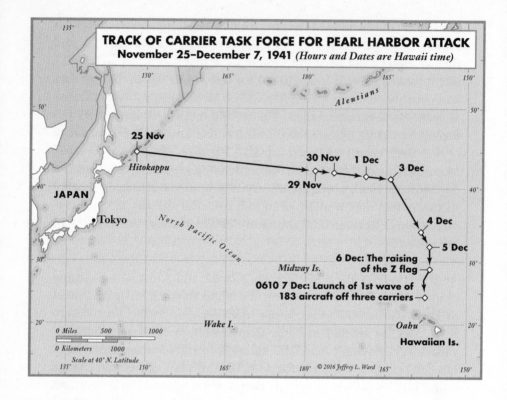

TRACK OF CARRIER TASK FORCE FOR PEARL HARBOR ATTACK
November 25–December 7, 1941 *(Hours and Dates are Hawaii time)*

was the approximate distance and course of the submarine that you sighted?' and she said, 'The course was about what we were steering at the time, 020 magnetic, and about a thousand yards from the entrance apparently heading for the entrance.' Well, I knew then that we had been searching in the wrong direction. We went to westward, and . . . just kept on searching in our area, in the restricted area outside of the buoys."

Giving up the search at 0443, *Ward* released her crew from battle duty; many, including Outerbridge, went back to bed.

The watch crew manning the antitorpedo net guarding the entrance to Pearl Harbor opened the gate to let *Crossbill* in at 0447. Since her sister ship *Condor* was then due in, the gate was left open, but after *Condor* entered at 0532, the watch crew saw that tug *Keosanqua* was scheduled to exit at 0615, and decided to leave the gate as it was. In the ensuing chaos, the one crinoline in use under Kimmel—the net keeping full-size submarines and enemy ships from firing torpedoes up the channel—would remain open from 0458 until 0840, giving

Japan's midget subs plenty of opportunity to sneak inside and search for prey.

In all of fifteen minutes, 183 planes of Genda's first attack wave had launched (with six fails) and now, in the middle of the buzzing cloud of warplanes, at 9,800 feet, were the ten arrowheads of horizontal high-altitude bombers directly commandeered by Mitsuo Fuchida. To their left were Takahashi's divers, at 11,000 feet; to the right, Murata's torpedoes, at 9,200 feet; and above them all sped Itaya's fighters, at 14,100 feet. The high-levels each carried only one bomb, a modified eight-hundred-kilogram, sixteen-inch shell from battleship *Nagato*. Fuchida was so pessimistic about their chances that he was hoping for a 20 percent hit rate. If the task force then came under American counterattack, the carrier crews would have to switch out the ordnance on all the high-level bombers to torpedoes, but if the US Fleet offered no resistance, they would instead convert torpedo planes to horizontal bombers and launch a third strike on Oahu.

At 0725 the second attack wave—having been frantically raised to the decks by elevators and then lined up for the runway as quickly as the first wave departed from each of the ships—lifted off; 171 warplanes, with four fails. Zenji Abe: "As we flew, I thought many thoughts. If we could not find the carriers, our secondary targets would be cruisers. I wondered if the special midget submarines had arrived in the harbor. They were to wait until the air attack started. Could we ask a man to have patience like this? I worried that one of our bombs would be dropped by mistake on their back."

Watching the sun rise at the horizon so reminded Fuchida of his nation's emblem that he could only crow, "Oh, glorious dawn for Japan! . . . After the clouds began gradually to brighten below us after the brilliant sun burst into the eastern sky, I opened the cockpit canopy and looked back at the large formation of planes. The wings glittered in the bright morning sunlight. . . . But flying over the clouds, we could not see the surface of the water and, consequently, had no check on our drift. I switched on the radio direction finder to tune in to the Honolulu radio station and soon picked up some light music. By turning the antenna, I found the exact direction from which the broadcast was coming and corrected our course. . . . In tuning the radio a little finer, I heard, along with the music, what seemed to be a weather report. . . . 'Averaging partly cloudy, with clouds mostly over the mountains. Cloud base at thirty-five thousand feet. Visibility good. Wind north, ten knots.' What a windfall for us! No matter how careful the planning, a more favorable situation could not have been imagined."

Fuchida now told his fellow pilots to home in on Honolulu's KGMB, which meant that the same radio station paid to broadcast all night by the US Army Air Corps for their B-17s coming in from California was simultaneously serving as a homing beacon to bring Japanese squadrons to Pearl Harbor.

Supply ship *Antares*, towing a barge about a hundred yards to her rear, was waiting just outside Pearl Harbor for an escort pilot to bring her to berth when her skipper, Commander Lawrence Grannis, saw at 0630 "about fifteen hundred yards on starboard quarter" an odd-looking submarine "obviously having depth-control trouble and . . . trying to go down." He notified *Ward*, where seaman H. E. Raenbig also saw this odd black object through his binoculars. To Raenbig the thing looked as if it were attached to the tow rope that *Antares* was using on her barge. He brought it up with helmsman Goepner, who thought it looked like a buoy, but various others on watch became convinced it was the conning tower of a sub trying to position itself behind the barge with the oldest sub trick in the book: following an enemy's boat into her own harbor to evade detection.

When Goepner then noticed a navy patrol bomber circling in position overhead, he became convinced his men were right and again rang Outerbridge, then sleeping on a chart-room cot. Quickly throwing a kimono over his pajamas and returning to the deck, Outerbridge thought that, whatever this thing was, it was suspicious: "We didn't have anything that looked like it in our navy, and they had never seen anything like it. . . . I was convinced it was a submarine. I was convinced it couldn't be anything else. It must be a submarine and it wasn't anything that we had, and we also had a message that any submarine operating in the restricted area not operating in the submarine areas and not escorted should be attacked. We had that message; so there was no doubt at all in my mind what to do."

At 0640 he again ordered general quarters; shells were broken out, guns loaded, and as Outerbridge called for "all engines ahead full," the destroyer surged from five to twenty-five knots, running full bore. Overhead, that navy patrol bomber PBY's pilot, Ensign William Tanner, dropped two smoke pots, marking the submarine's location. Tanner, however, believing that the sub was an American in distress, was only trying to help. In what would be the first American shots of World War II, when *Ward* reached within fifty yards of the target, her crew began to fire. Boatswain's Mate A. Art, the captain of *Ward*'s No. 1 gun, knew they were too close to use the sights, so he tried aiming as he did when he was out rifle hunting. At 0645 Art missed, his shell whistling high and hitting the water far behind the tower. Captain Russell Knapp, on the No. 3 gun housed on *Ward*'s galley roof, fired thirty seconds later, scoring a hit "at the waterline . . . the junction of the hull and conning tower." The captain gave four whistle blasts, and Chief Torpedoman W. C. Maskzawilz unrolled four depth charges—bombs inside oil cans with various methods of detonation—off *Ward*'s stern. *Ward* sailor Russell Reetz: "Suddenly, it rose out of the water, and I could see it was a sub. I saw not just the periscope but the whole conning tower. And then number three gun fired, and I saw the splash of the water at the waterline of the conning tower as the shell hit. There were 250 pounds of TNT in each depth charge. So that would be 1,000 pounds of TNT exploding. It was so close to the submarine that I'm almost sure there was enough damage to sink it." Maskzawilz was pleased to report that the enemy sub "seemed to wade right into the first" of four exploding geysers of foam. Rear Admiral T. B. Inglis: "As a result of these attacks, the submarine is believed to have gone down in twelve hundred feet of water. A large amount of oil came to the surface."

Ensign William Tanner, overhead in the PBY, now understood what was happening and followed his orders to "depth bomb and sink any submarines found in the defensive sea area without authority." He reported the strike to Kaneohe Naval Air Station. His report reached Commander Knefler McGinnis, in charge of PatWing (Patrol Wing) 1 at Kaneohe, who decided Tanner had to be wrong.

At 0648, *Ward*'s lookouts spotted a sampan sailing in the restricted area. This was common; local Japanese fishermen knew where the schools were. But what happened next was odd; the sampan took off on a run, and when *Ward* caught up with her, the Japanese skipper shut down his engines and waved a white flag. Perhaps he had heard the gunfire attacking the submarine earlier and wanted to make sure he wasn't fired at, but still, it was odd. *Ward* took the renegade sampan to Honolulu, where she would be dealt with by the Coast Guard. When the Fourteenth Naval District's chief of staff John B. Earle heard about this, he thought, What is the *Ward* doing escorting sampans when an enemy submarine is supposedly on the prowl? He now discounted the whole of that day's warnings.

At 0653, Outerbridge radioed the watch officer of the Fourteenth Naval District, "We have attacked, fired upon, and dropped depth charges upon submarine operating in defensive sea area." At 0703, Outerbridge "dropped four depth charges on another submarine in the area. . . . We bombed them until we ran out of depth charges and went in and got some more."

Receiving *Ward*'s message, Lieutenant Commander Lex Black called War Plans Officer Commander Vincent Murphy, who had coincidentally just gone over the latest procedure to follow if an attack occurred, which was to bring the carriers and their task forces back to Pearl Harbor and execute the appropriate war plans. Murphy told Black, "While I'm finishing dressing, call [headquarters duty officer Harold] Kaminski and see what he's doing about it and whether or not he's called Admiral Bloch." Though Black tried again and again, Kaminski's line was always busy; when he told Murphy this, the commander said, "All right, you go to the office and start breaking out the charts and positions of the various ships; I'll dial one more time and then I'll be over." Murphy tried, but again the line was still busy, so he called the operator and told him to break in on any conversation "unless it was of supreme importance," and have Kaminski return Murphy's call as soon as possible.

Kaminski's phone was busy, it turned out, because he was overwhelmed. After receiving *Ward*'s 0653 message at 0712, Kaminski had no doubt "we were in it." He tried phoning Admiral Bloch's aide and couldn't get hold of him, so next he tried the district's chief of staff, Captain John Earle, at home. Earle was certain it was another false alarm, so told Kaminski to get verification, and then inform Kimmel's duty officer as well as the district's operations officer, Commander Charles Momsen. Momsen told Kaminski to send a message to ready-duty destroyer *Monaghan* to "get under way immediately and contact USS *Ward* in defensive sea area."

By 0715, Earle was talking to Bloch, and the two men couldn't decide if the *Ward* had actually seen anything or not, so they decided "to await further developments."

War Plans Officer Vincent Murphy entered his office to a ringing phone. It was Patrol Wing 2's operations officer, Lieutenant Commander Logan Ramsey, calling from home to report that one of their PBYs had "sunk a submerged submarine one mile off the entrance to Pearl Harbor." Murphy told Ramsey, "That's funny, we got the same sort of message from one of the DD's on the inshore patrol." Ramsey thought something was up: "You had better get going and I'll be down at my Operations Center soon."

Ramsey's daughter, sixteen-year-old Mary Ann, remembered being woken up that day: "It was quiet on [Ford] island that particular morning because our carriers were at sea. And the next thing I knew, [my dad] was rushing out of our house and into our car and going down to command headquarters. I went into my mother's bedroom and said, 'What in the world has happened?' She said that they'd knocked out a Japanese sub just outside the net of Pearl Harbor."

Kaminski called Murphy back to give him the details of what had happened on the *Ward*. Murphy asked, "Have you any previous details or any more details about this attack?" "The message came out of a clear sky," Kaminski insisted. Murphy decided he'd better call Admiral Kimmel anyway. The admiral was scheduled to play golf with General Short that day and hadn't yet dressed or shaved, but he said, "I will be right down."

Husband Kimmel: "Between seven thirty and seven forty, I received information from the staff duty officer of the *Ward*'s report, the dispatch of the ready-duty destroyer to assist the *Ward*, and the efforts then under way to obtain a verification of the *Ward*'s report. I was awaiting such verification at the time of the attack. In my judgment, the effort to obtain confirmation of the reported submarine attack off Pearl Harbor was a proper preliminary to more drastic action in view of the number of such contacts which had not been verified in the past."

At 0733, the Honolulu office of RCA finally received General Marshall's warning. This was 1:03 p.m. in Washington—three minutes past Togo's deadline—and the First Air Fleet's first attack wave was at that moment thirty-five miles north of Oahu. The cable was handed to RCA messenger boy Tadao Fuchikami, who mounted his motorbike and took off to make his rounds of deliveries. Since Marshall's cable wasn't marked urgent in any way, it was just one of many being delivered to Fort Shafter.

At the Japanese consulate in Washington, Nomura saw how much his typists had left to finish, so he called Cordell Hull to reschedule the time of their meeting. Since Hull had already read part fourteen through MAGIC and interpreted this as merely a formal announcement of the end of diplomatic talks, he agreed.

That Sunday morning was especially dreary at the US Army's Opana radar station hard by Kahuku Point at Oahu's northern tip. One of six small units deployed at strategic locations across the coastline, the stations' radarscopes were erratic, having just begun operations two weeks before, but when they worked, they tracked any plane within 150 miles. The six remote units then radioed in their information to the men at Fort Shafter's information center, who collated it to move small arrows, representing aircraft, across a wood table kitted out as a plotting map.

Lieutenant General Short testified after the war that he considered radar something for training purposes, and never thought it could be real. Indeed, the general did not understand what radar was, or what it was good for, but since the War Department had given him the equipment, he arranged for privates to be trained on it. In one particularly damning example, the Hawaiian Department brass did not mentally coordinate that the radar's 150-mile radius gave an hour's warning of approaching enemy planes, while the territory's main defense against such an enemy, her fighters, required four hours to be readied. The Signal Corps officers in charge of the radar equipment, meanwhile, were more worried about its being overused and worn-out than they were about its being employed to actually spot something. A private who worked at the Fort Shafter information center, Richard Schimmel, summed up the local officers' opinion of this new technology: "It seemed that if you got in trouble in the army, a radar unit was mostly likely in your future."

Opana's trainees that morning, Privates Joseph Lockard and George Elliott, usually found about twenty-five planes during their three hours working the scope, but today, the skies were bare. Before Marshall's war warning of November 27, their hours had been 0700 to 1600, but as part of his Alert No. 1, General Short had them reassigned to daybreak's 0400–0700, and to guard against Short's feared legion of saboteurs, the post included a .45 pistol. All this resulted in Opana's being the only radar station in Oahu staffed and operating on December 7 at 0700.

The station was remote, with her crew of six bivouacked nine miles away at a little camp in Kawaiola, and daily commuting in by pickup truck. They were originally divvied up into three-man teams, but that morning, the third man assigned wanted to sleep in, and it was decided that two could easily handle a Sunday's workload. Lockard operated the radarscope, while Elliott did the plotting and the driving.

That morning nothing at all happened, until a little flicker of tiny flashes appeared from the northeast, 130 miles off, at 0645.

At 0654, a superior phoned to say they were relieved of duty and could shut the scope down. But the truck to carry them back to camp for breakfast hadn't arrived yet, so the two decided to keep working until it did.

At 0702, Elliott decided he wanted more practice, and started turning the oscilloscope's dials. Lockard was leaning over him, explaining the radar's echoes, when suddenly a huge blip appeared, something bigger than either man had ever seen before. It was so remarkable, they assumed that the scope, which regularly broke down, was busted again. Lockard had Elliott get up so he could take over, but soon realized that nothing was wrong; they had spotted "something completely out of the ordinary on the screen . . . an enormous amount of aircraft. It moved at a speed which we knew to be aircraft. It couldn't be a ship, it was moving too fast. So we called the switchboard operator at the information center."

Dawn is not slow to rise over the islands of the Pacific. It hits fast, and bright. But as the airmen of the First Air Fleet soared overhead, the skies continued to be dreary and occluded. Fuchida worried about whether his men would be able to find their targets, and when they did, would they be so obscured that they couldn't be hit. Finally the clouds parted, and directly ahead and below them was a white skirt of ocean surf striking the dark green shore against the mist-draped and saw-toothed mountain range of Oahu. They had reached the island's northernmost shore, Kahuku Point.

By Japan's home islands, the Pacific was gray with a bare hint of green, and the First Air Fleet's journey across the ocean's frigid north had been especially hard, as Japan's temperate climate is similar to the American Carolinas, with capital Tokyo sharing the same latitude as Nashville, Tennessee. Now below the Japanese attackers were golf-course-green lands touched by a Windex-blue ocean; skimming over Oahu's sugarcane, torpedo bomber Heita Matsumura smelled the odors of caramel and mown lawn while feeling "the warm air of an unending summer land." Bomber pilot Toshio Hashimoto was so charmed by the beautiful jungle and tiny houses that he pulled out his camera to take souvenir pictures. Zero pilot Yoshio Shiga fondly remembered when he'd been in Honolulu for a 1934 training cruise. The wonderful memory crashed against the feelings he was having now, and it was upsetting.

West Virginia bugler Richard Fiske: "Just before I was sounding reveille, this was around six, a little after six it was, we saw this floatplane come over, similar to one of our [Grumman Goose] JRFs. But nobody paid any attention to it. And it just circled Pearl Harbor, it circled a couple of times and then went back up north." It was the Kido Butai's reconnaissance, which radioed a target report at 0735—"Enemy formation at anchor; nine battleships, one heavy cruiser, six light cruisers, are in the harbor"—and the weather at 0738: "Wind direction from eighty degrees, speed fourteen meters, clearance over enemy fleet seventeen hundred meters, cloud density seven." The other floatplane, meanwhile, radioed, "The enemy fleet is not in Lahaina anchorage."

At Opana, Elliott went to the plotting table to set the position of the giant blip they saw on the radar—137 miles north, three degrees east—and at 0706, strapped on the headphones to report their findings to Fort Shafter. The line was dead, since at precisely 0700, everyone at the information center had quit work for breakfast. So when Elliott followed protocol and then used the phone, he was connected to the information center's switchboard, operated at that moment by Private Joseph McDonald. Elliott told McDonald, "There's a large number of planes coming in from the north, three degrees east." Since McDonald thought he was alone, he wrote down the message and looked to the big clock in the plotting room to get the time right. There he saw that one man was still on duty, Lieutenant Kermit Tyler, and so gave him the message, with the comment that he'd never gotten a report like this before.

Kermit Tyler was a pilot with no training as a pursuit officer and one day of experience at the information center who had been ordered to remain until 0800 even though the operation was closed and even though "I did not know what my duties were. I just was told to be there and told to maintain that work." Tyler had only recently learned of the existence of radar, and his duties were "to assist the controller in ordering planes to intercept enemy planes or supposed enemy planes, after the planes got in the air." He assumed Lockard and Elliott's discovery was nothing, so McDonald went back to his switchboard and called Opana. Lockard picked up this time and excitedly reported that the blips had grown in size and were moving fast. He calculated that it was at least fifty planes coming in over Oahu at 180 miles an hour. McDonald told him that Lieutenant Tyler had insisted there was nothing to worry about, but Lockard said he had to talk directly to Tyler, since he'd never seen anything like this before.

While Tyler was listening to Elliott's report, he remembered that Halsey's *Enterprise* task force was out on assignment, so if the scope wasn't malfunctioning, the blip must be navy planes. Then "I happened to have the radio on and I heard Hawaiian music," he later recalled. "Well, this told me that some B-17s were coming in, 'cause a bomber-pilot friend of mine who'd flown B-17s over there said the only time they operated the radio station after midnight was when the B-17s were coming in."

Tyler insisted to Lockard that there was nothing to worry about.

In one way, Tyler was correct, as Landon's B-17s from California were arriving a mere five degrees off Opana's data. Like many other officers in Hawaii that morning, Tyler was quick to discount an alarm, and just as the navy hadn't told the army about its suspicious submarines, so now the army wouldn't tell the navy about its peculiar radar sighting. If Tyler had passed the information over to Fourteenth Pursuit Wing operations officer Major Kenneth Bergquist, at least perhaps American planes would have been eventually sent in the right direction to find Nagumo's fleet. But Lockard and Elliott also erred in not telling Tyler that they knew their blip meant over fifty planes, which would have indicated even to Tyler that this could not possibly be planes from an American carrier or Flying Fortresses arriving overseas from California. Kermit Tyler would try to defend himself at the army board hearing by discounting the entire system: "If the AWAS service had been operating under twenty-four-hour basis, under the most favorable conditions, it would probably [have] provided a forty-five-minute warning to the army and perhaps a thirty-minute warning to the navy." But wouldn't any warning be better than none?

Naval Reserve Officer William E. G. Taylor had worked piloting fighters for a year with the British navy and another with her air force. His knowledge about the use of radar in the Battle of Britain got him assigned as an advisor to the army's radar warning system for Oahu.

Unfortunately he determined that that "the communications between the fighter-director officers', or controllers', positions, and the fighter aircraft were totally inadequate to control fighters more than five miles off shore." Even so, he concluded, "I feel, and felt then, that these stations should have been operating twenty-four hours a day, and the air warning system fully manned."

Like every dawn of every day on every island in that reach of the world, there was a cool wind, a hint of rain, and the empty, endless yaw of the bright blue Pacific.

The clouds had parted and the shores of Oahu had appeared with such imminence that Fuchida had to immediately call out, *"Tenkai!"*— Prepare to attack!—and remind his pilot, Lieutenant Mitsuo Matsuzaki, to be on the lookout for American fighters. He then raised his flare gun. As he and Genda had planned, if it was clear the attack was going to be a complete surprise, he'd fire once, bringing the torpedo planes to the fore, as well as fighters to destroy the enemy's aircraft and bases, followed by divers and horizontals. But if American defenses were alerted and ready, the torpedo planes would be vulnerable, so he'd fire twice, meaning, divers, fighters, and high-levels striking first to take out American air forces and antiaircraft defenses.

By the time of their arrival, Fuchida had not yet been informed of *Chikuma*'s reconnaissance report that Pearl Harbor was unaware of what was to come. But he saw no defenses up and ready whatsoever on the entire flight in, so he decided that surprise had been won. At 0740, just as he arrived at Kahuku Point, he fired his flare. As the pilots swerved southwest to follow the shore, they recast, to attack. Fuchida carefully watched his planes jockey into position, then he noticed that the fighter group headed by Masaharu Suganami had not taken formation. He waited a bit, then decided that Suganami's men hadn't seen his signal and so fired a second "black dragon." But these two shots were taken as the "two-shot" alert by Takahashi, who brought his dive-bombers to the fore to annihilate American air defenses at Ford Island and Hickam. When Murata saw what Takahashi had done, he knew his torpedo planes needed to get to their targets as soon as possible before they were obscured by clouds of bomb bursts, so he charged forward with his team as well

It was now 0749. Zero hour. Fuchida had his radioman order all pilots, *TO TO TO!*—Charge! While the forty-nine horizontals held formation at 9,800 feet, the forty torpedoes fell to a mere 50 feet, skimming just above the water, leading the force. The fifty-one divers rose to 13,000 feet, while eighteen fighters fell to 6,500 feet, and the other twenty-five cruised at 12,500. As Fuchida stewed that the careful tactics he'd devised with Genda had utterly failed, the whole of the Japanese assault force dove pell-mell to its targets.

One of Hawaii's beaches least known by tourists and much favored by locals is Haleiwa, on Oahu's legendary north shore. The Mann family was spending that weekend at their Haleiwa beach house when, first thing Sunday morning, they were all woken up by the frantic barking of their two pug dogs and the low rumble of airplane motors. Mrs. Mann assumed that the racket was another stick-happy pilot from Wheeler Field, maybe that notorious Lieutenant Underwood, who so enjoyed swooping low over the coastline. James Mann and his son, Junior, were astonished to go outside and see over a hundred planes circling above their heads. Junior, though all of thirteen years old, knew enough about aircraft to point out, "They've changed the color of our planes."

Haleiwa was directly beneath the attack route to the army's airfields and the navy's Pearl Harbor—the point where Fuchida's attack force split apart, the bombers winging off to their assigned targets, as the fighters pulled to the fore to protect against an American counterstrike—but the island was so swarming with soldiers, sailors, and pilots that a squadron of hundreds of planes sparked little notice. Those out on the golf links, on their way to church, surfing at Waikiki, fishing off the western coast, or even servicemen on a Sunday morning's duty roster, just naturally assumed they were American aircraft and paid little notice. Both Takeo Yoshikawa and General Short would believe it was all just another drill, Short thinking that either the navy had forgotten to mention it, or maybe he'd just forgotten himself. What everyone remembered, however, was what a beautiful day it was.

The last of that tropical winter's morning fogs lifted, and through his binoculars Fuchida could see the enormous and majestic United States Pacific Fleet. He was at first confused, since the consulate's spies had reported nine battleships, while he could only see seven; this was because *Pennsylvania* was dry-docked, and Yoshikawa had included *Utah* as a battleship; she was instead retired and used for target practice. And to the great disappointment of this naval airman, not one of America's aircraft carriers was anywhere to be seen.

At 0753, Fuchida's radioman tapped, *To Ra To Ra To Ra*. *To* is the first syllable of *totsugeki*—"charge" or "attack"—and *ra* the first of *raigeki*, "torpedo." That *tora* means "tiger," the animal of Fuchida's birth year, was a bright omen. This message, eventually relayed to the whole of Japan's navy, informed the empire that Operation Z had come as a complete surprise to the armed forces of the United States of America.

On *Akagi*, Nagumo was dumbstruck at hearing the news, and Kusaka silently wept tears of joy. They could barely believe that Yamamoto and Genda's outrageous plan had actually worked.

At around 0730, a Matson line passenger ship, the SS *Lurline*, was crossing the Pacific on its northeasterly route to San Francisco when the officer of the watch, "Tiny" Nelson, heard an SOS over the radio and showed it to chief officer Edward Collins. The SS *Cynthia Olson*, a 2,140-ton steam schooner ferrying lumber to Hawaii from Tacoma for the American army was being attacked by a submarine.

Commander Minoru Yokota, captain of Imperial Japanese Navy submarine *I-26*, was with sister sub *I-10* monitoring the Aleutian Islands between Russia and Alaska until December 5, and then reporting on military shipping to Hawaii between the fifth and the seventh. After the start of Japan's East Asian conquest signaled by Fuchida's call of *To Ra To Ra To Ra*, they were now to begin taking down American ships. Yokota's first sighting by periscope of one of these targets was the *Cynthia Olson*, which the sub followed until the very moment of X-day's zero hour, when *I-26*—a hundred feet longer and four hundred pounds heavier than the ship, armed with six torpedo tubes, two 25 mm machine guns, and a 140 mm deck cannon—surfaced directly before the schooner, at about a thousand meters.

Yokota fired eighteen rounds into *Cynthia Olson* from his deck gun, then submerged and launched a torpedo. It missed, so he resurfaced, to give her twenty-nine more shells from his gun. As *Cynthia Olson* began to sink, *I-26* left to prowl America's West Coast, looking for more prey.

Cynthia Olson radioed *Lurline*, "All crew abandoning ship in lifeboats." The following day, Japanese submarine *I-19* reported surfacing to give food to some of the ship's survivors, and that report is the last we know of *Cynthia Olson*'s merchant marine crew of thirty-three and her two army privates, radio operator Samuel Zisking and medical technician Ernest Davenport. Those thirty-five bodies were never found.

PART II

STRIKE!

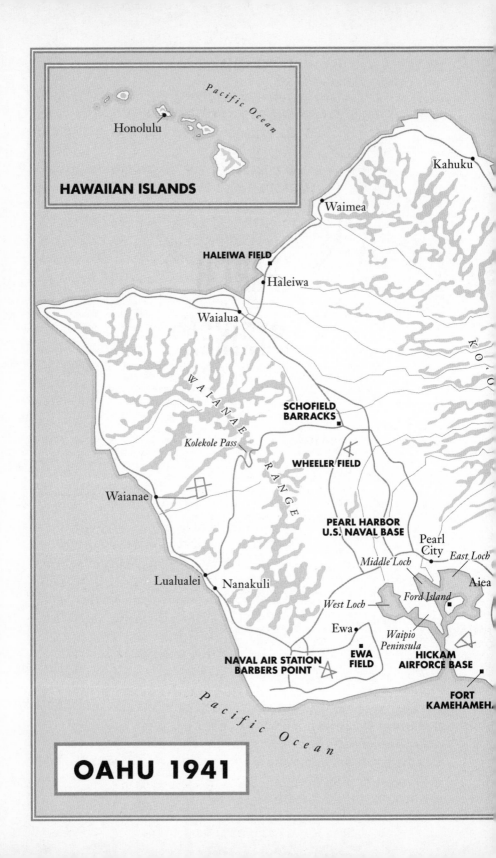

Pacific Ocean

HAWAIIAN ISLANDS

Honolulu

Kahuku

Waimea

HALEIWA FIELD

Haleiwa

Waialua

K O 'O

W A I A N A E

Kolekole Pass

**SCHOFIELD
BARRACKS**

WHEELER FIELD

R A N G E

Waianae

**PEARL HARBOR
U.S. NAVAL BASE**

Pearl
City

East Loch

Middle Loch

Aiea

Lualualei

Nanakuli

West Loch

Ford Island

Ewa

Waipio
Peninsula

**NAVAL AIR STATION
BARBERS POINT**

**EWA
FIELD**

**HICKAM
AIRFORCE BASE**

**FORT
KAMEHAMEH.**

Pacific Ocean

OAHU 1941

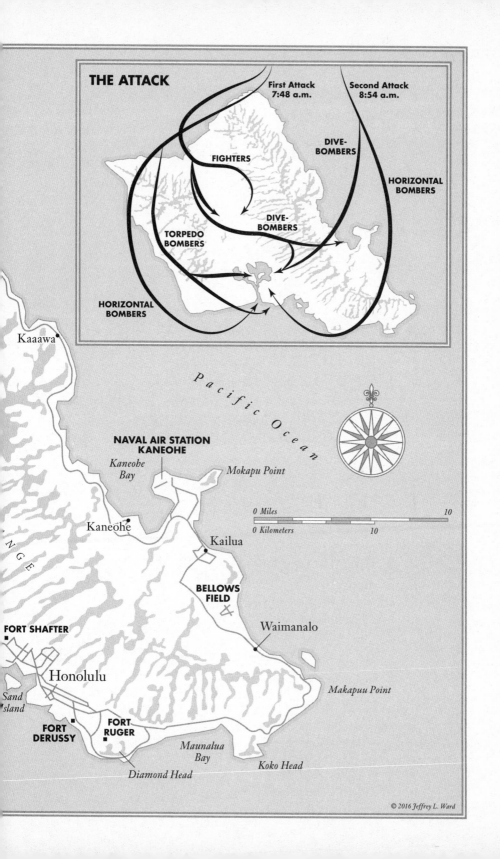

CHAPTER SIX

FROM THE AIR

Though December 7, 1941, is remembered as the worst defeat in American naval history, a significant part of Genda's and Fuchida's strategy was how to take out, with bombers and fighters, American air forces so they could not defend the territory or attack Nagumo's fleet. The story of the first victims of the Japanese attack on Hawaii has seldom been told, as it began on the other side of Oahu from the great naval base of Pearl Harbor.

At 0740, Fuchida's armada was just north of Kahuku Point when forty-three Zeros cut away to come in north and west of Wheeler Field at the dead center of Oahu. Five minutes later, dive-bombers from *Soryu* and *Hiryu* turned hard, to approach Wheeler from the south. Eleven *Shokaku* and *Zuikaku* Zeros flew east to pass north of Pearl Harbor and its neighboring airfields on Ford Island and at Hickam to attack the naval air station at Kaneohe (*kahn-a-o-hay*) Bay, while eighteen *Akagi* and *Kaga* Zeros headed toward the US Marines' Ewa (*a-vah*) Mooring Mast Field on the southwest coast.

Seventeen-year-old Fred Kamaka was attending Kamehameha High School, studying advanced woodworking to benefit his family's ukulele-manufacturing business. After breakfast, Fred stood on a campus hillock with a commanding view of the great panorama of Oahu, from the ridge of Diamond Head across Waikiki, the volcanic crater Punchbowl, the city of Honolulu with its harbor marked by the Aloha Tower, and to the west, the rustling sugarcane and pineapple fields of Ewa Plantation, with the Waianae Mountains behind her. He noticed a squadron of planes approaching in V configuration between the Army Air Corps field at Hickam and the navy's stronghold of Pearl Harbor. The planes began diving, one after the next, in single file. Lieutenant

Ainsley Mahikoa had pulled up in his car; now he explained to the students gathering to watch, "The planes are probably from the carrier fleet, which is absent from Pearl Harbor. Holes are dug into the ground and dynamite set off to simulate bomb bursts, and they are using smoke pots on the Hickam Field area instead of burning airplanes to make the action more realistic." This all made perfect sense as, the week before, everyone had watched the army and navy conduct interservice war games, which included a mock bombing of Honolulu Harbor. Then Fred Kamaka pointed out something really exciting: "Look, we're shooting down our own planes!"

What they saw falling from the sky was likely a civilian plane. At that moment under General Short's anti-sabotage alert, a mere four of Oahu's thirty-one antiaircraft batteries were in position, with none of their ammunition at hand; it all needed to be trucked over from locked-up depots. Of the island's 780 antiaircraft cannon, only a quarter were staffed, with three GIs from the California National Guard's 251st Coast Artillery Regiment who had spent the previous year deployed in Hawaii—twenty-year-old Sergeant Henry Blackwell, twenty-one-year-old Corporal Clyde Brown, and twenty-one-year-old Sergeant Warren Rasmussen—among the men with that day off. Blackwell and Brown had gotten their flying licenses after taking the Civilian Pilot Training Program from Robert Tyce of Honolulu's K-T Flying Service, and they'd convinced Rasmussen to come along that morning of December 7 to John Rodgers Airport to join them in renting a pair of K-T's taxi-yellow Piper Cubs, and soaring over paradise. Bob Tyce himself and his wife, Edna, were on their way to the airport at that moment because they had gotten friendly with Blackwell and Brown and wanted to say good-bye. The two young men were set to return to California on December 8, and this would be an aerial aloha to their memorable time in Hawaii.

The three guardsmen lifted off at the crack of dawn, soared over Waikiki and Diamond Head, and then turned to follow the coastline west, flying between five hundred and eight hundred feet in altitude and around two miles offshore. At 0755, forty-one-year-old navy Machinist's Mate 1st Class Norman Rapue was working aboard the *YT-153*, a sixty-five-foot tugboat heading out into Pearl Harbor's channel with a harbor pilot to man incoming cargo ship USS *Antares*. Rapue watched as two bright yellow Piper Cubs were attacked in the skies just south of Fort Weaver. The little props were hardly a priority for the arriving Japanese warplanes, but the First Air Fleet's crews were ordered to attack any and all targets of opportunity. "They didn't have a chance," Rapue said. "Both were cruising about two and a half miles offshore at about five hundred feet altitude when seven Japanese planes swooped down. . . . One of the yellow planes plummeted straight down into the ocean while the other circled for a moment and then plunged down." By 0830, an army rescue boat was out searching for Rasmussen, Blackwell, and Brown, but never found them, or any sign of their planes.

At the same time as the guardsmen were being slaughtered, twenty-six-year-old flight instructor Tommy Tomberlin and his student, James Duncan, were flying a neon-orange Aeronca 65TC north of Laie's landmark Mormon Temple when two red tracers shot into the canvas fabric of their rear fuselage. As the teacher took back the plane's controls from the student to quickly descend, two Japanese continued firing at them . . . but missed. After swooping down to skim just over the water, Tomberlin flew southeast, following a pass through the Ko'olau hills back home to John Rodgers. He was hoping for protection, but found none. The civilian airport was just to the southeast of one of Genda's main targets, Hickam Field, and the two men arrived to find the sky now filled with attacking planes.

Also in the air at that moment, twenty-two-year-old flying teacher Cornelia Fort was giving a lesson to a student pilot in an Interstate S-1A Cadet when she saw two planes headed their way, one on course to crash directly into them. She yanked the yoke and punched the throttle, furious at another hotdogging Army Air Corps pilot. She looked down to get his registration number so she could file a complaint, which was when she saw the red balls on the wings and knew that "the air was not the place for our little baby airplane." She set down as fast as she could and ran into Andrew Flying Service, machine-gun bullets strafing the ground around her feet, yelling, "The Japs are attacking!" Everyone on the ground laughed at this silly woman.

At about 0750, Bob and Edna Tyce arrived at the K-T Flying Service hangar at John Rodgers. While his wife did a little work in the office, Bob decided to go out and get some sun on the ramp. He yelled for Edna to come outside, pointed out some smoke in the distance, and said, "I think Hickam Field is having some kind of an accident." The couple then saw an airplane coming toward them. The plane that had fired on Cornelia Fort now buzzed the Tyces. Edna remarked, "They're flying too low over a civilian airport."

As Bob, puzzled, turned to say something to his wife, a machine gun's bullet entered the back of his head and out the side of his throat, leaving, Edna later said, a hole big enough to "put a golf ball through." Bob fell to the ground. Edna knelt beside him. She had previously worked as a nurse and immediately began taking his pulse. He was dead.

The Japanese crew that killed Bob Tyce then machine-gunned a Hawaiian Airlines DC-3 passenger plane waiting to depart for Maui. Shells tore into her wing, cockpit, twin engines, and passenger cabin, but when the airline's ground staff realized something was terribly wrong, they quickly got their customers out of the plane and back into the hangar, and no one was hurt.

Lawyer Roy Vitousek and his seventeen-year-old son, Martin, meanwhile, were out on a sightseeing trip, also in an Aeronca Tandem. Roy was so busy piloting he didn't even notice all the planes appearing around them until his son yelled out, "Look! P-40s!" The father looked over to see the red ball on one plane and yelled, "P-40s hell! They're Japanese!" The Vitouseks were fired on but their little Tandem escaped. Roy pulled out into a steep climb and headed south, to circle over the ocean until he saw things quiet down a little. An hour later, Edna Tyce realized the three servicemen from California who'd rented two of her Piper Cubs had never come home. Blackwell, Brown, and Rasmussen from the 251st went down in history as the first Americans killed in World War II.

The California National Guards' F Battery was stationed at Camp Malaloke, which is where the Japanese appeared next. "Captain Lemon came running around the end of the mess hall," Corporal Warren Hutchens remembered. "His pants were half-unbuttoned, and holding a pistol above his head, he yelled, 'Come on, get with it, a war is on!' We could not believe what he said until Japanese planes started strafing the camp. I started running messages from Colonel Sherman to Captain Lemon. While on a run to headquarters, I stopped at Battery E latrine to do my regular routine. While [I was] sitting on the toilet, a Jap plane strafed through the tin roof, cutting the bowl next to me in half! There was an eighteen-inch distance between bowls. Luckily I did my thing so I pulled up my pants and lay under the urinal thinking they might come back."

The Japanese continued to strike on the way to their primary targets. "In the movies, an airplane attack always has the *rat-tat-tat* of

guns as the plane dive-bombs its target," Dorinda Stagner Nicholson said. "But when these Japanese planes flew directly over us, the
sound of the bullets was muffled by the roar of the engines. Even
though we couldn't hear them, the incendiary bullets found their targets. Our kitchen was now on fire, and parts of the roof were gone.
The front door of our next-door neighbor was so bullet-ridden from
the strafing that it fell from its hinges." Dorinda was six years old at
the time. "Within an hour or so, Dad put the family in the car. We
got on Lehua Avenue and just kept following it all the way up into the
hills and hid there in the sugarcane fields. When we were waiting out
the attack in the cane field, I wasn't thinking about the dive-bombers
returning. I was thinking about my dog, Hula Girl. She was a black-
and-white mix, the kind of dog known in Hawaii as a poi dog. What
if she had been hit by a bomb or bullet? It was then for the first time
that I began to cry."

On the road between the gates of Pearl Harbor and the town of
Honolulu lies Hickam Field, a state-of-the-art base that had just
opened in 1939 with rolling lawns, four-lane avenues, administration
buildings with art deco terra-cotta façades, a Moorish water tower, the
world's biggest barracks—ten wings sleeping three thousand—and a
mess hall that could feed two thousand soldiers at once. Hickam was
home to bombers—six B-17s, twelve A-20s, and thirty-three B-18s—
with interservice rivalry regularly illustrated by the army's buzzing its
sailor neighbors and, when the carriers were in port, the navy's crack
pilots returning the favor.

Private Ira Southern woke up in Hickam barracks to what sounded
like artillery guns blasting. Then came the jagged roar of a plane
directly overhead, and a detonation. A dive-bomber had sliced a bomb
though a barracks window, filling the air with shrapnel and the screams
of wounded and frightened men. Southern went to get his gas mask,
but was in such shock he couldn't open his combination lock. Finally
he got his mask and joined others to get some guns out of the supply
room, which was locked. The door was broken open, but the guns
inside were all locked up, too. The men were able to release some old
Springfield rifles and a few Colt .45 semiautomatics, then had to lie flat
on the floor to load up on ammo since bomb strikes were now throwing shrapnel into that room, too.

They went back out with their weapons to bring down some goddamn enemy planes. One soldier hid behind a group of bushes with

his bolt-action rifle; another fought back with a submachine gun from under a truck. They were joined by two men trying to fight back with a gun on a tripod next to home plate on the camp's baseball field, along with Sergeant Stanley McLeod and Corporal William Anderson blasting away with a Thompson submachine gun on the parade ground. All four were cut down by strafer fire. A hundred of Hickam's civilian employees were arriving at work just then, including purchasing clerk Phillip Eldred, who was killed in a hail of Japanese bullets while driving to the base.

Captain Gordon Blake, Hickam base operations officer, was in his office getting ready for those twelve B-17 Flying Fortresses arriving from California. Working with him was operations officer Major Roger Ramey, since Ramey's good friend, Major Truman Landon, was leading the squadron.

Everyone at Hickam who knew the score wanted to see those Fortresses; they were big and exciting and spanking brand-new. A bunch of air buffs, including two of the base's mechanics, Jesse Gaines and Ted Conway, had gotten up early to watch. They saw the formation of bombers, in a perfect V, begin to peel, and Conway said, "We're going to have an air show!" Others nearby, though, said something was strange; they looked more like navy fighters than B-17s. Then Gaines saw something falling out of the lead aircraft. An oil tank exploded; followed by the mess hall of Hickam barracks; thirty-five men died instantly. Back on the field, Japanese machine guns strafed the startled watchers, who scrambled away in zigzag terror.

The approaching Fortress crews saw the heavy pall of smoke over the island and wondered if the fires were sugarcane fields getting cleared. Truman Landon's bombardier, Second Lieutenant Erwin Cihak, saw a formation of planes in single file heading his way and assumed it was the navy. Cihak then remembered hearing warnings about Japan from Hap Arnold, as well as that he had only a single .50-caliber machine gun on board. It was packed aboard in Cosmoline and stored in a crate.

Captain Blake and Major Ramey heard a tremendous blast and ran out to see a diver with red circles on its wings pulling up after bombing the Air Depot. Fearing for his B-17 pilots, who he knew had little remaining gas and were likely unarmed, Blake ran to the tower to help bring them in safely. He found his controllers giving the Fortresses all they needed to know—their assigned runway, the wind's direction, its velocity—along with reports that the airfield was being attacked by "unidentified planes."

When, at the tail end of their thirteen-hour trans-Pacific journey, an exhausted Major Truman Landon saw a group of pilots coming toward him, he, too, assumed they were friendly. But then those planes coming in at a higher altitude dove into a turn and swerved to attack while a voice on the intercom yelled, "Damn it, those are Japs!"

Landon was able to get away, but as he came around to landing position, Blake radioed a warning from the tower: "You have three Japs on your tail."

As Zeros were trying to take down Landon from the rear, American soldiers manning antiaircraft guns on the ground—either in a panic, or mistaking the B-17 for an enemy plane—were firing at him from the fore. That Landon got her down with no one killed or injured was a remarkable achievement and a shot of pure damn luck.

The next Fortress pilot coming in was Captain Raymond Swenson. As he first tried setting her down, a Zero's attacks made him overshoot, and when he came around to try again, a Zero's bullets struck some magnesium flares, which erupted, injuring one of Swenson's crewmen, Lieutenant William Schick, in the leg. Within seconds, the back half the B-17 was on fire, and while everyone was moving forward to escape, another Zero, strafing the airfield, hit Schick in the face. Swenson finally landed and was met by emergency crews as well as bikers from the Honolulu Motor Club, who, hearing of the attacks, had ridden down to help. The injured Schick was taken to Hickam Hospital. Acting commander Captain Frank Lane: "I suppose the reason my attention was called to him was that he was dressed in a winter uniform, which we never wore in the islands, and had the insignia of a medical officer on his lapels. He had a wound in his face, and when I went to take care of him, he pointed to the casualties on litters on the floor and said, 'Take care of them.' I told him I'd get him on the next ambulance, [but] the next day I heard that he died."

The six B-17s of the Eighty-Eighth Reconnaissance Squadron heard what was happening to their fellow pilots at Hickam and were ready. Three landed there and two others, headed by Captain Richard Carmichael and Lieutenant Harold Chaffin, detoured to Oahu's north shore. Sergeant Robert Barnard: "By then the sky was thick with puffs of antiaircraft fire. 'The Japs have hit Pearl Harbor!' was the word that came over the intercom. At this instant I looked through the radio hatch and saw six Mitsubishis go over us. The antiaircraft fire from the ground seemed to have no particular target, just aircraft. As we neared Hickam Field, we heard another pilot ask for landing instructions and he got an immediate reply. 'Land east to west, runway two, wind five mph—look out, there's a Jap on your tail!' We circled Hickam three times and saw the great battleships burning, smoke and flames everywhere. Antiaircraft fire kept us from landing. Our pilot, Lieutenant Harold 'Newt' Chaffin, from Arkansas, told the copilot and engineer he did not like the looks of it down there. He repeated it three times. 'Okay, let's get the hell out of here then,' said the engineer. 'Where to?' asked the pilot. 'You know we only have fifteen or twenty minutes of fuel left, if we're lucky.'" The engineer recommended Haleiwa Auxiliary Field, which had a shorter runway than ones built for a B-17, but their load was pretty light, and they were running out of gas. Captain Carmichael followed Chaffin over the mountains. Both bombers landed unharmed.

"An unfamiliar-sounding aircraft engine startled us, and we heard a lot of yells to head for the ditch," Barnard said. "A Japanese fighter plane came down the length of the field with guns blazing as it strafed the old P-36 trainer planes parked on the edge of the strip. The aircrews and the men at the field had only sidearms and rifles to shoot with, but they did fire at the Japs with gusto. One Japanese Val-type dive-bomber came in and strafed us. As he passed us, he did a chandelle, stood on his tail for an instant and then headed out to sea. In just a few seconds a P-40 came by and went after the Val. Shortly after we heard the crackle of fifty-caliber machine-gun fire, a huge ball of smoke plummeted into the sea. One less Val."

First Lieutenant Robert Richards was so overtaken by Japanese gunfire on his Fortress that he had to give up on coming in and flew back out to sea. Chased by Zeros, he finally saw the short strip at Bellows Field, which he thought he could handle by riding his four-engine giant into the wind. But at that moment, crew chief Earl Sutton was moving a P-40 on the runway, forcing Richards to pull up and come around. Bellows's Sergeant Covelesky: "Our asphalt landing strip at Bellows was hardly long enough to accommodate our P-40s, much less a B-17; and when he made an approach from the ocean downwind, we knew we were in for a breathtaking crash landing. Even though his wheels were down, he flared out and touched down halfway on the strip, knowing he wouldn't be able to stop, retracted the wheels, and slid off the runway over a ditch and into a cane field bordering the strip." Rescued by firemen and ambulance workers, the Fortress crew refused to leave the plane until making sure their Norden bombsight was pulled from the wreckage. If the Japanese invaded, it was one piece of American know-how that no one wanted falling into enemy hands.

First Lieutenant Frank Bostrom was so repeatedly attacked that he couldn't set down at any airfield and was forced to bring his B-17 in on the Kahuku Golf Course. It was a smart choice; the plane was damaged but fixable, and everyone aboard was alive and uninjured.

The Japanese continued to bomb and strafe the American airfields, spreading havoc and death. Hickam's William Melnyk was talking on a stairway landing with a group of servicemen when the force of a bomb striking Hangar 7 threw them all to the ground. A sergeant began screaming orders to get out. Since it looked as though the enemy was targeting buildings, everyone thought it would be safer to be outside, so a group gathered on the parade grounds along with men fleeing the barracks, many in their Skivvies. They heard *pah pah pah pah pah* and then saw a bomber dive in to strafe them with its cowling guns. Everyone began running in all directions; some fell to their deaths. One remembered thinking at that moment: He'd come to Hawaii with the idea that he was more or less getting a vacation paid for by the US government. Now he'd be lucky to get out alive. Another group, including Leon Webster, found cover under a building by the post exchange and became enraged when one crewman used the chaos to loot a case of beer and cartons of cigarettes out of the PX. But, loaded down with booty, he couldn't run and was taken down.

Fires now erupted everywhere. When a plane took a hit, it exploded, the flames both leaping to anything nearby they could ignite, and erupting from high-octane avgas tanks onto tarmacs to flow as lava-like streams of flame. William Melnyk went from building to building, followed by the whistle of falling bombs, the shock of explosions, and the terror of whizzing bullets. A man came in and said, "I need help; the lieutenant has been hit!" First Lieutenant Malcolm Brumwell had been seriously wounded by shrapnel. William Melnyk: "We carried him to the supply room and laid him on the counter. He was bleeding across the chest and moaned from the pain. At this time, there were about five people in the supply room, and one called the hospital for an ambulance. In a short time it came to the front of the building and we were told to bring the lieutenant out. The driver and another fellow slid him in and they turned toward me. The driver, thinking I was wounded also because of all the blood on my shirt, said, 'Take it easy now and get into the ambulance.' I said, 'There is nothing wrong with me.' He replied, 'I know, I know,' and began to force me inside where the lieutenant was lying. I went into the vehicle, crawled over the driver's seat, and went out through the door. As I walked away from the ambulance, the driver, thinking I was in shock, began chasing me, yelling for me to come back. He soon gave up, returning to the ambulance, and drove the injured man to the hospital. We later learned that he died from the injuries he received in the chest. I turned and saw a man from our squadron named Bernard Mulcahy. He looked at me and said, 'You know, Bill, we lived more in the past two hours than we did in our last nineteen years.'

"There was talk around about another raid and an invasion. We walked into the mess hall and it was a shambles. Someone mentioned that we would have to move into the mountains and fight off the Japanese. I noticed someone brought out a five-gallon pail of maraschino cherries in syrup, and several five-pound packages of American cheese. Thinking we would have to go to the mountains to fight, we both took a piece of the cheese, and I placed two handfuls of the syrupy cherries in my pocket."

Private Edward Hall, a truck driver who volunteered for KP duty first thing Sunday morning to earn some extra spending money, had heard the explosions and was hiding under a sink. He came back outside to find an enemy plane coming right at him, guns blazing. Hall froze, but suddenly the plane pulled up. The pilot had to avoid some power lines, and Hall's life was saved.

Dodging more bullets, Hall and a group of men took cover under a supply building's roof overhangs. When Hall walked out to see what was going on, someone grabbed his shirt and pulled him back. "Get outta there! You'll get killed!" He had indeed been spotted, and immediately strafer fire tore out chunks of the building they were hiding in.

"At this time our lieutenant called us together and assembled us on the edge of the parade ground and made the great statement 'Men, we are at war,' as if we did not already know it," Nineteenth Transport Squadron's George Gabik said. "He then posted a couple of men on east and west sides of the parade ground [as lookouts]. He no sooner said that than they were upon us. We lost several men because of this. The rest of us scattered and hid under or behind a building. Everything was now fine until the bombing started. I did not know what to do or where to go as we had no foxholes to jump into. So I just stayed where I was, and as the bombs came closer and hit, I dove for the ground. One hit across the road in front of me where a bunch of cars were parked, and they took most of the shrapnel. The piece that got me hit behind me and about thirty feet away in the dirt, and being on the ground I guess saved my life. The piece traveled along the ground and hit my left leg above the knee and below the hip and rolled me over. The first thing I thought of was this old movie *All Quiet on the Western Front*, where this one soldier was carrying another who had got hit in the leg and was being taken to the hospital. At the hospital he lost the leg. That was the only thought I had at this time, had I lost my leg, so I reached down and found the leg still there and what a great feeling it was."

There was courage, and there was fear and panic. A second lieutenant emotionally collapsed and was found hiding and sobbing, while another officer "went all to pieces after the attack and had to be sent back to the States on a stretcher." Fifth Bomb Group ground crewman Harold Fishencord said he could never forget the horrible screams of a man, trapped in the nose of a B-18 that had caught fire, as he burned to his death. Private 1st Class Gabriel Christie noticed fellow PFC James Lewis lying on his back in a warehouse. Christie was impressed that Lewis was so calm and courageous when Christie was scared and didn't know what to do. He later learned that Lewis had taken a lot of shrapnel in the back and was dead.

Carl Brown, a civilian, was standing near the airstrip when it looked as though one of the few surviving planes was about to be attacked. Brown heard someone yell, "For God's sake, save that plane!" Though he wasn't a pilot or even a mechanic, Brown started the plane and taxied her in a zigzag manner to avoid both Japanese strafers and American antiaircraft counterfire. After he drove her out of harm's way, an angry recruit screamed at the civilian, "Get the hell out of here! Don't you know this is a combat area?"

First Sergeant Carlos McCuiston: "After the last explosion, I jumped up and turned to run, hoping to find better shelter before the next bombs fell. As it turned out, that was the last of the bombing. As I turned, I saw two airmen lying facedown just a few feet from me. One had both legs severed at the buttocks. His blood had soaked the ground where he lay. The second had a massive head wound. Some object had passed through his head from the left temple area to just above the right ear. His brains were lying on the ground. Both were dead."

The army's Twenty-Ninth Car Company asked for volunteers to assist with the wounded. Someone took a bedsheet and painted a big red cross on it and laid it over the top of a truck. The Japanese bombed and strafed it anyway.

Second Lieutenant Monica Conter was one of Hickam's six nurses at a hospital that had only been open for three weeks and didn't yet have mattresses for all the beds: "There were just all kinds of wounds and blood and dust from the building that exploded on them. Some had machine-gun and bomb-fragment wounds. They were just butchered. We were trying to relieve their pain and their shock. We just went around giving that morphine in those ten cc syringes, filling them up from the flask, just going from one to the other. We did try to tag them. Then they would just load them in trucks and ambulances and off they would go. They were in terrible condition and may have died. Some were brought in dead, and we put them out at the rear of the hospital and covered them up.

"We heard this plane. It was losing altitude, and . . . we both just stopped suddenly and stared at each other. . . . There was a *bang*! I saw the rising sun on the planes. The bombs were getting closer and closer. . . . One five-hundred-pound bomb fell on the hospital lawn. . . . The whole hospital shook! In a split second someone yelled. 'Down everybody!' And we fell wherever we were, crouching, waiting for the next minute—the next bomb to kill us all!"

When Nurse Conter hit the floor during a strike and used a garbage-can lid to cover herself, someone tried to take it away from her, but she held on to it. Lieutenant Philip Sprawls: "She, nor any of them, had had any rest for over thirty hours. They laid victims on the porch floor for first aid. Many died, even while she was extracting the hypo needle! The blood actually ran on the floor. She showed me where it came up over the soles on her shoes. Marie [a nurse at Tripler] said many came in holding his arm or leg!—completely severed, but hating to leave it! Others came with an arm or leg off; both legs and an arm; and some with all limbs gone! All these fellows were still conscious and cussing the Japs!" George Gabik: "I got to Tripler [Hospital] about eleven a.m. and still had my .45 with me and would not give it up. I looked up and saw a Japanese doctor getting ready to work on me. I don't recall, but they said I tried to find my .45 so I could shoot him, and everyone was saying, 'No, no, he is one of us.'"

Carlos McCuiston: "Lieutenant Turner and I visited the morgue to try and identify the squadron dead. The dead were in plain wooden boxes, naked; many with no obvious wounds. This would support the belief that some were killed by concussion. As I walked among the dead, the thought occurred to me that perhaps in view of the expected invasion, they were better off than those of us who survived the initial attack."

The Honolulu fire department's Kalihi station was told to respond to a hangar fire at Hickam. There was no mention of the attack that had begun. They arrived to find one of the base's fire trucks bombed out in the station. In the other, twenty feet away, the driver, having been strafed, was now hanging over the steering wheel, dead. Three of the city's firemen would die in the attack on Hickam, while five more would be wounded.

At Makalapa senior officers' housing, Mrs. Mayfield took her maid, Fumiyo, with her next door when she went to join Mrs. Earle in sheltering together. They decided to turn the living room's bamboo couches upside down and pile the cushions on top. In the middle of this, Fumiyo asked, "Mrs. Mayfield, is it—is it the Japanese who are attacking us?" Mrs. Mayfield had to answer yes. At Hickam's NCO housing, Mrs. Walter Blakey knew the safest defense against bullets was a bathtub, while over at Ford, Mrs. Claire Fonderhide, married to a submarine officer, sat in her living room with a .45 automatic and waited.

Wheeler Field, at the center of Oahu, was home to the Air Force's Fourteenth Pursuit Wing—ninety-nine P-40s, thirty-nine P-36s, and an assortment of older craft. Just before 0800, armorer Private Wilfred Burke was in the tent area's quadrangle, talking with a bunch of airmen. Burke was up and out at that time on a Sunday because he had promised to go to church service with his boss, Sergeant Forest Wills. At 0802 a squadron of planes shot past, heading to Pearl Harbor.

Wheeler's aircraft were that Sunday morning guarded by one PFC Fusco, armed with a 1903 Springfield rifle. Fusco, however, immediately recognized the red balls on the wings and ran to the nearest hangar for a machine gun. The armory's door was locked; he had to break it down. The ammunition was locked up in a hangar, and that hangar was now on fire. Since General Short had set his department on sabotage alert, it would take four hours to get any of Wheeler's planes ready to fight.

"I was thirteen years old and living in army housing close to Wheeler Field—home of the P-40," Helen Griffith Livermont remembered. "My sister and I were in bed when it all started and discussed how terrible it was to stage a sham battle on a Sunday morning. The noise from the bombs grew louder, so we got up and joined our parents in the kitchen. My mother was in a frantic state. She was a German war bride of World War I and knew the sound of bombs. She headed out the door for the safety of the concrete housing across from us—ours was made of wood. My sister followed her, and I thought I had better get out, too. We lost track of our mother, but my sister and I ran between houses, dodging bullets for what seemed like an hour."

Just waking up in Wheeler's barracks, Gus Ahola was trying to decide if he should wash his car or go play golf. He heard an odd-whining plane engine, getting louder and louder, which meant trouble. He hoped the pilot could recover, but then the whole building shook with an explosion, and Gus knew the man must be dead. He looked out the window, hoping to see a parachute, but instead saw a pillar of smoke from the runway. Ahola assumed it was the "damned navy" practicing with their Betty Crocker bombs made from flour sacks. Then Ahola saw the rising-sun meatballs glinting on the wings. "Navy, hell!" he yelled out. "Those are the goddamn Nips!"

Base commander Colonel Flood was in front of his quarters nearby when he saw a bomb hit and assumed the explosion was an accident, but it was in fact a strike on the base's engineering shops at Hangar 1. Those nearby thought the building had lifted into the air, so powerful was the explosion. Bigger detonations followed, as the flammable storage dump, filled with drums of lacquer, turpentine, and aviation-grade fuel, thundered, followed by the ammunition depot, where all the aircraft machine-gun belts cracked like the Fourth of July.

In the mess hall at the food line, someone looked out the window and saw an explosion. "Boy, that lieutenant sure hit hard!" he said. "That's no crash," Private Henry Woodrum shouted. "It's the Japs!" The crowd inside rushed to get out, so clogging the doors that Woodrum had to jump over a steam table, run through the kitchen, and get out the back. He stopped on the loading dock, looked up, and saw a plane coming right at him. Then a bomb fell from its belly, the shock of its explosion so close and so huge it threw him back inside the building and into a pantry, where vegetables rained down on his body.

Many of the Chinese cooks tried to protect themselves in the freezer room. Another bomb hit, killing them all.

Bugler Private Frank Gobeo didn't know how to play the call to arms, so he blew pay call. The men swarmed from the barracks. Another strafing run was so low that an attacking plane's landing wheels got wrapped up in telephone wires and power lines. Wheeler's commander said one was so close that when the pilot smiled at him, he could see the gold, shining, in his teeth.

Switchboard operator Private 1st Class Robert Shattuck was driving in for duty when he was hit. One of his legs was chopped up by shrapnel, and he died quickly.

Master Sergeant Arthur Fahrner was trying to get dressed and report to base from his house in Pearl City, but he couldn't find a collar insignia. His wife kept insisting he put on a tie. "We're at war," he told her. "You don't wear a tie to war."

Wheeler's antiaircraft defense was a couple of guys from the base fire department who'd spent six hours learning how to operate a .50-caliber antiaircraft machine gun mounted on top of the firehouse. Since they were busy fighting fires, that gun was manned by a guard from Wheeler's stockade, helped by its prisoners.

Having dropped their loads, the dive-bombers now joined the fighters to strafe. Nineteen dived from the west, and then from the east, and then from both directions at once, crack-shot targeting the hangars and the barracks. Wheeler recruits who had heard one disparaging remark after another about the Japanese now got a firsthand look at their abilities when another group of planes appeared, directly over their heads. Wilfred Burke: "It was the first time I had ever seen a plunging dive-bomber, and it was an awesome sight. Nothing in warfare is more frightening. Hurtling down on us was the dive-bomber being followed by another, while six or seven more were in echelon awaiting their turn. The leader pulled out right over us in a spectacular climbing bank." First Lieutenant Frederick Cooper of the Seventeenth Air Base Group was also impressed: "The formation was perfect, and the timing on the dropping of the bombs are so perfect that I could follow them down in the formation right to the ground, right to impact."

Private Henry Woodrum got up and ran toward the Fourteenth's headquarters and came across a building site, with trenches dug for the foundations. Clouds of bullets kicked up just before his feet. He found some refuge behind a pile of lumber and turned back to look. Woodrum: "Down the ramp to my left, a P-36 exploded, hurling flaming debris upon an operations tent, which blossomed with petals of flame. A man ran from the tent, jumped into an old Plymouth, but drove only a hundred feet or so before a strafing aircraft machine-gunned it into another flaming hunk of metal. The GI jumped out of the car, his clothes smoking, and ran into a building unharmed."

Other men joined Private Woodrum in using the wood for cover. One of them, "a skinny crew-cut kid about twenty years old, crawled to the end of the pile with his upper body protruding beyond it, exposed," Woodrum remembered. "'You better get back here, you'll get hit out there!' I said. 'Naw, I can see 'em coming from out here. I'm all right.' He began to laugh, treating the newborn war as a joke, but a few minutes later, he suddenly gasped and rolled half over, his body rigid, quivering before he flopped back on his belly and died, gagging on unspoken words and blood, the toes of his shoes kicking bare places in the dirt alongside my head. We tugged his body slowly back toward us, behind the lumber, protection he no longer needed. The dead body's muscles relaxed, emitting strange gurgling sounds. The smell of fresh, warm blood merged with other smells."

Japanese gunners had seen the men hiding and were now targeting them. The barracks were about thirty yards away, and they decided to run there. One was cut down by strafer fire, but Woodrum made it to safety and survived.

Wilfred Burke was heading for the noncommissioned officers' quarters, where he could take shelter behind a house's wall away from the clear targets, when a bomb hit just behind him, killing several men. When he reached relative safety, Burke looked back to watch the methodical strafing of his wing's planes. The air was filled with the smoke of burning oil, which grew so thick the Japanese couldn't see some P-36 fighters parked at the end of the line.

When the first wave of the Japanese attack ended, Burke ran to his tent to get his helmet—a World War I tin hat with a lining that took half an hour to lace in—and on the way there passed by the spot where the bomb had exploded right next to him. At least six or seven men had died there, eviscerated on what had been just another sidewalk. A corporal ordered Burke to help with the wounded, who were being brought to a tent that had been riddled with gunshot. The men Burke tried to help included one with part of his head missing, and another whose belly had such a huge hole in it, his intestines were visible.

Every building on base now seemed either to be on fire or to have exploded in ruins. Operations officer Major Kenneth Bergquist realized that there was little to be done, so he arranged for a car and driver to get him to Fort Shafter and give General Davidson a full accounting. On the road, a string of planes strafed the car until it was forced to stop and pull over. As the driver hid in the brush, Bergquist crouched behind the rear axle, but the driver hadn't set the brake and the car started rolling, so Bergquist duck-walked behind it, to stay undercover. The car was sprayed with bullets, but the major was safe. Finally during a lull, Bergquist jumped back into the car and drove off, forgetting all about the driver, who lay beside the road, wounded in the leg.

Wheeler's casualties: thirty-nine killed and fifty-nine wounded. The base's commander, Colonel William Flood, summed up one reason why the military was so shocked and unprepared: "To think that this bunch of little yellow bastards could do this to us when we all knew that the United States was superior to Japan!"

Adjacent to Wheeler was the army's massive Schofield Barracks. Since Takeo Yoshikawa and his fellow Axis spies had not found any significant aircraft or other matériel there, the Japanese did not consider Schofield a priority target, but since it was so close to Wheeler, Japanese divers and fighters opportunistically strafed Schofield's officers' quarters, her hospital, and her quadrangles in an attack memorialized in the book and movie *From Here to Eternity*. Author James Jones: "On Sunday morning in those days there was a bonus ration of a half-pint of milk, to go with your eggs or pancakes and syrup, also Sunday specials. Most of us were more concerned with getting and holding on to our half-pints of milk than with listening to the explosions that began rumbling up toward us from Wheeler Field two miles away. 'They doing some blasting?' some old-timer said through a mouthful of pancakes. It was not till the first low-flying fighter came skidding, whammering low overhead with his MGs going that we ran outside, still clutching our half-pints of milk to keep them from being stolen, aware with a sudden sense of awe that we were seeing and acting in a genuine moment of history."

Second Lieutenant Francis Gabreski had spent the night at a

Schofield Barracks Officers' Club dance and woke up around 0800. As he thought about getting to church, he heard a whine, an explosion, and then "something like machine-gun fire at a distance, and, well, that didn't sound too pleasant. I heard an airplane flying over the rooftops so I ran out to look. The rear gunner was spraying the buildings with bullets. And I says, 'Oh, my God.' I says, 'We're at war.' It dawned on me and the other dumbfounded men that this was an actual bombing and our airplanes and hangars were being hit. Our second thought was, what we could do to help save the planes. So I immediately ran up and down the hallway trying to get the pilots out of bed and tell them that we're at war, to get out of here and put on your flying suits and get down the line.

"Only partly dressed, we ran toward the flight line when a couple of pursuits came down on us with blazing guns. We hit the dirt until they'd passed over, got to the line, and physically began pushing and shoving planes away from burning aircraft and buildings. Altogether, we managed to salvage about thirty planes. One hangar that was set afire held .30-caliber ammunition. Inside the heat was so intense that cartridges exploded, sending tracers around men and planes. The last hangar held all the refueling trucks, completely filled with gasoline. We tried to move them but found no keys. So we had to leave them to the mercy of whatever set them off first, planes or fire. Nobody knew what was going on. We took off in twelve airplanes and went out over Pearl Harbor, which is about eighteen minutes away. Every antiaircraft fire that was still intact was up shooting at us, which logically they should have been!" Francis Gabreski would survive Pearl Harbor, transfer to the European theater, and in time become America's greatest living ace.

"As long as I live, I shall never forget my feelings and emotions when I saw and realized that these were Jap planes and that we were in for the real thing," Schofield Army Hospital surgeon Major Leonard Heaton later said. "Something we never thought could ever happen to us here due to primarily our great naval force and implicit faith in such. There were many planes by now all over and around us. I remarked as must have many others before us in situations like this, 'Where are *our* planes?' Whereupon another Jap plane came down our street spraying everything and everybody with machine guns.

"We were now in the driveway of the hospital. The scene could have been lifted from the Atlanta hospital scene in *Gone With the Wind*. The hospital was already filled, and the overflow was lying all over the hall-ways and lawn. The horseshoe driveway was filled bumper to bumper with trucks and ambulances, all filled with the dead and wounded. The small new hospital had just opened and had neither equipment, doc-tors, or nurses to handle this flood. Little, if anything, could be done for the scores of wounded who sat or lay quietly around. Many were airman who walked in from the field after their planes were destroyed.

"A young doctor and nurse came out of the hospital door and shouted, 'Don't unload any more, we are full.' He was clearly fran-tic from the impossible task facing him and the small staff on duty. The planes were still pounding the hangar and barracks area. Their machine guns never seemed to run out of bullets. Fortunately, by now, most of the men had found some form of protection. To the everlast-ing credit of the Japanese pilots, they did not bomb the hospital, which was clearly marked with a huge red cross on the roof. If they had, it would have been a terrible slaughter, since all the wounded and many rescuers were congregated in and around it.

"A medical sergeant came running out of the hospital door shout-ing, 'Take them to Tripler, take them to Tripler.' Tripler General Hos-pital was in Honolulu and was the largest military hospital in the islands. The lead trucks and ambulances in the driveway started pull-ing out. About four vehicles back, the line stopped. An ambulance was not moving. The doctor and I ran up to urge him to go on and get the line moving. The doctor stuck his head in the door. The redheaded young driver had his head in his arms resting on the steering wheel. The doctor grabbed him by the hair and pulled his hair up. No won-der he didn't pull out. His face looked like raw hamburger. Blood cov-ered his khaki shirt to his waist. One look and the doctor ordered two nearby men to pull the driver in with the wounded he had brought in the ambulance. He did not say a word or make any expression. I believe he was in shock. The driver lay limp on top of the others in his own ambulance without the benefit of a stretcher.

"We left the airman we brought in on the grass. I could not bear to look at him as I felt he was going to die.

"I ran toward a burning Ford sedan. The burning smell of flesh should have told me I could not help the men inside. The passen-ger was bent over forward. His clothes were burned off and his skin in a condition I shall not attempt to describe here. The driver will leave a picture in my mind forever. The car had been strafed and set afire. The driver was sitting behind the steering wheel still clutching a Thompson machine gun. His face was burned horribly and burned black skin outlined his facial bones. At my feet was a section of his skull and black hair. The wood stock of his gun was burned almost off and was still burning. If a report had to be made, it would simply be 'Two soldiers in a black Ford sedan; one had black hair, both burned beyond recognition.'"

A great many of America's servicemen at this moment were teen-agers or young men, untried by life and untested by combat—of the forty thousand enlisted men on Oahu in 1941, the average age was nineteen. Novelist John Steinbeck would write of such raw troops, "They lack only one thing to make them soldiers, enemy fire, and they will never be soldiers until they have it. No one, least of all themselves, knows what they will do when the terrible thing happens. No man there knows whether he can take it, whether he will run away or stick, or lose his nerve and go to pieces, or will be a good soldier. There is no way of knowing and probably that one thing bothers you more than anything else. . . . Every man builds in his mind what it will be like, but it is never what he thought it would be."

At 0930, during the middle of the second wave, Private Bob Kinzler's company was ordered into trucks to defend the shore against a Japanese invasion. The recruits started discussing what it would be like to be hit by a bullet. One said, "Hey, I've heard the Japs only have .25-caliber ammo. Do you think that would hurt as much as being hit by a .30-caliber?" Many thought the smaller the bullet, the less the pain. But how much less would that pain in fact be? On the way to the battery, on a rise in the Kamehameha Highway, everyone could see Pearl Harbor, destroyed. Kinzler: "We wore World War One pie-plate hats, were lightly armed, and our average age was nineteen. We all thought we were going to die."

All this confusion may be hard to comprehend but it certainly makes sense. When George Bicknell called Fort Shafter to report that Pearl Harbor was under attack, the man who answered the phone said, "Go back to sleep, you're having a bad dream." When destroyer *Reid*'s Lieutenant Commander Harold Pullen first saw the carnage, he told a fellow officer, "My God, it looks like a movie set." In his testimony before Congress, army engineer foreman Charles Utterback said, "The only thing I heard that morning, sir, was 'They caught them asleep, by God.' I think I heard that comment fifty times that day."

In both the book and the film of *Eternity*, Schofield is portrayed as having been strafed by three planes for an hour, with a number of casualties. In fact, antiaircraft fire from Pearl Harbor dropped a dud shell into the kitchen's flour barrel, some casings fell into the quadrangles, and perhaps one Japanese pilot, seizing a target of opportunity, fired some rounds on the men below. With two killed and seventeen wounded, Schofield was comparatively lucky that day.*

Protected by the sawtooth range of Koʻolau and far from the hustle and bustle of Honolulu and Pearl Harbor, Kaneohe Bay Naval Air Station housed thirty-six PBY-5 Catalinas—the navy's signature reconnaissance seaplane—in the three squadrons of Patrol Wing 1. Early on that quiet Sunday morning, VP-14 division leader Lieutenant Murray Hanson got a phone call: "Lieutenant, this is the Comm Office. You'd better come up here. One of your pilots just sent a message to the commander in chief that he bombed a submarine one mile south of Ford Island. CINCPAC sent him a jig on it."

The pilot was Ensign William Tanner, who'd helped USS *Ward* in attacking the midget sub by the entrance to Pearl Harbor at dawn. Murray Hanson: "I told him I'd be right up. I had just launched my planes to search at first light. I was killing time in our hangar, reading the morning paper, until the planes returned. I [was to] debrief the crews, service the aircraft, and secure the hangar. In naval communications parlance *jig* means 'verify and repeat your message.' The encoded contact report from my plane was so startling in its import that CINCPAC wanted him to recheck the encoding to make sure it had been done accurately and then repeat the message to him.

"The communications duty officer and I chatted and looked out the window toward Kaneohe Bay with the beautiful Koʻolau mountains in the background. It hadn't entered our minds that the message wasn't just a garble. Not until ten seconds later. As we waited, we saw and heard aircraft flying low over the station. Then as one of the planes flew down past Lieutenant Northrup Castle's station boathouse and over our seaplane operating area, one of our aircraft anchored out

*Barracks museum curator Herb Garcia: "Remember, the soldiers who witnessed this were not trained observers, just excitable Depression-era kids. Then rumors got bigger in the telling and were reinforced by *From Here to Eternity*. Now, ninety percent of the veterans who return here say, 'Yeah, I was bombed, I was strafed.' If I argue, they say, 'Look, buddy, I was here and you weren't.'"

there burst into flames. Almost simultaneously the intruding plane did a chandelle, and as it rolled away from us, I clearly saw the meatball—the rising-sun insignia of the Japanese naval air arm—on the wing of the deadly Zero! It was now seven fifty-two a.m. in Hawaii on December seventh, 1941, and the dreaded but somehow expected moment had arrived—we were at war with Imperial Japan.

"The Naval Air Station, Kaneohe, was new. Many of the military had not yet heard of it. Obviously the Japanese had. Some of the buildings were still incomplete, and the station roads had not yet been paved. I ran downstairs to the station OOD's [Officer of the Day] office shouting, 'Japanese airplanes are attacking the station. Sound the alarm and call our commanding officer.' It wasn't news to the OOD, but he found that we had no working alarm on station. Our makeshift general alarm was the workmen's steam whistle on the contractor's timekeeper shack. Since it was Sunday, the shack was padlocked, and there was no steam for the whistle. No alarm! When I called my squadron commander, Lieutenant Commander Thurston B. Clark [not the historian Clarke, who was born in 1946], he was already awake and aware of the attack. He drove from his quarters to join me, his car strafed repeatedly all the way. He commandeered some guns from the OOD's armory and went outside. Never will I forget the spectacle of the squadron commander and me crouching behind the administration building, trying to shoot out of the sky with our heavy, awkward, and inaccurate .45-caliber automatics, those four-hundred-mile-per-hour Zeros."

Aviation Machinist Mate 3rd Class Guy Avery was sleeping on a bungalow's porch and woke up to the roar of a plane. All Gus could think was "To hell with the army." But the sound of this plane was odd, so he went to the window and saw "Zeros just beginning to fan out over the heart of the station and opening fire promiscuously." He yelled to the rest of the men in the house, "The Japs are here! It's war!" One said, "Well, don't worry about it, Avery. It'll last only two weeks." Guy Avery: "We were struck first of all and about seven minutes before Pearl Harbor. Our OOD called nearby Bellows Field to warn them and ask for help, but his call was regarded as a practical joke." Kaneohe contractor Sam Aweau also called Bellows and Hickam to warn them, but no one took him seriously.

Kaneohe's commander, Harold "Beauty" Martin, worried about how his brand-new staff—303 sailors and 95 marines—would react under fire, but he was impressed: "It was remarkable. There was no panic. Everyone went right to work battling back and doing his job."

Lieutenant Cy Gillette was showering at home in Kailua. The phone rang; his wife said it was his duty officer, ordering him to base on a Sunday. Gillette thought it was nothing and took his time shaving. Then a second call told him Kaneohe's planes were on fire. He jumped into his convertible and raced over to find the only planes not destroyed were the three out on patrol. His men were running away from Japanese machine gunners, pieces of pajama showing from under their uniforms.

He joined a group of sailors smashing the locks on the armory, grabbed a Thompson submachine gun, and ran across the runway, getting strafed every time he found himself out in the open. An ensign right next to him was killed. Gillette: "One moment we were running next to each other, and the next he was down on the tarmac."

Seaman "Squash" Marshall outran a Zero's guns for a hundred yards. His friends cheered when he survived.

Five pilots jumped into a car, caroming through strafing attacks to get to their planes and fight back. They reached the airfield and jumped out of the car to see that every one of their planes had been destroyed. Then, their car exploded.

Oswald Tanczos: "Suddenly, I noticed the gunner sitting behind the pilot had spotted us standing in a group. He turned his machine gun toward us. I yelled, 'Let's get out of here! I think that guy is going to shoot at us.' We turned and ran to take cover in the mess hall as he sprayed the ground right on our heels. Luckily he didn't hit any of us. . . . I took cover under a double sink about six feet long and the bottom about sixteen inches off the floor. I filled the sink with six to eight inches of water to deflect any bullets. . . . I guess about twenty to thirty minutes had passed since it all started when I heard one of our trucks stopping on the street outside. I said to the guys, 'I believe they're dropping off the rifle ammunition.' So about six or eight of us went out. Sure enough, there it was. We picked up a bandolier of ammo, which was about a hundred rounds, five to a clip, and walked across the street to our tent where our rifles were hanging on our cots. . . .

"All at once a bunch of Jap planes from the Pearl Harbor area appeared over the horizon coming straight at me. They seemed to sway from side to side, then opened up with all of their guns. I tell you it sounded like a hailstorm concentrated right on me. White tracer bullets were whizzing by me all around. Some were so close it was like popping a whip in my ear. It shook me up. I felt that I was trapped out there. Each time they flew over, I would empty my gun of the five rounds it held. Don't think I wasn't scared. I guess this is when I started praying for my life. In my simple way I asked the Lord to look after me, and it seemed like immediately I felt at ease or like a shield had come over me. After that I had no fear when I saw and heard all those bullets passing by me.

"One plane to the far left was bearing down directly in line with me. When he turned on his guns, the incendiary shells were coming out of the propeller shaft at the rate of one per second. The shell shots left a red trail, and I calculated that the fourth one was going to hit me in the right shoulder. I stepped aside to let it pass. It exploded about twenty feet behind me as it hit the ground.

"I heard a whining, like bombs falling. I decided to lie down and curl up into a ball to make myself the smallest target. . . . Later I learned that someone in the nearby area was shooting antiaircraft shells [and] instead of the antiaircraft shells hitting the planes or exploding in the air, they were falling on us. On top of that, someone had goofed. They forgot to arm those shells before they shot them.

"After the last of the three shells dropped, I started to shiver and shake. I thought how stupid I had been to put myself in the line of fire! Yet, I felt a certain satisfaction that I had stood up to them and come out of it without a scratch."

Eyewitnesses remembered that five or six Japanese fighters led by Lieutenant Tadashi Kaneko attacked the control tower, and then the four planes floating in the water. Five or six more Zeros, led by Lieutenant Masao Sato, destroyed the planes housed on the ramp.

Chief Aviation Ordnanceman John Finn, the son of a California plumber, had signed up for the service at the age of seventeen and was now a veteran of fifteen years and chief petty officer in charge of Kaneohe's munitions. He was in bed with his wife, Alice, when he heard airplanes, saw one out the window, and then heard machine-gun fire. He dressed and drove to the base, at first sticking with the 20 mph limit until "I heard a plane come roaring in from astern of me. As I glanced up, the guy made a wingover, and I saw that big old red meatball, the rising-sun insignia, on the underside of the wing. Well,

I threw it into second, and it's a wonder I didn't run over every sailor in the air station."

Finn immediately saw that someone needed to take charge, and so he did. With no antiaircraft guns, Kaneohe was nearly defenseless, but no one could tell Finn that. When it became clear that the base's planes couldn't be saved, he oversaw taking out the burning aircrafts' .50-caliber machine guns, then ordered metalsmiths to create tripod mounts so the guns could be used to defend the station. He ended up blasting away with a .50-caliber gun on a teaching bench for nearly two hours, trying to take down as many enemy planes as he could: "I was hoppin' mad; I wanted to shoot every damned plane out of the sky. It was so thick in places you could almost walk on it. All our planes were burning. And then this plane comes down and disappears in the smoke. I said to myself, 'When he gets out of that smoke, I'm going to let him have it.' I swung my gun around to the center of that smoke, and that guy came barreling out of it. I was shooting right down and hit the propeller hub. I got off maybe eight rounds. I think he came to get me but his plane slammed into a hillside. . . . I had tons of ammunition, everybody kept bringing me more ammunition to shoot. I could've shot for six months and never reloaded!"

When, at 0830, the second wave of two strikes from nine horizontals and assorted fighters appeared, Finn was caught, exposed, on the parking ramp. "I can still remember walking around that gun cussing everything in the world, kicking and screaming and hollering. I was not the cool, calm, collected hero. I was madder than hell. . . . I got shot in the left arm and shot in the left foot, broke the bone. I had shrapnel blows in my chest and belly and right elbow and right thumb. Some were just scratches. My scalp got cut, and everybody thought I was dying: 'Oh, Christ, the old chief had the top of his head knocked off!' I had twenty-eight, twenty-nine holes in me that were bleeding. I was walking around on one heel. I was barefooted on that coral dust. My left arm didn't work. It was just a big ball hanging down." Even so, John Finn refused to leave his post until given a direct order, then refused anything more in treatment than basic first aid, so that he could oversee rearming crews when the three VP-14 then on patrol returned. "The worst was little tiny pieces in my knuckle joint, elbow here and there. Tiny little things, you couldn't see 'em, and oh my God, did they hurt. But basically . . . it just wasn't my day to die.

"You've got to give those Japs credit. They did a wonderful job militarily. And just 'cause they sneaked in on us . . . I grew up with the idea, I think some old Southern general said, you get there first and you don't tell nobody you're coming!"

Admiral Chester Nimitz would award John Finn the Medal of Honor for his valor at a ceremony aboard the USS *Enterprise*.

Zero Lieutenant Fusata Iida was piling bullets into the naval air station's armory when he saw, from a side door, ordnanceman Sands trying to fight back with a Browning automatic rifle. Running out of ammo, Sands yelled out, "Hand me another BAR! I swear I hit that yellow bastard!" Using the building as a shield—a shield now peppered with Japanese bullets—Sands was able to keep just out of Iida's fire, which enraged the Japanese pilot, who headed straight at the American, determined to kill him. Instead, Sands filled the oncoming Zero with lead, hitting at just the point of weakness in the acclaimed fighter—its gas tank.

From the smell, and from his gauges, Iida knew he was going down. He had lectured his fellow airmen that any plane that failed should be used as a bomb, and now he was going to follow through. He would suicide-crash directly into Sands and the armory.

Pilot Iyozou Fujita: "Lieutenant Iida communicated with hand signs. He pointed to his mouth, which meant fuel, and he pointed down and waved 'Good-bye.' And he did a half roll and went down." But Iida missed the building and smashed into the road. Arthur Price: "We managed to recover some paperwork from his plane. Included was a map. . . . We later learned that it indicated our water tank was a fuel farm. Those pilots had just peppered the hell out of that tank during the attack but couldn't set it on fire."

After the war, Iyozou Fujita would fly for Japan Air Lines, sometimes piloting the popular Tokyo–Honolulu run. He said that coming into Oahu gave him "uneasy memories."

Directly to the southeast of Kaneohe was the Air Corps' Bellows Field, home to the Eighty-Sixth Observation Squadron and, at that moment, hosting the Forty-Fourth Pursuit Squadron for gun class. Around dawn, the sleeping tents were roused by a sergeant yelling that Kaneohe was "blown all to hell." At 0810 a phone call from Hickam said that they "were in flames" and needed a fire truck. But like so many others on December 7, these warnings were ignored.

At 0830, Lieutenant Tadashi Kaneko, having used up his Zero's cannon fire, strafed Bellows's tents with his machine guns. Aerial gunner Private 1st Class Raymond McBriarty saw the strike and saw the Japanese markings on the plane, which started a heated argument among the men. But since no officers gave any orders and no one even pulled the air-raid siren, McBriarty and the others went to church. Then a B-17 from California crash-landed on the runway, plowing into a knoll, followed by nine Japanese planes strafing the base. The air-raid alarm finally sounded and the men scrambled from their tents, looking for shelter. McBriarty and his fellow churchgoers ran from the chapel to their posts.

A group made it to the armament building to load up on Springfield bolts and Browning automatics. They couldn't find the ammo belts for the machine guns, but they did find a gun on a scout plane, as well as two .30-caliber antiaircraft guns on the runway. The army's Pearl Harbor report would judge trying to fight Zeros and Vals with Springfield rifles "ineffective."

Raymond McBriarty and William Burt mounted a gun to the rear cockpit of the squadron commander's O-47 plane. When the strafing Zeros targeted them, they fell to the ground, but when there was a lull, they pulled themselves into the cockpit and fired back 450 rounds. They were awarded Silver Stars.

Due to a series of commands and coincidences, only four officers were at Bellows that morning, and the P-40s that could have been used for counterstrikes were nearly empty on fuel and had most of their guns disassembled for cleaning. But three fighter pilots of the Forty-Fourth and the squadron's ground crew did all they could to refuel and rearm three planes to fight back. At first, when the three wanted to immediately get their P-40 Warhawks into the air, armament officer Lieutenant Phillips ordered that all six .50-caliber guns needed to be loaded before anyone could fly. When nine Zeros flew in and began strafing, the three decided to overturn this decision.

As Second Lieutenant Hans Christensen started to get into the cockpit of his plane, he was hit in the back by a bullet. The wound killed him.

Second Lieutenant George Whiteman ran up to a Warhawk and told the ground crew to get off the wing and stop loading the ammo, so he could fly. He taxied out so fast that the workers couldn't get the cowlings back over the wing guns, and on liftoff, he was spotted by two

Zeros. Whiteman tried evading, but didn't yet have enough speed, and his Warhawk was hit in the engine. It burst into flames.

First Lieutenant Samuel Bishop began to lift off behind Whiteman, and when he saw Whiteman shot down and burning, he became enraged. He tried to shoot down Whitman's attackers, but couldn't outmaneuver the Zeros, which shot him down into the ocean, half a mile off the beach.

"I was in a very excited state of mind when I saw the fighter headed straight onto me," Zero pilot Lieutenant Iyozou Fujita remembered. "I thought I would crash into him. But at the last minute the enemy pulled up to avoid the collision. And then it happened. He had exposed the belly of his plane right in front of me. And I started shooting. And he went down."

With a bullet in his leg, Bishop got out of his plane, inflated his Mae West, and swam home.

Tech Sergeant Henry Anglin was taking pictures of his three-year-old toddler, Hank, at the US Marines' Mooring Mast Field at Ewa, when he heard the "mingled noise of airplanes and machine guns." They went outside, joined by others, all assuming it was an American pilot . . . so much so that, when machine-gun bullets made puffs of dirt in the road, someone said, "Look, live ammunition. Somebody'll go to prison for this."

Diving as low as twenty feet, Akagi's Lieutenant Commander Shigeru Itaya and Kaga's Lieutenant Yoshio Shiga led eighteen Zeros against the base, striking at 0755 with their mix of incendiary, explosive, and armor-piercing rounds . . . first demolishing aircraft, and then killing men.

In all the ruckus, little Hank Anglin had run off. Now the puffs were clearly real. Henry found his son and threw himself over his body to protect him. They crawled together for thirty-five yards, surrounded by strafing fire, back to the photo tent. Henry told his son to hide under a wood bench and got his camera to take pictures. But when he went back outside, he was shot in the arm, and then when he went back in the tent to his boy, Hank pointed out a bullet on the floor next to him and said, "Don't touch that, Daddy. It's hot."

A group of Americans including Corporal Earl Hinz were in camp a half mile from the base when they heard the "Assembly for Colors" call to arms. Hinz had joined the Marine Reserves from Minneapolis and was called to active duty on December 16, 1940, when he was shipped from San Diego to Hawaii aboard *Enterprise* as part of Marine Air Group (MAG) 21, which cleared cane to build Ewa, a base still under construction on December 7. The Mooring Mast name came from an American navy of the 1930s that was busily assembling dirigibles and needed a global network of masts to anchor their great floating airships. Now, Ewa's hundred-foot mast was topped by a flight control tower.

MAG 21's commanding officer, Lieutenant Colonel Claude A. "Sheriff" Larkin, was at home in Honolulu when the attack started. He jumped into his 1930 Plymouth and was pedal to the metal when a Zero strafed him. Larkin pulled over and hid in a ditch until the fighter left; then he got back in the car and made it to Ewa by 0805. While helping defend his base, he was machine-gunned and seriously injured, but refused to leave his post.

Earl Hinz started up the fire truck and drove the crew chief to the operations building next to Ewa's runway, where forty-eight planes were parked. Just as their minds grasped that nearly all of their planes were on fire and beyond what they could save, a Zero shot at them, hitting the rear tires. They stopped and jumped out, hiding under the truck.

Having finished strafing Wheeler, Lieutenant Akira Sakamoto's dive-bombers now joined in the attack. The base ambulance took fifty-two bullets as it tried to help the dying and the injured. After eight strafing runs, nine of Ewa's eleven F4F fighters and eighteen of her thirty-two SBD-1 scout/bombers were destroyed.

Lieutenant Commander Howard "Brigham" Young had been 215 miles west of Oahu when he launched his Douglas Dauntless SBD-3 from the deck of the USS *Enterprise* at dawn. In an hour, a mix of SBD-2s, and -3s from Scouting and Bombing Squadrons Six led by Lieutenant Commander Hallsted Hopping would be surveilling in pairs to the southwest of the Hawaiian archipelago. Instead of returning to the carrier's deck that morning, Halsey had told them to land at the Naval Air Station on Ford Island, refuel, run an afternoon search, and then come home to *Enterprise* for dinner.

Though eventually their pilots would call them "Slow but Deadly," Douglas's SBDs, with a two-man crew that worked in pairs, could scout or dive-bomb, and were the American navy's most significant plane in the opening years of the war. The SBD's radioman/gunner sat in the rear cockpit, where he could swivel his seat 360 degrees to fire his machine gun; the newest SBD-3 was far more capable in a dogfight, with the gunner having twin .30-caliber guns and the pilot, two .50-caliber machine guns in the nose.

Eighteen planes, following Halsey's orders, would now try to land, like those B-17 Flying Fortresses, in the thick of the battle on December 7. Lieutenant Commander Hopping: "When a short distance from Barbers Point, heavy smoke was visible. At this time a report was heard over the radio: 'Do not attack me. This is six baker three an American plane,' and the same voice continued on telling his gunner to break out the boat as he was landing in the water.

The voice on the radio was *Enterprise*'s Bombing Squadron Six Ensign Manuel Gonzalez; flying five hundred yards to his right and another five hundred over his head was Ensign Frederick Weber. Around twenty-five miles before reaching the shores of Oahu, Weber had noticed a strange bunch of planes "milling around" at three to four thousand feet. He assumed they were American Army Air Corps—they were in fact first-wave dive-bombers on their way back to Nagumo's ships—when suddenly he realized that Gonzalez was missing. Weber circled in a roll and made four or five turns trying to spot his friend and finally saw another plane on the same course. He assumed this must be Gonzalez and tried to catch up, but at two thousand yards the other pilot pulled a 180, so Weber slid to turn as well, to follow the leader. Then suddenly the other plane spilled forward, the American pilot saw its meatballs, cracked his throttle full open, reversed into a diving turn, then an inverted dive, to evade, leveling off a mere twenty-five feet over the ocean.

Arriving halfway between Ewa and Ford Island, Brigham Young saw bursts of antiaircraft fire directly in front of him, and then was immediately attacked from the rear by "low-wing monoplane fighters with retractable landing gear." He dove to the ground in a zigzag to escape fire. Directly behind Young was Perry Teaff, whose own Dauntless got shot up, but as neither Teaff nor his gunner Jinks were injured, they continued to follow Young. As he skimmed over the cane field north of Pearl City and its algaroba trees with their three-inch spikes, Young realized they were also getting shot at by American antiaircraft defenses. He tried to radio Ford Island's control tower to establish their planes as friendly, but in the chaos he couldn't communicate with Ford.

Hopping radioed his fellow SBDs that Oahu was under attack, but almost no one heard his call. He rolled into an escape dive and set down at Ford, alive and well even though he was engulfed by American bullets all the way in.

One pilot who could hear Gonzalez's plea was Ensign Edward Deacon, flying in with Ensign William Roberts. They had arrived at 0833 over Barbers Point, and on hearing Gonzalez, each climbed to a thousand feet. Now Ford Island couldn't even be seen because of all the smoke from the fires at Ewa, so they headed elsewhere, only to find twenty enemy dive-bombers directly in their flight path. Deacon and Roberts then dove to land at Hickam, where American soldiers on the ground barraged them with .50-caliber and 20 mm gunfire. Both planes were hit. Roberts was able to land but Deacon's motor started to sputter, and his lift to stall out. He was at two hundred feet, too low for a chute, and he decided to try to land in the ocean. Deacon brought her in just fine; he and his radioman/gunner 3rd class, Audrey "Jerry" Coslett, were both amazed to have survived. Then someone on the beach two hundred yards off started firing at them, hitting Deacon in the thigh and Coslett in the wrist and in the neck. Deacon got out of the life raft and paddled them both to a boat in the channel, which took them to Hickam, and then an ambulance carried them to the hospital.

Ewa's commander, Claude Larkin, saw a midair collision of Ensign John Vogt's SBD with a Japanese bomber. Vogt, with his radioman/gunner 3rd class, Sidney Pierce, were able to bail out, but at too low an altitude. Falling, they crashed into trees and were killed.

Lieutenant Clarence Dickinson radioed Ensign John McCarthy to join him in a climb to four thousand feet and assumed that they were safe, but instead they were "very shortly attacked by two Japanese fighters as we headed towards Pearl Harbor." When McCarthy tried to maneuver so as to get a better line of sight to take down the Zeros, they strafed him raw, igniting his engine and main tank. Dickinson saw him drop and try to recover, then fall, crashing into the ground.

Then, a parachute appeared. McCarthy had a broken leg, but had survived. Radioman/Gunner 3rd Class Mitchell Cohn went down with the plane, however, and did not live; he would be one of many Pearl Harbor casualties buried in the Punchbowl as "unknowns." Two others whose fates are still unknown were Ensign Walter Willis with Coxswain Fred Ducolon, whose SBD vanished on the approach to Luke Field.

Dickinson and Radioman/Gunner 1st Class William Miller, mean-

while, now came under fire from four or five warplanes simultaneously, one a mere hundred feet off. Miller said that he was hit and "I
think it was just as the wing caught fire." Dickinson asked, "Are you all
right, Miller?" He said, "Mr. Dickinson, I've expended all six cans of
ammunition." Then Dickinson heard Miller scream "as if he opened
his lungs and just let go. I have never heard any comparable human
sound. It was a yell of agony. I believe Miller died right then. When I
called again there was no reply."

Their left fuel tank was on fire, and their Dauntless was out of control. Dickinson ordered Miller to bail. The radioman didn't answer.
The SBD went into a spin. Dickinson bailed, falling to the ground
with the spit of luck that the Japanese weren't able to fire on him or
his chute nor did the marines at Ewa open fire. He landed on the soft,
recently graded dirt of a road under construction and hitched a ride
back to base with a couple out for a Sunday picnic.

When Clarence Dickinson later told his story, he began to sob. Just
before they had taken off from *Enterprise*, William Miller had said,
"Mr. Dickinson, my four years' tour of sea duty ends in a few days
and there's a funny thing about it." "What's that, Miller?" "Out of
twenty-one of us that went through radio school together, I'm the
only one who hasn't crashed in the water. Hope you don't get me wet
today, sir."

Scouting just to the south of Dickinson and McCarthy were Lieutenant (jg) Hart Hilton with Radioman/Gunner 2nd Class Jack Leaming. When Leaming heard, *"Don't shoot! This is an American plane!"* and
then "Get out the rubber boat, we're goin' in!" he was shocked, thinking, "What the hell is wrong with that crazy SOB? He's breaking radio
silence! He had forgotten to keep his transmitter switch off! What was
wrong?" Naval aviators were trained to keep quiet on the radio and, if
they had to, pulled close enough to see each other and, patting their
heads with the palm for a dash and a closed fist for the dot, used Morse
code to communicate. Then Leaming smelled gunpowder. They were
arriving at Pearl Harbor, now engulfed in two columns of smoke.

Seven *Enterprise* planes were still in the air and approaching the
island at about four hundred feet when they noticed, at four thousand
feet, enemy fighters. But these did not attack. Knowing how unfair
a fight between their Dauntlesses and a Zero would be, the Americans didn't start anything. So, they circled. Finally there was a lull at
around 0845. Deciding Ford was too risky, they landed back to back

at Ewa, only to be told by the marines there that, since the Japanese had destroyed nearly all of Ewa's own planes, the SBDs should get out while they could. All seven took off, heading again for Ford.

Coming over the channel, a US destroyer hit them with her 1.1-inch, .50-caliber, and .30-caliber guns. Enraged by this friendly fire, Jack Leaming grabbed his Aldis lamp and used its pistol grip to flash Morse code to the destroyer. Hilton rolled bank right so its bridge could see the American stars on his wings and headed in. Finally he decided to forget Pearl Harbor; they were going back to Ewa. Four others followed him, and all landed just fine.

After an hour and forty-five minutes, General Short's Hawaiian Department had lost 163 killed, 336 wounded, and 43 missing. Of 231 aircraft, 64 were destroyed, 93 were irrevocably damaged, and 74 were fixable. Of Halsey's *Enterprise* air crews, six of eighteen planes were lost, with eight men dead and two wounded.

As it turned out, rough weather and mechanical troubles delayed *Enterprise*'s own return to Pearl Harbor by a day, to December 8. Marine Ernest Phillips was part of Halsey's Task Force Two, serving on *Northampton*:

"We'd been practicing towing a carrier when a line snapped and became wrapped around the propeller shaft. We had to send divers over the side to unravel the mess. It was then too late to enter Pearl Harbor. They had submarine netting in place and a dispatch that said, 'Delay entering Pearl until 10 a.m., December 7.'

"Some of the destroyers kept making submarine contacts. According to the dispatches, they said, 'You are in error. We do not have any submarines in the area. Please instruct your operators on the proper use of equipment,' or words to that effect. The admiral was very put out they were making the contacts where they shouldn't be.

"Right around eight o'clock we were called to general quarters. We were told the Japanese were attacking Pearl Harbor. Of course we had been doing these exercises before and assumed this was just another drill.

"We were not spotted by the Japanese. We weren't that close in. We could see the smoke but couldn't see the harbor. We turned the ship in the other direction. Occasionally we could see a plane shot down and we cheered. We later learned that many of those were our own planes taking off from Hickam Field."

CHAPTER SEVEN

PEARL HARBOR

Nestled in the center of Oahu's south coast is the inlet of Pearl Harbor with Ford Island at her heart. The navy's carrier planes and seaplanes were housed at hangars, aprons, and airfields, while her carriers anchored to the island's northwest, and battleships lay to its southeast. December 7, 1941, counted ninety-six ships, including cruisers *Detroit*, *Baltimore*, and *Raleigh*; seaplane and aircraft tenders *Tangier*, *Swan*, and *Curtiss*; repair ships; minelayers; leftovers from Teddy Roosevelt's Great White Fleet good only for target practice; and the queens of Pearl, the mighty tenants of Battleship Row: *Pennsylvania*, *Nevada*, *Arizona*, *Tennessee*, *West Virginia*, *Maryland*, *Oklahoma*, and *California*.

The first light of a Sunday morning started with the loading of perishables—USS *Chew* received ten gallons of milk; the *Conyngham*, six gallons of ice cream; the *Maryland* hauled in two thousand pounds of ice. Along with Pearl City, the harbor was home to forty thousand soldiers and sailors on December 7; most were looking forward to a relaxing day far from chores and commanders. Many sat around in their cabins, in pajamas, robes, or kimonos, just starting the Sunday comics. A number were sleeping off a Saturday-night tour of Honolulu's red-light Hotel Row. Signalman John Blanken on *San Francisco* planned on swimming at Waikiki; Ensign Thomas Taylor, on *Nevada*, had a tennis game scheduled; the marines of *Helena* were going to play softball; a group of old navy hands on *St. Louis* were looking forward to a round of checkers. Yeoman Durrell Conner spent his morning on *California* wrapping Christmas presents; there were, after all, only seventeen shopping days left.

• • •

Flying toward the harbor, Lieutenant Commander Shigeharu Murata ordered his torpedomen to assume attack formation at 0751. Just northwest of Ewa, they split in half, with two groups of eight planes each descending to Pearl Harbor from the west and two groups of twelve planes each flying southeast in an arc over Hickam to attack Ford Island from the east. "A faint haze of kitchen smoke from houses preparing breakfast hung over the water," pilot Zenji Abe remembered. "It was a peaceful scene. Fuchida was observing through his field glasses, and as the wave drew nearer, the basket [crow's nest] and tripod masts of the battleships *Nevada*, *Arizona*, *Tennessee*, *West Virginia*, *Oklahoma*, *California*, and *Maryland* appeared through the haze."

Worried that smoke from the dive-bombing attacks on Hickam and Wheeler might prevent his men from hitting their targets, at 0757 Murata ordered his crews to as quickly as possible drop their torpedoes against the dreadnoughts anchored east of Ford Island. In formations of twos and threes, *Akagi*, *Kaga*, *Soryu*, and *Hiryu* airmen descended to the attack altitude of fifty feet, preparing, as instructed, to risk their lives closing in on their targets. The dive-bombers and torpedo planes flew so low that it often looked as if they were about to crash into the American ships' superstructures.

Raleigh Ensign Donald Korn saw a line of planes coming in from the northwest. *Arizona* Seaman "Red" Pressler noticed another string, coming over the mountains to the east. Helm Quartermaster Frank Handler saw a group coming in from due south, flying directly into the harbor's entrance and coming up the channel known as Southeast Loch, only a hundred yards from where he stood. One of the pilots gave Frank a wave, and he cheerfully waved back. *Helena* Signalman Charles Flood thought their approach was strange, but it reminded him of something. He'd been in Shanghai in 1932 when the Japanese had invaded. Their planes had dived and glided in this exact same manner.

"It must've been about seven forty-five, seven fifty, we saw a bunch of airplanes coming in, but they were coming in from all over the place," *West Virginia* marine bugler Richard Fiske said. "So we thought this was going to be a regular drill like we normally had. And nobody got too excited about it until we saw these planes start forming around. The torpedo planes went around the mountain, and they were coming right down the channel there, and they were aiming right for the battleships."

At 0755, the Ford Island Navy Yard's signal tower atop the water tank raised a blue flag meaning "prepare," and the men assigned to each ship's morning colors took their places, fore with the navy's jack flag—the USN's first official jack had as its insignia a rattlesnake and the legend DON'T TREAD ON ME—and aft with the Stars and Stripes. At 0800, the blue flag fell, and the two flags rose to the sound of a boatswain's whistle, or a bugler's colors, or a band of horns and woods playing the national anthem.

Even after a Japanese plane screamed above their heads to drop a torpedo against *Arizona*, the USS *Nevada*'s brass band continued playing to the very last note of "The Star-Spangled Banner." After its sole torpedo missed, the Japanese returned to strafe the band, tattering its flag. One sailor on *Arizona* watching the whole thing smiled in appreciation, telling his friends that surely "This is the best goddamn drill the Army Air Force has ever put on."

Aviation Metalsmith 2nd Class Adolph Kuhn had spent the night playing poker and drinking with some friends and his cousin Andy Herrman at their barracks in the cane fields just outside the Pearl Harbor gates. Andy and Adolph woke up to bullets whizzing through their roof and assumed it was just another daredevil pilot from Hickam. They started playing poker again. Andy said, "Adolph, I wonder what it would be like to be in a real war." Another strafer came by, some of his bullets hitting their score pad.

Ford Island's Bloch Recreation Center, which had hosted "The Battle of the Bands" on Saturday night, was the site of a Catholic mass at 0800. Those waiting outside for the service to begin heard a popping sound, then watched planes flying a bare two dozen feet over their heads. For some reason, a sailor, and then a woman, fell to the ground, bleeding and screaming in pain. While some ran to hide, others ran to help. Ripping a strip from the woman's petticoat to make a tourniquet, Pharmacist Mate 3rd Class Joseph Honish stanched her leg wound and got a man with a car to take her to the Naval Hospital.

Ford Island not only housed airstrips and command centers, but also neighborhoods of officers' wives and kids. At naval housing next to Bloch Recreation, the family of Lieutenant Robert Littmann, the communications officer for minelayer *Oglala*, was getting ready to attend services downtown at Honolulu Cathedral. They heard a big blast. A sixteen-year-old cousin went out to see what had happened. A plane went right over his head, and he knew what its red circles meant;

he ran inside to tell everyone. Littmann's thirteen-year-old daughter, Peggy, then went out to see the excitement for herself. Another big plane went right over her, and a piece of metal fell out of the sky, and landed a few feet away. She ran inside to find her mother and her aunt on their knees, saying the rosary: "Hail Mary, full of grace, blessed be thy name and blessed is the fruit of thy womb, Jesus. Holy Mary, mother of God, pray for us sinners, now, and at the hour of our death . . ."

Patrol Wing 2 commander Rear Admiral Patrick Bellinger—of the Martin-Bellinger Report warning of a aerial attack on Hawaii, and the winner of the Navy Cross in 1919 for his epic transatlantic crossing from Newfoundland to the Azores—had a thirteen-year-old daughter, Patricia. She had arrived in Hawaii the year before, thrilled to have elaborate flower leis draped over her neck as she walked down the plank of the luxury liner *Lurline*. Living on Ford Island was so isolated, but Patricia quickly made friends, such as Joan and Peggy Zuber, whose dad, Adolph, commanded the marine barracks (and whose mother, Alice, didn't think Hawaii was a safe place to raise a family), and sixteen-year-old Mary Ann Ramsey, whose father, Lieutenant Commander Logan Ramsey, worked as Bellinger's operations officer. The Ramsey house was so close to the *Arizona* that when the battleship projected movies on her deck, Mary Ann could sit in her front yard and follow along to the dialogue and music. The house's other unusual feature was that it was built over a Great War gun battery, which had been turned into a garage, next to which was a cave that had once been a military dungeon, which the little girls thought spooky, and fun. In the spring of 1941, when the island began running air-raid drills every week, their neighborhood's assigned shelter was the cave dungeon. The Zuber girls thought that if an attack came and they were forced to live there, it would be good idea to have fudge and lemonade.

Mary Ann Ramsey: "On Saturday night, 6 December, we had dinner guests. As our friends were leaving, Dad called out, 'Well, let's hope the Japs wait until after Christmas before they start raising hell in the Pacific.'" Miriam Bellinger and her daughters had spent that day at the circus in Honolulu. Coming home to Ford and passing the fleet, Miriam said, "Isn't it beautiful? There are so many ships in the harbor."

On Sunday morning, Mary Ann woke to a ringing phone. Her father answered and in a shocked voice asked, "Are you sure?" Mary Ann Ramsey: "Within a few minutes, I caught just a glimpse of Dad, dressed in an aloha shirt and slacks, rushing past my bedroom door. He was gone from our carport before I could reach my parents' room, where I found Mother sitting up in bed, confused. Incredulous, she told me a submarine had been sunk just outside the harbor net, and before she had finished speaking, the first bomb fell. We looked at each other in disbelief."

Lieutenant Commander Logan Ramsey: "Approximately five or ten minutes after I reached the Command Center, I saw, together with the staff duty officer, a single plane making a dive on Ford Island. The single plane appeared at the time to both the staff duty officer and myself in the light of a young aviator 'flathatting' [flying low in a reckless manner], and we both tried to get his number to make a report of the violation of flight rules. He completed his dive, pulled up and away. We were commenting together on the fact that it was going to be difficult to find out who the pilot was when the delayed-action bomb which he had dropped, and which we had not seen drop, detonated, and I told the staff duty officer, 'Never mind; it's a Jap.'

"I dashed across the hall into the radio room, ordered a broadcast in plain English on all frequencies, 'Air Raid, Pearl Harbor. This is No Drill.'" Sent out under the name of his commander at Patrol Wing 2, Rear Admiral Patrick Bellinger, some of Ramsey's radiogram versions were famously printed as "This is Not Drill," perhaps from a transcription or Morse code error.

The Zuber family was making pork roast for Sunday lunch when Joan saw a rising column of smoke outside. She told her mother, "Look out the window! Please look out the window!" Adolph ordered his wife and daughters to get to the shelter as quickly as they could. As Alice in her nightgown ran down the street with Joan and Peggy in their bathrobes, a Japanese airman fired his machine guns at them. "They're strafing us!" Alice screamed, and tried using her arms to shield her daughters. A man gestured to the loading dock by the bachelor officers' quarters and yelled at them to get inside. They hid under tables and behind the kitchen sink. A huge blast shook the whole building. Alice began to pray silently, *Dear God, please let my children die instead of being maimed*. Then she told her frightened daughters, "Don't cry. Marines don't cry. Don't ruin the morale of the men." Finally, a man herded them into a truck and drove them to the safety of the dungeon cave.

Military families in the Pacific were well aware of the Imperial Japanese Army's reputation for raping and murdering women and children. Before medical officer Lieutenant Commander Cecil Riggs sent his wife and German shepherd, Chief, to the cave, he gave her a pistol and said that, faced with any Japanese soldiers, she needed to shoot the dog first and then herself. One military wife told the marine guarding the dungeon that he needed to save some bullets so that "when I am sure my children are dead, then you will shoot me."

Twelve-year-old Thompson Izawa had biked with his dad that morning to Pearl Harbor where the two were fishing, using tiny shrimp as bait, right next to the USS *Utah*. "It sounded like the hum of bees swarming," Thompson said. "Hundreds of airplanes were speeding toward us. They came over the Waianae Range like bees and all hell broke loose. At first, I thought they were making a movie. We saw a torpedo bomber come right overhead—with a long torpedo. I wish I had a machine gun—I could have shot some of those planes down—seriously! They were so low, especially the torpedo bombers. As my dad and I sat there, we heard a high-pitched whistle and then saw the torpedo that slid through the water and blew up the battleship *Utah*. Not one American gun fired back.

"My dad grabbed me by my earlobe. 'Get home, boy. We are in big trouble—those are Japanese airplanes!' I wanted to stay and see the action, but my father took off pedaling for home."

"When I looked up in the sky, I saw five or six planes starting their descent," *Utah* Pharmacist's Mate 2nd Class Lee Soucy remembered. "Then when the first bombs dropped on the hangars at Ford Island, I thought, 'Those guys are missing us by a mile.' It occurred to me and to most of the others that someone had really goofed this time and put live bombs on those planes by mistake. In any event, even after I saw a huge fireball and cloud of black smoke rise from the hangars on Ford Island and heard explosions, it did not occur to me that these were enemy planes. It was too incredible! Simply beyond imagination! 'What a snafu,' I moaned."

The torpedoes were carried naked below the plane's fuselage. Their clamps released, they crashed into the water and began to run, their wooden fins jerking away and left behind, the froth of their wakes visible to those about to die. As some ships exploded from torpedoes below, others were set ablaze by machine-gun fire from above, the bullets' trails bursts of color from arcing tracers.

"The torpedo bombers released their torpedoes, which splashed into the water," Zero pilot Yoshio Shiga wrote. "The bombers were like dragonflies skimming over the surface of the water. When I saw all this, I knew the attack was going to be successful." The blurred white splashes of torpedoes hitting the bay, followed by the flurried wakes of their runs, soon filled Pearl Harbor. "It was lovely," pilot Tatsuya Otawa said. "We were about to change an island of dreams into a living hell."

Squadron leader Lieutenant Heita Matsumura had specifically ordered the men of his torpedo squadron not to waste their ordnance on the old battleship *Utah*, which was sitting in a berth usually taken by an aircraft carrier. *Utah* had been pulled from service and was now used for target practice, her decks shielded in timber to deflect Betty Crocker practice bombs made of flour.

But excited young Japanese airmen on that morning ended up torpedoing everything in their path, perhaps mistaking *Utah* for a prize due to her location and to what looked like a teak deck. "The *Enterprise* was slated to tie up next to the *Utah*," *Northampton* marine Ernest Phillips explained. "That's why the Japanese threw twenty-seven torpedoes into the *Utah*. Their information said that the *Enterprise* would be tied right beside it. Apparently their information was pretty good, but it just wasn't current enough."

In a bare four minutes, *Utah* was listing forty degrees. The crew struggled to save her, and each other. They had nothing to fight back with since, as a radio-controlled target ship, *Utah*'s AA guns were covered in housing, and her machine guns were dismantled.

Can there be a more ignominious death for a sailor than to be bombed and torpedoed while in port? When you are supposed to defend, but instead are defenseless? Carl Johnson decided he could at least dog down the bilge manhole cover and was going to do that when the second strike threw him onto *Utah*'s deck. The crash broke sixteen of Johnson's teeth, but he was in such shock that he felt nothing and continued heading toward the bilge. A voice over his head asked, "Where you going?" When Johnson tried to explain about the bilges, the man above said, "Don't go down there. You will be killed!" This snapped Johnson out of his shock and saved his life.

Mess Attendant 2nd Class Clark Simmons: "Things were breaking loose. Furniture was sliding around. We heard the bugler blow the call for 'Abandon ship.' The ship was beginning to list when I was in the captain's cabin with two officers. We felt the ship lifting and beginning to roll over. We had picked up life jackets, but we didn't put them on. So, we could squeeze through a porthole about eighteen inches in diameter and jump into the water.

"We all were frightened. We didn't know what was going on, but we knew the ship was taking water and there was no way to close the watertight doors. And we knew it was just a matter of time before the ship was going to sink.

"In eight minutes [at 0812] the ship was history. She had turned turtle in eight minutes.

"We began to swim toward Ford Island. They were machine-gunning us from two directions. I saw fellows yelling and screaming. I really didn't know what was going on. I got hit in the head, a shoulder, and a leg. But I got to shore, and a navy medical corpsman gave me first aid. Every year, December seventh feels like my birthday. I feel like I was reborn on that day, because it was such a miracle I wasn't killed."

Lee Soucy: "After a minute or two below the armored deck, we heard another bugle call, then the bosun's whistle followed by the boatswain's chant, 'Abandon ship. . . . Abandon ship.' We scampered up the ladder. As I raced toward the open side of the deck, an officer stood by a stack of life preservers and tossed the jackets at us as we ran by. When I reached the open deck, the ship was listing precipitously. I thought about the huge amount of ammunition we had on board and that it would surely blow up soon. I wanted to get away from the ship fast, so I discarded my life jacket. I didn't want a Mae West slowing me down.

"I was tensely poised for a running dive off the partially exposed hull when the ship lunged again and threw me off-balance. I ended up with my bottom sliding across and down the barnacle-encrusted bottom of the ship. After I bobbed up to the surface of the water to get my bearings, I spotted a motor launch with a coxswain fishing men out of the water with his boat hook. I started to swim toward the launch. After a few strokes, a hail of bullets hit the water a few feet in front of me in line with the launch. As the strafer banked, I noticed the big red insignias on his wingtips. Until then, I really had not known who attacked us. At some point, I had heard someone shout, 'Where did those Germans come from?' I quickly decided that a boat full of men would be a more likely strafing target than a lone swimmer, so I changed course and hightailed it for Ford Island.

"I reached the beach exhausted, and as I tried to catch my breath, another pharmacist's mate, Gordon Sumner, from the *Utah*, stumbled out of the water. I remember how elated I was to see him. There is no doubt in my mind that bewilderment, if not misery, loves company."

Though he knew the ship was capsizing, Chief Watertender Peter Tomich, a Slavic immigrant, stayed below, making sure the boilers were secure and that all of his crew had evacuated. Finally, it was Tomich's turn to leave. It was too late. He was trapped. Peter Tomich was posthumously awarded the Medal of Honor and joined at least fifty-three other men, either trapped in the overturn like Tomich or strafed by Japanese machine guns, who died on *Utah*.

Having gone to bed at eleven the night before, General Walter Short and his wife were eating breakfast and reading the Sunday newspaper that morning with nothing more on the calendar that day than the general's twice-a-month golf game with Admiral Husband Kimmel. Hearing the roar of propeller planes and rocketing explosions—the sound of torpedo strikes against *Utah* and *Helena*—Short strolled to his back porch for a look. He then ran as fast as possible to his office. Even so, he couldn't see the explosions, only the rising pillars of smoke. One of the first men he found on the base was intelligence officer Lieutenant Colonel George Bicknell. Short asked, "What's going on out there?"

"I'm not sure, General," Bicknell said, "but I just saw two battleships sunk."

"That's ridiculous!" Short erupted.

At about 0803, after chief of staff Colonel Walter Phillips told Short "that it was the real thing," Short "immediately told him to put into effect Alert No. 3. That's all the order we needed. And by 8:10 that had been given." His troops were now to switch from defending against saboteurs to defending against an armed invasion. His Alert No. 1 had been so directed at the enemy from within that it handicapped his army in fighting the enemy from without. Alert No. 3 also meant that Short and his command staff evacuated to the army's underground post at Aliamanu Crater.

Axis spy Takeo Yoshikawa was having breakfast when the first bombs fell. He and Kita rushed to the consulate to destroy their codebooks and classified documents. The spy remembered smoke "pouring out of the chimney."

A mere five hundred yards away from Robert Littmann's *Oglala*, Third Torpedo Attack Unit commander Lieutenant Takashi Nagai released a torpedo. *Oglala*'s crew watched its wake as the missile charged straight at them. Then, as they all expected to die, nothing happened. The torpedo had plummeted under *Oglala*'s fifteen-and-a-half-foot draft to hit her moored neighbor, *Helena*. *Helena* exploded on her starboard in a blast so strong it blew out some of *Oglala*'s plates. Nagai rose over the two ships' superstructures so his rear gunner could strafe the decks with his machine gun. "The plane's canopy was open, and the pilot was hanging his head over the side to look at us," *Oglala*'s Robert Hudson said. "On his approach, we saw red flashes from his wings. I thought that it was a drill and that the flashes were from a camera taking pictures of the harbor. When the bullets started ricocheting off the bulkhead around us, I knew the plane was not there to take our picture. Looking out from the steel sheets after the plane had passed, I saw a man dressed only in tennis shorts come running down the dock, yelling for volunteers to man a destroyer. He had a tennis racket in his hand, so I assumed he was a junior officer. It was truly a nightmare to see shipmates from both the *Oglala* and *Helena*, in anger and frustration, throwing potatoes and wrenches at low-flying planes." One master sergeant was seen following the Zeros on his bicycle, shooting at them with a pistol.

Robert Littmann had thrown on his uniform and raced to his ship. On the same road to Pearl Harbor, *Arizona*'s Ensign Malcolm was driving hell for leather with Captain D. C. Emerson. When the speedometer hit eighty, the captain calmly said, "Slow down, kid; let's wait'll we get to Pearl to be killed."

By the time Littmann reached her, *Oglala* was already capsized, dead in the water, but at least none of her men were lost. His wife and daughter watched the horror from their living-room window. Thirteen-year-old Peggy Littmann would forever remember the bodies flying. They reminded *Helena*'s Ensign David King of the circus, when cannons shot clowns through the air. This time was different, he thought; no one would land, happily, in a safety net.

Even after taking a torpedo hit and losing all of her power, the first American ship to fire back against the Japanese was *Helena*. Below-decks, Warren Thompson found himself in shock and flailing about in the pitch black. Suddenly a light came straight at him; it was three men, with their hair on fire. The emergency bought Thompson back to the present, and he quickly found a blanket and used it to smother their flames.

By 0755, the .30- and .50-caliber machine guns of USS *Tautog* and *Hulbert*, moored at the island's submarine base, were firing even though *Tautog*, having just returned from a forty-five-day patrol, had only a quarter of her crew aboard. Within three minutes, an aircraft estimated to be 150 feet to the stern of *Tautog* exploded in flames, and later in the attack the subs' guns brought down at least one more enemy plane.

USS *Breese*'s Horace Warden: "The plane we had shot down landed right near us in the water. The pilot was still alive, so they got a whale-boat to go rescue him. Apparently he made a move, put his hand under his vest or something, and so they killed him and then didn't have a live pilot to question. The sailor who shot him was told that he was going to get court-martialed. But later that all was quashed and there was no court-martial."

Oiler *Ramapo* was in the middle of ferrying brand-new PT boats to the Philippines. Ensign Niles Ball gave orders to fight back by running the air compressors, firing up the power of their .50-caliber machine-gun turrets. *PT-26*, sitting on the dock waiting to be raised aloft onto the tanker, was empty on gas for her compressors. So that crew yanked off the hoses, and one man pushed the turret while another triggered the guns. One of the grand old men of the navy, Commander Duncan Curry, stood on the *Ramapo* bridge, firing away at enemy planes with a .45, sobbing uncontrollably.

A Japanese high-altitude bomb fell to the south end of Ford Island, missing its target, the concussion making Lieutenant (jg) Howell M. Forgy, chaplain of heavy cruiser *New Orleans*, imagine a tug was nudging his ship. *New Orleans* was having her engine fixed, and Forgy, a hearty six-foot-two athlete from Philadelphia, was still in his bunk, contemplating the sermon he was to deliver at church that morning. Next Forgy heard something that sounded like a kid "running a stick along one of those white picket fences back home." This was followed by the shriek of the bosun's pipe and the uproarious clang of the ship's general alarm. The chaplain "wondered why the officer of the deck could never get it through his head the fact that the general alarm was not to be tested on Sundays," and when he next heard, "All hands to battle stations! All hands to battle stations! This is no drill! This is no drill," he thought it "must be some admiral's clever idea of how to make an off-hour general quarters drill for the fleet realistic."

Edward Sowman explained that both *New Orleans* "and her sister ship the USS *San Francisco* were tied up across the dock from each other in the navy shipyard when the Japanese made their first attack. Both cruisers were undergoing machinery repairs and were taking all utilities from the dock, which included water, air, electricity, etc. Our antiaircraft battery had begun firing immediately after being manned, but suddenly all power from the dock was cut off and the gunners had to go to local control. This meant they would aim and fire from the mount itself without any additional assistance. At the same time it meant that the ammunition hoist would not operate, and on-deck ammunition was in limited supply." Between a gunner's mate shouting, "Get those goddamn lines down the hatch to the magazine!"—and Lieutenant Edwin Woodhead ordering the men, "Get over by that ammunition hoist, grab those five-inch shells [each weighed just under a hundred pounds], and get them to the guns!"—the cruiser's men formed into ammo trains to hoist shells from their magazine storage belowdecks through their handling quarters to their batteries above. While one faction of gunners raised and lowered the guns with hand cranks to follow a target, another loaded, fired, and cleared them by hand, both groups having to dodge strafer fire and shrapnel.

Chaplain Forgy's battle station was sick bay, which meant he had to force his way down the ladders against a tide of marines rushing up to the deck to their eight .50-caliber machine guns and their nine eight-inch and eight five-inch antiaircraft batteries. He saw a "tiny Filipino messboy, who weighed little more than a shell, hoist it to his shoulder, stagger a few steps, and grunt as he started the long, tortuous trip up two flights of ladders to the quarterdeck." Forgy wanted to help defend the ship, but as he explained, "A chaplain cannot fire a gun or take material part in a battle," so the man of God would instead become an epochal figure in Pearl Harbor history. Lieutenant Woodhead: "I heard a voice behind me saying, 'Praise the Lord and pass the ammunition.' I turned and saw Chaplain Forgy walking toward me along the line of men. He was patting the men on the back and making that remark to cheer them and keep them going. I know it helped me a lot, too." In 1942, this memory would inspire Frank Loesser to write "Praise the Lord and Pass the Ammunition," one of the great anthems that inspired Americans to win the war.

USS *Argonne* crewman Charles Christensen: "I was in my Skivvies— that's sailor slang for underwear—and putting on my white uniform. Next to my bunk was a small suitcase that I kept my roller skates in. Friends had introduced me to a young Japanese woman the night before. She said she liked roller-skating, so we made a date to go skating. I was supposed to meet her at nine Sunday morning. An explosion slightly shook the ship and I thought, 'Oh! That was a bad explosion!' I wondered what had happened. And I opened my porthole and stuck my head out. And, oh, boy, was there ever a fire on Ford Island! I thought, 'Wow! I'd better go take a look.' . . .

"Shrapnel was just bouncing all over. . . . I tried to pick up a piece. It was still hot! I dropped it. The only time I got scared was when a high-altitude bomber came over and dropped a bomb. When you look up, you don't know that the bomb is traveling the same speed as the plane, and you think it's coming straight down. And I thought my time had come, right then. But where are you going to run? You just have to stand there and watch it. And it misses.

"I just couldn't believe all of this was happening in this short length of time. With all of these planes coming in, it looked like bees coming back to the hive. There were so many of them in there at one time it was amazing that they didn't collide."

In all the horror, there were some remarkable moments. "We had a first-class electrician's mate on the *Worden* named Charles Ross, from Baltimore," John Beasley said. "While in East Asia, Charley had been living with a Japanese girl he called Peachy. Peachy had a brother in the Japanese naval air force. During the Pearl attack, whenever a Japanese plane would come very close, Charley would point at it and say, 'Don't shoot that one down—he might be my brother-in-law!' "

One example of Kimmel's command failure in the face of the November 27 war warning was that on nearly every ship in the harbor, only one boiler was kept lit, which meant a strike in the right compartment would destroy electrical power and, in turn, firepower. The thousands of man-hours of drilling at sea, with war games and task forces and gunnery and zigzag and the insistence of the navy for bigger guns and bigger battleships—all of that, in this moment, meant nothing. The most helpless of Pearl Harbor's ships were those in dry dock. Not only could they not move, but various of their power systems were shut down, meaning nearly the whole of their defenses were out of commission.

In Dry Dock One lay flagship *Pennsylvania* and two destroyers, *Cassin* and *Downes*. *Downes* took three bombs to the aft; *Cassin*, two to her stern and two at her superstructure; and *Pennsylvania*'s hull was collateral-damaged by one of the hits on *Cassin*. Then at 0906, a bomb crashed through *Pennsylvania*'s deck, killing twenty-eight men. Medical Corpsman Hank Lachenmayer: "The events about to be related here are still somewhat vague. Perhaps due to the fact that one could and would not imagine them in one's most horrid and imaginative nightmares.

"We, the band on the *Pennsylvania*, proceeded to the quarterdeck in preparation for morning colors. At exactly three minutes of eight, looking over toward the naval air station on Ford Island, we could see a group of planes proceeding gently from a high altitude and then leveling off about 150 feet from the ground.

"A plane that looked half like a Stuka and half like one of our own dive-bombers was just leveling off, and I could see the bombs dropping out of its bottom. It was a silver-gray plane with a reddish gold ball or sun painted on its side. I still don't know how I got my instrument in my case and back to the shelf in the band room, but I must have made Superman's speed look amateurish. By this time all hands were manning their battle stations, and I proceeded towards mine, stopping on the way to get my gas mask.

"A fire had broken out on the second deck and had to be attended to with haste. The fire was precipitated by the bursting of a five-hundred-pound bomb in the casemate [a warship's armored chamber for guns] and the main deck. The havoc created by this one bomb hit can never be exaggerated. The one bomb hit pierced the boat deck abreast of No. 7 AA gun and tore through the No. 9 casemate and down to the main deck. All this area exploded with vigor. The marine division suffered the severest losses. First Lieutenant Craig, standing near the three-inch gun, had both legs blown off and received other injuries; he died almost on the spot. Dr. Rall, a lieutenant junior grade, and a pharmacist's mate were mangled and killed instantly.

"I wandered around the dressing station, my eyes not believing what they saw. I gave a drink here and loosened an article of clothing there; there was not much else I could do. Many were badly burned and screamed for relief of pain; they had already received drug injections, and a glass of water to the lips was in many cases the only human assistance possible. Later in the day I assisted in taking the dead off the ship and in bringing on board many rounds of ammunition."

There was no water pressure to fight the fires that erupted everywhere, but *Pennsylvania* quickly got her foremast AA machine guns blasting. She was also helped in defense by yard worker George Walters, a crane operator working fifty feet in the air over the dry dock when the Japanese arrived. The dreadnought's enormous guns were designed to shoot at enemy ships over the horizon line, not fast-moving aircraft over a sailor's head. The best defense would be other planes but in the wake of the attack, few of these remained. Instead, George Walters marshaled his beast to block low-flying planes while American gunners followed his movements to target against an enemy they couldn't actually see. A record player in one of the ship's repair shops was left on to play over and over, during this early-morning nightmare, the rousing melody of Glenn Miller's "Sunrise Serenade."

Shaw was having just as much trouble in her floating dry dock to the west. A bad hit around 0912 started a massive fire, which spread toward the forward magazine. In fifteen minutes, it made contact, unleashing a tremendous explosion with a huge ball of fire ballooning into the air. Bits of flaming material arched and snaked across the sky, trailing white streamers of smoke.

At that moment, *Downes* and *Cassin* both ordered their men to abandon ship, while in the *Curtiss*'s transmitter room, four radiomen stayed tethered to their battle phones and transmitters, hearing the nightmare outside, but knowing little of what was happening. Suddenly a hole appeared right in front of James Raines. It was so confusing. Then he realized that the crewman sitting behind him, Benny Schlock, was dead, while Dean Orwick was seriously injured. R. E. Jones came over, and while the two were trying to help Orwick out the door, Jones asked, "My foot's gone, isn't it?" Raines nodded, but he assured the man that everything was going to be okay. Later, Raines found out Orwick died, and that his own back had been broken in the explosion.

An officer phoned Admiral Husband Kimmel at home with the news that Japanese planes were attacking his fleet. The admiral was still buttoning his white uniform as he ran out of his house and onto the neighboring lawn of the district's chief of staff, Captain John Earle, which had a panoramic view of Battleship Row. Mrs. Earle said later that Kimmel stood "in utter disbelief and completely stunned," his face "as white as the uniform he wore."

"The sky was full of the enemy," Kimmel said later. He saw the *Arizona* "lift out of the water, then sink back down—way down."

Mrs. Earle saw a battleship capsize and said, "Looks like they've got the *Oklahoma*."

"Yes, I can see they have," the admiral numbly responded.

Arriving at his base, Kimmel radioed the Pacific Fleet and CNO Stark that "hostilities with Japan commenced with air raid on Pearl Harbor," and at 0817, he ordered Patrol Wing 2 to "locate enemy force." One officer remembered, "I ran over to my offices and I happened to be standing alongside the commander in chief himself, Admiral Kimmel. We were glumly watching the havoc, the carnage that was going on. And suddenly he reached up and tore off his four-star shoulder boards, which indicated his rank and title as commander in chief, Pacific Fleet. He stepped into his adjacent offices and, realizing he was going to lose command, donned two-star rear-admiral shoulder boards."

According to other accounts, at this moment an errant bullet ricocheted against Husband Kimmel's chest and fell to the floor. He picked it up and said, "I wish it had killed me."

As vast as Pearl Harbor and her sister military installations then were, in many ways the US Navy was a small town. Sailors might spend an entire thirty-year career aboard one ship; officers would meet as young men at Annapolis, then work together for decades. All were bonded by that special tick of the heart that marks a life of duty. After seeing thousands of his men perish, so many of whom he knew personally, when Admiral Husband Kimmel said he wished that he, too, had died, it couldn't have been more heartfelt.

Twelve days before, Admiral Kimmel had asked naval war plans officer Rear Admiral Charles McMorris, "What do you think about the prospects of a Japanese air attack?" McMorris had categorically replied, "None, absolutely none." Now, running into intelligence officer Edwin Layton in the office halls—Layton having been one of the few naval officers in Hawaii who insisted they needed to prepare for just such an attack—McMorris whined, "If it's any satisfaction to you, you were right and we were wrong."

West Virginia's Ensign Roland Brooks thought he saw an explosion aboard *California* and set off the alarm for Away Fire and Rescue Party, sending hundreds of men running to the decks. Though Brooks had made a mistake—it wasn't *California* but a Ford Island hangar—his mistake saved hundreds of lives, since now arriving overhead were *Hiryu* torpedo planes led by Lieutenant Heita Matsumura, with their primary targets the American aircraft carriers anchored to the west of Ford Island. Since the flattops, as reported by Yoshikawa, were missing, the squadron instead attacked its secondaries. Pilot Takeshi Maeda: "We saw the water channel and we turned left. And right in front of us was Battleship Row. We aimed at the battleship. Our original order was to hit a *California*-class battleship, but at the time we didn't know we hit the *West Virginia*."

Marine bugler Richard Fiske had just finished playing for *West Virginia*'s raising of colors. He and his best friends from high school, Charles Jones and William Finley, had joined the marines together; Finley and Jones were assigned to *Arizona*, barely a hundred yards away. When the first planes appeared, Fiske was thinking about the girl he was going on a date with later that day in Honolulu. Guessing they were army pilots from Wheeler, Fiske told his friend Stanley Bukowski, "I guess we're going to have an exercise. We'd better get to our battle stations." "No, wait," Bukowski said. "They're going to drop some dummy torpedoes. Let's go over to the port side and see them."

"I saw two objects fall from their craft making a tremendous splash," Fireman 3rd Class Ed Carstens remembered. "Suddenly I spotted two wakes heading for the ship and surmised they were torpedoes. By the time I got the word *torpedoes* out of my mouth, they had hit and exploded. . . . I learned later that we had been hit with eight, plus two bomb hits."

"After they dropped their torpedoes, they would have to climb to clear the superstructure of the battleship," Fiske said. One flew so close with his canopy open that "we made eye contact, and I've dreamed about that son of a gun for more than fifty years."

Joseph Paul: "I was sleeping in the plotting room. That is the control center for all gunfire systems, especially the main battery of sixteen-inch guns. I was shaken by a tremendous explosion followed by six or more in close succession. The ship began to list badly. I tried to make my way up to topside. I heard water coming in huge amounts above me and the ship began tilting worse and worse. I tried to get back to the plotting room where my friends were, figuring out that I was not going to get out this way. As the water continued to rise, someone at the watertight door yelled, 'Anyone else?' I yelled right back, 'Wait for me!' He said, 'Hurry, I have to close the door!' . . . He managed to help me get through and close the door just in time. We're now in a sealed compartment with no air or lights. . . . We went into the control center, which was in the next compartment, and climbed up a ladder inside an escape tube that emptied into the conning tower on the bridge. I thought how lucky I was and how smart the designers of the ship were to install such an escape tube."

In *West Virginia's* conning tower, Ensign Victor Delano was looking for someone to help him fight back with two .50-caliber Browning machine guns. He came across a man with no gunnery experience, Mess Attendant Doris Miller. A fullback on the Moore High School football team in his hometown of Waco, Texas—his friends called him Dorie—Miller worked on his dad's twenty-eight acres of sharecropper before signing up in 1939 at the age of nineteen. The kitchen was the only part of the US Navy where an African-American was allowed to serve, but Miller liked it better than farming in Texas. He was stationed to the *West Virginia*—known by her crew as WeeVee—in 1940 and became WeeVee's heavyweight boxing champion, as well as spending a month at Secondary Battery Gunnery School. He was gathering laundry when general quarters struck and ran to his battle station—the midship AA battery—to find it destroyed by torpedoes. Doris Miller's courage would in time make him a civil rights hero.

Victor Delano thought the right thing to do at that moment was for Miller to pass him the ammo, and he would shoot the guns. Doris Miller thought the right thing to do was for each of them to take a gun and let the Japs have it. Doris Miller: "It wasn't hard. I just pulled the trigger and she worked fine. I had watched the others with these guns. I guess I fired her for about fifteen minutes. I think I got one of those Jap planes. They were diving pretty close to us." Delano later said that this was the only time he'd seen Miller smile since the day he'd won a boxing match.

Lieutenant Claude V. Ricketts: "The captain had a serious abdominal wound, a large piece of metal or other similar object apparently having passed through his abdomen. Leak, chief pharmacist's mate, arrived with a first-aid kit and dressed the wound as best he could. We put the captain on a cot and moved him under shelter just aft of the conning tower. He remained here during the second air attack. We had no stretcher but we obtained a wooden ladder about eight feet long and put the captain on it and lashed him to it and tied a line on each corner intending to lower him over the port or starboard side of the conning tower down to the boat deck. By that time however a serious oil fire had started, apparently in the galley, and heavy black smoke poured up over the bridge and boat deck forward. The boat deck had to be evacuated, so we could not lower the captain there. Neither could we lower him aft of the bridge because it was covered with fire. By this time the fire had spread to the life-jacket stowage under the after part of the bridge, and flames were coming up through the bomb hole in the port side of the flag bridge deck."

Nearly disemboweled and in great suffering, Captain Bennion ordered everyone to forget about him and save themselves. They succeeded in getting him to the safety of the bridge, but soon after, he died.

Marine bugler Richard Fiske had joined the rescuers, pouring buckets of sand on men who were on fire. The next day, he would have to play taps for his captain's burial.

Signalman Gene Merrill: "I volunteered to join the ten-hand rescue party to go below and rescue those wounded by the torpedoes. I have no idea how many we rescued. With no instructions, each of us used his own discretion. My modus operandi was to quickly examine the body for signs of life. If none was apparent, I moved on to the next one. However, questionable cases I rescued. . . . I stayed below until the flooding salt water and oil forced me to evacuate. When I emerged to the topside, the battle was over. The ship was sitting on the bottom with the port listed as burning. . . . The motor launch took us across the channel to the submarine base, where we boarded a flatbed truck that took us to the receiving-station barracks. I went into one of the buildings that seemed to be overrun with women wearing Red Cross armbands. I was naked as a newborn chicken, covered with oil, and practically surrounded by these women. Under normal circumstances, I would've been greatly embarrassed, but in this situation, not at all. None of these 'angels of mercy' seemed to pay me any attention. Under normal circumstances, I might've been insulted."

Lieutenant Commander T. T. Beattie, *West Virginia*'s navigator: "Just then the USS *Arizona*'s forward magazines blew up with a tremendous explosion, and large sheets of flame shot skyward, and I began to wonder about our own magazines and whether they were being flooded. I got hold of a chief turret captain to check immediately on the magazines and to flood them if they were not flooded at this time. Large sheets of flame and several fires started aft. Burning fuel oil from the USS *Arizona* floated down on the stern of the ship [then] a large oil fire swept from the USS *Arizona* down the port side of the USS *West Virginia*. We had no water on board as the fire mains and machinery were out of commission, and we were unable to do any firefighting at all. I got into a motor launch to go to the stern of the ship to investigate the fire. The smoke was so heavy that I could not see aft of the bridge. As I got into the boat, a sheet of flame swept on top of us and we barely managed to get free of the fire. I realized then that the ship was lost."

Between five and eight eighteen-inch torpedoes detonated against *West Virginia*'s port, while two armor-piercing bombs crashed through her deck. With an inclinometer marking list at fifteen degrees, Commander Roscoe Hillenkoetter and Lieutenant Commander John Harper gave orders for counterflooding to keep her from turning turtle. She had lost so much power, that no one could hear their commands; however a team of shipfitters, led by senior gunnery officer Lieutenant Claude V. Ricketts and Boatswain's Mate 1st Class Garnett Billingsley, did it on their own. Saved by her men, *West Virginia* sank on an even keel.

Of the 1,541 aboard *West Virginia* on December 7, 1941, 130 were killed and 52 wounded. Three of the dead were found, weeks later, in a sealed compartment, having lived in the dark without food or water until December 23, when the air ran out and they suffocated.

The USS *Oklahoma* had arrived at Pearl Harbor on December 5 after spending two weeks on maneuvers. With her crew of fifteen hundred, she was a true "city of the sea." American engineers believed that her system of watertight bulkheads made her unsinkable, and they imagined that the thirteen inches of steel armoring her hull made her impenetrable.

On the morning of December 7, *Oklahoma*'s Albert Ellis of Portland, Oregon, was in his bunk, playing "A String of Pearls" on his battle group's communal record player. Nineteen-year-old apprentice seaman Garlen Eslick, an actual Oklahoman from Bristow, was assigned to KP. Ensign Adolph Mortensen had watch duty the night before; relieved at 0345, he took the spyglass to his room, which marked his status as junior officer on deck—JOD.

Since senior officers lived ashore, most of those aboard that Sunday were junior in rank, and Admiral Kimmel had seen no reason to change this arrangement even in the wake of a series of alarming cables from Washington culminating in a war warning.

Ensign Mortensen had slept maybe three hours when the alarms went off. He ran out of his cabin shirtless, in pajama bottoms, with slippers and his hat, to designate he was an officer: "I felt foolish, but didn't have much of a choice." He saw a sailor assigned to the forward boiler control running to his post: "As he opened the hatch and stepped into the air lock, I watched the spinner handle spin and lock the hatch. I wondered to myself, 'What is he going to find down there? What are the others doing down there? Can they possibly light off the burners, and even if they could, what good would it do? How could this ship possibly get under way?'"

Mortensen came across another sailor sitting where the bulkhead met the deck, "a good worker who usually came back from liberty with a split lip, bloody nose, black eye, or disheveled uniform with his friend from another division. They seemed inseparable. Here he was, sitting on the deck with his friend's head in his lap, his body stretched out on the deck. I couldn't see what was wrong, but he seemed to be unconscious. When our eyes met, I said, 'You better get out of here.' He gave me an anguished look as he answered, 'No. I'm not going to leave my friend. He's hurt.'"

Quartermaster Herbert Kennedy, a nineteen-year-old from Seattle: "I heard this noise, a popping noise, and I looked up and there was a Japanese fighter plane, coming in ahead of the torpedo planes, strafing the decks. The boy that was directly across from me, it just tore him in half. Blood spattered all over me and I didn't know what to think. I couldn't believe what I was seeing." Ensign John Landreth worked in antiaircraft ops and summed up this strange feeling of shock: "What is this really? A dream, perhaps, or is it really me shooting at other men and they shooting at me? What is this really?"

Senior Reserve Ensign Herb Rommel grabbed the PA system mike on his way to his battle station to holler, "Man your battle stations! This is no shit!" Commander Paul Backus explained, "Only under the most unusual circumstances would an officer personally make an announcement in those days of formal battleship routine, and the use of obscene language by anyone over the announcing system was just unheard of. [And] right after the last word of the announcement, the whole ship shuddered. It was the first torpedo hitting our port side."

Adolph Mortensen: "The ship was lifted rapidly straight up a considerable distance. On reaching the B Division quarters, I found an incredible mess. . . . Berths attached to the bulkhead had come loose and were swinging on their chains, making walking difficult. The remainder of breakfast food, coffee, pots, dirty dishes and food trays, platters of uneaten sliced baloney covered with the usual tomato sauce, had spilled and made an incredible slippery mess through which we had to walk."

No one could man the antiaircraft batteries since "the boxes containing the ready ammunition were padlocked, and there was no compressed air for the rammers," Backus said. "The padlocks were broken and the ammunition was hand-rammed into the breeches. There were no firing locks on the breech blocks. They had been removed and were down in the armory being cleaned for a scheduled admiral's inspection. . . . Not a shot was fired from these guns before the ship rolled over." As part of that inspection, "some of our blisters [bulges of dead-air space that take the hit of a mine or torpedo without letting it penetrate] were open when the attack took place. The manhole covers had been removed in some instances so that the blisters could be aired out for a later cleaning. Obviously, our resistance to flooding was minimal when the torpedoes hit. When the blisters dipped under, flooding had to be massive. [Then] lines securing the *Oklahoma* to the *Maryland* had started to pop as the list on the ship increased rapidly."

Another torpedo slipped through the air and smashed into the bay. As marine Private Raymond Turpin of Waterloo, Alabama, and five others ran to their gun, the sound of a plane roared just over their heads; Ray looked up to see the Japanese pilot jerk her up to keep from colliding into one of the battleships' superstructure. Just then the man running behind him yelled, "Were you hit?" Ray said, "No, why'd you ask?" And the man said, "He strafed us!"

The bomber was *Akagi* squadron commander Lieutenant Jinichi Goto: "I was about twenty meters above the water . . . when I released my torpedo. As my plane climbed up after the torpedo was off, I saw that I was even lower than the crow's nest of the great battleship. My observer reported a huge waterspout springing up from the ship's location. *Ararimashita!* [It struck!] he cried. The other two planes in my group also attacked *Oklahoma*."

Sailor James Huston: "When a torpedo hits, that water goes up in the air way higher than the length of that ship! And that comes down on you—and you go onto your knees when that water comes down. You can't stand up. Just tons of water. When the torpedoes hit, it just rolled over like that. I couldn't walk across the deck. 'Cause the water and everything was over top of it—it was slippery. But they hung cargo nets up on this poop deck. I slid down those lines and swam over to the shoreline and crawled up and went on the *Maryland*."

"The first alarm came and I immediately ran up the ladder to the starboard side of the upper deck to go to the conning tower after calling for the crew to go to battle stations," USS *Oklahoma*'s Commander Jesse Kenworthy Jr. said. "As I reached the upper deck, I felt a heavy shock and heard a loud explosion, and the ship immediately began to list to port. Oil and water descended on deck, and by the time I had reached the boat deck, the shock of two more explosions on the port side was felt. In the meanwhile, general quarters had sounded and the crew had gone to battle stations and started zed closures [the dogging down of doors, hatches, ports, and valves marked with a *Z*]."

"I was five foot three and, at the age of seventeen, the youngest sailor on ship," remembered *Oklahoma* crewman George Smith. "My battle station was a loader on a five-inch gun, and I was so small I couldn't even pick up the shells. So they had me load the powder instead, because the powder bags didn't weigh as much. Well, I was young, and I disobeyed some orders. The captain put me in the brig and told me to read *The Bluejacket's Manual*, the navy's book on how a sailor is supposed to behave. Now, on that Sunday I was out [on his fourth day after spending thirty days in the brig], and I was getting ready for a day off the ship—liberty we call it. Then over the loudspeakers I heard, 'All hands, man your battle stations.' I was really scared. Then I heard, 'Abandon ship.' The ship was already rolling over on us. We jumped into the water. It was only about a five-foot jump. I saw the ship and the big gun turrets coming down on me, and I began to swim as fast as I could."

Robert West's battle station was three decks below: "A torpedo hit, and then another one, and then another one. The ship listed a little bit more, and then a little bit more, and it got so bad you couldn't walk over to the other side."

Now listing at forty-five degrees, the unsinkable, impenetrable *Oklahoma* took one more missile strike right at her deck line—the fatal blow. Eslick was in the middle of trying to help the injured when "the lights blackened out and the ship completed its roll. And that's the last I remember 'cause I was rendered unconscious."

The commander gave the order to abandon ship. The crew running Turret 4 had pitched in to buy themselves a phonograph. A torpedo knocked the volume dial to full blast, and in another incongruous musical accompaniment, it played Gene Krupa's "Let Me Off Uptown."

Five more torpedoes slammed into *Oklahoma*. Power systems failed, tanks exploded streaming oil across the floors, and seawater poured in. Sailor George DeLong: "The lights went out and water rushed in through the air vent. Furniture and equipment in the compartment started crashing around the deck. I realized my head was where my feet had been."

On Ford Island, Chief Albert Molter watched as she rolled completely over in the water, exposing her belly, "slowly and stately . . . as if she were tired and wanted to rest." It was eight minutes after the first assault of torpedo planes, and now this once-great ship of the American fleet was completely overturned, her mast dug into the mud. In her roll, *Oklahoma*'s ammunition handling rooms' fourteen-hundred-pound, fourteen-inch shells went into free fall, crushing to death several of the men, pinning one against a bulkhead and popping out his tongue and eyes.

Of 1,353 men aboard, 461 were now trapped inside. Robert West: "The water came rushing in like a flood, coming up to your knees and then your hips, and all of a sudden it got to a point where you were treading water. And it stopped." Garlen Eslick: "Evidently the cool water brought me to. I remembered hollering for help." Albert Ellis: "We had four flashlights, which we used very sparingly until they all ran out of power. Thank God we knew the area as well as we did. We got to the highest point. And we were dogged in; we couldn't get out. The hatch was armor plated and probably weighed in excess of two thousand pounds." West: "There was some light coming from some place, I don't know where, but we could see a ladder, and we could see the water was rising. So we went up to the top of the ladder and there was another door with a hatch on it, locked. So we just took the wrench and beat that lock until it broke. We opened the door. It was black in there, but it was dry." They shoved clothes into the air vents, trying to plug the flood of water from coming in.

George Smith: "There were a couple of other sailors still in the brig, which was set up in the carpenter shop. I found out later that when one of the torpedoes hit, it broke the carpenter's workbench loose, pinned the guard against the wall—the bulkhead—and he could not release the men in the brig. Everyone drowned."

"I helped a partially incapacitated man [up] to the second deck and then joined in a line passing injured men along to the ladder by the dental office," Assistant Pay Clerk Daniel Westfall remembered. "I lost all knowledge of time while here, but after some minutes, Ensign

[Thomas] McClelland, who was beside me in the line, said he was feeling faint and then collapsed. I noticed other men dropping around me. I stooped over to pick up McClelland but when I stooped over, I got dizzy and fell. I seemed to be paralyzed from the waist down, had great difficulty breathing, but had enough strength in my arms to drag myself to the ladder and up a couple of steps [toward the main deck] before collapsing completely [likely from breathing oil fumes]. After passing out I had only flashes of consciousness until midafternoon."

Ensign Adolph Mortensen saw "Chaplain Schmitt pushing one person out [through a porthole]. Two more were beside him. I understand he tried to squeeze through but was unable to fit so came back inside and spent the last few minutes of his life helping others escape. I don't think more than one more could have gotten out because shortly thereafter the ship rolled and he and the others were trapped in the rising waters."

Ray Turpin was one of those helping the trapped men struggle to escape through that fifteen-inch porthole. He helped get five out, but the sixth was in bad shape; he was just too big to fit though and got stuck. As Ray and some others pulled on the man's arms and chest and rocked him back and forth, Father Al was pushing as hard as he could from below. The men could hear the man's ribs pop as they manhandled him through and saw the black marks of bruises on his body, but even though he was suffering, he shouted, "Don't stop! Keep pulling!" Finally, he was free, but so injured by the effort it looked as if he'd been beaten. "I was amazed at his composure and jovial attitude, despite his horrible and painful wounds," his friend Adolph Kuhn remembered.

Then came Ray Turpin's worst memory of World War II as he had to watch through a porthole as a compartment flooded with water, and the man on the other side of that window, *Oklahoma* chaplain Lieutenant (jg) Father Aloysius Schmitt, refused his hand of help. "Someone tried earlier to pull me out and I couldn't get through," Schmitt insisted. "I'm going to see if there are others needing a way out."

Four weeks later, at a Protestant church in California, a Jewish sailor would testify that he was alive because a Catholic chaplain had pushed him through a porthole.

Now it was time for Raymond Turpin to save himself. He slid into the harbor. The water around him was covered in three inches of oil. He found a mooring line from *Oklahoma* to *Maryland* and started shimmying up it to safety. But the force of *Oklahoma*'s sinking was pulling *Maryland* away from her quay, and just as Turpin neared the ship, he heard an officer aboard *Maryland* yell, "Cut the line!" A chief petty officer approached with a fire ax. He looked and shouted back, "But, sir, there are guys on the line!" The order came down: "Cut the god-damn line!" With four whacks of the ax Turpin fell fifteen feet into the murk, the rope's coil landing on top of him. He came to the surface, sputtering for breath, and started swimming to the *Maryland* all over again. But he was exhausted, and failing, and then a big sailor pulled him forward to a line hanging near her bow and boosted him up so he could climb to the deck.

There he found a crew attacking the Japanese with a new 1.1-inch, four-barrel antiaircraft machine gun, and he was thrilled to see that three of them were fellow marines he knew from *Oklahoma*. "Can I help?" he asked. "Yeah, grab some clips, load 'em, and drop 'em in the guns when the others empty!" It was thrilling to finally be able to fight back, to give those Japs just what they deserved.

There was a tap on his shoulder. *Maryland's* senior medical officer, Lieutenant Commander John Luten, had just come on deck since the attack's start and asked, "What happened to you?"

"Sir, I just came off the *Oklahoma*."

"*Oklahoma*? What happened to the *Oklahoma*?"

Ray pointed. "It's sunk."

"My God!" Luten insisted that Ray, covered in oil, go get checked at the primary aid station. There, Luten ordered a medic to examine Ray's injuries, but the medic ignored him, so Ray went back to the deck and rejoined the gun crew. Dr. Luten found him again and again took him to the station and reprimanded the corpsman. He told Ray to take a good shower and throw his clothes into the trash.

Ray said, "What am I going to wear?"

"When you get out of the shower, I'll give you a pair of pajamas."

George Smith: "I swam around the *Oklahoma*, heading for the *Maryland*, which was moored alongside. They threw cargo nets over the side we could climb aboard. But there were so many men from the *Oklahoma* on the *Maryland* that they ordered us to get into the water again and swim to Ford Island."

Now safely ashore, Smith "couldn't stand looking over there, seeing my ship upside down. I cried that night. I kept saying to myself, 'What am I doing here? I could be home in Seattle going to high school with my buddies. I just quit high school to join the navy—for this.' I was scared. But I knew I grew up that day."

Having warned others of danger, Ensign Mortensen now found himself trapped. "As I treaded water, the ship continued to roll and I was carried into the pharmacy. As the door rolled over me, the glass-faced doors of the medicine cabinets on the bulkhead opened, and I was showered with a deluge of medicine bottles both small and large. . . . The light disappeared almost, but not quite, to zero."

"It was scary," Musician 1st Class Robert West said. "It scared the life out of me. And it knocked you around. And the water just kept rising up. We had to tread the water to keep your head above, and there was only about a foot, maybe a foot and a half, between your head and the water. But we knew we had to get out of that compartment because maybe the water would be coming up again. . . . One more hit and that would be it. So we decided to dive under the hatch. We followed each other into the other compartment. . . . There was so much that was going through your mind. If you were going to get out. And you thought of the good things that had happened to you before. I remember talking to this person next to me, you think about having a milk shake in Walgreens drugstore. . . . We used to talk about little things like that."

Now wearing only pajama bottoms and a hat—he'd lost his slippers—Mortensen was trapped in the pharmacy with about thirty men in all, and about forty cubic feet of air. For about an hour they assumed help was on the way and had no idea that the boat had turned over and that they were far below the water's surface. The only one with a flashlight was carpenter John Austin, who discovered one way out: an underwater porthole. Finally Mortensen kicked it open. It was positioned the wrong way, and that's when they realized the ship had upended, with the tiles on the ceiling being the dispensary's floor.

Some of the men swam down to investigate. Everyone knew that a number of portholes on the ship led to void space, which would be a trap. But when the air started running out, they had no other choice.

The hatch's reversed hanging meant that one man had to hold the door open while another man swam through the fourteen-inch opening. It took seaman George Murphy three attempts to get out; Mortensen ended up pushing him through the port.

Finally, only two men remained behind in the dispensary: Mortensen and the portly John Austin. Mortensen: "John must have known he had no chance. He did not say a word but moved over the few feet necessary and just reached down and held the port. I looked at his face but cannot describe the look of anguish it contained. It is a look that has never left me."

Swimming out, Mortensen could see the "golden brown glow above and I knew the surface was up there somewhere. It never occurred to me that the normal color should have been bluish." The harbor water was now covered with three to four inches of burning oil. The ensign was again shocked when he reached the surface and saw the devastation, since the whole time below, all the men assumed the only ship struck was theirs.

As the swimmers were picked out of the water by a launch, Mortensen realized that he'd lost his pajama bottoms and hat and was now completely naked. A marine working the launch looked him over and thought for a minute. Then without saying a word, he took off his pants and his Skivvies, gave Mortensen his underwear, and put his pants back on.

"We continued pulling men out of the water," Ensign Herb Rommel later reported. "It was difficult due to the oil making everyone slippery. Men with undershirts could be pulled into boats by grabbing the shoulder piece and sleeve on each side, while men who had stripped were very slippery. It is recommended that men be instructed not to remove undershirts when abandoning ship."

Mortensen wouldn't see his *Oklahoma* roommate until six months later, when he was working on the USS *Mackinac* in the Samoan harbor of Pago Pago. A motor launch puttered by. "I called out, 'Morey,' and he looked up at me and said, 'I thought you were dead.'"

Back on *Oklahoma*, eleven men were still trapped in the lucky bag, the hold for duffels, overcoats, and other personal items. The only escape would be to swim while holding your breath down five stories and then across the main deck, to where you could rise up to the surface. Russell Davenport made it so far he could feel the main deck's teak, but couldn't make it all the way and had to give up and go back.

Boatswain's Mate 1st Class Howard Aldrich said that, to save air, they needed to stay as quiet as possible, and anyone who could sleep should do that. A few more hours went by, and their one source of light, a lantern, died. Hours passed by in the pitch black. Did anyone even know they were there? Would they all suffocate to death?

Electrician's Mate Irvin Thessman, at twenty-five, was the oldest of eight men trapped in the aft steering compartment and felt responsible for the other men. They had followed the zed closure protocol as ordered, but it didn't make their compartment watertight, and the sea began leaking in through the ventilation lines. When they tried to tighten that fitting, it broke, so they stuffed rags into the inlet and covered it with a checkerboard to hold the rags in place.

As the hours passed, they heard tapping, coming from two directions. Using wrenches, hammers, or anything they could get to bang on *Oklahoma*'s hull or her plumbing, the men caught in the lucky bag and Radio Four were talking to each other in Morse code. One of the men in Radio was Seaman 1st Class James Bounds: "There's no way you could get out because in our space there was one of those big spring-loaded hatches up above in the carpenters' shop. So when they dropped that hatch, we were there, unless somebody opened from the topside. Sort of felt like a dark, cold, damp coffin. That's the only way I can describe it. And it felt like it was sealed, and you were just ready to suffocate."

The eight sailors trapped in aft steering voted on every decision that might mean life or death. They tried various doors to get out, but each time, a flood of water rushed in. They decided to wait it out, which led to much thinking about their lives. William Beal, age seventeen, couldn't stop remembering all the mean things he'd done to other people.

Trapped right next to them in No. 4 turret's handling room were thirty men who discovered their only exit was a hatch to the top deck. Getting out would mean holding your breath, pulling yourself thirty feet down to the hatch, swimming across the deck, and up to reach the water's surface. Like Russell Davenport, some tried and failed and came back, defeated. But one succeeded—a Brooklyn boy named Weisman, remembered by his colleagues for his poor physique—who, reaching the surface, could show the cutting teams of rescuers where to drill. But no one below knew about this. Seaman Stephen Young bet his friend Wilber Hinsperger that their air would run out, and they would suffocate. Hinsperger insisted instead that they would drown.

No one bet they would live.

Outside, teams from *Maryland*, *Widgeon*, *Rigel*, *Solace*, the Navy Yard, and even *Oklahoma* herself tapped back encouraging words while trying to figure out as quickly as possible where to cut into the armored hull. The trapped men's knocks, though, would echo, especially across the hollow of the keel, and every rescuer had a different opinion as to where it was coming from, and where they should drill.

It was a terrible education. They first tried burning through the hull plate with acetylene torches, but the flames ignited the caulking sealant. The first two men they found had been suffocated to death by the burning sealant's fumes. When they switched to air hammers and drills, the holes they cut to free the trapped sailors also let out the remaining breathable air. The men might drown in the minutes before they could be rescued.

The huge problem in using torches was that they might ignite the great ship's fuel tanks. *Maryland*'s Commander E. Kranzfelder: "I obtained a copy of the *Oklahoma* booklet of plans for use in connection with the cutting of holes in the *Oklahoma*'s hull. Lines were rigged from the bilge keel at intervals along the bottom; telephone communication was established with the *Maryland*; an air-supply line was quickly rigged from the *Maryland* to the *Oklahoma*. Since, with the exception of the reserve feed bottoms, practically the entire bottom of the *Oklahoma* consists of oil tanks, considerable care had to be exercised in cutting holes with an oxyacetylene torch in order not to open holes in the bottom which would permit the egress of oil with the attendant fire hazard."

The trapped men felt the hull over their heads getting hotter and hotter. One insisted it was a form of Japanese torture, but in fact the heat was from the cutting torches of rescue workers. Garlen Eslick and his group were one of the first out: "I don't know how long it took them, but it seemed like forever. They had three ends cut, and finally they took a sledgehammer and were beating that end towards us. Then they hoisted us up through the openings they had cut."

James Bounds was now with Thessman's group in the aft steering compartment: "I could see the light. Somebody reached down and got my arms and pulled me up. Then somebody was pushing me from below. They had to handle us up through these holes with lots of jagged edges."

Stephen Young pounded out SOS with a dog wrench, until he heard a voice yelling through the bulkhead. Most of the captives had been trapped inside for twenty-eight hours; Russell Davenport remembered swallowing a gulp of water before he was brought up into the sun and air at noon on December 8. Coming out, they were given cigarettes, and oranges. Brought aboard hospital ship *Solace*, no one who had been entombed wanted to sleep belowdecks.

Nineteen-year-old Herbert Kennedy was saved, but remembered

from that moment not freedom, but horror: "There were still bodies floating in water covered in oil, turning white from the salt water. A sight I never want to see again." George Smith would make it his mission to meet every single one of the *Oklahoma*'s thirty-two survivors who were rescued on the eighth. Four hundred and twenty-nine did not survive. Their tombstones read UNKNOWN. DECEMBER 7, 1941.

When it appeared that the USS *Raleigh* would also capsize like *Oklahoma*, "orders were given for all men not at the guns to jettison all topside weights and to put both airplanes in the water first," her commanding officer, R. E. Simons, reported. "Both planes were successfully hoisted out by hand power alone and were directed to taxi over to Ford Island and report for duty, along with all the aviation detail on board. The senior doctor was directed to report to the USS *Solace*, to aid in caring for the injured and wounded from other ships (we had no dead and only a few wounded on this ship). An oxyacetylene outfit and crew were sent over to the capsized USS *Utah* to cut out any men in the hull. One man was rescued, and this man, as soon as he took a deep breath, insisted on going back to see if he could rescue any of his shipmates."

At 0817 on December 7, destroyer *Helm* plowed through the burning waters and the black smoke to reach the open sea. As she exited the channel, lookouts spotted an odd submarine that had run aground on a reef. The destroyer fired, missed, and the sub dove. At about 0828, men on the *Perry* spotted an unidentified craft "heading toward the Middle Loch and swinging toward the moorings of *Medusa* [and] *Curtiss*" but *Perry* was moored between *Zane* and the sub in such a way that *Zane* couldn't fire her guns. *Perry* fired her four-inch cannon; the first shell missed, but the second appeared to strike the sub enough to sink it, and by then *Medusa* was also firing away. *Monaghan*'s Gun No. 2 joined in; one of her shells missed and ignited a fire on a derrick barge. *Burford* then charged toward the sub trying to ram it with "all engines ahead flank speed and full right rudder." The submarine shot a torpedo at 0840 that breached into the air, heading at *Monaghan*, but missed, plowing into the bank and throwing up a two-hundred-foot geyser. As *Burford* passed over the sub, her chief, G. S. Hardon, dropped two cans of depth charges, which both exploded at 0844. It was decided that the enemy had been destroyed.

• • •

In Washington, Navy Secretary Frank Knox's office received the "Air Raid, Pearl Harbor. This is No Drill" radiogram at around one thirty that afternoon. Knox immediately called the White House, first getting ahold of Harry Hopkins. Like so many officers in Hawaii who couldn't believe their eyes and ears, Knox and Hopkins were at first certain it had to be wrong, that the attack must have been on Manila. But President Roosevelt's immediate reaction was to yell, *"No!"* Secret Service agent Mike Reilly remembered seeing FDR just after he had gotten the news, thrusting forward in his wheelchair to the Oval Office, looking like a prizefighter: "His chin stuck out about two feet in front of his knees and he was the maddest Dutchman I—or anybody—ever saw."

Before that moment, Hopkins remembered the president had "really thought" the Japanese were capable of doing anything, except something that might explicitly draw the United States into the war; that she would go after more territory in China, Thailand, French Indochina, or even the Soviet Union, but directly attacking the United States? After hearing about the cable, though, "the president thought the report was probably true and thought it was just the kind of unexpected thing the Japanese would do, and that at the very time they were discussing peace in the Pacific, they were plotting to overthrow it."

Roosevelt called Cordell Hull at State, where, at that moment, Ambassadors Nomura and Kurusu were waiting to present Dispatch No. 907—the fourteen-point cable. Since Togo had ordered that only senior consular staff in Washington could know the details of the dispatch, and since none of those officials knew how to type, the two ambassadors had arrived at Hull's office at 2:05, missing their 1:00 deadline. The president suggested the secretary make no mention of the attack, but only greet them "formally and coolly and bow them out," just in case the air raid cable was wrong.

The ambassadors in fact had no idea that their country had launched its war against the world, but "coolly" was not the way of Cordell Hull. After ushering them in at 2:20, the secretary pretended to read the cable. Its fourteen points included that the United States had "resorted to every possible measure to assist the Chongqing regime so as to obstruct the establishment of a general peace between Japan and China," had "attempted to frustrate Japan's aspiration to the ideal of common prosperity in cooperation with these regions," and "may be said to be scheming for the extension of the war" with American demands for Japan's "wholesale evacuation of troops . . . [which] ignored the actual conditions of China and are calculated to destroy Japan's position as the stabilizing factor of East Asia." The Hull Note also ignored "Japan's sacrifices in the four years of the China affair, menaces the Empire's existence itself, and disparages its honor and prestige." The fourteenth point concluded that the Japanese government "cannot but consider that it is impossible to reach an agreement through further negotiations."

Though he'd already been informed of all of this hours before through MAGIC, Hull's hands shook with rage at both Tokyo's duplicity and at his own failures in reaching a diplomatic victory. He finished pretending to scan the pages and turning to the two unsuspecting emissaries, he announced: "I must say that in all my conversations with you, I have never uttered one word of untruth. This is borne out absolutely by the record. In all my fifty years of public service, I've never seen a document that was more crowded with infamous falsehoods and distortions—infamous falsehoods and distortion on a scale so huge that I never imagined until today that any government on this planet was capable of uttering them."

Nomura and Kurusu bowed and left, speechless and confused; they were then surprised by a group of reporters waiting outside, peppering them with questions on a Sunday. As their embassy's gates swung open and closed to let their car pass through, policemen formed a cordon to keep an angry and growing American mob from surging inside. Only then were the two admirals told how they had been used by their government. Admiral Yonai had in fact warned his fellow admiral Nomura of exactly this outcome when he'd first left for Washington, saying, "The gang around today are the kind who won't hesitate to pull the ladder out from under you once they've got you to climb up it." When a Japanese consular staff member told his wife the news of Japan's attack on Oahu, he concluded, "Oh, it's terrible! Why did they do such a terrible thing? Japan is doomed."

Though Cordell Hull would be the first to call the Pearl Harbor attack treacherous, he later came to believe that Nomura and Kurusu's delay in announcing the end of negotiations was due to "ineptitude" since, for over the next six decades, beginning at the Tokyo war crimes tribunal, Japan would present this incident as an honorable mishap, claiming that her government had tried to follow the terms of the 1907 Hague Convention and give notice before an attack—thirty minutes'

Assistant Secretary of the Navy Franklin Roosevelt watches on March 16, 1914, as the Brooklyn Navy Yard lays the keel for the ship that would be christened USS *Arizona* and attacked by the Japanese twenty-seven years later.

1

2

Admiral Isoroku Yamamoto was so conflicted about Tokyo's rush to war that he proselytized against fighting the Allies publicly while at the same time privately threatening to resign if the navy didn't approve his plans to attack Pearl Harbor.

Vice Admiral Chuichi Nagumo led the First Air Fleet in its strike on Oahu, even though he'd repeatedly opposed Yamamoto's plan and would forever after be vilified as being timid for not ordering a third strike.

3

Details of the strike force's targets were provided by Honolulu spy Takeo Yoshikawa. The teahouse he used for surveillance is still open for business.

4

America's military commanders in Hawaii, General Walter Short, *left*, and Admiral Husband Kimmel, *right*, met with Britain's Lord Mountbatten in 1941. Short and Kimmel would shoulder the burden of blame for the Hawaiian debacle, but were never court-martialed, only retired.

5

American secretary of state Cordell Hull, *center*, met regularly with Japanese ambassadors Kichisaburo Nomura and Saburo Kurusu to try to negotiate an accord between Tokyo and Washington. Afterward, Hull won the Nobel Prize as a founder of the United Nations, and *double Kurusu* became American slang for "betrayal."

6

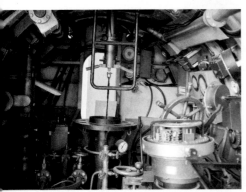

7

8

Japan's advanced technologies, including its battery-powered midget submarine, would fool Admiral Kimmel, who refused to believe torpedoes could be launched in the shallow waters of Pearl Harbor. Of the ten midget sub crewmen assigned to this mission, however, nine would die, and the only survivor would become America's first World War II POW.

9

Japan's First Air Fleet prepares to launch its surprise attack on Oahu. The profound success of this battle will end the era of dreadnoughts and launch the ascendancy of flattops, aircraft carriers capable of projecting massive firepower over great distances.

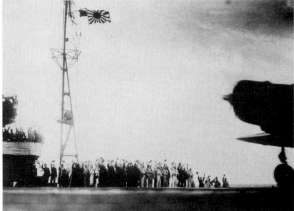

10

11

The attack was launched at 7:48 a.m. In less than thirty minutes, Hickam Field lay in ruins.

12

The first minutes of the attack caught by Japanese cameras. The background smoke is Hickam in flames; *left*, a torpedo is visibly porpoising; *dead center*, a shock wave emanates from a strike on *West Virginia*. Moored by Ford Island, *left to right*: *Nevada*, *Vestal* outbound to *Arizona*; *West Virginia* outbound to *Tennessee*; *Oklahoma* outbound to *Maryland*; *Neosho* and *California*. The explosion in the second picture is a torpedo strike on *Oklahoma*.

Ford Island Naval Air Station under fire. 2,403 Americans died in the attack.

Hell on earth: firefighters try to save *West Virginia*, while a small boat attempts to rescue her crew from the water. Some trying to escape by jumping into the harbor would be suffocated or burned alive by the fuel fires raging at the water's surface.

17

Arizona collapses. Of more than 1,400 crewmen, merely 334 survived.

18

19

The smoke of the burning harbor waters finally clears, revealing *Arizona* completely destroyed, and *Oklahoma* fully capsized.

20

21

The corpse of a Japanese airman is hoisted from the water.

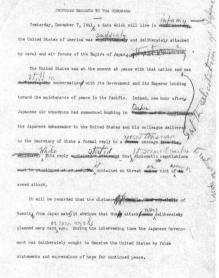

22

President Roosevelt appears before a joint session of Congress on December 8 to give one of the greatest speeches in American history and ask for a declaration of war. His handwritten revisions show his desire to properly convey the momentousness of the attack.

23

Admiral Chester Nimitz, Kimmel's replacement, awards the Navy Cross to *West Virginia*'s Cook 3rd Class Doris Miller on May 27, 1942. The heroic Miller will die in action, but his valor at Pearl Harbor will make him a civil rights hero.

On June 1, 1942, James Doolittle appears before America's great secret weapon of World War II— working men and women—at the Inglewood, California, site of North American Aviation's B-25 assembly line. When America learned that Japan had executed a group of his Raiders, the country bought more war bonds than at any other time in history.

25

Navy divers at work on a heroic effort of salvage as *Oklahoma* is righted to ninety degrees by March 29, 1943, and *Nevada* is fully restored.

26

27

Today's Pearl Harbor, and the *Arizona* Memorial with its pool of black tears.

28

notice, but so be it—and sadly, the incompetence of the consular staff in Washington prevented this warning from arriving in time.

In fact, the Foreign Ministry had drafted a Final Memorandum on December 3 that had far more ominous language than the fourteenth point's tepid conclusion of "impossible to reach an agreement through further negotiations." That draft announced that "we are forced to terminate negotiations" and that Washington "would be held responsible for any and all the consequences that may arise in the future." But during the December 4 liaison conference, the general staffs of the army and the navy rejected that language and insisted on the far milder conclusion that appeared in the radioed cable, language so vague that, of the dozen or so Americans allowed to read MAGIC, only Franklin Roosevelt and Rufus Bratton are recorded as having interpreted it as meaning war. The December 6 Imperial Japanese Army war diary admitted all this with the note: "Our deceptive diplomacy is steadily proceeding toward success." Additionally, the same Major Morio Tomura of the Army General Staff Communications Section who had delayed Roosevelt's cable to Hirohito for ten hours had also succeeded in delaying the final transmissions of the fourteen-part cable from Togo to Nomura. But Foreign Minister Togo was not without blame; he used the cable to Nomura to give a delayed notice, instead of directly speaking with Joseph Grew.

After getting confirmation of the attack, the president called White House press secretary Steve Early at home. Roosevelt and Early had been working together for almost thirty years, and they began an Oval Office tradition of getting ahead of the news. At his home, Early jotted down FDR's statement, then called the national wire services to brief them, before heading over to 1600 Pennsylvania Avenue.

At two thirty, James Roosevelt arrived to help his father in any way he could. He remembered the president's aura of "extreme calmness—almost a sad, fatalistic, but courageous acceptance of something he had tried to avert but which he feared might be inevitable." The man told his son simply, "It happened." The first lady agreed with James, noting her husband's "deadly calm. . . . I thought that in spite of his anxiety Franklin was way more serene than he had appeared in a long time. I think it was steadying to know finally that the die was cast. One could no longer do anything but face the fact that this country was in a war. . . . I remember when he was told he had polio, he seemed really relieved that he knew the worst that could happen to him."

Claude Bloch in Hawaii was finally able to reach Harold Stark on the phone that afternoon, but was wary of discussing horrific details on a conversation that could be intercepted. But Stark insisted on knowing everything, so Bloch finished his report and then warned any eavesdroppers, "If any unauthorized person has heard the remarks that I have just made to the chief of naval operations, I beg of you not to repeat them in any way. I call on your patriotic duty as an American citizen."

Just before leaving for the White House at 3:00 p.m., George Marshall cabled General Douglas MacArthur in Manila to warn, "Hostilities between Japan and the United States . . . have commenced. . . . Carry out tasks assigned in Rainbow Five."

Moored at Berth F-7, the 600-foot long, 31,400-ton *Arizona* was tied, bow to stern, on her port to the 466-foot, 12,585-ton repair ship *Vestal*. As Minoru Genda had predicted, US ships such as *Arizona* that were anchored inbound had suffered little damage from his dive-bombers and torpedo planes. *Vestal*'s Warner Fahlgren: "We're supposed to weld up the portholes on the *Arizona*, we were the repair ship. I was in the rec room addressing Christmas cards to send home when general quarters rang. They were coming down dropping torpedoes and strafing at the same time. I can remember seeing them drop a torpedo [at 0755] and it coming toward our ship—it looked like it was coming right where I was at. You could see the wake of the torpedo and it looked like it was coming to you. The torpedoes that hit the *Arizona*, they went underneath our ship."

Aboard *Arizona*, Ensign Jim Miller felt that strike and thought it was a mistaken firing of the catapult. Jim Lawson, enjoying *Flash Gordon* in the Sunday paper, didn't think anything of the thumps since the army had been doing so much construction work next door. When he heard general quarters, he raced to his battle station at Turret 4: "It was just a few minutes when the people down in the lower handling room, where the powder magazines were, started yelling, 'We're hitting water and it's coming pretty fast.' We didn't have any power or any communications whatsoever with the rest of the ship, so we had no idea what condition she was in. The guys there in the lower handling room kept getting water, water up to their knees, water up to their waist. Pretty soon it was up to their chins."

The division officer approved an evacuation to the turret's upper level, but when sea water hit the unit's batteries, the room filled with chlorine gas. Lawson: "The fumes were so bad. I was sitting there in the pointer's chair with a T-shirt over my nose saying, 'What do we do next?' The division officer was absolutely worthless—he didn't know what to do either. We had no communications with the bridge, we couldn't ask anybody what was going on. We were just sitting there in limbo. We knew we'd been hit bad."

Vernon Olsen was hauling himself up *Arizona*'s after mast to his battle station, the crow's nest: "They were strafing and bombing, but it don't take you long. You crawled up the ladders as fast as you could. I was scared. Everybody was scared. Anybody said they weren't scared were crazy." But as for so many others, a problem kept Olsen from firing back at the Japanese with his .50-caliber machine gun: "The ammunition was stored below the platform, but the guy with the key never got there. [So] we just stood there and watched them fly right between the masts and bomb us. You could see their faces. You could see them laughing when they were firing at us. They flew right between the two masts. Our machine gun nest must've been two hundred, three hundred feet high, so we had a bird's-eye view of it. We could see them bombing Ford Island. We felt pretty vulnerable."

Jim Foster was alone at his antiaircraft-gun battle station when he saw Admiral Isaac Kidd and Captain Franklin Van Valkenburgh sprinting to the bridge. Kidd turned to Foster and said, "Man your battle station, son." Jim Foster: "He hit me on the shoulder. I think he called me son. I don't know why. Man your battle station—one man on a sixteen-man gun!" Worth Ross Lightfoot and John McCarron then joined him. They loaded in a shell and pulled the trigger, but nothing happened. Then, Jim Foster was knocked unconscious. He came to and found that his legs and feet were all burned to hell, and his nose was broken: "We were blown off the gun. We went over the gun shield and landed on our hats over there. I was on the bottom of the admiral's boat." He looked up at the bridge, now in flames, to see what had happened to the admiral and the captain: "It was like pouring molten metal in there. It must've been the powder coming up out of the stack on the bridge. They died in that fire."

Lieutenant Commander Samuel Fuqua: "We found the admiral's body on the boat deck, or we found a body which I believe to be the admiral's body on the boat deck, just at the foot of the flag bridge ladder. The captain's body was never found. However, the captain's ring and some coat buttons were found on the flag bridge." Divers eventually found Admiral Kidd's wedding ring in the water. It had melted.

Foster, meanwhile, went to look for shelter in the galley deck: "I stuck my head in and it was full of gas or something. I couldn't breathe. I couldn't see anybody, but I heard them hollering all down below. They were screaming and pounding. Cursing. And the noise of the bombs was deafening. Bang! Bang! Boom! Bang! The ship would jerk and toss every time a bomb hit."

"After the torpedo attacks, horizontal bombers, in *V*s of five planes, came in from southward at twelve to fifteen thousand feet, in close formation and unhindered except for AA fire," *Jarvis*'s Ensign W. F. Greene reported. "Horizontal attacks were regularly spaced at rather long intervals, though I cannot be sure of the exact time, at about ten-to-fifteen-minute intervals." Greene was observing Mitsuo Fuchida and his high-level bombers in their formations of five, six, and nine, the nine made of three *V*s of three planes each, a tactic that had resulted in their best trial-run hit ratio: 33.5 percent. Just as he'd sent the dive-bombers in for the kill, Fuchida ordered his radioman to flash *Tsu, tsu, tsu* on the telegraph, which told his horizontals to begin their deadly run. Fuchida: "Dark gray puffs burst all around. Suddenly a cloud came between the bombsight and the target, and just as I was thinking that we had already overshot, the lead plane banked slightly and turned right toward Honolulu. We had missed the release point because of the cloud and would have to try again." One pilot released his 800-kilogram (1,763-pound) bomb anyway. It fell into the water, completely worthless. Fuchida let the pilot know his feelings with a shake of his fist; the bombardier responded that American antiaircraft fire had shook the bomb loose.

After the Japanese circled around for another attempt, Fuchida's plane was hit by American shells. He asked if everything was all right, and a crewman reported that it was just "a few holes in the fuselage."

Fuchida: "We were about to begin our second bombing run when there was a colossal explosion in Battleship Row. A huge column of dark red smoke rose to one thousand meters. It must have been the explosion of a ship's powder magazine. The shock wave was felt even in my plane, several miles away from the harbor."

"A spurt of flame came out of the guns in [*Arizona*'s] number two turret, followed by an explosion of the forward magazine," said a mechanic on nearby tanker *Ramapo*. "The foremast leaned forward, and the whole forward part of the ship was enveloped in flame and smoke and continued to burn fiercely."

Lieutenant Commander Samuel Fuqua: "I glanced up. I saw a bomb dropping, which appeared to me was going to land on me or close by. The next thing I remember I came to on deck in a position about six feet aft of the starboard gangway. I got to my feet and looked around to see what it was that had knocked me down. Then I saw I was lying about six feet from a bomb hole in the deck. . . . I would judge about eight fifteen or eight twenty I saw a tremendous mass of flames, the height of three hundred feet, rise in the air forward and shook the ship aft as if it would fall apart like a pack of cards."

Pilot Heita Matsumura: "A huge waterspout splashed over the stack of the ship and then tumbled down like an exhausted geyser . . . immediately followed by another one. What a magnificent sight!"

Pilot Otawa: "Now we had given this world-famous American navy the first blow. And I was the one who had made this first strike. I had been trained all the way for this moment. Now all this training was rewarded. Since the bomb weighed eight hundred kilograms and the weight of the plane itself was two and half tons, the plane suddenly lifted when we released that heavy bomb. At that moment, all of my feelings of joy rushed up. I did it!" The single bomb strike that took so many American lives in that instant would officially be credited to one of Fuchida's high-level bombers from *Hiryu*, Tadashi Kusumi.

As over a thousand American boys were incinerated, drowned, or eviscerated by shrapnel, five-hundred-foot-high towers of flame erupted into the sky. An immense fireball roared across the city of the sea's vitals, then the 32,600-ton dreadnought lifted out of the water, cracked her back, and sank back down, her enormous superstructure enveloped in vicious and immense oil-black clouds, her forward compartments flooding with both water and oil.

Japan's air commander couldn't take his eyes away from *Arizona*'s fiery death throes. After he had become a Presbyterian missionary, Fuchida would remember it as "a hateful, mean-looking red flame, the kind that powder produces, and I knew at once that a big magazine had exploded. Terrible indeed."

"A red fireball shot up and spread into a mushroom of death nearly a thousand feet high," said *California* sailor Theodore Mason. "A mighty thunderclap of sound, deep and terrible, rode over the cacophony of planes and bombs, and now-awakening guns."

A *West Virginia* sailor: "Ships on fire, ships burning, explosions going on all over the place. I saw the *Arizona* blow up and she just rained sailors. And of course those were the ones that were fortunate enough to live—the ones that were blown off the ship."

Burning *Arizona* crewmen ran aft or into the water, thinking they would find relief. Instead they found six-inch pools of fiery fuel oil covering the sea, turning them into matchsticks. Clint Westbrook: "All of the oil tanks on all of the battlewagons had been ruptured, most of them, and you could just about almost get out and walk on it, it was that thick. And around those ships that had fire on it was on fire as well, so a lot of these people jumping off the ships were jumping right into burning oil. We had just loaded the day before 'cause we were going back to the States for Christmas. The admiral had told us, so we had filled the tank Saturday."

The burning oil's smoke created an impenetrable black fog floating ten feet over the surface. One witness said, "These people were zombies. . . . They were burned completely white. Their skin was just as white as if you'd taken a bucket of whitewash and painted it white. Their hair was burned off; their eyebrows were burned off; the pitiful remains of their uniforms in their crotch was a charred remnant; and the insoles of their shoes was about the only thing that was left on these bodies. They were moving like robots. Their arms were out, held away from their bodies, and they were stumping along the decks." The teakwood decks, once holystoned into a rich glow, now "looked like a boneyard" from all the body parts. Adolph Kuhn: "The most vivid recording in my memory bank of that ordeal was the hundreds of white sailors' hats floating in the salty brine, with their black stenciled names in full view."

In the US Navy's final accounting, USS *Arizona* was struck by eight bombs. Like all the great battleships of Pearl Harbor, *Arizona*'s powder and ammunition magazines, as well as her fuel tanks, were full; the latter with about 660,000 gallons of oil. Similar to the unbelievable series of events that had exploded the *Shaw*, one Japanese bomb had penetrated to an *Arizona* powder magazine, igniting it into a chain reaction that turned the ship itself into a bomb. The explosion in her forward magazine of 308 fourteen-inch shells, 350 five-inch rounds, 5,000 powder cans, and over 100,000 rounds of bullets was so forceful it blew out some of her hull's armored plates until they were pancake-flat horizontal. The *Tennessee* was more damaged by *Arizona*'s debris than she was by the direct strikes of two Japanese bombs.

Arizona sank in nine minutes. The souls of 1,177 sailors and marines were lost, more than died in the Spanish-American War and the First World War combined. It was the highest mortality in the sinking of a single vessel in American naval history, and of human beings killed by a single explosion in the history of war . . . until Hiroshima.

Six months later, when Lieutenant Wilmer Gallaher dove his Dauntless to pay back *Akagi* with a fatal blow at Midway, he remembered the horror at Pearl Harbor. As *Akagi* exploded, he whispered to himself, "*Arizona*, I remember you."

Arizona's explosion was so immense it blew crewmen off the neighboring *Vestal*'s deck, including Captain Cassin Young. He swam back, countermanded the crew's collective decision to abandon ship—"You don't abandon ship on me!"—and ordered them back to their posts to defend Pearl Harbor. Young found two bodies on the afterdeck: "These men may have been either *Arizona* personnel blown over by magazine blast or members of *Vestal* after gun crews: they were burned beyond recognition."

As *Vestal* began firing back with her three-inch and her machine guns, two bombs struck, one exploding in a lower hold, cutting power cables and igniting a fire that burned toward the forward magazine, which held seven hundred rounds of ammunition. *Vestal* saved her own self from detonation by flooding that magazine, but could do little about the second bomb, which hit to port and farther aft, breaking tanks. The ship began to flood with both fuel and sea water.

Sailor Warren Law: "I've never seen anything like it in my life since, and I hope I never do. The devastation was just unbelievable on those battleships. You think they're big, heavy, lotta heavy steel and all that. When you see those superstructures just twisted—big hunks of steel that were twisted just like you take a straw and twist the thing. I couldn't believe the amount of devastation that I saw."

On *Arizona*, Boatswain's Mate 2nd Class John Anderson "was standing on gun turret number four when I saw a bomb hit the side of it. It scooped out the side of the turret. It went right past me, a big mound of molten steel. I got my people out and went to look for my brother." Anderson's twin, Delbert, was stationed at Turret 3, and John tried to find him, but between the wreckage left behind by the explosion, and the number of dead and dying men on the deck, John couldn't make it to 3. So he went in search of an officer to get some direction and came across his ensign "dead on deck, his back split open like a watermelon."

The force of a bomb then blew Anderson down a quarterdeck's hatch. He recovered and joined a group working to fight back with an antiaircraft gun, but when the ship lost power, that gun was unusable, so he joined the rescue operation: "By now the ship had settled some in the water. We were passing down the wounded hand over hand into the lifeboats as fast as we could. We weren't any too gentle, as you can imagine."

When Anderson's turn came to get in the boat, he announced that he was going back aboard to rescue Delbert. Samuel Fuqua set him straight: "He's gone, they're not going to make it. And we better get off before everyone else is killed, too." Anderson accepted this, and as his boat left for Ford Island, he took one last look at lost home: "Everything was on fire. The ship was on fire, the water was on fire, and there were people in the crane . . . and I saw them as we went and they were up in this fire. I thought, 'God Almighty, how are they going to make it?'"

Now reasonably safe on Ford, all John Anderson could think about was getting back to *Arizona* to rescue more men: "I looked around and saw a boat floating in the water. I saw a kid named Rose, Chester Clay Rose from Kentucky, and I said, 'Hey, Rose, are you game?' . . . He said yes, so we dived in, got in the lifeboat, and went back to the ship." They found the 250-pound body of *Arizona*'s cook: "I don't know how he got blown out of the galley to the outside. He was dead, with a kitchen knife stuck in him from the force of the explosion."

It was so hard to find the living among such a floating mass of corpses that Anderson decided to stop making guesses and just bring in everybody. Anderson and Rose rescued as many as they could out of the water, filling the boat with both the dead and the injured. On their way back to Ford's naval hospital, "we moved on into the middle of the stream, got hit by a shell, and lost everybody. I even lost Rose. I was the only survivor."

By the end of the week, he'd learn that his brother, Delbert, was trying to fix a jammed AA gun when he was killed.

William Goshen was a pointer for Turret 3's five-inch gun, but when he got there, no one else was around, and he couldn't find any ammunition. The strafing scared him, so he sat against a locker where there was some cover. Next thing he knew, he was swimming; the explosion had thrown him in the water. He had escaped with his life by sitting in that little corner; his turret was mere yards from the bomb strike: "All that was between me and that bomb was two canvas sheets. Evidently it burnt the canvas off and carried right on into the compartment where I was at, and the concussion happening inside blew me out." Struggling to the surface of the water, "I looked over at the ship, and I knew there was no need going back there. I looked up at the boats; they were all on fire. The *Arizona* was on fire. I heard the buzzing of planes, the cracking of cannons, the machine guns they were strafing with." He was taken to the Ford Island dispensary with burns on 70 percent of his body.

Galen Ballard's life was saved because, instead of going to bed the night of December 6 in his own bunk, he fell asleep in Honolulu, not waking up until a little after 0800. After starting the day with some Ink Spots on the record player, he turned on the radio and heard, "Seek cover. Personnel, report to your stations." He was out of uniform, so he had to go back to the Navy Center to get it, and on a Sunday the building was locked: "I had to scale a wall to get to my locker and change into uniform and call a cab." As he and the cabbie got close enough to see Pearl Harbor, "at first I thought from all the smoke they'd hit some oil reserves, but as we got going, I realized it was more than that. The bombers were going over and there was a lot of antiaircraft fire. We could see the *Arizona* was up in flames, and the *Oklahoma* was capsized. All we could see was smoke and flames. I was numb. Frightened. Confused. . . . Everything I owned was on the *Arizona*—all I had left was what I had on my back."

Samuel Fuqua: "As I was running forward on the starboard side of the quarterdeck, approximately by the starboard gangway, I was apparently knocked out by the blast of a bomb, which I learned later had struck the faceplate of number four turret on the starboard side and had glanced off and gone through the deck just forward of the captain's hatch, penetrating the decks and exploding on the third deck. When I came to and got up off the deck, the ship was a mass of flames amidships on the boat deck, and the deck aft was awash to about frame ninety. The antiaircraft battery and machine guns apparently were still firing at this time. Some of the *Arizona* boats had pulled clear of the oil and were lying off the stern.

"At this time I attempted, with the assistance of the crews of number two and number four turrets, to put out the fire which was coming from the boat deck, and which had extended to the quarterdeck. There was no water on the fire mains. However, about fourteen CO_2s were obtained that were stowed on the port side and held the flames back from the quarterdeck, enabling us to pick up wounded who were running down the boat deck out of the flames. I placed about seventy wounded and injured in the boats which had been picked up off the deck aft and landed them at the Ford Island landing. This was completed about 0900 or 0930. All personnel but three or four men, turrets number three and number four, were saved. About 0900, seeing that all guns of the antiaircraft and secondary battery were out of action and that the ship could not possibly be saved, I ordered all hands to abandon ship."

Ensign G. S. Flannigan: "When that bomb hit, it made a whish with a gust of hot air and sparks flew. There followed a very nauseating gas, and smoke immediately afterwards.

"Before this time, condition zed had been set in the lower room of Turret three, and the men in the passage and I were unable to get out of the passageway. I beat on the door for some minutes before someone inside the turret opened the door. We got all the men that we could find in the passageway into the lower room and then dogged down the passageway door.

"The air in the turret was fairly clear for a while, but finally gas or smoke starting coming in. The men made quite a bit of confusion at first but they were very obedient when Ensign Field and I ordered them to keep quiet. About this time we got a flashlight and saw the turret was very misty with smoke. Just after this, we heard hissing noise, which was later discovered to be air leaking from holes in the forward transverse bulkhead of the lower room.

"Conditions from smoke were getting worse and worse. It was then that we decided that we would have to leave the lower room. I took charge of the men in the pits, and Ensign Field went out on deck to help Lieutenant Commander Fuqua. We saw smoke entering the pits through the pointers' and trainers' telescope slots. I urged the men to take off their shirts, and we closed the openings with the clothes."

US marines Sergeant John Baker, Corporal Earl Nightingale, Major Alan Shapley, and Second Lieutenant Carleton Simensen were climbing the mainmast when one of Minoru Genda's eight-hundred-kilogram, armor-blasting shells hit Turret 4, bounced up, and hit the deck, exploding into shrapnel. Corporal Nightingale: "I was about three-quarters of the way to the first platform on the mast when it seemed as though a bomb struck our quarterdeck. I could hear shrapnel or fragments whistling past me. As soon as I reached the first platform, I saw Second Lieutenant Simensen lying on his back with blood on his shirt-front. I bent over him and, taking him by the shoulders, asked if there was anything I could do. He was dead, or so nearly so that speech was impossible. Seeing there was nothing I could do for the lieutenant, I continued to my battle station.

"When I arrived in secondary aft I reported to Major Shapley that Mr. Simensen had been hit and there was nothing to be done for him. There was a lot of talking going on and I shouted for silence, which came immediately. I had only been there a short time when a terrible explosion caused the ship to shake violently. I followed the major down the port side of the tripod mast. The railings were very hot, and as we reached the boat deck, I noted that it was torn up and burned. The bodies of the dead were thick, and badly burned men were heading for the quarterdeck, only to fall apparently dead or badly wounded."

Surrounded by the corpses of their friends and the destruction of their home, Shapley, Nightingale, and Baker finally got to the boat deck, where Fuqua, as senior officer present afloat, was in the middle of this scene of incomprehensible horror, leading shocked crewmen—many of them teenagers, or nearly so—in the abandonment of his ship. Aviation Machinist's Mate 1st Class D. A. Graham: "There were lots of men coming out on the quarterdeck with every stitch of clothing and shoes blown off, painfully burned and shocked. Mr. Fuqua set an example for the men by being unperturbed, calm, cool, and collected, exemplifying the courage and traditions of an officer under fire. It seemed like the men painfully burned, shocked, and dazed became inspired and took things in stride, seeing Mr. Fuqua, so unconcerned about the bombing and strafing, standing on the quarterdeck. There was no 'going to pieces' or 'growing panicky' noticeable." John Baker said that Fuqua's "calmness gave me courage, and I looked around to see if I could help," but Fuqua ordered him to join the others in the boats. Private Cory remembered Fuqua quietly urging them on: "Over the side, boys! Over the side!" Grabbing life rafts, they jumped overboard. The commander's leadership had such a profound impact that it saved countless lives beyond the seventy that are his official credit.

"I was the second-to-last man off the ship," Private Cory said. "Fuqua was the last guy. Those rafts immediately started drifting and floating into the burning oil, so those were quickly abandoned. The two or three guys that actually got on one were going right into the fire so they had to get off immediately. The currents were taking them right into the fire."

Marine Corporal Earl Nightingale: "Charred bodies were everywhere. I made my way to the quay and started to remove my shoes when I suddenly found myself in the water. I think the concussion of a bomb threw me in. I started swimming for the pipeline which was about one hundred and fifty feet away. I was about halfway when my strength gave out entirely. My clothes and shocked condition sapped my strength, and I was about to go under when Major Shapley started to swim by and, seeing my distress, grasped my shirt and told me to hang to his shoulders while he swam in. We were perhaps twenty-five feet from the pipeline when the major's strength gave out and I saw he was floundering, so I loosened my grip on him and told him to make it alone. He stopped and grabbed me by the shirt and refused to let go. I would have drowned but for the major. We finally reached the beach, where a marine directed us to a bomb shelter, where I was given dry clothes and a place to rest."

For these actions, Major Shapley would be awarded the Silver Star.

Argonne's Charles Christensen: "The oil was on fire and [the men] were trying to swim out of it. They'd come up and try to get their breath. The whites of their eyes were red. Their skin was coming off. At the hospital, oil was all over everything and everybody. I never saw any panic. I was always proud of the navy after that."

One man in the water didn't know how to swim. Jim Lawson tried to help, but it would have meant drowning for both: "I was making no progress, just treading water with him, and the breeze and the current were taking us into the fire. I went ahead and let him go." Finally Lawson was picked up by Fuqua, running a barge. Lawson got the sailor who couldn't swim to dog-paddle over, tied a T-shirt to the man's ankle, and they towed him to Ford Island. "There was a guy standing on the dock, how he got there I don't know. He looked like he just got off the grill. He was burned to a crisp. The poor guy, what kept him alive I don't know. He kept asking for help and no one could help. What could you do?"

"A friend of mine was crying and asking me for help," *Arizona* crewman Carl Carson wrote. "I looked at him in horror. His skin was hanging off him. There was nothing in the world I could do for him. He was dying. They gave us the word to abandon ship. I started to swim to Ford Island. I must have passed out and gone down in the water. Everything was peaceful and nice. It would have been so easy to just let go. And I saw this bright light, and something made me come to. And there was oil all around. And fire all around. A man saw me down there and he reached down and pulled me up to the surface."

Jim Foster jumped into water to get away: "When I came up, I was gagging. I was really busting water trying to get away from that thing before it blew up. I wasn't a very good swimmer, but I really busted water for about ten feet and realized I was giving out. I was giving plum out. The planes were still coming in, and they were strafing all the men in the water."

Finally he reached a pipe sticking out on the beach on Ford Island, and he and two others held on to it until they could get help. Foster and John McCarron survived; with Foster's feet so burned up it was months before he could wear shoes.

Worth Ross Lightfoot died after a couple of weeks.

"Both my legs were burnt pretty bad," *Arizona* Seaman 1st Class Donald Stratton said. "My legs, arms, face, my hair. Lost my hair. Lost a couple of tattoos . . . don't recommend that way to get rid of 'em. . . .

"I seen everything that went on there, and I tell you what. There was more courage and more heroics and more valor and more sacrifice that day than a human being ought to see in ten lifetimes."

CHAPTER EIGHT

DESCRIBING THE INDESCRIBABLE

Honolulu radio station KGMB interrupted its morning broadcast at 8:04 to announce that all military personnel were ordered back to duty, followed by calls for area policemen and firemen and, at 0840, the first American broadcast of World War II: "Calling all nurses! Proceed to Pearl Harbor! Oahu is being attacked! The sign of the rising sun is to be seen on the wings of the attacking planes!"

Soon after, one of Oahu's leading citizens, Allan Davis, made a private call to that morning's on-air personality, Webley Edwards. Davis told Edwards that he was making a mistake announcing the attack, that this was all just maneuvers, and America was still at peace. Edwards, having heard so many others insist that the reports were wrong, blew up, saying, "Hell, no, this is the real McCoy!" Davis was so shocked that he just mumbled and hung up, but Edwards realized his audience needed to be shocked into the reality of what they were facing and repeated again and again that this was the "real McCoy."

Just like so many servicemen, civilians in Hawaii had trouble believing the news, or even their own eyes. Perhaps the most common reaction was that of Yee Kam York, who followed much of the attack with binoculars from just outside Honolulu. He told his wife, "These Americans, when they have maneuvers, they certainly make it realistic." KGMB listeners heard the word *sporadic* used to describe the attacks and thought it was *simulated*, a common announcement in Honolulu. Others had trouble taking the warning seriously since a popular record getting much radio play at the moment was "Three Little Fishes," meaning war bulletins were interspersed with *down in the meadow in a iddy biddy poo thwam thwee little fishies and a mama fishie too.*

When Ethelyn Meyhre heard Webley Edwards's announcements,

she woke her dad, who laughed, said it must be a joke, and went back to bed. When Federal Bureau of Investigation agent Robert Shivers called director J. Edgar Hoover with the news, Hoover was so incredulous that Shivers held his telephone out the window, so the director could hear the bomb strikes and machine guns.

By 0930 the *Honolulu Star-Bulletin* had an edition hitting the street with the headline *"WAR! OAHU BOMBARDED BY JAPANESE PLANES."* A policeman called editor Riley Allen to warn that some of his more enterprising newsboys had gone out to Pearl Harbor to sell their papers and were in serious danger.

Besides breaking news of the attack as it happened, KGMB warned its listeners: "The United States Army Intelligence has ordered all civilians stay off the streets. Do not use your telephone. The island is under attack. Stay off the streets. Keep calm. Keep your radio turned on for further news. Get your car off the street. Drive it on the lawn if necessary, just so you get it off the street. Fill water buckets and tubs with water, to be ready for a possible fire. Attach garden hoses. Prepare to take care of any emergency. Keep tuned to your radio for details of a blackout, which will be announced later. In the event of an air raid, stay under cover. Many of the wounded have been hurt by falling shrapnel from antiaircraft guns. If an air raid should begin, do not go out of doors. Stay under cover. You may be seriously injured or instantly killed by shrapnel falling from antiaircraft shells."

Over Pearl Harbor, Mitsuo Fuchida and his squadron of horizontal bombers circled again. The commander needed to make detailed sightings for his damage reports to Nagumo, Genda, and Yamamoto, while his pilots needed to take down the USS *California*. Fuchida: "A warm feeling came with the realization that the reward of those efforts was unfolding before my eyes. I counted four battleships definitely sunk and three severely damaged, and extensive damage had also been inflicted upon other types of ships. The seaplane base at Ford Island was all in flames, as were the airfields, especially Wheeler Field."

It was now, however, no longer dawn, and the Americans were no longer sleeping. Antiaircraft fire so damaged Fuchida's steering gear that the wire connecting the stick to the ailerons was a bare thread; twenty holes had been drilled into his fuselage, and he was in trouble: "Suddenly it was as though a giant hand had smashed at my plane. A gaping hole appeared on the port side. The steering mechanism was damaged." Fuchida would not be deterred; while his bombers joined their torpedo brothers in attacking *California*, Fuchida went after *Maryland*: "I immediately lay flat on the cockpit floor and slid open a peephole cover in order to observe the fall of the bombs. The target—two battleships moored side by side—lay ahead. In perfect pattern [the bombs] plummeted like devils of doom. They became small as poppy seeds and finally disappeared just as tiny white flashes of smoke appeared on or near the ship."

Commander W. F. Fitzgerald Jr.: "While on the starboard side of the flag bridge I felt the *Maryland* shudder from what was apparently a near miss off the port bow. Within a second or two I saw a bomb land on the forecastle of the *Maryland* and shortly thereafter (a matter of a few seconds) a large geyser of water sprung up on the starboard bow of the *Maryland* apparently from another near miss. By this time the guns of both the port and starboard batteries were firing continuously at the enemy planes. The fires on the *Arizona* and *West Virginia* seemed to be increasing, and frequently the *Maryland* was entirely covered with heavy black smoke."

Two of *Maryland's* men were killed and one was injured by the falling shells; one "poor fellow had a hole right in his forehead where he'd been hit," Vice Admiral Walter Anderson remembered. "There was the bottom of the overturned *Oklahoma* facing me, and the sunken, blasted *Arizona*. Great clouds of black smoke were billowing up from the oil afire on the water. There was the most comprehensive antiaircraft fire I had ever seen, and yellow Japanese planes were flying back and forth, almost literally hedgehopping. I thought to myself, 'Dante's Inferno never looked like this.'"

Besides rescuing fallen sailors, the men of *Maryland* and *Tennessee* fought back with real strength. "Outstanding was the action of Leslie Vernon Short, seaman first class," *Maryland's* commanding officer, D. C. Godwin, reported. "Short, a machine-gun striker twenty-two years old, truly demonstrated the spirit of men behind the navy guns. Though he had not been called to duty at his gun station, upon seeing our country being attacked, he immediately manned a machine gun, opened fire on two approaching torpedo planes, downing the first one and injuring the second."

California's bulkheads were so torn by the first two torpedoes that knifed through her port that rivets popped out and were ricocheting around the lower compartments. She would be hit by two more

torpedoes, followed by two high-level bombs, and was especially vulnerable, since a number of watertight chambers had not been dogged
down. "After the second torpedo hit, we began to get large quantities
of smoke down the ventilator blowers, so we secured the ventilators,"
Ensign W. A. J. Lewis said. "Smoke still came down, and word was
received that gas was present. We could detect nothing but powder
gases so did not put on gas masks. Later on the smoke became thicker,
so I directed some of the men to put on their masks. The smoke began
to take effect on the crew, so I ordered all hands except the talker on
the upper level to go down to the lower level, where air was somewhat
better. The forward part of the engine room had become very hot,
and the metal in some places was too hot to touch. This accounted for
some of the paint fumes, as the paint had begun to blister."

Caught in a burning hallway, Chief Radioman Thomas Reeves kept
passing heavy shells forward by hand until he passed out and died. The
fires spread, and the rest of the men had to flee, many around the body
of wounded ensign Herbert Jones. Two friends tried rescuing Jones,
but he told them that it was all over for him, that they must leave and
save themselves.

Chief Yeoman S. R. Miller: "We obtained a line and lowered Ensign
McGrath through the trunk to Central Station, which was then being
flooded with fuel oil coming from vents and various other places. The
oil fumes were so strong that we feared Ensign McGrath would be
overcome with the fumes before the trapped men could be rescued.
At this time the ship was burning fiercely, and there was also danger
of the ship turning over as it was listing badly. Ensign McGrath completed his investigation and returned up the trunk to Flag Conn and
reported that these men were in a compartment under Central Station
and might be rescued by cutting a hole through the deck of Central
Station. He reported that the deck of Central Station would soon be
flooded with oil and that when this occurred, it would be too late to
cut the hole through the deck. A cutting torch was quickly obtained
and volunteers called for. Ensign McGrath and Campbell were both
nearly overcome by fumes before the job was completed. The first who
worked with the cutting torch was overcome by fumes and had to be
replaced with another experienced man. During the time this hole was
being cut, there was great danger of fire as the fuel oil was gradually
working its way close to where the hole was being cut. In addition to
this danger, there was danger of the ship turning over as it was strain-

ing the mooring lines badly. The hole in the deck was just cut in time before fuel oil flooded Central Station."

Gunner Jackson Pharris smartly ordered *California*'s shipfitters to counterflood. This equalized her weight and saved her from *Oklahoma*'s fate. He then oversaw teams of men plunging through the fumes to ferry ammunition from the magazines below to the deck guns above. He would be awarded the Medal of Honor, as would be Machinist's Mate 1st Class Robert Scott, who refused to evacuate while he ran the forward air compressor that fed power to *California*'s antiaircraft cannon. He said, "As long as I can give these people air, I'm sticking," and sacrificed his life.

California's John McGoran remembered the first thing he heard about the attack was when he was taking dirty dishes to be washed and a sailor darted past, maniacally singing, "The Japs are coming! Hurrah, hurrah!" Someone asked for help with a wounded man, and McGoran immediately thought to himself, "If on December 6 anyone had asked me to help save the life of this offensive guy, I would have answered, 'To hell with him.' I had known this fellow since boot camp, and he was one of the most overbearing individuals I had ever met. But now, unconscious, he had no personality. His was a life to be saved." Then "this crazy thought struck me. 'No one will believe all this when I tell them someday. And since I have no memory for dates, it will really sound silly.' So I sat down and with my pocketknife scratched on the back of my wristwatch 'Pearl Harbor Dec. 7, 1941.'"

Fires on *California* had to be fought with water from Ford Island's swimming pool because as *Arizona* sank, her body settled on the water main and broke it. Likely for the first time in naval history, two garbage-scow crews received formal commendations for their courage in firefighting.

A motor-driven whaleboat arrived from Honolulu harbor to immediately make repeated trips to the edge of the floating fire to help extinguish it or at least keep it from spreading. Just as repeatedly, the whaleboat itself caught fire, and as soon as it could put out its own flames, it would return to fight the burning water.

The night before, *California* musician Warren Harding had been delighted by the sight of a meteor shower. Then he remembered something his grandfather had said . . . that, when you see a shooting star, someone you know will die. "My God," Harding thought, "how many people do I know that are going to die soon?"

Ninety-eight died on his ship.

• • •

While Mitsuo Fuchida felt contempt for the US Navy that hadn't even installed torpedo crinolines around their battleships, his fellow aircrews in the second attack wave were impressed by the Americans, who were now fully alert and fighting back. Dive-bomber pilot Zenji Abe:

"As we crowded the shoreline, a group of black puffs of smoke appeared to our right front, and then another group appeared quite near our formation—about two hundred in all.

"Antiaircraft fire! Except for scattered shots in China, it was the first time I had experienced that. I watched the puffs come closer and closer. The thought flashed across my mind that perhaps our surprise attack was not a surprise at all. Would we be successful? I felt awful.

"[Then] there was a feeling of calm. It was very clear. Not many clouds. And I could see the large ships. I knew that they were the targets. I knew that they were what we needed to hit.

"I banked as a signal to my men and headed down. From the ground, thousands of tracer bullets soared upward, seeming to gain speed as they passed close by my plane. My altitude was three thousand meters and my speed two hundred knots. I applied my air brake and took the cover off my bombsight. I was diving at about a fifty-degree angle. There were no aircraft carriers in the harbor, so I decided to attack a cruiser.

"I caught my target, a big cruiser, squarely in the middle of the range scale of my sight. Warrant Officer Saito began to call the altitude. A strong northeast wind was blowing the plane to the left. I corrected for the drift as the target drew nearer and nearer until it almost filled my sight. 'Six hundred meters,' Saito called. 'Ready . . . release!'

"I released my bomb and at the same time pulled back on the stick. I almost blacked out for a moment, but I pulled out at fifty meters to the sound of Saito's voice in the voice tube. My observer was excitedly calling out the results of our bombing. 'Formation leader short. Second plane short. Third plane hit! Adjustment correct. Second echelon successful!' I was later able to identify our target as an Omaha-class light cruiser, *Raleigh*."

Tennessee sailor Millard McDonald: "My thoughts were to make an act of defiance to show the enemy that, although we were badly battered, we were not defeated. We climbed as fast as we could, for the steel of the mast was hot from the nearby fires and beginning to burn our hands.

We climbed through a thick smoke cloud, and Oscar then climbed to the yard in order to put the new halyard through. The moment he signaled everything was ready, I attached the nation's colors and hoisted them along the mast. At the very moment we completed our task, general quarters once again sounded. We turned to look at the sky and saw another wave of Japanese planes strafing his way to our position."

Projectiles decimated *Tennessee*'s Turret 2's center gun and killed four men running Turret 3. Signalman 2nd Class Richard Burge: "One Jap plane was hit and exploded over Ford Island, and the pilot landed just fifty feet from the USS *Tennessee*. We left his body in the water for three weeks before we picked it up."

Even after the Japanese second wave had left, the ship was still in danger. "The *Tennessee* was moored inboard of the *West Virginia* at berth F-6," as Executive Officer Commander Colin Campbell reported. "The *West Virginia* had been sunk and was on fire. The *Arizona*, about seventy-five feet astern of the *Tennessee* had been sunk and was on fire, and oil was burning on the water. The stern of the *Tennessee* was on fire, and fires were raging on the *Arizona* and *West Virginia*, threatening destruction of this ship. When the captain came aboard, he directed me to go aft and take charge on the quarterdeck, where I remained practically continuously supervising the firefighting on this ship and against the oil fires on the water coming from the *Arizona*, until about sundown Tuesday the ninth, by which time the oil fires on the *Arizona* had been extinguished by this ship and yard tugs."

As Campbell reported, it would take three days to stop the burning fires of Pearl Harbor. Seaman Jimmy Anders: "All this time, our cooks had been busy preparing sandwiches, nice big thick ham sandwiches. . . . In times like this, I was amazed how so much attention was paid to eating."

Of the many remarkable Pearl Harbor stories, one began in a farmhouse outside Odebolt, Iowa, that produced eight brothers and a father—the Pattens—who all signed up with the US Navy, collectively giving the nation 124 years of service. On December 7, six of them—Gilbert, Marvin, Bick, Allen, Ray, and Bruce—were working in the engine room of the USS *Nevada*. Allen remembered that morning's breakfast was "a 'dog' sandwich and beans. Then some of the other B Division sailors and I sat around drinking tea and coffee and discussing the Rose Bowl, and who would win the football game, Duke or Oregon. Then something strange started happening, and we couldn't figure out what was going on. It was just past eight a.m., we were three decks down, and the *Nevada* started shaking like a three- or four-scale earthquake. The porthole was open and I heard a rat-a-tat-tat sound, like a machine gun. We were all very confused; it had been such a nice serene morning. We thought it odd that someone might be practicing with their guns. Then the B Division mess cook, Henry, he was just a kid, eighteen years old, yelled down to us, 'Hey, you guys, we're being attacked.' "

"The planes are coming in," Steward 1st Class Ben Holt remembered. "The *Nevada* is getting hit. Our gunners are now manning the guns. I'm trying to secure cans on the side to keep them from rolling across the deck. I saw only one officer, Ensign Taussig. I remember him very vividly."

Joseph Taussig: "I caught a glimpse of a torpedo plane flying from the east and very low over the water. . . . The bomb-bay doors were open, and out dropped a 'fish.' My reaction was merely to think of the welcome break in the Sunday-morning tedium that we would have watching the salvage operation of digging the torpedo out of the mud under forty feet of water, the controlling depth of Pearl Harbor."

"On the way to my battle station, I found one of my brothers arguing with a chief petty officer," Boiler Tender Bruce Patten remembered. The officer said he was sick of hearing about rumors that they were under attack. "Then the first bomb hit and ended the argument."

According to Captain Charles Medinger, *Nevada* was originally set to spend the weekend of December 5–7 at sea. But when alien-submarine contacts were reported, she returned early to Pearl Harbor. She normally moored at one particular berth, but as *Arizona* was there, she had to tie up elsewhere.

"All guns were soon roaring," Robert Thomas Jr. said. "As I watched, the USS *Arizona*, just three hundred feet ahead of us, erupted in an enormous flash and thunderous blast that knocked me twenty feet backwards onto my back. I knew that German and British ships could explode, but I couldn't believe that an American ship could blow up like that. It was heart-wrenching to see the few tattered survivors abandon ship."

Joe Taussig: "I felt a very sharp blow on the bottom of my feet, and very shortly after that I felt a blow on my hip. And I looked down and my left foot was under my left arm. I was standing in a doorway so I wasn't knocked down. I was hit by a missile which passed completely through my thigh and through the case of the ballistic computer of the director, which was directly in front of me. The intercom called. It was the chief quartermaster, named Robert Sedberry. And he said, 'Mr. Taussig, aren't you the officer of the deck? You better get down here because we've got a signal to get under way.' And I said, 'Sedberry, you've been on that bridge seventeen years. If anybody can get the ship out, you can get her out.'"

Allen Patten: "Part of the crew was on liberty, and only one of the ship's six boilers was lit and on line. Thick ropes held the ship tightly in place. An ax cut through the hemp mooring lines, and by eight eighteen a.m., we had all six boilers off in ten minutes—record time. The *Nevada* was under way in eighteen minutes, steaming through billowing smoke, which was pouring from the *Arizona*."

Even though she'd been hit by a torpedo to her hull and two bombs to her deck, *Nevada* set sail. Ben Holt: "How could the ship move? It took hours to get up enough steam to get the ship to go. And this ship was moving! And all of us were just kind of 'Hallelujah!'"

As American servicemen across the devastated Pearl Harbor—which to so many looked like the end of the world—watched, thrilled and amazed, Robert Sedberry did the impossible, piloting *Nevada* across the notoriously narrow Pearl Harbor around the burning *Arizona*, the sinking *West Virginia*, and the capsized *Oklahoma*. Robert Thomas: "The chief quartermaster took the controls in an attempt to get to sea where we could maneuver and fight. There were no senior officers on board. They were all on land. As we cleared the burning *Arizona*, the harbor became visible to us. Good God! The *West Virginia* was awash and burning, the *Oklahoma* had capsized, the *California* was listing and afire, and the *Pennsylvania*, in dry dock, was burning. I thought, 'We are the only ones left!'" Joe Taussig: "We'd had a torpedo hit us on the port side by number two turret, so we were flooded pretty bad. But Sedberry got the ship out, which is probably one of the greatest seamanship maneuvers of all times because the *Arizona* had blown up ahead of us."

Just as the *Nevada* reached the channel, the First Air Fleet's second wave of warplanes appeared overhead. Pilot Yonnekichi Nakajima: "A battleship had survived and was navigating its way toward the mouth of Pearl Harbor. We all started to bomb it." *Nevada*'s drive to the sea was the opportunity Fuchida had been praying for. A capital ship, sunk in the channel, would seal Pearl Harbor for months, striking a perhaps fatal blow against American naval power in the Pacific. Originally, one squadron of dive-bombers had targeted *Helena* and another had their sights set on Dry Dock One, but seeing this remarkable target of opportunity, they curved up and set about to destroy *Nevada*.

Robert Thomas: "As we passed down the channel, I heard a shout, 'Dive-bombers! Dive-bombers!' I looked up and saw them in an echelon formation beginning to peel off, and then down they came. We were their targets. Through our firing they came, the pilots and other details clearly visible. Each carried a single bomb lodged between its fixed-wheel landing gear. As each bomb was released, I could tell from the relative motion as to whether it would be a hit or a miss. The first two or three missed just starboard. The next bomber released and his bomb just grew larger. I knew it was a hit. I said to myself, 'Mother, I am sorry.'"

Surrounded by the explosions of water columns from Japanese misses, *Nevada* seemed to be one of the lucky ones. It was like a dream. She was going to make it out and use her great guns to strike back at the Japanese! But then a bomb hit home and exploded, first shaking *Nevada*, then crippling her. Another hit to the starboard killed so many on the deck that Chief Gunner's Mate Robert Linnartz had to work as rammerman, sight-setter, and pointer to keep his gun running, even though he himself was seriously injured. Likewise, Ensign Thomas Taylor continued running the port antiaircraft battery, even though he was burned and deaf, his eardrums having been cracked open by a blast. Ben Holt: "People were being blown over the side. The ship was listing. People were saying, 'Abandon ship! Abandon ship!' And that's when I said, 'It's time to go over the side.'"

Artis Teer was working his five-inch gun when a bomb exploded in the casemate next to him, killing two men, knocking Teer unconscious, and showering his back with shrapnel. He was so wounded that the rest of his crew abandoned the gun and left Teer behind, assuming he was dead. He came to, saw his gun on fire, and, though delirious, remembered a round was inside that would explode. So he crawled to the gun, pointed it to sea, and fired.

Machinist Donald Ross was running the forward dynamo. When the room became overwhelmed by smoke and heat, he ordered his crew out and kept running the power, until he passed out. Ross was pulled out, came to, and went over to the aft dynamo, which he ran until he once again passed out. Carried out and brought to, he again returned to running that machine, until he was directly ordered to abandon ship.

Robert Thomas: "I ordered, 'Take cover,' and turned my back before the bomb struck. I was engulfed in a storm of blast, fire, smoke, and debris. A moment later, I noticed that I was still standing. I looked around to see a large crater in the deck just a few feet away and in the general vicinity of the now-empty main powder magazine. The bodies of my men were strewn about. I spotted one of my shipmates lying near the edge, and he was on fire. I took a step towards him and collapsed. That's when I realized that my leg was broken. My right wrist and hand were shot through as well, rendering it useless. I then noticed blood spurting from my arms and legs and I couldn't stop the bleeding. That worried me more than the rest of my physical condition. I crawled over to the edge of the crater and realized that I wasn't able to pull the man to safety. It became a nightmare as I yelled at the top of my lungs to several sailors just a few yards from me on the deck below. Despite their proximity, they couldn't hear me due to the deafening roar of the battle."

Robert Thomas would receive the Legion of Valor, the Purple Heart, and the Navy Cross. But another officer fell to his fears and started beating on the conning tower while begging, "Make them go away!" A very young seaman waited by a five-inch gun with a bag of powder next to his chest. He wasn't going to be injured, he explained, only killed.

Seaman 1st Class William Rodda: "When I got to the top of the first ladder, there was a Filipino sailor lying on his back. All his arms and legs were broken and bent the wrong way. I stepped over him, and at the top of the next ladder, there was a sailor on his back with a handful of guts sticking out through his T-shirt. After I stepped over him, I looked around. There were dead sailors lying everywhere. I got a hose and started putting water on the fire. After a while the water stopped. I was on the quarterdeck when our captain came aboard. He had an expression on his face you would not believe."

After being asked to send half of his crew topside to help in defense, Captain Charles Medinger "felt that those men who were singled out to go topside thought they were going to their deaths, and the ones who were staying thought they staying to their deaths, because it looked as though we might get trapped down there."

Nevada was now beginning to list, sinking at her bow. Commander

Thomas steered her to the floating dry dock off Hospital Point. There, he ran her aground. Fuchida's great dream of sealing the channel died with that one tactic.

"Some of us were given new, clean, shined galvanized buckets to pick up the isolated, fragmented parts of fallen shipmates," Seaman 2nd Class Charles Sehe remembered. "In two of the Fifth Division five-inch/fifty-one gun casements were portions of the bulkheads which consisted of Cyclone security linked fences. One noticed numerous body parts which seemed to have been strained through these partitions from the force of the explosions. I recall picking up several knee joints, shoulder pieces, and several torn and burned torsos that were unidentifiable because of their blackened and burned condition. The tremendous force of those explosions seemed to have literally strained the soft tissue through the chain-linked fencing, leaving the bony elements behind."

Miraculously, all the Patten brothers survived Pearl Harbor, and Bruce Patten would become one of the few servicemen to participate in both the attack on Hawaii and in the Japanese surrender when he served on destroyer *Wren*, which accompanied the USS *Missouri* into Tokyo Bay on September 2, 1945.

Back at the dungeon on Ford Island, as machine-gun bullets strafed across the Bellingers' front yard, sixteen-year-old Mary Ann Ramsey, thirteen-year-old Patricia Bellinger, and the little Zuber girls were now confronted by horribly wounded men seeking to join them in the sheltering cave. A medic told Patricia to give one of these men a blanket; she said he already had one. Then she realized what she thought was a blanket was the poor man's skin, hanging from his shoulders like a burnt drape. Another medic asked the families to give spare cloth to help clean the oil off the injured men; the Zuber daughters donated their bathrobes.

If the Pearl Harbor attack devastated Americans, it had a remarkable impact on these young girls. Mary Ann Ramsey: "A young man, filthy black oil covering his burned, shredded flesh, walked in unaided. He had no clothes on, his nudity entirely obscured by oil. The skin hung from his arms like scarlet ribbons as he staggered toward my mother for help. Looking at me, he gestured to his throat, trying to speak: he must have swallowed some of the burning oil as he swam through the inferno. His light blue eyes against the whites, made more so by the oil clinging to his face, were luminous in visible shock at what they had seen and experienced that awful morning.

"We gave cigarettes to those who wanted to smoke and held them for others who could not use their hands. We covered the men with sheets and tried to reassure them that transport to sick bay was forth-coming. There wasn't much else we could do except listen if they wanted to talk. A sailor told me, tears streaming down his cheeks, how his best friend was blown apart in front of him; another was grieving over the loss of his brother. From many there was only the deadly silence of shock or the soft moaning of pain."

When the second wave of attacks began, the dungeon's power and water failed, including its only toilet, creating an unimaginably grim atmosphere. The marine guards decided that now was a good time to eat and passed out cans of emergency-ration food. Everyone tried not to think how this might be his or her last meal. Miriam Bellinger got a can of sweetened yams, and the woman beside her, a can of clams. One woman thought a sing-along would help their spirits. Since Christmas was coming, she started up with "Jingle Bells."

The young children were quiet and seemed fine, under the circum-stances, until news arrived that Rear Admiral Isaac Kidd, a wonderful man they all knew from his daily jogs through the neighborhood, his pockets filled with signature matchbooks from each capital ship, had been killed on *Arizona*. The little girls began to wail.

Mary Ann Ramsey: "Turning my attention to my mother for the first time, I realized her face had become an ashen mask. I had been so preoccupied with the wounded, and she with the children, that the initial fear for self had disappeared. For her, it was back. As the noise increased, we looked at each other almost like strangers. I had no fear at all. I believe now that this was simply the difference in our ages. When I saw that first sailor, so horribly burned, personal fear left me. He brought to me the full tragedy of that day, drastically changing my outlook. At sixteen, the idea that any man could be the instrument of such desecration of another, in so hideous a manner, had been incom-prehensible."

After sending out his morning radiogram warning, "This is No Drill," Mary Anne's father, Patrol Wing 2's Logan Ramsey, called his commander, Admiral Bellinger, who was at home suffering from the flu, to get permission to order all of the navy's patrol planes to their assigned sectors to search for enemy ships. He then told Bellinger's operations and plans officer, Vice Admiral Charles Coe, "to get on the operational telephone, call Army Air, and find out where the hell the Japanese planes were coming from and try to get any other information." Coe did his best, but the same lack of preparation that had undercut the warnings from Opana and Outerbridge now sabotaged a chance for striking back. "Lines were not manned," Coe said, "and I could not get through to anybody, [besides which] we were simply not in a position to retaliate." Ramsey then turned to Kaneohe's Patrol Wing 1's PBYs, but they had been too decimated to now operate as a surveillance force. Ramsey's own seaplane apron at Ford had been so thoroughly strafed that barely any aircraft were left.

Still available to fly were the planes of Utility Squadron One, used for mail deliveries and target tows. Radioman 2nd Class Harry Mead was assigned to a search mission aboard an antique Sikorsky JRS-1, a parasol wing amphibian, and he remembered the selection process. Chief G. R. Jacobs pointed to various men in the room and said, "I want three volunteers—you . . . you . . . and you." To defend themselves against Nagumo's mighty fleet, they had Springfield rifles. The squadron searched in a broad circle, found nothing, and reported back that the Japanese had left the area. But this information seems to have gone nowhere, and its facts diminished no one's fears of enemy invasion.

In time, reports from the B-17 crews and the Opana radar station clearly indicated that the Kido Butai was to the north of Oahu. At 1018, Kimmel's office signaled his ships at sea that there were "some indication" of a Japanese force there. Then at 1030 the navy's antenna at He'eia intercepted a signal between Nagumo and Yamamoto, but could only get a reciprocal bearing, which meant the location could be interpreted as either due north or due south. Since someone had insisted they'd seen the enemy thirty miles southwest of Barbers Point—they had in fact seen American cruiser *Minneapolis*—Kimmel's office ordered *Minneapolis* to launch float planes to scout south and told Halsey to search there as well. When *Minneapolis* then responded that no enemy craft were to be found, her message was misread by headquarters as that two ships were seen.

The destroyers that had succeeded in avoiding torpedoes, bombs, and fire to sortie from Pearl Harbor—*St. Louis, Blue, Phelps,* and *Lawson*—were ordered to now group together and join Halsey's Task Force Two. As they prepared to do that, they were instead ordered to sail for Barbers Point and attack the First Air Fleet. *Blue*'s Ensign Nathan

Asher assembled a group of officers to decide on a strategy in confronting what they knew damn well was a far greater foe. Their decision was to speed to the location, fire torpedoes from port, lay down a smoke screen, make a 180, and fire starboard torpedoes, all interspersed with gunfire to protect their maneuvering. It was the best they could do, but no one believed it would work, and each man assumed he would not survive. Then as they rocketed through high seas at full throttle to war, one of *Blue*'s torpedoes started running in its tube, throwing itself out onto the deck. A group heaved it overboard, saving the ship. But it seemed like a bad omen.

At about 1100, six Seagull scouts—little biplanes—were launched from three of Halsey's cruisers. Forty minutes later, two from *Northampton*, piloted by Lieutenant Malcolm Reeves and Ensign Fred Covington, found themselves a hundred miles north of Kauai and under attack by a Zero. In six dives, the Japanese fighter piled fourteen hits into Reeves's little plane and eleven into Covington's, but on each strike, the two Americans kept a low altitude and pulled a diving turn. After twenty minutes, the Zero gave up, and the men escaped. Their bravery, though, went unappreciated by Halsey, since Reeves and Covington didn't break radio silence to report the sighting until after they'd already landed back at Ford.

Enterprise's Scouting Squadron Six's Lieutenant Commander Hopping ordered the Dauntless SBDs that had survived landing at Ford Island that morning be refueled and rearmed, and when Japanese ships were reported twenty-five to forty miles west or southwest of Barbers Point, Hopping was sent to scout: "At 1030 took off in 6-S-1, and from Barbers Point flew tracks west 30 miles, south 20 miles, east 60 miles and back to Ford Island. There were no contacts except with our own ships and sampans. During the return, orders from the *Enterprise* were received to 'refuel, rearm and rejoin.' These orders were acknowledged and passed on to 6-S-7 who was in the air with three other planes."

The surviving Dauntless crews now looking for Nagumo meant a small squadron "of us against an unknown number of surface ships and aircraft," remembered radioman Jack Leaming. "Every second in the air was fraught with anxiety, apprehension, anger, and searching the skies for the enemy. The situation grabbed our whole being, your thoughts and feelings. The past alternates with the present. The determination to destroy and obliterate the men and force that wreaked this havoc upon our fleet and shipmates superseded even personal safety.

All of a sudden you seem to realize that life itself is a defeat, a constant, incessant losing game. But, somehow, you summon the courage to continue, to accept what is, run with it, and hope the future will be brighter. If ever there was a suicide mission, this was one."

When some *Enterprise* SBDs spotted the American destroyers, they radioed back that they'd found enemy ships. *St. Louis*, *Blue*, *Phelps*, and *Lawson* were told they were hot on the trail. It turned out they were hot on the trail of themselves. Hopping: "At 1145 landed at Ford Island and reported to ComPatWing Two that there were no Japanese surface craft within rectangle covering area 100 miles west and 60 miles south of Barbers Point and informed him of my orders from *Enterprise*. ComPatWing Two then directed me to search sector 330° to 030°, attack enemy forces encountered, and return to Ford Island. At 1210 we took off with 9 VSB armed with 500 lb. bombs. No contacts were made."

A Japanese pilot shot down near Fort Kamehameha had been found carrying a map with ten courses flowing north, so Hawaiian Air Force commander General Frederick Martin ordered planes off in that direction. Private Earl Schaeffer had gotten emergency furlough to visit his dying father back on the mainland and was scheduled to depart on December 8. Instead he was assigned as turret gunner to one of Captain Waldron's two B-18s in the northern search for Nagumo's fleet. After flying for seven and a half hours and spotting nothing but whales, which, thinking they were enemy subs, they almost bombed, the squadron gave up. Waldron later said that if they had found the Japanese carriers, "I wouldn't be here." A B-18 didn't have the firepower to battle such a foe.

By the time Waldron and his crews returned, Oahu was under blackout, and they couldn't see to land and were fired upon. Waldron had to break radio silence to beg, "This is Gatty, your friend! Please let me land!" Finally someone turned on a searchlight, and they used that to set down. They were then told that the Japanese had poisoned the local water supply, so the only thing safe to drink was soda pop.

The failure of any American response ended in finger-pointing. Halsey said that the contradictory information from Kimmel's headquarters "succeeded only in enraging me. It is bad enough to be blindfolded, but it is worse to be led around the compass." The navy's Bellinger commented, "I never did know actually what the Army Air had available, and I never did know what they had actually done," while the army's Harold

"Beauty" Martin said that the navy didn't provide search missions to the army until late in the afternoon, when the surviving B-17s were sent south on yet another false alarm. Command errors were then exacerbated when Martin had a nervous breakdown and had to be hospitalized. Kimmel insisted that the many false alarms being reported to his headquarters must be the work of Axis agents, telling General Short, "The fifth column activities added great confusion," and being so adamant on this point that Navy Secretary Frank Knox would tell reporters, "The most effective fifth column work in this war was done in Hawaii, with the exception of Norway." Yet, Halsey later had to admit, "Suppose that the enemy was located, and suppose that I could intercept him: What then? A surface engagement was out of the question, since I had nothing but cruisers to oppose his heavy ships. In addition, we were perilously low on fuel. . . . On the other hand, my few remaining planes might inflict some damage, and by the next forenoon the *Lexington* task force would reach a position from which her aircrew could support an attack."

One American success at Pearl Harbor happened because there was a place where nobody wanted to be. Ten miles north of Wheeler lay the auxiliary field Haleiwa (*holly-eva*). Since no aircraft were stationed there permanently, Haleiwa apparently escaped the notice of Yoshikawa and the other Japanese agents. It did not appear on Genda and Fuchida's target list and was only mildly strafed around 0830 from a passerby. The ground crew there was ready to fight.

On the night of December 6, Second Lieutenants Kenneth Taylor and George Welch went to a formal dance at the Wheeler Officers' Club, followed by an all-night game of poker, getting back to barracks to fall asleep in their tuxedos. Kenneth Taylor: "When you're awakened suddenly, as I was, you generally jump into the first pants that you can find. Mine happened to be tuxedo pants.

"The Japanese had already bombed the field and they were busy strafing it. There was a lot of excitement in the quadrangle. But basically there were no officers, so the sergeants began to give their commands. I called my buddies and told them to arm a couple of planes and we were in the air maybe fifteen minutes after the attack started. . . . They were machine-gunning all around while we were driving for the post."

Taylor and Welch were so quick to get into the air with their P-40s that they hadn't picked up any .50-caliber ammo. They were looking for bear with just their four wing-mounted .30-caliber guns. Welch: "We got over to Easy [Barbers Point] and didn't see any planes. We didn't get a radio, so we went around by Wheeler and saw a B-17 and saw Japanese strung out, strafing Ewa."

Taylor and Welch dove in and started to fire. Each took down one enemy plane, even after one of Welch's guns stopped working. His cockpit was then hit by an incendiary and started to smoke, and he had to take shelter in a cloud bank, to see if it was critical. The plane was okay to fly, but by that time both Taylor and Welch needed to set down at Wheeler to refuel and rearm.

Welch: "We had to argue with some of the ground crew. They wanted us to disperse the airplanes and we wanted to fight. I got ammunition and gasoline. Just as they were loading some .50-caliber, the Japs came back again. We took off directly into them and shot down some."

Taylor: "As I was rearming at Wheeler, the second wave suddenly came up the valley. I would say this time they were going very low over Pearl Harbor. I turned on the grassy field and took off right into them so they could not run me down too easily." As their ground crew ran for cover, Welch and Taylor lifted directly into strafing attacks. Taylor: "Then I got in the middle of their line . . . a string of six or eight planes. The P-40 was very good at dogfighting. I was on one's tail as we went over Waialua, firing at the one next to me, and there was one following firing at me, and I pulled out. I don't know what happened to the other plane."

The plane following Taylor shot him in the left arm, and in the leg. But he would get his. Welch: "I shot down one right on Lieutenant Taylor's tail. I went back to Ewa and found some more over Barbers Point and engaged them there."

Taylor: "We had absolutely no trouble at all finding plenty of targets. We caught up with them at Ewa, a Marine base. They were in a strafing lineup, and I merely got into the line. There was a whole string of planes looking like a traffic pattern. We went down and got in the traffic pattern and shot down several planes there. I know for certain I had shot down two planes or perhaps more; I don't know." As the air filled with the firecracker pops of machine guns, the two young pilots twisted and spun to avoid fire, then climbed, backflipped, and dropped straight behind the enemy for speed. When they got a strike, the enemy plane suddenly sprouted a ball of fire and plummeted into the sea, leaving behind a soaring black-and-white trail.

Following right behind Welch and Taylor in driving through strafer bullets from Wheeler and then flying into battle out of Haleiwa were

Lieutenant John Dains in another P-40, and Lieutenants Harry Brown and Robert Rogers, both in P-36s, while First Lieutenant Lewis Sanders organized members of Wheeler's Forty-Sixth Pursuit Squadron to counterstrike. Lieutenant Othniel Norris started up, but found his chute was no good and left his plane, with the engine running, to get another. Instead, Second Lieutenant Gordon Sterling of the Forty-Fifth jumped into her and taxied right out with the rest of the group. No one noticed until they were at eleven thousand feet and Sanders spotted Sterling on his right wing, with nine Japanese planes below. The Americans pulled into formation and dove, Sanders firing on the leader, which started to smoke. As Sanders then made a 360, he saw the young and inexperienced Sterling bring down one of the enemy. Almost immediately, a Zero was on his tail, and the little P-36 was no match. His plane exploded in fire, and Sterling fell to his death.

At Kaena Point, Rogers got himself cornered by two Zeros, but bluffed one and fired on the other from fifty feet. Confronted with nearly a dozen enemy craft, Brown swooped straight at them like an American kamikaze. He was perhaps the luckiest American in the story of Pearl Harbor, for this was the very moment that the Japanese were under orders to withdraw back to their carriers. Brown's courage and Genda's timeline saved his life.

The American pilots reported getting some hits on the enemy, but none reported actually downing any. Kaaawa radar station operators, however, reported a P-40 took down a Zero, and the only man unaccounted for was John Dains. Dains flew two missions in a P-40, then switched to a P-35 for a third sortie, in the company of George Welch.

War Department records credit Welch and Taylor with dropping an incredible seven enemy planes, nearly a quarter of Japan's twenty-nine losses for the day. But Schofield antiaircraft guns blasted away at the returning US airmen, and John Dains was killed trying to come home.

Admiral Nagumo's First Air Fleet, meanwhile, remained on radio silence about two hundred miles north of Oahu, undetected and unharmed. Sailor Iki Kuramoti: "The deck is now transformed into a whirlpool of excitement. As the glorious battle results are announced one after another by the pipes of the hurrying orderlies, shouts of joy are raised on all sides, all gloom is completely swept away. Meanwhile, the fleet moves swiftly onward at a high speed of twenty-six knots.

"In this moment we are repaid for all our painstaking labors. The gods themselves will bear witness to the glory of our great enterprise!

"About 0900 the welcome shapes of the returning raiders begin to appear through the clouds. One by one, like fledglings longing for their nest, they come to rest on the decks of the carriers. Well done! But have they all come back? At this moment, my most earnest hope is that our losses my be small.

"Within an hour, all the planes were brought aboard. We had lost only twenty-nine planes. It was an incredibly small number when compared with our glorious battle results; nevertheless, when their heroic end was announced, the hearts of the crew were filled with sorrow for those men and/or the fate of our special submarines."

Commander Mitsuo Fuchida was one of the last airmen to set down, as he'd stayed behind, circling over the skies of Oahu to ensure the safe return of as many of his crews as possible, as well as to determine what damage the Japanese had wrought. The harbor's burning oil was churning up such huge pillars of smoke that Fuchida couldn't see much. Returning to *Akagi*, he landed and went to the bridge, where, after being given a cup of tea and a slice of bread, he reported to Ryunosuke Kusaka, Minoru Genda, and Chuichi Nagumo that the mission was an even greater success than anyone could have predicted.

"Four battleships sunk," Fuchida announced with pride. "I know this from my own personal observation."

"Four battleships sunk!" Nagumo exulted. "Good! What about the other four?"

Fuchida unrolled a chart of the Pearl Harbor moorings, prepared from Yoshikawa's reports: "There hasn't been time to check results precisely, but it looks like three were seriously damaged, the other somewhat damaged, although not quite so badly."

Nagumo then asked, "Do you think that the US fleet will be able to operate out of Pearl Harbor within six months?" This was the whole point of their mission after all; to protect the flank of Operation Number One, keeping the Americans out of the Pacific until the resource-rich Asian colonial territories could be conquered, occupied, and integrated into the Japanese economy.

"The main force will not be able to come out within six months," Fuchida first said with conviction. Then he hedged: "A lot of light cruisers and other vessels remain in the harbor. It would be worthwhile to launch another attack."

Kusaka: "What do you think the next targets should be?"

Fuchida: "The dockyards, the fuel tanks, and an occasional ship."

Kusaka then asked about the threat of an American counterstrike on the Japanese ships. Both Genda and Fuchida insisted that the Japanese were masters of the air between the fleet and Hawaii. But when a senior staff officer asked about dangers to the task force a second time, Fuchida honestly replied, "I believe we have destroyed many enemy planes, but I do not know whether we have destroyed them all. The enemy could still attack the fleet."

"Where do you think the missing US carriers are?" Nagumo asked. Fuchida said he wasn't sure, but assumed that, since they were not at Pearl Harbor, they must be out on training exercises, and "by this time no doubt they know about the attack, and they're searching for us."

Commander Tamotsu Oishi asked Genda for his opinion, which was pure Genda: "Let the enemy come! If he does, we will shoot his planes down. Stay in the area for several days and run down the enemy carriers."

While Fuchida went to his command post to enjoy a celebratory dessert—sweet rice cake with red adzuki-bean paste—Genda, Kusaka, and Nagumo continued discussing what to do next. They considered the percentage of losses between the two strikes, where the first was a surprise, and the second was not. They wondered where the Americans could have sent their carriers. Perhaps they had trailed a plane back to the task force? Nagumo pointed out that the planes for a third strike had already been armed to defend against an American attack. The weather was turning against them, making both launch and recovery more difficult. And the tankers were waiting due north, and in a battle might the entire First Air Fleet run out of fuel?

Even though many Japanese thought Operation Z was an overwhelming success, the returning airmen had mixed feelings. "There were seven planes of the *Kaga* torpedo squadron behind me. And five of them were shot down by antiaircraft machine guns," Haruo Yoshino said. "Fifteen men were lost, three in each plane. When I got back to the *Kaga*, my senior officer was under the bridge. He said dejectedly, 'We had terrible damage.' And because the American aircraft carriers were not there, it was hard for me to say that we had a big victory." After coming home to the *Akagi*, Zenji Abe remembered, "I was still in a dazed and dreamy state when I returned to my quarters. I entered the tiny room and began to remove my flying clothes. In the center of my otherwise clean desk lay the envelope containing my will, addressed to my father. Suddenly, my spirits lifted. It was good to be alive." "It was my first experience in battle," Iyozou Fujita remembered. "I thought I was going to fight such a powerful country. I thought I was going to die bombing Pearl Harbor. I didn't expect to come back. It's a wonder that I returned. They were ready for us, so three out of nine planes never returned. I only did my duty. It is not for me to say whether that strategy was good or bad. We were just pawns on a chessboard."

Back on *Akagi*'s bridge, Nagumo made his decision: "We may conclude that anticipated results have been achieved." He ordered, "Preparations for an attack canceled."

For this withdrawal, Admiral Chuichi Nagumo would be judged by Japanese military history as timid, his decision known in classic battle theory as "failure to pursue." Ugaki said it had "the quick pace of a fleeing thief and also as being contented with a humble lot," and by the end of 1942, a rueful Yamamoto said, "Events have shown that it was a great mistake not to have launched [another] attack against Pearl Harbor."

But Nagumo was right. A third strike would have been excessively risky. American defenses were awake and looking to kill. Even if a decent percentage of Japan's pilots in a third strike survived the anti-aircraft fire, the Americans could plausibly have followed a plane and discovered the location of the ships. Minoru Genda later admitted that his and Fuchida's bravado was excessive; that, without knowing the location of the American carriers, "Nagumo would have been a standing joke for generations if he had attacked Pearl Harbor again."

One remarkable piece of luck for the United States was that Pearl Harbor's 4.5-million barrel petroleum tank farm was untouched. One of the central reasons for the war between Japan and the United States—oil—would also be a crucial resource for Americans fighting in the Pacific theater. As Admiral Kimmel explained, "If they had destroyed the oil, which was all aboveground at the time and which could have been destroyed, it would have forced the withdrawal of the Fleet to the coast because there wasn't any oil anywhere else out there to keep the Fleet operating."

Even taking into account the unexpected consequences, the Japanese achieved a profound victory with Operation Z. In thirty minutes, all eight of the Pacific Fleet's battleships had been bombed and torpedoed until inoperable, and in another twenty minutes two-thirds of US military airpower in Hawaii—180 planes—had been left in ruins.

At 1330, signal flags were raised on *Akagi* giving an order to the whole of the First Air Fleet: "Withdraw."

The Hawaiian archipelago arcs from southeast to northwest, with its northwestern point the island of Ni'ihau. On December 7, 1941, the whole of Ni'ihau was a privately owned cattle and sheep plantation that the Robinson family maintained as a preserve of Polynesian culture staffed by two hundred native borns still speaking the Hawaiian language. The island was also the site selected by Yamamoto's Sixth Fleet for submarine *I-4* to lie in wait as an emergency rescue for any First Air Fleet crew who couldn't make it back to their carriers.

Two pilots headed for Ni'ihau after the attack, arriving just in time for church service at the island's sole village, Puuwai. The locals watched in surprise as one plane crashed and burned, and the other, flown by Shigenori Nishikaichi, set down just outside the village. Nishikaichi was taken into custody by one Hawila Kaleohano; though the news of Pearl Harbor had yet to make it to Ni'ihau, Kaleohano knew that diplomatic talks were not going well between Washington and Tokyo, and the sudden appearance of a Japanese warplane, shot up with bullets, made him suspicious. The Hawaiian confiscated the pilot's pistol, map, and documents and took the prisoner to his house, where Kaleohano's wife, Mabel, made everyone breakfast.

Three people of Japanese descent lived on Ni'ihau. Shintani raised bees for the Robinsons, but he refused to help Kaleohano translate Nishikaichi's pleas, so Hawila turned to the Haradas, a married couple who, besides assisting Shintani with the apiary, did housework and oversaw salaries. After the couple arrived at Kaleohano's house, pilot Nishikaichi told the Haradas in Japanese that Pearl Harbor had been attacked and asked for their help in getting his things back and escaping. The Haradas did not tell their neighbors any of this. However, news quickly spread across the small community that an exciting visitor had shown up, and soon enough there was something of a to-do. The locals decided that the right thing to do now would be to keep the pilot under custody until the issue could be decided by the island's controller, Aylmer Robinson, who lived twenty miles to the east on Kauai, and who visited Ni'ihau on Mondays.

On Monday the eighth, a group brought their hostage to the dock at Kii Landing, but neither Aylmer Robinson nor any other visitor appeared. Tuesday, Wednesday, and Thursday also brought no Robinson, and no supplies, perhaps due to General Short's shutting down local boat traffic as a security measure. As the Ni'ihauans became more and more alarmed, Harada offered to calm things down by keeping the prisoner at his place at Kie Kie instead of bringing him all the way back to town, where he was a source of unease. Everyone agreed to this, and on Friday after work, they set off to build a signal fire to alert Mr. Robinson on Kauai, leaving Nishikaichi at Kie Kie in the custody of a man named Haniki. The captive told Haniki that he could read and write some English, and that he considered Ni'ihau such a beautiful and perfect place, he would like to live here someday. After warming Haniki up, Nishikaichi begged him for a favor. He needed to talk to Yoshio Harada; couldn't they go and see him?

At the honey house, Nishikaichi and Harada had a brief talk in Japanese. Then Harada, armed with the Robinson's pistol and shotgun, locked up Haniki in the supply room, and Nishikaichi made his escape. They came across a horse and carriage, forced the passengers out at gunpoint, and ordered the girl leading the horse to take them as quickly as possible to Puuwai. There the two ransacked Kaleohano's house, but couldn't find the pilot's papers. They went back to the Zero, pulled out its machine gun, and walked thorough the village, threatening the locals with bursts of gunfire. Then they went through the house another time and finally found the map and pistol, but still not the other papers. So at three o'clock in the morning, they set the house, and the plane, on fire.

The whole of Ni'ihau meanwhile was hiding from the Japanese in the bush, except for the men working on the signal fire. After getting no response from Kauai, Kaleohano convinced some of the men that the situation was so serious that they should go to Kauai for help. Six of them rowed a whaleboat for sixteen hours, docked, and found Mr. Robinson, who, along with fourteen soldiers under the command of First Lieutenant Jack Mizuha, loaded into the tender *Kukui* and made their way back to Ni'ihau.

In Puuwai, a shepherd named Bene Kanahali snuck up behind the two renegades and took away their machine-gun ammo belt. At dawn, Bene and his wife, Ella, came out of the bush and returned to the village to see what had happened. The Japanese caught them and took them hostage. Bene told Harada enough was enough, that it was time to get the gun away from Nishikaichi and accept that nothing good could come of this. Harada said he just couldn't do it. So Bene jumped the pilot, who shot the Hawaiian twice before being overpowered. The shepherd grabbed the airman by the leg and the neck—as he'd done so often with sheep—and bashed his head against a stone wall. Harada used the gun to shoot himself in the stomach.

Robinson, Kaleohano, and the rest arrived from Waimea at about 7:30 a.m. on Sunday. At the Puuwai schoolhouse, Mizuha conducted an inquiry, which eventually led to Irene Harada being interned and then banned from Ni'ihau; Kanahali being awarded a Purple Heart; and Mizuha being appointed a state Supreme Court justice.

For all of General Short's and the local FBI's obsession with fifth columnists, Harada was the only instance of any person of Japanese descent living in Hawaii who assisted enemy forces.

On Oahu, the B-17s from California, the SBD-3s from *Enterprise*, and John Dains weren't the only Americans who had faced friendly fire. The worst collateral damage wouldn't be uncovered for two years. Many in Honolulu and the suburbs around Pearl Harbor assumed they, too, were attacked on December 7 by Japanese bombs. But in 1943, an ordnance investigation at a closed-door hearing of the Army Pearl Harbor Board revealed that, except for one strike on an electric-power station, US antiaircraft shells "whose time fuses had failed to function in the air" were the source of the thirty-nine explosions that killed forty-eight Hawaiian civilians. Seven-month-old Eunice Wilson died in her mother's lap in a rocking chair that morning; her father was killed by the same shell blast. Twelve more of the dead were younger than nineteen; the youngest was three-month-old Janet Yumiko Ohta. The investigator said that they "were navy five-inch shells. I went out and dug up the fragments and looked at the markings on them. I know they were navy shells; so does the navy." It wasn't anyone's fault. Besides bad fuses, if a US gunner missed, his shell had to land somewhere and hit something.

Hit especially hard were Pearl Harbor's neighbors, the next-door sugar plantations of Waipahu and Ewa, where four fires ignited in the cane fields, with shrapnel and shells killing two and injuring thirty-seven at Waipahu. A Japanese plane crashed into Schofield Barracks' neighbor, the town of Wahiawa, the resulting fire demolishing five houses before being doused by a bucket team of Boy Scouts.

Rose Wong: "I was a teenager at that time and lived right in the center of town. One plane flew over the house and dropped a bomb which landed about a hundred yards or so away. The way the bomb fell, I thought the house had been hit. The entire house shook. There was a group of teenaged boys who were on their way to the gym on that Sunday morning. They were all killed by the blast. Upon impact, the flesh and body parts just flew and hung up in one of our trees. My uncle was out in the road and came running into the house and told us not to go outside. He didn't want us to see what had happened. That's when we looked out the window and saw the flesh in the trees. It was still burning."

These "forgotten victims of Pearl Harbor," as their historian, Nanette Purnell, described them, have been poorly treated. The government refused to grant them any form of reimbursement, even funeral costs, and until the fiftieth anniversary in 1991 they were excluded from official Pearl Harbor events. During the congressional investigation of the attack, a civilian-casualty memorandum was prepared; it has vanished from the National Archives.

On the afternoon of December 7, General Short and his staff were evacuated to the underground bunker of the Red Hill ordnance depot at Aliamanu Crater. With over twenty rooms and six-hundred-foot tunnels, the bunker was well protected, but dank and remote. That day, hearing one report of catastrophe and loss after the next, the general became more and more enraged, slamming phones and swearing like a sailor.

As Hawaiian radio stations went off the air to keep them from being used as directional beacons by the enemy, Governor Joseph Poindexter declared a state of emergency, shutting down the archipelago's schools and initiating a nighttime blackout. He then called President Roosevelt, with Secretary of the Territory Charles Hite listening in to take notes: "Gov. managed to inform President Japs had attacked and about fifty civilians killed. Badly needed food and planes. Roosevelt marvelous—said he would send ships with food, and planes already ordered. Gov. said Short asked for martial law and he thought he should invoke it. President replied he approved."

Poindexter was wary of giving up civilian governance, but was shocked by the devastation and believed the military would move quickly and efficiently to return life on Oahu to a semblance of normal. When the governor then met with the general, Short "requested and urged Martial Law, saying for all he knew landing parties en route. . . . Said attack probably prelude to all-out attack—said otherwise all government and business functions to continue as usual. Gov. said he would accede and asked Short how long in his opinion such status would continue. Short said he unable to say, but if it developed this was a raid only and not the prelude to a landing, Martial Law could be lifted within a reasonably short time. Trouble was he didn't have complete reports, he himself in the dark and could not afford to take chances. Short obviously under great strain—Gov. calm and collected. Gov. signed Declaration. When Short left Gov. said never hated doing anything so much in all his life."

Poindexter later said he thought "reasonably short time" meant about thirty days. Instead, martial law—suspending habeas corpus and placing the police and courts under the jurisdiction of the US Army—was the rule of law in Hawaii for three years. Short's orders to his new civilian charges were published that afternoon in the *Honolulu Star-Bulletin*: "If you are ordered by military personnel to obey a certain command, that order must be obeyed instantly and without question. Avoid the slightest appearance of hostility in words or act. Civilians who go about their regular duties have nothing to fear. All citizens are warned to watch their actions carefully, for any infraction of military rules and regulations will bring swift and harsh reprisals. Prisoners when captured, will be turned over to the nearest military patrol, military guardhouse, police patrol or police station. Information regarding suspicious persons will be telephoned to the provost marshal at Honolulu. A complete blackout of the entire territory will go into effect at nightfall tonight. Anyone violating the blackout by showing a light will summarily be dealt with. All civilian traffic except in case of dire emergency, will cease at dark. In this emergency, I assure you that the armed forces are adequately dealing with the situation and that each and every one of you can best serve his country by giving his wholehearted cooperation to the military and civilian governments."

The general's staff worked with FBI agents to find and capture enemy operators. Honolulu policemen immediately raided the Japanese embassy on Nuuanu Avenue to find the staff burning papers. By the following day, 482 German, Japanese, and Italian suspects were in custody at the detention camp on Sand (previously Quarantine) Island.

Consul Nagai Kita and his employees were confined to quarters for ten days, then sent to Phoenix for interrogation. Under oath, Takeo Yoshikawa insisted his various outings were merely those of a tourist. In August 1942 during one of the thirty-three prisoner exchanges between Rome, Tokyo, and Washington, Yoshikawa returned to Japan aboard Swedish ship *Gripsholm*, where he continued working for naval intelligence. When he retired and asked for a pension, he was told, "You must be one kind of child to think that we will ever acknowledge your activities in Honolulu. The government of Japan never spied on anyone." At least Yoshikawa could tell himself, "In truth, if only for a moment in time, I held history in the palm of my hand."

A similar chain of events happened to journalist Masuo Kato in Washington, DC. Kato was outside the Japanese embassy when "I smelled acrid smoke. Overhead, above the embassy roof, white puffs were curling upward in the calm air. I hastened back to warn the Embassy staff that something was burning. They laughed at me. The smoke was from the papers that were being burned before the American authorities should arrive to take over."

Kato was taken into custody and shipped to Hot Springs, Virginia, to be interned with other enemy aliens: "There were about two hundred or three hundred of us in internment there, including Germans and Italians as well as Japanese. We realized that in some respects we were quite well off. We could take a hot shower every day. Daily newspapers were delivered to us, and we were free to listen to the radio as much as we liked. We were permitted to write letters and receive them without limitation, subject to censorship. When we inquired about using the golf course, we were told that there were a number of people in the district [of Hot Springs] obsessed with a desire to shoot Japanese on sight, and therefore golfing might come under the heading of hazardous occupations."

Two of Kato's fellow detainees were Japan's now-disgraced ambassadors, Kichisaburo Nomura and Saburo Kurusu. "That old man," Kurusu said of Secretary Hull, "had no wish to go to war with Japan. He did his utmost to preserve peace. The trouble is, both the United States and Japan were just like two children. Diplomatically they are not mature. The United States has always had a theoretical and academic approach, and Japan knows nothing of diplomacy. Japan's diplomats have never been allowed free exercise of their own judgment. If we had negotiated with England, things could have developed in an entirely different way. Now the two children are playing foolish war games." He was keenly aware that, just as the name *Quisling* had come to mean "traitor," so his own had been used to coin a new slang term: *the double Kurusu*.

Kato remembered that "Nomura was himself bitter about the position in which he had been placed by the Pearl Harbor attack. 'I am just like a living dead man,' he told me once during one of our frequent strolls on the hotel grounds. So far as he was concerned, he had failed in his mission, and there was very little left in life."

Oahu's Shuncho-Ro teahouse, meanwhile, made famous as a hotbed of espionage by Takeo Yoshikawa, changed its name to Natsunoya and today provides Japanese tourists with romantic details on where their famous spy did his business. One detail the teahouse omits is that, even with a good pair of binoculars, Pearl Harbor is too far away to be accurately observed from its infamous terrace.

By 2:25 p.m. on December 7 in Washington—less than half an hour after the secretary of the navy first told the president the news—UPI had a bulletin out on its wire service, and CBS news was getting reports from Hawaii affiliate KGMB. Just after 3:00 p.m., Stimson, Marshall, Knox, Hull, Hopkins, Grace Tully, Steve Early, and White House doctor Ross McIntyre, seated in a circle of leather couches and tufted club chairs, met with the president in his Oval Study. Roosevelt unleashed a torrent of questions at Stimson, Marshall, and Knox to find out just how the Gibraltar of the Pacific was so clueless and unprepared. Even facing the chief executive's wrath, "the conference met in not too tense an atmosphere," Hopkins noted, "because I think that all of us believed that . . . sooner or later we were bound to be in the war and that Japan had given us an opportunity."

Their main focus was trying to determine where Japan would strike next. FDR admitted he was worried about the Panama Canal. He was also concerned that American citizens would be demoralized if they knew the full extent of the devastation. He ordered naval intelligence to listen in on radio broadcasts and telephone calls from Hawaii and cut short anyone discussing details of the attack.

The group then discussed Roosevelt's message to Congress, when he would officially inform the American people of what had happened and call for a declaration of war. Cordell Hull urged an elaborate and extensively detailed explanation of the events leading up to the attack, and how wholly innocent the United States was in the face of Japan's treachery. Roosevelt preferred a simple and direct message, something similar to his radio chats, which he wrote while imagining an intimate group of Americans sitting with him before a fireplace.

Steve Early announced that Roosevelt had decided that the press would be handled by the White House, not the War Department. Early's office set the first Pearl Harbor casualty estimate as 104 dead and 300 wounded and did not update those numbers as the day progressed. When reporters said their sources were reporting the damage as far more severe, FDR advised that publishing the worst of the news would only aid the enemy.

The American response as shown in the press was steady and consistent. *New York Times:* "a military clique in Tokyo whose powers of self-deception now rise to a state of sublime insanity." *Philadelphia Inquirer:* "Army jingoes in Tokyo threw reason to the winds and went berserk in an insane adventure that for fatalistic abandon is unsurpassed in the history of the world." *Los Angeles Times:* "The act of a mad dog." *Chicago Tribune:* "An insane clique of Japanese militarists who apparently see the desperate conduct into which they lead their country as the only thing that can prolong their power." *New York Herald Tribune:* "Since the clash now appears to have been inevitable, its occurrence brings with it a sense of relief. The air is clear. Americans can get down to their task with old controversies forgotten." *Chicago Daily News:* "Thanks now to Japan, the deep division of opinion that has rent and paralyzed our country will swiftly yield. It cannot be otherwise."

"My greatest fear was that a Nazi undercover agent or saboteur might be willing to sacrifice his own life if he could assassinate our president," Secret Service chief Frank Wilson said. "I immediately decided to intensify to a high degree the protection extended to him." That afternoon, Wilson began to arm the roofs of the White House and other nearby federal buildings with snipers. Wilson's boss, Treasury Secretary Morgenthau, wanted a hundred soldiers patrolling the White House grounds and ordered a Treasury vault turned into a bomb shelter, with a 761-foot tunnel connecting it to the White House.

At 9:00 p.m. in England (4:00 p.m. in Washington), Roosevelt's special envoy to Britain, Averell Harriman, along with his wife, Marie, and American ambassador Gil Winant, were eating dinner with Winston Churchill at the British prime minister's residence Chequers. The meal over, Churchill lifted the lid of his radio, a present from Harry Hopkins (which, like a music box, powered on when you opened its top), to hear the BBC's nightly news. The lead story: "President Roosevelt has announced that the Japanese have bombed the Hawaiian base of the United States fleet at Pearl Harbor."

The British did not yet know that their own Malaya and Hong Kong were being invaded, but even so, Churchill gruffly announced, "We will declare war on Japan!" Winant pointed out that one should not "declare war on a radio announcement" and recommended first hearing directly from the White House.

The PM headed to the phone. "Mr. President, what's this about Japan?" Churchill asked.

"It's quite true," Roosevelt said. "They have attacked us at Pearl Harbor. We are all in the same boat now."

"To have the United States at our side was to me the greatest joy," Churchill later wrote. "I do not pretend to have measured accurately the martial might of Japan, but at this very moment I knew the United States was in the war, up to the neck and in to the death. So we had won after all! . . . Hitler's fate was sealed. Mussolini's fate was sealed. As for the Japanese, they would be ground to powder. . . . Being saturated and satiated with emotion and sensation, I went to bed and slept the sleep of the saved and thankful."

Adolf Hitler thought the attack meant the United States would turn its back on Europe to fight in Asia and announced that it was "the turning point! We can't lose the war at all. We now have an ally which has never been conquered in three thousand years." Mussolini proclaimed that it would be easy to win a war against "a country of Negroes and Jews," especially considering that "never in history has a people been ruled by a paralytic. There have been bald kings, fat kings, handsome kings, and even stupid ones, but never a king who when he wants to go to the toilet or to dinner must be assisted by other men."

At 4:50 p.m. in Washington, the president asked Grace Tully to take dictation and began, "Yesterday comma December 7 comma 1941 dash a day which will live in world history dash the United States of America was simultaneously and deliberately attacked by naval and air forces of the Empire of Japan." Tully later noted, "The entire message ran under five hundred words . . . a cold-blooded indictment of Japanese treachery and aggression . . . delivered to me without hesitation, interruption, or second thoughts." She read back this first draft, and FDR replaced *world history* with *infamy* and *simultaneously* with *suddenly*.

At 6:30 p.m., First Lady Eleanor Roosevelt began her Sunday NBC radio broadcast, offering steadying words of encouragement to 45 million American listeners:

"I am speaking to you at a very serious moment in our history. The cabinet is convening and the leaders in Congress are meeting with the president. The State Department and army and navy officials have been with the president all afternoon. In fact, the Japanese ambassador was talking to the president at the very time that Japan's airships were bombing our citizens in Hawaii and the Philippines and sinking one of our transports loaded with lumber on its way to Hawaii. By tomorrow morning the members of Congress will have a full report and be ready for action.

"In the meantime, we the people are already prepared for action. For months now the knowledge that something of this kind might happen has been hanging over our heads, and yet it seemed impossible to believe, impossible to drop the everyday things of life and feel that there was only one thing which was important—preparation to meet an enemy no matter where he struck. That is all over now and there is no more uncertainty.

"We know what we have to face and we know that we are ready to face it.

"I should like to say just a word to the women in the country tonight. I have a boy at sea on a destroyer, for all I know he may be on his way to the Pacific. Two of my children are in coast cities on the Pacific. Many of you all over the country have boys in the services who will now be called upon to go into action. You have friends and families in what has suddenly become a danger zone. You cannot escape anxiety. You cannot escape a clutch of fear at your heart, and yet I hope that the certainty of what we have to meet will make you rise above these fears.

"We must go about our daily business more determined than ever to do the ordinary things as well as we can, and when we find a way to do anything more in our communities to help others, to build morale, to give a feeling of security, we must do it. Whatever is asked of us I am sure we can accomplish it. We are the free and unconquerable people of the United States of America.

"To the young people of the nation, I must speak a word tonight. You are going to have a great opportunity. There will be high moments in which your strength and your ability will be tested. I have faith in you. I feel as though I was standing upon a rock and that rock is my faith in my fellow citizens."

Her radio audience knew well that Eleanor had her heart in what she said. The Roosevelt's son James was a marine; his brothers Franklin Jr. and John were in the navy; and Elliott was in the Army Air Corps. In the space of a year, all four would be in combat, and Roosevelt would become the only wartime president in American history besides Abraham Lincoln with children in the service.

Back at the Ford Island cave, the families were finally allowed to leave around noon. Mary Ann Ramsey went to the marine barracks, where the sixteen-year-old did all she could to give comfort to dying men. Around the neighborhood, marines were taking down all the signs identifying the homes of officers, since it was assumed that when enemy troops invaded, military leaders would be targeted for assassination. The Zubers found a dead Japanese man in their yard. The little girl Joan wanted to kick the corpse.

The only water they had to drink was scooped out of the swimming pool and boiled.

Many in the military's upper echelons who weren't assigned quarters on Ford Island lived in suburbs terraced into the hills above Pearl Harbor, and their wives and children ended up watching the attack from their living-room windows or front yards. Mrs. Arthur Gardiner and her two children joined some other families hiding in a ravine behind the junior officers' quarters. Mrs. Gardiner had brought along a blanket, a can of orange juice, a butcher knife, and the book *Pinocchio*. Reading the book to the children was interrupted at times by the roar of planes overhead, and the sound of crashes and explosions. Then, some cane workers came running toward them. Fearing these were Japanese invaders, Mrs. Gardiner picked up the butcher knife to defend her children. But the Japanese Americans, seeing the Caucasians, ran off, terrified that they themselves were going to die.

Eight hours after Fuchida broadcast his *To Ra To Ra To Ra* message, Japanese radios played the solemn notes of the national anthem, meaning an important announcement was coming. Moments later, the oddly lilting voice of Premier Tojo read an Imperial rescript:

"We by grace of heaven, Emperor of Japan . . . hereby declare war on the United States of America and the British Empire. The men and officers of Our army and navy shall do their utmost in prosecuting the war. . . . The entire nation with a united will shall mobilize their total strength so that nothing will miscarry in the attainment of Our war aims.

"It has been truly unavoidable and far from Our wishes that Our Empire had now been brought to cross swords with America and Britain. . . . These two powers, inducing other countries to follow suit, increased military preparations on all sides of Our Empire to challenge us. They have obstructed by every means Our peaceful commerce and finally resorted to a direct severance of economic relations, menacing gravely the existence of Our Empire. . . . They have intensified economic and military pressure to compel thereby Our Empire to submission. This trend of affairs would, if left unchecked, not only nullify Our Empire's efforts of many years for the sake of stabilization of East Asia but also endanger the very existence of Our nation. . . . Our Empire for its existence and self-defense has no other recourse but to appeal to arms and to crush every obstacle in its path.

The reverent citizens of Japan then heard the strains of the song "Umi Yukaba," which included the chorus:

> Across the sea,
> Corpses in the water;
> Across the mountain,
> Corpses heaped upon the field;
> I shall die only for the Emperor,
> I shall never look back.

The White House cabinet met again at eight that night, according to Frances Perkins's notes: "Number of maps up. President sitting at his desk with his back to the wall. Frank Knox sitting close to him and showing him something. . . . It was obvious to me that Roosevelt was having a dreadful time just accepting the idea that the navy could be caught unaware." The president was still angry and disturbed at the American military response, asking Knox twice, "Find out, for God's sake, why the ships were tied up in rows."

According to Attorney General Francis Biddle, the president called this the most significant cabinet meeting since 1861 and the birth of the American Civil War, and that there was "no question but that the Japanese had been told by the Germans a few weeks ago that they were winning the war and that they would soon dominate Africa as well as Europe. They were going to isolate England and were also going to completely dominate the situation in the Far East. The Japs had been told if they wanted to be cut in on the spoils, they would have to come in the war now." Roosevelt said he was certain that the attack was engineered by the Nazis, and Henry Stimson said these details should be in the speech to Congress, and that war should be declared on both Japan and Germany. FDR said he could save such details for his radio speech two days later, on the tenth.

Cabinet members were disturbed to learn that, after all the warnings sent to Hawaii, surveillance had been minimal. Also, they couldn't understand why so few officers were aboard their ships, with so much of the leadership in the crisis having passed to such junior men. Perkins: "We just got scraps of information, an episode here and there. We got a picture of total confusion. Nobody knew where the planes had come from. Why didn't our patrols find out? . . . We had all been trained to think of the US as invincible, and now we were faced with the fact that our navy had cracked."

That night, Franklin Roosevelt ate dinner at his Oval Study desk, with Grace Tully and Harry Hopkins eating from folding tray tables. While serving their meal, White House butler Alonzo Fields remembered the president, still very much in shock, saying, "My God, how did it happen? I will go down in disgrace." Hopkins gave him a line to add to his speech: "With confidence in our armed forces—with the unbounding determination of our people—we will gain the inevitable triumph—so help us God."

A group of leading congressmen, invited by Roosevelt, had assembled in the Red Room and were now ushered into the study. Roosevelt told them that the United States had lost perhaps four battleships, that the army had estimated three hundred dead, and that he didn't know the full extent of the navy's casualties, but that they "will undoubtedly be very heavy." He asked them to keep all this to themselves, which he knew was out of the question, so told them only what he thought the public should know.

Senate Foreign Relations Committee chairman Tom Connally was incensed that the military had responded so poorly, demanding, "Where were our forces—asleep? Where were our patrols?"

As FDR continued with the news that Japan was now invading Guam, Wake, and Shanghai, he was handed the latest report, of two hundred American marines in China forced to surrender. He then asked Congress to call a joint session at 12:30 p.m. the next day. What was he going to say? they wanted to know. Would he want war declared against both Tokyo and Berlin? Roosevelt said he hadn't made up his mind yet about Hitler, but "that it would be necessary to strangle Japan rather than whip her and that it took longer. He once spoke about two or three years being required."

Franklin and Eleanor had plans for dinner that night with broadcast journalist Edward R. Murrow and his wife. When Murrow called to say he assumed the meal was canceled, Eleanor said, nonsense, come on over and eat with me; she would make them her Sunday-night special of scrambled eggs. Then Roosevelt sent word that he wanted to talk to Murrow, so while his wife went back to their hotel, just after midnight Murrow went to see FDR. Waiting outside, he observed the comings and goings of various American leaders: "There was ample opportunity to observe at close range the bearing and expression of Mr. Stimson, Colonel Knox, and Secretary Hull. If they were not surprised by the news from Pearl Harbor, then that group of elderly men were putting on a performance which would have excited the admiration of any experienced actor. . . . It may be that the degree of the disaster had appalled them and that they had known for some time. . . . But I could not believe it then and I cannot do so now. There was amazement and anger written large on most of the faces."

Inside the Oval Study, the journalist found the president with Colonel William "Wild Bill" Donovan—who would become head of the CIA's predecessor, the Office of Strategic Services—noshing on sandwiches and beer. The president, agitated, was incensed the army had so many planes destroyed "on the ground, by God, on the ground!"

At the railings before the executive mansion on Pennsylvania Avenue, a crowd gathered. Even on this wet and chill December night, people wanted to be together. The crowd sang "My Country, 'Tis of Thee" and "God Bless America."

At Pearl Harbor, the surviving dinghies, barks, ketches, gigs, lighters, skiffs, and tugs now slipped between the sinking ruins of ships and the rising pillars of oil-fired smoke to beat back the flames and collect the dead. One crew working especially hard to rescue swimmers from the burning sea were the men of a water barge with a bad reputation. It was their tradition to pipe ten thousand gallons of freshwater above quota in exchange for treats, such as what had been worked out on December 6 with the USS *Curtiss*—a holiday turkey and sixty dozen eggs. The turkey was roasting for Sunday supper when Nagu-mo's First Air Force attacked. Now the barge's guilty and embarrassed men were doing all they could to help.

Moored at Pearl's submarine base, the eighteen ships of Lieu-tenant Commander William Specht's Motor Torpedo Boat Squadron were still in working order, and their crews began rescue operations. Seventeen-year-old Mal Garcia was working dock detail during the attack when an officer yelled, "Hey, coxswain, get that whaleboat out of here." Mal considered telling the superior he was actually a radio-man on submarine tender *Argonne*, but then remembered that you can't argue with a commander and spent the rest of the day helming an eighteen-footer, ferrying the dead and the wounded. He later said that Pearl Harbor aged him from seventeen to maybe thirty-five, and that later he tried to remember what it was like to be a teenager, but couldn't. He would spend in time twenty-two years with the US Navy.

"I remember one fella that—I never will forget this one—about him reaching up for the gunnel, trying to get out with his hand coming up," Bert Davis remembered. "And I reached down to help him, and I grabbed him right around his arm and I started pulling, and all the skin came right off in my hand. But that's the thing that sticks in my mind all the time, and I have nightmares sometimes about it. But you try and you do your best."

"That afternoon of course, anybody that was in the water was gone," *Vestal* machinist Arnold "Max" Bauer remembered. "They had floating bodies. They brought them up. And as time went on, peo-ple would come to the surface. They'd be bloated. They'd tie a rope around the foot. I saw boats haul fifteen, twenty men at a time with ropes on the legs, towed behind the boats." *Raleigh*'s Boatswain's Mate 2nd Class Nick Kouretas: "We would lasso a leg, an arm, a head, and maybe towed four, five, or six bodies behind us slowly in the launch over to the landing." There, corpsmen "would jump in the water with sheets . . . and scoop up the bodies." On day three, *Utah*'s Karl Johnson said, "They brought [the bodies] out in a dump truck. They would pull the chain just like it was a load of dirt and dump them out."

Officially, 1,178 were wounded. The number overwhelmed the mil-itary's care facilities, many of which had been damaged in the attack. Medics had to turn anything with a roof and a floor—barracks, school, canteen—into a hospital, while some hospitals bedded their over-flow of patients on the lawn. Everything and everywhere became a critical-care post, starting with the sick bays and dressing stations of the still-operational capital ships, the hospital ship *Solace*, and the Mobile Base Hospital, all still afloat on the burning harbor waters. The next stop was the dock itself, where 150 cots were arrayed under fire from strafing and shrapnel; this "hospital" was eventually transferred to the Navy Yard's Officers' Club. Pharmacist's Mate 2nd Class Lee Soucy:

"A line officer came by to inquire how we were getting along. We told him that we had run out of everything and were in urgent need of bandages and some kind of solvent or alcohol to cleanse wounds. He ordered someone to strip the beds and make rolls of bandages with the sheets. Then he turned to us and said, 'Alcohol? Alcohol,' he repeated. 'Will whiskey do?'

"Before we could mull it over, he took off and in a few minutes he returned and plunked a case of scotch at our feet. Another person who accompanied him had an armful of bottles of a variety of liquors. I am sure denatured alcohol could not have served our purpose better for washing off the sticky oil, as well as providing some antiseptic effect for a variety of wounds and burns.

"Despite the confusion, pain, and suffering, there was some gusty humor amidst the pathos and chaos. At one point, an exhausted swimmer, covered with a gooey film of black oil, saw me walking around with a washcloth in one hand and a bottle of booze in the other. He hollered, 'Hey, Doc, could I have a shot of that medicine?' I handed him the bottle of whichever medicine I had at the time. He took a hefty swig. He had no sooner swallowed the 'medicine' than he spewed it out along with black mucoidal globs of oil. He lay back a minute after he stopped vomiting, then said, 'Doc, I lost that medicine. How about another dose?' Perhaps my internal as well as external application of booze was not accepted medical practice, but it sure made me popular with the old salts. Actually, it probably was a good medical procedure if it induced vomiting. Retaining contaminated water and oil in one's stomach was not good for one's health."

The tide of the gruesomely injured kept coming, and coming, and coming. Thousands of bullet wounds. Hundreds of shell and shrapnel wounds, of bomb-fragment wounds, of broken bones of every kind. Men with their arms and legs forcibly amputated, their torsos disemboweled. Lieutenant Elizabeth Elmer at Fort Shafter's Tripler General Hospital remembers such an avalanche of patients that doctors had to amputate on stretchers; there weren't enough tables to operate. By the end of a day spent disposing of body parts, her hose and shoes were soaked in blood. Then a group of Honolulu's working girls arrived at the hospital to volunteer. Elmer didn't know what to do, but the chief nurse reasoned that since the men "spend enough on them, now it's their turn to spend some money on the boys."

Radioman Jack Leaming: "There were screams of men still hurt, unattended, still dying . . . men running around crying like babies, in a state of shock, cussing, screaming, 'Let me at those yellow bastards!' or 'They killed my best buddy!' Every second that stretched into minutes reflected and affirmed that the unquenchable struggle for life is timeless, and the hope and faith that bind men together in their most hopeless hour is of the divine. War pumps you up. A uniform suddenly becomes radiant, and destruction is the goal. It is easy to do and gets easier the more you do it. The squadron, your buddies, the ship, become more important than yourself. You become more vindictive and brutal."

For a great many severely wounded and dying men, all the nurses and medics could do was give morphine, then mark their foreheads with a lipstick *M*. In the middle of all this great horror came moments of great humanity. Schofield Barracks nurse Myrtle Watson remembered "another fellow I was helping who looked up at me, saw my nail polish, and said, 'Nail polish . . . on an officer . . . in the middle of a war.' Two hours later, he was dead."

Sixty percent of Pearl Harbor casualties were second- and third-degree burns. There had been fires at every airfield; both on and within the *Arizona*, *California*, *Curtiss*, *Downes*, *Nevada*, *Pennsylvania*, *Shaw*, and *West Virginia*; and on the oil that floated on the water of Pearl Harbor. Many of those burned had escaped through that water and were coated in marine fuel. To get to Ford, thousands of survivors had stumbled through roiling black clouds of smoke, many naked, dripping oil, sheathed in blood, screaming in pain. "The only thing I could see were their eyes, lips, and mouths," a survivor said. "Their mouths were reddish; their eyes looked watery. Everything else was black." With no time or enough equipment to clean off that oil, treatment proceeded anyway. Burned skin was cut away with scissors. To draw out the heat, tannic acid was sprayed on with Flit guns. Saltwater baths drew out the liquid. All of this was gruesome to perform, and excruciating to endure.

In an odd coincidence, New York surgeon John Moorhead, who had served in the army in the Great War, was in town giving a lecture on the subject of "Burns." Picked up at his hotel that morning by a Dr. Hill, when Moorhead mentioned hearing on the radio that Pearl Harbor had been attacked, Hill said, "Oh, you hear all kinds of stories around this place." Dr. Moorhead had to interrupt his presentation from time to time because of the many explosions. Finally Dr. Jesse Smith ran in, shouting that a dozen surgeons were needed at Tripler Hospital immediately, and the speech was over. Moorhead would spend the next eleven hours continuously operating. He said to a young man, "Son, you've been through a lot of hell, and you're going into some more. This foot has to come off. But there's been many a good pirate with only one leg!" To the hospital commandant, Colonel Miller, Dr. Moorhead suggested that perhaps he should be returned to active duty. After two hours, Miller returned to congratulate Colonel Moorhead with "You're in the army now!"

Herbert Louden, a pharmacist 3rd class on the navy hospital ship *Solace*, was "ordered to take care of one boy in particular that I stayed with eight days and nights and never left him. His name was James T. Lackey from Beeville, Texas. He had been a seaman first class aboard the USS *Curtiss*, which received the only kamikaze bombing plane. It smashed into the *Curtiss* and blew up the powder room where this young man was passing ammunition. He was burnt all over his body except from the left knee to the left hip with first-, second-, third-, and fourth-degree burns. Because of his condition he had been given one-half gram of morphine soleplate and a half hour later another one-half gram of morphine soleplate, which was eight times the normal dosage.

"When the medical team of doctors came through the ship checking various patients, they advised me to make him as comfortable as possible, realizing that not all of the patients would make it. The following day a nurse, Agnes Shure, and a doctor whose name I believe was Carlton, came by to check on the patient. The patient said, 'I hope I can be as good a man as my daddy,' and he went into unconsciousness again. The doctor turned to me and said, 'He has a will to live, and whether he lives or dies depends on the care you give him.' Being a young Christian man of twenty-four, I believe in prayer and prayed many times for his recovery. When he finally came to, he said he did not believe in prayer or God and thought he was an atheist.

"I forced fluids on him and had a heat cradle over the top of him, which had thirty-two lights to help control his temperature. To begin with, he came aboard with tannic acid jelly all over his body, and this tannic acid jelly causes an eschar or scab under which infection grows. So everything, all of his skin had turned black and had to be removed. So I really skinned the man alive in order to save his life. I had to remove that to cleanse his proud flesh and do pin grafting. That is where you stick a pin through some of his skin, raise it up, and cut it off with a scalpel and put it on top of the proud flesh. This would start growing and spread.

"This grew new skin all over the young man. Some of the intravenous injections or fluid, feeding, and medications had to be done through the soles of his feet because of the eschar over his arms and other parts of his body. It was hard to find blood vessels."

Sterling Cale oversaw six men boarding the charnel house that had once been the USS *Arizona*, to collect the dead. In hip waders and elbow-length black leather gloves, the workers came across a giant mass of bodies so charred that individual human beings could not be distinguished. Cale's strongest memory was of the piles of ashes by the antiaircraft guns, which floated in the winds, eddying around his legs, and drifting onto his boots. These, he realized, were once men. He bagged up all he could—the heads, the torsos, and even that dust—for a week, pausing every so often to vomit.

Dental officer Lieutenant James Justice did what he could to identify corpses through dental records so the headstones of the dead would have names. Charles Brewer took fingerprints and remembered that in some cases of the severely burned and waterlogged, the skin would "just pull off" the fingers. One marine sergeant devised a solution; he'd take the skin from a body's fingers and put it on his own to get a good print. Others, however, saw opportunity. Brewer: "Somebody had stripped a lot of our boys, officers and sailors, would take their rings and watches, and you could tell by the white spots on their arms that weren't tan."

With military efficiency the Chaplain Corps, assisted by two volunteer civilian priests, a marine guard to fire salutes, and a marine bugler to blow taps, processed burials in Honolulu's Oahu and Halawa cemeteries. There would be a week of nearly constant memorial services, funeral corteges, and grave digging, with the many unknown buried as numbers. Since war had not yet been declared at the time of their deaths, none of the dead had dog tags, and the manner of their deaths, from fires and explosions, resulted in 670 "unknowns" buried in 252 different locations at Honolulu's Punchbowl cemetery. Of that 670, 669 remain unknown to this day, and not surprisingly, casualty figures for an event so devastating are estimates. The army has at various times reported 218, 228, 229, and 240 deaths. In building the *Arizona* memorial's marble wall, the navy listed 1,103 names, but forgot one, which had to be added after the wall was erected.

Today's generally accepted numbers—2,403 dead, 1,178 wounded—mean that a great majority of the navy and marine casualties were from *Arizona*, while over 75 percent of the army's toll were Air Corps men from Hickam and Wheeler. The numbers also reveal one of the most lopsided battles in military history. Against the US loss, the Japanese lost 55 naval airmen, 9 midget-sub crewmen, and the 65-man crew of one destroyed submarine. The United States lost 18 warships; the Japanese, 0. The United States lost 188 planes, with another 159 severely damaged; the Japanese, 29.

There were in all this some miracles. Fire Control Man 3rd Class Dean Derrow was blown off *West Virginia*'s deck wearing only his sneakers, life preserver, and Skivvies. He was found floating in the water unconscious. Fished out and carried to *Solace*, he awakened to doctors telling him everything was fine and that he needed to return to duty. In January he went swimming, passed out, and slept for ten days. Doctors performed an appendectomy. Finally on March 7, 1942, X-ray tech Robert Rule found that an inch-and-half-long bullet had been stuck in Derrow's heart for three months, mostly likely from the strafing attack on the boat that first carried him to *Solace*. On April 7, a California naval surgeon sawed away part of Derrow's rib, then pulled out the bullet with forceps. Derrow married his nurse, Alice, and lived a good, long life. His funeral service on January 4, 1992, was conducted by Herb Louden—the corpsman who'd pulled him, unconscious, out of the water on December 7, 1941.

Charles Christensen would for the rest of his life remember one shining moment. Just as in the 1814 battle described by America's national anthem, "The Star-Spangled Banner," Christensen saw that, in the middle of a devastated Pearl Harbor, on the mast of the USS *California*, destroyed, sunk, and abandoned, his nation's flag still waved.

CHAPTER NINE

INFAMY

On Oahu, the night of December 7 was cold and wet and dark with fear. While sheltering themselves under anything available—ragged tents, dilapidated hangars, roadside ditches—the survivors of the Pearl Harbor attack weren't unreasonable to collectively imagine the Japanese, at any moment, returning to finish them all off. It was as logical as math.

The armed forces in Hawaii ached for revenge, feared the enemy's return, and were determined to not be caught unprepared a third time. Troops at Kaneohe that night shot at each other and then, when civilians came out to see what was happening, shot at them. A man lost his hat in the wind, and when he tried to grab it by sticking his arm through a fence, he was shot dead. Soldiers along the shore of windward Kaaawa beach thought the stars were enemy signals and shot at them. Japanese American fishermen, coming home from work, were strafed by US machine gunners. A US submarine was attacked by the USS *Gamble*.

Radio reports announced invading forces overtaking Waikiki . . . amphibious troops landing at Diamond Head . . . forty enemy army transports surging across the western shores . . . thousands of paratroopers, in blue coveralls, descending into the fields of cane. Saboteurs swimming onto the beaches at Oahu's north coast had US money and Honolulu bus tokens. Arrows had been cut out of the pineapple fields directing the way to Pearl Harbor.

The *Helm*'s crew was informed that the whole of Halsey's task force had been sunk, while *Tangier* heard that both *Enterprise* and *Lexington* had been taken out. *Nevada* was told that America's Panama Canal had been invaded, sealing up the Atlantic Fleet, and that right now California was under attack. The *Rigel* heard that San Francisco had fallen to the Japanese, while on *Pennsylvania*, Long Beach had fallen, with expeditionary forces heading toward Los Angeles right this minute. And not just Japanese but Nazi aircrews were part of the attack on Hawaii, with a confirmed sighting of a big blond who spoke pure German.

Kaneohe Naval Air Station ordered everyone to change to khakis. Many no longer owned a full set of uniform, so Mess Attendant Walter Simmons helped boil strong coffee to dye their whites to nearly the right color. Then the rumor came that Japanese marines were landing in khakis, so everyone needed to be in whites. It was then insisted that the invading forces were in whites, so everyone needed to be in blues. Simmons later guessed that the nervous twitching sounds of animals in the fields just outside the base led to a massive execution of mongooses.

Wheeler's Henry Woodrum: "I saw and heard other men whose closest friends were suddenly and shockingly dead. They walked around in profound helplessness, dazed, enraged, and shouting, or mentally berserk and deathly quiet, but each of them driven by one thought—revenge. It hit the old-timers the worst, I thought, as I watched the face of a first sergeant, dressed in fresh khakis as he strode past us, hands clenched into fists, his eyes staring, unseeing, tears streaming down his face as he muttered an endless string of curses because he somehow thought it was all his fault. . . .

"A young woman issued two packs of cigarettes, scrounged from the damaged PX, to every GI who stopped. I took the cigarettes she gave me, standing alone, watching as she served other men. Her presence there seemed wrong, like the whole day. She looked fresh and clean, in the midst of all that destruction with guys in fatigues, or stripped to the waist, still carting dead men from the lawn across the street.

"All over the island, men sat in the darkness, wondering what was going to happen, thinking that whatever did happen might be worse than what they already had experienced. The unanswered questions and the boredom of nothing to do but wait combined with the darkness of night to create the worst foe of all—apprehension. It was as if a cloak of darkness had settled over all our lives to eliminate awareness, assurance, and the security of orderly existence; we realized now that the word we had been given was wrong."

Of over 1,400 crewmen, *Arizona* counted a bare 334 survivors, who were now in various stages of injury, shock, and grief. Everyone had lost a friend; John Anderson had lost his twin brother. Some had watched their buddies burn to death, unable to do anything to help. Others couldn't stop thinking about the ones who had been trapped and drowned beneath the sea. Besides being homeless, they wondered when the next attack would come, and this time, would Hawaii be invaded?

Ralph Byard worked the chow line: "I went to work in the butcher's shop and it was dark and no lights. I worked from daylight to dark. And at night I laid five or six orange crates in a row and laid down on the orange crates and slept all night and got up at daylight and started butchering again. . . . Birdsell said that I behaved as if things were normal. He said he took strength from that and felt that if I could be so undisturbed that he would try to do likewise. He said that I set an example for him. It was three days before I got emotional about it."

After arriving safely on Ford Island, Bronx-born Clint Westbrook found an armory giving out guns: "We pulled over and stopped and went in and got some, too. I thought to myself, 'I'm going to go Jap-hunting.' I grabbed handguns. I'd love to have had a picture that day, 'cause I had a .30-06 [Springfield] slung over my shoulder, two bandoliers of ammunition crisscrossed, and two .45s strapped on my hips with extra clips. And we found a light machine gun. We set it up in the back of the truck and were prowling Ford Island looking for Japs. We saw one parachute, but he landed out in the water."

Chief Gunner's Mate Hendon dove into *Arizona* to get the contents of the paymaster's safe, assisted by John Rampley: "He got all the money and all the pay receipts for the quarter, and I took them down into the furnace room of the receiving station and spread the pay receipts out on the deck. They were so hot there that they'd dry in just about the length of time it took you to lay them out. . . . I took them up and we reconstructed the payroll for the quarter and figured out what each man had still coming to him. We transferred that to wherever they had gone if they survived, and we transferred the information to Washington for those who were dead or missing."

The rumors continued to swirl. Japanese spies were everywhere, landed by flotillas of sampans, disguised as an army of milkmen, or as all-American boys next door. Sailor Frank Lewis heard that a Japanese corpse had been found wearing a University of Oregon ring; marine Private E. H. Robison heard the same story, but that it wasn't Oregon, but USC; while Lieutenant William Keogh was warned that a squadron was casually walking the streets disguised in McKinley High School sweaters.

Local saboteurs, it was said, had poisoned the reservoirs and water towers and had trained dogs to bark in a secret dog-code. Honolulu police were forced to investigate such reports as "a fifth columnist transmitting intelligence via shortwave radio"—a man listening to the radio; "a man up a telegraph pole signaling Japs at sea"—a telephone repairman; "spies signaling with blinker lights"—two men smoking cigarettes. A light was spotted flashing off and on; obviously a signal. It was a flashlight that a man had dropped and was rolling downhill.

Albert Finkel was part of a group repairing *Pennsylvania*: "It was just as dark as inside a cat stomach, and of course they had marines stationed everywhere with their guns ready, and you better sing out real loud and clear when you moved on that ship because if you showed a light or you just made a wrong move or a wrong noise, you didn't know if you were going to take a bullet or not."

When men putting up antiaircraft batteries on the *San Francisco* tried to use a spotlight, they were swamped in bullets, which set off other trigger fingers, until the harbor was ablaze in gunfire. Two groups at Schofield, each convinced the other was Japanese, kept up a fusillade until a soldier got hurt and cussed as only an American soldier could cuss, which made the other side realize these weren't Japs. One sentry at a sub base kept firing at his relief, so his commander kept him on duty for the whole night.

Hawaii's Japanese Americans heard their own terrifying rumors. First it was universally confirmed that the US Army was coming at any minute to slaughter them all. This was clarified: the soldiers were only going to kill the men; they would leave the women and children behind, to starve to death.

"When the military truck came by and told us, 'You can't take anything—get in the truck just as you are,' that's when we got scared," Hazel Kobashigawa, who was fifteen on December 7, later wrote. "Then the truck went down the street and got the other Japanese families from their homes—only the Japanese families. They took us up Waimano Home Road to a sugarcane field and told us, 'Don't move around, because you could get shot.'"

Five Japanese Americans were walking on a road in the hills when they were seen by a group of sailors trucking some ammo from Lualualei Depot to Pearl. The driver slammed to a halt. One sailor said,

"Let's shoot them all," some others agreed, but then one piped up, "We are not beasts; these people had nothing to do with the attack." The crisis was over, and the truck went on its way.

A Japanese maid told the woman she worked for, "I am so ashamed, I wish I could change my face."

Back on Task Force Two just off the Oahu coast, Halsey needed to bring home the six F4F Wildcats of Fighter Squadron Six, which, along with the scouting and bombing Dauntlesses, had futilely searched for the Japanese task force. But Halsey now had a problem: if he lit up his flight deck so his boys could land, *Enterprise* might be spotted by enemy aircraft or submarines. Finally the admiral was able to get through to command at Ford Island to tell them that the six fighters would be landing at their airstrip instead of on his deck. Ford in turn ordered its men on the ground to hold their fire.

To keep from being spotted by the enemy, the Wildcats flew with lights out and radios off and approached a blacked-out Oahu to find the island's only lights were the still-raging fires from the attack. It was so black that some pilots couldn't get their bearing and flew all the way to the eastern shore before coming about and finding their way to Ford.

SBD ace Brig Young had landed on Ford Island earlier that day and was trying to call Halsey from the control tower. When that radio wasn't strong enough to reach *Enterprise*, he tried again from his own plane's radio.

The *Enterprise* planes were approaching Ford from the south, which meant coming in over Hickam. Lead pilot Lieutenant (jg) Fritz Hebel radioed that they planned to circle around, to land from the north, but Brig Young, at the control tower radio, urged them repeatedly to come straight in. Either Hebel didn't hear him or didn't agree with that call.

As the Wildcats tried to set down, it seemed as if every piece of American firepower on Oahu was exploding in their faces, the bullets and tracers "so thick you could walk on it," as Captain Jim Daniels described it. While an officer ran up and down the sandbags at Ford Island shouting, "Hold your fire! Hold your fire! Those are our planes," the "sky was lit up like daytime" remembered Dick Girocco, watching from Hangar 56, and the sound was deafening.

Henry Woodrum: "Two of our own .50-caliber machine-gun positions north of the highway began chattering away as several planes swept low overhead and continued on, but further back, in a momentary glimmer of moonlight, we had a glimpse of an aircraft as it began to slowly roll over before it nosed down into the pineapple patch. A horrendous thumping sound filled the air as the engine sound stopped abruptly. The aircraft skidded through the soft earth of the field as a second aircraft crashed somewhere farther up the gully. It began to skid, shredding parts and pieces here and there until it pitched up and came to rest in the pineapple field not far from the highway.

"We all started running towards the crash sites. When we reached the plane in the gully, we found it almost on its back. The canopy was smashed and the pilot hung suspended through the opening. As each man arrived at the site, he stopped abruptly, immediately seeing the insignia on the fuselage and tail, which identified the plane as US Navy. Several men eased the pilot from the aircraft and laid him down. They felt for a pulse but couldn't be sure if he was alive or not."

Ensign Herbert Menges was shot down, crashing into Pearl City's Palms Hotel, and died. Fritz Hebel pulled away from Ford to try landing at Wheeler, but he was shot down and died of head injuries the next day. Lieutenant (jg) Eric Allen's Wildcat was so riddled with bullets he bailed out. His parachute only half opened, and then he took a .50-caliber bullet to the chest. Still, he was able to swim through the water to the minesweeper *Vireo*. But Allen also died the following day.

Ensign Gayle Herman's plane was struck eighteen times, then a five-inch shell blew the engine out. Herman crashed onto the Ford Island golf course. Astonishingly, he walked away, uninjured. Ensign David Flynn also bailed out, his chute opening fully and bringing him down safely into a cane field. There, soldiers immediately assumed he was a Japanese paratrooper and unleashed a barrage of fire. Flynn was finally able to convince them he was an American and survived.

Ensign James Daniels was now the only Wildcat pilot still in the air. He clicked off his lights and dove for the field's flood lamps, trying to blind the defenders, but this didn't stop the gunfire. So Daniels followed the channel toward Barbers Point and circled there for about ten minutes, until the firing settled down a bit. Then he again asked the tower for landing instructions, and this time the controllers tried the opposite of what they'd told Hebel, telling Daniels to come in low, fast, with no lights. He was going to land just like an enemy pilot would.

He lowered the wheels, hit his flaps, and started coming in, not at 85 knots, but at 120. It worked. He turned around at the edge of the runway and started taxiing to the hangar. A marine with a machine gun then started firing at the Wildcat in the dark, barely missing the plane. Gayle Herman came up from behind and hit the marine in the back of the head with his rifle butt to save his friend.

After then flying 110 combat missions from World War II to Korea, Jim Daniels commanded the carrier *Ticonderoga* during the early days of Vietnam. Gayle Herman, though, would die in a launch accident at the Battle of Midway.

Between 0600 and 0700 on the morning of December 8, 1941, army air patrols were getting ready to again search for the Japanese task force when a Bellows control tower message arrived with the news that someone had spotted "something strange in the water, out by the reef, on the beach end of the runway." An O-47 was dispatched to circle overhead with a crewman in the "greenhouse," its windowed surveillance belly, who quickly confirmed the sighting of an enemy submarine. At the same time, Sergeant David Akui and Lieutenant Paul Plybon were patrolling Waimanalo Beach when Akui, scanning with binoculars, sighted a body rolling in the surf. They pulled a Japanese man in uniform out of the water, determined he was not dead but unconscious, and drew their pistols. He finally came to and explained that he was the sub's commander, Ensign Kazuo Sakamaki, who had so struggled to get to shore that he had passed out. He and his engineer, Kiyoshi Inagaki, Sakamaki said, "had fully expected to die in battle. Then something went wrong."

That something was the gyrocompass malfunction, which had plagued the midget ever since they had detached from their mother submarine. Their mission was to get inside Pearl Harbor, lie submerged until the attack was under way, and then fire their two torpedoes at any suitable target. Instead, the erratic gyroscope interfered with their trim, meaning that after running around in circles in the harbor unable to get their bearings, they'd run aground onto a reef. There, destroyer *Helm* had seen their periscope and fired on them but missed. The shell had instead broken up the reef, allowing them to submerge, but as they tried to again enter the harbor, they were depth-charged, the blow knocking both men out. Coming to, they found their battery had ruptured, filling the tiny compartment with noxious gases, and Sakamaki decided they would suicide-crash into *Pennsylvania*. Instead, their power failed entirely, they could only drift about in the channel entrance, and both fell unconscious again. They came to and discovered they were stuck, quite visibly, on a reef by Bellows Field.

Sakamaki now decided that Petty Officer 2nd Class Inagaki should swim to shore, while Sakamaki would set explosives to scuttle the sub. Instead, Inagaki drowned—his body would wash ashore in three days' time—and the sub's charges failed to detonate. Completely humiliated, Sakamaki, a twenty-four-year-old Imperial Naval Academy graduate, was now America's first POW of World War II. He begged the Americans not to tell the Japanese he had been captured, said that his "honor as a soldier has fallen to the ground," and asked them to kill him. Instead, he was taken into custody at Sand Island by naval intelligence, and his submarine was hauled away on an eighteen-wheel flatbed.

After the navy learned all they could about the midget submarine's technology, it was outfitted with mannequins dressed as Japanese sailors and sent on a tour of forty-one states to help sell war bonds. An unwilling prisoner, Sakamaki burned his face with the lit ends of cigarettes, but after arriving at a mainland prison camp, he gave up thoughts of suicide, he later explained, because the American landscape was so pretty, and the guards treated him with such kindness. Repatriated back to Japan after the war, Sakamaki became as famous as his nine fellow midget-sub crewmen, who had spent the war years after their deaths lionized as great heroes of the nation and memorialized on Shinto shrine portraits. American POW number one, however, received either proposals of marriage or demands that he kill himself to make amends for his shameful behavior. For the whole of his life, Sakamaki refused to be interviewed by Pearl Harbor historians or journalists, and in time he became president of Toyota Brazil.

In 1960, students of the US Navy's deep-sea diving school found another midget, sunk at the harbor's mouth, with warping that made it appear she had been depth-charged. The US Naval Institute investigated this historical curiosity and concluded, "Little doubt exists that her two-man crew left the submarine. Whether or not they survived remains a mystery. . . . If they were able to swim the mile to shore across placid Keehi Lagoon, they could have easily melted into the local populace of Hawaii with its many Orientals. . . . Their devotion to Japanese ideology would likely have caused them to reveal to no one, either during or after the war, that they had failed in their mission. Therefore, it is a remote possibility that one or both may be alive today." The historian of Pearl Harbor's Naval Submarine Base, Ray de Yarmin, said, "It's not impossible that they're alive because the dishonor of having survived would have kept them hidden. The truth will never be known, but there are things people have overlooked."

At about 7:00 p.m. in Washington that December 7 night—0800 in Manila; 1400 in Hawaii—General Gerow finally got General MacArthur on the phone to repeatedly warn him that the Japanese were coming for him next. MacArthur said he was ready for them: "Our tails are up in the air."

At 1030 and 1230, General Lewis Brereton, air commander of the Philippines, asked permission to send his B-17s on bombing runs against Japanese bases on nearby Formosa. MacArthur's chief of staff, Richard K. Sutherland, refused to allow Brereton to speak with the commander.

1257: From their Saipan base, Japanese naval bombers attacked the five hundred marines and sailors posted to Guam, who had no weapons beyond a few machine guns and pistols. After destroying the local barracks and the USS *Penguin*, the planes departed, only to be succeeded by an invasion force of transports and destroyers.

1300: With only fifteen seconds of warning, the Americans on Wake atoll couldn't get their fighters into the air or their antiaircraft guns ready to defend against thirty-six Japanese bombers arriving from the Marshalls. The planes just delivered by *Enterprise* were destroyed, along with the island's fuel-storage tank. As Pan Am's flying boat *Philippine Clipper* took off with airline personnel and Allied wounded, the captain radioed that he saw Japanese cruisers and destroyers heading for Wake.

1400: Thirty-five hell divers arrived over Hong Kong, destroying the *Hong Kong Clipper* and the China National Aviation fleet, as ground forces advanced on the British mainland territory of Kowloon. Allied defenses consisted of a few Canadian and Indian infantry battalions, one antique destroyer, and eight PT boats.

1530: Brereton called MacArthur again for permission to launch an assault and again was told to wait. Brereton finally received an approval and by 17:20, orders for the attack were sent by Teletype to Clark Field.

1730: The Philippines' Iba Field radar operator tried to send Teletype, radio, and telephone warnings to Clark that he had detected two hundred Japanese warplanes heading toward them. The radio didn't work, the Clark teletypist was out to lunch, and the lieutenant who answered the phone promised to spread word of the impending attack "at the earliest opportunity," but never did.

1750: Brereton's planes were still on the ground being fueled, checked, and loaded when, a good fifteen hours after Pearl Harbor, fifty-four Mitsubishi horizontal bombers and seventy-nine Zero fighters from Formosa attacked Clark Field, destroying half of the American air forces in the Philippines and killing over one hundred men. In less than an hour, the Japanese had won the victory that would enable them to launch their ground assault on the Philippines. Hearing the news, MacArthur refused to believe the attackers could be Japanese, insisting they must be German or Italian mercenaries.

Grace Tully woke President Roosevelt at seven on the morning of the eighth with more terrible updates. Midway, Wake, and Hong Kong were under attack, and even after all the warnings sent to Douglas MacArthur, he'd been caught on the ground at Manila, losing over half of his air force, most of his fleet, and a great deal of his supplies. The death toll on Oahu, meanwhile, was now estimated at twenty-eight hundred. The president continued to keep this information as private as possible, not wanting the Japanese to know the magnitude of their victory—a great success, after all, might inspire them to invade Hawaii, or even the West Coast—as well as not wanting Americans to panic or feel defeated even before they had begun to fight.

After breakfast, at 11:00 a.m. valet Arthur Prettyman arrived to dress the chief executive for his appearance at the joint session of Congress. He removed Roosevelt's pajamas and slid each leg into a heavy metal brace, strapping in his knee, thigh, and hip to keep his legs rigid and make it appear as if the leader of the United States of America could walk. Then the valet dressed his president in formal wear, the last touch being the black armband Roosevelt continued to wear in memory of his mother Sara's death on September 7. Prettyman then lifted the American leader into his wheelchair, and Roosevelt wheeled himself to the North Portico, where a limousine he'd never seen before was waiting. Secret Service chief Mike Reilly had determined that in wartime the president required additional protection.

FDR asked, "What's that thing, Mike?"

"Mr. President, I've taken the liberty of getting a new car. It's armored, I'm afraid it's a little uncomfortable, and I know it has a dubious reputation. It belonged to Al Capone. The Treasury Department had a little trouble with Al, you know, and they got it from him in the subsequent legal complications. I got it from Treasury."

At 12:20, ten black limousines entered the Capitol grounds, three of them—*Leviathan*, *Queen Mary*, and *Normandie*—filled with Secret Service guards. Jimmy Roosevelt, in his Marine Corps uniform, helped his father, in his US Navy cape, out of Capone's leviathan and into a wheelchair.

The House chamber, where the meeting would take place, could seat 86 members of the press; 590 appeared.

At 12:15, the Speaker of the House of Representatives, Sam Rayburn, rapped his gavel, bringing the session to order, and Doorkeeper Joe Sinnott announced that the Senate had passed House Concurrent Resolution 61, to convene a joint session. Vice President Henry Wallace then brought the Senate into the chamber, while Cordell Hull, Henry Stimson, Harold Stark, George Marshall, and the justices of the Supreme Court took seats in the audience.

At 12:29, to an explosion of applause, Sinnott announced, "The president of the United States." For the first time in as long as any legislator could recall, even Republicans stood for Franklin Delano Roosevelt. Only two refused to stand: Montana's Jeannette Rankin and Michigan's Clare Hoffman; Rankin would be the only representative or senator voting nay to the president's call for war against Japan.

Holding on to his son James's arm, the crippled man forced himself to walk in an Olympian effort, as the son recalled: "His uppermost thought was that he get one braced foot after the other in the right position; that he hold his balance over his hips and pelvis just so; that he shift his great shoulders forward, left, and right just so; that he not fall down. This concentration caused him to break out into a sweat as, indeed, it always did."

At the podium, Roosevelt fiddled with his glasses, then took a look for the ages, slow and long, at everyone assembled, before he began. He spoke for six minutes and thirty seconds, to the biggest audience in radio history. His "face appears to be carved in granite," the *New York Times* reported. "Gone is the almost happy-go-lucky air of early New Deal days; gone is the latter-day fatigue and occasional irritability. He stands more firmly than for some time, his head held higher, his chin thrust out."

Franklin Delano Roosevelt: "Mr. Vice President, Mr. Speaker, members of the Senate and the House of Representatives:

"Yesterday, December seventh, 1941—a date which will live in infamy—the United States of America was suddenly and deliberately attacked by naval and air forces of the Empire of Japan.

"The United States was at peace with that nation, and, at the solicitation of Japan, was still in conversation with its government and its emperor looking toward the maintenance of peace in the Pacific. Indeed, one hour after Japanese air squadrons had commenced bombing in the American island of Oahu, the Japanese ambassador to the United States delivered to our secretary of state a formal reply to a recent American message. And while this reply stated that it seemed useless to continue the existing diplomatic negotiations, it contained no threat or hint of war or of armed attack.

"It will be recorded that the distance of Hawaii from Japan makes it obvious that the attack was deliberately planned many days or even weeks ago. During the intervening time the Japanese government has deliberately sought to deceive the United States by false statements and expressions of hope for continued peace.

"The attack yesterday on the Hawaiian Islands has caused severe damage to American naval and military forces. I regret to tell you that very many American lives have been lost. In addition, American ships have been reported torpedoed on the high seas between San Francisco and Honolulu.

"Yesterday the Japanese government also launched an attack against Malaya.

"Last night Japanese forces attacked Hong Kong.

"Last night Japanese forces attacked Guam.

"Last night Japanese forces attacked the Philippine Islands.

"Last night the Japanese attacked Wake Island.

"And this morning the Japanese attacked Midway Island.

"Japan has therefore undertaken a surprise offensive extending throughout the Pacific area. The facts of yesterday and today speak for themselves. The people of the United States have already formed their opinions and well understand the implications to the very life and safety of our nation.

"As commander in chief of the army and navy I have directed that all measures be taken for our defense, that always will our whole nation remember the character of the onslaught against us.

"No matter how long it may take us to overcome this premeditated invasion, the American people, in their righteous might, will win through to absolute victory.

"I believe that I interpret the will of the Congress and of the people when I assert that we will not only defend ourselves to the uttermost but will make it very certain that this form of treachery shall never again endanger us.

"Hostilities exist. There is no blinking at the fact that our people, our territory, and our interests are in grave danger.

"With confidence in our armed forces, with the unbounding determination of our people, we will gain the inevitable triumph. So help us God.

"I ask that the Congress declare that since the unprovoked and dastardly attack by Japan on Sunday, December seventh, 1941, a state of war has existed between the United States and the Japanese Empire."

For Americans listening at home, Roosevelt's speech echoed with memories of America's other historic days of infamy: the Alamo massacre and Custer's Last Stand. In those two instances, terrible setbacks were followed up by heroic victories, and the Texas cry of "Remember the Alamo" soon became "Remember Pearl Harbor."

With its attack on Hawaii, Japan erased the isolationist argument that had held sway over American politics for two decades. By 1:06 p.m. the Senate had voted unanimously, and by 1:26 p.m. the House had voted 388 to 1. Congress had declared war in all of fifty-two minutes. This would be the last war declared by Congress, and its unanimous sentiment was felt across the country, with isolationist icon Charles Lindbergh announcing, "Our country has been attacked by force of arms and by force of arms we must retaliate," and FDR antagonist Herbert Hoover concurring, "American soil has been treacherously attacked by Japan. Our decision is clear. It is forced upon us. We must fight with everything we have." Later that day, Roosevelt cabled Churchill, "Today all of us are in the same boat with you and the people of the Empire, and it is a ship which will not and cannot be sunk."

Elsewhere in Washington, DC, enraged Americans chopped down four of the Potomac River's cherry trees, gifts from the mayor of Tokyo in 1912. Archibald MacLeish, librarian of Congress, shipped the Declaration of Independence, the Constitution, the Bill of Rights, a Gutenberg Bible, and a copy of the Magna Carta to Fort Knox for safekeeping.

• • •

Back on Ford Island, Mary Ann Ramsey had spent all afternoon and the night of December 7 taking care of the dead, the dying, and the horribly wounded. On the eighth, she walked outside and found herself drawn to the smoldering hulk that was the *Arizona*. For the first time, she broke down in sobs. Others were at the Bellinger home at that moment, also in tears, after hearing President Roosevelt's speech to Congress, the declaration of war, and the now-poignant trumpeting of "The Star-Spangled Banner."

Mary Ann Ramsey: "Even the children were pin-drop quiet as he talked. When it was over, the national anthem was played. Without a word, every woman and child rose, standing as I had so often seen the smallest of the Navy Juniors do at taps, when the flag was taken down at sunset. Even Chuckie Coe's young face was somber as he placed his hand over his heart. Adults wiped away tears."

There were other points of view. "Since the war, I have confiscated about $500 worth of radio equipment, soda, beer, cigarettes, and seventeen cars," Hickam Private 1st Class Nicholas Gayno later wrote his family. "Some fun! I conked a Jap in the Sears-Roebuck in Honolulu and had him turn over a shortwave receiver. Boy, was he scared. I hadn't shaved, changed clothes or washed since Sunday. I had two revolvers, one huge bolo knife—about twenty-six inches long—and a mean look on my face. I was sure having fun scaring hell out of these civilians."

Rigel's Lieutenant Commander Ed Seiser tells a very different story: "Cowboy, a sailor from Texas, had brought along his dog, Brandy, which he offered as the ship's mascot, and who was accepted as such and named Captain Brandy. He took off to visit other ships and shore facilities and made many new acquaintances. It took him about two weeks to make the rounds; at least he was gone that long before he returned to the ship. Of course, he was under no obligation to return at all, but he had to come aboard to see how Cowboy was getting along and to check in with his orderly.

"A few days before the attack, one of the smaller ships had to make a run to San Francisco, and Brandy just happened to be aboard at the time of departure. So away he went on a trip to the mainland. The word of Brandy's departure was passed along to Cowboy, so that he wouldn't worry too much.

"When his ship arrived in San Francisco, Brandy immediately took off to do some visiting and shopping up and down the Embarcadero. . . . Under normal conditions, whenever a ship was about to depart, she would sound her siren and give certain blasts on her whistle to signal what she was going to do. . . . But now, with the country at war, all sirens and whistles were silenced, so Brandy had no way of knowing that his ship was about to get under way. She sailed and left him stranded on the beach. He spent a couple of days wandering up and down the docks before he was recognized by a sailor from another ship, who took him in tow temporarily until he could decide what to do with him.

"News of Brandy's plight finally reached the ears of the captain of the *Lurline*, flagship of the Matson Line. . . . So the skipper of the *Lurline* invited Brandy to be his guest and to share his cabin on a run he was preparing to make to Honolulu. . . . News of Brandy's arrival preceded him by some unknown means, for all radio communications were silenced. When the *Lurline* arrived in Honolulu, a navy brass band was on hand to head a greeting party. Brandy was mounted on an elevated seat in the stern of a jeep for a parade through the city and out to Pearl Harbor. The dog's picture along with a story about his escapade appeared on the front page of one of the daily newspapers."

As central a role in American history as Pearl Harbor continues to hold, in Japanese history, it was only a small moment in a cavalcade of victories, the foundation of a great Asian empire. Twenty-three hundred miles west of the Hawaiian archipelago lay the three coral islets of Wake, home to scrub and rats and a *China Clipper* runway with an adjacent motel, the Pan Am Inn; for their guests' recreation, the inn provided air rifles to go rat hunting. On December 7, Japanese horizontal bombers destroyed the Wildcats just delivered to the marines at Wake by *Enterprise* as well as the inn, killing half the army's troops and fifty Morrison-Knudsen construction workers. On December 16, Admiral Kimmel sent an armada to support Wake's defenders, but when on December 22, two thousand Japanese soldiers invaded and the island's commander cabled Hawaii, "The Enemy is on the Island. The Issue is in Doubt," the carrier armada retreated back to Hawaii, and the sixteen hundred remaining Americans surrendered.

On December 18, the Japanese took Kowloon and began their assault on the island of Hong Kong, and on the twenty-second, 109 Japanese transports launched almost ten thousand men into the Philippines, not at the heavily defended southern end of Lingayen Gulf, but miles up the coast near the town of Aganoo, and miles south in Lamon Bay. They poured down the cobblestone highway to Manila, where they expected MacArthur to lie in wait. But by now the general had snapped out of his shock and torpor, and the brilliant soldier within awakened to execute a strategic retreat that saved his fifteen thousand American and sixty-five thousand Filipino troops from the invaders and united them on the Bataan Peninsula, where, across the whole of Southeast Asia, they became the only resistance to Japanese attacks. The battling bastards of Bataan repulsed three enemy assaults and believed that they might indeed win their war, once they received American reinforcements as Marshall had promised. But those reinforcements never arrived, and the logistics of getting supplies, weapons, and food from the beaches and cities to them immediately faltered into chaos. While MacArthur stayed in the relative comfort of Corregidor's tunnel defense, the nearly hundred thousand people on the peninsula ran out of food, water, and medicine, falling prey to dysentery, scurvy, malaria, and beriberi. The shock of their abandonment created a misplaced nickname for MacArthur—Dugout Doug—as well as the brutally honest chant:

> We're the battling bastards of Bataan:
> No mama, no papa, no Uncle Sam,
> No aunts, no uncles, no nephews, no nieces,
> No rifles, no planes, or artillery pieces,
> And nobody gives a damn.

MacArthur himself expected to die there, and he expected that his wife of a soldier and his four-year-old son of a soldier would die there, too. He risked a court-martial by refusing Washington's order to evacuate, but when his staff said that a great army awaited in Australia that would allow him to return and take back the Philippines, he agreed. Sneaking across two thousand miles of enemy-held territory, he arrived in Australia to discover that, in fact, her troops had been ordered to Egypt to battle Rommel. "God have mercy on us," he said, collapsing, stunned and flabbergasted, in what was his "greatest shock and surprise of the whole war."

It took the arrival of an additional twenty-two thousand Japanese to force the battling bastards into the largest surrender in American history. As POWs, between seven thousand and ten thousand then perished on the sixty-five-mile forced death march to prison camps, another of Japan's notorious war crimes. An American civilian in Luzon studying Filipino anthropology, a full-edged isolationist who played swing tunes on the accordion, got caught by the Japanese and set for execution. His last act was to play, on his accordion, "God Bless America."

December 25: Hong Kong surrendered to the Japanese, whose airmen sank Britain's battleship *Prince of Wales* and cruiser *Repulse*. Churchill was flabbergasted: "In all the war I never received a more direct shock. As I turned and twisted in bed the full horror of the news sank in upon me. There were no British or American capital ships in the Indian Ocean or the Pacific except the American survivors of Pearl Harbor who were hastening back to California. Over this vast expanse of waters Japan was supreme and we everywhere were weak and naked."

December 28: Borneo surrendered, while off the coast of Java, the Japanese Navy engaged Dutch, British, and American sailors fighting in ancient craft left over from World War I.

January 22: Mitsuo Fuchida led a squadron of ninety fighters and an equal number of bombers from *Akagi*, *Kaga*, *Shokaku*, and *Zuikaku* in an attack on Rabaul, the Australian air base on New Britain Island.

January 31: The Malay Peninsula was now under Japanese control and the assault on Singapore began. Defended by eighty-eight thousand British, Australian, Indian, and Malay soldiers and volunteers, the city fell to the Japanese in two weeks. When Chinese and Indian civilians tried to resist the Imperial Japanese Army, they were immediately executed, their heads left as warnings along the streets. After the conquest, the people of Singapore and Malaya found swinging from their trees the corpses of tortured Englishmen, their mouths stuffed with their severed genitals.

February 19: Fuchida and his squadron attacked the harbor of Darwin, Australia, destroying dozens of Allied planes and ships and so obliterating the town that it had to be abandoned.

March 8: Rangoon fell to Japanese ground troops, along with Sulawesi, Bali, and Sumatra. The news from the Philippines was so relentlessly negative, meanwhile, that George Marshall became convinced the Japanese would capture MacArthur, one of America's great World War I heroes, and parade him through the streets. On March 11, under orders from Washington, MacArthur, his wife, his son, and his officers were evacuated from Corregidor on *PT-41*, slipping through enemy lines to the Philippines' southernmost island of Mindanao. As he passed his men, now known as "the battling bastards of Bataan," "I could feel my face go white," MacArthur remembered, "feel a sudden, convulsive twitch in the muscles of my face." After his safe arrival in Alice Springs, Australia, Roosevelt awarded him the Medal of Honor.

March 9: Java surrendered to the Japanese, who now controlled the entire Netherlands East Indies.

April 3: Fifty thousand Japanese troops with 150 guns, howitzers, and mortars arrived at Bataan to face seventy-eight thousand starving Americans and Filipinos, three-quarters of them half-dead from malaria. At 1000, a rain of bombs and shells exploded against the Allied front lines. The jungle burst into flame, and the defenders ran pell-mell in retreat. Tanks and infantry, coming in from all directions, poured through. The Japanese commander originally estimated it would take a month to win the territory; instead, Bataan fell in six days.

The Japanese force-marched their POWs, running out of water, food, and medicine, sixty-five miles through the jungle to prison camps at the peninsula's base. Ten thousand died along the way, with thousands more subsequently perishing in the camps.

April 5: Fuchida led an attack on the British port of Colombo, Ceylon, sinking the carrier *Hermes*, the destroyer *Vampire*, and two heavy cruisers, *Dorsetshire* and *Cornwall*.

April 29: On his forty-first birthday, the news of one military success after the next was so rapid and so astounding that Hirohito told his closest adviser, "The fruits of victory are tumbling into our mouths too quickly."

In a mere five months, the entire Pacific Ocean west of a line drawn from the Aleutian Islands to Hawaii and Australia had come under the control of Dai Nippon Teikoku. The Japanese Empire stretched six thousand miles from the home islands to Korea and down eastern China to Taiwan and Hong Kong, across today's Vietnam to Burma, down Malaysia to Singapore, and then across all of Indonesia to most of New Guinea. What Tokyo named the Greater East Asia Co-Prosperity Sphere spelled the end of Western control over Sarawak, Borneo, Sumatra, Java, Celebes, the Moluccas, western New Guinea, the Solomons, the Philippines, Malaya, Indochina, the Andamans, Guam, Wake, the Gilberts, and the Marshall Islands and included a vast amount of the world's oil, rice, tin, and rubber. The bucktoothed, nearsighted race of American cartoons had unceasingly

defeated England, Australia, and the United States in battle after battle. The tally: 15,000 killed and wounded Japanese; 320,000 killed,
wounded, and captured Allied soldiers.

Originally planned merely to protect Japan's flank and very much a
side show to the main event, her attack on Pearl Harbor was a signal
moment in military history. Its victorious element, for the first time
in that history, were planes launched from ships carrying explosives.
Overnight, battle strategies would be changed forever.

"What's going to happen at war is a deep mystery until it happens," *Tennessee* sailor Warren Law concluded. "To a degree we didn't
nearly think it was going to happen, we thought that the Japs would
be chicken and would back out. That was kind of the general feeling
of it, that they just weren't up to it and they weren't going to fight, and
if they did, we had the misconception that they weren't worth a hoot.
We soon found out how wrong we were on that. They were very good
fighters and very good navigators and extremely good tacticians."

When news of the success in Hawaii spread across Japan, the nation
was exuberant. Politesse, so admired as a national trait, collapsed, as
thrilled strangers on the streets spontaneously shook hands. At the great
public square before the Imperial Palace, legions gathered to kowtow
in thanks to the great leadership of the Emperor Showa, and longtime
critics of the China War now wholly reversed course. "Until this very
moment, we feared that Japan, hiding behind the beautiful slogan of
'Building East Asia,' was bullying the weak," China scholar Takeuchi
Yoshimi announced. Yoshimi said that he and his colleagues now realized that "our Japan was not afraid of the powerful after all. . . . Let us
together fight this difficult war." Poet Kotaro Takamura created a verse:

> Remember December eighth!
> On this day the history of the world was changed.
> The Anglo-Saxon powers
> On this day were driven back on East Asian land and sea.
> It was their Japan that drove them back,
> A tiny country in the Eastern Sea,
> Nippon, the Land of the Gods
> Ruled over by a living God.

Not everyone was ebullient. Yamamoto's chief of staff, Rear Admiral Ugaki, wrote in his diary, "It is almost certain that the US, after

reorganizing their forces, will come against us in retaliation. . . . Tokyo should be protected from air raids; this is the most important thing to be borne in mind." Then at a celebratory banquet, Yamamoto presented Fuchida with a ceremonial scroll—a kakemono—written in the admiral's distinctive calligraphy: "Message of 'ATTACK!' reaches my ears from more than three thousand miles away—a message from Hawaii. Thinking of Flight Leader Fuchida's brilliant action on the early morning of 8 December, so writes Yamamoto Isoroku." Yet, the most famous reaction of the reluctant admiral to news of his profound victory in Hawaii was "We have awakened a sleeping giant and instilled in him a terrible resolve."*

*Much cited, this quote is now in dispute by historians who favor instead a phrase from a letter cited in Agawa by Yamamoto to Taketora Ogata on January 9, 1942: "A military man can scarcely pride himself on having 'smitten a sleeping enemy'; it is more a matter of shame, simply, for the one smitten. I would rather you made your appraisal after seeing what the enemy does, since it is certain that, angered and outraged, he will soon launch a determined counterattack."

CHAPTER TEN

RESURRECTION

On the night of December 7, Secretary of War Henry Stimson and Army Chief of Staff George Marshall ordered an investigative team headed by Colonel Charles Bundy and Major General Herbert Dargue—with Dargue having been named to replace Short—to fly to Hawaii. But in bad weather over the Sierras, Bundy and Dargue's plane crashed, and they were killed. Secretary of the Navy Frank Knox had decided independently that he himself must go to Oahu to see, first-hand, how such a tragedy could have occurred, and what needed now to be done; Knox's visit would become the first of eight federal investigations of Pearl Harbor.

Departing Anacostia Naval Air Station outside Washington on December 8 and arriving at Kaneohe on the eleventh, Knox was immediately given a tour by commander "Beauty" Martin, who said his officers and men were "trying to salvage something." Knox next met with Kimmel at the Royal Hawaiian Hotel on Waikiki; the admiral had offered quarters for the civilian secretary but Knox declined, explaining that due to the "investigative nature of his visit . . . he would not be the guest of any senior officer on Oahu."

Knox and his team from Washington were horrified by the incalculable human suffering on their tour of the harbor—the corpses still being pulled from the water, the survivors at Ford Island's naval hospital "so terribly burned and charred as to be beyond recognition"—and noticed the Hawaiian commanders having many conversations "carried on in whispers" with "much glancing around lest their words be overheard."

Kimmel and Short straightforwardly admitted to Knox that they had "regarded an air attack as extremely unlikely because of the great distance which the Japs would have to travel to make the attack and the consequent exposure of such a task force to the superior gun power of the American fleet. Neither the army nor the navy commander expected that an attack would be made by the Japanese while negotiations were still proceeding in Washington." Knox did, however, find Kimmel's and Short's saboteur theories credible, telling FDR, "The activities of the Japanese fifth columnists immediately following the attack, took the form of spreading on the air by radio dozens of confusing and contradictory rumors concerning direction in which the attacking planes departed, as well as the presence in every direction of enemy ships."

After preparing his report on the long flight back to Washington, Knox immediately delivered a copy to the White House, and then appeared before the press, saying that "between one hundred and fifty and three hundred planes took part in the attack, too many to have come from a single aircraft carrier," that "apparently none was land based [and] none was flown by Germans." He also said that "a rumor that the navy had been forewarned" was just a rumor and false. He concluded, "In the Navy's gravest hour of peril, the officers and men of the fleet exhibited magnificent courage and resourcefulness," but that the "services were not on the alert against surprise air attack on Hawaii. This fact calls for a formal investigation, which will be initiated immediately by the president. Further action is, of course, dependent on the facts and recommendations made by the investigating board. We are entitled to know it if (A) there was any error of judgment which contributed to the surprise, (B) if there was any dereliction of duty prior to the attack."

In Hawaii after December 7, the FBI and military police took into custody 1,441 Japanese who had dual citizenship, worked for the consulate, were Shinto or Buddhist priests, or who taught the language. One of these was May Namba, who recalled, "[First] there was a curfew; we had to be in by eight o'clock and not leave the house till six. And the Chinese wore 'I'm Chinese' buttons. Well, my brother borrowed a Chinese button, and he used to go out at night, but I don't know whether my mother knew he snuck out, but he always came home safely. There were rumors every day. That we were going to be put in camps, and we thought, 'Well, we're citizens. We don't have to go.' But that was our firm belief at that time, but things changed, and we were soon rounded up and left for camp."

Those 1,441 were less than 1 percent of Hawaii's Japanese population of 155,000. Washington had ordered Short's replacement, Delos Emmons, to intern 40,000 Japanese aliens on the island of Molokai, and the Joint Chiefs "suggested" he evacuate Hawaii's Japanese to mainland detention camps. Emmons ignored both the order and the suggestion, instead recommending on April 6, 1942, that a regiment of Japanese American soldiers be sent to North Africa or Europe where "their physical characteristics will not serve to confuse our other troops." On May 28, Marshall agreed, eventually creating the One Hundredth Infantry Battalion, whose performance was so impressive that it led to a much larger Japanese American force, the 442nd Regimental Combat Team, which won 18,143 individual decorations, including 9,486 Purple Hearts—the most highly decorated unit per man in army history. In time, over thirty-three thousand Japanese Americans would fight for the United States in World War II, with nearly eight hundred giving their lives to their country.

Meanwhile, after the news of Pearl Harbor first reached the American mainland, panic spread across the West Coast. On the morning of December 8, General John DeWitt, the region's commander of defenses, told reporters that enemy planes had been spotted overhead, that "they were tracked out to sea. Why bombs were not dropped, I do not know. . . . Death and destruction are likely to come to this city at any moment." Marine-held machine-gun emplacements popped up overnight across the Federal District, and Treasury Secretary Henry Morgenthau urged FDR to have tanks standing by on Pennsylvania Avenue. Roosevelt declined.

After a series of incidents of mob violence against anyone who looked Asian (both physical attacks and the ransacking of homes and businesses), the first lady felt compelled to point out in her nationally syndicated newspaper column that not every person of Japanese descent living in America was a traitor or a spy. The *Los Angeles Times* replied, "When she starts bemoaning the plight of the treacherous snakes we call Japanese, with apologies to all snakes, she has reached the point where she should be forced to retire from public life." On the twenty-fifth, that newspaper's headline was "L.A. Area Raided! Jap Planes Peril Santa Monica, Seal Beach, El Segundo, Redondo, Long Beach, Hermosa, Signal Hill."

On December 16, the army relieved Generals Short and Martin and the navy relieved Admiral Kimmel. Short was replaced on the next

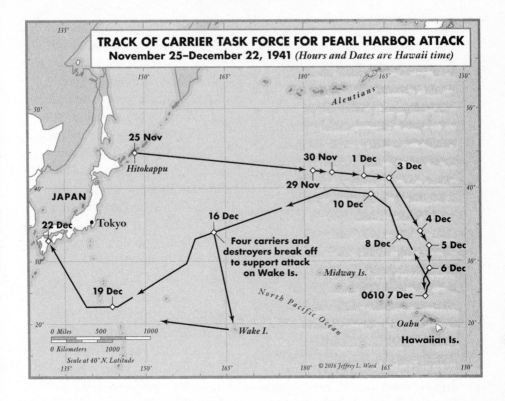

TRACK OF CARRIER TASK FORCE FOR PEARL HARBOR ATTACK
November 25–December 22, 1941 *(Hours and Dates are Hawaii time)*

25 Nov

Hitokappu

30 Nov   1 Dec

3 Dec

29 Nov

JAPAN

10 Dec

16 Dec

4 Dec

22 Dec   • Tokyo

8 Dec   5 Dec

Four carriers and
destroyers break off
to support attack
on Wake Is.   Midway Is.   6 Dec

19 Dec

0610 7 Dec

North Pacific Ocean

Oahu

Wake I.

Hawaiian Is.

Aleutians

0 Miles   500   1000
0 Kilometers   1000
Scale at 40° N. Latitude

© 2016 Jeffrey L. Ward

day by the Army Air Force's Lieutenant General Delos Emmons, while, after seventeen hours of flying from San Diego, Chester Nimitz replaced Kimmel on Christmas Day. But when Kimmel, Short, and Martin were cashiered, the press made note that their counterparts in the Philippines—Hart, MacArthur, and Brereton—weren't similarly relieved of duty and demanded answers, as did various members of Congress. Roosevelt created an executive commission headed by Supreme Court justice Owen Roberts, whose reputation had been forged in the Teapot Dome scandal. Roberts's commission determined that "the effective causes for the success of the attack" were Kimmel's and Short's "errors of judgment," errors so grave that they could only be judged "dereliction of duty" in not adequately reacting to the various cables warning of trouble, culminating with the war warning of November 27. The Roberts Commission blamed Washington for "causes contributory to the success of the Japanese," including Chief of Naval Operations Harold Stark's addenda cables that Japanese aggression would be focused not on Hawaii but on the Far East, and George Marshall's lack of responsiveness to Short's cable that he was on anti-sabotage alert, as well as the delay in getting Marshall's last-minute warning to Oahu.

When the Roberts findings were publicly released at the end of January 1942, they included a few vague comments about Japanese American saboteurs operating in Hawaii. Picked up by the press, this small mention triggered a renewed outburst of paranoia. On February 12, national columnist Walter Lippmann wrote, "The Pacific Coast is in imminent danger of a combined attack from within and from without. . . . The Japanese navy has been reconnoitering the coast more or less continuously. The Pacific Coast is officially a combat zone; some part of it may at any moment be a battlefield. Nobody's constitutional rights include the right to reside and do business on a battlefield. And nobody ought to be on a battlefield who has no good reason for being there."

Congressmen from Oregon, Washington, and California wrote the White House demanding "immediate evacuation of all persons of Japanese lineage." Their great supporter was the alarmist local army chief, General John DeWitt, who insisted that national security urgently required alien internment. FDR's Justice Department tried to calm things down, and a range of Washington insiders, from J. Edgar Hoover to Eleanor Roosevelt, made clear their opposition, but both Secretary of War Stimson and Secretary of the Navy Knox agreed with DeWitt, as did the attorney general of California, Earl Warren, who argued that, if the United States did not incarcerate tens of thousands of Japanese Americans in camps, the nation risked a massive surprise attack from within. A memo from Assistant Secretary of War John McCloy summed up the paranoia: "If it is a question of the safety of the country and the Constitution . . . why, the Constitution is just a scrap of paper to me."

Roosevelt finally decided that, if relocation and internment were the considered judgments of American military leaders, he would not stand in their way and issued Executive Order 9066 on February 19, 1942, allowing military commanders to determine territories "from which any or all persons may be excluded," notably those of "Foreign Enemy Ancestry." As Attorney General Francis Biddle noted, across US history "the Constitution has never greatly bothered any wartime president." On March 2, DeWitt's Western Defense Command issued a proclamation certifying the western halves of California, Oregon, and Washington and the southern third of Arizona as military areas, with all persons of Japanese descent needing to be excised. On March 18, FDR established the War Relocation Authority, headed by Milton Eisenhower, Dwight's brother. Over 110,000 Japanese Americans, two-thirds of them US citizens, were sent to "relocation centers" in California, Arizona, Idaho, Wyoming, Colorado, Utah, Texas, and Arkansas.

Japanese orphans were carted off, as were the adopted Japanese children of Caucasian parents, and transported in trains, with shades drawn so they would not know where they were going, to makeshift camps in the mountains or the desert, fenced in by barbed wire and guard towers. When an inmate needed to visit the outhouse at night, he or she was lit up by a searchlight. Actor George Takei: "I'd just turned five years old, but I still remember that day when my parents dressed my brother, my baby sister, and me. They got us up very early in the morning and dressed us hurriedly. We were in the living room, my brother and I, looking out the window, and we saw two American soldiers, marching up the driveway, with bayonets on their rifles. They stomped up the front porch, banged on the door, and my father answered it. We were literally ordered out of our home at gunpoint.

"My parents told us that we were going on a long vacation to a place called Arkansas. That sounded exotic: Arkansas! A vacation! So when we were put on these trains with armed guards at both ends of each car, being treated like criminals, I thought everyone took their vacations with guards like that.

"We were behind those barbed-wire fences for the duration of the war. There were ten camps altogether. All in the most desolate places. Hellish places. Two on the blistering-hot desert of Arizona, if you can imagine that. We were sent to the swamps of Arkansas. There were others in the wastelands of Wyoming, Idaho, Utah, Colorado. It was a dark chapter of American history.

"Every morning at school in the barracks we started the day with the Pledge of Allegiance to the flag. There was the American flag waving in the middle of the camp, but I could also see the barbed-wire fence with the sentry towers and the machine guns pointed at us from my schoolhouse window as I recited the words "with liberty and justice for all."

Internee Peter Yoshida: "When we had to leave in such a hurry, and people knew we had to leave, they didn't come by and ask, 'How much?'—referring to a price for a property, equipment, tools, etc. Friends, or those we thought were friends, came by with their trucks and asked, 'What can I have?'—referring to refrigerators and stuff like that. We gave away everything, basically. That hurt my father, I think. He had lots of farm equipment and just had to give it all away.

"We ended up in a holding area in Santa Anita—the racetrack. We had a central toilet and place for washing. When we arrived, we were given sewn sheets. There was hay in the streets, so we basically had to make our own mattress. Some people did this at night and really couldn't see what they were doing. Later while lying there, they could feel something moving around in their mattress. When they investigated, they found that there were snakes living in there."

While the story of Pearl Harbor has a number of heroes, some of the most significant have to date remained unsung. War workers joined enlisted men immediately after Pearl Harbor's fires were extinguished to begin the business of salvage . . . of saving. A temporary town—Civilian Housing Area III—bloomed into a population of twelve thousand, becoming Hawaii's third-largest city after Honolulu and Hilo, with its own stadium, post office, theater, police force, and train station. Pearl's shallow waters, which had lulled Kimmel into thinking he was immune from torpedoes, now meant that his stricken ships had sunk a mere fifteen to twenty feet and then sat there, ready for repair. Kimmel's replacement, Admiral Chester Nimitz, even claimed that "it was God's mercy that our fleet was in Pearl Harbor on December 7," since if Kimmel "had advance notice that the Japanese were coming, he most probably would have tried to intercept them. With the difference in speed between Kimmel's battleships and the faster Japanese carriers, the former could not have come within rifle range of the enemy's flattops. As a result, we would have lost many ships in deep water and also thousands more in lives."

The USS *Oklahoma*, flipped with its belly exposed, was righted by a fantastical arrangement of cables and winches out of *Gulliver's Travels*. And "when the subject of the *West Virginia* is mentioned to the men who worked on its salvage, they seldom say anything. They just whistle," reported Robert Trumbull in a series of articles that War Department censors refused to allow the *New York Times* to publish for forty years:

> The engineers decided to use cofferdams, watertight chambers that could be built and attached to the ship. So huge cofferdams were built, their wooden sections braced with steel. They were lowered, bolted to

the hull as on other ships, and meeting so as to form one tremendous outwall. . . . Hundreds of tons of Tremie concrete were poured from hoppers into funnels high above the water. This quick-setting cement, which hardens under water, oozed through thick pipes and formed about the *West Virginia*'s uneven crevasses far below. It hardened and made the cofferdam part of the ship watertight. As the pumps strained to suck out the fouled sea inside, the *West Virginia* rose, inch by inch. Each new day disclosed a new surface ring of oil and black muck from the harbor bottom marking on the cofferdam the laborious progress of the ship's flotation. . . . During ensuing repairs, workers located the remains of seventy *West Virginia* sailors who had been trapped below deck. In one compartment, a calendar was found, the last scratch-off date being 23 December 1941.

When navy divers Ed Raymer and Bob "Moon" Mullen arrived to work salvage in Hawaii, they were warned by diving officer Lieutenant H. E. Haynes that "because of the floating oil, sediment, and debris in the water, underwater lights would be useless," Raymer recalled. "Diving inside the ships would be done in complete and utter darkness. This would require us to develop a keen sense of feel, great manual dexterity with tools, and a high degree of hand-to-brain coordination. Since the navy had no safety precautions for such a situation, we would be required to devise our own."

Wearing a rubberized suit with thirty-six-pound lead-soled shoes, an eighty-four-pound lead-weighted belt, and a heavy copper helmet with small port window to see, Raymer was tethered to the surface by a lifeline of coupled rubberized telephone wire and air hose. Before submerging, divers familiarized themselves with the general layout of a route from blueprints, while telephone talkers used the details of the ship's plan to direct the diver on his path. Besides the telephone talker, the only sound Raymer heard was the air pumping into his helmet.

On January 12, 1942, Ed Raymer dove into *Arizona*: "The dense floating mass of oil blotted out all daylight. I was submerged in total blackness." The large hatch door was stuck and couldn't be opened, perhaps because a gasket had melted in the attack. But the door to the trunk hatch opened, and Raymer descended to the third-level deck.

"Suddenly I felt that something was wrong. I tried to suppress the strange feeling that I was not alone. I reached out to feel my way and touched what seemed to be a large insulated bag floating overhead.

As I pushed it away, my bare hands plunged through what felt like a mass of rotted sponge. I realized with horror that the 'bag' was a body without a head. I fought to choke down the bile that rose in my throat. That bloated torso had once contained viscera, muscle, and tissue. It had been a man."

As he made his way through the ship, Raymer was confronted again and again by floating bodies that he had to push aside to get through doorways and compartments. "Then, as if someone had thrown a switch, my air supply stopped. 'What's wrong with my air supply?' I yelled. No answer. The topside phone key was depressed, but all I could hear was panic-stricken shouting. I quickly closed the exhaust valve in my helmet before all the air escaped from my helmet and suit. 'Take in my slack, I'm coming up,' I yelled, fear rising in my voice.

"Back came a rapid reply: 'Your lifeline is hung up. Retrace your steps and clear it as quickly as you can.' I knew the oxygen remaining in my helmet could not sustain life for more than two minutes. By now the air had escaped from my suit, causing the dress to press tightly against my torso, the pressure from the surrounding water flattening it. As the pressure increased, I felt the huge roiling mass of panic surge into my throat. I tried desperately to hold back the growing anxiety within me. I had seen what terror could do to a man.

"I grabbed the lifeline and started back, pulling hand over hand toward the access trunk. The 196 pounds of diving equipment on my shoulders became an incredible weight. Without buoyancy in my suit, it became a heavy burden dragging me down. I finally felt where a loop in my air hose was caught on the handwheel of a lathe. I cleared my lines and yelled, 'Take up my slack!' 'It's free,' someone shouted over the phone. 'Stay calm. We'll have you up in a minute.'

The salvage crews next moored their barges to *California*, where divers had built a cofferdam around the bow and quarterdeck and were closing off all bulkheads and valves, covering damaged manholes and portholes with metal blanks, and filling the ship's cracks and tears. Shipyard workers removed the above-water conning tower, mainmast, catapults, cranes, anchors, and boats. Dewatering pumps, operating 24-7, then flushed water out of the cofferdam and, just like *West Virginia*, *California* began to rise.

The salvage work required five thousand individual dives totaling twenty thousand hours underwater, and though these men couldn't bring the dead back to life, through a miracle of muscle and engineering, they restored almost everything else with such speed, and such fury, that the material effects of Japan's attacks were almost wholly reversed in a matter of months. By December 20, less than two weeks after the attack, *Maryland*, *Pennsylvania*, and *Tennessee* were back in service. *Nevada* was restored by the end of 1942; *California* at the end of 1943; *Oglala*, *Downes*, and *Cassin* were sailing by February 1944; *West Virginia* on July 4, 1944. The *Arizona*'s five-inch antiaircraft guns were salvaged to defend Oahu. If any more enemy planes appeared, the *Arizona*'s own guns would help bring them down.

A few months after the attack, "we gathered on the barge to watch as a strange-looking ship sailed by on her way around Ford Island making a triumphant sweep through the anchorages to show the fleet she was proudly sailing for home," Ed Raymer said. "The strange ship was the destroyer USS *Shaw* [seen in cataclysmic eruption on this book's cover]. Regardless of how she appeared, all the assembled divers express a sense of pride in our country as we watch the first heavily damaged ship sailed back to America under her own power, knowing she would be able to fight once more."

Shaw was back on full duty by the following autumn. In all of the destruction at Pearl Harbor, only three ships were judged to be beyond the astonishing feats of America's salvage crews, but they would live on in a new way.

At nearly three million square miles, Dai Nippon Teikoku, the Great Empire of Japan, was now a colossus even more vast than the Third Reich, covering one-seventh of the surface of the earth and uniting most of urban China with Hong Kong, Formosa, the Philippines, French Indochina, British Burma and Malaya, the Dutch Spice Islands of Sumatra, Borneo, Java, and Celebes, the Kuriles, the Bonins, Ryukyus, Marianas, Carolines, Palau, Marshalls, Gilberts, northern New Guinea, two Aleutians, and almost all of the Solomons. And at every encounter over the first months starting with December 7, the Japanese triumphed. When IJA troops invaded Britain's Crown Colony of Hong Kong on the morning of December 8 and the garrison surrendered on the twenty-fifth, the Japanese reported 2,754 casualties; the British, 11,848. After the siege of Singapore, 85,000 British troops surrendered to 30,000 Japanese in a mere seven days, with the battle for Malaya ending on February 15 after 138,708 British were killed, wounded, and captured, versus 9,824 Japanese.

Hawaii now found herself on the front lines of the Pacific war, with enemy submarines over the last two weeks of December repeatedly shelling her towns. Japanese wolf subs brought down the Matson freighter *Lahaina* eight hundred miles from Oahu on December 11, then sank oiler *Neches* on January 23 and army transport *Royal T. Frank* on January 28.

On the other side of the world, believing that war was distant and tourists near, the Eastern Seaboard towns of New York City, Atlantic City, and Miami refused Washington's call for blackouts. Their bright lights could be seen ten miles from shore, where U-boats gathered nightly to bring down American merchant trade. In twelve hours one January night, the Nazis sank eight ships, including three tankers. On April 10, a surfaced Nazi sub used her deck gun to sink *Gulfamerica* as the tourists of Jacksonville Beach, Florida, watched in horror. "All the vacationers had seen an impressive special performance at Roosevelt's expense," Commander Reinhard Hardegen triumphantly wrote. "A burning tanker, artillery fire, the silhouette of a U-boat—how often had all of that been seen in America?" The same spectacle assaulted the sunbathers of Virginia Beach, Virginia, when two American freighters were torpedoed in broad daylight on June 15. By July, Nazi forces had sunk 4.7 million tons of Allied shipping. "The U-boat attack was our worst evil," Churchill wrote, "the only thing that ever really frightened me during the war."

Back in the Pacific, on March 3, 1942, two Kawanishi H8K1 Type 2 flying boats, each with four 550-pound bombs, lifted off from bases in the Marshalls, refueled from two submarines at French Frigate Shoals—islands located about halfway between Midway and Kauai—for Operation K: the third strike against Pearl Harbor. At the end of 1941, those same subs had launched Yokosuka E14Y1 folding-wing biplanes from their waterproof deck hangars to survey Oahu's recovery efforts, and now they would be targeted. The enemy flying boats were caught by Kauai radar on March 4, just after midnight. Though the Japanese air crews radioed "surprise attack successful," overcast skies meant they missed their targets entirely, dropping bombs on Oahu's Mount Tantalus and into the ocean, causing no harm. The Americans assumed they were carrier based and, besides sending out four P-40s to attack them, sent five torpedo-armed PBYs to attack their ships, but the Japanese airmen, once again, escaped unharmed.

PART III

VICTORY

CHAPTER ELEVEN

VENGEANCE

The Pearl Harbor attack set in motion a series of events that rippled across the Pacific. If the Holocaust defined evil for the Americans of World War II, December 7 was the embodiment of malignant treachery and their response would be, as historian John Dower has called it, a war without mercy, a series of such savage, gruesome, and inexorable battles so unlike the "band of brothers" memorialized in Europe that it would be known by Norman Mailer as *the naked and the dead*.

Between the eyewitness accounts of Japanese airmen gloating while killing Americans, the destruction of *Oklahoma*, and the massive deaths on *Arizona*, most Pearl Harbor survivors had one overwhelming feeling: rage. An *Oklahoma* gunner's mate said there was "a deep, powerful thirst for revenge on the part of every enlisted man," while Pat Morgan said, "We were all consumed with an urge to do something violent." Kathy Cooper felt "an utter feeling of horror, helplessness, and anger, consuming anger. If a Japanese pilot had walked into the house, I would have tried to kill him." After replacing Husband Kimmel as commander in chief of the Pacific Fleet, William Halsey announced that the Japanese language would be spoken only in hell and urged his men, "Kill Japs, kill Japs, kill more Japs."

The very first American response to December 7, however, was a little-known military quid pro quo that was just as unexpected, just as tactically brilliant, just as symbolic, and just as devastating to an enemy's confidence as Pearl Harbor had been. It started with the men of the Seventeenth Bombardment Group, Army Air crews spending their daylight hours circling repeatedly in their Mitchell B-25s over the same strips of America's West Coast, searching for enemy subs. Then "I got a call from Major Ski York, who was Group Ops, to meet him at Wright-Patterson airfield," Group Officer Davey Jones remembered. "Ski and I climbed to the very top of one of the hangars there, to get away from everybody else." When he got back, Jones called his men together in his hotel suite to report, "Captain York wanted me to talk to you and see how many of you would volunteer for a special mission. It's dangerous, important, and interesting." Hearing this, twenty-four-year old bombardier Bob Bourgeois thought, "*Dangerous* is a pretty bad word when you're talking about airplanes."

"He said, 'Some of you fellows are going to get killed. How many of you will volunteer?'" thirty-year-old bombardier Jacob DeShazer remembered. "Well, I thought, 'Boy, I don't want to do that.' We went around and he said, 'Would you go? Would you go? Would you go?' And they all said, 'Yes.' I was right down at the end of the line, so because all the others said they'd go, I said I would, too."

The commanders selected 140 pilots, copilots, navigators, bombardiers, and gunners, who were then sent to Eglin Air Corps Proving Ground just outside Pensacola, Florida. "The reason Eglin was chosen," said ops officer Ski York, "was because it had about seven or eight satellite fields out in the swamps and the woods, and it was pretty secure from prying eyes." Strange modifications had been made to their B-25 bombers. The radios were gone, black broomsticks were attached to the tail (imitating .50-caliber guns), deicer boots had been added to the wings, a 160-gallon rubber fuel bag was the crawl space between the tail gunner and the cockpit, ten five-gallon cans of gas took up the crewmen's storage space, and the bomb bays were stocked with a 225-gallon leakproof tank. "Special five-hundred-pound demolition bombs were provided by the Ordnance Department," the commander noted. "These bombs were loaded with an explosive mixture containing 50 percent TNT and 50 percent amatol. They were all armed with a one-tenth-of-a-second nose fuse and a one-fortieth-of-a-second specially prepared tail fuse. The one-tenth-of-a-second nose fuse was provided in case the tail fuse failed. Eleven-second-delay tail fuses were available to replace the one-fortieth-of-a-second tail fuse in case weather conditions made extremely low bombing necessary. The Chemical Warfare Service provided special 500 incendiary clusters, each containing 128 incendiary bombs. A special load of .50-caliber ammunition was employed. This load carried groups of one tracer, two armor-piercing, and three explosive bullets."

The volunteers next learned that their training would be even stranger than their modified Mitchells. The man in charge wasn't even a soldier but a sailor, Lieutenant Henry Miller, who announced they would be lifting off from a five-hundred-foot taxi at fifty miles an hour. Since a Mitchell, fully loaded, required a thousand feet to launch, the pilots asked Miller if he had ever done this himself. Hank admitted that he'd never even seen a B-25 before.

The technique was harrowing: wheel brakes on, elevator trim tabs at three-fourths, then blow the throttle all the way. While the B-25 reached full power and shook on its tricycle struts, the wing flaps were turned down, and then the brakes released. The plane tilted back, skidding on its tail as it zigzagged down the runway before wobbling into the air, so lacking in grace that it inspired Ted Lawson to call his plane *The Ruptured Duck*. "At around four or five hundred feet, the airplane would leap in the air, and the copilot—who was in charge of the gear—pulled it up," said Brick Holstrom. "Actually, it was stalling on and off, and then recovering from the stall, that was the trouble [a stall being when the wind, speed, and position of an aircraft combine to make it suddenly falter in altitude]."

A select few of the mission's officers knew its destination, as well as that in Washington, it was known only as Special Aviation Project #1. One of those in the know was Ski York, who "was fairly well convinced that none of us would come out of this thing alive. I was surprised that, with such a conviction, my excitement and nervousness was replaced by a deep and unusual, for me, calm. My only real thought was that I had not been as good a husband as I could have been, and I blamed myself for being such a bastard at times."

On Tuesday, March 3, 1942, the Special Aviation Project #1 volunteers were called to the Eglin Ops Office to meet their commander; for these airmen to learn that he was none other than the world-famous pilot Lieutenant Colonel James Harold Doolittle . . . the thrill was indescribable. Hearing Doolittle's introductory speech, one said, "Within five minutes, we were his . . . we'd have followed him anywhere. . . . I don't think there was any doubt in anybody's mind that as long as he was with us, whatever he wanted to do, we'd go ahead and do it."

Perhaps if the volunteers had spent a little time thinking about how Doolittle had spent his adult life, though, they would have had second thoughts. The man chosen by the chief of the Army Air Corps to lead this team was no stranger to death-defying stunts and hopeless causes, and that this lieutenant colonel had survived to the age of forty-five was remarkable, since nearly every one of his professional colleagues had been killed on the job.

In the aftermath of Pearl Harbor, CNO Harold Stark was demoted to lead US Naval Forces–Europe and moved to London; his official biographer reported this new assignment as voluntary. Stark's replacement as CNO, Ernest King, insisted he'd been fired, and wanted to know why Marshall hadn't been demoted too, since surely the army shared blame with the navy for the Pearl Harbor fiasco? A daughter called King "one of the most even-tempered men in the navy. He is always in a rage."

When Navy Secretary Frank Knox made King commander in chief of the US Fleet on December 23, 1941, one of King's first orders of business was to change the acronym CINCUS to COMINCH. He admired Marshall—"I don't know what the hell this logistics is that Marshall is always talking about," he said, "but I want some of it"—but had as little as possible to do with inferior-in-rank Army Air Corps chief Hap Arnold. That army-navy camaraderie was reciprocated; Eisenhower found the admiral "the antithesis of cooperation, a deliberately rude person . . . a mental bully. . . . One thing that might help win this war is to get someone to shoot King."

The last time that the United States Army and Navy had cooperated was during the Civil War. When it came to unity of command in the Pacific, Marshall wanted his General MacArthur in charge, King insisted that it must be his Admiral Nimitz. The *Washington Post*'s analysis of the Roberts Commission Report pointed out how this history helped lead to December 7: "The Army thought the Navy was patrolling. The Navy thought the Army had its detection service operating. Neither bothered to check with the other—or maybe they were not on speaking terms. . . . The two services were totally uncoordinated, and neither knew what the other was doing—or in this case, not doing. And the air force, so supremely important in the new warfare, apparently was regarded by both as a minor auxiliary."

Thrilled that the might of America had finally been enlisted against Hitler and Mussolini, British military chiefs had been shocked to discover during the Arcadia Conference of Christmas 1941 how independently the American service chiefs operated. George Marshall's counterpart, Sir John Dill, wrote of American military power that "the whole organization belongs to the days of George Washington, who was made Commander in Chief of all the forces and just did it. America had not, repeat not, the slightest conception of what the war means, and their armed forces are more unready than it is possible to imagine."

Who in America at that moment didn't want revenge for Pearl Harbor? In the wake of December 7, every member of Congress was deluged with telegrams and phone calls insisting on a counterstrike and suggesting how to do it. Few knew that Roosevelt had been covertly fighting the Japanese for some time. That covert action began on December 23, 1940, when the president ordered 120 Curtiss P-40 fighters and three hundred men to Asia as volunteers for China's air force, training in Burma. Headed by Louisiana-bayou-bred Claire Chennault, the American Volunteer Group was known as the Flying Tigers, "a rough bunch," Herb Macia said; "the pilots were paid on the basis of kills." Tigers got $300 a week and a $500 bounty for every Japanese plane shot down; after the war, a group of Flying Tigers would start a motorcycle club—the Hells Angels.

Cordell Hull was gung-ho about the operation, telling Treasury Secretary Morgenthau, "What we have got to do, Henry, is get five hundred planes to start from the Aleutian Islands and fly over Japan just once. . . . That will teach them a lesson. . . . If only we could find some way to have them drop some bombs on Tokyo." On July 23, 1941, Roosevelt approved a Second American Volunteer Group of sixty-six Lockheed Hudson and Douglas DB-7 bombers shipped to Nationalist China and from there to bomb Tokyo. By December 7, 1941, however the SAVG's crewmen were still training and its planes were still being assembled at Lockheed.

After Pearl Harbor, FDR would demand that US military leaders "find ways and means of carrying home to Japan proper, in the form of a bombing raid, the real meaning of war." Stimson dismissed it as a "pet project," and Marshall thought it was implausible. But no American wanted revenge for Oahu as much as the navy, notably Ernie King, who discussed the idea with his key officers.

On Saturday, January 10, 1942, King's ops man, Captain Francis "Frog" Low, was in Norfolk, Virginia, inspecting the navy's newest carrier, the USS *Hornet*, which would be a significant part of rebuilding America's Pacific Fleet. Low was sitting in the plane for the trip back to Washington when out the window he noticed one of the runways had the dimensions of an aircraft carrier's flight deck painted on it, used for training carrier pilots. Just then, as two fat army bombers came in for a landing, their shadows fell across the flight deck.

In Washington, Low went to his commander's flagship, the *Dauntless*, to offer King an unorthodox idea: "If the army has some plane that could take off in that short distance, I mean a plane capable of carrying a bomb load, why couldn't we put a few of them on a carrier and bomb the mainland of Japan?" King replied, "That might be a good idea. Discuss it with Duncan and tell him to report to me."

A detail-oriented perfectionist who'd eventually become vice chief of naval operations, Captain Donald "Wu" Duncan heard Low out but had an immediate objection: army bombers could never land on a carrier deck. Low said that maybe they could land elsewhere, perhaps in the sea, picked up by destroyers. What about the rest of the idea? The two looked over the specs of the army's midrange bombers. The B-23 Dragon's ninety-two-foot wingspan meant it was too wide; the B-26 Marauder needed a takeoff that was too long; but the B-25 Mitchell might just fit. Duncan then had two submarines, *Trout* and *Thresher*, look into weather patterns between Midway and Japan. The subs noted that the Pacific's monsoon season would begin at the end of April, meaning a hot crisis deadline. After discussing all these details with King, the CNO said, "Go see General Arnold about it, and if he agrees with you, ask him to get in touch with me. But don't mention this to another soul."

Army Air Corps chief Hap Arnold was immediately taken with Low and Duncan's plan since on January 4, the Allies had been working out the preliminaries of Operation Torch—the invasion of North Africa—when Admiral King had suggested that his carriers ferry air corps planes across the Mediterranean. General Arnold greatly appreciated Duncan's mind for details, and thought the army needed someone of equal caliber to work with the navy on planning this mission, an officer who could face the short timetable needed, and who had the guts to rattle the service's slow-moving bureaucracy and whip the operation right out of it. Only one man in the AAC could do all that—Jimmy Doolittle—and he worked down the hall.

On February 2, in a cold and foggy dawn, crewmen from fo'c'sle to fantail watched as *Hornet*'s deck crane lifted aboard two fat B-25s. At 0900, tugs pulled the carrier away from her berth, freed her lines, and watched as she roared down Hampton Roads in the snow. Her captain ordered full power into the wind—launch position. Who aboard didn't hold their breath as army pilots climbed into their planes and revved their engines?

The Mitchells would have only six feet of starboard clearance to keep their right wings from hitting the tower. *Hornet*'s flagman watched the rise and fall of the bow for the exact moment when he would drop his flag and instantly fall prone to the deck. The first Mitchell then rumbled, shaking down the runway. The navy men, especially the air wing, so used to their sleek SBDs, had only one thought: *He's a sinker.* The B-25 powered itself harder and faster, just barely missing the island with its right wing, and just before the end of the deck . . . she was airborne.

At 3:00 a.m. on Tuesday, March 24, telephones rang out across Eglin Field in Florida, ordering twenty-two crews to assemble. The mission was on. On April 1, the volunteers arrived at Alameda Naval Air Station outside San Francisco, where the *Hornet* was now anchored. Her deck was 809.5 feet long, 127 feet wide, lined with 20-millimeter and 1.1-inch light guns, and painted in Measure Twelve Camouflage. Beneath the deck was a 565-foot hangar bay enclosed by steel roller curtains, which could be raised to ventilate the fumes from the eighty planes warming up their engines before being lifted, by three elevators, onto the deck. Her forty-foot-high, midship starboard island housed the navigation bridge, chat house, captain's deck, admiral's quarters, signal bridge, flight control, and gun director's platforms. Fully loaded, a *Yorktown*-class carrier such as *Hornet* displaced twenty-five thousand tons, was manned by a crew of three thousand, and cost $32 million. Her commander—who'd had REMEMBER PEARL HARBOR painted in huge white letters on the ship's stack—was fifty-four-year-old Captain Marc "Pete" Mitscher. Often described as Lincolnesque for his height and tight-lipped demeanor, a truer mark of Mitscher's character might be found in his pioneering of a captain's wearing a baseball cap, which quickly became a navy tradition.

That April Fools' Day (the perfect moment for launching this mission, one raider would later come to believe), the Mitchells were winched aboard *Hornet* and tied down to the open deck with wheels chocked. All the airmen, even those whose planes didn't make the cut, were then ushered aboard this giant city of steel.

Two carrier groups would be employed for Special Aviation Project #1; one to carry the men and their planes from the continental United States, and the other to provide defense in enemy waters;

together they would be known as Task Force 16. The defenders—carrier *Enterprise*, cruisers *Northampton* and *Salt Lake City*, oiler *Sabine*, and destroyers *Balch*, *Benham*, *Ellet*, and *Fanning*—would depart from Pearl Harbor to meet with *Hornet* and her convoy in the middle of the Pacific.

Aboard, tensions ran high. Colonel Horace "Sally" Crouch said that "the marine personnel in particular resented our being there and treated us with contempt. When they would see you in the passageways or otherwise like that, there was a very active minority group who made it very apparent that it was an insult for their ship to be used as a transport vehicle." Hank Miller had warned the airmen not to talk about their mission, a silence that led to sailor scuttlebutt so serious that Marine Sergeant George Royce told his detachment that while he didn't know any more about all this than they did, if they were smart, they'd take out government life insurance immediately. When Corporal Larry Bogart learned that the commander was the infamous Jimmy Doolittle, he paid out enough in premiums to quintuple his benefits.

On April 2 at 1018, *Hornet*, *Vincennes*, *Nashville*, *Gwin*, *Grayson*, *Meredith*, *Monssen*, and *Cimarron* weighed anchor and set off under a heavy fog, the USS *Hornet* destined never again to see the continental United States. As the task force cleared the Golden Gate Bridge, the bosun's whistle sounded, and Captain Mitscher announced over *Hornet*'s loudspeakers and simultaneously via semaphore to the other ships: "The target of this task force is Tokyo. The army is going to bomb Japan, and we're going to get them as close to the enemy as we can. This is a chance for all of us to give the Japs a dose of their own medicine."

Cheers broke out across the decks of every ship as the army and the navy united to strike a blow of vengeance. "The sailors I saw were jumping up and down like small children," said Mac McClure. "It was like you were at a football game and somebody has just kicked a goal at the last second," bombardier Bob Bourgeois remembered. "People went wild. I rejoiced just like everyone else. I was glad to see somebody was going to retaliate for Pearl Harbor." A ditty soon swept across the ships: "Heigh-ho! Heigh-ho! We're off to Tokyo! We'll bomb and blast and come back fast, heigh-ho! Heigh-ho!"

At a meeting with his fliers, Doolittle outlined the industrial and military targets that American army intelligence had chosen in Tokyo, Yokohama, Osaka, Kobe, and Nagoya; the crews were allowed to pick their strikes. Everyone wanted to take out Emperor Hirohito and the

Imperial Palace, so they cut cards to see who would claim the prize. But Jimmy Doolittle had seen the whole of England unite in common cause after the Luftwaffe's strike on Buckingham Palace, and vetoed an attempt on the palace. Later in life he'd consider this one of the best decisions he'd ever made.

The plan was to launch at dusk, arriving over Japan at night. Flying three hours ahead of the rest, Doolittle would drop incendiaries over the wooden cities of Japan. The fires would serve to light up the targets, and the men could then see their way clear.

As the days passed, the thrill of this history-making endeavor and the visceral joy of giving payback for December 7 wore away, and serious thought as to what they would be facing began to occupy the airmen's minds. Military intelligence had concluded they would be greeted over Tokyo by three hundred 75 mm antiaircraft guns and five hundred Japanese planes. The men knew how horribly the Japanese treated their POWs and feared capture. "Personally, I know exactly what I'm going to do," Doolittle said. "I don't intend to be taken prisoner. If my plane is crippled beyond any possibility of fighting or escaping, I'm going to bail my crew out and then drive it, full throttle, into any target I can find where the crash will do the most damage." He'd already thought through the odds and come up with his own professional estimate of their chances: fifty-fifty.

Though Task Force 16 took a zigzag course across the Pacific to avoid detection, what US military intelligence hadn't learned was that Japan had a flotilla of fishing boats posted six hundred miles off its coastline, radio-equipped and on round-the-clock lookout for enemy forces. It would be Task Force 16 that discovered this picket line, at dawn on April 18.

The sky that morning was a dark gray murk. At 0508, eleven scouts were launched, one of them a Dauntless piloted by Lieutenant O. B. Wiseman. The lieutenant came out of cloud cover directly over an enemy ship forty-two miles directly before Task Force 16. Returning over *Enterprise*, Wiseman's rear gunner slid open the tail hatch and dropped a beanbag with a note detailing the enemy ship's position, and that they'd been spotted.

Dive-bombers from *Enterprise* joined with the fleet's guns and after twenty-nine minutes of attack and 924 six-inch shells fired, the picket boat, *Nitto Maru*, raised a white flag, The ship's radioman had, however, already sent a message to Japan's Fifth Fleet: "Three enemy carriers sighted at our position 650 nautical miles east of Inubo Saki [central Japan's historic lighthouse] at 0630." Commander in Chief of Combined Forces, Rear Admiral Matome Ugaki, ordered all ships within a day's run on a course to the *Nitto Maru*. Five carriers, 6 cruisers, 10 destroyers, 9 submarines, 90 fighter planes, and 116 Japanese bombers now headed toward Task Force 16.

The original goal was to get within 450 miles of Japan. At 550 miles, the air crews could still make it, but with little margin for error. Instead, six hundred and eighty-eight miles from Tokyo and over two hundred miles from the launch site, the mission had been compromised. "We knew that the pilots really didn't have a Chinaman's chance of getting to China," said Hank Miller. At 0800, *Enterprise* blinker-lit a message: LAUNCH PLANES. TO COL. DOOLITTLE AND GALLANT COMMAND: GOOD LUCK AND GOD BLESS YOU.

Hornet turned into a twenty-seven-knot wind and chief engineer Pat Creehan pushed the turbines to their maximum. The seas continued rough. "This was zero weather conditions. Zero. *Zero!* That means you can't see across the table," recalled bombardier Bob Bourgeois. "Have you ever seen a thirty-foot sea? I never had. It's seventy feet from the water to the top of the ship. And the bow of the ship was going down and picking up water and throwing it over the deck. I have never been in worse weather in my life. The rain! Oh, the rain! I've been in a bunch of hurricanes right here in Louisiana. And they were tame compared to this thing."

Airdales—sailors assigned to work with the carrier's planes—unslipped the ropes holding the bombers down, yanked the chocks away, crewed a donkey to maneuver the Mitchells into position, and topped off their fuel tanks, rocking the planes wing by wing to shake out the air bubbles and load the maximum. As Doolittle's men prepared, so did the crew of Commander John Ford. The Oscar-winning director would capture the moment for the nation's movie-house newsreels. The men who would be known by history as the Doolittle Raiders were as ready as they could possibly be, which was hardly ready at all.

At 0815, flight-deck signal officer Ozzie Osborne whirled a checkered flag in broader and broader, faster and faster eights over his head. First in line, Lieutenant Colonel James Harold Doolittle turned down his wing flaps and revved up his throttle. The heavy plane shook against the brakes. Jimmy had under five hundred feet of taxi before him and a mere six feet of clearance between his right wing and the tower. Even after their Eglin training, the runway looked awfully small to the army fliers, while the waves crashing over the deck seemed mountainous.

Osborne felt in his bones the *Hornet*'s rise and fall, waiting for precisely the right moment. "You knew how long it would take them to run down the deck, and you wanted to start them as the bow started down because it would take them that length of time to get to within fifty or seventy-five feet of the bow, and then, as the deck started to come up, you'd actually launch them into the air, or at least horizontal but on the upswing, in fact giving them a boost," said Steven Jurika. This meant that pilots spent most of taxi heading straight at the waves.

Osborne's flag shot down, Doolittle yanked his feet from the brakes, the carrier tilted, and the lead B-25, filled to the max with fuel and bombs, began its slow shuffle. "He won't make it! He can't make it!" one navy pilot shouted over the din, but when Doolittle was asked later how he felt at that moment, he said, "Confident." The man flying number two to Doolittle, Dick Cole, remembered thinking: "It'd be a pretty bad feeling for everybody behind us if we took off and dropped into the water."

Ted Lawson saw it all: "We watched him like hawks, wondering what the wind would do to him, and whether he could take off in the little run toward the bow. If he couldn't, we couldn't. . . . Doolittle picked up more speed and held to his line, and just as the *Hornet* lifted itself up on the top of a wave and cut through it at full speed, Doolittle's plane took off. He had yards to spare. He hung his ship almost straight up on its props until we could see the whole top of his B-25. Then he leveled off, and I watched him come around in a tight circle and shoot low over our heads—straight down the line painted on the deck."

The entire task force cheered in relief, a shout so loud that the Mitchell crews could hear it above their engines' roar. Every four minutes, another B-25 nosed into position, gunned its engines, and wobbled from the runway. The sky now hummed with a black stream, a sixteen-plane, eighty-man squadron heading due west, the protection of the task force far behind them and their targets, their escape route, and their allied territory far, far ahead.

April 18, 1942—four months and eleven days after December 7, 1941—was a bright, hot Saturday in central Honshu. Sunbathers on the beach were the first to see the solid, snub-nosed planes painted OD (olive drab), that soared just overhead. Everyone assumed they were Japan's famous navy fighters and many, especially the children, looked up, and waved. Not until the squadron reached central Tokyo did the Japanese notice the gleaming red, white, and blue emblem of stars on their wings.

Cruising at thirty feet, Doolittle pulled up to twelve hundred so bombardier Fred Braemer could get to work. At 1215, a red cockpit light blinked four times, confirming that all four bombs had left the bay. It was odd that North American Aviation had included this lamp as everyone aboard could feel each bomb snap from its shackles, the release leaving a B-25 two thousand to three thousand pounds lighter, the plane suddenly jumping in the air like a stallion.

Decorated with such messages as I DON'T WANT TO SET THE WORLD ON FIRE—JUST TOKYO! and YOU'LL GET A BANG OUT OF THIS, the five-hundred-pound bombs and thousand-pound incendiaries struck. Explosion after explosion rang out; then after a brief silence came the unmistakable ack-ack of antiaircraft fire, and the wail of air-raid sirens.

Back at Task Force 16, radio rooms intercepted Japan's propaganda station, JOAK, announcing: "A large fleet of enemy bombers appeared over Tokyo this afternoon. . . . The known death toll is between three thousand and four thousand so far." This news was loudspeakered and semaphored across the American ships; elated cheers and whoops roared from deck to deck. Pearl Harbor had been avenged, and the army and the navy had done it together.

The only other time a foreign nation had attacked Japan was seven hundred years before, when Mongolia's Kublai Khan sent an armada. The fleet was destroyed by a typhoon, and ever since the Japanese believed their homelands were safeguarded by a supernatural *kami-kaze*—a "divine wind." The endangered American airmen, however, would now get their own *kamikaze*—a thirty-mile-an-hour tailwind pushing them toward the safety of Nationalist China—providing an extra 250 miles or so of thrust. The change in the wind that eased their way, however, had at the same time undermined the work of those coordinating their ground support. The question that Wu Duncan and Frog Low had never answered—if the fliers couldn't land on a carrier, where would they go?—was still, four months later, unresolved.

On April 13, Major E. N. Backus and Lieutenant Colonel E. H. Alexander had flown from Chongqing to oversee thirty thousand gallons of avgas and five hundred gallons of oil arriving from India as well as to ensure that lights, landing flares, and DF (direction-finding) signals were in place for Special Aviation Project #1. Backus and Alexander, however, were prevented from flying in by the same *kamikaze* now giving the Doolittle volunteers a heaven-sent push. The airfields were never set up.

Already flying on a prayer, the airmen would find that some prayers go unanswered. The navigators listened for their beacons, but heard nothing. As the gas needles knocked against "empty" pegs, most of the pilots yoked their Mitchells up so the crews could bail out, pulling rip cords into the unknown, falling at 180 miles an hour, in the dead of the night, through thunderstorm and fog, into enemy-held territory on the other side of the world.

One pilot had decided to try for the Soviet Union instead of Nationalist China, and that plane would be the first to land. Doolittle had ordered them not to go to Russia, but Ski York felt he had no choice. Navigator Nolan Herndon determined their course from his vague maps that didn't really match what he saw out the window and dead-reckoning guesses. Praying they hadn't ended up in Japanese-run Korea, the Mitchell set down in Kamchatka. "At last," thought Bob Emmens, "dry, good ground. It was a wonderful feeling."

Over a dozen Russians came over to have a look at the B-25. One of them started talking in rapid Russian and the fliers picked up a word: *Americanski*. The crew immediately replied "Americanski!" again and again, and the Russians laughed. After a nap, the men were brusquely awakened and told to hurry; the plane was ready and waiting. They rushed out to discover that it wasn't their Mitchell, but a DC-3, which flew them to meet General Stern of the Far Eastern Red Army. After they were interrogated, Stern's translator announced, "The general has asked me to tell you that according to a decision reached between our two governments and by direction of orders from Moscow, you will be interned in the Soviet Union until such a time as further decisions are made in your case. Do you have any requests to make at the present time?"

Instead of bailing out into the unknown, Ted Lawson tried to land *Ruptured Duck*, but the engine conked out as he was coming in and the struts hit a wave at 100 mph. Gunner David Thatcher was knocked out, then came to. Water was pouring in. He put on his Mae West and started to climb out the hatch, but couldn't fit. Dave then realized that the plane, filling with water and sinking, was upside down; he had been trying to squeeze through the turret blister.

He got out to find Bob Clever seriously gashed up and bleeding out in buckets. Mac McClure had tried to help, but Mac's shoulders were wrenched out of their sockets. Ted Lawson was severely injured and seemed unlikely to survive.

Eight Chinese farmers came down to the beach where they washed up. The peasants took the men to a shack about half a mile away. Morning came, wet and gray. Dave Thatcher could hear a motor. He saw an idling patrol boat. From its stern waved the blood red flag of Japan.

But as they had promised, the Chinese arrived with bamboo poles, ropes, and strips of palm that they used to make litters to carry the injured men to safe territory. "I swung between them," Lawson said, "like a butchered hog." The men were taken by boat to a town where the entire crew of plane fifteen, including gunner Doc White, appeared. They'd ended up in the water and their raft had sunk, but Doc salvaged two tubes of morphine, which he would use to save Lawson's life.

Ted Lawson: "Doc stepped away and walked back quickly with a silver saw. It made a strange, faraway soggy sound as he sawed through the bone. Except for the tugging fear that I was coming back too soon, the actual amputation was almost as impersonal to me as watching a log being sawed."

All night long as the other Americans bailed out across the southeastern provinces, the Chinese heard the explosions of crashing planes, saw the rising plumes of smoke, and watched the broad white-circle ghosts descend through the clouds.

In the morning the raiders discovered that they had fallen into a rugged terrain similar to the foothills of the American West, but with valleys of rice paddies and citrus groves. Though few in that part of China had telephones or radios, news of the big-nosed men who had bombed Japan and had fallen from the sky traveled across the territory with remarkable speed. Almost every American would be amazed at how soon the Chinese learned the news and by how well they were treated.

Dick Knobloch and Mac McElroy were following a river. A young boy ran out, shook his head no, made a gun with his hand, shouted,

"Bang! Bang!," and pretended to die. Japanese troops were just minutes away. The boy took them to a Chinese squadron whose Captain Wong could speak some English. Soon the whole crew was reunited and brought to the outskirts of a town in Nationalist-held territory. Wong told them to wait, and for over an hour they sat there, with no explanation. It was mysterious, and unsettling. Were the Chinese going to turn them in to the Japanese? The Americans were so tired and so dirty and so hungry. Should they try to run away? No one could figure out what to do. Then, from far off in the distance, came a noise, which grew louder, and closer, until the Americans found themselves in the middle of a glorious and enthusiastic parade, led by an eight-piece marching band.

"There was this Chinese band who'd stayed up all night long, learning to play 'The Star-Spangled Banner,' " said Bob Bourgeois. "There was an American flag, and I tell you, there were five guys from crew thirteen, listening to them play 'The Star-Spangled Banner,' well, we had tears running down our faces." The city of three hundred thousand was festooned with banners: WELCOME BRAVE AMERICAN FLIERS. FIRST TO BOMB TOKYO. UNITED STATES AND CHINA RULE THE PACIFIC! They were fed a dinner of mashed potatoes, pie, and wine, and the next morning they were taken to have hot baths, in a tub.

On Saturday, April 18, in Hyde Park, New York—April 19 in China—Franklin Roosevelt was working at his home office with secretary Grace Tully and speechwriter Sam Rosenman when a call came in from the White House: Radio Japan was broadcasting a report of Americans bombing Tokyo.

Smiling broadly and chain-smoking, a thrilled president told Grace and Sam the entire story. Rosenman had an idea: "You remember the novel of James Hilton, *Lost Horizon*, telling of that wonderful, timeless place known as Shangri-La? It was located in the trackless wastes of Tibet. Why not tell them that's where the planes came from? If you use a fictional place like that, it's a polite way of saying that you did not intend to tell the enemy or anybody else where the planes really came from."

Roosevelt called a press conference for April 21. There he made an extremely cryptic announcement confirming that American bombs had fallen on Japan, the planes having come "from our new base in

Shangri-La," and refused to take questions. FDR became so enamored with this allusion that he renamed the chief executive's Maryland country getaway Shangri-La; today it is known as Camp David.

The great majority of Doolittle Raiders eventually arrived in Chongqing, the capital of Free China, in what could only be considered a miracle. Eighty airmen had bombed the heart of Japan, with seventy-five of them crashing into enemy-controlled territory and then smuggled across a quarter of China. One was dead; five were in Russia; five were healing in Linghai; ten were MIA. Considering the history of Special Aviation Project #1, it seemed like providence.

In an amazing turnabout, Doolittle and his men had mirrored Admiral Yamamoto's December 7 strategy, with Special Aviation Project #1 just as much of a surprise to the Japanese as Operation Z had been to the United States. Mitsuo Fuchida: "Headquarters spokesmen sarcastically pooh-poohed the attack as not even a 'do-little' but rather a 'do-nothing' raid. In point of physical damage inflicted, it was true enough that the raid did not accomplish a great deal. But the same could not be said of its impact on the minds of Japan's naval leaders and its consequent influence on the course of the war at sea. The fighting services, especially, were imbued with the idea that their foremost duty was to protect the emperor from danger. Naturally, they felt that it would be a grave dereliction of this duty if the emperor's safety were jeopardized by even a single enemy raid on Tokyo."

After the war, MacArthur's occupying forces uncovered data on the effects of the Doolittle Raid: 50 dead, 252 wounded, 90 buildings damaged or destroyed. It seems like so little, especially when compared to the deaths of Pearl Harbor, but the repercussions were immense. Not only was this act of retaliation the first US victory of World War II, but after month after month of defeat and humiliation in Europe, North Africa, and the Pacific, it was also the first real victory for the Allies as a whole. Many Americans would remember for the rest of their lives where they were when they learned Tokyo had been bombed, especially the majority of citizens who were convinced at the time that Germany, Italy, and Japan were going to win the war. The raid proved, at a crucial moment, that the Axis powers weren't invincible.

An enraged Japan exacted vengeance on the Chinese who'd helped Doolittle and his men. On April 20 Hirohito signed an order "to destroy the air bases from which the enemy might conduct air raids on the Japanese homeland. The captured areas will be occupied for a period estimated at approximately one month. Airfields, military installations, and important lines of communication will be totally destroyed." The Imperial Japanese Army ripped up American church missions and Christian graveyards while sending over six hundred sorties to bomb the southeastern provinces, ultimately killing an estimated 250,000 Chinese. "We fed the Americans and carried them to safety so that they could bomb Tokyo again," one Chinese schoolteacher said. "Then, the [Japanese] dwarf invaders came. They killed my three sons; they killed my wife, Angling; they set fire to my school; they burned my books; they drowned my grandchildren in the well. And I crawled out of the well at night, when they were drunk, and killed them with my own hands—one for every member of my family they had slaughtered."

Even after being awarded the Medal of Honor, Brigadier General Doolittle never thought of his raid as victorious: "The raid had three advantages, really. The first advantage was to give the people at that time a little fillip. The news had all been bad until then. The second advantage was to cause the Japanese to worry and feel that they were vulnerable, and the third and most useful part of the raid was that it caused a diversion of aircraft and equipment to the defense of the home islands which the Japanese badly needed in the theaters where the war was actually going on. It, for me, was a very sad occasion because, while we had accomplished the first part of our mission, we had lost all of our aircraft, and no commander feels happy when he loses all of his aircraft. And of course, we lost some of the boys."

Green Hornet arrived over China having run out of gas four minutes before making landfall and at an altitude of only a hundred feet—too low for bailing out. When Dean Hallmark tried to bring her down in the water, the plane slammed against a wave with such force that it was thrown back up and then crashed in a nosedive. Bob Meder tried to revive gunner Don Fitzmaurice and bombardier Bill Dieter, but nothing could be done for them.

Discovered by peasants, Hallmark, Chase Nielsen, and Meder were taken to a Chinese camp but then were captured by the Japanese, as were the five crewmen from *Bat out of Hell*. Though Doolittle had explicitly ordered his men not to bomb the Temple of Heaven, a raid on the home islands was seen by many in Tokyo as an attack on the emperor, and the POWs would be dealt with accordingly.

The Americans were imprisoned by the Kempeitai, the Japanese Gestapo who believed truthful confessions could be extracted from prisoners taken as near to death as possible. "I was given what they call the water cure," Chase Nielsen said. "I was put on my back on the floor with my arms and legs stretched out, one guard holding each limb. A towel was wrapped around my face and put across my face and water was poured on. They poured water on this towel until I was almost unconscious from strangulation, then they would let up until I'd get my breath, then they'd start all over again. I felt more or less like I was drowning, just gasping between life and death."

Even though the Japanese had already retrieved enough evidence to tell them all they needed to know about the Doolittle Raid, they simply could not believe that American bombers had successfully attacked the empire and were determined to beat the truth out of their captives. For two months, the torture and interrogation would continue, and thoughts of suicide naturally occurred in the minds of these young men. The Americans would think, what could be worse than this? Why not end it now? Then they would remember, they had no means; they didn't even have the power to kill themselves.

When he first heard that Tokyo had been bombed, Isoroku Yamamoto was so filled with shame that he took to quarters aboard battleship *Nagato* and refused to come out. Day after day, he ignored his staff's pleas, crippled by anxiety and depression. When finally Yamamoto emerged, he was determined that such a violation of his beloved country could never happen again.

When Doolittle struck, Japan's armed forces were engulfed in bitter conflict on strategy in the wake of Operation Number One. The navy general staff wanted to consolidate and expand their Pacific conquests, eventually cutting off Australia's sea lanes to the United States. Yamamoto and his Combined Fleet officers wanted to instead finish the job they'd started at Pearl Harbor by destroying the rest of America's Pacific Fleet.

Yamamoto proposed solving two concerns with one battle. Since the Doolittle Raid must have been launched by a carrier near Midway, the American-controlled atoll eleven hundred miles west of Hawaii, then Midway must be the next target. With a victory at Midway, Japan could protect the home islands from future attacks and lure the US Navy into a battle that, in the face of Japan's vastly superior Pacific naval power, it was guaranteed to lose. Additionally Japan would have a military base from which to launch the eventual conquest of Hawaii, and then a full retaliatory strike against the American West Coast.

Yamamoto's strategy was approved.

Most of the men who survived the Doolittle Raid spent the rest of World War II in CBI/SEAC (China-Burma-India/Southeast Asia Command, known by wags as Confused Bastards in India and Saving England's Asian Colonies). As they were thrown by war across the globe, another group of men, also not as honored and remembered as they deserve, were spending their combat years in Hawaii as self-imposed prisoners of the windowless basement in Pearl Harbor's Naval District Administration Building. The Japanese attackers missed this building entirely on December 7, an oversight that was one of their greatest strategic errors.

The men in that basement were Station HYPO, the local branch office of OP-20-G, the Communications Security Section of the Office of Naval Communications. Their chief, Joseph J. Rochefort Jr., felt so responsible for December 7 that he rarely left the basement and he almost never slept. HYPO team was charged with cracking the latest Imperial Japanese Navy code—JN-25. If it weren't for Rochefort, HYPO, a series of Japanese missteps, and the Kantai Kessen triggered by the Doolittle Raid, the Japanese Asian empire of Dai Nippon Teikoku might remain to this day.

On May 5, 1942, HYPO intercepted, decoded, and translated an order to strike the Aleutian Islands of Attu and Kiska on June 3, as well as a target code named "AH" on June 4. Rochefort guessed that AH was Midway, a notion his superiors dismissed. Why would Tokyo want to simultaneously hit opposite ends of the Pacific, and why would the Japanese make such efforts over Midway's two negligible specks of atoll? Even so, Rochefort's superiors approved his plotting a trick. Rochefort had Midway officers openly broadcast a false distress call that their distillation plant was broken. Almost immediately, Japanese forces on Wake informed Tokyo of AH's water troubles.

The Americans had another secret Japan didn't know, in that Japanese pilots had reported sinking two American aircraft carriers during May's Battle of the Coral Sea. Instead, *Yorktown* had struggled into Pearl Harbor on May 27 and Nimitz was informed it would take three weeks to return her to service. He ordered the repairs done in three days. In the same miracle of sweat and engineering that had restored so many of the Queens of Pearl, on May 30, she sailed out, her band playing (in another of World War II's great mysteries) "California, Here I Come."

As Yamamoto began to assemble his mission, HYPO was able to decrypt the date, location, time, and details of this battle. After an assault on Alaska's Aleutians drew away some of America's fighting force, Midway would be attacked by a group of four carriers led by Chuichi Nagumo, the hero of Pearl Harbor, followed by an invasion of Japanese troops. A third armada, which included three of Japan's greatest battleships, would meanwhile wait nearby for the American navy to rush to Midway's defense. It was a strategy that combined Mahan with Mitchell; a Kantai Kessen starring naval aviation.

On May 24, Rochefort handed the exact Japanese battle plans to Edwin Layton, CINCPAC's intelligence officer, who studied the transcriptions, the Pacific charts, tides, winds, and weather, and informed Nimitz that the Japanese would "come in from the northwest on bearing 325 degrees and they will be sighted at about 175 miles from Midway, and the time will be about 0600." It was, word for word and point by point, exactly what would happen and was the most significant intelligence in the history of World War II's Pacific theater. Yet, even with this key advantage, Nimitz only had three task groups to send against Yamamoto's ten battleships, twenty-four cruisers, seventy destroyers, eighteen tankers, fifteen submarines, eight aircraft carriers, and assorted transports—185 ships in all. Additionally, one of America's greatest admirals had been sidelined; the stress and exhaustion of the first months of war had finally caught up with Bill Halsey, who succumbed to an attack of eczema that sent him to the hospital. In his stead, Rear Admiral Ray Spruance became temporary head of *Enterprise*, joined by Rear Admiral Frank Jack Fletcher on *Yorktown*, and Pete Mitscher on *Hornet*.

June 4 turned out to be a typical Pacific summer day, with flat water, a few scattered white clouds, and wind so mild a carrier would need full-out power to launch its air. At 0534, scout planes radioed back to *Enterprise* that enemy carriers had been spotted. Ray Spruance ordered his airmen to attack.

At 0615, Vice Admiral Nagumo ordered seventy-two bombers and thirty-six fighters to strike the Americans on the twin atolls of Midway. They were met by twenty-five obsolete fighter planes, which they downed. From 0630 to 0650, the Japanese destroyed Midway's hospital, fuel tanks, and Marine command post, killing another twenty men. They were met by heavy antiaircraft fire however; thirty-six Japanese planes were taken, and thirty more made it back to their carriers too damaged to fly again.

At 0702, *Enterprise* and *Hornet* together launched twenty Wildcat fighters, sixty-seven Dauntless dive-bombers, and twenty-nine Devastator torpedo planes, keeping behind only the airpower needed for defense. At 0838, *Yorktown* sent out seventeen Dauntlesses, twelve Devastators, and six Wildcats—in sum, pretty much everything the Americans had to throw.

At 0705, ten Devastators from Midway attacked. Their torpedoes missed, and seven of them were shot down. Since the Japanese hadn't yet vanquished the atoll and there was no sign of an approaching American fleet, Nagumo changed strategy against Yamamoto's plans and ordered another assault on Midway. This meant doing what he'd forgone in not making a third strike on Pearl Harbor—an hour-long process of lowering planes below, replacing their torpedoes with bombs, and raising them back to the flight deck.

At 0728, the very last of Nagumo's patrol planes sent a message: "Sight what appears to be ten enemy surface ships . . . 240 miles from Midway." The reported position established that they were well within air range, so Nagumo reversed direction, ordering that all planes that hadn't yet been switched to bombs should now keep their torpedoes. Yamamoto's double-edged strategy of invading Midway while simultaneously destroying the American fleet had bottlenecked. Nagumo's decks were full of land bombers and a few dive-bombers, not the right equipment for a naval aerial assault, and he had planes returning from Midway unable to land, since the decks were too crowded.

Almost immediately, twenty-seven dive-bombers and fifteen B-17 Flying Fortresses attacked, dropping 322 bombs—over 120,000 pounds of explosives—which missed. Ten were shot down. "We had by this time undergone every kind of attack by shore-based planes—torpedo, level bombing, dive-bombing—but were still unscathed," Mitsuo Fuchida, watching from the *Akagi* deck while recovering from an appendectomy, remembered. "Frankly, it was my judgment that the enemy fliers were not displaying a very high level of ability. It was our general conclusion that we had little to fear from the enemy's offensive tactics."

Hornet's Torpedo Squadron Eight meanwhile followed John Waldron's hunch straight to the Japanese fleet. At 0918, they were spotted by cruiser *Chikuma*, who signaled her closest destroyer. The two opened fire and blew out smoke screens. One by one, Zero attackers appeared in the sky above the American fliers, quickly swooping down to maul the Devastators. Of the fifteen planes of Torpedo Squadron Eight, fourteen caught enemy fire, burst into flames, and fell into the sea. The sole survivor was Ensign George Gay. During the assault, the electric release for his torpedo jammed, so he had to do it manually. His target, carrier *Soryu*, saw his missile's wake, moved, and the American torpedo missed. Ensign Gay then tried strafing the carrier's deck with his guns, but they didn't work. Now, five Zeros were after him. They disintegrated his rudder. They killed his crewman. They shot off one of his wings. His plane crashed, but the ensign, though hit in the leg and seriously wounded, was still alive. George grabbed his seat cushion and rubber life raft out of the cockpit and hid under the floats from Japanese patrols.

At 0920, Wade McCluskey and his *Enterprise* SBD dive-bombers arrived at the last reported Japanese position before the withdrawal. At an altitude of twenty thousand feet, McCluskey could see for sixty miles or so, and no ships were to be found in any direction. His gas gauge gave him two choices. Everyone in his squadron could give up, salvo their ordnance into the water, and return to *Enterprise*, or they could immediately fly in exactly the right direction and just as immediately attack. Wade was a fighter pilot who'd never dropped a bomb before, and he began a box search starting in the most likely direction he thought Nagumo might have taken: the northeast. Finally McCluskey sighted a Japanese destroyer—the *Arashi*, which had unsuccessfully been chasing and rolling depth charges against American sub *Nautilus*—running north at flank speed, and decided it must be heading toward the Japanese fleet. *Enterprise* Bombing Six followed it.

At 1005, pilots in McCluskey's squadron reported seeing "curved white slashes on a blue carpet"—the wakes of more ships than any US naval airman had ever seen.

At 1020, all four Japanese carriers turned into the wind, to begin a devastating assault on the American fleet. Simultaneously, McCluskey's force of thirty-seven dive-bombers met up with *Yorktown's* remaining fighters and torpedo planes directly overhead. The Americans rose to position and began their assaults. "I saw this glint in the sun and it looked just like a beautiful silver waterfall; these dive-bombers coming down," remembered James E. Thach, leader of the *Yorktown* fighters. "I'd never seen such superb dive-bombing."

The first three bombs aimed at *Kaga* missed, but the fourth struck directly in the middle of her launch line. Two more missed, but the seventh and eighth struck forward, exploding on the hangar deck below. *Kaga* burst repeatedly into flames; even her paint caught fire. Three bombs then hit their mark on *Soryu*; its fire was so intense that the hangar doors warped. By 1915, both had sunk.

On *Akagi*, "the plump silhouettes of the American Dauntless dive-bombers quickly grew larger, and then a number of black objects suddenly floated eerily from their wings," Fuchida recalled. "Bombs! Down they came straight toward me! . . . The terrifying scream of the dive-bombers reached me first, followed by the crashing explosion of a direct hit. There was a blinding flash and then a second explosion, much louder than the first. . . . Looking about, I was horrified at the destruction that had been wrought in a matter of seconds. There was a huge hole in the flight deck just behind the midship elevator. The elevator itself, twisted like molten glass, was drooping into the hangar. Deck plates reeled upward in grotesque configurations. Planes stood tail up, belching livid flame and jet-black smoke. Reluctant tears streamed down my cheeks as I watched the fires spread."

A bomb from *Enterprise* Bombing Six's Lieutenant Richard Best, had struck the dead center of *Akagi*'s flight deck, crashed through to the hangar deck beneath, and exploded. Just as on *Arizona*, that single strike chain-reacted with the ship's own bombs and fuel, blowing crewmen overboard and destroying *Akagi*, the lead flattop of what was once the world's mightiest naval force, with a single blow. Jumping to the escape boats when the ship was abandoned, pilot Fuchida broke both of his legs.

At 1040, eighteen dive-bombers and six fighters launched from *Hiryu* immediately found *Yorktown*. She was hit on the flight deck, down the smokestack, and four decks below, with an armor-piercer, as well as with two Japanese torpedoes. Dead in the water, at 1458 she was abandoned.

Shortly after 1600, *Enterprise* and *Hornet* sent out the rest of their aircrews to mop up. At around 1700, twenty-four *Yorktown* Dauntlesses scored four hits on *Hiryu*, sinking her. Nagumo's airmen reported sinking three American carriers, and he ordered a pursuit, thinking he could incite a night battle, at which the Japanese now excelled. But as time went on and more reports came in, he realized that his pilots' first calls were exaggerated, and that he could be heading up against a surprisingly powerful American fleet. At 0815 on June 5, the order was given to withdraw. That night, George Gay, sole survivor of *Hornet*'s Torpedo Squadron Eight, was found by an American flying boat, rescued, and taken home.

The Americans knew they had repelled a great force, but it was a while before either side understood that this was a true Kantai Kessen, the decisive battle that was the turning point in World War II's Pacific theater. If the attack on Pearl Harbor had been wildly successful in so many ways, its effect on American morale was the exact opposite of what Yamamoto had predicted. The Americans might be mystified, grief stricken, humiliated, and in shock after December 7, but they were not ready to grant Tokyo any peace treaties; they were ready to wreak vengeance.

For Japanese leaders however, Operation Number One (which included Pearl Harbor) infected them with a fatal dose of victory disease. At Midway, "for reasons that will always defy rational analysis," military historian H. P. Willmott noted, "Yamamoto insisted upon a tactical deployment that incorporated every possible risk and weakness and left his forces inferior to the enemy at the point of contact, despite their having what should have been an irresistible numerical and qualitative superiority." As for the Imperial Japanese Army, he noted, "One cannot ignore the simple fact that not a single operation planned after the start of the war met with success."

Roosevelt had sent the Doolittle Raiders as vengeance for Pearl Harbor; Yamamoto responded by attacking Midway; and the American triumph in that battle, using the secrets of HYPO, would cost the Japanese four of the six carriers that had attacked Oahu a mere six months before, along with 322 planes and 700 pilots, crewmen, and schooled naval officers. Their feared navy would never forcefully strike again, and the Japanese would from then on be on the defensive from a greater US naval power.

The American vengeance had just begun. After the heroic work of salvage at the cofferdams and dry docks of Pearl Harbor, *Nevada* participated in Midway, the Aleutians, Normandy, Iwo Jima, Okinawa, and operations against the Japanese home islands. *California* was awarded seven battle stars for its numerous campaigns. *West Virginia* fought in Surigao Strait, Leyte, Luzon, Iwo Jima, and Okinawa; on September 2, 1945, she entered Tokyo Bay as witness to the formal Japanese surrender aboard the USS *Missouri*. Meanwhile, the thirty-one Japanese ships in the First Air Fleet that had attacked Hawaii were all hunted down by the US Navy and fully destroyed. The Midway victory sunk carriers *Soryu*, *Kaga*, *Akagi*, and *Hiryu*. *Shokaku* was destroyed on June 19, 1944, at the Battle of the Philippine Sea, after which, on July 6, Admiral Chuichi Nagumo shot himself in the head. *Zuikaku* was sunk off Cape Engano on October 25, 1944; and *Tone* was destroyed at her Inland Sea moorings on July 24, 1945. Eventually, Isoroku Yamamoto's captured flagship *Nagato* was towed to Bikini Atoll and used as a nuclear-test target.

CHAPTER TWELVE

TRIUMPH

On April 28, 1942, Prime Minister Hideki Tojo called a special conference to resolve the question of what Japan should do with its eight captured Doolittle Raiders. Tojo felt ambivalent; he believed the American bombing "contrary to international law. It was not against troops but against noncombatants, primary-school students. . . . it was homicide." But he also feared that other countries would judge POW executions as barbarous, and that such an act could endanger Japanese prisoners of war.

By June, the Kempeitai realized that they were making no progress in extracting the confessions they wanted from the Raiders. All eight captives from *Bat out of Hell* and *Green Hornet* were reunited and after being forced to sign "confessions," were sent to Shanghai's Bridge House, one of World War II's most notorious prisons. "At night we would hear this beautiful, beautiful American music with all of the popular tunes that we had heard in the States," Bob Hite said. "That was hard to understand. . . . One of the tunes they played when I think we all kind of wanted to cry a little bit was 'Smoke Gets in Your Eyes.' It was hard to take and think that here we were, we could hear music like that, and then to realize where we were, and what had happened to us."

The miracle of muscle and engineering that restored the American fleet at Pearl Harbor would continue on a grand scale in the United States, where a secret group of heroes now began turning the tide of war. The most brilliant of generals, the most inspiring of admirals, and the greatest of battlefield troops would pale in significance to the thousands of American Rosie and Ronnie the Riveters who outproduced both the

Axis and the other Allied powers combined, contributing nearly three hundred thousand planes, 2 million trucks, eighty-seven thousand warships, and one hundred thousand tanks to Roosevelt's arsenal of democracy in 1943. Like all wars, the winners of World War II were the guys with the most ships, guns, and planes; in 1944, Joseph Stalin even proposed a toast to the productivity of the American assembly line.

Over the last two years of war, Japanese shipyards issued six new fleet carriers, while the United States produced seventeen fleet, ten medium, and eighty-six escort carriers. *Wasp*, *Hornet*, *Yorktown*, and *Lexington* were all reincarnated, joining *Enterprise*, *Essex*, *Intrepid*, and *Bunker Hill* in the Pacific, each bristling with five-inch, 40 mm, and 20 mm guns while carrying almost a hundred planes, most crucially a new fighter specifically engineered to beat Zeros: the F6F Hellcat. The Department of Ordnance was finally manufacturing torpedoes that could hit something, and these new eels allowed American subs to launch obliterating assaults on the Japanese merchant marine. Just as Nazi U-boats had crippled Atlantic shipping at the start of the war, now Chester Nimitz's 150 Pacific wolves destroyed the economy of an island nation by making it incapable of importing or exporting anything at all.

In response to the attack on Pearl Harbor, the USA would build the mightiest navy in the history of the world—including forty aircraft carriers, twenty-four battleships, and twenty-four thousand planes—powered by 3.3 million sailors and 480,000 marines, while from September 1939 to December 1941, she increased her army troops by 435 percent and then, from 1941 to 1945, another 492 percent, totaling 8,291,336 men in eighty-nine divisions. By July 1944, the Army Air Forces included 2,403,056 men and women at 1,479 airfields in sixteen air forces, eight air divisions, and ninety-one wings . . . and besides "Praise the Lord and Pass the Ammunition," these millions of men and women sang, "Let's remember Pearl Harbor as we go to meet the foe. Let's remember Pearl Harbor as we did the Alamo."

In the first week of October, Prime Minister Tojo and Army Chief of General Staff Sugiyama met at the Imperial Palace with Lord Privy Seal Kido. Sugiyama wanted all of the Raiders shot immediately, while Tojo urged leniency, believing that only those guilty of slaughtering innocent civilians should be executed, such guilt to be determined by their "confessions." Questioned on this point after the war by the

International Military Tribunal, Tojo explained, "Since I had known of the humane nature of the Emperor, it would be to his wish that the death penalty be applied to the smallest possible number of prisoners. For this reason, only the three who had killed a schoolchild were to receive the death sentence. I consulted the Emperor regarding this matter, for he was the only authority who could issue the reduction of the sentence. . . . He was very generous."

On October 14, twenty-eight-year-old Lieutenant Dean Hallmark of Robert Lee, Texas, twenty-three-year-old Lieutenant William Farrow of Darlington, South Carolina, and twenty-one-year-old Sergeant Harold Spatz of Lebo, Kansas, were informed that they had been found guilty of war crimes and sentenced to execution. That night, Japanese carpenters nailed together three wooden crosses and three boxes. The crosses had been sunk into the turf of a newly mown field, and each condemned man was ordered to kneel. Twenty feet away, a six-man firing squad was waiting in front of a Shinto altar of burning incense. Warden Tatsuta announced, "Your lives were very short, but your names will remain everlastingly. . . . When you die on the cross, you will be honored as gods."

The prisoners' wrists were tied behind them to the crosses. White cloths were draped over their faces, and then black marks were etched onto them, at the center of each man's forehead. The first line of Japanese riflemen were ordered to fire. Each shot was accurate. The second line of riflemen was not required to assist. Blood soaked into the newly mown grass.

The remaining POWs were still held in solitary and for some time had no idea Dean Hallmark, Bill Farrow, and Harold Spatz had been killed. Eventually they were marched into a courtroom, where the judge announced, "The tribunal, acting under the law . . . hereby sentences the defendants to death. . . . but, through the graciousness of His Majesty the Emperor, your sentences are hereby commuted to life imprisonment . . . with special treatment." When prison trusty Caesar brought the Americans their rations, he sometimes tried to help by hiding notes inside. Later that week, he explained their verdict's "special treatment": "If the Americans win the war, you are to be shot, and if the Japanese win the war, you are to be kept as slave labor."

After Midway, a host of Japan's naval officers offered to commit suicide. Yamamoto refused, saying, "I take full responsibility. If anyone is to commit hara-kiri because of Midway, it is I." By now, his navy had lost almost every ace pilot, and his new aircrews were novices, so their strikes accomplished little. In their zeal, they would report one great victory after the next back to Tokyo, which only spurred on the country's drunken war fever. When Hirohito was told on September 21, 1943, that the Allies were invading New Guinea and that Japanese defenses were ready, he exclaimed, "Being ready to defend isn't enough. We have to do the attacking!" When told that Saipan would fall, giving the United States a base close enough to bomb Tokyo, Hirohito ordered, "Rise to the challenge; make a tremendous effort; achieve a splendid victory like at the time of the Japan Sea battle [Tsushima]." When Japan, after suffering defeat after defeat, clearly had no hope of victory, Hirohito told his senior statesmen on February 14, 1945, "If we hold out long enough in this war, we may be able to win, but what worries me is whether the nation will be able to endure it until then."

In April 1943, Admiral Yamamoto flew to Bougainville (a Solomon island in the north fork of what is now Papua New Guinea) to give an inspirational speech to his men. Radio messages from nearby Japanese bases carried details of his travel plans, which were intercepted by the basement team of HYPO, and Roosevelt ordered, "Get Yamamoto." After talks with Nimitz and Halsey, it became clear that navy fighters didn't have the range for the mission. It would have to be done by Hap Arnold's Army Air Forces.

On the morning of April 18, 1943, the one-year anniversary of the Doolittle Raid, Isoroku Yamamoto's plane approached southern Bougainville, escorted by nine Zeros. Eighteen P-38 Lightnings swooped in; fourteen took on the Zeros; the other four attacked the Mitsubishi G4M transport bomber ferrying the admiral. Captain Thomas Lanphier Jr. and his wingman, Rex T. Barber, both strafed the craft with 20 mm cannon and machine guns. The plane exploded in flames and crashed into the jungle.

Yamamoto's death shook every member of the Combined Fleet, many of whom saw this as an omen, even the always-optimistic Mitsuo Fuchida, who "believed now that the war was entirely lost." Two months later, General Sugiyama had to tell his emperor that those same positions in the Solomons were now imperiled. Hirohito replied, "Isn't there some place where we can strike the United States? . . . When and where on earth are you ever going to put up a good fight? And when are you ever going to fight a decisive battle? . . . After suffering all these defeats, why don't you study how not to let the Americans keep saying, 'We won! We won!'" Lanphier and Barber, meanwhile, spent the rest of their lives confronting each other in federal court over who deserved credit for the kill.

Journalist Masuo Kato: "For many years the Japanese people had been taught to believe that their national misfortunes were due to lack of access to raw materials and restrictions on free immigration, which might have relieved the congestion in one of the most congested spots on the face of the earth. The solution, they had been told, was to drive out Western imperialism, to become the savior of the oppressed peoples to the south, to establish Asia for the Asiatics, and then reap the just reward of such a policy. The poorest Japanese believed that it was only a matter of time until the advance to the south would result in great wealth to the Japanese nation as a whole and concrete benefits to himself. A number of private companies were created with the purpose of profiting from the South Seas trade, but none of these companies was able to convert its prospects into profits because the area failed to be stabilized as promised. The Co-Prosperity Sphere [would soon be dubbed] in Japan, the Co-Poverty Sphere."

Three days after Yamamoto's assassination, President Roosevelt announced in a radio broadcast, that the Japanese had executed some of their captured Doolittle Raiders. The American public's reaction was overwhelming. On the day following the news, they bought more war bonds than on any other day of World War II.

By the fall of 1943, Meder's constant dysentery, which had left him weak and thin for months, took a severe turn for the worse. On December 1, Lieutenant Robert J. Meder of Cleveland, Ohio, died at the age of twenty-six. The one crewman who always had hope in his heart, who was always so confident they would get out of this all right in the end, had been starved to death.

"We thought, 'Well, any of us can die at any time,'" Bob Hite said. "'We could all die, and they could do away with us, and nobody would ever know the difference.' No one knew we were there. It was sort of an eerie feeling." Hite asked the prison authorities to be given a Bible, and they agreed. The Americans shared it; when Jake DeShazer had his turn, the words came to life, as though they were written just for him. On June 8, 1944, Jake started praying: "Lord, though I am far from home and though I am in prison, I must have forgiveness." As he thought deeply about the message of the Christ, he was overcome with a tremendous sensation: "My heart was filled with joy. I wouldn't have traded places with anyone at that time."

Jake realized that his sins had been forgiven and that, as a Christian, he, too, would have to forgive. He started treating the sadistic man who guarded him politely, until finally the guard came over and spoke with him through the door. DeShazer asked about his family, and the Japanese man smiled.

A few mornings later, he saw the guard pacing, his hands folded in prayer. The man later said that he was talking to his mother, who had died when he was a boy. From that moment on, he treated Jake well, never shouting, kicking, or beating him. In fact, "one morning he opened the slot and handed in a boiled sweet potato. I was surprised and thanked him profusely. Later he gave me some batter-fried fish and candy. . . . How easy it was to make a friend out of an enemy because I had just tried."

In the first four months of the appalling six that it took to win Guadalcanal, the men of the First Marine Division became heroic legends equal to the Spartans at Thermopylae, living on weeds and roots and suffering malarial fevers while killing over twenty thousand Japanese soldiers and holding their territory until victory. Churchill was inspired to say, "Long may the tale be told in the great Republic." Guadalcanal would also be remembered as the front line where one leatherneck yelled to the other side, "Hirohito eats shit!" and soon came the reply, "Eleanor eats shit!"

"There was nothing macho about the war at all," said one marine, E. B. "Sledgehammer" Sledge. "We were a bunch of scared kids who had to do a job. The Japanese fought by a code they thought was right: Bushido. The code of the warrior: no surrender. You don't really comprehend it until you get out there and fight people who are faced with an absolutely hopeless situation and will not give up. I was afraid so much, day after day, that I got tired of being scared."

On the front lines at Peleliu and Okinawa, Sledge watched American soldiers collect souvenirs: hands, ears, and gold teeth from Japanese corpses. "The fierce struggle for survival . . . eroded the veneer of civilization and made savages of us all," he thought. When Charles Lindbergh came back from New Guinea, one of the questions asked by US customs was "Do you have any bones in your luggage?" Follow-

ers of Shinto, believing ancestral remains are sacred, were disgusted to
see *Life* magazine's story of a thrilled American girl posing with what
her boyfriend had brought back home from his tour of duty—a Japanese skull. The followers must have forgotten when Japanese troops
invaded Korea and brought back one hundred thousand Korean noses
and ears, today buried outside Kyoto in what is known as the Ear
Mound.

This brutality would last for the whole of the war. While the Japanese created a national pun for American—*Mei-ri-ken*, "misguided
dog"—American soldiers in the Pacific invented a new term for when
men lost their minds: *going Asiatic*. Samuel Eliot Morison said the
Pacific theater echoed "the primitive days of fighting Indians," while
Harry Truman said it was okay to use nuclear weapons against the Japanese since "when you have to deal with a beast, you have to treat him
as a beast," while author William Manchester concluded, "War is literally unreasonable. Today's youth cannot understand it; mine, I suppose, was the last generation to believe audacity in combat is a virtue.
And I don't know why we believed it."

Winning Guadalcanal meant a cost of 4,123 American lives, but
when the Pacific war's tide turned, it was nothing less than a tsunami.
In November 1943 on Betio in the Tarawa chain, 1,026 marines died
fighting over five thousand Japanese for an atoll half the size of New
York's Central Park. In taking the island of Truk on February 16, 1944,
Vice Admiral Marc Mitscher lost about thirty planes and had a carrier
damaged, while the Japanese lost two light cruisers, four destroyers,
two submarines, five auxiliaries, and twenty-four merchant ships.

After a year of waiting for his legs to heal from jumping into the
lifeboat at Midway, Mitsuo Fuchida was appointed air operations
officer of the Combined Fleet on April 20, 1944, just in time for the
devastating losses at the Battle of the Philippine Sea. In what American forces called "the Marianas Turkey Shoot," 395 of the Combined
Fleet's 430 planes were taken down, along with carriers *Taiho, Soikaku*,
and *Hiyo*. Many of Fuchida's friends from his Imperial Naval Academy
days, from Operation Z and from Midway, were killed that month,
along with every member of the First Air Fleet, either by enemy fire
or suicide. As 1944 drew to its close, Fuchida would become one of the
few surviving Japanese airmen from the attack on Pearl Harbor.

On October 20, 1944, the general who was perhaps the most complicated man in American army history, Douglas MacArthur, rode

aboard cruiser *Nashville* as the first of his two hundred thousand soldiers landed on the east coast of Leyte. In a drenching rain, he came
ashore to announce, "People of the Philippines, I have returned. . . .
Rally to me. . . . As the lines of battle roll forward to bring you within
the zone of operations, rise and strike. Strike at every favorable opportunity. For your homes and hearths, strike! For future generations
of your sons and daughters, strike! In the name of your sacred dead,
strike!"

For the next three days, two hundred thousand sailors and pilots
from 282 ships fought over one hundred thousand square miles of
ocean in history's biggest naval battle. On October 25, Admiral Thomas
Kinkaid used the same tactical maneuver that Admiral Togo employed
in his historic win at Tsushima, positioning his fleet at the neck of
Surigao Strait to cross Japan's *T*. If that weren't sweet enough revenge
for the Americans, of the six dreadnoughts sinking the Japanese navy,
five—*West Virginia, Tennessee, Maryland, California*, and *Pennsylvania*—
had been "destroyed" by Genda's airmen at Pearl Harbor. At Surigao
the Imperial Japanese Navy lost two battleships, three cruisers, and
four destroyers, while American losses were one PT boat. For the Battle of Leyte Gulf as a whole, American losses were a light carrier, two
escort carriers, and three destroyers. Japan lost four carriers, three battleships, six heavy cruisers, three light cruisers, eight destroyers, and
sixty-five thousand men, meaning that the Imperial Japanese Navy had
lost its war.

The closer American forces got to the Japanese home islands, the
more appalling was the carnage. At Iwo Jima, the entire Japanese
force of nearly twenty thousand men fought to their deaths, while
about seven thousand Americans were killed and nineteen thousand
wounded. Of this battle, Navy Secretary James Forrestal said, "I can
never again see a United States marine without feeling a reverence."

After the loss of Saipan, a Japanese territory since 1919, Hirohito
said, "Hell is on us." Even so, the Japanese armed forces continued
to operate with such contempt for the nation's civilian leaders that
Prime Minister Hideki Tojo—simultaneously a general on active
duty—wasn't told about the catastrophic losses at Midway for over a
month. Tojo, in the wake of "an unprecedentedly great national crisis,"
resigned, and the Imperial Japanese Navy did not tell the new prime
minister that the Combined Fleet had been destroyed at Leyte Gulf
until after the nation had surrendered.

It would take five months to win Okinawa, a battle marked by a new tactic: suicide attacks. Fighter pilot Captain Motoharu Okamura is credited with what he called the Hornet Corps—meaning when a hornet stings, he dies, but so does his victim. Much like the midget submarines that had taken part against Pearl Harbor, the MXY7 Ohka ("cherry blossom," symbol of the young warrior who gives his life for his country) was a small glider with a twenty-six-hundred-pound bomb in the nose and a missile in its tail that was ferried to its target by a mother plane. Ohka crews, known as the Divine Thunderbolt Corps (Jinrai Butai), flew in the ferrying bomber until it was their time, then climbed out of a belly hatch and into their bomb. Simultaneously in the Philippines, navy Zero crews began to use suicide-diving of their own planes into the enemy, calling themselves the Shinpu Tokubetsu Kogekitai (Divine Wind Special Attack Squad). Imperial Japanese Navy airmen now signed a contract saying they were willing volunteers in the Special Attack Corps. About one in thirty-three suicide bombers successfully sank their targets, and it's believed that their use extended the war into 1945.

Okinawa meant 82,000 Allied casualties, with over 14,000 dead, while Japan lost over 77,000 servicemen. The civilians on Okinawa had been told that American GIs routinely raped and murdered Asian women, and that if any American wanted to become a marine, he had to first murder his parents. A high percentage of the estimated 42,000 to 150,000 of the island's residents who perished committed suicide.

It had taken almost three years since Pearl Harbor for Nimitz and MacArthur to fight their way close enough to directly bomb the enemy's home islands. The task would be assigned to B-29s based in the Marianas under Curtis LeMay. For these crews, a round-trip to Tokyo ran three thousand miles, meaning fuel could run out on the way home, forcing a ditch into the ocean. If LeMay failed, however, and Japan had to be invaded by land forces, military intelligence estimated that half a million Americans would die.

Over Nazi Germany, the air forces had learned to come in at extremely high altitude, in formation, with guns and fighters blazing, to precisely bomb specific targets in daylight. This technique hadn't worked at all in the Pacific war, and LeMay was ordered to craft a solution. Tokyo now had few fighters trained in nighttime operations, no more barrage balloons, and few antiaircraft guns aimed at low-altitude targets. So "Iron Ass" LeMay (a name inspired both by the Bell's palsy that kept him from being physically able to smile and by his bellicose demeanor) went with the opposite of everything that had been tried and refined so far. His B-29s sortied at night, at a mere five thousand feet, one at a time. Instead of explosive ordnance, their bays were filled with napalm and phosphorous.

On the nights of March 9–10, 1945, 334 B-29s fire-bombed the capital of Japan with two thousand tons of incendiaries. Fourteen of those planes were lost at sea; five of the fourteen were rescued by the navy. At midnight on the eleventh, reconnaissance photographs were finally printed, and what they revealed stunned the American air force chiefs. Over sixteen square miles of Tokyo had been destroyed, a greater area of damage than what nuclear weapons would inflict on Hiroshima and Nagasaki combined. The fires produced with this early form of napalm were so hot that window glass melted, and victims trying to escape the conflagration by jumping into canals, sewers, and streams were boiled alive. One-quarter of the capital was gone, with 267,171 buildings demolished and over a million left homeless. It would take almost a month to excavate the dead—almost eight-four thousand men, women, and children.

"I heard the huzzle-huzzle of something falling, and I ducked and crouched in a corner," Gustav Bitter, a priest living in Tokyo, remembered. "It struck beside me, with a noise like a house falling, and I leaped a fine leap into the air. I must have shut my eyes, for when I opened them again, I was in a world of fairyland. On every tree in the garden below, and on every tree so far as the eyes could see, some sort of blazing oil had fallen, and it was dancing on the twigs and branches with a million little red and yellow candle-flames. On the ground in between the trees and in all the open spaces, white balls of fire had fallen, and these were bouncing like tennis balls. . . . [Watching the firebombs from a distance] was like a silver curtain falling, like . . . the silver tinsel we hung from Christmas trees in Germany long ago. And where these silver streamers would touch the earth, red fires would spring up . . . and the big fire in the center sent up a rising column of air which drew in toward the center the outer circle of flame, and a hot, swift wind began to blow from the rim toward the center, a twisting wind which spread the flames between all the ribs of the fan, very quickly. Thus, everywhere the people ran there was fire, in front of them and in back of them, and closing in on them from the sides. So that there were only a very few who escaped."

The Japanese would call these days the Raid of the Fire Wind and the Raid of the Dancing Flames. Eight-year-old Japanese survivor Haruyo Nihei: "The bombs were falling like rain. The wind was very strong, like a typhoon, and the fire was like a tornado crawling around the ground. My father, my mother, my sister, and I held hands and ran away through the fire. Then a gust of wind blew me away and I was on my own in a sea of fire." She fell in a crowd of people and passed out. "I heard a voice: 'Japanese don't die like this. Japanese must survive. You must not sleep.' I was pulled out of the bottom of a pile of people, and I discovered that the person talking to me was my father. Then I looked at where I had been. There was a mountain of black, dead bodies. I was the only survivor under all those dead people." On the twelfth, LeMay used the same weapons on Nagoya; on the thirteenth on Osaka; on the sixteenth, on Kobe; on the nineteenth, again on Nagoya. By mid-June, urban Japan had been completely annihilated.

One of those involved in incendiary planning, Robert McNamara—who would become secretary of defense for both the Kennedy and Johnson administrations—remembered, "LeMay said if we'd lost the war, we'd all have been prosecuted as war criminals. And I think he's right. He, and I'd say I, were behaving as war criminals. LeMay recognized that what he was doing would be thought immoral if his side had lost. But what makes it immoral if you lose and not if you win?"

The summer would bring mop-up operations, with certain key targets precision-bombed beyond recognition, sixty smaller cities firebombed into oblivion, and the Japanese coastal waters so extensively filled with mines dropped by LeMay's B-29s that her naval traffic was entirely halted. One ship that took its place at the forefront of this assault was the new USS *Hornet*, which served in the forward combat zone, often a mere forty miles from Japan, for fifteen continuous months. Her new flyboys knocked out 1,410 Japanese planes, a World War II record, with 72 destroyed in one day, a US Navy record. On June 18, President Harry Truman approved Operation Downfall, an invasion of the Japanese home islands. He asked about projected casualty figures and was not given a meaningful answer.

After their cities were destroyed and their sea-lanes shut down, military leaders in Tokyo met to discuss their next course of action. None of them could even consider the possibility of surrender. In the Pacific war, not one Japanese unit had surrendered, ever; the most popular slogan in the Imperial Japanese Army canon was "Duty is a heavy burden, but death is light as a feather." The Japanese government instead decided to inspire every man, woman, and child in Japan to resist to the very end, to fight to the last survivor of Yamato blood. Newspapers and radio stations announced this new policy; planes dropped leaflets over rural areas promoting it. The horrors of an American invasion were described in lurid detail, and the leaders of what was left of Dai Nippon Teikoku created a new slogan: *Ichioku gyokusai!*—"One hundred million die for the country!"—telling every Japanese man, woman, and child to give their lives for the nation and perish "like shattered jewels."

The Japanese military still believed that they could negotiate with the Americans for better terms than unconditional surrender, with the nation's military leaders remaining in power. Major General Masakazu Amano said, "The geographical advantages of the homeland were to be utilized to the highest degree, the enemy was to be crushed, and we were confident that the battle would prove to be the turning point in political maneuvering."

Operation Downfall meant the Allies would have to subdue 4–5 million Japanese soldiers and 27 million civilians. The campaign would start with poison gas dropped on twenty-five cities, producing 7–8 million deaths, and causing mass panic. Operation Olympic then invaded the southern island of Kyushu on November 1, her beaches getting code names from the Pentagon as a tribute to the American automobile industry: Buick, Chrysler, Chevrolet, Pontiac, and Cadillac. Operation Coronet, the invasion of Tokyo, was planned for March 1, 1946. General MacArthur estimated he would need seven hundred thousand men for all of Downfall, a number that seemed wildly optimistic when Japan sent six hundred thousand men to defend Kyushu—nearly as many as the Allies were planning on using for the whole country.

Would an invasion at a tremendous cost of Allied lives mean victory in any real sense? After the horror of Okinawa, Nimitz told King that he did not support Olympic, and King in turn told Marshall and Stimson that planning could proceed, but the US Navy could not agree to these operations.

In June 1945, the captured Raiders were moved to Peiping. DeShazer's health had by now so rapidly deteriorated that he came to believe he, too, would die at any moment: "I got out of bed and sat on the little bench one morning after I had prayed it all out with God. I was so weak that my heart could have stopped very easily. . . . I didn't know what to expect. I just prayed that God would make me better. I made up my mind to sit there until I either passed out or God healed me. It was not long before the voice of God broke into my thoughts. This was different from anything I had experienced before. . . .

" 'It is the Holy Spirit who is speaking to you,' the mysterious voice said. 'The Holy Spirit has made you free!' I immediately began to wonder if I was going to get out of prison. The voice said, 'You are free to do as you please. You can go through the wall or jump over the wall. You are free.' I couldn't figure that out."

On August 10, DeShazer was told by the mysterious voice to "start praying. . . . I asked, 'What shall I pray about?' 'Pray for peace, and pray without ceasing,' I was told. I had prayed for peace but very little, if at all, before that time, as it seemed useless. At two o'clock in the afternoon, the Holy Spirit told me, 'You don't need to pray anymore. The victory is won.' I was amazed. I thought this was quicker and better than the regular method of receiving world news. . . . At this time the voice of the Holy Spirit spoke to me clearly: 'You are called to go and teach the Japanese people and to go wherever I send you.' "

Jake was frightened by this idea. He had no talent or skills as a public speaker; he couldn't even tell a joke that well. He was short and lacked a commanding, inspiring presence and had no training as a theologian, or education as a preacher.

The day before Jacob DeShazer was told that the war was over, *New York Times* journalist Bill Laurence was part of a crew flying over one of the few Japanese cities that had spared LeMay's firebombing campaigns—Nagasaki:

> Despite the fact that it was broad daylight in our cabin, all of us became aware of a giant flash that broke through the dark barrier of our arc-welder's lenses and flooded our cabin with intense light.
>
> Observers in the tail of our ship saw a giant ball of fire rise as though from the bowels of the earth, belching forth enormous, white smoke rings. Next they saw a giant pillar of purple fire, ten thousand feet high, shooting skyward with enormous speed.
>
> Awestruck, we watched it shoot upward like a meteor coming from the earth instead of from outer space, becoming ever more alive as it

climbed skyward through the white clouds. It was no longer smoke, or dust, or even a cloud of fire. It was a living thing, a new species of being, born right before our incredulous eyes.

At one stage of its evolution, the entity assumed the form of a giant square totem pole, with its base about three miles long, tapering off to about a mile at the top. Its bottom was brown, its center was amber, its top white. Then, just when it appeared as though the thing has settled down into a state of permanence, there came shooting out of the top a giant mushroom that increased the height of the pillar to a total of forty-five thousand feet. The mushroom top was even more alive than the pillar, seething and boiling in a white fury of creamy foam, sizzling upward and then descending earthward, a thousand Old Faithful geysers rolled into one.

It kept struggling in an elemental fury, like a creature in the act of breaking the bonds that held it down. In a few seconds it had freed itself from its gigantic stem and floated upward with tremendous speed. But no sooner did this happen when another mushroom, smaller in size than the first one, began emerging out of the pillar. It was as though the decapitated monster was growing a new head.

As the first mushroom floated off into the blue, it changed its shape into a flowerlike form, its giant petal curving downward, white outside, rose-colored inside. It still retained that shape when we last gazed at it from a distance of about two hundred miles.

On June 22, Hirohito had announced to the Supreme War Leadership Council that it was time to end the war, but it took the dream to end all dreams—the atomic bombings of Hiroshima on August 6 and of Nagasaki on August 9, as well as the collapse of talks with the Soviet Union and that nation's declaring war against Japan—before Japanese leaders could stop thinking they should fight to the end, and start thinking that this was the end. Later the emperor explained, "I was told that even Tokyo cannot be defended. I thought that the Japanese race will be destroyed if the war continued," and of the warmongering fascists who claimed he was a god, "I told them I am not a god, for the structure of my body is no different than that of a normal human being. I continued to tell them that it is a nuisance to be called such." Hirohito had one condition for the surrender—that he remain in power—and he did. The nation's grossly ineffectual leader in the rush to war could, it turned out, be effective after all.

On the morning of August 15, 1945, the entire population of Japan, including the farmers laboring in distant fields and citizens living overseas, were told that, at noon, they must stop whatever they were doing and listen to the radio. Though everyone hurried to make ready for this once-in-a-lifetime event, most already knew what the announcement would be. The great empire that Dai Nippon Teikoku had won for itself in the first half of the twentieth century was now entirely gone, and the foreign barbarian hordes would be invading their homeland at any minute. The broadcast would give instructions and inspiration so that all those of Yamato blood could sacrifice their lives fighting against the incoming Anglo-Saxon wave.

What the people of Japan heard that day at noon was not just unexpected, it was unimaginable. First, the national anthem played. Then a voice spoke, a voice they'd never heard before. The voice was strange, high-pitched, thin and nasal, and it spoke an odd form of Japanese, a dialect hundreds of years old that few could understand clearly. For the first time in the history of the Chrysanthemum Throne, the emperor was speaking directly to his mortal people.

The voice told them *senso owari*, "the war is over." It said that the emperor was no longer the Son of Heaven, but an ordinary man. It said that events "did not turn in Japan's favor, and trends of the world were not advantageous to us. . . . The enemy has for the first time used cruel bombs to kill and maim extremely large numbers of the innocent, and the heavy casualties are beyond measure. To continue the war further could lead in the end not only to the extermination of our race but also to the destruction of all human civilization. . . . My vital organs are torn asunder." The voice said it was time for the Yamato race to "endure the unendurable, and bear the unbearable."

Just before the announcement, an urgent Japanese army telegram had been sent to all camps and bases, recommending that anyone who had mistreated prisoners or local populations immediately vanish into anonymity. Over the next four weeks 1,066 Allied planes would fly over nine hundred sorties, dropping forty-five hundred tons of supplies over 150 POW camps across Japan and East Asia. Along with medicine, food, cigarettes, magazines, chocolate, and chewing gum, the bursting canisters included leaflets that implored, "Do not overeat."

After arriving in Japan aboard a C-54 Skymaster named *Bataan* on August 30 the sixty-five-year-old General Douglas MacArthur and his

American contingent were indignant to see, on every street corner, Japanese sentries with their backs turned to the Allied convoys. What Americans thought of as an insult, however, the Japanese considered a sign of honor. Shamed by defeat, the soldiers of Dai Nippon Teikoku were not worthy enough to look directly into the face of the American victors.

On September 2, accompanied by 260 Allied warships, MacArthur appeared on the last of the great American dreadnoughts, the USS *Missouri*—Admiral Halsey's flagship—to accept the Japanese Empire's surrender in Tokyo Bay. The general had postponed the ceremony so that officials from China, Russia, England, the Philippines, and other countries involved in the Pacific theater could attend. The flag raised at morning colors was the same Stars and Stripes that had flown over the Capitol in Washington on December 7, 1941, while the bulkhead overlooking the ceremony displayed the thirty-one-star banner Commodore Matthew Perry had flown on his *Powhatan* in 1853, when he initiated the gunboat diplomacy that forced Japan into America's embrace. Narrow enough to fit through the 110-foot-wide Panama Canal and twenty-two stories in height, the USS *Missouri* was sent to Tokyo Bay since the president was from that state, and his daughter, Margaret, had christened the battleship on January 29, 1944, in Brooklyn (*Missouri* now sits at anchor in Pearl Harbor at Ford Island; Perry's flag is still there, under glass). Since the onetime greatest naval power in all the world no longer had a single seaworthy vessel, destroyer *Landsdowne* had to ferry the Tokyo delegation to the signing.

Attending the ceremony were Mitsuo Fuchida, Joseph Stilwell, James Doolittle, and Japanese Foreign Office secretary Toshikazu Kase, who had been assigned to prepare a report on the surrender for his emperor. *What would the Americans do now?* everyone in Japan wondered. Of the 7 million Tokyo residents who'd survived the Raid of the Dancing Flames, 5 million were so overcome by fears of Allied vengeance that they'd fled to the country to hide.

MacArthur instead announced, "It is my earnest hope and indeed the hope of all mankind that from this solemn occasion a better world shall emerge out of the blood and carnage of the past—a world founded upon faith and understanding—a world dedicated to the dignity of man and the fulfillment of his most cherished wish—for freedom, tolerance, and justice."

About this speech, Kase wrote Hirohito, "Here is the victor

announcing the verdict to the prostrate enemy. He can exact his pound of flesh if he so chooses. He can impose a humiliating penalty if he so desires. And yet he pleads for freedom, tolerance, and justice. For me, who expected the worst humiliation, this was a complete surprise. I was thrilled beyond words, spellbound, thunderstruck. For the living heroes and dead martyrs of the war this speech was a wreath of undying flowers. . . . [Would it] have been possible for us, had we been victorious, to embrace the vanquished with a similar magnanimity? . . . [W]e were not beaten on the battlefields by dint of superior arms. We were defeated by a nobler ideal. The real issue was moral beyond all the powers of algebra to compute." That same week, Hirohito would explain to his son, Crown Prince Akihito, that Japan had lost because "our people . . . knew how to advance, but they didn't know how to retreat." As the signatures dried across the official documents, four hundred B-29 bombers and fifteen hundred Navy fighters drew a curtain across the sky. The Pacific war had endured just under four years; the American occupation of Japan would last almost seven.

The night before he could be taken into custody by US forces, Prince Fumimaro Konoye committed suicide with poison. Next to his body lay Oscar Wilde's *De Profundis*, marked in red pencil: "I must say to myself that I ruined myself, and that nobody great or small can be ruined except by his own hand. . . . Terrible as was what the world did to me, what I did to myself was far more terrible still. . . . People used to say of me that I was too individualistic. . . . My ruin came not from too great individualism of life, but from too little."

The Japanese had regularly and publicly announced that, if they lost the war, they would kill every POW under their control. Two days before American troops landed on Luzon with Douglas MacArthur in the campaign to retake the Philippines, Allied intelligence had uncovered information that the Japanese had massacred every captive on Palawan Island. Consequently, the OSS's Special Ops forces hurried behind enemy lines before the announced surrender to ensure that no more POWs would be summarily executed.

Parachuting into Peiping on August 17, 1945, from a B-24 bomber, the seven members of MAGPIE touched down in the middle of what was, a few days' past, the heart of enemy territory. Special Ops agent Dick Hamada: "A flatbed truck with six Japanese soldiers, armed with bayonets and guns and led by an officer, approached us. The soldiers dismounted and surrounded our team. Major [Ray] Nichols told the lieutenant, 'The war is over and we are here to get the prisoners.' The lieutenant stated emphatically, 'The war is not over yet.' " After another day of negotiations, Nichols announced the Americans would go to the POW camps with or without Japanese consent. The Japanese capitulated. Hundreds of prisoners were released, but Major Nichols learned that some Americans, convicted of war crimes, were still being held at Fengtai. The major insisted that the Japanese confess to their own crimes, and release these prisoners immediately.

On the evening of August 20, 1945, guards opened the cells of Jacob DeShazer, Chase Nielsen, George Barr, and Robert Hite, and took them to shave and shower—the first hot water they'd had in three years and four months. A prison official said, "The war is over. You can go home now."

Home. One airman's wife remarked, "After the war ended, these men had time to think. The fact that they killed other human beings started to prey on their minds. My husband said again and again, 'I pushed that lever. What if the bomb killed some kids? They had nothing to do with the war. I can't stop thinking about it. I couldn't forgive myself if it were true.' " An army psychiatrist who spent his entire professional life studying the effects of combat said, "One thing I've noticed in the interviews I've done is that these men cut off their feelings, and they almost were aware of it. They couldn't feel anything after a certain point. And yet they did have feelings. If a friend was killed, they would still be overwhelmed, but in order to go on, they would see things, and it would almost be like looking at a photograph. It's called emotional numbing. . . . Often the only feelings they can feel are more intense feelings of rage, and when they're very stimulated, like a lot of vets who are numb are drawn to more daredevil activities as a way of feeling something. . . . We don't know whether that numbing is due to a natural occurring opiate which is released in the body . . . but the fact is that this is a very common complaint, and it's a common complaint of the families, that these men are cut off from their feelings. They say that they just can't feel closeness for anyone, they can't really be touched, although when they talk about World War II vets and losses there, they get very flooded emotionally. Somehow that overwhelms them.

"War is one of those experiences that most people, unless you've been in war, you don't have a parallel experience to relate to, and a lot of combat vets, whether it's World War II or Korea or Vietnam, they feel that either there's not going to be an interest in what they have to say, or they'll be judged by their activities, or they're just simply not going to be understood, so there is a lot of withholding. I think as the World War II vets are aging and they're becoming more aware of their mortality as they see their numbers decrease, I see them reaching out more and feeling a need to talk more about their experiences with their families."

Six days after Japan's surrender, Supreme Commander Allied Powers (SCAP) Douglas MacArthur, a descendant of Matthew Perry, began to transform a destroyed state of 70 million into a modern democratic nation. Daily outside the American embassy, forty to fifty people went through the garbage, scavenging for food. When the US Congress was chary about giving foreign aid to the starving Japanese, MacArthur, worried about civil order and rioting, said, "Give me bread or give me bullets."

Soon after assuming command, the general was photographed with the emperor at the imperial palace; MacArthur, dressed informally, towered over Hirohito. The picture had two messages: the war is over and Japan lost; but the Americans in charge are standing by the emperor. Hirohito's desire to remain on the throne aligned with military theory of what should now be done. Army Chief of Staff Eisenhower was informed that "as complete a research as was possible" looked for evidence linking Hirohito to war crimes, but nothing was found, and that if the United States indicted him, the country would collapse. MacArthur's domestic strategy was to present the emperor as having been betrayed by militarist fascists, with Hirohito now leading the way to democratic reform and such American ideals as broadening education, emancipating women, shutting down the secret police, encouraging labor unions, and promoting agricultural reform. Because so many of the Japanese people were sick of fourteen years of war, the American aid was welcomed, and the reforms exceedingly popular. The emperor, meanwhile, attended a ceremony at Hiroshima's ground zero, dressed not in divine imperial robes but in a black suit and homburg, to pledge to his people that the nation would never again pursue policies that would lead to another Great East Asia War.

Thirty-nine Japanese leaders were arrested and charged with war crimes on September 11. When American MPs arrived at Hideki Tojo's house with his warrant, they heard a gunshot. A doctor had used charcoal to mark his chest so Tojo could shoot himself in the heart, but the bullet landed in his stomach. As the Americans rushed in, Tojo, thinking he was dying, said, "I am very sorry it is taking me so long to die. The Greater East Asia War was justified and righteous. I am very sorry for the nation and all the races of the greater Asiatic powers. I wait for the righteous judgment of history. I wished to commit suicide but sometimes that fails." Given surgery at an army hospital, Tojo recovered and was detained at Sugamo Prison, where he was also given a new set of dentures. The American dentist who cast them arranged for "Remember Pearl Harbor" to be written on his teeth in Morse code.

Allied military courts held over 2,200 legal proceedings to prosecute an estimated 5,600 Japanese, convicting 4,400, and executing close to a thousand, the main venue being the eleven-nation, eleven-judge International Military Tribunal for the Far East (IMTFE), which ran for two and a half years from April 29, 1946, to November 12, 1948. Twenty-eight Japanese military and political leaders were charged with Class A "crimes against peace," and more than 5,700 Japanese nationals were charged with Class B and C crimes, mostly entailing POW abuse. Justice Radhabinod Pal issued a 1,235-page dissent in which he held that the IMTFE was nothing but a victor's idea of justice, a form of institutional revenge.

China held thirteen tribunals of its own, resulting in 504 convictions and 149 executions. The Soviet Khabarovsk War Crime Trials indicted some members from Unit 731, Japan's biological and chemical warfare unit, but MacArthur granted immunity to unit chief Shiro Ishii and those of his team who surrendered to the Americans, in exchange for their germ weapon research, which Ishii had conducted on living human beings.

At one point in the tribunals, Tojo was asked about the Son of Heaven's role on the road to war and empire. He admitted that nothing in Japan could be done, by either the government or the military, without Hirohito's consent. That afternoon, US Army officers sent Japanese workers to the onetime prime minister's cell to make sure he corrected this testimony the next day.

One serviceman forced to testify against many of his colleagues was Mitsuo Fuchida. During reconstruction, the hero of Pearl Harbor had bought land just outside Osaka from his father-in-law to became a farmer, raising wheat, rice, vegetables, fruit, grapes, chickens, rabbits, and ducks. This new life wasn't going well; his only success was in selling eggs to a nearby American army camp.

In wartime, Fuchida had been nationally famous, regularly speaking to crowds of cheering countrymen. Now, they treated him like a leper. He was disgusted by the military tribunal, especially the hangings of those convicted of mistreating POWs. This, he thought, was an entirely trumped-up charge, as weren't all POWs treated horribly around the world?

After Jacob DeShazer had recovered somewhat from his years as a POW, he decided to get an education in religion and public speaking and then return to Japan as a missionary. At college, he wrote an essay, "I Was a Prisoner of Japan," explaining what had happened to him during the war. He and his new wife, Florence, were accepted by the Free Methodist Church for missionary service and arrived in Japan on December 28, 1948, having no idea that Christian organizations in Japan had distributed over a million copies of "I Was a Prisoner of Japan." Prince Takamatsu invited DeShazer to the Temple of Heaven, where Jake was able to thank the prince for the emperor's sparing of his life, and over the next thirty years, the DeShazers would build twenty-three churches, helped in part by their association with a Japanese celebrity, a story that would make headlines around the world.

CHAPTER THIRTEEN

LEGACY

"After the attack of Pearl Harbor, there were still about four more years of the war," *Raleigh*'s Yeoman 2nd Class Gene Telecky said. "I had a job to do and I didn't give Pearl Harbor much thought at the time." After serving in Australia, New Guinea, and Okinawa, Telecky retired from the navy in 1960, but it took many years before he could talk about what had happened to him on December 7: "Our kids were already married before I could even tell them about it."

San Francisco's Mal Middlesworth was an eighteen-year-old marine during the attack: "I saw the *Oklahoma* roll over, and I saw the *Arizona* blow up. I looked over, and the officer of the deck had tears running down his cheeks. But it was too much for my mind to understand." Middlesworth was asked by his grandson about his moment in history, and when he started describing his experience, his son sat down. "I said, 'What are you doing?' And he said, 'Dad, you've never told me anything about what you saw.'"

Many have stories like Telecky's and Middlesworth's. For a great number of World War II veterans, the war was both the greatest moment in their lives and a horror that would scar them for the rest of their days. After surviving *Arizona*, Vern Olsen volunteered for aircraft carrier *Lexington*, which was blown up at the Battle of the Coral Sea: "[After December 7] I was pretty shook up. Shook up for two years. I lost a lot of weight. I was a bundle of nerves. Then I got sunk again in the Coral Sea. Then I lost everything all over again on the *Lexington*— money, billfold, all down below in the lockers."

Something little discussed alongside America's championing of the "greatest generation" is this suffering that they carried, in silence, for decades. Novelist J. D. Salinger told his daughter, "You really never get the smell of burning flesh out of your nose entirely . . . no matter how long you live."

Sterling Cale had spent three hours on December 7 swimming in the stew of body parts that was Pearl Harbor, hauling the dead and wounded onto a barge. Six years later at a family picnic, a sudden wave came in, grabbing their plastic picnic table and their two-year-old son and pulling them out to sea. Cale jumped into the ocean to save his boy, the first time he'd been swimming since December 7, and immediately went into shock, freezing, unable to move his shoulders, his arms, his legs. Luckily the family's dog, a K-9 Corps veteran, heard the child's screams and swam out, grabbed his pants in its teeth, and brought him to safety. For the rest of his life, Cale would get nauseated if he even came close to a shoreline and could never take a walk along a beach or ever go swimming again.

For over fifty years, Ensign Ike Sutton would wake up in the night, screaming. He had run Admiral Bloch's launch, pulling the dying and the injured out of the flaming water and ferrying them to Hospital Point. His lifetime of nightmares came from remembering the faces of those who'd died because he'd waited for the boat to be full before making his way to the hospital.

Servicemen weren't the only ones scarred by the war. By June 1942, the man overseeing the War Relocation Authority, Milton Eisenhower, said he couldn't sleep at night and quit. On December 17, 1944, after the presidential elections that year had concluded, the government announced that the nation's security no longer required the internment of Japanese Americans and ended the WRA. But when the camps closed down, many of the internees did not want to leave since now they had nothing to go home to—their property had been stolen in many cases, and they were afraid they would be beaten or killed wherever they went. Internee Peter Yoshida: "We went to the Japanese church to retrieve our furniture and found that people had pried open the building and looted all of the contents. As a result, we had nothing. Everything we owned was gone, except the suitcases we were allowed to take with us." In 1971, when Chief Jusice Earl Warren was asked about the internment policy for an oral history project, he burst into tears.

Bomber crewman Mark Ferris survived Hickam barracks on December 7, then spent the rest of the war as an army reporter. After V-J Day he became editor of the *Gardena Tribune*, and in 1957, Ferris was assigned an article on the meaning of December 7. A *Tribune* reporter asked forty-two people on the street what had happened on that date. No one knew. An outraged Ferris told other Pearl Harbor survivors about this and asked them to get in touch. One year later, he and ten men began the Pearl Harbor Survivors Association, with Ferris as the PHSA's first president. At its peak, the association counted eighteen thousand members, and it could easily be said that Pearl Harbor would not today hold the special place it does in American hearts if not for their efforts.

For all the American engineering miracles of resurrection at Pearl Harbor, three ships could not be brought back to life. Starting July 15, 1942, crews spent nearly eleven months parbuckling USS *Oklahoma* using twenty-one derricks attached by steel cables to shore-mounted hydraulic winching machines. After cofferdams encircled the hull and she was dewatered and refloated, *Oklahoma* made it to dry dock on December 28, where she was judged too old and too beat-up for any use by the navy. Her cannon and superstructure were chopped off and she was sold to a California scrap company, but on her way across the Pacific, the convoy was hit by a bad storm and *Oklahoma* sank all over again on May 17, 1947. The USS *Missouri* has taken her place at the Ford Island docks as a museum, and a memorial to *Oklahoma*'s 429 lost crewmen can be found just outside the *Missouri*'s entrance.

USS *Utah*, born in 1909, had served in Mexico and Ireland before being converted into a target ship in 1931. When she was torpedoed, turned turtle, and sank on December 7, *Utah* took sixty-four men with her. *Utah* was parbuckled with seventeen winches, but she, too, had little value, so after freeing her from berth, the wreckage was allowed to remain in Pearl Harbor as a war grave, and in 1972 a white concrete walkway leading to a brass plaque at her sunken hull was erected as a memorial.

During efforts in 1942 to resurrect *Arizona*, meanwhile, divers discovered a foot-wide crack in her back, meaning she would be impossible to raise. *Arizona*'s superstructure was excised and her remains left—including nine hundred or so crewmen, with twenty-three sets of brothers—to rest in peace.

On December 7, 1946, Honolulu businessman Tucker Gratz rode out to where the *Arizona* wreckage lay to memorialize her dead with a wreath. Gratz was upset to find, floating there, the exact same wreath he had laid the year before and began actively politicking the navy to create a memorial. The American military prefers to commemorate victories, not defeats, so it took five years for Gratz to get just a simple flagstaff at the site. Over the years, the flagpole was followed by a platform, and on the platform was set a plaque, and then next to the plaque, an obelisk. Finally in 1958, a memorial design was approved by President Eisenhower, and that same year Rear Admiral Samuel Fuqua, who had won the Medal of Honor for his profound bravery aboard *Arizona*, appeared on the television program *This Is Your Life*. His story spurred Americans to give money, and the USS *Arizona* Memorial at Pearl Harbor was dedicated on Memorial Day 1962 by the Pacific War Memorial Commission, whose chief was the patient, but relentless, Tucker Gratz.

The architect chosen for the memorial was a refugee from Hitler's Austria, Alfred Preis, whose first idea included an undersea viewing chamber for visitors to contemplate the wreckage directly, but this was considered too gruesome. His revision was the present swoop of concrete wave floating over the hull, which Preis said "sags in the middle but stands strong and vigorous at the ends, express[ing] initial defeat and ultimate victory. . . . The overall effect is one of serenity. Overtones of sadness have been omitted to permit the individual to contemplate his own personal responses . . . his innermost feelings. At low tide, as the sun shines upon the hull, barnacles which encrust it shimmer like gold jewels . . . a beautiful sarcophagus."

Each day, a flag is raised and lowered on the *Arizona*. Since all of Kimmel's fleet's fuel tanks had been filled to the brim on December 7, about a quart of fuel bubbles up each day and, on reaching the surface, spreads into floating, iridescent rings. Otherwise strong-willed military historians will often describe these as "black tears," and the drops' eternal release make the ship seem, in a way, still alive.

A number of *Arizona* survivors have had their cremains placed in the wreckage to rejoin their December 7 brothers. Only those who were stationed on her that day can be interred within the ship itself, inside Turret 4; those who served with her but weren't crew on December 7 can have their ashes scattered in the water. The two exceptions have been Joe James Custer, onetime executive secretary of the Pacific War Memorial Commission, and the memorial's architect, Alfred Preis.

Others cannot even bear to visit. *Arizona*'s Ralph Bayard: "I've never dared to go near the *Arizona* Memorial. I was in and out of Pearl Harbor for years after the *Arizona* was out there, but the memorial was built after I retired from the navy. I don't think I could go aboard it. But I have the layout of that ship indelibly in my mind. I'll never forget it."

Today, the most Japanese city outside Japan is Honolulu. Hawaii's top employers are the military and tourism. The state's number one tourist attraction is Pearl Harbor. Two million visit the *Arizona* each year. Of the many who are Japanese, a local guide said, "For them this was a great victory, one of the greatest in their history." It seems peculiar: Do British World War II enthusiasts, after all, visit Dresden on vacation, or Germans, Warsaw?

Research on four-hundred-odd National Park Service questionnaire replies by Japanese visitors showed that a majority saw the memorial as a peace monument similar to the many built across Japan, nearly all of which portray the Japanese as victims. One comment summed up this point of view: "Even though it was an unavoidable war, it is regrettable that young lives were destroyed in the water. I hope the peace will last." A few Japanese did feel some shame. "Up until now, I had a bit of grudge [against America] for dropping the A-bombs," a fourteen-year-old wrote. "But I saw this from the Americans' perspective for the first time and realized that our ancestors did a very bad thing. I am so ashamed and want to apologize." Others thought the Americans needed to understand that Japan, too, suffered, and that the National Park Service movie—which is remarkably evenhanded for a war memorial—should also include footage of Hiroshima and Nagasaki. "The most impressive place I visited so far is the *Arizona* Memorial," one wrote. "I even recommended my friend from ukulele class to go there. When I saw the film, I just could not hold back my tears. . . . [It] should also be shown in Hiroshima and Nagasaki. In turn, the memorial should also show a film on the A-bombs. This to show that both nations suffered a great deal and there is no happiness in wars."

This Japanese perspective has remained constant for decades. When MacArthur's troops first arrived in August 1945, Prime Minister Naruhiko Higashikuni offered that, if the Americans made an effort to forget about Pearl Harbor, the Japanese would do the same for Hiroshima and Nagasaki. But if Pearl Harbor's visitor center included reference to Hiroshima and Nagasaki, it would be hard to imagine that they would be portrayed as a reason for American shame, as the Japanese imagine, but instead as moments of triumph and retribution. Of course, nothing about the Ear Mound, the rape of Nanking, the horrible crimes unleashed against the Chinese peasants who helped the Doolittle Raiders, or any of Japan's many war atrocities are mentioned at their own peace memorials.

To the Japanese, Pearl Harbor is a horror that led to more horror. To Americans, it is a rallying cry for a nation, and a horror that led to triumph. The Japanese see no parallels between December 7, 1941, and September 11, 2001. US visitors to Pearl Harbor dramatically escalated in numbers after 9/11, showing that Americans do feel a resonance.

Before one takes the launch to *Arizona*'s viewing platform and marble cenotaph, a documentary narrated by Stockard Channing tells those who lost their lives that day, "Your future has been taken from you, but with this memorial, you will never be forgotten." It concludes, "How shall we remember them, those who died? Mourn the dead. Remember the battle. Understand the tragedy. Honor the memory."

> Most Holy Spirit! Who didst brood
> Upon the chaos dark and rude,
> And bid its angry tumult cease,
> And give, for wild confusion, peace;
> Oh, hear us when we cry to Thee,
> For those in peril on the sea.
> —"Navy Hymn"

When General George MacArthur died on April 15, 1964, at the age of eighty-four, former presidents Eisenhower and Truman did not attend the funeral, but former prime minister Yoshida of Japan did.

After a thirty-three-year career with the navy, Rear Admiral Samuel Fuqua died on January 27, 1987, at the age of eighty-seven and was buried in Arlington National Cemetery.

Hirohito remained on the Chrysanthemum Throne for sixty-two years, the longest reign in all of Japanese history, until his death, in 1989. That same year, on August 15, the eighty-four-year-old General Minoru Genda died. Of the war, he said, "I thought we would win, but we misjudged America's real strength. We lacked war matériel, and our national leadership was not up to the task." He also said that Japanese troops should have occupied Hawaii and turned it into a base for attacking the American mainland, and that the Japanese can feel no moral superiority over Hiroshima and Nagasaki since, if Japan had developed nuclear weapons, it would certainly have used them against the United States. In 1962, the American government awarded him the highest honor it can grant a foreigner, the Legion of Merit, for his rebuilding of Japan's air forces, and that year he was elected to Japan's parliament, where he would remain until 1986, and become a leading figure in the Liberal Democratic Party.

Ellen Lawson: "In the last years of his life, Ted Lawson was in a great deal of pain and required painkilling medication, but his mind was still as bright as ever. He was limited in what he could do, though, because every time he moved, he was in pain. He thought amputees just had to suffer, but in fact it turned out he'd broken his back, which for many years we didn't know. On January 19, 1992, Ted had a pulmonary aneurysm and died. He was interred at Chico Cemetery Mausoleum in Chico, California. Today, I still live on our acre of walnut trees. And I just finished the harvest; it went well, in spite of the winds and the rain. All I can think is 'Finished!'"

In 1993, Lieutenant General James Doolittle's own silver Raider cup was turned over. The daredevil-may-care flying ace, known for his risky, outrageous stunts, a man who called himself "a crackpot pilot," had lived to the ripe old age of ninety-six, passing away at his son John's home in Pebble Beach, California. Just before the general died, even after all his achievements and acclaim, he told a reporter, "There has never been a time when I've been completely satisfied with myself." Jimmy and his wife, Joe, are buried side by side in Section 7-A of Arlington National Cemetery.

On November 25, 2006, ace pilot Kenneth Taylor passed away in Tucson. His partner in history, George Welch, had died in October 1954 while working as chief test pilot for North American Aviation in California's Antelope Valley.

On May 26, 2010, John Finn, the last surviving Medal of Honor bluejacket from Pearl Harbor, died at the age of one hundred. In 2001, Finn had been one of the vets invited to Hawaii to see the premiere of Disney's *Pearl Harbor*. "It was a damned good movie," he insisted. "It's helped educate people who didn't know about Pearl Harbor and what happened there. I liked it especially because I got to kiss all those pretty little movie actresses."

While Ford Island's Luke Field is now a meadow, and its forty-two-thousand-square-foot seaplane hangar that survived December 7 is now home to the Pacific Aviation Museum, Hickam and Wheeler still have some .50-caliber bullets stuck in their peach-colored concrete walls. We can also be certain that remaining in *Arizona* are what we know can survive in such a watery tomb: human teeth. By the tens of thousands.

Sailor Donald Raymond: "I seen the *Arizona* blow up. I seen the *California* on fire and I seen her sink. I seen the *Oklahoma* roll over. The whole harbor was nothing but a big sheet of black smoke. I never want to go through it again, I know that. And they say—ya know, whenever we go to these schools—they all say 'the heroes' and that. Well, the real heroes are the ones that's still over there. The *Arizona*. The *Utah*. The *Utah* was on the other side of Ford Island, and you don't hear very much about it. But five hundred men went down on her. I say those fellas are the heroes. We're the lucky ones, that's all."

At Pearl Harbor's fiftieth anniversary ceremony in 1991, President George H. W. Bush, who had served in World War II as a navy pilot and had been shot down by the Japanese, told the two thousand survivors in the audience that it was time to move on: "I have no rancor in my heart toward Germany or Japan—none at all. I hope you have none in yours. This is no time for recrimination. World War Two is over. It is history. We won. Americans did not wage war against nations or races. We fought for freedom and human dignity against the nightmare of totalitarianism. We crushed totalitarianism, and when that was done, we helped our enemies give birth to democracies."

At the ceremony, Ford Island's A. M. Geiger teared up when asked if this would be his last trip to Pearl Harbor. "Don't talk about that," said Mr. Geiger, who walked with a cane and wore a pacemaker. "I don't have any friends left." "You never get over it: I've been crying," said *Salt Lake City*'s Haile Jaekel. "But I'm going to keep coming till I drop."

Japanese television produced a series of historical dramas and documentaries that year telling a very different story from the one Americans know. A typical and especially popular drama was *Defeat in Showa 16*, a tale in which ordinary citizens working with the Planning Board try to stop a small band of military hard-liners from driving the country to war. Blaming Hideki Tojo and his compatriots while absolving the great majority of Japanese citizens, though, sounds awfully similar to the 1950s German viewpoint that basically said, "It wasn't us, it was Hitler." When onetime deputy defense minister Seiki Nishihiro admitted, "Of course the military had much of the power, but the mass media and everyone else followed, so not only the military was responsible," politician Masayuki Fujio countered, "Why should we fling mud at the history of Japan?"

Foreign Minister Michio Watanabe had hoped to honor the fiftieth anniversary in Hawaii by offering a "milestone" resolution of regret from Japan's parliament, but the vote failed, with senior legislator Takashi Hasegawa explaining, "There is no need now for the loser to apologize to the victor." Instead, Emperor Akihito expressed his regrets, Prime Minister Kiichi Miyazawa said that his countrymen "feel a deep sense of responsibility for the unbearable damage and grief" that the war brought to the world, Foreign Minister Watanabe expressed "deep remorse about the unbearable suffering and sorrow," and Hiroshima mayor Takashi Hiraoka visited Pearl Harbor to lay a wreath of solidarity. Japanese psychiatry professor Susumu Oda theorized that the country's inability to take responsibility and make amends "relates to the mentality of ancestor worship. Some Japanese feel that it would be sinful to apologize for World War II, because they would be blaming their ancestors."

I went to Japan to try to understand their side of this story. At the very center of Tokyo, surrounded by parkland, stands the low-slung Temple of Heaven, home to the emperor, and just up the street on a small hill overlooking the palace can be found a very different kind of building. Overseen by dozens of busy Shinto priests and attendant maidens dressed in stark red skirts and billowing white blouses, its grounds dotted by the brilliant white of its specially bred doves, Yasukuni-jinja (Empire at Peace Shrine) is perhaps the most controversial site in all of Japan. Fronted by two rows of ginkgo and cherry trees, the normal wooden torii gate here is bronze, while the temple's entryway is draped in purple curtains marked in the facet emblem of the Chrysanthemum Throne—the emblem for which the 2,466,000 *kami*, "soldier-gods," memorialized here sacrificed their lives. Suppli-cants appear before the cedar altar and honor the deities of departed soldiers by bowing and clapping their hands. In 1978, the urn of Tojo's ashes, along with the remains of other Pacific war leaders hanged as war criminals, were clandestinely brought to Yasukuni to be housed in its inner sanctum. The Japanese believe that the world's most beautiful *sakura* ("cherry blossoms," whose brief and vivid blooms are symbols of fallen warriors) are found here.

Before Yasukuni's entryway stands Yushukan—the Hall for Com-muning with Noble Souls—a museum surveying the country's entire history of warfare concluding with the Great East Asia War. Inside are swords, maps, medals, an Ohka kamikaze cherry-blossom attack glider, various bits of Yamamoto memorabilia, a midget submarine, a Kaiten suicide torpedo, a carrier minibomber, a light tank, field guns, antiair-craft guns, and naval shells. Two rooms are dedicated to the six thou-sand suicide fliers who died in the war's last days, with the highpoint a panorama of the Jinrai Butai, the Divine Thunderbolt Corps, in its final heroic moment—Okinawa.

Yushukan holds one of the four main Great East Asia War archives in Japan. The others are at Hiroshima, Kure, and Etajima. I was warmly received everywhere, as expected in the most gracious and hospitable nation on earth . . . except at the Imperial Japanese Naval History Museum of Etajima, which includes the school attended by every military figure on the Japanese side of this story. There, each time I or a Japanese trying to help me called to arrange a visit, we were given a different reason for why I couldn't go. They were closed. They weren't closed, but they weren't for sightseers. Maybe I wasn't a sight-seer, but if so, I would need an appointment. No, they wouldn't make an appointment since they couldn't assist an English speaker. When I offered to bring my own translator, the response was that it didn't mat-ter, they were closed. It went round and round.

I showed up at Etajima anyway. People were working there, the lights were on, and the parking lot was busy. I asked to speak to some-one in charge. Mr. Masuko appeared, and again he refused to let an American writer work at a Japanese history archive. I asked if, after seventy-five years, the Japanese navy was still fighting this war. Did they have something to hide? Before leaving, I told him that this is not how writers from his country are treated in the United States, and that he was an embarrassment to our nations' friendship. I was angry at how the Etajima staff treated me, but at the same time, I know that, if American veterans of World War II have trouble talking about their wartime experiences, Japanese veterans are doubly afflicted since they lost. Yet there is a renewed interest among the Japanese about this history, and what levels of pride, and remorse, they should feel. Every Pacific-war museum I saw in Japan was mobbed.

On June 22, 2001, the Walt Disney Company rented the Tokyo Dome and invited the thirty thousand winners of a video-store lottery to watch the Japanese premiere of its movie *Pearl Harbor*. Disney's newspaper ads did not mention that all the villains were Japanese; they instead described the story as "The world starts moving; the world is caught in a tide of history. With hope for the future and love in their hearts, young heroes battle against the opposition of the times." One lottery winner was nineteen-year old Chikako Inomata, who said, "It is normal that Pearl Harbor would be seen differently from a Japanese and an American viewpoint, but sometimes I felt a little bad that the Japanese people were simply portrayed as evil." A thirteen-year-old, however, "was moved to tears at the point when Danny died. . . . I learned more about human relations than I did about history." Disney's *Pearl Harbor* was a hit in Japan, the country's sixth-highest grosser at the time.

In polls taken at Pearl Harbor's fiftieth anniversary in 1991, 55 percent of the Japanese and 40 percent of the Americans thought that Japan should apologize for Pearl Harbor, while 73 percent of the Japanese and 16 percent of the Americans said that the United States should apologize for Hiroshima and Nagasaki. If Japan apologized for Pearl Harbor, though, 50 percent of the Americans thought the United States should then apologize for its atomic bombs. "Fifty years of pain and hatred is long enough; the time has come for reconciliation," said Hawaii's US senator Daniel K. Inouye at a Japan-America Society of Honolulu dinner on the fiftieth anniversary. (As a boy in Honolulu on December 7, when Japanese American Inouye learned who was behind the attack, he screamed, "You goddamn Japs!") This anniversary took place when the American economy had sagged for two decades while Japan's had soared. Southeast Asia and Hawaii were now financially dominated by the Japanese, whose businessmen worked to influence local politics. Americans of Japanese ancestry, known as AJAs in Hawaii, are now 23 percent of the population and wield tremendous power through grassroots politics and business investment. Similarly, 20 percent of Hawaii's tourists are Japanese, but on average they spend five times as much as American tourists. Many in Europe saw that the Germans were behaving similarly on that continent and wondered, Were the losers of World War II now economically dominating the globe? By the nineties, Japan's economic boom and her preference for American investments was a daily topic of conversation in the US business community, with rancor over Tokyo's unequal trade protectionism. Her financial success was often referred to in the press as an economic Pearl Harbor, while the American reaction can be seen in the movie *Rising Sun*, with its immaculately suited villainous Japanese businessmen and talk of "financial samurai."

The Pearl Harbor Survivors Association banquet in 1991 was held at the Sheraton Waikiki Hotel, which the Japanese owned. No representatives of Japan were invited to attend the ceremonies, however. "We did not invite the Japanese fifty years ago and we don't want them now," said PHSA president Gerald Glaubitz. "This is our own thing. We've been planning for almost five years. I've had widows call me and say, 'You mean they are going to invite the people who killed my husband?'"

In October 1948, Mitsuo Fuchida was consumed with thoughts about the path his life had taken. He had been a hero of the nation, and now he was nothing. After emerging from Tokyo's Shibuya subway station, he saw an American giving out pamphlets written by a fellow airman. After hearing its title—"Watakushi Wa Nippon No Horyo Deshita"—Fuchida immediately read the four pages. He then bought a Bible to confirm Jacob DeShazer's claims about human forgiveness. At the end of the Gospel of St. Luke, he found himself riveted when the tortured Christ said, "Father, forgive them, for they know not what they do." "It was," Fuchida said, "like having the sun come up."

Fuchida decided right then he had to become a Christian, and wrote to the publisher of DeShazer's pamphlet, the Pocket Testament League. The letter shocked, Glenn Wagner, PTL's president, who arranged to meet Fuchida in Osaka. There, the American minister told the Japanese convert that to be a Christian, he needed to read the Bible daily and to bear witness.

The two drove to the middle of Osaka in Wagner's Chevy truck, which had been converted into a portable stage with a loudspeaker and a podium. After setting up, the frightened man, not knowing how the crowd would react, leaned forward into the microphone to announce: "I am Mitsuo Fuchida, a former navy captain who commanded the air attacking forces against Pearl Harbor on eight December 1941. But now I'm a Christian, and I want to let you know how I became one. All Japanese want peace, I'm sure of that. No one wants war again, no one less than I, who engaged in war as a naval officer for almost four years. I know the brutality and the cruelties of war better than many people. Now I want to work for peace. But how can mankind achieve a lasting peace?" As Fuchida continued, a large crowd gathered, and the one-time admirer of Adolf Hitler found a new purpose in life.

In 1950, Jacob DeShazer was speaking in Osaka when Fuchida approached to say how he had been affected by Jake's pamphlet. The two then preached together in Osaka, converting almost five hundred Japanese to Christianity. The story of how the hero of Pearl Harbor had converted to faith was carried by every major Japanese newspaper.

The strength of his newfound faith notwithstanding, Fuchida would have difficulties adjusting to the tenets of Christianity. "Fuchida had two women; one was his concubine and one was his wife," DeShazer said. "Some of the fellows didn't think he was much of a Christian that he didn't start straightening out and become a moral man: 'You've got to get rid of one of those women.' But it was a big problem for Fuchida. I guess eventually he realized it was wrong, and he got so he only had one wife, or one woman. I think he took the best-looking one."

Eighteen years after the war ended, Fuchida met the B-29 pilot who had dropped the atomic bomb on Hiroshima. Paul Tibbets recalled that a man "walked up to me, stuck out his hand, and he said, 'I'm Fuchida. Shall we talk about it?' I looked at him; he saw I didn't understand; he said, 'Man, I led the attack on Pearl Harbor.' I said to him, 'You sure did surprise us,' and he said, 'What do you think you did to us?' We talked for thirty to forty minutes, and he said, 'You did exactly the right thing because Japan would've resisted an invasion using every man, woman, and child, using sticks and stones if necessary. That would've been an awful slaughter.' "

On May 30, 1976, after living for many years in America, Fuchida died of complications from diabetes at the age of seventy-three. Today, his children and grandchildren reside in California.

Fuchida's story wasn't the only remarkable turn in the tide of this history. Fellow pilot Zenji Abe had been the leader of the *Akagi* dive-bombing squadron attacking Pearl Harbor. He next took part in the raid on Dutch Harbor in the Aleutians and in battles over both the Indian and Pacific Oceans, and in 1944 during the Battle of the Philippine Sea, he crash-landed onto a Pacific island, was taken prisoner, and spent fifteen months as an POW.

After the war, Abe became an officer with Japan's National Police Reserve. On learning years later that his country had not officially declared war before attacking Pearl Harbor, he "was shocked and mortified to know that. To conduct a successful mission, the attack had to be made in an unexpected way to the enemy, but delaying the declaration is immoral and against the Bushido spirit." In the 1980s, he traveled across Japan in search of surviving First Air Fleet pilots and convinced them to sign a letter apologizing to the Americans at Pearl Harbor. He then flew to the United States, landed in Atlanta, and hired a taxi to drive him for the two hours it took to reach the home of a Pearl Harbor Survivors Association senior officer. He rang the doorbell, explained who he was in halting English, and showed the man the letter. The American sailor said that the Japanese pilot could take his letter and shove it up his ass and slammed the door. Crushed, Abe flew back home to Japan, but refused to give up. Instead he began the Japan Friends of Pearl Harbor and convinced a small group to go to Hawaii for Pearl Harbor's fiftieth anniversary.

Zenji Abe: "The wartime leaders at that time told people to commit suicide if we were captured. They should have committed seppuku [suicide by disembowelment] when the war ended as they had the responsibility for causing the suffering of so many people. Their attitudes were immoral. I believe Japan and the world would have changed for the better if the Pearl Harbor attack did not happen, and the relationship between Japan and its neighboring countries would have been different if wartime leaders had acted morally. There was no ill feeling or hate before the war against the United States. Why did we make such a mistake? No more Pearl Harbors and no more Hiroshimas should be the watchword for those who believe in peace. Those persons who lost husbands and fathers and sons, of course, can never forget that day, and I am afraid that even [my] small story is like opening an old wound. I pray from the bottom of my heart for those who were killed in action and their bereaved families."

In Hawaii, three Japan Friends of Pearl Harbor—Zenji Abe, Takeshi Maeada, and Heita Matsumura—met USS *West Virginia* marine bugler Richard Fiske, who not only survived Pearl Harbor, but also the battle of Iwo Jima, which killed sixty-eight hundred Americans and nineteen thousand Japanese. Fiske called Iwo Jima "thirty-six straight days of Pearl Harbor." He had spent his postwar decades so filled with loathing for the Japanese that thinking about them made him physically ill.

Then Fiske met the men who had been his lifelong enemies in person and suddenly saw them as human beings, as soldiers like himself. Takeshi Maeda: "Mr. Fiske suddenly hugged me. He was maybe as tall or a little taller than me. And I saw tears coming out of his eyes. And I told him, 'I'm sorry for sinking your ship.' But he said, 'No, don't say sorry, because it was a war between two nations. And we were soldiers, and it was our duty to fight. And there is no need for you or I to be sorry.'"

Richard Fiske: "We didn't even shake hands, we just hugged each other. I'll never forget that. Bringing the Japanese veterans and the American veterans together . . . I think it's one of the greatest things that ever happened. Because it shows the world that here are two opposites, and now they've clasped their hands in friendship."

Before they departed, Abe put his arm around Fiske's shoulders and said, "Richard-san, please do me this favor. Take this three hundred dollars and buy two roses and take them out to the *Arizona* every month and blow taps. This is my simple way of saying I am so very sorry." Across the following decade, Abe sent Fiske money for flowers, and each month Fiske bought one white and one red rose to lay at the memorial's wall of names, then blew both the American and the Japanese taps. Invited by the three pilots, Fiske then visited Japan, where he blew his bugle at the Hiroshima Memorial and met the engineer who designed Pearl Harbor's shallow-water breakaway torpedo fins.

In 1996, Emperor Akihito awarded Richard Fiske the Order of the Rising Sun for promoting Japanese-American friendship. At the last PHSA reunion he was able to attend before dying in 2004 at the age of eighty-two, a Japanese tourist touched Fiske's arm and said in broken English, "I am so sorry," then burst into tears. "The war's over now," Fiske replied. "Besides, my daughter married a Japanese boy, so what can I do?"

Fiske's fellow sailor aboard *West Virginia*, Mess Attendant Doris Miller, received a commendation from Secretary of the Navy Frank Knox and the Navy Cross from Chester Nimitz, with Nimitz saying, "This marks the first time in this conflict that such high tribute has been made in the Pacific Fleet to a member of his race, and I'm sure that the future will see others similarly honored for brave acts." *Utah's* Clark Simmons pointed out what many felt about this at the time: "This was a very courageous young man, and it was always believed that he should've gotten the Congressional Medal of Honor. And the only reason why he didn't get the Congressional Medal of Honor was because he was black." After news of Miller's heroism reached the continental United States, the African-American community began a campaign to pressure President Roosevelt to allow Miller admittance to the Naval Academy. In his follow-up letter to Navy Secretary Knox, the NAACP's Roy Wilkins pointed out that "the greatest honor that could be paid Mess Attendant Miller by the United States Navy would be for it to abolish forthwith the restrictions now in force against the enlistment of members of Mess Attendant Miller's race so that black Americans can serve their country and their Navy in any capacity." Such a step "would serve dramatic notice that this country is in fact a democracy in an all-out war against anti-democratic forces."

Instead of being enrolled in the Naval Academy, Doris Miller was promoted to cook 3rd class and, in the spring of 1943, was assigned to escort carrier *Liscome Bay*. By November, *Liscome Bay* was battling in the Gilbert Islands when, at 5:10 a.m. on the twenty-fourth, she was torpedoed. The shell ignited her bomb magazine, and she sank. Of her crew, 272 survived, and 646 died, including Doris Miller. But that is not the end of his story. By combining the story of his heroism with the stories of other black military heroes over the years (such as the Revolutionary War's Crispus Attucks), civil rights organizations were able to battle segregation as being both contrary to American values and a hindrance to the nation's war efforts. The campaign was so successful that poet Langston Hughes was able to say, after Truman desegregated the military in 1948, "When Dorie Miller took gun in hand, Jim Crow started his last stand." In 1973, frigate USS *Miller* was named in his honor (with Dorie's mother in attendance at its christening), and in 2001, Disney's *Pearl Harbor* movie cast Oscar winner Cuba Gooding Jr. in the role of Doris Miller. Today, a group in Waco, Texas, is trying to raise $1.35 million for a Miller memorial; their plans can be seen at http://www.dorismillermemorial.org.

The story of Pearl Harbor is the story of a hundred *what ifs*? What if FDR's partial embargo hadn't been secretly manipulated into a total embargo? What if one Japanese leader had succeeded in forcing the belligerents to make peace in China and give up their fantasy of Dai Nippon Teikoku? What if Prime Minister Konoye had held his summit with President Roosevelt? What if the American president had succeeded in negotiating at the last minute with the Japanese emperor?

The answer to the key and eternal American questions—Why didn't the United States know? Why didn't our intelligence work? Why couldn't our military defend us?—is that in the end, Japanese emotion won out over rational action. Starting with the fundamental theory—that killing thousands of Americans in a surprise attack would trigger the United States to falter and surrender—and ending with the decision to wage war—during which dozens in Tokyo, from graduate students to finance, foreign, naval, and prime ministers, told the army that fighting the United States was nonsensical—Japan's course to Pearl Harbor was irrational in the extreme. Sense, in the end, did not carry the day.

Two cognitive psychologists, Daniel Kahneman and Amos Tversky, used clinical research to understand how human beings make decisions. They found that people are overwhelmingly irrational instead of rational, and their findings have upended cornerstone beliefs about economics, politics, and sports. As Michael Lewis explained, "In their most cited paper, cryptically titled 'Prospect Theory,' they convinced a lot of people that human beings are best understood as being risk-averse when making a decision that offers hope of a gain but risk-seeking when making a decision that will lead to a certain loss. In a stroke they provided a framework to understand all sorts of human behavior that economists, athletic coaches, and other 'experts' have trouble explaining: why people who play the lottery also buy insurance; why people are less likely to sell their houses and their stock portfolios in falling markets; [and even why] professional golfers become better putters when they're trying to save par (avoid losing a stroke) than when they're trying to make a birdie (and gain a stroke)."

Pearl Harbor, along with 9/11, has proven that intelligence agencies and defense departments need to expand their thinking about future threats, the greatest of which will be just as out of the blue as these two tragedies. How do we plan for an irrational outburst that defies logical analysis? Can we defend ourselves with emotional intelligence?

The history of Pearl Harbor is as remarkable as any moment in a nation's memory, but the history of the American reaction to Pearl Harbor is the founding force of the United States today. The impact was so profound that it could easily be said that the America we live in was born, not on July 4, 1776, but on December 7, 1941, a transformation so remarkable that by 1950, *Life* magazine said, "In retrospect Pearl Harbor seemed clearly the best thing that could have happened to the US." Publisher Henry Luce's 1941 essay "The American Century" predicted that, by the war's end, America's values and point of view would be spread across the planet. The *New York Times* concluded: "The world changed because, with the lockstep of history, the first Japanese bomb became the Hiroshima bomb, the death of the battleship age led to the birth of the nuclear age, the thrust of Asian imperialism destroyed Western empires, and most of all because a world in which a nation might be defeated and survive became inexorably a world in which a nation might conquer and die. . . . History is a sequence of ironies and of these one of the greatest is that a nation that did not want world power, that did not understand and perhaps still does not understand world power, was thrust into world power by the very nations—the Germans in Europe and the Japanese in Asia—for whom it was their sustaining dream."

Before Pearl Harbor, many Americans were convinced that they was protected by two oceans and a hemispheric distance from wars in Europe and Asia. President Calvin Coolidge proclaimed, "Our borders are unfortified. We fear no one; no one fears us." In the years preceding Pearl Harbor, America's international role was essentially that of Great Britain's uncertain and conflicted little brother, knowing he had to do something about totalitarianism, but wishing it were otherwise.

After December 7, even onetime fervent isolationist Senator Arthur Vandenberg accepted "that oceans are no longer moats around our ramparts. We learned that mass destruction was a progressive science which defies both time and space and reduces human blood and flesh to cruel impotence." The attack on American soil galvanized and united a United States torn apart by partisan squabbling and helped Americans to start thinking of themselves as citizens of the country and of the world. Being forced to wage war on two oceans and three continents meant an end to America's Great Depression—1933's unemployment rate of 24.9 percent became 1942's rate of 1.2 percent—as well as a transformation of the country from a timid and withholding isolationist into a global superpower. In 1940, the American State, War, and Navy Departments were all housed together in a small building next to the White House. By January 15, 1943, War and Navy had moved into the world's largest building—the Pentagon. Today's US Department of Defense employs 2 million people and annually spends about $600 billion—more than the next eight largest defense services combined.

December 7 created the democratic alliance that ultimately defeated Italian, German, Japanese, and Soviet totalitarianism, saving the world from dictatorship. Rage against the Japanese for Pearl Harbor led the United States to destroy Japan's oil shipping, merchant fleet, and military forces, excise her colonial territories, firebomb her cities into dust, and in the final episode of World War II's enormous cost in human suffering, unleash nuclear weapons for the only time in the world's history of warfare. After the Japanese slaughtered between 5 million and 20 million Asians over a decade of imperial conquest, the global cataclysm killed over four hundred thousand Americans, over 2 million Japanese, over 5 million Poles, over 5 million Germans, nearly 6 million Jews, and over 26 million Russians, for a total of between 60 million and 80 million.

After Congress finished investigating what had gone wrong at Pearl Harbor—investigations detailed in the appendix below—legislators joined with President Truman to reform the nation's security, Truman saying that Pearl Harbor might not have happened "if there had been something like coordination of information in the government. . . . The military did not know everything the State Department knew, and the diplomats did not have access to all the army and navy knew." Their answer was the National Security Act of 1947, merging the Departments of War and Navy; making the air force independent of the army; and creating the first peacetime intelligence bureaucracies in American history. Army's underfunded and understaffed Signal Intelligence was transformed into the immense National Security Agency, while Roosevelt's Office of Strategic Services became the Central Intelligence Agency.

There is however an entirely forgotten legacy of December 7—its inspiration to American leaders to make sure such a cataclysm could never happen again. In a speech prepared for Jefferson Day on April 13, 1945 (which he was never to give), Franklin Roosevelt wrote, "Today we are part of the vast Allied force—a force composed of flesh and blood and steel and spirit—which is today destroying the makers of war, the breeders of hatred, in Europe and in Asia. . . . We, as Americans, do not choose to deny our responsibility. Nor do we intend to abandon our determination that, within the lives of our children and our children's children, there will not be a third world war. We seek peace—enduring peace. More than an end to war, we want an end to the beginnings of all wars."

This legacy of Pearl Harbor was reiterated in the proclamations that Douglas MacArthur gave from the decks of the USS *Missouri* during Japan's surrender, the start of Japan's transformation from one of America's greatest enemies to one of her greatest allies:

"It is my earnest hope, and indeed the hope of all mankind, that from this solemn occasion a better world shall emerge out of the blood and carnage of the past—a world dedicated to the dignity of man and the fulfillment of his most cherished wish for freedom, tolerance, and justice. . . .

"Today the guns are silent. A great tragedy has ended. A great victory has been won. . . . We have known the bitterness of defeat and the exultation of triumph, and from both we have learned there can be no turning back. We must go forward to preserve in peace what we won in war.

"A new era is upon us. Even the lesson of victory itself brings with it profound concern, both for our future security and the survival of civilization. The destructiveness of the war potential, through progressive advances in scientific discovery, has in fact now reached a point which revises the traditional concepts of war.

"Men since the beginning of time have sought peace. . . . Military alliances, balances of power, leagues of nations, all in turn failed, leaving the only path to be by way of the crucible of war. We have had our last chance. If we do not now devise some greater and more equitable system, Armageddon will be at our door. The problem basically is theological and involves a spiritual recrudescence and improvement of human character that will synchronize with our almost matchless advances in science, art, literature, and all material and cultural development of the past two thousand years. It must be of the spirit if we are to save the flesh."

The course Douglas MacArthur pursued to ensure peace in Asia was simultaneously followed by another American general to bring peace and stability to Europe. In 1947, President Truman used General Eisenhower as an intermediary to ask George Marshall to be his secretary of state and Marshall replied, "My answer is in affirmative if that continues to be his desire. My personal reaction is something else." At that moment Europe was destroyed, the Soviet empire was gobbling up territory, and regional Communist Parties were growing in popular support among citizens desperate to survive. Secretary of State Marshall presented his solution at a June 5 speech—an economic reconstruction of Europe backed by American financing: "It is logical that the United States should do whatever it is able to do to assist in the return of normal economic health to the world, without which there can be no political stability and no assured peace. Our policy is not directed against any country, but against hunger, poverty, desperation, and chaos. Any government that is willing to assist in recovery will find full cooperation on the part of the USA."

Marshall got Congress to pass 1948's Economic Cooperation Act, which would over the next four years send Europe $13.3 billion—$130 billion in 2015 dollars—and be known as the Marshall Plan; another $6 billion would be sent to Asia. Besides keeping devastated nations from again collapsing into fascism or communism, most of this money was used to buy American-made products, adding to the United States' own postwar economic boom.

The four years of the Marshall Plan unleashed the fastest economic growth in Europe's history, with industry boosted by 35 percent, agriculture surpassing prewar conditions, and two decades of continuous growth. For this great success, George Marshall won the Nobel Peace Prize in 1953, becoming the first professional soldier Peace Prize laureate.

Starting with the news of Hitler's invasion of Poland in 1939, meanwhile, Cordell Hull's State Department began outlining a global organization that could succeed where the League of Nations had failed by providing a counterforce that could stop future Hitlers in Europe, Mussolinis in Africa, or Tojos in Asia. Three weeks after Pearl Harbor on December 29, 1941, Roosevelt and Churchill expanded Hull's State-drafted Atlantic Charter into the "Declaration of United Nations," which pledged to fight the fascists through mutual defense as well as begin a new global peacekeeping organization. The declaration was signed on New Year's Day 1942 by the United States, Great Britain, China, and the Union of Soviet Socialist Republics, and the next day by twenty-two other countries. The following year, Hull and Roosevelt drafted a "Charter of the United Nations," and to overcome deep-seated American isolationism, State sent officials across the country to appear at over five hundred meetings to raise popular support. On October 24, 1945, the United Nations was founded with fifty-one members and grew in time to 193.

Some are quick to criticize the United States' behavior on the global stage; they were answered by Barack Obama in his last year as president: "For all of our warts, the United States has clearly been a force for good in the world. If you compare us to previous superpowers, we act less on the basis of naked self-interest, and have been interested in establishing norms that benefit everyone. If it is possible to do good at a bearable cost, to save lives, we will do it. . . . We should be promoting values, like democracy and human rights, because not only do they serve our interests the more people adopt values that we share—in the same way that, economically, if people adopt rule of law and property rights and so forth, that is to our advantage—but because it makes the world a better place. [Yet] I also believe that the world is a tough, complicated, messy, mean place, and full of hardship and tragedy. And in order to advance both our security interests and those ideals and values that we care about, we've got to be hardheaded at the same time as we're bighearted."

Others are quick to find fault with the United Nations. In his memoirs, Cordell Hull answered these critics by saying that the UN is "a mirror of the world, and if we don't like what we see, let's not blame the mirror." Franklin Roosevelt called Hull "the one person in all the world who has done his most to make this great plan for peace [the United Nations] an effective fact," and for this work Cordell Hull was awarded the Nobel Peace Prize in 1945.

In the years directly after 1945, half of the world's industrial production was American, as was eighty percent of its gold. Yet at the height of its preeminence, America became a victor like no other in the history of the world. Instead of demanding territory and treasure such as had concluded nearly every other great military conflict, the United States created, through the United Nations, through such alliances as NATO, SEATO, and the European Union, through global financial diplomacy such as the World Trade Organization, the International Monetary Fund, the International Bank for Reconstruction and Development, and foreign aid, and through the threat of the world's largest military force, seven decades of Pax Americana—a world at peace—described by John F. Kennedy on June 10, 1963: "What kind of peace do I mean and what kind of a peace do we seek? Not a Pax Americana enforced on the world by American weapons of war. Not the peace of the grave or the security of the slave. I am talking about genuine peace, the kind of peace that makes life on earth worth living, and the kind that enables men and nations to grow, and to hope, and build a better life for their children—not merely peace for Americans but peace for all men and women, not merely peace in our time but peace in all time."

With a rage ignited by Tokyo, a confidence born with Doolittle, and the great idealism of ensuring such a thing would never happen again, Pearl Harbor's greatest legacy is our nation's continuing struggle to make sure that there will never be a World War III. Whatever you think of the United States of America, its foreign policy, its military, and its actions overseas, the world at overall peace since 1945 has been an American goal and an American triumph. What could be a greater legacy to those who served and died in World War II, beginning at Pearl Harbor?

JUDGMENT AND CONTROVERSY

Six weeks after the attack on Oahu, the Roosevelt Administration–convened Roberts Commission, the first Pearl Harbor investigation after Frank Knox's preliminary report, released its conclusions on January 24, 1942:

> The Commission examined 127 witnesses and received a large number of documents. All . . . who were thought to have knowledge of facts pertinent to the inquiry were summoned and examined under oath. . . . The oral evidence received amounts to 1,887 typewritten pages, and the records and documents examined exceed 3,000 printed pages in number. . . .
>
> The Commanding General, Hawaiian Department [Short], the Commander in Chief of the Fleet [Kimmel], and the Commandant 14th Naval District, their senior subordinates, and their principal staff officers, considered the possibility of air raids. Without exception they believed that the chances of such a raid while the Pacific Fleet was based upon Pearl Harbor were practically nil. . . . On November 27 each responsible commander was warned that hostilities were momentarily possible. The warnings indicated war, and war only. Both of these messages contained orders. The Commanding General was ordered to undertake such reconnaissance and other measures as he deemed necessary. The Commander in Chief of the Fleet was ordered to execute a defensive deployment in preparation for carrying out war tasks.
>
> Other significant messages followed on succeeding days. These emphasized the impending danger and the need for war readiness. In this situation, during a period of ten days preceding the Japanese attack, the responsible commanders held no conference directed to a discussion of the meaning of the warnings and orders sent them, and failed to collaborate and to coordinate defensive measures which should be taken pursuant to the orders received. . . .

Had orders issued by the Chief of Staff and the Chief of Naval Operations on November 27, 1941, been complied with, the aircraft warning system of the Army should have been operating; the distant reconnaissance of the Navy, and the inshore air patrol of the Army, should have been maintained; the antiaircraft batteries of the Army and similar shore batteries of the Navy, as well as additional antiaircraft artillery located on vessels of the fleet in Pearl Harbor, should have been manned and supplied with ammunition; and a high state of readiness of aircraft should have been in effect. None of these conditions was in fact inaugurated or maintained for the reason that the responsible commanders failed to consult and cooperate as to necessary action based upon the warnings and to adopt measures enjoined by the orders given them by the chiefs of the Army and Navy commands in Washington.

The commission was especially taken aback by General Short's interpretation of the November 27 war warning, asking him, "In other words, there were no troops in your command ready for war at that moment?" General Short: "No, sir. They were ready for uprisings. They were—we were definitely organized to meet any uprising or any act of sabotage." Short's other response to the war warning was to order his radar service, the Aircraft Control and Warning System—whose Opana station sighted the arriving enemy forces—to mildly expand their hours. Originally operating from 0700 to 1100 for routine training except Sundays and from noon to 1600 for training and maintenance except Saturdays and Sundays, the system now additionally ran from 0400 until 0700—three extra hours a day—seven days a week. But Short, like many high-ranking officers, didn't understand this nascent technology's value, saying, "At that time we just got machines and set up. I thought this was fine training for them. I was trying to get training and was doing it for training more than any idea that it would be real."

After being vilified by the public, Admiral Kimmel demanded a court-martial to clear his reputation, but no one except Kimmel wanted a public investigation into December 7 during the war. The solution was December 1943 legislation extending the statue of limitations for responsibility at Pearl Harbor, and a June 1944 joint resolution of Congress that instructed both services to further investigate Pearl Harbor. The Army Pearl Harbor Board of 1944 found General Short responsible, but additionally censured George Marshall and War Plans Division chief Leonard Gerow for failing to keep General Short adequately informed of the collapsing diplomatic relationship with Tokyo, for not making the November 27 war warning clear enough, for not getting him Marshall's last-minute warning in time, and for failing to correct Short's alert for sabotage. That same year's Navy's Court of Inquiry criticized Chief of Naval Operations Harold Stark for inadequately warning Kimmel in a failure "to display the sound judgment expected," but essentially absolved everyone in Hawaii, concluding that "no offenses have been committed nor serious blame incurred on the part of any person or persons in the naval service."

Even so, the navy's court was astonished by the army's reaction to the war warning: "General Marshall had told the commanding general of the Hawaiian Department much earlier, with emphasis and clarity, that the function of the Army in Hawaii was to defend the fleet base. Despite this fact, when warned that Japan's future action was unpredictable but hostile action was possible at any moment and when his attention was called to the necessity for reconnaissance, General Short proceeded to institute an alert against sabotage only. This was done although there had not been one single act of sabotage on the islands up to that time; for that matter, there were no acts of sabotage thereafter. . . . General Short has stated that the silence and failure of the War Department to reply to his report of measures taken constituted reasonable grounds for his belief that his action was exactly what the War Department desired. He has pointed out that if the action taken by him was not consistent with the desires of the War Department it should have informed him of that fact."

Short testified that he didn't go to an ALL-OUT alert after receiving the war warning since it had specifically said not to alarm the local civilians. But his predecessor, Herron, had told Short that he had run an ALL-OUT during the war games of June 17, 1940, without the locals becoming concerned.

War Department Secretary Henry Stimson was particularly enraged by the general's explanations:

> When General Short was informed on November 27 that "Japanese action unpredictable" and that "hostile action possible at any moment," and that the policy directed "should not comma repeat not comma be construed as restricting you to a course of action that might

jeopardize your defense," we had a right to assume that he would competently perform this paramount duty entrusted to him. . . . The very purpose of a fortress such as Hawaii is to repel such an attack, and Short was the commander of that fortress. Furthermore, Short's statement in his message that "liaison" was being carried out with the Navy, coupled with the fact that our message of November 27 had specifically directed reconnaissance, naturally gave the impression that the various reconnaissance and other defensive measures in which the cooperation of the Army and the Navy is necessary, were under way and a proper alert was in effect. . . .

To cluster his airplanes in such groups and positions that in an emergency they could not take the air for several hours, and to keep his antiaircraft ammunition so stored that it could not be promptly and immediately available, and to use his best reconnaissance system, the radar, only for a very small fraction of the day and night, in my opinion betrayed a misconception of his real duty which was almost beyond belief. . . .

From some of the comments quoted in the public papers, one would get the impressions that the imminent threat of war in October and November 1941 was a deep secret, known only to the authorities in Washington who kept it mysteriously to themselves. Nothing could be further from the truth.

Perhaps the most damning evidence against Husband Kimmel and Walter Short is that, even after all the warnings from Washington and even after all their own staff memos across 1941 warning of the possible attacks, the levels of reconnaissance that they conducted were cavalier to the point of comedy. Short's army was supposed to conduct regular overflights of Oahu through a range of twenty miles. It only did so during drills and exercises, with pilot training limited to daylight hours on weekdays. Supplementing this, Kimmel's navy was supposed to conduct distant surveillance of from seven hundred to eight hundred miles. This was also only achieved during drills and maneuvers, never through a full arc of 360 degrees, and rarely to seven hundred miles.

Admiral Kimmel told the court of inquiry that this reaction to the war warning wasn't ineptitude: "The omission of this reconnaissance was not due to oversight or neglect. It was the result of a military decision, reached after much deliberation and consultation with experienced officers, and after weighing the information at hand and all the factors involved." His belief was that, by sending Halsey and his task force to Wake on November 28, and Newton to Midway and Brown to Johnston with their task forces on December 5, as well as ordering a squadron on December 2 and 3 to survey the territory between Midway and Wake, around 2 million square miles of ocean were patrolled, so the surveillance he was supposed to maintain was unnecessary.

The court did not accept this since "nothing was done . . . to detect an approaching hostile force coming from the north and northwest, recognized as the most dangerous sector. . . . Admiral Kimmel has suggested that under the Joint Coastal Frontier Defense Plan, Admiral Bloch was responsible for distant reconnaissance, and had the latter desired planes, he could have called upon the commander in chief of the Pacific Fleet. This suggestion, apart from being incompatible with Admiral Kimmel's stating he made the decision not to conduct distant reconnaissance, is not tenable. Admiral Bloch had no planes with which to conduct distant patrols and Admiral Kimmel knew it." In fact, Kimmel didn't even discuss the matter or share the war warning message with Defense Air Force commander Admiral Patrick Bellinger, who oversaw eighty-one patrol planes. Indeed, Bellinger wasn't informed of the many alerts from either War or Navy during October, November, and December until after December 7.

About all this, General Marshall told Congress, "I never could grasp what had happened between the period when so much was said [by officers in Hawaii] about air attack, the necessity for antiaircraft, the necessity for planes for reconnaissance, the necessity for attack planes for defense, and the other requirements which anticipated very definitely and affirmatively an air attack—I could never understand why suddenly it became a side issue."

Henry Stimson pointed out to Congress that the warning of November 27 specifically ordered reconnaissance, and said, "This is to my mind a very important part of the message, not only because of its obvious desirability but also because we had provided the Hawaiian Department with what I regarded as the most effective means of reconnaissance against air attack and one to which I had personally devoted a great deal of attention during the preceding months. I refer to the radar equipment with which the Hawaiian Department was then provided. This equipment permitted approaching planes to be seen at distances of approximately 100 miles, and to do so in darkness and storm as well as clear daylight. In the early part of 1941, I had taken up earnestly the matter of securing such radar equipment for aircraft protection. I knew, although it was not generally known, that radar had proved of the utmost importance to the British in the Battle of Britain, and I felt in the beginning of 1941 that we were not getting this into production and to the troops as quickly as we should, and put on all the pressure I could to speed up its acquisition. By the autumn of 1941, we had gotten some of this equipment out to Hawaii, and only a few days before this I had received a report of the tests which had been made of this equipment in Hawaii on November 19th, which indicated very satisfactory results in detecting approaching airplanes. I testified at considerable length with regard to this before the Army Pearl Harbor Board. When we specifically directed the commanding officer at Hawaii, who had been warned that war was likely at any moment, to make reconnaissance, I assumed that all means of reconnaissance available to both the Army and the Navy would be employed."

The navy court also found Kimmel's reaction to the warning that Japan was destroying its code machines lackadaisical: "In strange contrast with the view of the code burning intelligence taken by Admiral Kimmel, virtually all witnesses have agreed that this was the most significant information received between November 27 and December 6 with respect to the imminence of war. Indeed, the overwhelming weight of the testimony is to effect that orders to destroy codes mean from a military standpoint only one thing—war within a very few days. While orders to burn codes may not always mean war in the diplomatic sense, it very definitely meant war—and soon—in a military sense after the 'war warning' of November 27. Admiral Kimmel received this intelligence less than four days before the attack; it gave him an opportunity to correct his mistake in failing to institute distant reconnaissance and effect a state of readiness commensurate with the likelihood of hostilities after the November 27 war warning. Nothing was done—General Short was not even informed." The court concluded that Kimmel "knew that the only effective means of detecting a surprise raiding force in adequate time to combat it was by distant reconnaissance. He knew the Japanese reputation for deceit and treachery. He knew the greatest danger to the Fleet at Pearl Harbor was the possibility of an air raid. . . . He had been categorically warned of war."

Yet even with all their flaws fully detailed, the case can be made that Kimmel and Short took too much of the blame, that they were in fact scapegoated, especially by the court of public opinion. In parceling out blame for Pearl Harbor, Washington had plenty of fingers to point at itself. If Kimmel and Short deserved courts-martial for their actions in Hawaii, and Harold Stark deserved demotion for his in Washington, then MacArthur deserved similar treatment for his behavior in the Philippines. The warning cables sent to admirals and generals triggered by the Nazi invasion of France, the start of Washington's embargoes, the announcement of Tojo as prime minister, and the Hull Note, which were considered so vigorous from the War Department's perspective, were exceedingly vague when seen from the perspective of Oahu. Each said that something, somewhere, might happen, so be ready, and three of the four sent from Stark to Kimmel included a side note that said more or less that this warning probably didn't apply to Hawaii. When Short told Marshall's office that he was going to sabotage alert only, no one from Washington replied that more was called for under the circumstances; Marshall himself later testified, "That was my opportunity to intervene and I did not do it." Admiral Stark reminded Congress of the number of times in 1940 and 1941 he had appeared before it to ask for the American navy to be strengthened and was refused, adding US legislators to the legion of those responsible for Pearl Harbor.

From July 20 to October 20, 1944, ten of those legislators (six Democrats and four Republicans) impaneled the Joint Congressional Committee on the Investigation of the Pearl Harbor Attack. After testimony from 151 witnesses, the committee produced over 10 million words on 9,754 printed pages with an attendant 469 exhibits. Researchers discovered some basic facts explaining the success of the attack: the Japanese had superior torpedoes, fighter planes, flashlights, gunpowder, warhead explosives, and optics, with sonar that was four to five times better than America's, and her pilots had been seasoned over the skies of China. General Short defended himself by reading a 61-page statement, and Admiral Kimmel read one of 108 pages. Then at a private lunch, Kimmel revealed to the committee's assistant counsel, Edward Morgan, the essence of what had happened: "I never thought those little yellow sons of bitches could pull off such an attack, so far from Japan." Back in 1941, two weeks after December 7, Kimmel's Japanese counterpart, Isoroku Yamamoto, had exactly this same rationale for Operation Z's success: "That we could defeat the enemy at the outbreak of the war was because they were unguarded and also they made light of us. 'Danger comes soonest when it is despised' and 'don't despise a small enemy' are really important matters. I think they can be applied not only to wars but to routine matters."

Two pieces of evidence were of particular interest to the committee. When General Short and Admiral Kimmel learned about the bomb-plot cable sent to Yoshikawa during the postwar investigations, they were enraged at not having been informed. "With the dispatch of September 24, 1941, and those which followed," Kimmel said, "there was a significant and ominous change in the character of the information which the Japanese government sought and obtained. . . . It was no longer merely directed to ascertaining the general whereabouts of ships of the fleet. It was directed to the presence of particular ships of the fleet. . . . These Japanese instructions and reports pointed to an attack by Japan upon the ships in Pearl Harbor. . . . No one had a greater right than I to know that Japan had carved up Pearl Harbor into subareas and was seeking and receiving reports as to the precise berthings in that harbor of the ships of the fleet." Congress's interrogation of G-2, chief of the army's Military Intelligence Service, Brigadier General Sherman Miles, reflected his outcry:

[Chief Assistant Counsel Gerhard] Gesell: It is really, is it not, looking at it as one message alone, and, if you will, from hindsight, a plan for laying out what amounts to a bombing plan for Pearl Harbor?

[Army Intelligence G-2] General Miles: That is exactly what it looks like now, sir, now that we know Pearl Harbor was bombed.

Mr. Gesell: Would it be a fair statement to say that one of the functions and responsibilities of a properly organized and functioning military intelligence division would have been to single out this message, recognize its difference from the other messages, and attempt to evaluate its significance?

General Miles: Yes, sir, but we did not give it the significance at that time that it now has in the light of subsequent events.

Mr. Gesell: Do I gather from what you have just stated, General Miles, that prior to December seventh you personally at least had not reached the conclusion in your own mind that there was an immediate possibility of hostilities between the United States and Japan?

General Miles: Oh, no, sir; that is not so. The crisis that resulted in General Marshall's telegram of November 27 certainly indicated that the possibility of a war between the United States and Japan had very much increased. By the third of December, when we knew that they were burning their codes, one would have rated that possibility, now well within the realms of probability, now even higher, so that if you are asking me on December seventh I am quite sure in saying that I would have rated quite highly the probability of an involvement immediate, or certainly in the fairly near future, of a Japanese-American war.

General Miles then explained why this particular cable triggered no special notice from his department: "It should always be remembered that it was well-known to everyone in the intelligence departments of the two services that the Japanese were following as closely as they possibly could the movement of all of our warships. I remember on several occasions going to Admiral Kirk's or Admiral Wilkinson's secret room in the Navy Department and looking at his big map of the positions of the Japanese warships. Everybody was doing it."

The director of the Office of Naval Intelligence, Admiral Ted Wilkinson, testified, "The Japanese for many years had the reputation, and the facts bore out that reputation, of being meticulous seekers for every scrap of information, whether by photography or by written report or otherwise. We had recently, as reported to me, apprehended two and I think three Japanese naval officers on the West Coast making investigations of Seattle, Bremerton, Long Beach, and San Diego. In the reports that we had gotten from them, there had been indications of movements and locations of ships; in the papers that they had, there were instructions for them to find out the movements and locations of ships except in Hawaii and the Philippines, the inference being that these fellows that were planted in America, these naval officers, were not to be responsible for movements in Hawaii and the Philippines because there were agencies finding that information there." To confirm or deny these assertions, congressional investigators produced a study, "Japanese Messages Concerning Military Installations, Ship Movements, etc.," which included fourteen pages of cables on Hawaii, seventeen on the Panama Canal, forty-three on the Philippines, seventeen on Southeast Asia, and four on the American West Coast. CNO Stark: "There was literally a mass of material coming in. We knew the Japanese appetite was almost insatiable for detail in all respects."

Later in his testimony, General Miles would boomerang Congress's attempts at scapegoating the military and the Roosevelt Administration:

> Vice Chairman Cooper: General, I understood you to say that for years it had been understood by the Army—I assume that means, of course, the high-ranking officers of the Army—that hostilities with Japan would involve an attack on Hawaii, and that a knowledge of the Japanese people caused the anticipation of a surprise attack. That is substantially and in essence your statement on that, isn't it?
>
> General Miles: That the possibility if not the probability of an attack on Hawaii was inherent in a Japanese war. You gentlemen of the Congress appropriated millions of dollars for that fortress. Against whom were you building it?

Another contentious piece of evidence was Tokyo's November 19 message about what its radio stations would broadcast in case of a diplomatic breakdown, which became known as "east wind, rain," as that was the code for trouble with the United States. OP-20-G's Captain Laurance Safford insisted that one of his radio operators intercepted a confirmation of "the winds message" on December 4:

"We knew that the Japanese ambassador in London had destroyed his secret codes three days previously: this was the only way that Tokyo could get news to him secretly. Reception or nonreception at other points was irrelevant. Tokyo knew full well, before the winds message was sent, that it probably would not be received in Washington or in Rio. That was immaterial—the winds message was intended for London. . . . I immediately sent the original of the winds message up to the director of naval communications [Rear Admiral Noyes] by one of the officers serving under me and told him to deliver this paper to Admiral Noyes in person, to track him down and not take no for an answer, and, if he could not find him in a reasonable time, to let me know."

But that intercept has never been found, and the Japanese, interrogated after the war, insisted that no such message was ever sent. The point is in fact moot. "East wind, rain" only meant "Japan-US relations in danger," which American leaders already knew.

Not only did no piece of MAGIC point directly to an attack on Pearl Harbor, since Operation Z's secrecy was so well maintained, but a great deal of MAGIC's trouble in raising alarm was that, by the closing months of 1941, when the worst was expected at any moment and when Japan's consular cable traffic was a deluge, the whole of Washington's decoding team was thirty-six analysts and six Japanese translators. "The agency was simply too small and too exhausted," one cryptanalyst explained. "Our eyes were red and glazed; exhaustion and dream consciousness had overcome us months before the event. . . . Had these [critics] been among us and seen how buried we were in stacks of messages through the Purple machine, which had . . . priority, they would not wonder that we failed to process and translate a few messages."

The Joint Congressional Committee on the Investigation of the Pearl Harbor Attack concluded on July 16, 1946, that Kimmel and Short were not guilty of derelictions of duty, but had committed errors of judgment, and that the War Plans Division had not warned either commander to the fullest extent necessary. The committee also found no evidence that Roosevelt, Hull, Stimson, Marshall, Stark, or Knox "tricked, provoked, incited, cajoled, or coerced Japan into attacking this Nation." Two Republicans on the committee issued a "Minority Report" that judged Roosevelt "responsible for the failure to enforce continuous, efficient, and appropriate cooperation among the Secretary of War, the Secretary of the Navy, the Chief of Staff [General Marshall], and the Chief of Naval Operations [Admiral Stark] in evaluating information and dispatching clear and positive orders to the Hawaiian commanders as events indicated the growing imminence of war." When it came to foreknowledge of the attack, the committee decided:

> Virtually everyone in Washington was surprised Japan struck Pearl Harbor at the time she did. Among the reasons for this conclusion was the apparent Japanese purpose to move toward the south—the Philippines, Thailand, the Kra Peninsula; and the feeling that Hawaii was a near-impregnable fortress that Japan would not incur the dangers of attacking. The latter consideration necessarily contemplated that Hawaii was alert and that the enemy would be met with the full weight of Army and Navy power provided for defense.
>
> It is apparent, however, that an attack on the fleet by Japan at some time was regarded as a distinct possibility. The warning messages sent the Hawaiian commanders contained orders requiring defensive measures against this possibility. Admiral [Richmond Kelly] Turner,

Director of War Plans in the Navy Department, is the only officer in Washington in the higher echelons who indicated a strong belief that Hawaii would be attacked—he testified that he regarded such an attack as a "50-50 chance." Asked if he had gained this impression around December 1 as a result of the Japanese ship-location reports, he testified: "No. That had been the opinion all along, expressed by the Navy Department, expressed in Hawaii, expressed by the War Department, expressed by everybody else, that there was a strong possibility that there would be an attack, a raid, that is, against Hawaii. That was merely following along the line the Navy officers and Army officers had been thinking about for twenty-five years or more. There was no change."

When asked why, around November 27, if the Navy felt in this way about the chances of an air raid on the fleet in Pearl Harbor, some further message was not sent suggesting this possibility, Admiral Turner stated: "That had been in correspondence right along. The dispatch of November twenty-seventh fully covers it, in my opinion. I think on the fifth, the afternoon of the fifth of December, after canvassing the situation with officers in my division, I went into Admiral Ingersoll's office and we talked for an hour as to what more the Navy Department could do to warn the forces in the field, the fleets, what ought to be done, should we send any more dispatches, or what. We came, both, to the conclusion that everything had been done covering the entire situation that ought to be done, and we then proceeded into Admiral Stark's office, discussed the same question with him for fifteen minutes, and it was the unanimous decision that the orders that we had sent out for Admiral Kimmel to take a defensive deployment there were sufficient."

In this connection Captain [Arthur] McCollum said: "I was not surprised at the Japanese attack, sir. I was astonished at the success attained by that attack, sir. I do not mean by that statement to imply that I had any knowledge that the Japanese were going to attack Pearl Harbor, and I wish to state categorically that there was no bit of intelligence that I had at my disposal that definitely to my mind indicated that the Japanese would attack Pearl Harbor, but I had for many years felt that in the event of an outbreak of hostilities between the United States and Japan that the Japanese would make a very definite attempt to strike the fleet at or near the commencement time of those hostilities. . . . There was historical precedent if the Japanese wished to start a war with us. Their war with China in 1895 was started that way; their war with Russia in 1907 was started that way; their war against Germany in Tsingtao in 1914 was started in that way."

The committee took special notice of the missed communications between Washington and Oahu, especially the point that, while everyone at Navy in DC apparently knew that Tokyo's cables to its consulates to destroy their codebooks meant war was imminent, Kimmel and his intelligence officer, Captain Edwin Layton, did not comprehend this. Congress recommended, "Supervisory officials cannot safely take anything for granted in the alerting of subordinates," and went on to describe this key failure: "Admiral Kimmel was ordered to execute an appropriate defensive deployment. Everyone in Washington in testifying before the committee seems reasonably certain as to just what this meant; Admiral Kimmel did not feel that it required his doing anything greatly beyond what he had already done, even though he knew that Washington knew what he had previously done. In using the words 'this dispatch is to be considered a war warning' everyone in Washington felt the commander in chief would be sharply, incisively, and emphatically warned of war; Admiral Kimmel said he had construed all the messages he had received previously as war warnings. Everyone in Washington felt that upon advising Hawaii the Japanese were destroying their codes it would be understood as meaning 'war in any man's language'; Admiral Kimmel said that he did not consider this intelligence of any vital importance when he received it."

Though this section of the public record paints Kimmel as somewhat dim, Washington did not escape criticism: "The committee feels that the practice, indulged by the Navy, of sending to several commanders an identical dispatch for action, even though the addressees may be located in decidedly different situations, is distinctly dangerous. In the preparation of messages to outposts the dispatch to a particular officer should be applicable to his peculiar situation. . . . It is believed that brevity of messages was carried to the point of being a fetish rather than a virtue. . . . The Magic intelligence was preeminently important and the necessity for keeping it confidential cannot be overemphasized. However, so closely held and top secret was this intelligence that it appears the fact the Japanese codes had been broken was regarded as of more importance than the information obtained from decoded traffic. The result of this rather specious premise was to leave large numbers of policy-making and enforcement officials in Washington completely oblivious of the most pertinent information concerning Japan."

Kimmel and Short's work together, meanwhile, was judged "the epitome of worthy plans and purposes which were never implemented. . . . They played golf together, they dined together—but they did not get together on official business . . . to effect coordination and integration of their efforts. . . . The people are entitled to expect greater vigilance and alertness from their Army and Navy—whether in war or in peace." The committee also concluded that both Kimmel and Layton had difficulty in admitting their mistakes.

Federal investigations into Pearl Harbor were not done. On June 13, 1944, a Joint Resolution of Congress instructed the secretaries of war and navy to investigate Pearl Harbor and initiate courts-martial. On August 29, 1945, Navy Secretary James Forrestal revealed the findings of Admiral Kent Hewitt's further inquiries. Hewitt determined that Kimmel and Stark "particularly during the period 27 November to 7 December, 1941, failed to demonstrate the superior judgment necessary to exercising command commensurate with their rank and assigned duties." After spending two years interviewing over one hundred servicemen and civilians for an eight-hundred-page report to Henry Stimson, Henry Christian Clausen of the Judge Advocate General's Department, a civilian Washington lawyer who'd made his bones with the Truman Commission's investigation into military fraud, decided that the United States had suffered an intelligence failure. Using the example of Lieutenant Colonel Kendall Fielder, Clausen found that the chief of army intelligence for Hawaii had no training in the field, was not cleared for top-secret information, and was appreciated by Walter Short more for his skills at golfing and magic shows than for anything he accomplished as an officer. Clausen learned that whenever General Short was busy and needed someone to escort his wife to her many social events, the man chosen was a good dancer—Kendall Fielder. "There was no relevant intelligence communications between Layton and Fielder, or between Kimmel and Short," Clausen determined. "The Pacific Fleet at Pearl Harbor had wanted to have everything its own way. It wanted to control intelligence information, and it did not share the information with Short's command, yet it wanted the Army to protect the fleet at Pearl Harbor. . . . All the

testimony . . . points to the conclusion that Kimmel was merely following the Naval practice of hoarding secret intelligence and using it for
his own purposes. This does not excuse Kimmel for what he did. But,
for the first time, it explains why he did it."

Clausen's other findings led to the Joint Congressional Committee's recommendation "that immediate action be taken to assure that
unity of command is imposed at all joint military and naval outputs."
Though this would lead to the merging of the navy and army under
the Department of Defense, no actual unity of command would occur
until 1991's Operation Desert Storm, which, as of this writing, remains
one of the Pentagon's more significant post–World War II victories.

Pearl Harbor's aftermath, which continues to this day, often reads like
a history of finger-pointing, beginning with Congress's joint committee, which spent little effort at attempting to understand what the Japanese did to succeed compared to the great effort it spent investigating
which American deserved blame. Republicans blamed Democrats,
Hawaii blamed Washington, admirals blamed other admirals, the navy
blamed the army, and intelligence blamed command.

Rear Admiral Robert "Fuzzy" Theobald, who had commanded
destroyers in December 1941 and who had offered to act as counsel for
Husband Kimmel during the Roberts Commission investigation, published *The Final Secret of Pearl Harbor* in 1954. By going through the
vast amount of evidence to highlight such incriminating documents as
the bomb-plot message and the winds code, Theobald concluded that
Washington deliberately withheld MAGIC intelligence from Kimmel
and Short, that the only reason to do so was to ensure Japanese success,
and that the only reason why anyone in Washington would want the
Japanese to succeed would be to drag America into the fight against
Hitler. After Theobald published his book in 1954, Rear Admiral Kimmel released his memoirs, which included the charge that Roosevelt,
Stimson, Marshall, and Knox had information showing an attack on
Hawaii was imminent that they did not share with him, and for which
"they must answer on the day of judgment like any other criminal."

Theobald and Kimmel began a popular theory that continues to
this day, the advance-knowledge or back-door-to-war theory, which
holds that President Roosevelt, his most senior cabinet members, and
various senior army and navy officials secretly colluded to instigate the
attack on Pearl Harbor. Japanese historian Takeo Iguchi has a clear

idea of how this thinking began: "The almost incredible success of the Japanese attack on Pearl Harbor also opened the eyes of the American people to the unpreparedness of the US military, and the conspiracy theory gained currency as a salve for the nation's wounded psyche."

In 1962, Roberta Wohlstetter's *Pearl Harbor: Warning and Decision* argued, "The United States was not caught napping. . . . We just expected wrong [in] a failure of strategic analysis [and] a failure to anticipate effectively." Due to her profound influence, the CIA and its cousins in military intelligence came to believe that the enduring lesson of December 7 was in separating "signals" from "noise." In this needle-in-the-haystack perspective, inspired again by the bomb-plot and winds messages, the Americans had plenty of information the attack was coming, but couldn't piece together these clues into a meaningful warning because they were buried by so much other data. But in fact no signal said specifically that Japan was going to attack Hawaii, and when a very few in command raised that possibility, they were dismissed.

On March 9, 1949, Walter Short died in Dallas, Texas, where he worked for Ford Motor. On May 14, 1968, Husband Kimmel died of a heart attack at the age of eighty-six. Two years before, he said, "They made me the scapegoat. They wanted to get the United States into the war. That was President Roosevelt and General George Marshall and others in the Washington high command. FDR was the architect of the whole business. He gave orders—I can't prove this directly—that no word about Japanese fleet movements was to be sent to Pearl Harbor, except by Marshall, and then he told Marshall not to send anything."

Japanese Imperial Navy commander Masataka Chihaya summed up the key weakness of the conspiracy theory: "Even if one admits . . . that President Roosevelt wanted to have Japan strike first, there would have been no need to have all the major ships of the US Fleet sit idly in the harbor to be mercilessly destroyed and many killed." A second major point comes from even a cursory knowledge of FDR: if he were involved in any sinister conspiracy, it wouldn't be anything detrimental to his beloved navy. A third is that Nazi submarines were at that time causing so much trouble with American merchant shipping in the Atlantic that FDR hardly needed to instigate Pearl Harbor to trigger American war fever; it would have arrived at any time on its own. And a fourth is that during the "day of infamy" speech Roosevelt asked

Congress to declare war only against Japan and did not include Germany or Italy.

George Marshall, meanwhile, insisted he had proof there that there was no back door to war since he couldn't even get enough money for troops to defend Alaska: "I remember in 1940, when [President Roosevelt] was trying to keep within a fifty-billion-dollar debt limit and was cutting out some of the defense measures I proposed. In 1940, before France fell, I advocated eleven million dollars for defense housing in Alaska. I couldn't even get this. Congress cut it out and President Roosevelt concurred. You don't remember what it was like then. The army had little or nothing. When I wanted that little eleven-million-dollar appropriation, newspapers and columnists came out against me. They said I was trying to drag this country into war."

As part of a defense appropriations bill for the year 2000, Congress requested that the president clear the names of Admiral Husband Kimmel and General Walter Short of responsibility for failing to defend Pearl Harbor since the two officers "were not provided necessary and critical intelligence that would have alerted them to prepare for the attack." Sponsored by Delaware senators Joe Biden and William Roth, the measure was one more effort by Kimmel's son, Edward, to clear his father's name, even though, as late as 1995, a Pentagon investigation (undertaken primarily through Edward Kimmel's efforts) had refused to do so, concluding: "The intelligence available to Admiral Kimmel and General Short was sufficient to justify a higher level of vigilance than they had chosen to maintain."

Kimmel and Short were indeed treated unfairly as scapegoats by the press and public opinion, but were they really mistreated by the Roosevelt administration? Officially, they were never charged with dereliction of duty, errors of judgment, or any other malfeasance; they were merely relieved of command and categorized as retired. Considering the American emotional reaction to Pearl Harbor, could either have served as a commander during World War II?

The need to assign blame for every great American tragedy, from Pearl Harbor to the Kennedy assassination to 9/11, is now a subject of social studies called conspiracism, first analyzed by historian Richard Hofstadter in a 1964 essay, "The Paranoid Style in American Politics," which includes, "Any historian of warfare knows it is in good part a comedy of errors and a museum of incompetence; but if for every error and every act of incompetence one can substitute an act of treason, many points of fascinating interpretation are open to the paranoid imagination."

One student of conspiracism, Fred Kaplan, said, "If horrible events can be traced to a cabal of evildoers who control the world from behind a vast curtain, that's, in one sense, less scary than the idea that some horrible things happen at random or as a result of a lone nebbish, a nobody. The existence of a secret cabal means that there's some sort of order in the world; a catastrophic fluke suggests there's a vast crevice of chaos, the essence of dread." Writer Robert McKee has noticed that, since conspiracism is now so widespread, "instead of the British mystery where the investigator narrows the focus to six possible suspects, in America a murder is committed, we start to investigate, and it turns out to encompass all of society." Harry Truman went so far as to pin the fault for Pearl Harbor on the United States of America as a whole: "The country was not ready for preparedness. . . . I think the country is as much to blame as any individual in this final situation that developed in Pearl Harbor."

With the passing of another half century, will the only thing the general public knows about 9/11 be conspiracy, and scapegoats? Do these kinds of national tragedies inflict a type of post-traumatic stress disorder on American leaders and thinkers, with endless investigations by the government, and accusations of conspiracy by civilians, no matter what information is revealed or judgments rendered? Will we ever accept the truth? If we accept it, will we be healed? Since the truth we have is clearly no balm.

THE MEDAL OF HONOR

Bennion, Mervyn Sharp.
Rank and organization: Captain, US Navy.
Born: 5 May 1887, Vernon, UT.
Citation: For conspicuous devotion to duty, extraordinary courage, and complete disregard of his own life, above and beyond the call of duty, during the attack on the Fleet in Pearl Harbor by Japanese forces on 7 December 1941. As Commanding Officer of the USS *West Virginia*, after being mortally wounded, Captain Bennion evidenced apparent concern only in fighting and saving his ship and strongly protested against being carried from the bridge.

Finn, John William.
Rank and organization: Lieutenant, US Navy.
Born: 23 July 1909, Los Angeles, CA.
Citation: For extraordinary heroism, distinguished service, and devotion above and beyond the call of duty. During the first attack by Japanese airplanes on the Naval Air Station, Kaneohe Bay, on 7 December 1941, Lieutenant Finn promptly secured and manned a .50-caliber machine gun mounted on an instruction stand in a completely exposed section of the parking ramp, which was under heavy enemy machine gun strafing fire. Although painfully wounded many times, he continued to man this gun and to return the enemy's fire vigorously and with telling effect throughout the enemy strafing and bombing attacks and with complete disregard for his own personal safety. It was only by specific orders that he was persuaded to leave his post to seek medical attention. Following first aid treatment, although obviously suffering much pain and moving with great difficulty, he returned to the squadron area and actively supervised the rearming of returning planes. His extraordinary heroism and conduct in this action were in keeping with the highest traditions of the US Naval Service.

Flaherty, Francis C.
Rank and organization: Ensign, US Naval Reserve.
Born: 15 March 1919, Charlotte, MI.
Citation: For conspicuous devotion to duty and extraordinary courage and complete disregard of his own life, above and beyond the call of duty, during the attack on the Fleet in Pearl Harbor by Japanese forces on 7 December 1941. When it was seen that the USS *Oklahoma* was going to capsize and the order was given to abandon ship, Ensign Flaherty remained in a turret, holding a flashlight so the remainder of the turret crew could see to escape, thereby sacrificing his own life.

Fuqua, Samuel Glenn.
Rank and organization: Lieutenant Commander (LCDR), US Navy, USS *Arizona*.
Born: 15 October 1899, Laddonia, MO.
Citation: For distinguished conduct in action, outstanding heroism, and utter disregard of his own safety above and beyond the call of duty during the attack on the Fleet in Pearl Harbor, by Japanese forces on 7 December 1941. Upon the commencement of the attack, LCDR Fuqua rushed to the quarterdeck of the USS *Arizona* to which he was attached where he was stunned and knocked down by the explosion of a large bomb which hit the quarterdeck, penetrated several decks, and started a severe fire. Upon regaining consciousness, he began to direct the fighting of the fire and the rescue of wounded and injured personnel. Almost immediately there was a tremendous explosion forward, which made the ship appear to rise out of the water, shudder, and settle down by the bow rapidly. The whole forward part of the ship was enveloped in flames which were spreading rapidly, and wounded and burned men were pouring out of the ship to the quarterdeck. Despite these conditions, his harrowing experience, and severe enemy bombing and strafing, at the time, LCDR Fuqua continued to direct the fighting of fires to check them while the wounded and burned could be taken from the ship and supervised the rescue of these men in such an amazingly calm and cool manner and with such excellent judgment that it inspired everyone who saw him and undoubtedly resulted in the saving of many lives. After realizing the ship could not be saved and that he was the senior surviving officer aboard, he directed it to be abandoned but continued to remain on the quarterdeck and directed abandoning ship and rescue of person-

nel until satisfied that all personnel that could be had been saved, after which he left his ship with the last boatload. The conduct of LCDR Fuqua was not only in keeping with the highest traditions of the US Naval Service but characterizes him as an outstanding leader of men.

Hill, Edwin Joseph.
Rank and organization: Chief Boatswain, US Navy.
Born: 4 October 1894, Philadelphia, PA.
Citation: For distinguished conduct in the line of his profession, extraordinary courage, and disregard of his own safety during the attack on the Fleet in Pearl Harbor by Japanese forces on 7 December 1941. During the height of the strafing and bombing, Chief Boatswain Hill led his men of the line handling details of the USS *Nevada* to the quays, cast off the lines, and swam back to his ship. Later, while on the forecastle, attempting to let go the anchors, he was blown overboard and killed by the explosion of several bombs.

Jones, Herbert Charpoit.
Rank and organization: Ensign, US Naval Reserve.
Born: 21 January 1918, Los Angeles, CA.
Citation: For conspicuous devotion to duty, extraordinary courage, and complete disregard of his own life, above and beyond the call of duty, during the attack on the Fleet in Pearl Harbor by Japanese forces on 7 December 1941. Ensign Jones organized and led a party, which was supplying ammunition to the antiaircraft battery of the USS *California*, after the mechanical hoists were put out of action when he was fatally wounded by a bomb explosion. When two men attempted to take him from the area which was on fire, he refused to let them do so, saying in words to the effect, "Leave me alone! I am done for. Get out of here before the magazines go off."

Kidd, Isaac Campbell.
Rank and organization: Rear Admiral, US Navy.
Born: 26 March 1884, Cleveland, OH.
Citation: For conspicuous devotion to duty, extraordinary courage, and complete disregard of his own life, during the attack on the Fleet in Pearl Harbor by Japanese forces on 7 December 1941. Rear Admiral Kidd immediately went to the bridge and, as Commander, Battleship Division One, courageously discharged his duties as

Senior Officer Present Afloat until the USS *Arizona*, his flagship, blew up from magazine explosions and a direct bomb hit on the bridge which resulted in the loss of his life.

Pharris, Jackson Charles.
Rank and organization: Lieutenant, US Navy, USS *California*.
Born: 26 June 1912, Columbus, GA.
Citation: For conspicuous gallantry and intrepidity at the risk of his life above and beyond the call of duty while attached to the USS *California* during the surprise enemy Japanese aerial attack on Pearl Harbor, territory of Hawaii, 7 December 1941. In charge of the ordnance repair party on the third deck when the first Japanese torpedo struck almost directly under his station, Lieutenant (then Gunner) Pharris was stunned and severely injured by the concussion that hurled him to the overhead and back to the deck. Quickly recovering, he acted on his own initiative to set up a hand-supply ammunition train for the antiaircraft guns. With water and oil rushing in where the port bulkhead had been torn up from the deck, with many of the remaining crewmembers overcome by oil fumes, and the ship without power and listing heavily to port as a result of a second torpedo hit, Lieutenant Pharris ordered the shipfitters to counterflood. Twice rendered unconscious by the nauseous fumes and handicapped by his painful injuries, he persisted in his desperate efforts to speed up the supply of ammunition and at the same time repeatedly risked his life to enter flooding compartments and drag to safety unconscious shipmates who were gradually being submerged in oil. By his inspiring leadership, his valiant efforts, and his extreme loyalty to his ship and its crew, he saved many of his shipmates from death and was largely responsible for keeping the *California* in action during the attack. His heroic conduct throughout this first eventful engagement of World War II reflects the highest credit upon Lieutenant Pharris and enhances the finest traditions of the US Naval Service.

Reeves, Thomas James.
Rank and organization: Radio Electrician (Warrant Officer), US Navy.
Born: 9 December 1895, Thomaston, CT.
Citation: For distinguished conduct in the line of his profession, extraordinary courage, and disregard of his own safety during the attack on the Fleet in Pearl Harbor by Japanese forces on 7 Decem-

ber 1941. After the mechanized ammunition hoists were put out of action on the USS *California*, Reeves, on his own initiative, in a burning passageway, assisted in the maintenance of an ammunition supply by hand to the antiaircraft guns until he was overcome by smoke and fire, which resulted in his death.

Ross, Donald Kirby.
Rank and organization: Machinist, US Navy, USS *Nevada*.
Born: 8 December 1910, Beverly, KS.
Citation: For distinguished conduct in the line of his profession, extraordinary courage, and disregard of his own life during the attack on the Fleet in Pearl Harbor, territory of Hawaii, by Japanese forces on 7 December 1941. When his station in the forward dynamo room of the USS *Nevada* became almost untenable due to smoke, steam, and heat, Machinist Ross forced his men to leave that station and performed all the duties himself until blinded and unconscious. Upon being rescued and resuscitated, he returned and secured the forward dynamo room and proceeded to the after dynamo room where he was later again rendered unconscious by exhaustion. Again recovering consciousness he returned to his station where he remained until directed to abandon it.

Scott, Robert R.
Rank and organization: Machinist's Mate 1st Class, US Navy.
Born: 13 July 1915, Massillon, OH.
Citation: For conspicuous devotion to duty, extraordinary courage, and complete disregard of his own life, above and beyond the call of duty, during the attack on the Fleet in Pearl Harbor by Japanese forces on 7 December 1941. The compartment in the USS *California* in which the air compressor, to which Scott was assigned as his battle station, was flooded as the result of a torpedo hit. The remainder of the personnel evacuated that compartment but Scott refused to leave, saying words to the effect, "This is my station and I will stay and give them air as long as the guns are going."

Tomich, Peter.
Rank and organization: Chief Watertender, US Navy.
Born: 3 June 1893, Prolog, Austria.
Citation: For distinguished conduct in the line of his profession,

extraordinary courage, and disregard of his own safety during the attack on the Fleet in Pearl Harbor by the Japanese forces on 7 December 1941. Although realizing that the ship was capsizing as a result of enemy bombing and torpedoing, Tomich remained at his post in the engineering plant of the USS *Utah* until he saw that all boilers were secured and all fire room personnel had left their stations, and by so doing lost his own life.

Van Valkenburgh, Franklin.
Rank and organization: Captain, US Navy.
Born: 5 April 1888, Minneapolis, MN.
Citation: For conspicuous devotion to duty, extraordinary courage, and complete disregard of his own life during the attack on the Fleet in Pearl Harbor by Japanese forces on 7 December 1941. As commanding officer of the USS *Arizona*, Captain Van Valkenburgh gallantly fought his ship until the USS *Arizona* blew up from magazine explosions and a direct bomb hit on the bridge that resulted in the loss of his life.

Ward, James Richard.
Rank and organization: Seaman 1st Class, US Navy.
Born: 10 September 1921, Springfield, OH.
Citation: For conspicuous devotion to duty, extraordinary courage, and complete disregard of his life, above and beyond the call of duty, during the attack on the Fleet in Pearl Harbor by Japanese forces on 7 December 1941. When it was seen that the USS *Oklahoma* was going to capsize and the order was given to abandon ship, Ward remained in a turret holding a flashlight so the remainder of the turret crew could see to escape, thereby sacrificing his own life.

Young, Cassin.
Rank and organization: Commander, US Navy.
Born: 6 March 1894, Washington, DC.
Citation: For distinguished conduct in action, outstanding heroism, and utter disregard of his own safety, above and beyond the call of duty, as commanding officer of the USS *Vestal*, during the attack on the Fleet in Pearl Harbor, territory of Hawaii, by enemy Japanese forces on 7 December 1941. Commander Young proceeded to the bridge and later took personal command of the three-inch

antiaircraft gun. When blown overboard by the blast of the forward magazine explosion of the USS *Arizona*, to which the USS *Vestal* was moored, he swam back to his ship. The entire forward part of the USS *Arizona* was a blazing inferno with oil afire on the water between the two ships; as a result of several bomb hits, the USS *Vestal* was afire in several places, was settling, and taking on a list. Despite severe enemy bombing and strafing at the time and his shocking experience of having been blown overboard, Commander Young, with extreme coolness and calmness, moved his ship to an anchorage distant from the USS *Arizona* and subsequently beached the USS *Vestal* upon determining that such action was required to save his ship.

ACKNOWLEDGMENTS

I'd like to thank Rick Kot at Viking for germination and Colin Harrison at Scribner for cultivation. Both are two of the best editors in the business, and over the course of this book's half decade, I learned that Colin can heroically pull authors out of the trough of despair, for which I'm especially grateful.

Colin's right hand is the terrifically professional Sarah Goldberg; my hardworking copy editor is Steve Boldt; my production editor, Dan Cuddy; and production manager, Olga Leonardo. Overseen by art director Jaya Miceli, the book's eye-catching cover is by Jonathan Bush, and its handsome interior design is by Erich Hobbing. I so appreciate all of your hard work and have such great feeling for the remarkable Scribner team: Jessica Yu in publicity, Kara Watson in marketing, publisher Nan Graham, and president Susan Moldow. It is an honor to be published by you.

My titan of an agent is Stuart Krichevsky, and his fantastic team includes David Gore and Ross Harris. Mary K. Elkins creates my website, and Johanna Ramos-Boyer was my incredible publicist.

Books such as this are made through research. Thanks so much to the great aid of Andrew Scott Lewis and Christie Thompson in New York; Dylan Tokar and Normal Gleason in Washington; Dorinda Nicholson, Ryan Troxel, Andrew Teigler, and Olav Holst in Hawaii; and Miko Yamanouchi, Laura Hagler, Kuniko Kaio, Kimiko Nakatsuka, Ayaka Kuroiwa, and Maho Kawachi in Japan.

They are also made in archives, and these librarians and archivists were extraordinary: Teri Sierra, Lewis Wyman, and Suzanne Legault at the Library of Congress, Washington; Adam Berenbak, Kate Mollan, Rod Ross, and Juliet Arai at the Center for Legislative Archives, Washington; Yukako Tatsumi and Amy Wasserstrom, the Gordon Prange

Collection, College Park, Maryland; Kate Flaherty, Still Picture Division, National Archives and Records Administration, College Park, Maryland; Raymond Teichman and Robert Parks, the Franklin D. Roosevelt Library, Hyde Park, New York; Yvonne Kinkaid, US Office of Air Force History, Bolling Air Force Base, Washington; and Lynn Gamma, Archivist of the Air Force, Joseph D. Caver, and Essie Roberts, Air Force Historical Research Agency, Maxwell Air Force Base, Alabama.

NOTES

Abbreviations

AFHRA	Air Force Historical Research Agency, Maxwell Air Force Base, Alabama.
FDR papers	Franklin Delano Roosevelt Library, Hyde Park, New York.
Grew papers	Joseph Grew Papers, Harvard University, Cambridge, Massachusetts.
Hara	*Senshi sōsho*, the World War II History Collection of the National Institute for Defense Studies' Military Archives in Tokyo, also available as Shiro Hara, *Senshi sōsho* [The history of war], 102 vols. (Tokyo: Asagumo Shinbunsha, 1966–80).
Hoover Institution	Hoover Institution, Stanford University (papers of Short, Hornbeck, America First, etc.).
Hull papers	Cordell Hull Papers, 1908–56, and Memoranda of Conversations, 1933–44, Library of Congress Manuscript Division, Washington, DC.
NA	National Archives, College Park, Maryland.
PHA	Congress of the United States, "Hearings before the Joint Committee on the Investigation of the Pearl Harbor Attack," Seventy-Ninth Congress, 1946, Center for Legislative Archives.
Prange papers	Gordon W. Prange Papers, Hornbake Library, University of Maryland.
State	US Department of State, *Peace and War: United States Foreign Policy, 1931–1941*, National Archives, Maryland.
Stimson diary	Diaries of Henry Lewis Stimson, Yale University Library, New Haven, Connecticut.

Preface: Dreadnoughts and Holystones

1 "The cleanest bodies," "SAILORS AND DOGS": Raymer.
1 "I was just overwhelmed": Jasper et al.
2 "people could walk underneath it": Ibid.
2 "The [float] plane sat on top": Ibid.
2 "It was a thrill": Ibid.

3   "A man's name": Ibid.
3   "biggest fighting ship, built or building": "Lay Keel of Navy's New Dread-nought," *New York Times*, March 17, 1914.
4   "I am making a strange wish": Leckie.
4   "was in high spirits, for he loved the Navy": J. Richardson.
4   "should keep me in touch personally": Fromkin.
5   "I have always disliked him": Ibid.
5   "We are going to make a country": Perkins.
7   "Well, Mother," "I think I know what all you men want for Christmas": Jasper et al.
9   "bitterer than death to me": Michael Tighe, "Hawaii Marks Annexation," *Eugene Register-Guard*, August 9, 1996.
9   "An armada of 160 ships": Hanson W. Baldwin, "160 Ships Berthed at Pearl Harbor," *New York Times*, May 27, 1935.
10   "timid and ineffective": Prange et al., *At Dawn We Slept*.
10   "My objections for remaining there were": PHA.
10   "You are there because of the deterrent effect": McWilliams.
11   "Immediate alert. Complete defensive organization": Ibid.
11   "On October 7, I talked with Stark, Nimitz, Knox": Richardson testimony, PHA.
11   "Now, someone suggested that the government was trying to bluff": Hull testimony, PHA.
12   "The President asked me to have luncheon with him on October 8": PHA.
12   "Conversely, we're within striking distance": Ian W. Toll, "A Reluctant Enemy," *New York Times*, December 6, 2011.
13   "In early January, a dispatch came in ordering Richardson to be relieved": Vice Admiral George C. Dyer, "My God, They Can't Do That to Me," in Stillwell.
13   "After taking over command of Patrol Wing Two": Prange et al., *At Dawn We Slept*.
15   "Hawaii is on a far better basis": Ibid.
15   "Upon my meeting Short when he arrived," "Following my talks with General Short": Clausen report, PHA; Clausen and Lee.
15   "Cables from the Navy Department might have declared": Clarke.
16   "During the spring and summer of 1941 we saw a death ship," "Long about one o'clock": Jasper et al.
16   "We'd have a few beers at the Officers' Club": Brinkley.
17   "Nobody talked about the possibility of war": Verklan.
17   "It was actually my first time to have any distance": Brinkley.

Chapter 1: Conceiving the Inconceivable

23   "Japanese troops defeat Chinese at P'yongyang": Ienaga.
24   "In response to the warning": Koenig.
25   "The steel plates and superstructure": Ibid.
26   "Defeat is a common fate": Ibid.
26   "a legend that was to haunt Japan's leaders": For more of Regan's theory, see *The Guinness Book of Decisive Battles*.

27 "As far as I am concerned, war with America," "Ever since the ten:six ratio was imposed": Asada.

27 "Throughout the history of Japanese naval aviation": General Minoru Genda, "Evolution of Aircraft Carrier Tactics of the Imperial Japanese Navy," in Stillwell.

29 "In all games Yamamoto loved to take chances": Prange papers.

31 "incompetency, criminal negligence and almost treasonable," "with the advent of aircraft, the battleship has become window dressing": Cited in Smithsonian National Air and Space Museum's *General William "Billy" Mitchell and the Sinking of the* Ostfriesland*: A Consideration.*

31 "Anyone who has seen the auto factories in Detroit": Toll, "A Reluctant Enemy."

31 "Should hostilities break out between Japan and the United States," "on heaven's behalf": Prange papers.

32 "In case the enemy's main fleet is berthed": Costello.

32 "The general nature of the exercise was": Stillwell.

32 "War with Japan will be precipitated": PHA; Lord.

33 "In the 1920s and 30s": Batty.

34 "We planned exercises for these men": Cook and Cook.

35 "This situation reminds me strongly of the efforts of," "That we do not and never will recognize title": State.

37 "The national essence of Japan": Toland, *Rising Sun.*

39 "the four races of Japan," "Seven hundred million brethren": Ienaga.

40 "We have large emotional interest in China," Kennedy, *Freedom from Fear.*

41 "It seems clear to me": Northridge.

41 "Tell me of one case in history," "The danger of war is by far the greatest," "To get on with Japan": Iguchi.

42 "at a lower order of the human evolution": Batty.

42 "Our candid ideas at the time were that": Dower, *War without Mercy.*

42 "was very much like chasing a vagrant beam": Larrabee.

43 "If Cordell says, 'Oh, Chwist,' " "as crooked as a bundle of fishhooks": Perkins.

44 "a formally recorded expression": State.

45 "The Japanese would take any men": Chang.

45 "One by one the prisoners fell down": Yin and Young.

46 "Few know that soldiers impaled babies": Pitman.

47 "We always stabbed and killed them": Yin and Young.

47 "I personally severed more than forty heads": Cook and Cook.

50 "Tony, keep quiet," "not so much as the twitching": Kennedy, *Freedom from Fear.*

52 "Why are you crying about": Yin and Young.

52 "The man is saturated with hate": Kennedy, *Freedom from Fear.*

53 "war with America was to be avoided": Iriye.

55 "In both my talks with the President": Feis.

56 "action in showing surprise now": Kato.

56 "If you tell me that it is necessary that we fight": Fuchida and Okumiya.

58 "I reported to the State Department": PHA.

58 "Of all the world's statesmen": G. Terasaki.

59 "Our opposition to the alliance," "You must, therefore, share with me": Asada.

59 "You see, I am an Asian," "full of subtle twists": Hotta, *Japan 1941.*

60 "Taranto, and the night of November": Iguchi.

62 "If Great Britain goes down": Frank Freidel, "FDR vs. Hitler: American Foreign Policy, 1933–1941," *Proceedings of the Massachusetts Historical Society*, 3rd ser., 1987.

63 "it is impossible to rectify diplomatic relations": Morley, *The Fateful Choice*.

64 "would begin with an air attack on our fleet": For a thorough accounting of the Zacharias conundrum, see Pfeiffer.

65 "said that I had observed every phase of Hitler's conduct and utterances": Library of Congress.

66 "The draft understanding that came from America is appalling": Hotta, *Japan 1941*.

Chapter 2: A Sinister Wind

67 "A conflict with the United States and Great Britain": Prange papers.

69 "Should hostilities break out between Japan and United States": Ibid.

69 "Unless a technical miracle can be achieved": Ibid.

70 "Yamamoto's daring plan," "A new concept suddenly hit me": Stillwell.

71 "Since we cannot use a torpedo attack": Prange papers.

73 "Under present conditions I think war": Ibid.

73 "None of us was a volunteer": Kazuo Sakamaki, *I Attacked Pearl Harbor* (New York: Association Press, 1949).

73 "My Peruvian colleague": PHA.

74 "The Division of Naval Intelligence": Ibid.

74 "would have to expect to come into conflict": This exchange is in Heinrichs.

75 "We felt secure against a raid," "I never knew what the navy had": PHA.

75 "to sit absolutely quiet while two or three nations": Library of Congress.

77 "It first off involved what I call:" For a more detailed look at this story, see Kahn.

77 "Grotjan enters room, obviously excited": Recounted in Theodore Hannah, "Frank B. Rowlett—a Personal Profile," Declassified Asset Files, NSA.gov.

79 "According to a fairly reliable source of information": Prange papers.

80 "Since I had been studying English": A detailed account of Yoshikawa can be found in Savela.

81 "From there I saw the fleet in Pearl Harbor": Batty.

81 "It was a matter of common knowledge that": Prange papers.

82 "We all knew he was a spy": PHA.

82 "Go ahead, Mr. Kita": Stillwell.

83 "Personnel of your naval intelligence service": PHA.

83 "Japan is deathly afraid": Clarke.

83 "tell these people that Japanese aviators": Stillwell.

83 "With our heavy bombers and our fine new pursuit planes," "felt that Hawaii was impregnable": Stimson diary.

83 "The island of Oahu, due to its fortification": PHA.

84 "Practically every person on the island of Oahu": PHA.

85 "with few having thought through a detailed response": Ibid.

85 "Roosevelt is keen to go to war": G. Terasaki.

86 "The president shows evidence of waiting": Stimson diary.

87 "With the recent detachment of many of the most modern": PHA.

87 "were carrying on informal talks with certain Japanese": This conversation between Kimmel and FDR is from Kimmel's memo "Interview with the President, 1425–1550, Monday, June 9, 1941," NA.
87 "recent developments have shown that": PHA.
88 "aerial torpedoes could run in Pearl Harbor": Ibid.
88 "a very interesting piece of news": Stimson diary.
89 "Do you really think we can act," "You're telling me": Hotta, *Japan 1941*, citing Inose Naoki, *Showa Jurokunen Natsu no Haisen* (Bunshun Bunko, 1986).
90 "No new developments": *Kimitsu senso nisshi*, Hara.
91 "Operations against the United States were primarily the responsibility": Akira Fujiwara, "The Role of the Japanese Army," in Stillwell.
91 "Imperial conferences were a curious thing": *Showa tenno dokuhakuroku*, Hara.
91 "War preparations against," "How could you have endorsed": Asada.
92 "To embargo oil to Japan would be as popular a move," "sit on the fence and be more friendly": FDR papers.
92 "offering assistance to Germany's policy": State.
93 "That the Japanese Government did not understand": Ibid.
94 "Tell [Churchill] also in great confidence that": FDR papers.
94 "received the impression that some kind of an economic": Prange papers.
94 "We, myself included, thought that advancing": Toshitane Takada television interview, NHK, *Supersharu: Gozen Kaigi*, August 15, 1991, Hara.
94 "The vicious circle of reprisals and counter-reprisals": Grew papers.
95 "By the grace of heaven": Grew papers.
95 "Our Empire must immediately take steps": PHA.
95 "made up his mind that we have reached the end": Stimson diary.
95 "only a step this side of": Feis.

Chapter 3: Autumn 1941

96 "enemy ships or aircraft or ships of neutral": Kenshujo.
97 "You shall not resign your post": PHA.
97 "saddled with the responsibility for some": Grew papers.
97 "The invitation is merely a blind": Morley, *The Final Confrontation*.
97 "we could not think of reopening": State.
98 "I had the right information to forestall": Popov.
98 "Our most likely enemy, Orange": PHA.
99 "I didn't think [Japan] could": PHA.
99 "*Yamato-damashii* is what the United States": *Showa Jurokunen Natsu no Haisen*, Hara.
100 "Could we expect a big victory": Saionji.
100 "How many planes do we need": Prange, *God's Samurai*.
102 "We cannot rely only on torpedoes," "It was decided to make bombings only against them": Prange papers.
103 "I was in command of a bomber company": Schmidt.
104 "By occupying the necessary areas to the south," "That is correct": Sugiyama memo, Hara.
105 "Japan was like a patient suffering," "over and over again . . . striving to introduce," "filled with trepidation": PHA.

106 "arranged a meeting with me on September 6": State.

107 "there was any possibility that Japan might intervene": Kido.

107 "The war games cut through the year 1941": Prange papers.

108 "Henceforth, we would like to have you make reports": PHA.

108 "the Japanese were showing unusual interest," "Japanese intent to execute a submarine," "the fleet is not going to be there": PHA.

109 "Is the October fifteenth deadline," "You are the one who called": Hotta, *Japan 1941.*

109 "The key to peace or war": Hull papers.

110 "It is obvious that a war between Japan": *Gozen Kaigi*, Hara.

111 "Many Japanese, and he himself": Hull papers.

111 "I have no confidence": Morley, *The Fateful Choice.*

112 "If you die in this operation": Ibid.

112 "It is no longer time for discussion," "That sort of thing is called *scheming*," "The army is saying": *Gozen Kaigi*, Hara.

114 "We've lost two hundred thousand souls": Ibid.

116 "I realize that some do not think well": Prange papers.

116 "We must continue to seek a diplomatic": Gomikawa, Junpei. *Gozen Kaigi*, found in Hara and cited in Hotta, *Japan, 1941.*

116 "We are at the crossroads of pursuing": Ibid.

117 "I am greatly responsible for the China Incident": Ibid.

117 "For the past six months, ever since April": Ibid.

117 "Although I respect him for that": Ibid.

118 "I've got some awful news! Ozaki's been arrested": Saionji.

119 "Minister, you cornered Prince Konoye": *Showa Jurokunen Natsu no Haisen*, Hara.

120 "I have three things to say to you": Saionji.

120 "A soldier serves the emperor": Tsunoda and Fukuda.

121 "much more anti-American": Hull papers.

121 "The resignation of the Japanese Cabinet," "Personally I do not believe the Japs," "I am firmly convinced that I should retire": PHA.

122 "If you have made a mistake," "If this seems strange": Prange papers.

123 "The security of the Fleet," "Nearly all of the failures": PHA.

124 "We can defend anything": Bartsch.

124 "I have recently heard that there are some elements": Prange papers.

126 "A Nazi tin fish," "I was asleep when the torpedoes hit us": Hynes.

Chapter 4: November

128 "Could you explain to me": *Gozen Kaigi*, Hara.

129 "It was as though they had already decided to go to war": Ibid.

130 "Yes, until twelve midnight": Ibid.

131 "Perhaps it is unavoidable": Hotta, *Japan 1941.*

131 "Of course His Majesty is a pacifist": Hattori, citing Fujiwara.

132 "I was born a boy at the right time!": Prange papers.

132 "This time we are showing the limit": PHA.

133 "At the very outset of the beginning of hostilities": *Gozen Kaigi*, Hara.

133 "[American] policy, together with the impact": State.

134 "Things seem to be moving steadily towards a crisis," "The plain fact is that Japanese politics": PHA.

135 "If we just stand by with": *Taiheiyo Senso e no Michi*, in Hara.

135 "If things go as they are going now": Hotta, *Japan 1941*.

135 "a major calamity for the world," "I find my present position extremely odd": Larrabee.

135 "on the brink of chaos": PHA.

136 "relations had become extremely critical": Ibid.

136 "Do not let the talks deteriorate": Hull papers.

136 "At the present time the United States Fleet": PHA.

136 "There must be no behavior such as": State.

137 "not merely an expedient and temporary agreement": Ibid.

137 "This equipment is to enable you to haul": Prange papers.

137 "tiny, like a bean": Allen.

138 "We were told the altitude": Editors, "Remembering Pearl Harbor," *National Geographic*.

138 "would begin with an air attack": Pfeiffer.

139 "As relations between Japan and the United States": PHA.

139 "prepare them for the shock of war," "Nothing that I am telling you today": Baldwin.

140 "because the hazards would be": Bartsch.

140 "The American commander [Kimmel] is no," "The Empire is now going to war": Prange papers.

141 "In emphasizing the need for guarding": State.

141 "In this dangerous emergency": Hotta, *Japan 1941*.

141 "[Togo] said he had picked Mr. Kurusu": PHA.

142 "the chance of success in the negotiations": In Saburo Kurusu, *Homatsu no San-jugonen* (Tokyo: Chuko Bunko, 2007).

142 "There is no last word between friends": Hull papers.

144 "At the time of year when green leaves turn suddenly": From "The Southern Cross" by Iki Kuramoti in PHA.

144 "At six o'clock on the dark and cloudy morning": Mitsuo Fuchida, "I Led the Attack on Pearl Harbor," in Stillwell.

146 "Regarding the broadcast of a special message in an emergency": PHA.

147 "tiny ball of crumpled rice paper": Savela.

148 "We knew then that things were building": Ibid.

149 "condonement by the United States of Japan's": Hull testimony, PHA.

149 "Chances of favorable outcome of negotiations," "I have been in constant touch": PHA.

150 "If your bomb hits directly beside the turret": Genda.

151 "Achtung, Warning, Alerte": Bell.

152 "If I man these islands": This conversation is detailed in Gillon and in PHA.

152 "that we were likely to be attacked": Stimson diary.

153 "Hell no!": This conversation is detailed in Gillon and in PHA.

153 "G-2 that was very disturbing": Ibid.

153 "Those men over there do not believe me": Iguchi.

154 "The slight prospect of Japan's agreeing," "sincerely desired that the message": PHA.

154 "The Government of Japan will withdraw": State.

155 "told me he had broken the whole thing off": Stimson diary.

155 "Japan may attack the Burma Road": PHA.

155 "a cold bath": State.

156 "I was struck by despair," "This must be divine grace": Hotta, *Japan 1941*, citing Togo, *Jidai no Ichimen*.

156 "I knew at the same time as": PHA.

157 "This dispatch is to be considered a war warning": Ibid.

158 "We considered it an unequivocal war warning": Ibid.

159 "My impression of the Hawaiian problem has been": PHA

159 I would appreciate your early review": Ibid.

159 "The news this morning indicates": FDR papers.

159 "Excuse me for speaking my mind in crude": *Taiheiyo Senso e no Michi*, Hara.

160 "preparatory to an emergency situation": PHA.

161 "The most probable line of action for Japan": Ibid.

161 "a seat at the head of the table": Hull papers.

161 "They all come at me with knives": Ibid.

162 "I could see with my own eyes": Hara.

162 "With war, if you don't try it": Iguchi.

162 "the fact that service calls lasted only one month": PHA.

163 "I hope they would be sighted": Ibid.

163 "Niitaka yama nobore": Prange papers.

163 "If it was permitted": Brinkley.

164 "I am very sorry": Ibid.

164 "After we finished flight training": Editors, "Remembering Pearl Harbor," *National Geographic*.

164 "North America (including Manila)": PHA.

164 "serene after fully realizing the inevitability": Prange papers.

165 "If we begin on November": Spector.

165 "a hundred million Asians": Costello.

165 "will lead to a war in which": Prange papers.

166 "he had the Japanese running around": Hull papers.

166 "Circular twenty four forty four": PHA.

166 "without equivocation that Tokyo": Clausen and Lee.

167 "Highly reliable information has been received": PHA.

167 "We have received considerable": Ibid.

168 "At five forty-five this evening," FDR papers.

168 "approach the president": G. Terasaki.

169 "an especially trained espionage man": Ibid.

170 "If this is a blackfish": Prange papers.

170 "the movements of the fleet": PHA.

171 "With every hour that passes": Hull papers.

172 "No expression of concern": Perkins.

Chapter 5: December 6

173 "The problem is whether the Japanese," "Emphatically!": PHA.
173 "When they came out, Nomura had": Vice Admiral William R. Smedberg, "Aide to Admiral Stark," in Stillwell.
174 "I imagine you will receive it tomorrow": PHA.
174 "Japanese warriors never tried to assassinate": Brinkley.
175 "Hell, I didn't even know they were sore at us": LaForte and Marcello.
175 "in the late afternoon or early evening": PHA.
175 "Gentlemen, are they going to": PHA.
176 "firmly determined to fulfill the responsibility": Prange papers.
176 "I received your telegram": PHA.
177 "This needs a lot of work, Mrs. Edgers": Ibid.
177 "Shoot this to Grew": State.
178 "a very clever move on the part": PHA.
178 "This son of man": Ibid.
178 "left suddenly . . . undue alarm": Ibid.
179 "left and went home at about 9 p.m.": Clausen and Lee.
179 "If we are going into a war": Ibid.
180 "Corporal, what in the hell do you": Travers.
181 "We all knew war might break out," "My God, what a way to spend that evening": Clarke.
183 "What a target that would make": Ibid.
183 "The mood on the mother submarine": Allen.
184 "On to Pearl Harbor!": Ibid.
185 "a little farewell drink": Verklan.
185 "I slept soundly": Prange papers.
185 "The night before the attack": Brinkley.
185 It is my sole wish to serve: Costello.
185 "The Japanese Government regrets": PHA.
186 "to Secretary Hull's office at ten thirty": Stimson diary.
186 "received a very brief, urgent": PHA.
188 "I am going now": Schmidt.
189 "I would find a target on the ground": Ibid.
189 "Honolulu sleeps," "Admiral, I am sure the airmen": Friedrich.
191 "The ships pitched and rolled": Editors, "Remembering Pearl Harbor," *National Geographic*.
192 "Our fighting spirit was high": Allen.
193 "The wind was competing": Schmidt.
193 "From the decks of the aircraft carriers," "On my arrival there Colonel Bratton": PHA.
194 "immediately stunned," "I think that I immediately called": Ibid.
195 "very early in the morning in the Far East": Ibid.
195 "That's a periscope, sir": Lord.
195 "We searched for about an hour": PHA.
197 "As we flew, I thought many thoughts": Schmidt.
197 "Oh, glorious dawn for Japan!": Prange papers.
198 "about fifteen hundred yards on starboard quarter": PHA.

201 "You had better get going": Ibid.
201 "Have you any previous details": PHA.
201 "Between seven thirty and seven forty": Ibid.
202 "It seemed that if you got in trouble": Travers.
203 "something completely out of the ordinary": PHA.
203 "the warm air of an unending summer land": Blakeman.
204 "Just before I was sounding reveille": Ibid.
204 "Enemy formation at anchor": Genda.
204 "There's a large number of planes": PHA.
205 "If the AWAS service had been operating": Ibid.
206 "the communications between the fighter-director": PHA.
207 "They've changed the color of our planes": Lord.
208 "All crew abandoning ship": McWilliams.

Chapter 6: From the Air

215 "They didn't have a chance": McWilliams.
215 "the air was not the place": Harding.
216 "P-40s hell": Ibid.
216 "In the movies, an airplane attack": Author interview.
218 "We're going to have an air show": Spector.
219 "I suppose the reason my attention": McWilliams.
219 "By then the sky was thick with puffs": Stephens.
220 "Our asphalt landing strip": Ibid.
221 "We carried him to the supply room": McWilliams.
222 "At this time our lieutenant called us together": Gabik.
223 "After the last explosion": State of Hawaii.
225 "Mrs. Mayfield, is it": Ibid.
226 "I was thirteen years old": Richardson, *On the Treadmill.*
227 "We're at war": Lord.
227 "It was the first time I had ever": McWilliams.
228 "a skinny crew-cut kid": Ibid.
229 "To think that this bunch of little yellow bastards": Clarke.
229 "On Sunday morning in those days": James Jones, *WW II: A Chronicle of Soldiering* (New York: Ballantine, 1975).
230 "something like machine-gun fire": Editors, "Remembering Pearl Harbor," *National Geographic.*
230 "As long as I live": State of Hawaii.
232 "They lack only one thing": John Steinbeck, "Fear of Death as Green Troops Sail to Invasion," *New York Herald Tribune*, October 3, 1943.
232 "Hey, I've heard the Japs only": Clarke.
232 "Go back to sleep, you're having a bad dream": PHA.
235 "It was remarkable": Ibid.
235 "Suddenly, I noticed the gunner": Richardson, *Reflections.*
236 "I heard a plane come roaring in from astern": Goldstein, "John Finn."
238 "Lieutenant Iida communicated": Verklan.
240 "I was in a very excited state": Ibid.
242 "When a short distance from Barbers": Historic Wings.

244 "What the hell is wrong with that crazy SOB": Ibid.
245 "We'd been practicing towing a carrier": Richardson, *Reflections.*

Chapter 7: Pearl Harbor

247 "A faint haze of kitchen smoke": Schmidt.
247 "It must've been about seven forty-five": Brinkley.
248 "Adolph, I wonder what it would be like": Lord.
249 "Hail Mary, full of grace": Ibid.
249 "On Saturday night, 6 December": Ramsey.
250 "Approximately five or ten minutes after": PHA.
250 "Look out the window!": Tennant.
251 "when I am sure my children are dead": Ibid.
251 "It sounded like the hum of bees swarming": Nicholson.
251 "When I looked up in the sky": Naval History & Heritage Command.
251 "The torpedo bombers released their torpedoes": Verklan.
252 "We were about to change an island of dreams": Ibid.
252 "The *Enterprise* was slated to tie up next": Richardson, *Reflections.*
253 "After a minute or two": Ibid.
254 "What's going on out there": Lord.
255 "The plane's canopy was open": Richardson, *Reflections.*
255 "Slow down, kid": Slackman.
256 "The plane we had shot down": Naval History & Heritage Command.
256 "running a stick along one": McWilliams.
256 "and her sister ship:" Richardson, *Reflections.*
257 "tiny Filipino messboy": McWilliams.
257 "I heard a voice behind me": Ibid.
257 "I was in my Skivvies": Editors, "Remembering Pearl Harbor," *National Geographic.*
258 "We had a first-class electrician's mate": Richardson, *Reflections.*
259 "The events about to be related here": Molotsky.
260 "in utter disbelief and completely stunned": Gillon.
261 "I ran over to my offices": Batty.
261 "If it's any satisfaction to you": PHA.
262 "We saw the water channel and we turned left": Verklan.
262 "I saw two objects fall from their craft," "I was sleeping in the plotting room": Richardson, *Reflections.*
263 "It wasn't hard," "The captain had a serious abdominal wound": Naval History & Heritage Command.
264 "I volunteered to join the ten-hand": Richardson, *Reflections.*
264 "Just then the USS *Arizona's*": Naval History & Heritage Command.
266 "Man your battle stations! This is no shit!": Ibid.
266 "The ship was lifted rapidly": Richardson, *Reflections.*
267   "the boxes containing the ready ammunition": Ibid.
267 "I was about twenty meters": Verklan.
267 "When a torpedo hits": Editors, "Remembering Pearl Harbor," *National Geographic.*
268 "I was five foot three and": Ibid.

268 "the lights blackened out and": "Trapped in a Watery Grave."

269 "We had four flashlights": Ibid.

269 "I helped a partially incapacitated": Naval History & Heritage Command.

270 "Chaplain Schmitt pushing one person," "Someone tried earlier": Spiller.

271 "When you get out of the shower": Editors, "Remembering Pearl Harbor," *National Geographic*.

272 "As I treaded water": "Trapped in a Watery Grave."

274 "There's no way you could get out": Ibid.

275 "I obtained a copy of the *Oklahoma*": Naval History & Heritage Command.

276 "orders were given": Ibid.

276 "heading toward the Middle Loch": McWilliams.

277 "His chin stuck out": Michael F. Reilly as told to William J. Slocum, *Reilly of the White House* (New York: Simon and Schuster, 1947).

277 "the president thought the report": "Memorandum: December 7, 1941," Harry Hopkins papers, Georgetown University Library Special Collections Research Center.

277 "resorted to every possible measure": Hull papers.

278 "The gang around today": Ibid.

278 "Oh, it's terrible!": Prange, *Dec. 7, 1941*.

279 "we are forced to terminate negotiations," "Our deceptive diplomacy is steadily": French, "Pearl Harbor Truly a Sneak Attack."

279 "extreme calmness," "deadly calm": James Roosevelt, *My Parents* (New York: Playboy Press, 1976).

280 "If any unauthorized person": PHA.

280 "We're supposed to weld": Richardson, *Reflections*.

280 "It was just a few minutes": Jasper et al.

281 "We were blown off the gun": Wallin.

281 "We found the admiral's body": PHA.

282 "I stuck my head in": Jasper et al.

282 "Dark gray puffs": Fuchida and Okumiya.

283 "I glanced up": Gudmens.

283 "A huge waterspout splashed": McWilliams.

283 "Now we had given this": Brinkley.

283 "a hateful, mean-looking": Fuchida and Okumiya.

283 "A red fireball shot up": Clarke.

284 "Ships on fire, ships burning": Batty.

284 "All of the oil tanks on all of the battlewagons": Lord.

284 "These people were zombies": LaForte and Marcello.

284 "The most vivid recording": Spiller.

285 "*Arizona*, I remember you": Manchester.

285 "You don't abandon ship on me": McWilliams.

285 "was standing on gun turret": Jasper et al.

287 "at first I thought": Ibid.

287 "As I was running forward": Naval History & Heritage Command.

288 "When that bomb hit": McWilliams.

289 "I was about three-quarters of the way": Naval History & Heritage Command.

291 "When I came up, I was gagging": Ibid.

Chapter 8: Describing the Indescribable

292 "Hell, no, this is": McWilliams.

292 "These Americans, when": Larrabee.

293 "A warm feeling came with the realization": Iguchi.

294 "While on the starboard side": Naval History & Heritage Command.

296 "My God": Ibid.

297 "As we crowded the shoreline": Schmidt.

297 "My thoughts were to make a act of defiance": Naval History & Heritage Command.

298 "All this time, our cooks had been": Ibid.

298 "a 'dog' sandwich and beans": pearlharborsurvivorsonline.org.

303 "Some of us were given new": Ibid.

303 "A young man, filthy black": Ramsey.

304 "Turning my attention": Ibid.

305 "to get on the operational telephone": PHA.

305 "I want three volunteers": Lord.

306 "At 1030 took off in 6-S-1": Historic Wings.

307 "This is Gatty": Ibid.

307 "succeeded only in enraging me": PHA.

308 "Suppose that the enemy was located": Ibid.

308 "When you're awakened suddenly": Brinkley; Goldstein, "Kenneth Taylor."

309 "We had absolutely no trouble": Ibid.

310 "The deck is now transformed": PHA.

311 "Four battleships sunk": Hara.

313 "Nagumo would have been": Ibid.

313 "If they had destroyed the oil": PHA.

316 "whose time fuses had": Clarke.

316 "I was a teenager at that time": Richardson, *Reflections*.

318 "requested and urged Martial Law": PHA.

319 "You must be one kind of child": Clarke.

319 "I smelled acrid smoke": Kato.

320 "the conference met in": Hopkins papers.

321 "My greatest fear was that": Gillon.

322 "It's quite true": Ibid.

322 "To have the United States at our side was to me": Churchill.

322 "the turning point," "never in history has a people": Stanley Weintraub, *Long Day's Journey into War: December 7, 1941* (New York: Dutton, 1991).

322 "The entire message": Gillon.

323 "I am speaking to you": "Eleanor Roosevelt's Remarks: December 7, 1941," the first lady's weekly radio broadcast, *Pan American Coffee Bureau*, National Broadcasting Company, http://www.gwu.edu/~erpapers/teachinger/q-and-a/q21-pearl-harbor-address.cfm.

324 "We by grace of heaven": Bartsch.

326 "We just got scraps of information": Perkins.

326 "My God, how did it happen?": Alonzo Fields, *My 21 Years in the White House* (New York: Coward-McCann, 1961).

327 "that it would be necessary": Ibid.

327 "There was ample opportunity," "on the ground, by God": Sperber.
328 "Hey, coxswain": pearlharborsurvivorsonline.org.
328 "That afternoon of course": Verklan.
330 "The only thing I could see": Clarke.
331 "Oh, you hear all kinds of stories": Lord.
331 "ordered to take care of": pearlharborsurvivorsonline.org.

Chapter 9: Infamy

335 "I saw and heard other men": McWilliams.
336 "We pulled over and stopped": Naval History & Heritage Command.
337 "It was just as dark as": Slackman.
338 "Two of our own .50-caliber": Naval History & Heritage Command.
340 "something strange in the water": PHA.
340 "had fully expected to die": Editors, "Remembering Pearl Harbor," *National Geographic.*
341 "Little doubt exists": Captain Andrew Biache Jr., "Pearl Harbor: A Midget Sub in the Picture?," *Naval History Magazine*, December 2004.
342 "It's not impossible that they're": Ibid.
342 "our tails are up in the air": "Record of Telephone Conversation Between Gen. Gerow, WPD, and Gen. MacArthur in Manila, P.I., About 7:00 PM," December 7, 1941, FDR papers.
343 "What's that thing, Mike": Michael F. Reilly, *Reilly of the White House* (New York: Simon and Schuster, 1947).
344 "His uppermost thought": Roosevelt, *My Parents.*
346 "Our country has been attacked," "American soil has been treacherously": Minutes of the Special Meeting of the Advisory Board, December 8, 1941, America First Committee, Hoover Institution.
346 "Today all of us are in the same boat": FDR to "For the Former Naval Person," December 8, 1941, Map Room Papers, FDR papers.
347 "Even the children were pin-drop": Ramsey.
347 "Since the war, I have confiscated," "Cowboy, a sailor from Texas": Travers.
349 "God have mercy on us": PBS.org.
350 "In all the war I never received": Churchill.
351 "The fruits of victory are tumbling": Keene.
352 "What's going to happen at war": Editors, "Remembering Pearl Harbor," *National Geographic.*
352 "Remember December eighth!": Keene.
352 "It is almost certain that": Carroll V. Glines, *Doolittle's Tokyo Raider* (Princeton, NJ: C. Van Nostrand, 1964).

Chapter 10: Resurrection

354 "trying to salvage something": PHA.
355 "In the Navy's gravest hour": Ibid.
356 "[First] there was a curfew": Richardson, *Reflections.*
356 "their physical characteristics," "they were tracked out": PHA.
357 "the effective causes": PHA.

358 "immediate evacuation of all," "If it is a question of the safety": Jan Jarboe Russell, *The Train to Crystal City* (New York: Scribner, 2015).
359 "I'd just turned five years old": Jon Stewart.
359 "When we had to leave": Travers.
360 "it was God's mercy that our fleet": Wallin.
361 "because of the floating oil": Raymer.
363 "we gathered on the barge": Ibid.
364 "All the vacationers had seen," "The U-boat attack was": Kennedy, *Freedom from Fear.*

Chapter 11: Vengeance

367 "a deep, powerful thirst": PHA.
367 "I got a call from Major Ski York": Hasdorff, "Interview with York"; a detailed version of this story is in *The First Heroes.*
368 "The reason Eglin was chosen": Ibid.
368 "Special five-hundred-pound demolition": AFHRA.
369 "was fairly well convinced that none," "Within five minutes": Hasdorff, "Schultz."
370 "one of the most even-tempered": Larrabee.
370 "I don't know what the hell this logistics is": Spector.
370 "the antithesis of cooperation": Kennedy, *Freedom from Fear.*
370 "the whole organization belongs": Costello.
371 "a rough bunch": Hasdorff, "Macia."
371 "What we have got to do, Henry": Hull papers.
371 "find ways and means of carrying home": Reynolds.
372 "If the army has some plane": Ibid.
372 "Go see General Arnold": Hasdorff, "Schultz."
374 "the marine personnel in particular": Hasdorff, "Crouch."
374 "The sailors I saw were jumping up": Merrill.
375 "Personally, I know exactly what I'm": Author interview.
376 "This was zero weather conditions": Author interview.
377 "You knew how long it would take them": Steven Jurika interview, United States Naval Institute, March 17, 1976.
377 "It'd be a pretty bad feeling": Author interview.
377 "We watched him like hawks": Lawson.
379 "At last": Author interview.
379 "The general has asked me to tell you": Emmens.
380 "Doc stepped away and walked": Lawson.
381 "There was this Chinese band": Author interview.
381 "You remember the novel of James Hilton": Samuel Rosenman, *Working with Roosevelt* (New York: Harper and Row, 1952).
382 "Headquarters spokesmen sarcastically pooh-poohed," Fuchida and Okumiya.
383 "We fed the Americans": The Reverend Charles Meeus, "China Letter," *Reader's Digest*, May 1944.
383 "The raid had three advantages": Doolittle.
384 "I was given what they call": Author interview.

387 "Sight what appears to be ten," "We had by this time undergone": Larrabee.
388 "curved white slashes": *Reminisces of Vice Admiral James E. Thach*, US Naval Historical Center.
389 "I saw this glint in the sun": Ibid.
389 "the plump silhouettes of the": Larrabee.
390 "for reasons that will always": Willmott.

Chapter 12: Triumph

392 "contrary to international law": International Military Tribunal, Far East papers, NA.
392 "At night we would hear this beautiful": Author interview.
394 "The tribunal, acting under the law": International Military Tribunal, Far East papers, NA.
394 "If the Americans win": Hasdorff.
394 "I take full responsibility": Prange papers.
395 "Being ready to defend," "Isn't there some place where": Bix.
396 "We thought, 'Well'": Hasdorff, "Hite."
396 "Lord, though I am far": Watson.
397 "one morning he opened the slot": Ibid.
397 "Long may the tale be," "Hirohito eats shit!": Manchester.
397 "There was nothing macho": Terkel.
397 "Do you have any bones": Charles Lindbergh, *The Wartime Journals of Charles A. Lindbergh* (New York: Harcourt Brace Jovanovich, 1970).
398 "the primitive days of fighting Indians," "when you have to deal with a beast": Peter Wyden, *Day One* (New York: Simon and Schuster, 1985).
399 "People of the Philippines, I have returned": PBS.org.
399 "I can never again see": Manchester.
399 "Hell is on us": Bix.
401 "I heard the huzzle-huzzle": George Martin, "Black Snow and Leaping Tigers," *Harper's*, February 1946.
402 "The bombs were falling like": Webb.
402 "LeMay said if we'd lost the war": Morris, *The Fog of War*.
403 "Duty is a heavy burden": Dunnigan and Nofi.
403 "The geographical advantages of the homeland": Frank.
404 "I got out of bed": Hasdorff, "DeShazer."
404 "Despite the fact that it was": Laurence.
405 "I was told that even Tokyo": Bix.
406 "the war is over": Dower, *Embracing Defeat*.
407 "It is my earnest hope": PBS.org.
407 "Here is the victor announcing the verdict to the prostrate enemy": Toshikazu Kase, *Journey to the Missouri* (New Haven, CT: Yale University Press, 1950).
408 "our people . . . knew how to advance": Dower, *Embracing Defeat*.
408 "I must say to myself that I ruined myself": Kato.
408 "A flatbed truck with six Japanese": Author interview.
409 "After the war ended": Author interview.
409 "One thing I've noticed": Dr. Gerald Levine, Veterans Administration Hospital, East Orange, NJ, *Jimmy Doolittle and Me*, http://www.tankbooks.com/ptsd.htm.

410 "Give me bread or give me bullets": PBS.org.
411 "I am very sorry it is taking me so long to die": International Military Tribunal, Far East papers, NA.

Chapter 13: Legacy

413 "I had a job to do and I didn't give": Wu.
413 "I saw the *Oklahoma* roll over": McKinley.
413 "I was pretty shook up": Jasper et al.
413 "You really never get the smell": Cross.
414 "We went to the Japanese church": Richardson.
416 "sags in the middle": M. Miller, "Pearl Harbor 30 Years Later."
416 "I've never dared to go near": Jasper et al.
417 "For them this was a great victory": Blakeman.
417 "Even though it was an unavoidable war," "The most impressive place": Gallicchio.
418 "I thought we would win": Flint.
419 "In the last years of his life": Author interview.
420 "It was a damned good movie": Goldstein, "John Finn."
420 "I seen the *Arizona* blow up": Editors, "Remembering Pearl Harbor," *National Geographic*.
420 "I have no rancor": Robert Reinhold, "Pearl Harbor Remembered," *New York Times*, December 8, 1991.
420 "Don't talk about that": McKinley.
421 "Of course the military had much": Sanger.
421 "There is no need now": Associated Press, "Japan Declines to State Regret at Pearl Harbor."
421 "relates to the mentality of": Kristof.
423 "The world starts moving": French, " 'Pearl Harbor' in Japan."
423 "Fifty years of pain": Reinhold.
424 "We did not invite the Japanese": Ibid.
424 "It was . . . like having the sun": Prange, *God's Samurai*.
425 "Fuchida had two women": Author interview.
426 "was shocked and mortified": Schmidt.
427 "thirty-six straight days": Blakeman.
427 "I am so sorry": Ibid.
428 "This marks the first time": Cook 3rd Class Doris Miller, USN, at Naval History & Heritage Command.
428 "This was a very courageous young man": Editors, "Remembering Pearl Harbor," *National Geographic*.
428 "the greatest honor that could be paid": Chester.
428 "When Dorie Miller took gun in hand": Ibid.
429 "In their most cited paper": Michael Lewis, "The King of Human Error," *Vanity Fair*, December 2011.
430 "In retrospect Pearl Harbor seemed": *Life's Picture History of World War II* (New York: Time, 1950).
430 "Our borders are unfortified," "that oceans are no longer moats": Editors, "The Imprints of Pearl Harbor," *New York Times*, December 1, 1991.

431 "if there had been something like coordination": "The Impact of Pearl Harbor," *Intelligence throughout History*, US Central Intelligence Agency Archives.

433 "My answer is in affirmative," "It is logical that": Weintraub, "The Conscript."

434 "For all of our warts": Jeffrey Goldberg. "The Obama Doctrine." *The Atlantic*, April 2016.

434 "a mirror of the world": Cordell Hull, *Memoirs of Cordell Hull* (New York: Macmillan, 1948).

434 "the one person in all the world": Vandenbosch.

435 "What kind of peace": John F. Kennedy, "Peace Speech," American University, June 10, 1963.

Appendix 1: Judgment and Controversy

437 "The Commission examined 127": PHA.

441 "This is to my mind a very important part of the message": PHA.

443 "That we could defeat the enemy at the outbreak of the war": Weintraub, *Pearl Harbor Christmas.*

450 "There was no relevant intelligence communications": Clausen and Lee.

451 "that immediate action be taken": Ibid.

452 "Even if one admits . . . that President Roosevelt wanted": Prange papers.

454 "instead of the British mystery where": Wallace-Wells.

454 "The country was not ready for preparedness": Lutton.

SOURCES

Administrative History Section, Bureau of Medicine and Surgery. *The United States Navy Medical Department at War, 1941–1945.* Washington, DC: The Bureau, 1946.

Agawa, Hiroyuki. *The Reluctant Admiral: Yamamoto and the Imperial Navy.* New York: Kodansha International, 1969.

Alcott, Caroll D. "Why Remember Pearl Harbor?" *Antioch Review,* 1942.

Allen, Thomas B. *Remember Pearl Harbor: American and Japanese Survivors Tell Their Stories.* Washington, DC: National Geographic Society, 2001.

Anastas, Benjamin. "Atrocity Exhibition." *Los Angeles Review of Books,* July 24, 2014.

Anderson, Charles R. *Days of Lightning, Years of Scorn: Walter C. Short and the Attack on Pearl Harbor.* Annapolis: Naval Institute Press, 2005.

Armstrong, Alan. *Preemptive Strike: The Secret Plan That Would Have Prevented the Attack on Pearl Harbor.* Guilford, CT: Lyons Press, 2006.

Arnold, Henry H. "8.2, Doolittle Raid." Murray Green Donation, Air Force Archives.

———. *Global Mission.* New York: Harper and Row, 1949.

Asada, Sadao. *From Mahan to Pearl Harbor: The Imperial Japanese Navy and the United States.* Annapolis: Naval Institute Press, 2006.

Associated Press. "Adm. Husband E. Kimmel Dies; Pearl Harbor Navy Commander." *New York Times,* May 15, 1968.

———. "Japan Declines to State Regret at Pearl Harbor." *New York Times,* December 7, 1991.

Baker, Kevin. "The Guilt Dogging the Greatest Generation." *New York Times,* November 12, 2000.

Baker, Lieutenant Colonel Sue. "Remembering Granddad Doolittle." *AFMC Public Affairs,* February 1998.

Baldwin, Hanson W. "160 Ships Berthed at Pearl Harbor." *New York Times,* May 27, 1935.

Barr, George. "Rough draft of a story by Captain George Barr, pertinent to the trials in Shanghai of those Japanese officials held responsible for the execution of three Doolittle fliers who participated in the raid on Tokyo." March 30, 1946. In the papers of James Harold Doolittle, Library of Congress.

Bartsch, William H. *December 8, 1941: MacArthur's Pearl Harbor.* College Station: Texas A&M University Press, 2003.

Batty, Peter, writer and director. "Episode 6: Banzai! Japan, 1931–1942." *The World at War.* Thames Television, 1973.

Beinart, Peter. "Trump Is Right about 9/11." *Atlantic,* October 19, 2015.

Bell, Joseph N. "Mystery of Magazine Ads Hinting of Pearl Harbor Attack Lingers 48 Years Later." *Los Angeles Times*, December 7, 1989.

Bernard, Tom. "Japs Were Jumpy after Tokyo Raid," *Stars and Stripes*, April 27, 1943.

Biers, Dan. "Japanese Fighter Pilot Recalls Pearl Harbor." Associated Press, December 7, 1991.

Bigelow, Michael E. "A Short History of Army Intelligence." *Military Intelligence*, April 2009.

bin Laden, Osama. "Dispatch to Terror Agents on the Eve of 9/11." http://www.americanrhetoric.com/speeches/binladdendispatch.htm.

Bix, Herbert P. *Hirohito and the Making of Modern Japan*. New York: HarperCollins, 2000.

Blakeman, Karen. "R. I. Fiske, Pearl Harbor Survivor, Dead at 82." *Honolulu Advertiser*, April 5, 2004.

Bodnar, John. *The "Good War" in American Memory*. Baltimore: Johns Hopkins University Press, 2010.

Borch, Frederic L. "Comparing Pearl Harbor and 9/11: Intelligence Failure? American Unpreparedness? Military Responsibility?" *Journal of Military History* 67, no. 3 (July 2003).

Borg, Dorothy, Shumpei Okamoto, and Dale K. A. Finlayson, eds. *Pearl Harbor as History*. New York: Columbia University Press, 1973.

Brinkley, David, narrator. *Pearl Harbor: Two Hours That Changed the World*. NHK/ABC News Productions, May 26, 2001.

Bruck, Connie. "The Inside War: To Expose Torture, Dianne Feinstein Fought the C.I.A.—and the White House." *New Yorker*, June 22, 2015.

Bryant, Arthur. *Triumph in the West, 1943–1946*. London: Macmillan, 1959.

Lieutenant Colonel Burch, Major Fogelman, and Captain Tate. "Interview: Gen. James H. Doolittle." USAF Oral History Program, September 26, 1971.

Burns, Ken, director. *The Roosevelts: An Intimate History*. PBS, September 14, 2014.

Carter, K. C., and R. Mueller. "Combat Chronology, Army Air Forces in World War II." September 15, 1945. Albert F. Simpson Historical Research Center and the Office of Air Force History. Air Force Historical Research Agency, Maxwell Air Force Base, AL.

Carter, Shan, and Amanda Cox. "One 9/11 Tally: $3.3 Trillion." *New York Times*, September 8, 2011.

Castle, Terry. "Stockhausen, Karlheinz: The Unsettling Question of the Sublime." *New York*, August 27, 2011.

Central Intelligence Agency. *Intelligence throughout History: The Impact of Pearl Harbor*. December 2010. https://www.cia.gov/news-information/featured-story-archive/2010-featured-story-archive/pearl-harbor.html.

Chang, Iris. *The Rape of Nanking*. New York: Basic Books, 1997.

Chester, Robert K. " 'Negroes' Number One Hero: Doris Miller, Pearl Harbor, and Retroactive Multiculturalism in World War II Remembrance." *American Quarterly* 65, no. 1 (March 2013).

Churchill, Winston. *The Second World War*. New York: Houghton Mifflin, 1986.

Clarke, Thurston. *Pearl Harbor Ghosts*. New York: William Morrow, 1991.

Clausen, Henry C., and Bruce Lee. *Pearl Harbor: Final Judgement*. New York: Da Capo, 1992.

Congress of the United States. *Hearings before the Joint Committee on the Investigation of the Pearl Harbor Attack.* "Report of the Joint Committee on the Investigation of the Pearl Harbor Attack, pursuant of S. Con. Res. 27, 79th Congress, a concurrent resolution to investigate the attack on Pearl Harbor on December 7, 1941, and events and circumstances relating thereto, and additional views of Mr. Keefe, together with Minority views of Mr. Ferguson and Mr. Brewster." 79th Congress, 39 vols. Washington, DC: Government Printing Office, 1946. Nicknamed PHA by scholars, this Center for Legislative Archives collection includes the documents of the federal government's prior investigations: Roberts, Army Board, Navy Court, Clarke, Hewitt, and Clausen.

Cook, Haruko Taya, and Theodore F. Cook. *Japan at War: An Oral History.* New York: New Press, 1992.

Cooper, Colonel Merian C. "The Doolittle Air Raid on Japan Known as First Special Aviation Project"; "Report on Doolittle Raid on Tokyo, 18 April 1942, with Collection of Interviews, Messages and Maps"; "Reports on B-25 Aircraft"; "Assessment of Damage, Tokyo Raid"; "Report and Analysis on Tokyo Raid"; and "Interviews with Pilots and Air Crews Conducted after the Raid." Air Force Historical Research Agency.

Coox, Alvin D. "The Pacific War Revisited." *Pacific Affairs* 56, no. 1 (Spring 1983).

Costello, John. *The Pacific War.* New York: Rawson, Wade, 1981.

Countis, Sierra. "The Message on Tojo's Teeth." *Chico News & Review*, September 12, 2002.

Craig, William. *The Fall of Japan.* New York: Dial, 1967.

Cressman, Robert J., and J. Michael Wenger. "Infamous Day: Marines at Pearl Harbor, 7 December 1941." World War II Commemorative Series. Washington, DC: Government Printing Office, 1992.

Cross, Ian, director. "World War II in the Pacific." *Globe Trekker.* Pilot Productions, February 20, 2012.

Crowe, David M. *War Crimes, Genocide, and Justice: A Global History.* New York: St. Martin's Press, 2014.

"Crusade in the Pacific." *March of Time Television.* Time, 1951.

Davis, Kenneth S. *FDR, the War President: 1940–1943.* New York: Random House, 2000.

Daws, Gavan. *Prisoners of the Japanese.* New York: William Morrow, 1994.

de Lespinois, Pierre, director. Dennis Haysbert, producer. *Secrets of Pearl Harbor.* Discovery Channel, 2004.

Densho Digital Archive. "Pearl Harbor and Aftermath; Personal Recollections." http://archive.densho.org/main.aspx.

Didion, Joan. "Fixed Opinions, or the Hinge of History." *New York Review of Books,* January 16, 2003.

Dockrill, Saki. "Hirohito, the Emperor's Army and Pearl Harbor." *Review of International Studies* 18, no. 4 (October 1992).

Doenecke, Justus D. *Storm on the Horizon: The Challenge to American Intervention, 1939–1941.* Lanham, MD: Rowman and Littlefield, 2000.

Doolittle, General James H. "Jimmy," with Carroll V. Glines. *I Could Never Be So Lucky Again.* New York: Bantam Books, 1991.

Dower, John W. *Cultures of War: Pearl Harbor / Hiroshima / 9–11 / Iraq.* New York: W. W. Norton, 2010.

———. *Embracing Defeat: Japan in the Wake of World War II*. New York: W. W. Norton and Company, 1999.

———. "The Innocence of 'Pearl Harbor.' " *New York Times*, June 3, 2001.

———. *War without Mercy: Race and Power in the Pacific War*. New York: Pantheon, 1986.

Downes, Lawrence. "How a War Was Won and a City Vanished at Pearl Harbor." *New York Times*, December 7, 2006.

Dunne, John Gregory. "The American Raj." *New Yorker*, May 7, 2001.

Dunnigan, James F., and Albert A. Nofi. *Victory at Sea*. New York: William Morrow, 1995.

Edgerton, Robert B. *Warriors of the Rising Sun: A History of the Japanese Military*. New York: W. W. Norton, 1997.

Editors. "General William 'Billy' Mitchell and the Sinking of the *Ostfriesland*: A Consideration." Smithsonian National Air and Space Museum. http://blog.nasm .si.edu/aviation/general-william-%E2%80%9Cbilly%E2%80%9D-mitchell -and-the-sinking-of-the-ostfriesland-a-consideration.

Editors. "Lay Keel of Navy's New Dreadnought." *New York Times*, March 17, 1914.

Editors. "The 9/11 Encyclopedia." *New York*, August 27, 2011.

Editors. "9/11: The Reckoning." *New York Times*, September 8, 2011.

Editors. *Our Finest Hour: Voices of the World War II Generation*. Des Moines, IA: Life Books, 2000.

Editors. "Remembering Pearl Harbor." *National Geographic*, June 28, 2014.

Editors. "Stories of Valor Recited at Pearl Harbor Service." *New York Times*, December 8, 1996.

Eichenwald, Kurt. "The Deafness before the Storm." *New York Times*, September 10, 2012.

Eizo, Hori. *Daihonei Sanbo No Joho Senki (An IGHQ Staff Officer's Record of Intelligence Warfare)*. Tokyo: Bungei Shunju, 1989.

Elder, Sean. "The Sappiest Generation." *Salon*, July 31, 2000.

Emmens, Lieutenant Colonel Robert G. *Guests of the Kremlin*. New York: Macmillan Company, 1949.

Fackler, Martin. "Conservative Group Urges Changes at Japanese War Shrine." *New York Times*, October 28, 2014.

———. "Pressure in Japan to Forget Sins of War." *New York Times*, October 28, 2014.

———. "Rewriting War, Japanese Right Goes on Attack." *New York Times*, December 3, 2014.

Falkenberg, Jim. "Finding Forgiveness at Pearl Harbor." Columbus, OH: Bible Literature International, 2001.

Fallows, James. "The Tragedy of the American Military." *Atlantic*, January/February 2015.

Feis, Herbert. *The Road to Pearl Harbor*. Princeton, NJ: Princeton University Press, 1950.

Filkins, Dexter. *The Forever War*. New York: Knopf, 2008.

Fiss, Owen. *A War Like No Other: The Constitution in a Time of Terror*. New York: New Press, 2015.

Flint, Peter B. "General Minoru Genda, 84, Dies." *New York Times*, August 17, 1989.

Ford, Daniel, ed. *Glen Edwards: The Diary of a Bomber Pilot*. Washington, DC: Smithsonian Institution Press, 1998.

Frank, Richard B. *Downfall: The End of the Imperial Japanese Empire*. New York: Random House, 1999.

French, Howard W. "Japan's Resurgent Far Right Tinkers with History." *New York Times*, March 25, 2001.

———. "'Pearl Harbor' in Japan: Love or War?" *New York Times*, June 22, 2001.

———. "Pearl Harbor Truly a Sneak Attack, Papers Show." *New York Times*, December 9, 1999.

Friedrich, Otto. "Day of Infamy." *Time*, December 2, 1991.

Fromkin, David. *In the Time of the Americans*. New York: Knopf, 1995.

Fuchida, Mitsuo, and Masatake Okumiya. *Midway, the Battle That Doomed Japan*. Annapolis: Naval Institute Press, 2001.

Fujiwara, Akira. *Showō tennō no ju-go nen sensō* [The Shōwa emperor's fifteen-year war]. Tokyo: Aoki Shoten, 1991.

Fullilove, Michael. *Rendezvous with Destiny: How Franklin D. Roosevelt and Five Extraordinary Men Took America into the War and into the World*. New York: Penguin Press, 2013.

Gabik, George. Oral History of George J. Gabik, 19th Transport Squadron, 102 Eden Ave., Satellite Beach, FL 32937. http://hawaii.gov/hawaiiaviation/world-war-ii/december-7–1941/December%207%20Memories%20of%20George%20J.%20Gabik.pdf.

Gallicchio, Marc, ed. *The Unpredictability of the Past: Memories of the Asia-Pacific War in US-East Asian Relations*. Durham, NC: Duke University Press, 2007.

Genda, Minoru. *Shinjuwan sakusen kaikoroku*. Tokyo: Yomiuri Shinbunsha, 1973.

Gibney, Frank. *Senso: The Japanese Remember the Pacific War: Letters to the Editor of Asahi Shimbun*. London: M. E. Sharpe, 1995.

Gillon, Steven M. *Pearl Harbor: FDR Leads the Nation into War*. New York: Basic Books, 2011.

Glaser, April. "Long before Snowden, Librarians Were Anti-Surveillance Heroes." *Slate*, June 3, 2015.

Glenn, Beth. "The Shock of Pearl Harbor Undiminished." *St. Petersburg Times*, December 7, 1999.

Glines, Carroll V. *Doolittle's Tokyo Raiders*. Princeton, NJ: D. Van Nostrand, 1964.

———. *Four Came Home*. Missoula, MT: Pictorial Histories, 1981.

———. *Jimmy Doolittle: Daredevil Aviator and Scientist*. New York: Macmillan, 1972.

Goldberg, Jeffrey. "The Obama Doctrine." *The Atlantic*, April 2016.

Goldstein, Richard. "John Finn, Medal of Honor Winner, Dies at 100." *New York Times*, May 27, 2010.

———. "Kenneth Taylor, 86, a Key Pilot at Pearl Harbor, Dies." *New York Times*, December 7, 2006.

———. "Kermit Tyler, Player of a Fateful, If Minor, Role in Pearl Harbor Attack, Dies at 96." *New York Times*, February 25, 2010.

———. "Rex T. Barber, Pilot Who Downed Yamamoto, Dies at 84." *New York Times*, August 1, 2001.

Goodwin, Doris Kearns. *No Ordinary Time*. New York: Simon & Schuster, 1994.

Gopnik, Adam. "Stones and Bones." *New Yorker*, July 7, 2014.

Grew, Joseph C. *Ten Years in Japan*. New York: Simon & Schuster, 1944.

Grier, Peter. "Pearl Harbor Day 2011: Three Enduring Mysteries." *Christian Science Monitor*, December 7, 2011.

Gudmens, Jeffrey J. *The Staff Ride Handbook for the Attack on Pearl Harbor, 7 December 1941.* Fort Leavenworth, KS: Combat Studies Institute Press, 2009.

Haley, James L. *Captive Paradise: A History of Hawaii.* New York: St. Martin's, 2014.

Hankoff, Peter, writer and producer. *How It Was: Attack on Pearl Harbor.* 2006.

Hanyok, Robert J., and David Mowry. *West Wind Clear: Cryptology and the Winds Message Controversy.* Fort Meade, MD: Center for Cryptologic History, National Security Agency, 2008.

Hara, Shiro. *Taisenraku naki kaiser* [*Beginning a war with no great strategy*]. Tokyo: Hara Shobo, 1987.

Hara, Shiro, the National Institute for Defense Studies, et al. *Senshi sōsho* [The history of war]. 102 vols. Tokyo: Asagumo Shinbunsha, 1966–80.

Harden, Blaine. "Pearl Harbor's Old Men Find New Limelight Since Sept. 11." *New York Times*, December 7, 2001.

Harding, Stephen. "First Planes Down at Pearl." *History Net*, November 4, 2013. http://www.historynet.com/first-planes-down-at-pearl.htm.

Hasdorff, Dr. James C. "Interview of Lieutenant Colonel Horace E. Crouch"; "Interview of Reverend Jacob D. DeShazer"; "Interview of Lieutenant Colonel Robert L. Hite"; "Interview of Major General David M. Jones"; "Interview of Chief Master Sergeant Bert M. Jordan"; "Interview of Brigadier General Richard A. Knobloch"; "Interview of Colonel James H. Macia"; "Interview of Captain Charles J. Ozuk, Jr.,"; "Interview of Colonel Edward J. York." US Air Force Oral History Program, 1982–89. Air Force Historical Research Agency.

Hattori, Takushiro. *Dai toa senso zenshi* [The complete history of the Great East Asia War]. Tokyo: Headquarters, US Army Forces Far East, 1953–54.

Hayes, Grace P. *The History of the Joint Chiefs of Staff in World War II: The War against Japan.* Annapolis: Naval Institute Press, 1982.

Heinrichs, Waldo. *Threshold of War.* New York: Oxford University Press, 1988.

Herbers, John. "Survivors Reliving the Bombing of Pearl Harbor 30 Years Ago." *New York Times*, December 7, 1971.

Hinchey, Frank. "The Will to Survive Remembering Pearl Harbor." *Columbus (OH) Dispatch*, December 7, 1999.

Historical Section, Fourteenth Naval District. "History of Pearl Harbor." *Administrative History of the Fourteenth Naval District and the Hawaiian Sea Frontier.* Vol. 1. 1945. http://www.history.navy.mil/docs/wwii/pearl/hawaii.htm.

Historic Wings. "Scouting Squadron Six at Pearl Harbor. December 7, 2012. http://fly.historicwings.com/2012/12/scouting-squadron-six-at-pearl-harbor/.

Hofstadter, Richard. "The Paranoid Style in American Politics." *Harper's*, November 1964.

Holstrom, Lieutenant Everett W. "Personal Report, Chungking, China, May 14, 1942." Air Force Historical Research Agency, Maxwell Air Force Base, AL.

Hoover, Lieutenant Travis. "Personal Report, Chungking, China, May 15, 1942." Air Force Historical Research Agency, Maxwell Air Force Base, AL.

Hopkins, Harry L. "Report from the Commission created by Executive Order 'to ascertain and report the facts relating to the attack made by Japanese armed forces upon the Territory of Hawaii on December 7, 1941.'" January 24, 1942. Franklin Delano Roosevelt Library, Hyde Park, NY.

Horvat, William J. *Above the Pacific*. Fallbrook, CA: Aero Publishers, 1966.

Hotta, Eri. *Japan 1941: Countdown to Infamy*. New York: Alfred A. Knopf, 2013.

———. *Pan-Asianism and Japan's War, 1931–1945*. New York: Palgrave Macmillan, 2007.

———. "Understanding Pearl Harbor." *Guardian*, December 7, 2008.

Hoyt, Edwin P. *Japan's War: The Great Pacific Conflict, 1853–1952*. New York: McGraw-Hill, 1986.

Hull, Cordell. *Memoirs of Cordell Hull*. New York: Macmillan, 1948.

———. "Memoranda of Conversations, 1933–1944." Reel 31, containers 60–61. Cordell Hull Papers, 1908–56. Library of Congress Manuscript Division,

Hunt, Michael H., and Steven I. Levine. *Arc of Empire: America's Wars in Asia from the Philippines to Vietnam*. Chapel Hill: University of North Carolina Press, 2013.

Hylton, Wil S. "American Deserter." *New York*, February 23, 2015.

Hynes, Samuel, et al., Advisory Board. *Reporting World War II*. New York: Library of America, 1995.

Ienaga, Saburo. *The Pacific War, 1931–1945*. New York: Pantheon, 1978.

Iguchi, Takeo. *Demystifying Pearl Harbor: A New Perspective from Japan*. Tokyo: I-House Press, 2010.

Ike, Nobutaku. *Japan's Decision for War*. Stanford, CA: Stanford University Press, 1967.

Iriye, Akira. *The Origins of the Second World War in Asia and the Pacific*. London: Longman Group, 1987.

Irokawa, Daikichi. *The Age of Hirohito: In Search of Modern Japan*. Collingdale, PA: Diane Publishing, 1995.

Jansen, Marius. *The Making of Modern Japan*. Cambridge, MA: Belknap Press/ Harvard University Press, 2000.

Jasper, Joy Waldron, et al. *The USS* Arizona. New York: St. Martin's Press, 2001.

Johnson, Glen. "Probe Reconstructs Horror, Calculated Attacks on Planes." *Boston Globe*, November 23, 2001.

Joint Congressional Committee. "Pearl Harbor: Documents: The Attack." *Foreign Affairs* 70, no. 5 (Winter 1991–92).

Jones, Captain David M. "Narrative Report, Chungking, China, May 18, 1942." Air Force Historical Research Agency, Maxwell Air Force Base, AL.

Jones, James. *From Here to Eternity: The Restored Edition*. New York: Open Road, 1998.

Judt, Tony. "What Have We Learned, If Anything?" *New York Review of Books*, May 1, 2008.

Kahn, David. "The Intelligence Failure of Pearl Harbor." *Foreign Affairs* 70, no. 5 (Winter 1991–92).

Kakesako, Gregg K. "Baby's Ashes Rest aboard USS *Utah*." *Honolulu Star-Bulletin*, September 29, 2000.

Kaplan, Fred. "Killing Conspiracy." *Slate*, November 14, 2013.

Kato, Masuo. *The Lost War: A Japanese Reporter's Inside Story*. New York: Alfred A. Knopf, 1946.

Kean, Thomas H., Chairman. *The 9/11 Commission Report.* Washington, DC: Government Printing Office, 2004.

Keating, Joshua. "Ending the Forever War." *Slate,* December 10, 2014.

Keene, Donald. *So Lovely a Country Will Never Perish: Wartime Diaries of Japanese Writers.* New York: Columbia University Press, 2010.

Kennedy, David M. *Freedom from Fear: The American People in Depression and War, 1929–1945.* New York: Oxford University Press, 1999.

———. "Victory at Sea." *Atlantic Monthly,* March 1999.

Kennedy, Paul. *Engineers of Victory.* New York: Random House, 2013.

Kenshujo, Boeicho Boei. *Senshi sosho Hawai sakusen.* Tokyo: Asagumo Shimbunsha, 1967.

Kepel, Gilles. *Jihad.* Cambridge: Harvard University Press, 2000.

Kido, Koichi. *The Diary of Marquis Kido, 1931–45.* Washington, DC: University Publications of America, 1984.

King, Ernest J., and Walter Muir Whitehill. *Fleet Admiral King: A Naval Record.* New York: W. W. Norton, 1952.

Kirk, Robert, director. "Trapped in a Watery Grave." *The Great Escapes of World War II.* Greystone Television, 2004.

Kleinsasser, Joe. "Pearl Harbor, 9/11 Attacks Have Similarities, Differences." *Wichita State University News,* September 6, 2011.

Kluckhorn, Frank L. "US Declares War, Pacific Battle Widens." *New York Times,* December 8, 1941.

Koenig, William. *Epic Sea Battles.* London: Peerage, 1975.

Kotler, Mindy. "The Comfort Women and Japan's War on Truth." *New York Times,* November 14, 2014.

Kristof, Nicholas D. "Tokyo Journal: Why a Nation of Apologizers Makes One Large Exception." *New York Times,* June 12, 1995.

Kuramoti, Iki. "The Southern Cross." This account of an anonymous enlistee in the Imperial Japanese Navy was included as evidence for the Joint Congressional Committee on the Investigation of the Pearl Harbor Attack. Translation submitted July 25, 1945.

LaForte, Robert S., and Ronald E. Marcello, eds. *Remembering Pearl Harbor: Eyewitness Accounts by US Military Men and Women.* Wilmington, DE: Scholarly Resources, 1991.

Langewiesche, William. *American Ground: Unbuilding the World Trade Center.* New York: Farrar, Straus and Giroux, 2002.

Larkin, Sergeant George E., Jr. "Personal Diary, October 18, 1942." Filson Club Historical Society, Louisville, KY.

Larrabee, Eric. *Commander in Chief: Franklin Delano Roosevelt, His Lieutenants, and Their War.* New York: A Cornelia and Michael Bessie Book, Harper and Row, 1987.

Laurence, William L. "Atomic Bombing of Nagasaki Told by Flight Member." *New York Times,* September 9, 1945.

Lawson, Captain Ted W. *Thirty Seconds over Tokyo.* New York: Random House, 1943; and Cutchogue, NY: Buccaneer Books, 1943.

Leckie, Robert. *Delivered from Evil: The Saga of World War II.* New York: Harper and Row, 1987.

Leish, Kenneth W. "The Reminiscences of James Harold Doolittle." Aviation

Project Collection. Columbia University Oral History Research Office, 1960.

Leonard, Tom. "The 9/11 Victims America Wants to Forget: The 200 Jumpers." *Mail Online*, September 11, 2011.

Lewin, Tamar. "The Lessons." *New York Times*, September 8, 2011.

Lewis, Claude. "Dorie Miller Was a Pearl Harbor Hero, but He Never Escaped the Galley at the Start of World War II; the Only Jobs for Black Sailors Were in the Kitchen." *Philadelphia Inquirer*, December 9, 1991.

Library of Congress. "Pearl Harbor 70th Anniversary." Experiencing War: Stories from the Veterans History Project, 23 July 2013–6 June 2014. http://www.loc.gov/vets/stories/ex-war-pearlharbor.html.

Lindbergh, Charles A. *The Wartime Journals of Charles A. Lindbergh*. New York: Harcourt Brace Jovanovich, 1970.

Liptak, Adam. "Civil Liberties Today." *New York Times*, September 7, 2011.

Lloyd, Nigel. "Cloud over the Empire of the Sun." *Times* (London), July 29, 1995.

Lopez, Matthews, et al. "Remembering Pearl Harbor . . . 70 Years Later." *Prologue* 43, no. 4 (Winter 2011).

Lord, Walter. *Day of Infamy*. New York: Henry Holt, 1957.

Lowman, David D. *Magic: The Untold Story of US Intelligence and the Evacuation of Japanese Residents from the West Coast during WWII*. Washington, DC: Athena Press, 2001.

Lutton, Charles. "Pearl Harbor: Fifty Years of Controversy." Institute for Historical Review, Winter 1991–92. http://www.ihr.org/jhr/v11/v11p431_Lutton.html.

Madsen, Daniel. *Resurrection: Salvaging the Battle Fleet at Pearl Harbor*. Annapolis: Naval Institute Press, 2013.

Manchester, William. *Goodbye Darkness, A Memoir of the Pacific War*. Boston: Little, Brown, 1980.

Marshall, George. *Biennial Report of the Chief of Staff of the United States Army to the Secretary of War, July 1, 1939 to June 30, 1941*. Washington, DC: Government Printing Office, 1941.

Mayer, Jane. *The Dark Side: The Inside Story of How the War on Terror Turned into a War on American Ideals*. New York: Doubleday, 2008.

McKechney, John. "The Pearl Harbor Controversy: A Debate among Historians." Tokyo: *Monumenta Nipponica* 18, no. 1 (1963).

McKinley, Jessie. "Final Hawaii Reunion for Pearl Harbor Veterans." *New York Times*, December 8, 2006.

McWilliams, Bill. *Sunday in Hell: Pearl Harbor Minute by Minute*. New York: Open Road, 2014.

Mercado, Stephen C. "Japanese Army Intelligence Activities against the United States, 1921–45." *Studies in Intelligence*, US Central Intelligence Agency, Summer 1994.

Merrill, James M. *Target Tokyo: The Halsey-Doolittle Raid*. Chicago: Rand McNally & Co., 1964.

Michel, Frank. "Mystic Chords of Memory at Pearl Harbor." *Houston Chronicle*, December 7, 1998.

Miles, Donna. "Pearl Harbor Parallels 9–11." *Military.com*, December 7, 2006.

Miles, Sherman. "Pearl Harbor in Retrospect." *Atlantic*, July 1, 1948.

Military Intelligence Service, War Department. "Japanese Land Operations from Japanese Sources, December 8, 1941 to June 8, 1942." Campaign Study #3, November 18, 1942. Air Force Historical Research Agency (AFHRA), Maxwell Air Force Base, AL.

Miller, Edward S. *Bankrupting the Enemy: The US Financial Siege of Japan before Pearl Harbor.* Annapolis: Naval Institute Press, 2007.

Miller, Mike. "Funeral Held for Baby Entombed within USS *Utah.*" *www.navy.mil,* December 16, 2003.

———. "Pearl Harbor 30 Years Later." *New York Times,* December 5, 1971.

Mills, Nicolaus. "Images of Terror: Enduring the Scars of 9/11." *Dissent* 56, no. 4 (Fall 2009).

Mitscher, Marc A. "Report of Action, April 18, 1942, USS *Hornet.*" US Naval Historical Center, Annapolis, MD.

Mitter, Rana. *Forgotten Ally: China's World War II, 1937–1945.* New York: Houghton Mifflin Harcourt, 2013.

Molotsky, Irvin. "Pearl Harbor Diary: A Calm Sunday Abruptly Shattered." *New York Times,* December 7, 1998.

Morison, Samuel Eliot. "Pearl Harbor: Documents: The Rising Sun in the Pacific." *Foreign Affairs* 70, no. 5 (Winter 1991–92).

———. *The Two-Ocean War.* Boston: Little, Brown, 1963.

Morley, James William, ed. *Deterrent Diplomacy: Japan, Germany, and the USSR, 1935–1940 / Selected Translations from "Taiheiyo senso e no michi: Kaisen gaiko shi."* New York: Columbia University Press, 1976.

———, ed. *The Fateful Choice: Japan's Road to the Pacific War / Selected Translations from "Taiheiyo senso e no michi: Kaisen gaiko shi."* New York: Columbia University Press, 1980.

———, ed. *The Final Confrontation: Japan's Negotiations with the United States, 1941 / Selected Translations from "Taiheiyo senso e no michi: Kaisen gaiko shi."* New York: Columbia University Press, 1994.

———, ed. *Japan Erupts: The London Naval Conference and the Manchurian Incident, 1928–1932 / Selected Translations from "Taiheiyo senso e no michi: Kaisen gaiko shi."* New York: Columbia University Press, 1984.

Morris, David J. "Cancel Water-Boarding 101." *Slate,* January 29, 2009.

———. *The Evil Hours: A Biography of Post-Traumatic Stress Disorder.* New York: Eamon Dolan, 2015.

Morris, Errol, director. *The Fog of War.* Sony Picture Classics, 2003.

Mueller, John. "Pearl Harbor: Military Inconvenience, Political Disaster." *International Security* 16, no. 3 (Winter 1991–92).

Murnane, John R. "Japan's Monroe Doctrine?: Re-Framing the Story of Pearl Harbor." *History Teacher* 40, no. 4 (August 2007).

Naftali, Tim. "Did the CIA Go Rogue after 9/11? The Senate Intelligence Report Raises Painful Questions about Who Watches the Watchers." *Slate,* December 10, 2014.

Naoki, Inose. "Doubt Cast on Lead-Up to Pearl Harbor Attack." *Daily Yomiuri,* February 28, 2000.

Nathan, John. "Tokyo Story." *New Yorker,* April 9, 2001.

National Park Service, US Department of the Interior. "Timeline: Flight 93, September 11, 2001—Phone Calls from the Passengers and Crew of Flight 93." Flight 93 National Memorial.

Naval Historical Center. USS *Arizona*, USS *Bagley*, USS *Bobolink*, USS *Dale*, USS *Helena*, USS *Helm*, USS *Hull*, USS *Jarvis*, USS *Maryland*, USS *Nevada*, USS *Oklahoma*, USS *Perry*, USS *Raleigh*, USS *Ralph Talbot*, USS *Regal*, USS *Solace*, USS *Tangier*, USS *Tennessee*, USS *Utah*, USS *West Virginia*. *Report of Pearl Harbor Attack*. http://www.history.navy.mil/docs/wwii/pearl/.

Naval History & Heritage Command. *Oral History of the Pearl Harbor Attack*, 7 December 1941. http://www.history.navy.mil/faqs/faq66-3.htm.

Naval History & Heritage, Pearl Harbor Navy Medical Activities. http://www.history.navy.mil/faqs/faq66-5.htm.

Nelson, Craig. *The First Heroes*. New York: Viking, 2002.

Nicholson, Dorinda Makanaonalani Stagner. *Pearl Harbor Child*. Raytown, MO: Woodson House, 2008.

———. *Pearl Harbor Warriors: The Bugler, the Pilot, the Friendship*. Raytown, MO: Woodson House, 2001.

Nihon kokusai seiji gakkai [The Japan association of international relations]. *Taiheiyō sensō e no michi: Kaisen gaikōshi* [The road to the Pacific war]. 7 vols. Tokyo: Asahi Shimbunsha, 1962–63.

Noon, David Hoogland. "Operation Enduring Analogy: World War II, the War on Terror, and the Uses of Historical Memory." *Rhetoric & Public Affairs* 7, no. 3 (Fall 2004).

Northridge, A. R. "Pearl Harbor: Estimating Then and Now." CIA Historical Review Program, vol. 2, no. 4. Washington, DC: Center for the Study of Intelligence, September 22, 1993. https://www.cia.gov/library/center-for-the-study-of-intelligence/kent-csi/vol9no4/html/v09i4a07p_0001.htm.

Omata Yukio. *Reports and Recollections of Japanese Military Correspondents*. Tokyo: Tokuma Shoten, 1985.

Packer, George. "Dark Hours: Violence in the Age of the War on Terror." *New Yorker*, July 20, 2015.

Panic, Ray. "VF-6: The Deadly Night of December 7, 1941." Pacific Aviation Museum. http://www.pacificaviationmuseum.org/pearl-harbor-blog/vf-6-the-deadly-night-of-december-7-1941.

PBS.org. "MacArthur." *American Experience*. 2001. http://www.pbs.org/wgbh/amex/macarthur.

Pearl Harbor Survivors Association. Gunnery Sergeant James L. Evans, administrator.http://www.pearlharborsurvivor.net.

Pearl Harbor Survivors Online. http://www.pearlharborsurvivorsonline.org.

Perkins, Frances. *The Roosevelt I Knew*. New York: Viking, 1946.

Pfeiffer, David A. "Sage Prophet or Loose Cannon? Skilled Intelligence Officer in World War II Foresaw Japan's Plans, but Annoyed Navy Brass." *Prologue* 40, no. 2 (Summer 2008).

Pillar, Paul R. *Intelligence and US Foreign Policy: Iraq, 9/11, and Misguided Reform*. New York: Columbia University Press, 2011.

Pinkney, Captain J. "Untitled After-Action Interviews." Chungking, China-Headquarters, Army Air Forces, Washington, DC, June 15, 1942. Air Force Historical Research Agency, Maxwell Air Force Base, AL.

Pitman, Joanna. "Repentance." *New Republic*, February 10, 1992.

Plotz, David. "What You Think You Know about Sept. 11 . . . but Don't." *Slate*, September 10, 2003.

Popov, Dusko. *Spy/Counterspy: The Autobiography of Dusko Popov*. New York: Grosset & Dunlap, 1974.

Potter, J. D. *Yamamoto: The Man Who Menaced America*. New York: Viking, 1965.

Powers, Thomas. "The Failure." *New York Review of Books*, April 29, 2004.

Prange, Gordon W. Gordon W. Prange Papers. Hornbake Library, University of Maryland.

———. *December 7, 1941*. New York: Grand Central, 1989.

Prange, Gordon W., with Donald M. Goldstein and Katherine V. Dillon. *At Dawn We Slept: The Untold Story of Pearl Harbor*. New York: McGraw-Hill, 1981.

———, with Donald M. Goldstein and Katherine V. Dillon. *God's Samurai*. McLean, VA: Brassey's, 1990.

Ramsey, Mary Ann. "Only Yesteryear." *Naval History*, Winter 1991.

Raymer, Edward C. *Descent into Darkness*. Novato, CA: Presidio Press, 1996.

Reda, Lou, executive producer. *Unsung Heroes of Pearl Harbor*. A&E Television Networks, 2009.

Reddy, Lieutenant Kenneth E. "Personal Diaries, 4/6/42–5/9/42." Unpublished manuscript, courtesy Kenneth Reddy.

Regan, Geoffrey. *The Guiness Book of Decisive Battles*. Middlesex, UK: Guiness Publishing, 1992.

Reinhold, Robert. "50 Years after Pearl Harbor, Reconciliation Is Still Elusive." *New York Times*, September 1, 1991.

Reynolds, David. *From Munich to Pearl Harbor: Roosevelt's America and the Origins of the Second World War*. Chicago: Ivan R. Dee, 2001.

Rich, Frank. "Day's End. The 9/11 Decade Is Now Over. The Terrorists Lost. But Who Won?" *New York*, August 27, 2011.

Richardson, James O. *On the Treadmill to Pearl Harbor*. Washington, DC: Naval History Division, 1974.

Richardson, K. D. *Reflections of Pearl Harbor: An Oral History of December 7, 1941*. Westport, CT: Praeger, 2005.

Roberts, Sam. "Pearl Harbor Conspiracy Theory about 'Winds' Message Refuted." *New York Times*, November 7, 2008.

———. "Remembering Pearl Harbor; Lessons for the World Trade Center Memorial." *New York Times*, May 25, 2003.

Robinson, James J. "Surprise Attack: Crime at Pearl Harbor and Now." *American Bar Association Journal* 46, no. 9 (September 1960).

Rongstad, Richard. "Pearl Harbor Pilot to Tibbets: 'You Did the Right Thing.' " Sun Tzu's Newswire, September, 20, 1998.

Roosevelt, Franklin Delano. "Pearl Harbor Speech." December 8, 1941. http://www.archives.gov/publications/prologue/2001/winter/crafting-day-of-infamy-speech.html.

Rose, David. "9/11: The Tapping Point." *Vanity Fair*, September 2011.

Rosenberg, Emily S. *A Date Which Will Live: Pearl Harbor in American Memory*. Durham, NC: Duke University Press, 2003.

Rosenthal, A. M. "The Day That Changed the World Forever." *New York Times*, December 3, 1961.

Ross, Richard, director. "Myths of Pearl Harbor." *Unsolved History*. Military Channel, December 7, 2003.

Saionji, Kinkazu. *Saionji kinkazu kaikoroku*. Tokyo: Nihon Tosho Senta, 2005.

Sanburn, Curt, and John Corrales. "Decades after Pearl Harbor, a Mission to Honor the Unknowns' Gains Urgency." *New York Times*, August 14, 2015.

Sanger, David E. "In a Memoir, Hirohito Talks of Pearl Harbor." *New York Times*, November 15, 1990.

Savela, Edward. "The Spy Who Doomed Pearl Harbor." *Military History Quarterly*, November 2011.

Sayle, Murray. "A Dynasty Falters." *New Yorker*, June 12, 2000.

———. "The Kamikazes Rise Again." *Atlantic Monthly*, March 2001.

Schellstede, Sangmie Choi, ed. *Comfort Women Speak*. New York: Holmes & Meier, 2000.

Schlesinger, Arthur. "Today, It Is We Americans Who Live in Infamy." *Los Angeles Times*, March 23, 2003.

Schmidt, Warren R. "Lieutenant Zenji Abe: A Japanese Pilot Remembers." May 2001. http://www.historynet.com/lieutenant-zenji-abe-a-japanese-pilot-remembers .htm.

Schuessler, John M. "The Deception Dividend: FDR's Undeclared War." *International Security* 34, No. 4 (Spring 2010).

Schwartz, Matthias. "The Whole Haystack." *New Yorker*, January 26, 2015.

Shenon, Philip. "Senate Clears 2 Pearl Harbor 'Scapegoats.' " *New York Times*, May 26, 1999.

Sherma, Geraldine. "Japan's War Heroes Have Their Shrine." *Globe and Mail* (Canada), December 7, 1991.

Sherwell, Philip. "9/11: Voices from the Doomed Planes." *London Telegraph*, September 10, 2011.

Slackman, Michael. *Target: Pearl Harbor*. Honolulu: University of Hawaii Press, 1990.

Sledge, E. B. *With the Old Breed: At Peleliu and Okinawa*. Novato, CA: Presidio Press, 1981.

Smith, Carl. *Pearl Harbor, 1941: The Day of Infamy*. Oxford, UK: Osprey, 2001.

Smith, Patrick L. "Jill Abramson's Sad Admission." *Salon*, July 30, 2014.

Snyder, Timothy. *Bloodlands*. New York: Basic Books, 2010.

Spector, Ronald H. *Eagle against the Sun*. New York: Free Press, 1984.

Sperber, A. M. *Murrow, His Life and Times*. New York: Fordham University Press, 1998.

Sperry, Paul. "Inside the Saudi 9/11 Coverup." *New York Post*, December 15, 2013.

Spiller, Harry. *Pearl Harbor Survivors: An Oral History of 24 Servicemen*. Jefferson, NC: McFarland, 2002.

Staff, Central Intelligence Group. "Memorandum for the Director of Central Intelligence. Subject: Intelligence at Pearl Harbor." August 22, 1946.

State of Hawaii, Hawaii Aviation Archive. "Eye Witness Accounts of the Bombing of Hickam AFB. http://hawaii.gov/hawaiiaviation/world-war-ii/december -7–1941/first-hand-accounts-of-the-bombing-of-hickam-afb.

Steinbeck, John. "Fear of Death as Green Troops Sail to Invasion." *New York Herald Tribune*, October 3, 1943.

Stephan, John J. *Hawaii under the Rising Sun: Japan's Plans for Conquest after Pearl Harbor*. Honolulu: University of Hawaii Press, 2002.

Stephens, Glenn A. "Hot Reception at Pearl Harbor." *VFW Magazine*, December 1975.

Stewart, James B. "The Real Heroes Are Dead." *New Yorker*, February 11, 2002.

Stewart, Jon, producer. "George Takei." *The Daily Show with Jon Stewart*, July 23, 2014.

Stillwell, Paul, ed. *Air Raid: Pearl Harbor!* Annapolis: Naval Institute Press, 1981.

Stilwell, General Joseph. "Incoming Message From: Chungking To: Agwar For Ammisca, Attn Sec War and Chief Staff." April 1, 1942. Franklin Delano Roosevelt Library, Hyde Park, NY.

Stimson, Henry. *Diaries of Henry Lewis Stimson*. Yale University Library, New Haven, CT.

Stinnett, Robert B. *Day of Deceit: The Truth about FDR and Pearl Harbor.* New York: Free Press, 1999.

Streatfeild, Dominic. *A History of the World Since 9/11.* London: Atlantic Books, 2011.

Tanaka, Miya. "Pearl Harbor Was Mistake: Attack Vet, 89." *Japan Times*, December 6, 2005. http://www.japantimes.co.jp/news/2005/12/06/national/pearl-harbor-was-mistake-attack-vet-89.

Tanaka, Yuki. *Hidden Horrors: Japanese War Crimes in World War II.* Boulder, CO: Westview Press, 1996.

Taylor, Jay. *The Generalissimo: Chiang Kai-shek and the Struggle for Modern China.* Cambridge, MA: Belknap Press/Harvard University Press, 2009.

Tennant, Diane. "Pearl Harbor Survivors Will Reunite in Va. Beach." *Virginian-Pilot*, February 27, 2014.

Terasaki, Gwen. *Bridge to the Sun.* Chapel Hill: University of North Carolina Press, 1957.

Terasaki, Hidenari, and Mariko Tersasaki Miller, eds. *Showa tenno dokukakuroku.* Bunshun Bunko, 2010.

Terkel, Studs. *The Good War: An Oral History of World War II.* New York: New Press, 1984.

Thomas, Evan. "The Last Night." *Newsweek*, October 15, 2011.

Tojo, Hideki. "Prison Diary." *Journal of Historical Review* 12, no. 1 (Spring 1992).

Toland, John. *Infamy.* New York: Doubleday, 1982.

———. *The Rising Sun.* New York: Random House, 1970.

Tolischus, Otto D. *Tokyo Record.* New York: Harcourt Brace and World, 1943.

Toll, Ian W. "A Reluctant Enemy." *New York Times*, December 6, 2011.

Townsend, Timothy. "The First Hours." *Rolling Stone*, October 2001.

Travers, Paul Joseph. *Eye Witness to Infamy: An Oral History of Pearl Harbor.* Lanham, MD: Madison Books, 1991.

Trumbull, Robert. "A Day of Infamy, Two Years of Hard Work." *New York Times*, December 7, 2006.

Tsunoda, Jun, and Shigeo Fukuda. *Nichibei kaisen* [The beginning of hostilities between Japan and America]. Tokyo: Asahi Shimbunsha, 1963.

Tsunoda, Ryusaku, et al. *Sources of Japanese Tradition.* New York: Columbia University Press, 1958.

Tuchman, Barbara W. *Stilwell and the American Experience in China.* New York: Macmillan, 1971.

United States Department of State. *Peace and War: United States Foreign Policy, 1931–1941.* Washington, DC: Government Printing Office, 1943.

United States Navy. *Remembering Pearl Harbor.* June 6, 2014. http://www.navy.mil/navydata/rph.htm.

Van Deerlin, Lionel. "Who Really Shot Down Admiral Yamamoto?" *San Diego Union-Tribune*, March 20, 1996.

Vandenbosch, Amry. "Cordell Hull: Father of the United Nations." *World Affairs* 136, no. 2 (Fall 1973).

Verklan, Laura, writer and director. *Tora, Tora, Tora: The Real Story of Pearl Harbor.* A&E Television Networks, 2000.

Vidal, Gore, and Ian Buruma. "Pearl Harbor: An Exchange." *New York Review of Books,* May 17, 2001.

Virginia Law School. "The Tokyo War Crimes Trial: A Digital Exhibition." http://lib.law.virginia.edu/imtfe.

Wallace-Wells, Benjamin. "The Truly Paranoid Style in American Politics. From the JFK Assassination to Weather Control and the New World Order: 50 Years of Conspiracy Theory." *New York*, November 25, 2013.

Wallin, Homer N. *Pearl Harbor: Why, How, Fleet Salvage and Final Appraisal.* Washington, DC: Government Printing Office, 1968.

Warner, Denis. "Could Pearl Harbor Have Been Averted?" *New York Times*, December 8, 1998.

Warner, Michael. "The Creation of the Central Intelligence Group." *Studies in Intelligence*, Fall 1995.

———. "The Office of Strategic Services." CIA Publications, May 2000.

Watson, C. Hoyt. *The Amazing Story of Sergeant Jacob DeShazer.* Winona Lake, IN: Life and Light Press, 1950.

Webb, Andy, director. *X Day: The Invasion of Japan.* History Channel, August 15, 2005.

Weidhorn, Manfred. "The Fall of 1941: A Meditation on History." *Historically Speaking* 11, no. 4 (2010).

Weintraub, Stanley. "The Conscript: George Catlett Marshall." *Journal of Military History* 72, no. 3 (July 2008).

———. *Pearl Harbor Christmas.* New York: Da Capo, 2011.

———. "Pearl Harbor in the Mind of Japan." *New York Times*, November 3, 1991.

Weisman, Steven R. "Pearl Harbor Remembered: Japanese Think They Owe Apology and Are Owed One on War, Poll Shows." *New York Times*, December 8, 1991.

Wetzler, Peter. *Hirohito and War: Imperial Tradition and Military Decision Making in Prewar Japan.* Honolulu: University of Hawaii Press, 1998.

White, Geoffrey M. "National Subjects: September 11 and Pearl Harbor." *American Ethnologist* 31, no. 3 (August 2004).

Willmott, H.P. *Empires in the Balance: Japanese and Allied Pacific Strategies to April 1942.* Annapolis: Naval Institute Press, 2008.

Wohlstetter, Roberta. "Cuba and Pearl Harbor: Hindsight and Foresight, Memorandum RM-4328-ISA." Santa Monica, CA: Rand Corporation, April 1965.

———. *Pearl Harbor: Warning and Decision.* Stanford, CA: Stanford University Press, 1962.

Wolk, Herman S. *Cataclysm: General Hap Arnold and the Defeat of Japan.* Denton, TX: University of North Texas Press, 2010.

Woodrum, Henry C. "Cloak of Darkness." *Aerospace Historian*, December 1988.

Wright, Lawrence. *The Looming Tower.* New York: Alfred A. Knopf, 2006.

Wright, Mike. *What They Didn't Teach You about World War II*. Novato, CA: Presidio Press, 1998.

Wu, Julianne. "Veterans Bonded by Pearl Harbor." *St. Petersburg Times*, December 7, 1999.

Zegart, Amy B. *Spying Blind: The CIA, the FBI, and the Origins of 9/11*. Princeton, NJ: Princeton University Press, 2007.

Zinnemann, Fred, director, Daniel Taradash, scriptwriter. *From Here to Eternity*. Columbia Pictures, 1953.

INDEX

ABOUT THE AUTHOR

Craig Nelson is the author of *The Age of Radiance* and the *New York Times* bestseller *Rocket Men*, as well as several previous books, including *The First Heroes*, *Thomas Paine* (winner of the Henry Adams Prize), and *Let's Get Lost* (short-listed for WHSmith's Book of the Year). His writing has appeared in *Vanity Fair*, the *Wall Street Journal*, *Salon*, *National Geographic*, *New England Review*, *Popular Science*, *Reader's Digest*, and a host of other publications. He has been profiled in *Variety*, *Interview*, *Publishers Weekly*, and *Time Out*. Besides working at a zoo and in Hollywood, and being an Eagle Scout and a Fuller Brush man, he was a vice president and executive editor of Harper & Row, Hyperion, and Random House, where he oversaw the publishing of twenty national bestsellers. He lives in Greenwich Village.